Vietnam

A HISTORY IN DOCUMENTS

ABOUT THE EDITOR

GARETH PORTER, Ph.D., Southeast Asian Studies, Cornell University, is an associate at the Center for International Policy in Washington D.C. He was Bureau Chief for Dispatch News Service International in Saigon in 1971 and was co-director of the Indochina Resource Center from 1974 to 1976. Dr. Porter is the author of *A Peace Denied* and *Cambodia: Starvation and Revolution* and has been a professorial lecturer at the School of Advanced International Studies, Johns Hopkins University.

GLORIA EMERSON covered the Vietnam War as a foreign correspondent for *The New York Times*, 1971-72, for which she won the 1971 George Polk Award for Excellence in Foreign Reporting. Her largely acclaimed book, *Winners and Losers*, won a National Book Award. She is the author of numerous articles on Vietnam and other subjects appearing in: *Esquire, Harper's, Vogue, New York, Playboy, Saturday Review, Rolling Stone, New Times*.

Vietnam

A HISTORY IN DOCUMENTS

Edited by
GARETH PORTER

———

INTRODUCTION BY
Gloria Emerson

A MERIDIAN BOOK
NEW AMERICAN LIBRARY
TIMES MIRROR
NEW YORK AND SCARBOROUGH, ONTARIO

Copyright © 1979 Earl M. Coleman Enterprises, Inc., Publishers

Abridgment Copyright © 1981 by Gareth Porter

Introduction Copyright © 1981 by Gloria Emerson

All rights reserved. For information address Earl M. Coleman Enterprises, Inc.,
Publishers, P.O. Box 143, Pine Plains, New York 12567.

The two maps of Vietnam appearing in this volume are reprinted from
Fire in the Lake: The Vietnamese and the Americans in Vietnam by Francis
FitzGerald, Copyright © 1972 by Little Brown & Company, Inc., by permission
of Little Brown & Company in association with Atlantic Monthly Press.

This edition is an abridgment by the author of his two-volume work
entitled *Vietnam: The Definitive History of Human Decisions,* published in
hardcover by Earl M. Coleman Enterprises in 1979.

Library of Congress Cataloging in Publication Data
Main entry under title:

Vietnam, a history in documents.

An abridgment of the 2 volume work: Vietnam, the
definitive documentation of human decisions.
Includes bibliographical references and index.
1. Vietnam—History—1945-1975—Sources. 2. Viet-
namese Conflict, 1961-1975—Sources. 3. Vietnam—
Foreign relations—United States—Sources. 4. United
States—Foreign relations—Vietnam—Sources. I. Porter,
Gareth, 1942-   . II. Vietnam, the definitive documen-
tation of human decisions.
DS556.8.V532 1981   959.704   81-12
ISBN 0-452-00553-1

Contents

The Documents

1947

1948

1949

1950

1951

1965

1966

1975

INTRODUCTION

by Gloria Emerson

Many Vietnamese soldiers were comforted by writing in their diaries as they made the long voyage on foot coming down the Ho Chi Minh trail, which was our name for it, not theirs. The American soldiers, who would have scorned diaries, often wrote fierce, blunt sentiments across the camouflage linings over their helmets, using them like little notebooks that anyone could read. There were no photographs published in *The New York Times* of troops who had written "Fuck The Army" on their heads, for the editors did not want their readers to be exposed to the coarseness of enlisted men. Boys of fourteen who had seen the war on television at home grew up to find themselves fighting it and were not grateful.

And I, coming back from the field to Saigon to send off my stories of sorrow and loss and debasement, would sometimes need to write on the walls of our Saigon office, write things that other people would someday see and understand. Perhaps it was the four-thousandth-or-so-day of the war when I printed on a door these three lines in English: Although we have been at times strong/at times weak/We have no time lacked heroes. And the words had something to do with a dying Vietnamese soldier, a Northerner, too weak to peel the American orange I slipped him, and who was facing a most unpleasant death.

Some other reporters noticed the door and thought it was a little weird to quote Ho Chi Minh in *The New York Times* bureau. But these were the feelings expressed early in the sixteenth century by the Vietnamese patriot, Emperor Le Loi, who had started a resistance movement against the Chinese ruling his country, and was joined by an extraordinary writer named Nguyen Trai, who wrote these words. Inspired by Tran Hung Dao, who defeated the Mongols in 1284, Le Loi and his guerrillas carried out a nine year rebellion and, by the end of 1427, triumphed at last. What Le Loi won were ruined rice and farm lands and the allegiance of starving subjects. Among the extensive and harshly enforced reforms he imposed was the prohibition of large private landholdings. There was a street in Saigon named Le Loi, and another named Tran Hung Dao, but those names meant nothing to foreigners, and the city belonged to them.

When it came time to leave, to get out, I wrote high above a stucco wall in our office only this: Give Me Voice or Give Me Beeper. It was what American pilots said on the radio when an aircraft had gone down and they needed to know whether any of the crew had survived. It only means: Tell me if you are alive—speak, or make a sound. For many years after leaving Vietnam, wandering around America, it seemed a good question to put to yourself.

When our war with them was over, after April 1975, a Vietnamese visitor, one of the victors who was visiting New York, asked me in beautiful French: "Don't you want to return to see how high the fruits and flowers will grow?" My answer was no, there were too many ghosts for me in Vietnam, ghosts from all three armies, village ghosts as well, it would be better if other Americans went. In French, ghosts are *phantomes*, but I speak French with such a peculiar, flat accent that it came out sounding as if I was worried about the U.S. F-4 Phantom jets. But the Vietnamese official saw my eyes were wet and only touched my arm and said no more. (The Vietnamese know almost everything about grief, but Americans think it is unwholesome and should be immediately concealed or cleared up like a scalp disease.)

If you want to know how ghosts are made—millions of them—then these documents will tell you. I first saw Saigon in 1956, wanting to be a journalist and not knowing how you did it. It was only two years after the French had been defeated but enough of them were still there to hate the sight of the Americans pouring in, eager to carry out new projects, full of plans and programs on how to "make it work" in South Vietnam. The French had called it Cochin-China when, in the years 1884 to 1954, Indochina was part of the French Empire. It was Le Loi, that remarkable man, who said: "Our people long ago established Vietnam as an independent nation with its own civilization. We have our own mountains and rivers, our own customs and traditions . . ." But this profound Vietnamese attachment to their independence was not considered significant in Washington, for the decision was made to encourage France to maintain her sovereignty in Vietnam and to speed up the flow of military aid. *Our own mountains and rivers:* often at night, in the killing zone, you could hear American howitzers firing at the same hills and mountains they had hit years before, as if no one told the Army to stop, so the howitzers kept firing. Fifteen years after that first visit to Saigon, I came back and could not quite believe what had happened. Nothing was as it had been in Saigon, in Danang, in Hue, in Phan Thiet, in Nha Trang, or in Quang Tri where there had once been cattle and birds and flowers. Even the trees had been slaughtered. Villages that had been were no more, the addresses of friends in the countryside did not exist. And, here, in these pages are the voices of older Vietnamese trying to expel the French, and something of Le Loi and Nguyen Trai persists—the same conviction, the stubborn belief in their people and, always, the scrupulous analysis of themselves. "At present, most of our armymen only know how to fight bravely; they do not pay attention to the study of tactics . . ." This is from a study on the Vietnamese resistance in 1947—commonly called the Viet Minh, an abbreviation designating the political front headed by Ho, which directed the war against the French—to be found here. It pointed out that the Vietnamese fighters had *material* weaknesses, while the enemy's frailties were *moral*. And there is a terrible echo in the optimistic assertions made so often and so earnestly in Washington, that the French were doing well with their colonial war, when the reverse was true. Dr. Ellen Hammer wrote in 1954, in *The Struggle for Indochina*, with startling insight, that the French war in Vietnam "provided an unhappy testing ground for the new American doctrine of massive retaliatory power to be applied at places and with means of our choosing . . ."

La sale guerre, the French called it, and many of them in Paris called out for an end to it. Others were not so sure whether it was a war that could be stopped, just as ten years later many Americans would wonder. In *Le Monde* of April 1953—twenty-two years to the day that a new generation of Vietnamese soldiers, again led by General Vo Nguyen Giap, took back southern Vietnam from the Americans—J. J. Servan-Schreiber wrote: "The generally accepted theory is that the prolongation of the war in Indochina is a fatality imposed by events, one of the dramas in history which has no solution." He knew otherwise and said so. "The truth is that the facts now known seem to add up to a lucid plan worked out step by step in order to assure the prolongation without limit of the hostilities and of the military occupation." An American critical of our war in Vietnam in 1965 or 1966 need hardly have changed a word of what Servan-Schreiber wrote.

In 1956 in Saigon, Vietnamese vendors peddled books printed in Paris about the French war, bloody little records of immense effort and error and doom. One of them was called *Les Rescapés de L'Enfer, Les Heroes de Dien Bien Phu*, which has slightly muddy black-and-white photographs of troops of the two races dying for France, moving through punishing terrain. *The jungle, always the jungle*, said one caption. And under another picture of a patrol: *And always, always the hostility of a country defending itself.* I did not know then that those photographs were the first ghastly X-rays of what would happen to us, that there would be American faces to be seen in the elephant grass, the bamboo, the triple-layer-canopy jungle as they called it. That was the year, too, in which, lying at night under mosquito netting, three times I read Graham Greene's new novel, *The Quiet American*, which told us too much and upset some of the younger C.I.A. men as well as the emininent journalist, A. J. Liebling, who gave it a scorching review in *The New Yorker* and attacked Greene for insulting Americans in such a manner. It took me fifteen years to notice that in the foreward Mr. Greene quoted Byron: "This is the patent age of new inventions/For killing bodies, and for saving souls/All propagated with the best intentions."

There are so many records now of American desolation but nothing on what the Vietnamese knew, and still suffer. Some men learned that the Vietnamese who fought us were heroic and often young drafters, as the Americans were, who wanted their country back. In the end, it was as General Tran Van Tra said, when at last he was able to come back to

Saigon: "It is our country, the trees and leaves are ours, we know every-thing." And our own veterans are often weighted with such sadness and despair, that although still young, they have nothing to do with youth. It leaked away. The pitch of their sorrow, or loneliness, the struggle to understand the memories, darkens the poems of a former Marine named Gerald McCarthy who wrote:

> "... *The soldiers are coming home,*
> *They carry their sadness with them*
> *like others carrying groceries*
> *or clothes in from the line.*
> *There is no music in the parade;*
> *the sound of their coming*
> *waits at the bottom of rivers,*
> *stones rubbing against each other*
> *in the current."*

Some of the veterans I know still hate the Vietnamese and, even more, those who fought against the war at home. "The other side of the coin," a man said of the anti-war groups; there was no arguing the point. (He forgave me, I think, for marching and speaking and, yes, yelling, against the war because I had been a witness to it.) But some men should be told about Le Loi and some, perhaps not all, would be helped by reading these documents that led to the end of all their childhoods and pushed them into a country they had never imagined. The soldiers did not vote to go, were not told what policies were at stake, whose reputations in Washington had to be defended, what experts must be proven right at any cost, yet it is they who must now bear the punishment for the arrogance and criminality of our calling for that war. And, of course, aside from mutilated men, there are always the deformed children of veterans constantly exposed to the herbi-cide, Agent Orange, to remind us of our fine technology and efficiency in that war of attrition. I give you my friend, Gustav Hasford, a Marine combat correspondent who calls himself "an unreconstructed Vietnam vet-eran," and what he has to say on the subject. "For more than a decade now my friends have humored me in what they call my tireless obsession as I continue to work at understanding the roots and lessons of our involvement in Vietnam," he wrote in an article for *The Los Angeles Times,* "It is difficult for them to understand that I cannot forget the war because there's gunpowder in my cereal bowl."

Some of the Americans who declared war on the war have wounds of their own so deep and wide no cure yet exists. In October, 1977, a draft evader, who had been out of the country for seven years and seven months and was not yet thirty, decided to leave Canada and return to America, where he faced charges not only of refusing to comply with Selective Service laws but assault charges as well. He had taken sanctuary in a church, with the consent of the congregation, when it was stormed by FBI agents and other law enforcement fellows. While defending himself from the men trying to seize him, my friend inadvertently hit the nose of a man intent on dragging him outside. At any rate, the draft evader said he did not want to wake up one day and discover he had reached fifty and found himself still in exile. So when he decided to go home, and give himself up, quite a few of us assembled at a little hall in Fort Erie, Canada, to walk across Friendship Bridge to Buffalo, U.S.A. He wept a good deal and not just for himself. One of his escorts was a former Colonel, a Marine pilot who had spent five years as a prisoner of war, and was flown in from California to tell my friend how to get through prison, in case the sentence was severe. When we reached America, and the draft evader surrendered, he was asked, "Do you have anything to declare?" (But we all did—long stories of shame and lies and remorse that sent a thin steam out of our skins for years.)

Afterwards, the ex-Colonel came with me to New York because it had been arranged for him to meet the Vietnamese Ambassador to the United Nations. The Ambassador, who later died in an automobile accident when he was home in Vietnam, had fought the French as a very young man and had been critically wounded; I once asked him *where*—meaning the place— when he opened his shirt to show me the deep winding ruts that scarred him.

There was beer and tea, little cakes and fruit, and the Ambassador who spoke no English, and the former pilot who knew no French, but needed to speak and, in his gentle, simple way, sort his own life out. I never knew why, but the American, who believed the war was much more than a mistake, began to tell the older man a good deal about his life, perhaps hoping to illustrate why he had become a pilot. It was I who tried to interpret. "I was a poor boy," the ex-Marine said. *J'étais un pauvre garçon, vous savez, un orphelin qui etait élevé par une tante pas très jeune. . . .* Raised by an aunt, quite old, on a farm, my parents had died. The Ambassador sat quietly, nothing on his face to guide us. Only once, when the American was explaining how he had broken his back but it had healed in the POW camp and he was glad now he had not had American surgery, which would have made him less mobile, did the older man speak. "They had better food than our own soldiers," he said of the prisoners-of-war. Much else was said by the American, who wanted the Vietnamese to know that when he was flying over the South on bombing missions he could see what a beautiful country it was, he always loved looking down at it. The Ambassador understood but did not flinch or speak sarcastically; he only seemed faintly sad and a little fatigued.

We know that 57,661 Americans died, and we will probably never know what the death toll for the Vietnamese armies—on all sides—or the Vietnamese people really is. And the total of all the Indochinese killed must be in the millions. Many Americans, unable to forgive the Vietnamese for winning the war, hope to rewrite its history or put forth the claim that we only lost because our military was not "permitted" to win. There are those who say the boat people—the Vietnamese who escaped at such peril—are proof that we were right to go on, there are elderly Americans, with wax lining their brains, who tell us it was a "noble cause," and still more who point to the Vietnamese occupation of Cambodia as proof we were on the side of God to have taken on the yellow heathen, quite forgetting that by routing Pol Pot, the former Prime Minister who murdered—is it a million, perhaps twice that?—during his three year reign, the Vietnamese saved the lives of many. Whatever the Vietnamese government does, whatever mistakes they now make, hardly honors us for the damages we inflicted, the unbelievable destruction we inflicted so passionately for so long. I cannot imagine, given Vietnam's wreckage and postwar disorder, that in my lifetime I will see the fruits and flowers grow high and learn that the people have enough food, medicine, and schools. It is a country where not every family owns even a needle and thread.

"What have I learned about Vietnam from the Federal government?" asked Mr. Hasford in *The Los Angeles Times*. "I have learned, for one thing, that politics is a ballet of devils and that politicians, with paper roses falling out of their mouths, cannot conceal the blood from distant wounds that stains their neckties—but they do try, and millions do listen and believe and choose not to see."

It was a man in Bardstown, Kentucky, who once asked the question that endures. His son was killed at a place in Vietnam named Fire Support Base Tomahawk, twenty miles south of Phu Bai, in the province of Quang Tri. The Americans called the region I Corps, pronounced Eye Corps. Four men, who lived in or near Bardstown, died on that one day in June 1969, and a fifth died a week later. All were friends.

"If we had done it, if we had won, what would we have?" the father asked.

EDITOR'S PREFACE

To trace the thirty-five-year evolution of the Vietnam struggle in a single volume is obviously a task of interpretation. Of the thousands of documents available, only a tiny fraction could be included in this compilation. I have tried to select those documents that illuminate the ideologies, assumptions, and strategies of both the United States and revolutionary Vietnam. That choice, of course, reflects my own understanding of the attitudes and issues on each side that underlay the shifting political, military, and diplomatic struggle.

In selecting these documents I have also been guided by a few major considerations. First, I have tried wherever possible to present the internal documents of the two sides, rather than their published declarations, which often have a high propaganda content. Thanks to the Pentagon papers, diplomatic papers in the National Archives and presidential libraries, and other recently declassified documents, there is a vast documentary record of the internal communications of the U.S. government on Vietnam from which to draw.

This record unfortunately does not cover the entire period of the conflict. Few internal U.S. documents are available for the 1969–1975 period, in which policy making was tightly concentrated in the Nixon White House. The Nixon White House papers remain in a legal tangle, and few Freedom of Information requests have been made, so I have had to draw far more from the public record for this period than for earlier phases of the conflict.

Second, I have tried to the extent possible to keep a balance between American and Vietnamese documents. Documentation from the Vietnamese side remains meager, as the government of the Democratic Republic of Vietnam (now the Socialist Republic of Vietnam) has not yet published the Party Central Committee resolutions and other decisions for the period of the conflict. Nevertheless, it has published a number of documents in recent years that add to our understanding of Vietnamese Communist thinking and policies during the first Indochina War. There are also many captured Communist documents that reveal the content of high-level decisions as disseminated within the Party and army. Throughout the book I have made a special effort to present those Communist documents that have previously been unavailable in English.

Third, I have refrained from tracing the policies of other international actors in the conflict, presenting documents from China and the Soviet Union only where they represent a central development in the drama. Although the United States was not directly involved through most of the first Indochina War, I have treated U.S. policy during that war as a prologue to the American war in Vietnam. There is no effort to document in any detail French policy during the first war. Instead, the documents have been selected to show how the United States and revolutionary Vietnam were moving inexorably toward their decade-long military conflict.

Finally, I have been concerned with several broad historical themes, which emerge with particular force from reading these documents. The underlying reasons for the failure of the United States to support Vietnamese independence from France after World War II and the consequences of that failure, the relentless American drive to take up the burden in Vietnam from the faltering French, the eagerness of the Vietnamese Communist leadership to avoid war in South Vietnam in the late 1950s and early 1960s, and the disinterest of American officials in exploring diplomatic alternatives to war—all these are questions that seem to me central to an understanding of why and how the United States and Communist Vietnam went to war.

Of the major themes that are limned by these documents, one of the most significant is that the roots of U.S. support for French imperialism in Vietnam after World War II lay not in the cold war with the Soviet Union but in a set of attitudes and perceived interests regarding Asia and Africa that American officials held in common with the French colonialists. While President Franklin D. Roosevelt's wartime policy was strongly opposed to the restoration of French colonialism in Indochina, the State Department took a distinctly *realpolitik* approach in April 1945. It accepted as fact that colonialism would continue in Southeast Asia and that the United States could not afford to deny France its colonial role in Indochina, since France would be "weakened as a world power" (document 8). As soon as Roosevelt died, the State Department's views became U.S. policy. In this world view, the right of the "leading powers" to maintain hegemony in Asia and Africa was unquestioned. As Secretary of State George C. Marshall's telegram to Paris put it so succinctly, the United States was "in [the] same boat as French, also as British and Dutch" (document 44).

Despite the evidence that the Vietnamese population overwhelmingly supported the Ho Chi Minh government, reflected in the reports of U.S. in Vietnam (document 45), and despite Vietnamese pleas to the Truman Administration for support for Vietnam's independence from France (document 26), American officials were ideologically unprepared to question the legitimacy of French colonialism. While they recognized nationalism as a reality in postwar Asia, they saw it as a dangerous force the West would have to keep in check. Marshall's May 1947 telegram reflects the State Department's nightmare of "anti-Western Pan-Asiatic tendencies" becoming dominant in the region, whether under Communist or non-Communist auspices. The best "safeguard" against that threat, in the State Department view, was a "close association" between the imperialist powers and their former colonies—a formula derived from the U.S. relationship with the Philippines.

Also dear in these documents is the typical colonialist assumption that the Vietnamese were incapable of governing themselves, and that only a steadying European hand would prevent anarchy, followed by the extinction of all freedoms. The first draft memorandum on policy toward postwar Indochina took the position that the Vietnamese, though a "highly civilized people," would require further preparation of unspecified duration before being allowed to govern themselves (document 8). Marshall's 1947 telegram asserted that Vietnam would "for an indefinite period require material and technical assistance and enlightened political guidance," which meant, in effect, French control.

It was not Ho Chi Minh's ties with Moscow that prompted U.S. support for the French and opposition to Vietnamese independence in 1947. American consuls in both Hanoi and Saigon agreed in mid-1947 that there was no inevitability about a Communist-led Vietnam joining a Soviet bloc, and that the United States could have considerable influence in Ho's Vietnam if it supported independence (document 47). But both believed, as the consul in Saigon put it, that "without occidental check or control," Vietnam would degenerate into "chaos" and thus be ripe for Communism and Chinese expansionism.

When the United States extended its global anti-Communist policy to Indochina, it superimposed that policy on earlier attitudes toward the Vietnamese. This overlay of anti-Communism on the existing ideological justifications for postwar Western imperialism in Southeast Asia helps to explain the internal contradictions of U.S. policy toward Vietnam, and its drift away from political reality.

The central contradiction in that policy was that it suggested, on one hand, that the Vietnamese demand for independence had to be accommodated, while insisting, on the other hand, that France had to retain its political-military role. Americans believed these contradictory objectives could be reconciled by yielding "independence" not to those who were fighting against the French but to those who were ready to accept the French presence in order to crush the revolution.

One of the leitmotifs of U.S. policy during the first Indochina War was thus the idea that the transfer of legal sovereignty to a handpicked native regime would fatally weaken the anti-French resistance. This thesis did not question whether Vietnamese nationalists would trust a colonial power that suddenly claimed it was renouncing colonialism but had no intention of abandoning its military occupation of Vietnam. Nor did it wonder if poverty-stricken peasants might prefer a revolutionary regime to one consisting of landowners and *fonctionnaires* with no interest in improving their lives. The chief of the first U.S. economic mission to visit Vietnam pointed out in 1951 that the French-sponsored regime was a "relic of the past as much as French colonialism," (document 70) but his warning was ignored.

The notion that a formal transfer of sovereignty could somehow transform the political-military situation in Vietnam was divorced from the realities of a Vietnam caught up in both nationalism and revolution. But it was an accurate reflection of the consciousness of U.S. policymakers during the early phase of the transition from an imperialist-dominated international system in Southeast Asia to one of fully independent states.

The French performance in turning over "independence" to the government it had so carefully put together was never satisfactory. As a July 1949 policy paper put it, the French had been so "niggardly" in negotiation with ex-Emperor Bao Dai that "they have thus far failed to create an effective puppet regime capable of draining nationalists away from the Viet Minh" (document 53). The State Department authors thus implied that it should have been possible for a puppet government to win over nationalists from the Viet Minh. The French reluctance to yield complete, formal independence to the Bao Dai regime lasted nearly to the end of the war.

But by early 1950, American policy was already fixed on the aim of denying victory to the Viet Minh. The refusal of France to promise that it would eventually turn over all governing powers to its puppet regime did not discourage the State Department from supporting the French war effort. The American desire to remove the taint of colonialism from the venture was more than balanced by a dependence on the French military to maintain the Indochinese front in the global war against Communism. U.S. concern with satisfying the aspiration of Vietnamese nationalists therefore gave way to concern for satisfying the aspirations of France, so as to avert a French withdrawal from the war. Secretary of State Dean Acheson warned in a November 1950 telegram to the Embassy in Britain against political demands on France that would "remove whatever stake for [the French] in Indochina sufficient to assure their continued acceptance of 'primary responsibility' to [the] extent of proceeding with [its] present program" (document 64).

The shift of "primary responsibility" for Indochina from Paris to Washington was not complete until 1955. But there are glimpses in these documents of impulses in U.S. policy that adumbrated a readiness to assume the responsibility for defeating the Communists in Vietnam. As early as July 1949, the State Department's report on U.S. policy regarding Southeast Asia looked toward the day when the French had finally withdrawn from Vietnam and it would be "necessary" for the United States, "working through a screen of anti-Communist Asiatics, to ensure, however long it takes, the triumph of Indochinese nationalism over Red imperialism," (document 53).

Documents from the Vietnamese side also shed new light on how the second Indochina War began. The generally accepted view is that Hanoi gave orders to its cadres in the South in 1959 to launch a "People's War" aimed at toppling Diem. But the series of documents tracing the evolution of Hanoi's policy toward the South from 1956 through 1961, drawn from the collections of captured Communist documents assembled by Douglas Pike and Jeffrey Race, tells a more complicated story.

As shown by a 1956 policy directive to the Party branch in South Vietnam (document 122), the Party leadership had committed itself to a line of peaceful political struggle that ruled out the use of armed force, in conformity with the Soviet line of maintaining peace to strengthen the socialist camp. This line was highly unpopular in South Vietnam, where Diem's repression of resistance fighters and party members was in full swing. Hanoi even broadcast a lecture to Southern cadres on the dangers of a premature uprising (document 123). But even though some Party members began to carry out individual assassinations and organize for armed struggle on their own, the Party's line of peaceful political struggle was reaffirmed as late as the end of 1958 (document 125).

The Fifteenth Plenum of the Central Party Committee in January 1959 decided on a new policy in the South. But it was not, as has been generally believed, to mount a guerrilla war to overthrow the U.S.-supported regime. The Party's journal in the South (document 126) and a letter to local Party officials from the Regional Committee from the South (document 128) both make it clear that the policy authorized armed force only for self-defense, to support political struggle. It specifically ruled out a guerrilla war like the one against the French, asserting instead that Diem would be overthrown ultimately by a political uprising, not by military force.

As late as October 1961, after both sides had escalated the level of violence, the Party Committee in the South reaffirmed that it wanted to "avoid going down the road to total war such as the [anti-French] resistance war" (document 138). Because of the enormous disparity in size and material resources between the United States and Vietnam, and their knowledge of the human cost of the nine years of war against the French, the Vietnamese leaders understood far better than American officials what a war over South Vietnam would mean.

As is evident from reading the internal U.S. documents of the period, high American officials were unaware of Hanoi's efforts to avoid an escalating conflict in South Vietnam. This defensive North Vietnamese posture, which did not rule out a diplomatic agreement with Diem on peaceful coexistence and exchanges between North and South Vietnam (see documents 126 and 138), offered opportunities for political compromise that could have averted all-out war.

The unexplored possibility of compromise does not mean, of course, that the final outcome of the Vietnam conflict would have been different. It does mean, however, that it could have been postponed for some years, and that it would have spared both Vietnam and the United States the long years of carnage. Looking at the shifting political alignments of world politics that began during the war and have continued to the present, it seems evident that the significance of the conflict would have looked far different had the United States decided to try diplomatic compromise rather than pursuing a military solution.

But as these documents suggest, the North Vietnamese desire to avoid confrontation with the United States was not matched by a similar desire on the American side. This was a period when most high U.S. officials regarded Vietnam as a test of will and believed in the ability of the United States to manage the problem of "insurgency" by military means. Indeed, American willingness to become more deeply involved militarily in Vietnam was spurred not only by the shared perception of policy makers that they were involved in a historical show-down of long-term global significance there, but also that victory in Vietnam was important to American morale. William Bundy expressed that feeling explicitly in November 1961, when he commented that a successful suppression of Vietnamese insurgents with an eight-thousand-man U.S. force would be "excellent for domestic will and drive" (document 146).

The documents reflect the strong aversion of U.S. policy makers to the idea of diplomatic compromise. They portray an atmosphere in which the prospects for negotiating peace based on mutual concessions were systematically denigrated, while the ability of the United States to coerce North Vietnam to accept American terms was taken for granted.

Confronted with French President Charles de Gaulle's insistence that a major "diplomatic operation" was the only way out of Vietnam, Under Secretary of State George Ball argued that guerrillas in South Vietnam would never abide by a cease-fire (document 173). Yet at the same time, the United States was passing on to Hanoi a diplomatic message demanding flatly that it end the war in the South or face American air and naval attacks against North Vietnam (document 172). Thus, U.S. policy was based on the contradictory propositions that a cease fire based on a political compromise was impossible to achieve, while Hanoi's complete capitulation on South Vietnam was a realistic aim.

It was also argued that even the suggestion that the United States would negotiate on South Vietnam would result in what Ball called a "general failure of the will to resist" in the South. But if the weakness of the South Vietnamese government constituted a poor basis for a negotiated settlement, how could it constitute a stronger basis for attempting to defeat a revolutionary movement by military force, with or without American troops? The bizarre logic of official thinking about force and diplomacy suggest that powerful emotional impulses were at work as the United States went down the road to war.

Only after the deaths of fifty thousand Americans and more than a million Vietnamese would the United States finally end direct involvement in the war. As these documents show, the United States gradually scaled down its aims in Vietnam, adjusting slowly and painfully to the reality that it could not remain in Vietnam indefinitely and that the revolutionary forces, supported fully by the North, could be held in check temporarily by American military power but not defeated.

The Vietnam conflict was, in the issues it posed, the sacrifices it exacted, and the attention it claimed from the world, one of the great human dramas of modern history. It was a clash of wills between a small, backward peasant society and the world's leading power, in which a technologically advanced military machine pounded away at agricultural economies year after year. Ultimately, the deep divisions it provoked within American society were crucial to the final outcome.

As the conflict recedes into the past, what ought to emerge more clearly in the American consciousness about Vietnam is what a needless war it was. Future generations may understand better than those who lived through it that American leaders failed to see the longer and broader sweep of history, in which the Vietnamese revolution could not be denied its place and need not have been the test of American will or ability to make war. It is my hope that this collection of documents will contribute to that understanding.

The editor wishes to express his thanks to David Elliott, Tran Van Dinh, and Jean Sauvageot for assistance on specific problems of translation, and to William Turley for making available copies of captured Communist documents from his personal collection. Finally, I would like to express my gratitude to Prof. George McT. Kahin of Cornell University for his moral support and intellectual guidance in my own study of the Vietnam conflict.

Gareth Porter

Maps

Indochina

0 25 50 75 100
Statute Miles

0   50   100
Kilometers

Sam'l H. Bryant

South Vietnam
ADMINISTRATIVE DIVISIONS
- –·–·– National boundary
- ··········· Province boundary
- ⊕ National capital
- ▣ Autonomous municipality
- • Province capital

0 25 50 75 100 125 MILES

0 25 50 75 100 125 KILOMETERS

GULF OF TONKIN

Cease fire line, July 22, 1954

QUANG BINH
Dong Hoi
Vinh Linh
QUANG TRI
Quang Tri
Hue
THUA THIEN
Da Nang
Hoi An
QUANG NAM
Tam Ky
QUANG TIN
Quang Ngai
QUANG NGAI
KONTUM
Kontum
BINH DINH
An Nhon
Qui Nhon
Pleiku
PLEIKU
Hau Bon (Cheo Reo)
PHU BON
PHU YEN
Tuy Hoa
DARLAC
Cape Varella
Ban Me Thuot
KHANH HOA
Nha Trang
QUANG DUC
Gia Nghia
TUYEN DUC
Dalat
NINH THUAN
Cam Ranh
An Loc
BINH LONG
PHUOC BINH
LAM DONG
Bao Loc
Phuoc Binh
BINH THUAN
Hoa Da
Phan Rang
TAY NINH
Tay Ninh
BINH DUONG
Phu Cuong
LONG KHANH
BINH TUY
Moc Hoa
HAU NGHIA
GIA DINH
Xuan Loc
Ham Tan
Phan Thiet
KIEN PHONG
Cao Lanh
KIEN TUONG
BIEN HOA
PHUOC TUY
Saigon
LONG AN
Phuoc Le
KIEN GIANG
Rach Gia
CHAU DOC
Chau Phu
AN GIANG
VINH LONG
Can Tho
PHONG DINH
DINH TUONG
Truc Giang (Ben Tre)
GO CONG
KIEN HOA
Phu Vinh
VINH BINH
CHUONG THIEN
Vi Thanh
Khanh Hung
BA XUYEN
BAC LIEU
Quan Long
AN XUYEN
Vinh Loi
CON SON

LAOS

THAILAND

Thakhek
Savannakhet
Saravane
Ubon Ratchathani
Pakse
Attopeu

CAMBODIA

Kompong Preng
Lomphat
Siem Reap
Stung Treng
Battambang
Tonle Sap
Pursat
Kompong Thom
Kratie
Kompong Cham
Phnom Penh
Prey Veng
Kompong Speu
Takeo
Chau Phu
Kampot
Sihanoukville

GULF OF SIAM

SOUTH CHINA SEA

Mekong

104°   106°   108°   110°

17°   16°   14°   12°   10°

am H Bryant

1941

1. LETTER BY HO CHI MINH FROM ABROAD, JUNE 6, 1941

Following the outbreak of World War II, the Indochinese Communist Party (ICP), recognizing that there was a new opportunity for winning independence, emphasized that national liberation was the primary task of the revolution. In May 1941, the Eighth Plenum of the Party Central Committee met and founded the Vietnam Independence League (Viet Nam Doc Lap Dong Minh Hoi, *or* Viet Minh). *After the meeting, Ho Chi Minh's letter to his countrymen was issued by the Party (Ho was then in Southern China) as an inspiration to revolt against both Japanese and French overlords in Vietnam.*

Venerable elders!
Patriotic personalities!
Intellectuals, peasants, workers, traders and soldiers!
Dear fellow-countrymen!

Since France was defeated by Germany, its power has completely collapsed. Nevertheless, with regard to our people, the French rulers have become even more ruthless in carrying out their policy of exploitation, repression and massacre. They bleed us white and carry out a barbarous policy of all-out terrorism and massacre. In the foreign field, bowing their heads and bending their knees, they resign themselves to ceding part of our land to Siam and shamelessly surrendering our country to Japan. As a result our people are writhing under a double yoke of oppression. They serve not only as beasts of burden to the French bandits but also as slaves to the Japanese robbers. Alas! What sin have our people committed to be doomed to such a wretched fate? Plunged into such tragic suffering, are we to await death with folded arms?

No! Certainly not! The twenty-odd million descendants of the Lac and the Hong are resolved not to let themselves be kept in servitude. For nearly eighty years under the French pirates' iron heels we have unceasingly and selflessly struggled for national independence and freedom. The heroism of our predecessors, such as Phan Dinh Phung, Hoang Hoa Tham and Luong Ngoc Quyen and the glorious feats of the insurgents of Thai Nguyen, Yen Bai, Nghe An and Ha Tinh provinces will live forever in our memory. The recent uprisings in the South and at Do Luong and Bac Son testify to the determination of our compatriots to follow the glorious example of their ancestors and to annihilate the enemy. If we were not successful, it was not because the French bandits were strong, but only because the situation was not yet ripe and our people throughout the country were not yet of one mind.

Now, the opportunity has come for our liberation. France itself is unable to help the French colonialists rule over our country. As for the Japanese, on the one hand bogged down in China, on the other hampered by the British and American forces, they certainly cannot use all their strength against us. If our entire people

SOURCE: Ho Chi Minh, *Selected Writings* (1920-1969), (Hanoi: Foreign Languages Publishing House, 1977) pp. 44–46.

are solidly united we can certainly get the better of the best-trained armies of the French and the Japanese.

Fellow-countrymen! Rise up! Let us emulate the dauntless spirit of the Chinese people! Rise up without delay! Let us organize the Association for National Salvation to fight the French and the Japanese!

Dear fellow-countrymen! A few hundred years ago, in the reign of Tran, when our country faced the great danger of invasion by Yuan armies the elders ardently called on their sons and daughters throughout the country to stand up as one man to kill the enemy. Finally they saved their people, and their glorious memory will live forever. Let our elders and patriotic personalities follow the illustrious example set by our forefathers.

Notables, soldiers, workers, peasants, traders, civil servants, youth and women who warmly love your country! At present national liberation stands above everything. Let us unite and overthrow the Japanese, the French and their lackies in order to save our people from their present dire straits.

Dear fellow-countrymen!

National salvation is the common cause of our entire people. Every Vietnamese must take part in it. He who has money will contribute his money, he who has strength will contribute his strength, he who has talent will contribute his talent. For my part I pledge to follow in your steps and devote all my modest abilities to the service of the country and am ready for the supreme sacrifice.

Revolutionary fighters!

The hour has struck! Raise aloft the banner of insurrection and lead the people throughout the country to overthrow the Japanese and the French! The sacred call of the Fatherland is resounding in our ears; the ardent blood of our heroic predecessors is seething in our hearts! The fighting spirit of the people is mounting before our eyes! Let us unite and unify our action to overthrow the Japanese and the French.

The Vietnamese revolution will certainly triumph!
The world revolution will certainly triumph!

2. STUDY DOCUMENT BY SECRETARY GENERAL OF THE INDOCHINESE COMMUNIST PARTY TROUNG CHINH, SEPTEMBER 23–24, 1941 [Extracts]

ICP Secretary General and leading theoretician Troung Chinh wrote the definitive analysis and program for the new situation created by the world war. It

SOURCE: "The Party's New Policy," in Troung Chinh, *Cach Mang Dan Toc Dan Chu Nhan Dan Viet-Nam: Tac Pham Chon Loc* [*The Vietnamese People's National Democratic Revolution: selected works*] (Hanoi: Su That, 1976), 1:189–192, 196–199, 203–204, 206–208, 216–218. [Translation by the editor.] Hereafter cited as *The Vietnamese People's National Democratic Revolution*.

called for the subordination of the agrarian revolution in Vietnam to the task of winning independence and for preparations for the armed uprising to seize political power at the proper moment. The most notable feature of the analysis is the degree to which the Vietnamese leaders saw their strategy for winning independence as being linked with international developments.

How has the situation in the world and in Indochina changed?

For the past two years, the Second World War has passed through the first phase and begun to enter into the second phase. During the first phase, the German fascist imperialists attacked the French and British imperialists, aiming at dividing the world market. Exploiting the time gained by the imperialists attacking one another, the Soviet Union actively prepared for any unexpected development, strengthening their combat forces, striving to protect the first socialist government in the world, and looking for the opportunity to help the world's working class and the oppressed peoples turn the imperialist war into an internal revolutionary war or a liberation war. The Soviet Union had foreseen that the fascists would sooner or later definitely attack the Soviet Union and that the war between imperialists could easily become a war between fascists and the Soviet Union or between aggressive fascism, on one hand, and the Soviet Union and other antifascist forces on the other.

In Indochina, the situation has also changed profoundly. The French colonialists rule Indochina, but France itself has lost its country to Germany, and become a dependency of Germany. The ranks of French imperialism have disintegrated and divided into two factions: the traitorous Pétain faction, which kneels before Hitler, and the deGaulle faction, which follows Britain and occupies part of the French colonies. The French ruling Indochina belong to the Pétain faction. A fascist system has been established in Indochina. The Indochinese people must be slaves for slaves, an extremely painful situation. After the French lost their country, the Japanese imperialists invaded Indochina. The French imperialists in Indochina, kneeling before the Japanese Emperor, offered Indochina to Japan. The Indochinese people suffered the dual yoke of the Japanese-French fascists weighing heavily on their shoulders.

The French not only surrendered to Japan but also carved a tenth of Indochina's territory for the Thai militarists, the lackies of the Japanese. The Indochinese peninsula is like a piece of meat for them to cut up as they please, like merchandise for them to exchange with each other!

The Indochinese people not only must pay taxes to make the fascist militarists fat, but must also pay them in blood so that they can continue the war. The fascist war oppresses the lives of the Indochinese people very heavily. The fate of the Indochinese people hangs by a hair.

The Indochinese economy is declining. Dependent on the French economy, Indochina was disrupted after the French lost their country. The Japanese immediately exploited the opportunity, making themselves the masters of the Indochinese economy.

Our compatriots live in extremely bad conditions. Industry is stagnant, while agriculture is in decay. Many workers are unemployed, and peasants are being impoverished. The business of the national bourgeoisie, small landowners, and small merchants is falling off, because they lack the technical means, raw materials and markets, as well as having to face the competition of the Japanese economy.

War, critical economic shortages, the policy of devaluating the Indochinese piaster, and speculation and hoarding are causing the prices of goods to climb. All the Indochinese people are suffering because of the cost of living and heavy taxes, because of monopolies and subscription payments to the Japanese-French fascists.

In these circumstances, the revolutionary movement of the Vietnamese people is seething. Armed uprisings have taken place in Bac-son, in the South, and in Do-luong. After the uprisings were bloodily suppressed, the movement declined somewhat, but because the situation in the world and in the Far East is changing rapidly it can leap to a high level.

Prepare for the Armed Uprising

One extremely important and urgent mission of the party right now is to prepare for the armed uprising, and create all the conditions necessary to insure that the armed uprising is victorious. The world situation is changing rapidly. The world revolutionary movement is more and more on the rise, in rhythm with the Soviet Union's war of national defense and the resistance war of the Chinese people. Our party must urgently organize the political and military forces of the masses in order to seize the opportune moment in time, and begin the armed uprising.

Therefore we must:

First, establish, develop, and consolidate the national United Front against Japanese-French fascism everywhere.

Second, create a broad, resolute struggle movement in order to save the country and save the people.

Third, prepare armed forces, develop and consolidate self-defense units and guerilla units; establish, develop, and consolidate guerilla base areas. Propagandize soldiers of the imperialists: the red berets, green berets, French soldiers, soldiers from French colonies, and foreign legionnaires.

Fourth, arm the cadres and party members with the theory and practice of general uprising and seizing political power; research the experiences of the general uprisings in Bac Son, the South, and Do-luong; study the experience of the October Revolution and the experience of guerilla warfare in China, etc.

Fifth, consolidate and develop the party in all cities and in the countryside. We must definitely create party bases and national salvation bases in places where workers are concentrated and on strategic communications routes.

Recently due to the severe repression of the imperialists, the mass movement has declined to a degree. But because the Indochinese suffer many layers of heavy oppression and exploitation, they feel more and more that they must struggle to gain political power, so the party and the national salvation organizations not only can easily restore the organization but have conditions to develop rapidly. The world situation will change unexpectedly, creating a favorable opportunity for the

Indochinese revolution. With our own subjective efforts, the conditions for the armed uprising of the Indochinese people will rapidly ripen.

1943

3. MEMORANDUM OF CONVERSATION BETWEEN PRESIDENT FRANKLIN D. ROOSEVELT AND MARSHAL JOSEPH STALIN AT THE TEHERAN CONFERENCE, NOVEMBER 28, 1943 [Extract]

In a discussion of the future of Indochina at the Teheran Conference, Roosevelt agreed with Stalin that the French should not be permitted to reestablish control and raised the possibility of a trusteeship lasting twenty to thirty years.

Marshal Stalin expatiated at length on the French ruling classes and he said, in his opinion, they should not be entitled to share in any of the benefits of the peace, in view of their past record of collaboration with Germany.

The President said that Mr. Churchill was of the opinion that France would be very quickly reconstructed as a strong nation, but he did not personally share this view since he felt that many years of honest labor would be necessary before France would be reestablished. He said the first necessity for the French, not only for the Government, but the people as well, was to become honest citizens.

Marshal Stalin agreed and went on to say that he did not propose to have the Allies shed blood to restore Indo-China, for example, to the old French colonial rule. He said that the recent events in the Lebanon made public service the first step toward the independence of people who had formerly been colonial subjects. He said that in the war against Japan, in his opinion, that in addition to military missions, it was necessary to fight the Japanese in the political sphere as well, particularly in view of the fact that the Japanese had granted the least nominal independence to certain colonial areas. He repeated that France should not get back Indo-China and that the French must pay for their criminal collaboration with Germany.

SOURCE: *United States-Vietnam Relations, 1945–1967: Study Prepared by Department of Defense,* printed for the use of House Committee on Armed Services (Washington, D.C. Government Printing Office, 1971), Book 7, V.B. 1, p. 24. Hereafter cited as *U.S.-Vietnam Relations.*

1944

4. MEMORANDUM BY ROOSEVELT TO SECRETARY OF STATE CORDELL HULL, JANUARY 24, 1944

In response to Secretary Hull's query about his views in Indochina, Roosevelt reaffirmed his support of trusteeship for Indochina, calling the case "perfectly clear."

I saw Halifax last week and told him quite frankly that it was perfectly true that I had, for over a year, expressed the opinion that Indo-China should not go back to France but that it should be administered by an international trusteeship. France has had the country—thirty million inhabitants—for nearly one hundred years, and the people are worse off than they were at the beginning.

As a matter of interest, I am wholeheartedly supported in this view by Generalissimo Chiang Kai-shek and by Marshal Stalin. I see no reason to play in with the British Foreign Office in this matter. The only reason they seem to oppose it is that they fear the effect it would have on their possessions and those of the Dutch. They never liked the idea of trusteeship because it is, in some instances, aimed at future independence. This is true in the case of Indo-China.

Each case must, of course, stand on its own feet, but the case of Indo-China is perfectly clear. France has milked it for one hundred years. The people of Indo-China are entitled to something better than that.

5. SPEECH BY COMRADE VAN (VO NGUYEN GIAP) AT THE CEREMONY FOUNDING THE VIETNAM LIBERATION ARMED PROPAGANDA BRIGADE, DECEMBER 22, 1944

Former history professor Vo Nguyen Giap, as commander of the Armed Propaganda Brigade, chose thirty-four fighters—thirty-one men and three women—from among the best in the Cao-Bac-Lang guerrilla zone, to join the unit. In an inspirational speech at the unit's founding ceremony, Giap linked the fight for independence in Vietnam with both Vietnamese traditions of patriotic struggle and the world-wide national liberation movement that had begun to emerge during the

Source: *U.S.-Vietnam Relations*, Book 7, V.B.1, p. 30.

Source: General Vo Nguyen Giap, *Nhat Lenh, Dien Tu va Thu Dong Vien (1944–1962)* [Orders of the day, speeches, and mobilization letters], (Hanoi: Su That, 1963), pp. 5–10. [Translation by the editor.] Hereafter cited as Giap, *Orders of the Day*.

world war. The "organization" mentioned by Giap was the term then used to refer to the Indochinese Communist Party.

Comrades,

Today, December 22, 1944, in accordance with the order of the Organization, we have gathered in this spot of green jungle and red earth, between Tran Hung Dao canton and Hoang Hoa Tham canton in Cao-Bac-Lang interzone, in order to open the meeting founding the Vietnam Liberation Army Propaganda Unit. You comrades certainly know that the time we are meeting here is precisely the time that the battle between the fascist and democratic fronts is about to bring down the final curtain in Europe: German Nazism has been thoroughly destroyed. And as for East Asia, that battle has also entered a decisive phase with the Japanese attack on South China and the U.S. landing in the Philippines. Then our own Vietnam could very well be drawn into the war, and Japanese fascism will go down to defeat.

You comrades certainly know that the time that we are meeting here is precisely the time that from East to West, the wave of new democratic revolution, the movement of national revolution, is seethingly spreading, drawing in hundreds of millions of people in oppressed countries. From Yugoslavia to China, countless numbers of people are struggling gloriously to win independence, freedom and happiness.

At the same time, in our country, in the context of the most extreme repression and exploitation, the contradictions between France and Japan is growing deeper every day, and the Vietnamese national liberation, going along with the world stream, is about to enter the phase of direct armed struggle. Haven't our masses boiled up everywhere expecting the day of decisive struggle? Hasn't the flag of armed struggle been held high in Thai Nguyen?

In order to deal with the opportune moment and insure the success of the liberation revolution, the Vietnam Independence League has put forward a new task: armed propaganda. And in the Cao-Bac-Lang interzone, it has entrusted that task to us, to the Vietnam Liberation Armed Propaganda Unit, which today we meet to establish in a simple, rustic but solemn setting.

Comrades,

The mission which the Organization has entrusted to us is an important mission, a heavy mission. Politics is more important than military activities, propaganda more important than combat; that mission has the characteristic of being the mission of a transitional period: employ propaganda to appeal to the entire people to stand up, preparing political and military bases for the general uprising later on.

We must realize this clearly, in order to carry it out correctly and strive to the utmost to carry it out. For the Organization to entrust this mission to us is to put great faith and hope in us. We will carry out orders correctly in order to avoid being ungrateful to the Organization.

Thus, from this moment forward, we will advance together on the path of armed struggle. We raise high the spirit of bravery and sacrifice, never afraid in spite of hardship, never giving up in spite of suffering. And although our heads may fall, and blood may flow, we will still not retreat. We are determined to advance in order to complete our mission. So great is the anger of the nation, so many are the tragic atrocities that await a settlement of accounts. We will reveal clearly to the whole people that the way to life is the path of unity to prepare the armed uprising. The Liberation Army will show that it is a military unit of the people, of the country, going in the vanguard on the road to national liberation.

The Liberation army will be a military unit which is very respectful of discipline, absolutely obeying each order; it will be a military unit which is rich in the spirit of unity, sharing the bitter with the sweet. We shall be audacious and we shall be prudent, neither haughty in victory, nor discouraged in defeat. Our experience is still young, but only by doing can we gain experience, and if we do we will naturally gain experience. We have faith in our victory.

Yes, we will certainly be victorious. The Yugoslavian people have won back their fatherland with their bones and blood. The French people and the Chinese people also are exchanging their bones and blood for liberation and freedom. There is no reason why our people cannot do what the Yugoslav people, the French people, and the Chinese people have done. As the nephews of Tran Hung Dao and Hoang Hoa Tham, we will liberate our country and will be worthy of our ancestors. And certainly, it is not a surprise that today, our propaganda unit is founded right between Tran Hung Dao canton and Hoang Hoa Tham canton.

Remember, Comrades: to participate in the first unit of the Liberation Army is an honor for us, and we will show that we are worthy of that honor. You have waited for the hour of armed struggle. That hour has come.

In accordance with the order of the organization, under the red flag with the five-pointed gold star, I declare the Vietnam Liberation Army Propaganda Unit established and command you to advance on the road of armed struggle.

From this moment, you will follow the flag as we advance on the road of blood. We will advance, always advance until the day of the liberation of the entire people.

In order to hold high the spirit of suffering and sacrifice, and in order to demonstrate our desire to recall the glorious examples of national heroes who have gone before and our determination to follow them, I suggest that tonight our unit eat together a meatless meal without vegetables and without salt, and that throughout the night, we divide into platoons to attend to the flag and to recite the oaths of honor, near the guerilla fires that we will set here in the jungle. Tonight is the first guerilla night of our propaganda unit.

Finally, on behalf of the Organization and the entire unit, I would like to express thanks for the zealous support of the masses in the interzone, especially the brothers and sisters who ignored danger to come here to lend comfort to the soldiers and participate in the founding of our unit. We will destroy the invaders and save the country in order to repay the kindness of the masses.

I shout:
Determined to advance on the road of combat!
Long live the spirit of the Vietnam Liberation Army!
Long live the Vietnam Independence Alliance!
Long live independent Vietnam!

1945

6. INSTRUCTIONS OF THE STANDING BUREAU OF THE CENTRAL COMMITTEE OF THE INDOCHINESE COMMUNIST PARTY, MARCH 12, 1945 [Extracts]

When the Japanese launched their armed takeover in Indochina on March 9, 1945, the ICP Central Committee's Standing Bureau held an enlarged meeting to assess the new situation. Three days later, the bureau issued its instructions to the Party membership to concentrate on the Japanese as the "main, immediate and sole enemy" and to be ready to take advantage of the eventual arrival of Allied troops in Indochina. But the document indicated that the Party leadership would be prepared to launch a general insurrection before the arrival of Allied troops under any one of several circumstances.

II. New Conditions Created by the New Situation

1. Conditions not yet ripe for an uprising. The political crisis is acute but the conditions are not yet ripe for an uprising because:

a) French resistance was so weak and the Japanese *coup d'état* was relatively easy; though the division between the French and Japanese ruling cliques has reached its climax, and the French ranks in Indochina are in extreme confusion and are disintegrating; extreme division, confusion and indecision do not yet prevail among the Japanese ruling clique.

b) The "neutral" strata of the population must necessarily go through a period of disillusionment with the disastrous results of the *coup d'état* before they give way to the revolutionary forces and become determined to help the vanguard elements.

c) Except in localities where the natural features are favourable and where we have fighting units, in the country as a whole the vanguard, still engaged in preparations for the uprising, is not yet ready to fight nor resolved to make every sacrifice.

2. Circumstances favouring the rapid maturing of conditions for insurrection. Three circumstances are creating conditions for the rapid maturing of the insurrection and launching of a vast revolutionary movement:

a) The political crisis (the enemy's hands are tied, preventing them from dealing with the revolution)

b) The terrible famine (deep hatred of the people for the aggressors)

c) The war is entering the decisive phase (imminent Allied landing in Indochina to attack the Japanese).

SOURCE: *Breaking Our Chains, Documents of the Vietnamese Revolution of August 1945* (Hanoi: Foreign Languages Publishing House, 1960), pp. 7–17. Hereafter cited as *Breaking Our Chains*.

III. Changes in the Party's Tactics

1. Enemy's ranks and allied forces after the Japanese *coup de force*. The Japanese *coup de force* has brought about the following big changes.

a) French imperialism having lost its ruling power in Indochina is no longer our immediate enemy, although we still have to be on our guard against the manoeuvers of the Gaullist group, who are trying to restore French rule in Indochina.

b) After the *coup de force*, the Japanese fascists have become the main, immediate, and sole enemy of the Indochinese peoples.

c) The French who are conducting a resistance to the Japanese are, for the moment, objectively allies of the Indochinese peoples.

2. Main slogans change and whole tactics change. We must energetically renounce the old slogans and old forms of struggle and pass over to new forms of propaganda, organization and struggle. Particular attention must be paid to the following points:

a) We must replace the slogan "Drive out the Japanese and French!" by "Drive out the Japanese fascists!" We must use the slogan "Establish the revolutionary power of the Indochinese peoples" in the struggle against Japanese power and the puppet government of the pro-Japanese traitors.

b) We must switch the central point of our propaganda over to two themes:

1. The Japanese bandits will not liberate our people; on the contrary, they will increase oppression and exploitation.

2. The Japanese invaders cannot consolidate their power in Indochina and will certainly be annihilated.

3. We must change to forms of propaganda, agitation, organization and struggle which are best suited to the pre-insurrectionary period, intensively mobilizing the masses for the revolutionary front and training them to march boldly forward to general insurrection.

c) A powerful anti-Japanese movement for national salvation will be launched as a pre-requisite of the general insurrection. This movement could include actions ranging from non-cooperation, strikes in workshops and markets, and sabotage, to forms of a higher degree such as armed demonstrations and guerilla activity.

d) We must be ready to switch over to general insurrection when the right conditions are obtained (e.g. on the Japanese capitulation, or when the Allied troops have established a firm position and are advancing firmly on our territory).

*   *   *

VI. To Hold Ourselves in Readiness to Unite Action with the Allied Troops

1. We cannot launch the general insurrection immediately upon the arrival of the Allied forces in Indochina to fight the Japanese. We should not only wait for the Allied forces to get a firm foothold, we must also wait until they are advancing. At the same time, we must wait until the Japanese send forces to the front to intercept the Allied forces, thus relatively exposing their rear, before we launch the general insurrection; only then will the situation be favourable to us.

2. Wherever the Allied forces land, we should mobilize the people to organize demonstrations to welcome them and at the same time arm the masses, set up militia forces to fight the enemy side by side with the Allied forces. In localities where our guerillas are active, they should enter into contact with the Allied forces and together with them fight the Japanese according to a common plan. But in any case, our guerillas must always keep the initiative in the operations.

3. All over the country in the zones behind the enemy's line, we should mobilize the people to go out into the streets to welcome the Allied forces and especially to keep watch upon the least movement of the Japanese and to inform our troops and the Allied forces of any such movements. At the same time we should carry out sabotage where and when this is necessary. On the order for the launching of the general insurrection, everyone should rise up, cut off the enemy's communication lines (except where there are orders to the contrary), storm and seize the enemy's stores and garrisons, and extend guerilla warfare throughout the countryside and to the towns.

7. MEMORANDUM OF CONVERSATION WITH ROOSEVELT BY CHARLES TAUSSIG, ADVISER ON CARIBBEAN AFFAIRS, MARCH 15, 1945 [Extract]

During a conversation with his adviser on Caribbean affairs regarding trusteeship as it related to the United Nations conference, Roosevelt reaffirmed his position that France should not be permitted unconditional control over Indochina once again, although he relented on his previous insistence that Indochina be placed under United Nations trusteeship.

The Peoples of East Asia

The President said he was concerned about the brown people in the East. He said that there are 1,100,000,000 brown people. In many Eastern countries, they are ruled by a handful of whites and they resent it. Our goal must be to help them achieve independence—1,100,000,000 potential enemies are dangerous. He said he included the 450,000,000 Chinese in that. He then added, Churchill doesn't understand this.

The President said he thought we might have some difficulties with France in the matter of colonies. I said that I thought that was quite probable and it was also probable the British would use France as a "stalking horse."

I asked the President if he had changed his ideas on French Indochina as he had expressed them to us at the luncheon with Stanley. He said no he had not changed his ideas; that French Indo-China and New Caledonia should be taken from France and put under a trusteeship. The President hesitated a moment and then said—well if we can get the proper pledge from France to assume for herself the obligations of a trustee, then I would agree to France retaining these colonies with the proviso that independence was the ultimate goal. I asked the President if he

SOURCE: *Foreign Relations of the United States, Diplomatic Papers 1945,* (Washington, D.C.: Government Printing Office, 1969) Vol. I, p. 124.

would settle for self-government. He said no. I asked him if he would settle for dominion status. He said no—it must be independence. He said that is to be the policy and you can quote me in the State Department.

8. DRAFT MEMORANDUM BY G. H. BLAKESLEE, FAR EASTERN DIVISION, DEPARTMENT OF STATE, APRIL, 1945

While President Roosevelt was resisting pressures to assist the French military in positioning itself for the postwar reconquest of Indochina, bureaucrats in the State Department's Far Eastern Division were thinking in very different terms. In an annex to a draft memorandum on Indochina and the use of French military resources in Pacific operations, written prior to Roosevelt's death, the division found Vietnamese unready for self-government and cited antagonism between the Vietnamese and the Khmers and Cambodians as another argument against independence. It recommended against placing any conditions on restoration of French rule or pressure on France to agree to trusteeship, in order to preserve good relations with a friendly state which was expected to join the United States in exercising world power. Although the exercise was apparently cut short by Roosevelt's death, it offers insight into State Department views of the Indochina problem at that time.

United States Policy with Regard to the Future of Indochina

I. Possible Solutions

There are three possible solutions for the problem of the disposition of Indochina. It may be restored to France, with or without conditions; it may be granted independence; or it may be placed under an international trusteeship.

II. Restoration to France

1. Considerations in Favor of Restoration

a. The Global Situation

If France is to be denied her former position in Indochina she will be to that extent weakened as a world power. It will probably be necessary for the United States to take the lead in any move by which France will be denied her former position in Indochina. If the United States, especially in view of its many unequivocal statements favoring the restoration of the French overseas territories, is the spearhead for partial dismemberment of the French Empire, French resentment will be such as to impose a very serious strain upon our relations and thus tend to defeat basic elements underlying our policy towards France. A disgruntled, psychologically sick and sovereign-conscious France will not augur well for postwar collaboration in Europe and in the world as a whole.

If it is to be the active policy of the United States to seek and insist upon the adoption of measures by which the peoples of dependent areas

SOURCE: 851G.00/4-545, State Department Central Files, National Archives.

are to be lifted from their present social condition and are to be given in time opportunity for full self-determination, we should consider whether that aim can best be accomplished in the case of Indochina through cooperation with the French or through denial of any role to France, and operate through an international trusteeship. In reaching that decision we must determine whether it is of more interest to us and the world as a whole to have a strong, friendly, cooperative France, or have a resentful France plus having on our hands a social and administrative problem of the first magnitude.

b. Commitments of the United States Government

"The policy of the Government of the United States has been based upon the maintenance of the integrity of France and of the French Empire and of the eventual restoration of the complete independence of all French territories." (Department of State Press Release of March 2, 1942 [no. 85] relative to situation in New Caledonia.)

"The Government of the United States recognizes the sovereign jurisdiction of the people of France over French possessions overseas. The Government of the United States fervently hopes that it may see the reestablishment of the independence of France and of the integrity of French territory." (Acting Secretary of State in note to the French Ambassador at Washington, April 13, 1942 with respect to the establishment of a consular post at Brazzaville.)

"It is thoroughly understood that French sovereignty will be reestablished as soon as possible throughout all the territory, metropolitan and colonial, over which flew the French flag in 1939." (Mr. Murphy, the Personal Representative of the President, in an unpublished letter of November 2, 1942 to General Giraud.)

"It has been agreed by all French elements concerned and the United States military authorities that French forces will aid and support the forces of the United States and their allies to expel from the soil of Africa the common enemy, to liberate France and restore integrally the French Empire." (Preamble of unpublished Clark-Darlan Agreement of November 22, 1942.)

2. Restoration Subject to Conditions Accepted by Other Colonial Powers in the Pacific and Far East

Upon the liberation of Indochina and the termination of military operations in that area under the condition that the French Government accepts the following minimum commitments, which it is assumed will also be accepted by the other colonial powers in the Pacific and the Far East: (1) subscription to a colonial charter; (2) membership on behalf of Indochina in a regional commission; and (3) the submission of annual reports on the progress made in Indochina during the year in education, government, and social and economic conditions.

3. Restoration Subject to Additional Conditions

The considerations which favor placing additional conditions on France are: (1) French administration of Indochina has in general been less satisfactory and less considerate of the interests of the native peoples than have been the administrations of the other leading colonial powers in the Pacific and the Far East, and (2) the French authorities cooperated with the Japanese and permitted them to enter and to effect military control of the colony.

To remedy the more outstanding weaknesses of the French administration of Indochina the United Nations in the Far Eastern area might insist that France be permitted to return to Indochina only after giving commitments to carry out the following reforms:

1. Tariff autonomy for Indochina.

2. The establishment and development of local and central representative institutions; the extension of the franchise as rapidly as possible.

3. Access on equal terms to all occupations and professions by Indo-Chinese; adequate educational and training facilities for all elements of the population.

4. Abolition of compulsory labor and effective supervision of labor contracts.

5. The development of local industries and a more balanced economy.

The chief considerations against placing additional conditions on France are that such conditions would constitute a discrimination against France and, in view of the national sensitiveness of the French and their devotion to their colonial empire, would probably cause long-continued resentment against the United States, which might embarrass this Government in achieving all of the objectives of its global policies.

4. Restoration Subject to No Conditions

The French policy of commercial exclusiveness, the failure to develop representative institutions, the small use made of Indochinese in administration, and the failure of the French Indochinese Administration to resist Japanese demands, make unconditional restoration of French sovereignty over this strategic corner of Asia highly undesirable.

A possible consideration in favor of the unconditional restoration of French administration is that if the British and the Dutch should be unwilling to make any commitments in regard to the administration of their dependencies in the Pacific and the Far East, it might appear impolitic to make discriminatory demands on France, in view of the possible unfortunate effects of such demands on United States global policies.

III. Independence for Indochina

Over 17 million of the 24 million inhabitants of Indochina are Annamites. The Annamites are one of the most highly civilized peoples in southeastern Asia, and it would seem reasonable to suppose that, after a preparatory period, they would prove to be politically not less capable than the Thai, who have successfully governed Thailand for centuries, or than the Burmese who, before the war, had achieved the substance of self-government though not the title.

A nationalist movement of some proportions exists in Indochina. Although the French never favored the growth of an indigenous nationalism, the liberal principles of French political thought inevitably produced a desire for political liberty among educated native people. More particularly, the development of native political consciousness may be traced to grievances against the French rulers. Among these might be listed the contrast between the native standard of living and that of resident Europeans, discrimination in wage levels and in social and professional opportunities, the high cost of living which largely nullified the economic advantages produced by the French regime, in equality before the law, alleged abuses of its privileges by the Roman Catholic Church, unfilled promises of political liberties beyond the limited advisory councils in each colony, failure to train natives for progressive participation in administration, and the thwarted ambitions of the native intelligentsia.

However, a preparatory period for independence is necessary. At the present, the elements necessary for the early establishment of an independent Indochina are lacking. The French policy of permitting only restricted native participation in government has allowed no opportunity for the development of a trained and experienced body of natives capable of assuming full responsibility for the direction of governmental affairs. The nationalist movement has been weakened by factional strife and by lack of solid organization, and has left the great mass of the people unaffected. The antagonism of the Annamites toward the Khmers and Laotians and toward the resident Chinese also limits the possibilities of early native unity.

IV. An International Trusteeship

There are two considerations which might appear to favor an international trusteeship for Indochina: the interests of the natives and the interests of the United States.

The failure of France to provide adequately for the welfare of the native population might justify placing Indochina under the control of an international administration, which would follow certain prescribed standards designed to develop the basis for eventual independence and for a rising standard of living among the native population.

French administration of Indochina was not directed toward developing colonial self-government, but rather toward progressive integration of the dependency into a closely knit empire dominated by the mother country. French policy, therefore, deliberately restricted the opportunity for native participation in government. The subordinated officials in Cochin-China included a much smaller proportion of natives than would be found in a British or Dutch colony. French economic policy toward Indochina was formulated primarily in terms of the interests of the mother country, not of the colony.

The interests of the United States are opposed to imperialism and favor the progressive development, economically and politically, of dependent peoples until they are prepared for and are granted independence. The peoples in the Far East have a vigorous and emotional opposition to western imperialism and this opposition appears to have increased in strength as a result of Japanese promises and propaganda during the present war. It is to the interest of the United States to dissociate itself in every feasible way from the imperialism of the European powers in the Far East. If the United States should participate in the restoration of France in Indochina, with no conditions or provisions looking to the betterment of native conditions and the development of the people toward independence, it might well weaken the traditional confidence of Eastern peoples in the United States. If Indochina were a problem by itself the solution would appear to be the termination of French rule of an international trusteeship.

A trusteeship might be created by the projected international organization to function within the framework of the plan for international trusteeships which has been approved by the Department. Or, two or more of the leading powers might set up a trusteeship. The trustee powers would necessarily assume, in the name of the people concerned, all rights and responsibilities of sovereignty including security for the peoples, conduct of foreign relations, financial solvency of the administration, and responsibility and power for all acts of government—executive, legislative and judicial. A detailed plan for such a trusteeship has been drafted by an interdivisional committee of the Department, entitled "Draft Outline of an International Trusteeship Government for Indochina" (CAC-114 Preliminary).

The perplexing fact, however, is that France is not the only imperialist power in the Far East. Great Britain and the Netherlands also claim the return of colonies which are now under Japanese military occupation. Each of the colonial powers should give commitments to adopt measures of colonial administration, with some degree of international responsibility, which will further the development of their dependent peoples, along the path toward autonomy or independence.

The problem for the United States is whether it will be advisable, especially in view of the effect on United States global policies, to make demands on France in regard to Indochina when similar demands are not made on Great Britain and the Netherlands in regard to their Pacific and Far Eastern colonies.

9. RESOLUTIONS OF THE REVOLUTIONARY MILITARY CONFERENCE OF NORTH VIETNAM, APRIL 20, 1945 [Extracts]

To step up preparations for the general insurrection, the Standing Bureau of the Central Committee convened a Revolutionary Military Conference of North Vietnam in Bac Giang Province from April 15 to 20, under Truong Chinh's chairmanship. A Revolutionary Military Committee of North Vietnam was nominated which became the military high command for the entire country. The Conference anticipated an Allied landing in Indochina before the Japanese surrender and called for the general insurrection to take place once the Japanese had committed their troops to fighting the Allies. The Vietnamese plan did not take into account the American strategy of ending the war through the bombing of Japan's home islands, including the use of the atomic bomb.

IV. Eventual Allied Landing in Indochina

There are still people who hold that the Allies should take the war directly to the territory of Japan and that once the metropolis is defeated, the Japanese troops in the colonies would capitulate. The Conference estimates that sooner or later Allied troops will enter Indochina. First, because of the fairly important strategic position of Indochina and because the Japanese forces stationed here are relatively big. Second, because of the conflict of interests in Indochina between the French and British on the one hand and the Americans and Chinese on the other. This rivalry which came to light at the Hot Springs Conference, will prompt them to rush into Indochina to defend their respective interests. Thus, toward these two groups of allies, Chinese and Americans on the one hand and British and Gaullist French on the other, who all want to have their share of interests in our country, our attitude must be as follows:

In the diplomatic field:
a) To profit by the antagonism between the Chinese and Americans and the

SOURCE: *Breaking Our Chains*, pp. 23–34.

British and Gaullist French to obtain aid from the outside, sign agreements with the Allies and bring them to recognize our national independence.

b) In addition, our diplomats must struggle for Viet Nam to be represented at the international peace conferences.

c) To bring before world opinion documents relating to the atrocities and reactionary deeds of the French colonialists, and the Viet Minh policy of coopera- tion with the French who struggled actively against the Japanese.

At home:

a) Actively to prepare our forces; not to rely on others.

b) To develop guerilla units immediately and on a large scale and keep them ready to cooperate with the Allies.

According to our estimates, the Allied offensive could begin at various points. In the North: the border provinces of Cao Bang, Lang Son and Ha Giang. In the Eastern and Southern coastal areas: the Gulf of Tonkin, Cam Ranh Bay, and Saigon. In the West: Upper Laos and Dien Bien Phu (coming from Burma).

Having foreseen this, how should we receive the Allied forces and cooperate with them? At points where the landing takes place, we should mobilize the people to welcome them and appoint delegates to come into contact with them. On the other hand, local troops should be mobilized for the destruction of the communica- tion and supply lines of the Japanese and, together with the Allied forces, fight the common enemy. During this time we should strive to occupy the key positions and keep the initiative. But this does not mean that immediately after the Allied landing we should launch the general insurrection. On the contrary, we should wait until the Japanese have thrown in all their forces to ward off the Allied attack, until their rear lines are in disorder, before we launch the general insurrection. There is one point we must bear in mind: in case of abuses and extortions on the part of the landing troops (for example on the part of Chinese troops commanded by corrupt officers) we should use diplomacy to avoid all incidents likely to harm the common struggle against the Japanese.

10. DRAFT MEMORANDUM FOR THE PRESIDENT, DIVISION OF EUROPEAN AFFAIRS, APRIL 20, 1945

Following Roosevelt's death on April 12, 1945, the State Department began a review of policy toward Indochina. The process was initiated by the Division of European Affairs, which recommended that the United States not oppose restora- tion of Indochina to France.

Subject: Suggested Reexamination of American Policy with Respect to Indo-China

General Observations

1. The Japanese aggression against the French in Indo-China last month has brought about a marked increase in the number of proposals advanced by the French for the use of French forces and resources in the Pacific.

SOURCE: *U.S.-Vietnam Relations*, Book 8, V.B.2, pp. 6–8.

2. The consequences of these military developments make it clear that our last policy, which held that the disposition of Indo-China was a matter for postwar determination and that the United States should not become involved in military effort for its liberation, is in urgent need for reexamination and clarification. This is particularly so in order that American military and naval authorities may have guidance to enable them to take appropriate action with respect to the French proposals referred to above.

3. The United States Government has publicly taken the position that it recognizes the sovereign jurisdiction of France over French possessions overseas when those possessions are resisting the enemy and had expressed the hope that it will see the reestablishment of the integrity of French territory. In spite of this general assurance, the negative policy so far pursued by this Government with respect to Indo-China has aroused French suspicions concerning our intentions with respect to the future of that territory. This has had and continues to have a harmful effect on American relations with the French Government and people.

4. On April 3, 1945, the Secretary of State with the approval of the President issued a statement of which the following excerpt is pertinent to the present problem:.

> "As to territorial trusteeship, it appeared desirable that the Governments represented at Yalta, in consultation with the Chinese Government and the French Provisional Government, should endeavor to formulate proposals for submission to the San Francisco Conference for a trusteeship structure as a part of the general organization. This trusteeship structure, it was felt, should be defined to permit the placing under it of the territories taken from the enemy in this war, as might be agreed upon at a later date, *and also such other territories as might voluntarily be placed under trusteeship.*"

5. General de Gaulle and his Government have made it abundantly clear that they expect a proposed Indo-Chinese federation to function within the framework of the "French Union." There is consequently not the slightest possibility at the present time or in the foreseeable future that France will volunteer to place Indo-China under an international trusteeship, or will consent to any program of international accountability which is not applied to the colonial possessions of other powers. If an effort were made to exert pressure on the French Government, such action would have to be taken by the United States alone for France could rely upon the support of other colonial powers, notably Great Britain and the Netherlands. Such action would likewise run counter to the established American policy of aiding France to regain her strength in order that she may be better fitted to share responsibility in maintaining the peace of Europe and the world.

Recommendations

In the light of the above considerations, the following recommendations, which have been communicated to the War and Navy Departments, are submitted for your approval.

1. The Government of the United States should neither oppose the restoration of Indo-China to France, with or without a program of international accountability, nor take any action toward French overseas possessions which it is not

prepared to take or suggest with regard to the colonial possessions of our other Allies.

2. The Government of the United States should continue to exert its influence with the French in the direction of having them effect a liberalization of their past policy of limited opportunities for native participation in government and administration, as well as a liberalization of restrictive French economic policies formerly pursued in Indo-China.

3. The French Provisional Government should be informed confidentially that, owing to the need of concentrating all our resources in the Pacific on operations already planned, large-scale military operations aimed directly at the liberation of Indo-China cannot be contemplated at this time.

4. French offers of military and naval assistance in the Pacific should be considered on their merits as bearing upon the objective of defeating Japan, as in the case of British and Dutch proposals. The fact that acceptance of a specific proposal might serve to strengthen French claims for the restoration of Indo-China to France should not be regarded as grounds for rejection. On the contrary, acceptance of French proposals for military assistance in the defeat of Japan should be regarded as desirable in principle, subject always to military requirements in the theater of operations.

5. While avoiding specific commitments with regard to the amount of character of any assistance which the United States may give to the French resistance forces in Indo-China, this Government should continue to afford all possible assistance provided it does not interfere with the requirements of other planned operations.

6. In addition to the aid which we are able to bring from the China theater of operations to the French forces resisting the Japanese in Indo-China, the United States should oppose no obstacle to the implementation of proposals looking toward the despatch of assistance to those forces from the southeast Asia theater of operations, provided such assistance does not constitute a diversion of resources which the Combined Chiefs of Staff consider are needed elsewhere.

11. DRAFT MEMORANDUM FOR THE PRESIDENT, DIVISION OF FAR EAST AFFAIRS, APRIL 21, 1945

The State Department's Division of Far Eastern Affairs, while agreeing with the basic recommendation of the European Division, urged that the United States seek assurances from France that it would extend at least a measure of self-government to Indochina–though not necessarily complete independence.

Subject: American Policy with Respect to Indochina

General Observations

1. The Japanese aggression against the French in Indochina last month has brought about a marked increase in the number of proposals advanced by the French for the use of French forces and resources in the Pacific.

SOURCE: *U.S.-Vietnam Relations*, Book 8, V.B.2. pp. 9–17.

2. These proposals and recent military developments make it essential that the United States reach a definitive determination regarding its policy towards Indochina rather than, as heretofore considered, the disposition of Indochina a matter of postwar determination.

3. The joint State-War-Navy authorities have reached the decision that all American military efforts must be directed entirely to the major issue of defeating Japan in its homeland and that, for military reasons, American troops should not be used or equipment needed in American operations be utilized for the liberation of Indochina.

4. It is established American policy to aid France to regain her strength in order that she may be better fitted to share responsibility in maintaining the peace of Europe—where her chief interests lie—and of the world. However, in pursuing this policy, the United States must not jeopardize its own increasingly important interests in Southeast Asia.

5. The United States Government has publicly taken the position that it recognizes the sovereign jurisdiction of France over French possessions overseas when those possessions are resisting the enemy, and has expressed the hope that it will see the reestablishment of the integrity of French territory.

6. Until the last few weeks the French administration of Indochina has collaborated with the Japanese in marked distinction to the administrations of colonial areas belonging to our other Allies.

7. President Roosevelt recognized the future increasing importance to the United States of Southeast Asia. He saw the necessity of aiding the 150,000,000 people there to achieve improved social, economic and political standards.

He realized that dynamic forces leading toward self-government are growing in Asia; that the United States—as a great democracy—cannot and must not try to retard this development but rather act in harmony with it; and that social, economic or political instability in the area may threaten the peace and stability of the Far East and indeed the world.

8. As his solution of this problem, as it relates to Indochina, President Roosevelt long favored placing Indochina under a trusteeship. However, on April 3, 1945, the Secretary of State with the approval of the President issued a statement relative to the plans approved at Yalta which would indicate that Indochina could come under the trusteeship structure only by voluntary action of the French. It is abundantly clear that there is no possibility at the present time or in the foreseeable future that France will volunteer to place Indochina under trusteeship, or consent to any program of international accountability which is not applied to the colonial possessions of other powers. If an effort were made to exert pressure on the French Government, such action would have to be taken by the United States alone for France could rely upon the support of other colonial powers, notably Great Britain and the Netherlands.

9. The prewar French administration in Indochina was the least satisfactory colonial administration in Asia, both as regards the development and interests of the native peoples and as regards economic relations with other countries. Among the Annamites there is increasing opposition to French rule. The Chinese are giving active support to the independence movement. France will probably encounter serious difficulty in reimposing French control in Indochina.

10. If really liberal policies towards Indochina are not adopted by the French—

policies which recognize the paramount interest of the native peoples and guarantee within the foreseeable future a genuine opportunity for true, autonomous self-government—there will be substantial bloodshed and unrest for many years, threatening the economic and social progress and the peace and stability of Southeast Asia.

11. On several occasions in the past few years, French authorities have issued policy statements on the future of Indochina. These show a growing trend toward greater autonomy for the French administration of Indochina, but even the recent statement of March 24 is vague and, when examined with care, indicates little intention of permitting genuine self-rule for the Indochinese. The change in French attitude towards Indochina is believed to have been occasioned by clearer realization of the anti-French sentiment among the Annamites and a belief that American approval of French restoration can be won only by a liberalization of its policies towards Indochina.

12. China is exercised at the economic stranglehold which France formerly exercised through control of the Yunan Railroad and the port of Haiphong, and is particularly perturbed at the danger to its southwest flank first made visible by the surrender of Indochina to the Japanese.

13. It is stated American policy that the cession of territory by Indochina to Thailand in 1941 is not recognized and that this territory must be returned to Indochina. This territory, however, had in earlier years been wrested by the French from Thailand and its inhabitants are culturally akin to the Thai. Similarly, parts of Laos are Thai in character. Whatever the legalistic background may be, the entire border region between Indochina and Thailand will be a source of potential conflict unless a fair and appropriate frontier is determined by an impartial international commission. The Thai Government will accept any frontier so determined.

14. It will be an American victory over Japan which will make possible the liberation of Indochina. We are fighting to assure peace and stability in the Far East, and will, in fact, bear the major responsibility for its maintenance after the war. Encouragement of and assistance to the peoples of Southeast Asia in developing autonomous, democratic self-rule in close, willing association with major Western powers would not only be in harmony with political trends in that area, but would appear to be the one practical solution which will assure peace and stability in the Far East. If this policy is not followed, the millions who live in that area may well embrace ideologies contrary to our own—or ultimately develop a pan-Asiatic movement against the Western world. It is not unreasonable, therefore, for the United States to insist that the French give adequate assurances as to the implementing of policies in Indochina which we consider essential to assure peace and stability in the Far East.

Recommendations

In the light of the above considerations, the following recommendations, which have been communicated to the War and Navy Departments for their comment, are submitted for your approval:

1. The Government of the United States should not seek a trusteeship, international or French, over Indochina, unless it seeks similar trusteeship by the British and Dutch over Burma and the Netherlands Indies, nor should the United States

seek international accountability which is not sought for the adjacent colonial areas. It should not oppose restoration of Indochina to France, provided the French give adequate assurances that they will meet the following conditions:

  a. Development of a democratic national or federal government to be run for and increasingly by the Indochinese themselves with no special privileges for French or other persons who are not inhabitants and citizens of Indochina so that within the forseeable future Indochina may be fully self-governing and autonomous, except in matters of imperial concern in which Indochina should be a partner in the French Union.

  b. Maintenance of a policy of non-discriminatory treatment and of complete economic and commercial equality.

  c. Establishment of Haiphong as a free port with tax-free transit facilities between Haiphong and China.

  d. Acceptance of a frontier between Indochina and Thailand, to be determined by an impartial international commission.

  e. Acceptance of such international security arrangements, including American or international bases, as may be determined to be necessary for international security, including protection of China's southwestern flank.

2. For the present, the policy of the United States with respect to the postwar status of Indochina should not be communicated to the Provincial French Government.

3. The French Provisional Government should be informed, confidentially, that owing to the need of concentrating all our resources in the Pacific on operations already planned, American military operations aimed directly at the liberation of Indochina cannot be contemplated until after the defeat of Japan, nor will it be possible to make any commitments for the furnishing of military equipment or supplies to resistance groups in Indochina or to French military forces in the Asiatic theatres of war.

4. French officers of military and naval assistance in the Pacific should be accepted or rejected by the military authorities solely on their military merits as bearing upon the defeat of Japan, as in the case of British and Dutch proposals.

12. TELEGRAM FROM ACTING SECRETARY OF STATE JOSEPH GREW TO AMBASSADOR JEFFERSON CAFFERY IN FRANCE, MAY 6, 1945

Within days of Roosevelt's death, Secretary of State Byrnes, at the United Nations Conference on International Organization in San Francisco, discussed U.S. policy toward Indochina with French Minister for Foreign Affairs Georges Bidault. He assured Bidault that the United States did not question French sovereignty, thus reversing Roosevelt's policy of trusteeship for Indochina.

The subject of Indo-China came up in a recent conversation I had with Bidault and Bonnet. The latter remarked that although the French Government interprets

SOURCE: *Foreign Relations, 1945,* Vol. VI, p. 307.

Mr. Welles' statement of 1942 concerning the restoration of French sovereignty over the French Empire as including Indo-China, the press continues to imply that a special status will be reserved for this colonial area. It was made quite clear to Bidault that the record is entirely innocent of any official statement of this government questioning, even by implication, French sovereignty over Indo-China. Certain elements of American public opinion, however, condemned French governmental policies and practices in Indo-China. Bidault seemed relieved and has no doubt cabled Paris that he received renewed assurances of our recognition of French sovereignty over that area.

13. TELEGRAM FROM ACTING SECRETARY GREW TO AMBASSADOR PATRICK J. HURLEY IN CHUNGKING, JUNE 7, 1945 [Extract]

Responding to Ambassador Hurley's need for policy guidance on Indochina, the acting secretary, speaking for President Truman, reported that the United States would not insist on trusteeship for Indochina except with the consent of the French government, even though it would seek assurances from France on "increasing measures of self-government" for Indochina.

The President thanks you for your considered telegram in regard to the problems presented by the reestablishment of French control in Indochina and the British desire to reoccupy Hongkong and fully appreciates the difficulties in which you and General Wedemeyer may be placed on account of the lack of specific directives in respect to both of these problems which have been under careful study both here and in connection with the discussions at San Francisco.

I have also received your message No. 1548 of June 6 and regret that there has been delay in replying to your earlier one owing to the study which has been required of these matters in connection with present developments at the Conference. The President has asked me to say that there has been no basic change in the policy in respect to these two questions and that the present position is as follows:

The President assumes that you are familiar with the statement made by the Secretary of State on April 3, 1945 with the approval of President Roosevelt in which Mr. Stettinius declared that as a result of the Yalta discussions the "trusteeship structure, it was felt, should be defined to permit the placing under it of such of the territories taken from the enemy in this war, as might be agreed upon at a later date, and also such other territories as might voluntarily be placed under trusteeship". The position thus publicly announced has been confirmed by the conversations which are now taking place in San Francisco in regard to trusteeships. Throughout these discussions the American delegation has insisted upon the necessity of providing for a progressive measure of self-government for all dependent peoples looking toward their eventual independence or incorporation in some form of federation, according to circumstances and the ability of the peoples to assume

SOURCE: *U.S.-Vietnam Relations*, Book 8, V.B.2. pp. 30–32.

those responsibilities. Such decisions would preclude the establishment of a trusteeship in Indochina except with the consent of the French Government. The latter seems unlikely. Nevertheless, it is the President's intention at some appropriate time to ask that the French Government give some positive indication of its intentions in regard to the establishment of civil liberties and increasing measures of self-government in Indochina before formulating further declarations of policy in this respect.

14. PAPER ON POSTWAR POLICY TOWARD ASIA AND THE PACIFIC PREPARED IN THE DEPARTMENT OF STATE, JUNE 22, 1945 [Extract]

The State Department responded to Secretary of War Henry L. Stimson's request with a paper on policy in Asia and the Pacific that foreshadowed the postwar problem of reconciling the general American inclination to give an "increased measure of self-government" to former colonial peoples and the desire for good relations with France. The paper noted the likelihood of a violent struggle for independence by Vietnamese nationalists, led by the Viet Minh, but again concluded that the United States recognized French sovereignty over Indochina.

An Estimate of Conditions in Asia and the Pacific at the Close of the War in the Far East and the Objectives and Policies of the United States

I. Introduction

Aside from the traditional American belief in the right of all peoples to independence, the largest possible measure of political freedom for the countries of Asia consistent with their ability to assume the responsibility thereof is probably necessary in order to achieve the chief objective of the United States in the Far East and the Pacific: continuing peace and security.

Another condition on which peace and security depend is cooperation among the peace-minded states of the world. One of the foremost policies of the United States is to maintain the unity of purpose and action of all the United Nations, especially of the leading powers. Two of these leading powers are Great Britain and France, each of which has dependencies in the Far East in which there is an insistent demand for a greater measure of self-government than the parent states have yet been willing to grant.

A problem for the United States is to harmonize, so far as possible, its policies in regard to the two objectives: increased political freedom for the Far East and the maintenance of the unity of the leading United Nations in meeting this problem. The United States Government may properly continue to state the political principle which it has frequently announced, that dependent peoples should be given the opportunity, if necessary after an adequate period of preparation, to achieve an

SOURCE: *Foreign Relations,* 1945, Vol. VI, pp. 557–558, 567–568.

increased measure of self-government, but it should avoid any course of action which would seriously impair the unity of the major United Nations.

The United States, also, may utilize either the force of its example or its influence or both. Its treatment of the Philippines has earned a rich reward for this country in the attitude and conduct of both the Filipinos and the nationals of other Far Eastern states. The American Government influenced the British Government to take parallel action with it in the renunciation of extraterritoriality and other exceptional rights in China.

The solution which would best harmonize these two policies of the United States would be a Far East progressively developing into a group of self-governing states—independent or with Dominion status—which would cooperate with each other and with the Western powers on a basis of mutual self-respect and friendship. The interests of the United States and of its European Allies require that the Far East be removed as a source of colonial rivalry and conflict, not only between the Great Powers, but between the Great Powers and the peoples of Asia.

*   *   *

V. French Indochina

A. Estimate of Conditions at the End of the War

1. Political

At the end of the war, political conditions in Indochina, and especially in the north, will probably be particularly unstable. The Indochinese independence groups, which may have been working against the Japanese, will quite possibly oppose the restoration of French control. Independence sentiment in the area is believed to be increasingly strong. The Indochinese Independence League, representing some ten different native political groups, is thought to carry substantial influence with between one-quarter and one-half million persons. The serious 1930 insurrection, in which over 100,000 peasants actively participated, and similar insurrections which took place in the fall of 1940, indicate that the supporters of independence are neither apathetic nor supine and are willing to fight. It is believed that the French will encounter serious difficulty in overcoming this opposition and in re-establishing French control. What effect the Japanese declarations of independence for Annam, Cambodia, and Luang Prabang will have in the period immediately following the war cannot be estimated at this time, but clearly these declarations will make the French problem more difficult.

The French government recognizes that it will have very serious difficulties in reestablishing and maintaining its control in Indochina, and its several statements regarding the future of that country show an increasing trend toward autonomy for the French administration. Even the latest statement, however, shows little intention to give the Indochinese self-government. An increased measure of self-government would seem essential if the Indochinese are to be reconciled to continued French control.

Economically, Indochina has so far suffered least of all the countries involved in the war in the Far East. Bombing and fighting before the close of the war will probably, however, have resulted in the destruction of some of its railway system, key bridges, harbor installations, and the more important industrial and power plants. This will probably intensify already existing food shortages in the north and lack of consumer goods throughout the area.

Pre-war French policies involved economic exploitation of the colony for

France. Indochina had to buy dear in the high, protected market of France and sell cheap in the unprotected markets of other nations. The French realize that this economic policy, which was very detrimental to Indochina, must be changed. They have pledged tariff autonomy and equality of tariff rates for other countries. There is no indication, however, that the French intend to pursue an open-door economic policy.

B. International Relations

French policy toward Indochina will be dominated by the desire to reestablish control in order to reassert her prestige in the world as a great power. This purpose will be augmented by the potent influence of the Banque de l'Indochine and other economic interests. Many French appear to recognize that it may be necessary for them to make further concessions to Indochinese self-government and autonomy primarily to assure native support but also to avoid unfriendly United States opinion. Chief French reliance, however, will continue to be placed upon the United Kingdom, which is almost as anxious as the French to see that no pre-war colonial power suffers diminution of power or prestige. Friction between France and China over Indochina will probably continue. The Chinese government, at least tacitly, is supporting the Independence League and is thought by the French, despite the Generalissimo's disclaimer of territorial ambitions, to desire to dominate, if not annex, northern Indochina. French economic policies interfered with all nations trading with China through its access to the sea at Haiphong. China particularly will look for a complete reversal of French policy in this respect.

The Thai consider the territory acquired from Indochina in 1941 as theirs by legal and historic right, but they have indicated they will accept any border determined by an Anglo-American commission. The French consider the territory theirs and there will doubtless be border conflict unless a fair settlement is reached which eliminates causes for serious discontent.

C. United States Policy

The United States recognizes French sovereignty over Indochina. It is, however, the general policy of the United States to favor a policy which would allow colonial peoples an opportunity to prepare themselves for increased participation in their own government with eventual self-government as the goal.

15. TELEGRAM FROM PRESIDENT HARRY TRUMAN FOR GENERALISSIMO CHIANG KAI-SHEK, TRANSMITTED VIA AMBASSADOR HURLEY, AUGUST 1, 1945

At the Potsdam Conference, President Truman and British Prime Minister Clement Attlee reached an agreement that divided French Indochina at the sixteenth parallel for Allied military operations. That decision gave British Admiral Mountbatten operational control over the southern half of Vietnam and made possible the British assistance to the French that eventually led to the outbreak of Vietnamese resistance there.

SOURCE: *Foreign Relations,* 1945, Vol. II, p. 1321.

Top secret from the President to Ambassador Hurley.

Please deliver the following message from me to Generalissimo Chiang Kaishek.

"1. At the Potsdam Conference the Prime Minister of Great Britain and I, in consultation with the Combined Chiefs of Staff, have had under consideration future military operations in Southeast Asia.

"2. On the advice of the Combined Chiefs of Staff we have reached the conclusion that for operational purposes it is desirable to include that portion of French Indo-China lying south of 16 ° north latitude in the Southeast Asia Command. This arrangement would leave in the China Theater that part of Indo-China which covers the flank of projected Chinese operations in China and would at the same time enable Admiral Mountbatten to develop operations in the southern half of Indo-China.

"3. I greatly hope that the above conclusions will recommend themselves to Your Excellency and that, for the purpose of facilitating operations against the common enemy, Your Excellency will feel able to concur in the proposed arrangements.

"4. I understand that the Prime Minister of Great Britain is addressing a communication to Your Excellency in a similar sense."

16. GENERAL UPRISING ORDER BY VO NGUYEN GIAP, REPRESENTING THE PROVISIONAL EXECUTIVE COMMITTEE OF THE LIBERATED ZONE, AUGUST 12, 1945

On August 12, only one day after the Japanese asked to surrender, Vo Nguyen Giap, using the name "Van," signed the order on behalf of the Provisional Executive Committee of the Liberated Zone, calling on its troops and political cadres to go into action to seize power before the landing of the Allies in Indochina.

Unit chiefs, political cadres and members of Liberation Army units!
Self-defense units, peoples committees and the entire people!

On August 11, 1945, the Japanese invaders completely disintegrated and asked to surrender to Allied Forces. The Soviet, British, and American conference meeting in Moscow has accepted the surrender of Japán. Thus the Pacific war is about to end.

The hour and minute of the general uprising has arrived, the general struggle has come to a decisive time; you, comrades, must calmly and determinedly carry out the orders which follow:

1. Mobilize troops to strike into the cities where there are sufficient conditions for victory.

2. Deploy to attack and cut off withdrawing troops of the enemy.

Source: Giap, *Orders of the Day*, pp. 13–14. [Translation by the editor.]

3. Before acting, send an ultimatum to the Japanese army and security troops [Vietnamese troops under Japanese command, ed.]. If they do not surrender, they must be annihilated.

4. With regard to Japanese forces who have surrendered, they must be treated with all kindness, a large part of them must be put into concentration camps, and one part should be propagandized, then returned to the Japanese troops in various places to exert influence.

As for Vietnamese soldiers, let them go after propagandizing them.

5. When you have fought a battle, immediately reinforce your troops with weapons captured. Unless you receive special orders, one third of the troops should stay in the locality, while two thirds should prepare to move on to another place to fight.

6. After occupying the cities, all military provisions and foodstuffs which cannot be used right away should be taken immediately to our base for storage.

7. At this present moment, liaison must be tight, troops must always stay in touch with headquarters, and must immediately notify headquarters if there is a change in the situation.

8. Peoples committees and the whole people must with all their heart do their best to coordinate with the troops. The entire army and people must be prepared for all eventualities in order to continue the struggle for complete independence for the country.

9. With regard to the French of De Gaulle, continue to follow the previous announcement, and with regard to other foreigners, there will be a separate order.

10. This is a time of military action, so discipline must be very strict.

Dear comrades!

In order to insure the success of the general uprising, you should carry out these orders quickly, determinedly, heroically, and carefully.

—Annihilate the Japanese fascists!
—Long live completely independent Vietnam!
—Long live the Vietnam Liberation Army!

17. DECLARATION OF INDEPENDENCE OF THE DEMOCRATIC REPUBLIC OF VIETNAM, SEPTEMBER 2, 1945

After the Viet Minh uprising, which the Communist leaders called the "August Revolution," had succeeded in almost all provinces, the Standing Committee of the Indochinese Communist Party met in Hanoi for the first time under Ho's chairmanship and decided to promulgate the Provisional Government of the Democratic Republic of Vietnam (DRV) on the same day as its Declaration of Independence. Ho drafted the entire declaration himself during the five days preceding his public presentation of it at a mass meeting in Hanoi on September 2. The quotation from the American Declaration of Independence was part of the DRV effort to court American support.

SOURCE: Information Service, Viet-Nam Delegation in France, *The Democratic Republic of Viet-Nam* (Paris: Imprimarie Centrale Commercial, 1948), pp. 3–5.

"We hold truths that all men are created equal, that they are endowed by their Creator with certain unalienable Rights, among these are Life, Liberty and the pursuit of Happiness."

This immortal statement is extracted from the Declaration of Independence of the United States of America in 1776. Understood in the broader sense, this means: "All peoples on the earth are born equal; every person has the right to live to be happy and free."

The Declaration of Human and Civic Rights proclaimed by the French Revolution in 1791 likewise propounds: "Every man is born equal and enjoys free and equal rights."

These are undeniable truths.

Yet, during and throughout the last eighty years, the French imperialists, abusing the principles of "Freedom, equality and fraternity," have violated the integrity of our ancestral land and oppressed our countrymen. Their deeds run counter to the ideals of humanity and justice.

In the political field, they have denied us every freedom. They have enforced upon us inhuman laws. They have set up three different political regimes in Northern, Central and Southern Viet Nam (Tonkin, Annam, and Cochinchina) in an attempt to disrupt our national, historical and ethnical unity.

They have built more prisons than schools. They have callously ill-treated our fellow-compatriots. They have drowned our revolutions in blood.

They have sought to stifle public opinion and pursued a policy of obscurantism on the largest scale; they have forced upon us alcohol and opium in order to weaken our race.

In the economic field, they have shamelessly exploited our people, driven them into the worst misery and mercilessly plundered our country.

They have ruthlessly appropriated our rice fields, mines, forests and raw materials. They have arrogated to themselves the privilege of issuing banknotes, and monopolised all our external commerce. They have imposed hundreds of unjustifiable taxes, and reduced our countrymen, especially the peasants and petty tradesmen, to extreme poverty.

They have prevented the development of native capital enterprises; they have exploited our workers in the most barbarous manner.

In the autumn of 1940, when the Japanese fascists, in order to fight the Allies, invaded Indochina and set up new bases of war, the French imperialists surrendered on bended knees and handed over our country to the invaders.

Subsequently, under the joint French and Japanese yoke, our people were literally bled white. The consequences were dire in the extreme. From Quang Tri up to the North, two millions of our countrymen died from starvation during the first months of this year.

On March 9th, 1945, the Japanese disarmed the French troops. Again the French either fled or surrendered unconditionally. Thus, in no way have they proved capable of "protecting" us; on the contrary, within five years they have twice sold our country to the Japanese.

Before March 9th, many a time did the Viet Minh League invite the French to join in the fight against the Japanese. Instead of accepting this offer, the French, on the contrary, let loose a wild reign of terror with rigour worse than ever before against Viet Minh's partisans. They even slaughtered a great number of our *"condamnés politiques"* imprisoned at Yen Bay and Cao Bang.

Despite all that, our countrymen went on maintaining, vis-a-vis the French, a humane and even indulgent attitude. After the events of March 9th, the Viet Minh League helped many French to cross the borders, rescued others from Japanese prisons and, in general, protected the lives and properties of all the French in their territory.

In fact, since the autumn of 1940, our country ceased to be a French colony and became a Japanese possession.

After the Japanese surrender, our people, as a whole, rose up and proclaimed their sovereignty and founded the Democratic Republic of Viet Nam.

The truth is that we have wrung back our independence from Japanese hands and not from the French.

The French fled, the Japanese surrendered. Emperor Bao Dai abdicated, our people smashed the yoke which pressed hard upon us for nearly one hundred years, and finally made our Viet Nam an independent country. Our people at the same time overthrew the monarchical regime established tens of centuries ago, and founded the Republic.

For these reasons, we, the members of the Provisional Government representing the entire people of Viet Nam, declare that we shall from now on have no more connections with imperialist France; we consider null and void all the treaties France has signed concerning Viet Nam, and we hereby cancel all the privileges that the French arrogated to themselves on our territory.

The Vietnamese people, animated by the same common resolve, are determined to fight to the death against all attempts at aggression by the French imperialists.

We are convinced that the Allies who have recognized the principles of equality of peoples at the Conferences of Teheran and San Francisco cannot but recognize the Independence of Viet Nam.

A people which has so stubbornly opposed the French domination for more than 80 years, a people who, during these last years, so doggedly ranged itself and fought on the Allied side against Fascism, such a people has the right to be free, such a people must be independent.

For these reasons, we, the members of the Provisional Government of the Democratic Republic of Viet Nam, solemnly declare to the world:

"Viet Nam has the right to be free and independent and, in fact, has become free and independent. The people of Viet Nam decide to mobilise all their spiritual and material forces and to sacrifice their lives and property in order to safeguard their right of Liberty and Independence."

18. SPEECH BY GIAP, SEPTEMBER 2, 1945 [Extract]

Just after Ho read the Declaration of Independence, Vo Nguyen Giap predicted French efforts to reoccupy Indochina and expressed the hope that the Allies would

SOURCE: *Trang Su Moi* [A new page of history] (Hanoi: Hoi Van Hoa Cuu Quoc, 1945). Enclosure to dispatch no. 39, October 25, 1945 from Consul Philip D. Sprouse in Kunming, State Department Central Files, National Archives. [Translation by the editor.]

not support the restoration of the French colonial regime in Indochina. In an effort to neutralize the Kuomintang Chinese, who were then entering the country to disarm the Japanese, Giap treated them as allies against imperialism, even quoting Chiang Kai-shek's own anti-imperialist rhetoric.

As for the United States, it is a democratic country which has no territorial ambitions but has contributed particularly to the defeat of our enemy, Japanese fascism. Therefore we regard the U.S. as a good friend.

Of our foreign problems at present, the most important is the attitude of the French Government of De Gaulle toward our independence. Its propaganda aims at creating misunderstanding among the allied countries of the present situation in Indochina. Sometimes they say we are faithful to them, because it was they who fought Japan; sometimes they say we are the lackeys of Japan, and sometimes they accuse us of having killed French women and children. But we have enough proof to destroy those dark schemes. Politically, they have named a new Governor General and secretly incited French civil servants to plot to take back public offices. Militarily, they are preparing to bring troops back into Indochina. Generally speaking, from the information recently obtained, it is clear that they tend to reestablish their power in our country. We swear that we will defend our nation against them to the death. Our people have always desired peace, but when we must shed blood, we are also determined to do so.

Compatriots,

In the future in all fields, but especially in foreign affairs, we will meet many difficulties. We do not rely on anyone. We do not expect any such good fortune. We must take care of ourselves in order to determine our own fate. If we want an excellent domestic policy and foreign relations victories, we must quickly create the strength by unity, forged in struggle and sacrifice, by actions supporting the government in a realistic manner.

At this time, division, doubt, and apathy are all a betrayal of the country.

At this time, the mind of each person must be directed to the struggle for independence, the concern of each person must be to oppose foreign aggression. Only if there is such concern can we avoid the yoke of slavery.

Beloved compatriots, nephews of Tran Quoc Tuan, and of Le Loi, let us all stand up, close our ranks and await the orders of the Provisional Government.

To warn those who might decide on a repetition of plans for aggression, we repeat the words of Chiang Kai-shek on the attitude of the oppressed Asian peoples when this World War concluded: "If they are not given freedom and equality, a third World War will follow on the heels of this Second World War, just as this Second World War followed on the heels of the First World War."

The Vietnamese people must obtain independence, freedom, and equality. That is not the aspiration of the Vietnamese masses alone but of all democratic countries. The masses of those countries have sacrificed in the struggle to serve the cause of justice, not to serve oppression. Therefore the masses in those countries all earnestly hope to see the small and weak nations liberated, and they also believe with Chiang Kai-shek that: "When the war ends, imperialism must also be ended, because imperialism is the cause of war."

The Vietnamese people demand independence, freedom, and equality to the end. If demanding it by diplomacy and using moderate means does not work, then we must take up the sword. We are prepared for anything that might happen. We may not be as strong as the enemy but we will defeat the enemy as our ancestors in the time of the Tran dynasty.

In any case, if we are determined, and continue the struggle we will definitely maintain the victories of today. Just as Mr. Roosevelt has said, oppression and cruelty have made us know what freedom means.

Under the leadership of the Provisional Government and Chairman Ho Chi Minh, our people will give all their wealth, their bones and blood to build and beautify the fatherland, to make our beloved Vietnam bright, wealthy and powerful after so many years of misery and exhaustion.

Following the traditions of previous generations, our generation will fight a final battle so that generations to follow will forever be able to live in independence, freedom, and happiness.

19. MEMORANDA FOR SECRETARY OF STATE JAMES BYRNES FROM OSS DIRECTOR WILLIAM J. DONOVAN, SEPTEMBER 5 AND 6, 1945

Members of the U.S. Office of Strategic Services (OSS) team reported on the situation in Vietnam via Kunming. Through these reports, which were then passed on to the secretary of state, American policy makers became aware almost immediately of the existence of the independent Vietnamese government and the seriousness of its plans to resist the restoration of French power in Vietnam.

The OSS representative in Hanoi, who has been instrumental in communications concerning the Japanese surrender in Indo-China, has transmitted the following information, dated 1 September, via Kunming:

The Provisional Annamese Government in Indo-China is in full control and so well organized that several attempts by French from Calcutta to parachute into the country have been frustrated. The parachutists, although not maltreated, were held as prisoners. According to the Annamese Prime Minister, should the French attempt a return, the Annamese are determined to maintain their independence even at the cost of lives. They feel they have nothing to lose and all to gain. Meanwhile, however, the Prime Minister has promised the OSS representative in Hanoi that no organized violence against Europeans will occur until the Chinese assume control in the area.

The Japanese have been destroying, selling, and otherwise disposing of stocks of rice and miscellaneous equipment in addition to arms and ammunition from their dumps. The commanding Japanese general has promised that severe disciplinary measures would be taken against violators of his orders to safeguard all property belonging to or in the possession of the Japanese Army or Japanese administration in Indo-China.

SOURCE: 851G.0019-545, State Department Central Files, National Archives.

The OSS representative in Hanoi has transmitted, via Calcutta, the following information, which is a continuation of our memoranda of 21 August, 22 August, 31 August, and 5 September, concerning the Provisional Government in Indo-China:

On 2 September the head of the Provisional Annamese Government flatly refused an invitation to confer with Major Sainteny, the French representative in Indo-China. With this act, the Annamese apparently intended to close all negotiations with the French for an indefinite period. The French intend to carry on, however, and Sainteny will remain in the Governor General's palace, hoping to maintain France's prerogatives. Sainteny intends to organize an underground resistance group to work along subversive lines against the adamant Provisional Annamese Government. The Provisional Government now clearly seems to be composed of strictly left-wing elements. A strong element of the Annamese Kuomintang and certain republican factions are not represented.

The Chinese residents in Indo-China are becoming more and more politically aggressive because they believe that their Government in Chungking has prepared a puppet government with which to present the Annamese upon arrival. On the other hand, the Annamese are prepared to combat such a government openly or subversively. The French are once again becoming belligerent and are rebuking the Allies for not siding with them. Trouble seems to be brewing, and may break out after the armistice has been signed in Indo-China.

20. LETTER BY HO CHI MINH TO THE VIETNAMESE PEOPLE TO FIGHT FAMINE, SEPTEMBER 1945

At the first meeting of the cabinet of the Provisional Government of the Democratic Republic of Vietnam on September 3, President Ho told his ministers that the most urgent problem facing the new government was to do everything possible to prevent starvation. The corn and yam harvest, which would help somewhat to alleviate the famine, was still three or four months away, and it would take some time to increase rice production. The only way the new government could immediately reduce starvation was to distribute the existing grain supply as equitably as possible. It did not have the administrative resources to do so by administrative fiat, however, so Ho could only appeal to the population to spare one of its meals every ten days for the poor—and to pledge to do so himself.

Dear compatriots!

From January to July this year, in the North, two million people have starved to death.

Floods adding, the famine increased, plunging the people in utter wretchedness.

How painful we are at our meals when we think of those who are dying of hunger!

SOURCE: Ho Chi Minh, *Selected Works*, 4 Vol. (Hanoi: Foreign Languages Publishing House, 1962) Vol. III, pp. 40–41.

Therefore I propose to you, and I will do it first:

To do without a meal every ten days, that is three meals every month, and spare this rice (one tin each meal) for the poor.

Thus these people will have something to eat while waiting for the next crop, and escape death.

I am confident that all our compatriots out of charity are eager to respond to my proposal.

Thank you on behalf of the poor.

21. REPORT ON OSS "DEER MISSION" BY MAJ. ALLISON K. THOMAS, SEPTEMBER 17, 1945 [Extract]

In May 1945, the U.S. Office of Strategic Services decided to send two O.S.S. teams into Tonkin to sabotage the Hanoi-Langson road and railroad. The Americans were originally to work with French and Vietnamese troops but were informed that, contrary to French assurances, the Vietnamese would not collaborate with the French military. Since the Viet Minh were the only effective anti-Japanese guerilla organization in the region, the American teams found themselves training troops and working directly with Ho Chi Minh and Vo Nguyen Giap just at the time that key decisions were being made on the August Revolution. The report by one of the team leaders, Major Allison Thomas, indicates the warmth that the O.S.S. team felt toward the Viet Minh leaders and its conviction that it was a genuinely popular movement.

9 Sept–16 Sept: Our team left by foot, car, and boat and arrived at Hanoi about 4 PM. We obtained quarters through the VIETMINH party, which was authorized by the PATTI MISSION.

We spent the time from 9 Sept to 16 Sept seeing the city buying souvenirs, saying good-bye to our VIETNMINH friends, and making arrangements to return to Kunming. Hanoi was an extremely festive city for everyone except the French.

VIETMINH flags were flying from almost every house. Banners were stretched across the streets with various "slogans" in Annamese, English, Chinese, Russian, Indian, etc. French was noticeably absent.

Some of the slogans seen everywhere were as follows: "Welcome Allies," "Welcome Peace Commission," "Down with French Imperialism," "Let's kick out French Imperialism," "Independence of Death," "2,000,000 people died under French domination," "Vietminh for the Vietnamese."

Our friend of the forest, Mr. C. M. Hoo, now Mr. Ho Chi Minh, was President of the Provisional Government and Minister of Foreign Affairs. Another friend of the forest, Mr. Van, now Vo Nguyen Giap became Minister of Interior. Party members were appointed cabinet members. The new government seems to

SOURCE: *Causes, Origins, and Lessons of the Vietnam War*, Hearings before the Committee on Foreign Relations, U.S. Senate, 92nd Cong., 2nd Session, 1973, pp. 251–264.

be enthusiastically supported by the majority of the population in every province of Indochina. The new government was given strength by the resignation and abdication of Bao Dai, former puppet Emperor, who offered his services as friend and adviser.

The people know the French intend to come back but they keep saying if they come back with arms they will fight to the death.

The story of our experiences in IndoChina is melodramatic in the following sense. On July 16 we were living in the forests of Indochina with the Chief of the VIETMINH Party. Less than two months later, this same chief had become President of the new Provisional Government and was installed in the former home of the French "President Superior" in Hanoi.

22. LETTER FROM MAJ. GEN. PHILIP E. GALLAGHER IN HANOI TO MAJOR GENERAL R. B. McCLURE, KUNMING, SEPTEMBER 20, 1945

Maj. Gen. Philip E. Gallagher arrived in Hanoi following the Japanese surrender to assist the Chinese in their occupation of northern Vietnam. As this excerpt from his first report to the commanding general of the Chinese Combat Command in Kunming indicates, he was sympathetic to Vietnamese aspirations for independence but was forbidden to do anything to assist the Vietnamese cause. The letter indicates that the Vietnamese were still in the dark about American intentions regarding the return of the French in Indochina.

The Annamite party, Viet Minh, led by Ho Chi Minh who is the Prime Minister, is definitely in the saddle. This Ho Chi Minh is an old revolutionist and a political prisoner many times, a product of Moscow, a communist. He called upon me and welcomed us most profusely, gave me a very beautiful banner with my name on it and some remark about the "Great American nation," etc. His political party is an amalgamation of all lesser parties. There may be some smaller bandit groups, but they are negligible, his is the dominant force. They now claim their independence, and he has told me that, regardless of the decision of the big powers regarding whether France would or would not be permitted to come back in, his party expected to fight, that they are armed, well supplied, and will resist all French efforts to take over French Indochina. In this regard, it is well to remember that he is a revolutionist whose motto is "Independence or Death," and since all the chips are placed down, we should not put too much stock in his statement that he is going to fight the French. He looks upon America as the saviour of all nations, and is basing all of his actions on the statement in the Atlantic Charter that the independence of the smaller nations would be assured by the major powers. Of course we know that charter was never signed. He expects us to support him in his efforts, and

SOURCE: Original typescript in Gallagher Papers, Center for Military History, U.S. Army, Washington, D.C. Hereafter cited as Gallagher Papers.

it will be a great shock, of course, if the French are allowed to come back, either as a protectorate or otherwise. In my discussion with him, I pointed out frankly that my job was not as a representative of the State Department, nor was I interested in the political situation, and could neither offer my sympathy nor assurance of any help, that I was merely working with Lu Han. One thing that was worrying him was that he had been given the impression that Lu Han was going to establish complete military control over the entire area for which he was responsible, and that his sole purpose therein was to disarm the Japanese and maintain peace and order, that he undoubtedly intended to use, wherever practicable, existing constituted authority to run the country and to enforce peace and discipline; that Lu Han favored neither the French nor Annamites and would tolerate no violence on the part of either and would treat them as equals. I assured him that China had no territorial desires insofar as FIC was concerned. Here again I indicated to him that he must gain the confidence of Lu Han and deal with him altogether. Confidentially, I wish the Annamites could be given their independence, but, of course, we have no voice in this matter.

23. TELEGRAM FROM DRV FOREIGN MINISTER HO CHI MINH TO BRITISH PRIME MINISTER CLEMENT ATTLEE, SEPTEMBER 26, 1945

When the Supreme Allied Commander of all Allied Forces in Southeast Asia Command, Admiral Lord Louis Mountbattan, arrived in Saigon in September 1945 pursuant to the agreement at Potsdam, it was on the understanding between Britain and France that British forces would assist the French in resuming control over Indochina. But the British faced a determined Viet Minh government in Saigon. The response by the British command was to ignore the Vietnamese authorities and assert its authority in their place. The proclamation by General Douglas D. Gracey did so, however, on the promise of "strict impartiality" with regard to political affairs—a pledge that induced the Viet Minh officials to cooperate with the British authorities rather than openly resist.

On September 23, French prisoners of war, with the explicit consent of Major General Gracey, who freed them, carried out a coup d'état *in Saigon against the Viet Minh Executive Committee. British and Indian troops participated in the fighting to secure important positions in the city, meeting considerable Vietnamese resistance. Fighting continued for several days. The DRV reacted sharply to this violation of what they thought had been a policy of Allied neutrality on Indochina's political future with a telegram of protest to Britain, and ordered the people in the South to resist the reoccupation by French forces throughout the South. Ho Chi*

SOURCE: Great Britain, Parliament, Papers by Command, *Documents Relating to British Involvement in the Indochinese Conflict, 1945–1965,* (London: Her Majesty's Stationery Office, Cmnd. 2834), p. 53.

Minh, in his role as foreign minister, protested the British assistance to the French coup.

Foreign Minister of Viet-Nam Republic to Premier Attlee, London.

The release of French prisoners of war with arms and ammunition leading to the French attack against Saigon and the arrests of members of the People's Committee constitutes a great violation of our national rights and is an offense to our national dignity, a non-fulfillment of the mission placed on Commander British Forces in South Indo-China by the United Nations, a failure in the carrying of the Atlantic Charter and non-observation of attitude of neutrality by the British Disarmament Forces. We therefore lodge a most emphatic protest against such smoke-screening of French aggression and express earnest hope that you would interfere on basis full respect for the independence of Viet-Nam Republic.

24. MEMORANDUM FOR THE RECORD: GENERAL GALLAGHER'S MEETING WITH HO CHI MINH, SEPTEMBER 29, 1945 [Extract]

Shortly after receiving word from Kunming that the Chinese were to help the French recover power in Indochina, Gallagher met with Ho. The conversation centered on the delicate question of the Allied governments' attitude toward the DRV. Gallagher tried to soothe Ho's fears that Vietnam was being viewed as "conquered territory," despite his knowledge that the United States had assured the French of its acquiescence in French reconquest.

1. Conference, Friday 28 September 1945, 1830 hours. Present were General Gallagher, Colonel Hutson, Major Patti, Lt. Ungern and Prime Minister Ho Chi Minh.

2. Mr. Ho inquired regarding the surrender proclamation issued by Lu Han, and that part in particular dealing with military control of governmental administrative functions. He was referred to Lu Han for his exact interpretation, but was informed that spirit behind policy was to use constituted authority as much as possible to continue proper administrative functions, but, at the same time have a supervisory system set up capable of controlling certain key positions in case of disorder or unrest. In this regard, and in all matters arising regarding the occupation forces or their policies, Mr. Ho was urged to formulate a close working basis with Lu Han and cooperate with him and his decisions closely. When questioned, Mr. Ho stated that there had not yet been any interference with any local authorities or controls by the Chinese.

3. Mr. Ho expressed the feeling that the Allies considered Indo China as a conquered country and that the Chinese came as conquerors. He was reassured that

SOURCE: Gallagher Papers.

this was not the case, and section of surrender proclamation issued by Lu Han quoted directly as an indication of this. It was stated that the presence of the Chinese forces was hoped would have stabilizing effect and afford time for negotiation between the parties concerned. In the meantime, every effort will be made to avoid the outbreak of trouble and bloodshed.

4. Mr. Ho stated that the youth of the Viet Minh party wished to stage a large demonstration on 29 September, and asked advice as to whether he should give permission for the rally. He stated that probably anti-French posters would be displayed during the rally. He was referred in this matter to Lu Han for a decision, and urged to be honest and frank in stating the purpose of the rally and the fact that anti-French sentiment would be included.

25. TELEGRAM FROM ACTING SECRETARY OF STATE DEAN ACHESON TO CHARGE WALTER ROBERTSON IN CHINA, OCTOBER 5, 1945

In the first U.S. official policy response to the establishment of the Democratic Republic of Vietnam and its declaration of independence, Acting Secretary of State Dean Acheson repeated in a statement first sent out by the department on August 30, 1945, that the United States did not question French sovereignty over Indochina. He also suggested that the American position would be dependent upon evidence of popular support in Vietnam for French rule.

US has no thought of opposing the reestablishment of French control in Indochina and no official statement by US Government has questioned even by implication French sovereignty over Indochina. However, it is not the policy of this Govt to assist the French to reestablish their control over Indochina by force and the willingness of the US to see French control reestablished assumes that French claim to have the support of the population of Indochina is borne out by future events.

26. LETTER BY HO CHI MINH TO PRESIDENT TRUMAN, OCTOBER 17, 1945

Ho's first major diplomatic initiative was to appeal to the United States to support Vietnam's independence. In a letter to President Truman, Ho relied primarily on legal arguments to convince him that Vietnam, not France, should be represented on the United Nations Advisory Commission for the Far East. The letter, like those that followed from Ho, was never answered.

SOURCE: *U.S.-Vietnam Relations*, Book 8, p. 49.
SOURCE: *U.S.-Vietnam Relations*, Book 1, I.A.C., pp. 73–74.

Establishment of Advisory Commission for the Far East is heartily welcomed by Vietnamese people in principle stop. Taking into consideration primo the strategical and economical importance of Vietnam secundo the earnest desire which Vietnam deeply feels and has unanimously manifested to cooperate with the other democracies in the establishment and consolidation of world peace and prosperity we wish to call the attention of the Allied nations on the following points colon:

First absence of Vietnam and presence of France in the Advisory Commission leads to the conclusion that France is to represent the Vietnamese people at the Commission stop. Such representation is groundless either *de jure* or *de facto*. stop. *De jure* no alliance exists any more between France and Vietnam colon: Baodai abolished treaties of 1884 and 1863 comma, Baodai voluntarily abdicated to hand over government to Democratic Republican Government comma, Provisional Government rectorated [sic] abolishment of treaties of 1884 and 1863 stop. *De facto* since March ninth France having handed over governing rule to Japan has broken all administrative links with Vietnam, since August 18, 1945, Provisional Government has been a *de facto* independent government in every respect, recent incidents in Saigon instigated by the French roused unanimous disapproval leading to fight for independence.

Second France is not entitled because she had ignominiously sold Indo China to Japan and betrayed the Allies. Third Vietnam is qualified by Atlantic Charter and subsequent peace agreement and by her goodwill and her unflinching stand for democracy to be represented at the Advisory Commission. Stop. We are convinced that Vietnam at Commission will be able to bring effective contribution to solution of pending problems in Far East whereas her absence would bring forth unstability [sic] and temporary character to solutions otherwise reached. Therefore we express earnest request to take part in Advisory Commission for Far East. Stop. We should be very grateful to your excellency and Premier Attlee Premier Stalin Generalissimo Tchang Kai Shek for the conveyance of our desiderata to the United Nations.

27. SPEECH BY HO CHI MINH, ON THE RESISTANCE WAR IN SOUTH VIETNAM, NOVEMBER 1945

While the DRV tried to maintain good relations with the Chinese in the North in order to ward off the return of the French, it gave all-out support to the resistance war in the South. The government organized "Southward March" military units to supplement the efforts of the badly organized, ill-trained, and meagerly equipped resistance forces in the South, and they were already fighting battles with the French at Nha Trang and Kanh Hoa by the end of November 1945. That same month, President Ho rallied the people throughout the country behind the resistance in the South.

SOURCE: Ho Chi Minh, *Selected Works*, Vol. III, pp. 48–49.

Compatriots!

During the Second World War, the French colonialists twice sold out our country to the Japanese. Thus they betrayed the Allied nations, and helped the Japanese to cause the latter many losses.

Meanwhile they also betrayed our people, exposing us to the destruction of bombs and bullets. In this way, the French colonialists withdrew of their own accord from the Allied ranks and tore up the treaties they had earlier compelled us to sign.

Notwithstanding the French colonialists' treachery, our people as a whole are determined to side with the Allies and oppose the invaders. When the Japanese surrendered, our entire people single-mindedly changed our country into a Democratic Republic and elected a provisional Government which is to prepare for a national congress and draw up our draft Constitution.

Not only is our act in line with the Atlantic and San Francisco Charters, etc. solemnly proclaimed by the Allies, but it entirely conforms with the glorious principles upheld by the French people, viz. Freedom, Equality and Fraternity.

It is thus clear that in the past the colonialists betrayed the Allies and our country, and surrendered to the Japanese. At present, in the shadow of the British and Indian troops, and behind the Japanese soldiers, they are attacking the South of our country.

They have sabotaged the peace that China, the United States, Britain and Russia won at the cost of scores of millions of lives. They have run counter to the promises concerning democracy and liberty that the Allied powers have proclaimed. They have of their own accord sabotaged their fathers' principles of liberty and equality. In consequence, it is for a just cause, for justice of the world, and for Viet Nam's land and people that our compatriots throughout the country have risen to struggle, and are firmly determined to maintain their independence. We do not hate the French people and France. We are energetically fighting slavery, and the ruthless policy of the French colonialists. We are not invading another's country. We only safeguard our own against the French invaders. Hence we are not alone. The countries which love peace and democracy, and the weaker nations all over the world, all sympathize with us. With the unity of the whole people within the country, and having many sympathizers abroad, we are sure of victory.

The French colonialists have behaved lawlessly in the South for almost one and a half months. Our southern compatriots have sacrificed their lives in a most valiant struggle. Public opinion in the great countries: China, the United States, Russia and Britain, has supported our just cause.

Compatriots throughout the country! Those in the South will do their utmost to resist the enemy. Those in the Centre and the North will endeavour to help their southern compatriots, and be on the alert.

The French colonialists should know that the Vietnamese people do not want bloodshed, that they love peace. But we are determined to sacrifice even millions of combatants, and fight a long-term war of resistance in order to safeguard Viet Nam's independence and free her children from slavery. We are sure that our war of resistance will be victorious!

Let the whole country be determined in the war of resistance!

Long live independent Viet Nam!

1946

28. MEMORANDUM OF CONVERSATION BY RICHARD L. SHARP, DIVISION OF SOUTHEAST ASIAN AFFAIRS, JANUARY 30, 1946 [Extract]

General Gallagher returned from Hanoi in January 1946 and gave his assessment to State Department officials. Gallagher did not believe the Viet Minh, who he said were not "full-fledged doctrinaire Communists," could hold out against the French militarily, nor did he think Vietnam was ready for self-government, despite widespread demands among the Vietnamese people for independence.

The question was raised whether the French mission in Hanoi was in fact negotiating with Ho Chi Minh. General Gallagher replied that the Viet Minh Provisional Government was at first willing to negotiate; then in October, after de Gaulle's pronouncements on colonial policy, the Annamese refused to negotiate with the French and reacted vigorously against all French nationals in Hanoi. The Chinese may succeed in putting in a less anti-French Annamese government so that negotiation might go forward. All French efforts to stimulate a palace revolution against Ho were of no avail. Ho himself will not deal with the French. The Viet Minh is strong and, regardless of possible superficial changes in the Provisional Government, Ho will be behind any continuing Annamese movement. General Gallagher said that Sainteny had told him he expected peaceful agreement between the French and the Annamese would be reached by negotiation.

General Gallagher was asked how effective the Viet Minh administration would be with neither French nor Chinese forces present. He replied that on the whole he was impressed by the remarkably effective Annamese administration. There was an able personnel; they were all enthusiastic and young, but there were too few of them. Whatever their technical skill, they perhaps lack executive ability and experience since the technical services in Hanoi were at first very well run but gradually deteriorated. Trained people for the government and at the municipal level are lacking. In General Gallagher's opinion the Annamese are not yet ready for self-government and in full-fledged competition with other nations they would "lose their shirts." However, the demand for independence is widespread and even in the villages the peasants refer to the example of the Philippines.

Ho is willing to cooperate with Great Britain, USSR, or the United States and would perhaps even settle for French tutelage if that were subordinated to control by the other nations. French control alone, however, will be strongly resisted. The deep-seated hatred for the French has been fanned by exceedingly clever Viet Minh propaganda.

General Gallagher was asked whether the Annamese were realistic regarding their ability to stand up against French military force. While they are too enthusiastic and too naive, he said, they probably know that they will be licked. They are

---

SOURCE: *U.S.-Vietnam Relations*, Book 8, V.B.2., pp. 53–57.

strong on parades and reiterate their willingness "to fight to the last man," but they would be slaughtered and they have been told that and probably know it. The Annamese would be no match for forces with modern arms even if they themselves have some, which they may have since the Chinese found no Japanese rolling artillery and numerous Japanese anti-aircraft guns seem to have completely disappeared. United States Army representatives never did learn the extent of arms controlled by the Viet Minh. Certainly the Chinese are not turning Japanese arms over to them. Before V-J Day the Japanese undoubtedly had armed and trained many Annamese. A Japanese general claimed they had taken over on March 9 simply because the French could no longer control the Annamese, but this statement General Gallagher characterized as a lie. He had heard that under the pretext of arming Annamese gendarmes for police duty in Hanoi, the Japanese had actually armed three distinct contingents, dismissing each group when armed and bringing in a new one to be armed and trained. Furthermore, the Annamese had acquired Japanese arms from arsenals which had been opened. General Gallagher did not know whether or not Tai Li was sending arms to the Viet Minh.

29. PRELIMINARY FRANCO-VIETNAMESE CONVENTION, MARCH 6, 1946

After a Sino-French agreement was reached in February 1946 permitting the French to replace Chinese troops north of the sixteenth parallel, Vietnamese leaders were convinced that China, France, the United States, and Britain had reached a compromise at Vietnam's expense. They feared an attempt would be made to install a pro-Chinese government before Chinese troops left the country. So they decided to negotiate with France, to gain leverage against the Chinese and also to gain time to prepare for the ultimate fight against France. After tough negotiations in which the French refused to accept the word "independence," Ho himself proposed the phrase "a free state" as an ambiguous substitute, allowing a tenuous preliminary accord to be reached.

Following the preliminary convention of March 6, the military staffs of the two sides negotiated a more detailed agreement which not only imposed tight restrictions on the movements and activities of French troops but created a "Mixed Commission of Liaison and Control" that had ultimate authority for the application of the agreement. On paper, at least, the Vietnamese appeared to be in a strong bargaining position.

Between the High Contracting Parties designated below, the Government of The French Republic, represented by MR. SAINTENY, Delegate of the French High Commissioner, regularly commissioned by Vice Admiral Georges Thierry

SOURCE: Enclosure to Despatch No. 366 from Bangkok, April 24, 1947, "Transmitting Documents relative to recent developments in Indo China, received from Dr. Pham Ngoc Thack [sic], Vietnam Under-Secretary of State." F.W. 851.G.00/4-2447, State Department Central Files, National Archives. Translation of this and all other documents enclosed with this dispatch was done by the Department of State in 1947.

D'ARGENLIEU, French High Commissioner, depository of the powers of the French Republic on the one hand and the Government of the Republic of Viet Nam, represented by its President, MR. HO CHI MINH and the Special Delegate of the Council of Ministers, MR. VU HONG KHANH on the other hand, it is agreed as follows:

1—The French Government recognized the Republic of Viet Nam as a free state which has its government, its parliament, its army, and its finances, and is a part of the Indochinese Federation and of the French Union. So far as the union of the three Ky is concerned, the Government pledges itself to confirm the decisions reached by the populations consulted by means of a referendum.

2—The Government of Viet Nam declares itself ready to receive the French Army in a peaceful manner, when it relieves Chinese troops in accordance with international agreements. A supplemental agreement attached to the present Preliminary Convention shall fix the means according to which relief operations shall take place.

3—The stipulations formulated above shall enter into force immediately after the exchange of signatures, each of the high Contracting Parties shall take all measures necessary to bring about the cessation of hostilities immediately, to maintain the troops in their respective positions and to create the favorable atmosphere necessary for the immediate opening of friendly and frank negotiations. The negotiations shall concern particularly:

(a) diplomatic relations of Vietnam with foreign countries;

(b) the future status of Indochina;

(c) French economic and cultural interests in Viet Nam.

Hanoi, Saigon or Paris may be selected as the place for the Conference.

Agreement Supplemental to the Preliminary Convention Entered into Between the Government of the French Republic and the Government of Viet Nam:

The following is agreed upon between the High Contracting Parties designated in the Preliminary Convention;

1—The relief forces shall be composed of:

(a) 10,000 Viet Nam soldiers with their Viet Nam Cadres who are subject to the orders of the military authorities of Viet Nam.

(b) 15,000 French forces, including the French forces in the territory of Viet Nam at the present time, north of the 16th parallel. The said forces shall be composed solely of French soldiers of metropolitan origin, with the exception of troops charged with the guarding of Japanese prisoners.

All such forces shall be placed under the French High Command, assisted by Viet Nam delegates. The progress, installation and utilization of such forces shall be defined during the course of a General Staff conference between representatives of the French and Viet Nam Commands, which shall be held when the French units land.

Mixed commissions shall be created at all levels to assure, in a spirit of friendly collaboration, liaison between the French and Viet Nam troops.

2—The French members of the relief forces shall be divided into three categories:

(a) The units charged with the guarding of Japanese prisoners. These units shall be repatriated as soon as their mission becomes unnecessary following the evacuation of the Japanese prisoners; in any case within a maximum period of ten months;

(b) The units charged, in collaboration with the Viet Nam Army, with the maintenance of public order and the security of the Viet Nam territory. These units shall be relieved one fifth each year, by the Viet Nam Army, this relief therefore being effectively carried out within a period of five years.

(c) The units charged with the defense of naval and air bases. The duration of the mission entrusted to these units shall be defined at later conferences.

3—At places where French and Viet Nam troops are garrisoned, clearly defined cantonment zones shall be assigned.

The French Government pledges itself not to employ Japanese prisoners for military purposes.

30. NOTE FROM SECRETARY OF STATE JAMES BYRNES TO FRENCH AMBASSADOR HENRI BONNET, APRIL 12, 1946

Acting Secretary Acheson's earlier caveat about popular support for the return of the French was put aside as the United States officially gave its approval to the reversion of all Indochina to French control in a diplomatic note from Secretary Byrnes to the French Ambassador. The note ignored the fact that France had already signed an agreement recognizing Vietnam as a "free state."

The Secretary of State presents his compliments to His Excellency the French Ambassador and has the honor to refer to the Ambassador's note no. 167 of March 7, 1946, enclosing a copy of the Franco-Chinese Agreement with regard to the relief of Chinese forces in northern Indo-China by French forces and requesting the approval of the Combined Chiefs of Staff thereto.

The Secretary of State is pleased to inform the Ambassador that the Combined Chiefs of Staff have no objection to the relief of Chinese troops in northern French Indo-China by French forces, since they consider that such arrangements are a matter for determination by the Governments of France and China.

Since the Franco-Chinese agreement completes the reversion of all Indo-China to French control, the Combined Chiefs of Staff consider that the French military commander in Indo-China should act as a medium for the French Government for coordination with the Supreme Commander for the Allied Powers on matters relating to the repatriation of Japanese from Indo-China, and that the Chinese Supreme Commander and Admiral Mountbatten should be relieved of their duties and responsibilities for disarmament and evacuation of Japanese in Indo-China.

SOURCE: *U.S.-Vietnam Relations*, Book 8, V.B.2, pp. 64–65.

Current repatriation schedules envisage the completion of the evacuation of the Japanese from northern Indo-China by April 15. The Combined Chiefs of Staff consider that it is most desirable to have the French commander in Indo-China conform to present schedules.

Accordingly, Admiral Mountbatten has been directed to make the necessary arrangements with the French military commander in Indo-China regarding the transfer of his share of the above-mentioned responsibility at the earliest possible date.

The Supreme Commander for the Allied Powers and the appropriate Chinese authorities have been informed of the Combined Chiefs of Staff action on this matter.

It is understood that a memorandum has been addressed directly to the French Military Attache to the United States informing him of the above and requesting that appropriate instructions be issued to the French military commander in Indo-China.

31. LETTER FROM HO CHI MINH TO COMPATRIOTS IN NAM BO, MAY 31, 1946

Before leaving for France for the Fontainebleau Conference on Franco-Vietnamese relations, Ho reassured South Vietnamese that the unity of Vietnam would be upheld in the talks in France and urged them to be generous with fellow Vietnamese who might have opposed the resistance at first.

Dear fellow-countrymen in Nam Bo,

The news of my going to France with a delegation for official negotiation has caused concern to our people, especially in Nam Bo. What does the future hold for Nam Bo?

Please, don't worry. I pledge my word that Ho Chi Minh will never sell his country.

You in Nam Bo have been fighting self-sacrificingly for many months now to safeguard the territorial integrity of Viet Nam; for this, our entire people are grateful to you.

You in Nam Bo are citizens of Viet Nam. Rivers may dry up, mountains may erode; but this truth can never change.

I advise you to unite closely and broadly. The five fingers are of unequal length but they are united in the hand.

The millions of our fellow-countrymen are not all alike; but they are descended from the same ancestors. We must therefore be generous and broadminded and admit the fact that the offspring of the Lac and the Hong are all more or less patriotic. With regard to those who have gone astray, we must use friendly persuasion. Only in this way can we achieve unity, and broad unity will bring us a bright future.

Through this short message written before my departure, I wish to convey my cordial greetings to all of you, dear fellow-countrymen in Nam Bo.

SOURCE: Ho Chi Minh, *Selected Writings*, pp. 66–67.

32. MEMORANDUM BY THE CHIEF OF THE DIVISION OF SOUTHEAST ASIAN AFFAIRS, ABBOT L. MOFFAT TO THE DIRECTOR OF THE OFFICE OF FAR EASTERN AFFAIRS, JOHN CARTER VINCENT, AUGUST 9, 1946

The discussion between Vietnamese and French delegations at Fontainebleau revealed how wide the disparity was between their respective conceptions of Vietnam's status as a "free state within the French Union" in terms of both military and diplomatic autonomy. Relations between the French and Vietnamese delegations at Fontainebleau further deteriorated after France convened a conference at Dalat to which it invited representatives of the royal governments of Cambodia and Laos, the French-created "Republic of Cochinchina," the ethnic minorities of the highland region and even the politically and juridically nonexistent entity called "Southern Annam." In his analysis of French policy, the chief of the State Department's Southeast Asia Office supported the Vietnamese charges of French bad faith toward the March 6 accord.

Recent developments indicate that the French are moving to regain a large measure of their control of Indochina in violation of the spirit of the March 6 convention. The evidence, as set forth below, suggests that the French are attempting to gain their objective by manoeuvres designed to confine and weaken Viet Nam. In the event that Viet Nam decides to resist these encroachments, which is by no means unlikely, widespread hostilities may result.

The chief opposition to the reestablishment of French rule in Indochina has all along come from the Annamese, who inhabit the three east coastal provinces of Tonkin, Annam, and Cochinchina, which once comprised the Kingdom of Annam. The populations of the other two countries of Indochina—Cambodia and Laos—are not in a high state of political development or in any condition seriously to resist French control. A *modus vivendi* between the French and the Annamese was achieved in the preliminary convention of March 6, 1946, by which the Annamese "Republic of Viet Nam" was recognized as a free state within the Indochinese Federation and the Viet Nam Government declared its readiness to receive the French Army. The convention left for future settlement two crucial problems: the status of Viet Nam in its external relations, and the geographical extent of Viet Nam. On the former point, the provisional agreement states that "each contracting party will take all necessary measures . . . to create the favorable atmosphere necessary for an immediate opening of amicable and free negotiations. These negotiations will bear particularly upon diplomatic relations between the Viet Nam and foreign states, the future status of Indochina, French economic and cultural interests in Viet Nam." On the latter point the agreement stated that "with respect to the bringing together of the three (provinces), the French Government pledges itself to ratify the decisions taken by the populations consulted by referendum." The crux of

SOURCE: *Foreign Relations*, 1946, Vol. VIII, pp. 52–54.

the present situation lies in the apparent intention of the French to settle both matters to their own advantage and without reference to Viet Nam.

The hostility of the Annamese toward the French began to mount to its present intensity when the French on June 1 announced the inauguration of the Provisional Government of the Republic of Cochinchina. Annamese leaders had long emphasized their view that the inclusion of Cochinchina in Viet Nam was a matter of life and death to their country. Cochinchina, it may be mentioned, contains the important mercantile cities of Saigon and Cholon, includes the mouths of the Mekong, and is the richest province in Indochina. Called the Southern Province by the Viet Namese, it is racially indistinct from Tonkin and Annam. Statements by the French that the referendum in Cochinchina (as pledged in the March 6 convention) would still be held failed to reassure Viet Nam leaders, who pointed out that such a referendum could not possibly be fair owing to the suppression by the French of pro-Viet Nam political parties and of all anti-French opinion. SEA's information tends to substantiate this point of view.

Tension between the French and the Annamese reached its present pitch when the French on August 1 convened a conference at Dalat (in southern Annam) to which the Royal Governments of Cambodia and Laos, the Government of the autonomous Republic of Cochinchina, and the native peoples of southern Annam and high plateau of Indochina (but *not* Viet Nam, recognized by the French as part of the Indochina Federation and French Union) to send delegates to "study the framework of the French Union." Subsequently published agenda of the conference indicated that the salient aspects of the Indochina Federation would also be deliberated. As an immediate result of this conference, the Viet Nam delegation which had been discussing the future relation between France and Viet Nam with the representatives of the French at Fontainebleau since July 6 announced that they were suspending negotiations until the French should have cleared up the "equivocal" situation which had been created. The head of the Viet Nam delegation, who had opened the conference with a violent blast against French policies, charged that the French were now trying to engineer their own statute for the Indochinese Federation and their own settlement of the status of Cochinchina and other areas claimed by Viet Nam. The view of Consul Saigon is not very different. He gave as his opinion that a front against Viet Nam was in the making, that the states participating in the Dalat Conference were at least tacitly recognized as free states by the French, and that France and these free states are now determining the status of the Indochinese federation without reference to Viet Nam. In his view it indicated double-dealing on the part of the French, and he reported that the French Commissioner for Cochinchina had forced the issue by threatening to resign unless his policy is carried out. Nothing has been said at the conference about a referendum. Finally, Consul Saigon added that he had learned that representatives of the southern regions of the Province of Annam (which has always been claimed by Viet Nam) will petition for inclusion of their territories in Cochinchina. In view of the completeness of the agenda of the Dalat Conference, which covers the essential framework of the Indochinese federation, and in view of the deliberate exclusion of Viet Nam from the conference, the conclusion is inescapable that the French are endeavoring to whittle down Viet Nam and to settle the future form of organization of Indochina with those who may be expected to be amenable to French influence.

Annamese reaction to French moves has been sharp, and following the suspension of the Fontainebleau negotiations, there were pro-Viet Nam manifestations in Saigon. The ambush of a French supply column near Hanoi by Annamese soldiers, during which the French suffered 52 casualties (one of the worst of many incidents during the past several months), may have been related to the opening of the Dalat Conference.

33. FRANCO-VIETNAMESE *MODUS VIVENDI*, SEPTEMBER 14, 1946

In protest against the Dalat Conference, the Vietnamese delegation left France, but Ho Chi Minh remained behind, hoping to reach an agreement that would gain more time for Vietnam to consolidate its political, economic, and military strength. The result was a modus vivendi *that did not resolve the primary problem of Cochin-china but did give Viet Minh adherents in the South political freedom in return for guarantees of French cultural and economic interests.*

The Government of the French Republic and the Government of the Democratic Republic of Viet Nam have firmly decided to pursue, in a spirit of reciprocal confidence, the policy of concord and collaboration established by the Preliminary Convention of March 6 and outlined during the course of Franco-Viet Nam conferences at Dalat and Fontainebleau. Convinced that this policy alone represents the permanent interests of the two countries and the democratic traditions which they claim as theirs, the two Governments, while referring to the Convention of March 6 which continues in force, consider that the time has come to register new progress in the development of relations between France and Viet Nam, while awaiting the time when circumstances will permit the conclusion of a complete and definitive agreement. In a spirit of friendship and mutual understanding, the Government of the French Republic and the Government of the Democratic Republic of Viet Nam have signed a *Modus Vivendi* providing, within the framework of the limited agreements, provisional solutions of the main issues of immediate interest which arise between France and Viet Nam. So far as the referendum provided for in the Convention of March 6 is concerned, the two Governments reserve the right to fix later its date and form. They are convinced that all the measures contained in the *Modus Vivendi* will contribute to the establishment, in the near future, of an atmosphere of calm and confidence which will permit the carrying on of definite negotiations in the near future. They believe, therefore, that it is possible to anticipate for the resumption in January 1947 of the work which has just taken place at the Franco-Vietnamese conference in Fontainebleau.

Franco-Vietnamese *Modus Vivendi*

Article 1—Viet Nam nationals in France and French nationals in Viet Nam shall enjoy the same freedom of establishment as nationals, as well as freedom of speech, freedom to teach, to trade and to circulate in general all the democratic freedoms.

SOURCE: Enclosure to Dispatch 366 from Bangkok, April 24, 1947.

Article 2—French property and concerns in Viet Nam shall not be subject to a stricter regime than the one reserved for Vietnamese property and concerns, particularly with respect to taxation and labor legislation. This equality of status shall be granted reciprocally to the property and enterprises of Viet Nam nationals in the territories of the French Union. The status of the French property and concerns in Viet Nam may not be changed except by common agreement between the French Republic and the Republic of Viet Nam. All French property requisitioned by the Government of Viet Nam or of which persons or enterprises have been deprived by the Viet Nam authorities shall be returned to their owners and parties entitled thereto. A mixed commission shall be appointed to fix procedure for such restitution.

Article 3—For the purpose of the resumption of the cultural relations which Viet Nam and France are equally desirous of developing, French educational institutions representing different categories shall be able to function freely in Viet Nam and they shall apply official French programs. The institutions in question shall receive, by special agreement, the buildings necessary for their functioning. They shall be open to Vietnamese students. Scientific research, the establishing and functioning of scientific institutions shall be unhindered for French nationals throughout Viet Nam territory. Viet Nam nationals shall enjoy the same privilege in France. The Pasteur Institute shall be secured in its rights and property. A mixed commission shall regulate the conditions under which the "Ecole Francaise d'Extrême Orient" (Far Eastern French School) shall resume its activity.

Article 4—The Government of the Republic of Viet Nam shall call, first on French nationals, whenever it needs advisers, technicians or experts. The priority granted to French nationals shall cease to be in effect only in cases where it is impossible for France to furnish the required personnel.

Article 5—As soon as the present problem of monetary standardization is settled, one and the same currency shall have circulation in the territories under the authority of the Government of the Democratic Republic of Viet Nam and in the other territories of Indochina. The said currency shall be the Indochinese piaster.

Article 6—Viet Nam shall form a Customs Union with the other members of the Federation. Therefore, there shall be no customs barrier within the country and the same tariffs shall be applied everywhere for entry into and departure from Indochinese territory. A coordinating customs and foreign trade committee which, moreover, may be the same as the one dealing with currency and exchange shall study the necessary means of application and prepare the organization of the Indochinese customs service.

Article 7—A mixed communications coordinating committee shall study the measures which will re-establish and improve communications between Viet Nam and the other countries of the Indochinese Federation and the French Union: land, sea and air transport, postal, telephone, telegraph and radio communications.

Article 8—Until such time as the French Government and the Government of the Democratic Republic of Viet Nam conclude a definitive agreement regulating the question of the diplomatic relations of Viet Nam with foreign countries, a mixed Franco-Viet Nam Commission shall determine the arrangements to be made to ensure the consular representation of Viet Nam in neighboring countries and its relations with foreign consuls.

Article 9—Desirous of ensuring as soon as possible, in Cochinchina and in

Southern Annam, the restoration of public order as indispensable to the free development of democratic liberties as it is to the resumption of commercial transactions and aware of the fortunate effect that the cessation on the part of both of all acts of hostility or violence will have, the French Government and the Government of the Democratic Republic of Viet Nam have decided on the following measures:

(a) Acts of hostility and violence on the part of both shall cease.

(b) Agreements of the French and Viet Nam General Staff shall arrange the conditions of application and supervision of measures decided in common.

(c) It is specified that prisoners detained at the present time for political reasons shall be released with the exception of those prosecuted for crimes and offenses against the common law. The same shall apply for prisoners captured in the course of operations. Viet Nam guarantees that no prosecution shall be initiated and no act of violence tolerated against any person by reason of his attachment or loyalty to France; reciprocally, the French Government guarantees that no prosecution shall be initiated and no act of violence tolerated toward any person because of his attachment to Viet Nam.

(d) The enjoyment of the democratic freedoms defined in Article I shall be reciprocally guaranteed.

(e) Unfriendly propaganda on both sides shall be terminated.

(f) A person of note designated by the Government of the Democratic Republic of Viet Nam and approved by the French Government shall be accredited to the High Commissioner to establish the cooperation indispensable for the carrying out of the present agreements.

Article 10—The Government of the French Republic and the Government of the Democratic Republic of Viet Nam agree to seek in common the conclusion of special agreements concerning all questions requiring them in order to strengthen friendly relations and prepare the way for a general, definitive treaty. Negotiations shall be resumed again for that purpose as soon as possible and in January 1947 at the latest.

Article 11—All the provisions of the present *Modus Vivendi* drawn up in duplicate, shall enter into force on October 30, 1946.

34. PROCLAMATION BY HO CHI MINH TO THE PEOPLE UPON RETURN FROM FRANCE AFTER NEGOTIATIONS, OCTOBER 23, 1946 [Extract]

Upon his return, Ho discussed the modus vivendi *he had negotiated in France, emphasizing the importance of avoiding violence and reprisals and of correct behavior toward the French.*

The French Government has acknowledged the holding of a referendum by our southern compatriots to decide on the fate of the South.

SOURCE: Ho Chi Minh, *Selected Works*, Vol. III, pp. 71–76.

In the September 14 *Modus Vivendi*, the French Government agreed to implement the main points concerning the South as follows:

1—To release the political prisoners and those arrested for taking part in the resistance.

2—Our southern compatriots are to have freedom of organisation, of meeting of the press, of movement, etc.

3—Both parties are to stop fighting.

The French government will undoubtedly respect its signature and implement the above clauses.

Now, what must our southern compatriots have to do?

1—The Vietnamese army like the French army must simultaneously stop fighting.

2—Our compatriots must carry out political actions in a democratic way.

3—Close unity must be realized with no discrimination as to political parties, social classes and creeds. Unity means strength. Division means weakness.

4—Acts of reprisals are forbidden. Toward those who went astray, our compatriots must display a generous policy. We must let them hear the voice of reason. Everybody loves his country. It is only for petty interests that they forget the great cause. If we use the right words, they will certainly listen to us. Violent actions are absolutely forbidden. This is what you have to do at present to create a peaceful atmosphere, paving the way democratically to reach the unification of our Viet Nam.

35. ULTIMATUM OF COLONEL DEBÈS, FRENCH COMMANDER AT HAIPHONG, NOVEMBER 22, 1946

Although the modus vivendi *established mixed commissions for customs and foreign trade, the French unilaterally set up harbor controls on October 15. When Vietnamese militia took some French border patrolmen prisoner in Haiphong in November, the French tried to free them by force, setting off a serious clash. Ho Chi Minh had agreed with a French delegation from Saigon to open talks in Hanoi on the operation of the mixed commission on customs and foreign trade on November 24. But the French hawks in Paris and Saigon wanted to use the Haiphong incident to gain control of the entire city. General Jean Valluy, commander of all French troops in Indochina, went around High Commissioner for Tonkin General Morlière and received permission directly from Premier Bidault to unilaterally seize control of Haiphong. Thus, Colonel Debès, the local commander at Haiphong, presented the Haiphong Administrative Committee an ultimatum aimed at providing the pretext for an all-out French offensive on the city. A French official later said that "no more than 6,000" Vietnamese had been killed by French naval bombardments of the Vietnamese quarters of the city on November*

SOURCE: Enclosure to Despatch 366 from Bangkok, April 24, 1947

22. *See Ellen J. Hammer,* The Struggle for Indochina, 1940–1955 *(Stanford, Calif.: Stanford University Press, 1966), p. 183.*

By order of the General High Commissioner of the French Republic in Indo-China, I demand:

    1. That all Viet Nam military or semi-military forces evacuate:

        a) the Chinese quarter, that is, the quarter bounded on the north by the Rue de la Mission; on the west, by the Song Tam-Bac; on the south, by the Darse Bonnal; on the east, by the Blvd. Admiral Courbet;

        b) the quarters to the northeast of the Avenue de Belgique (including that Avenue);

        c) the villages of Lac-Vien.

    2. That all the Vietnamese who were in those quarters and villages, whether or not they have their present domicile there, be disarmed and that no depot of arms or ammunition be set up there.

I demand the pure and simple acceptance of these conditions before November 23, at 9 A.M.; failing which, I reserve for myself the right to take any measure which the situation calls for.

36. EXCHANGE OF LETTERS BETWEEN GENERAL MORLIÈRE AND GIAP, NOVEMBER 28–30, 1946

In response to Vo Nguyen Giap's inquiry to General Morlière about measures that might be taken to prevent the new battles from developing from relatively minor incidents, Morlière again demanded, on a nonnegotiable basis, complete French military control of Haiphong, its surroundings, the roads connecting Haiphong and Hanoi, and all French garrisons. Giap proposed a joint commission to discuss the issues raised, but Morlière again rejected negotiation on the French demands.

In pursuance of the communication which was sent to you yesterday through me, I have the honor to confirm to you the military conditions laid down by the French High Command for the purpose of preventing definitively the possible repetition of the serious incidents of which the Haiphong region has just been the scene:

    1. In the zone bounded on the south by the Cua Lach-Tray; on the west, by the Lach-Tray cut, the Haly cut, the Cua Cam ferry, and the Haiphong road to Nui Deo (that locality included); on the north, by the Nui Deo road to Quang-Yen; on the east, by the Cua Nam-Trieu to its mouth (all these boundaries included):

        a) Prohibition to station any Viet Nam military or semi-military formation (militia, *tu-ve*, etc.). Safety in this zone will be assured entirely by the French troops.

SOURCE: Enclosure to Despatch 366 from Bangkok, April 24, 1947

b) Transit of Viet Nam military formations or armed boats across this zone, whatever may be the method of transportation (overland or river) will be subject to French military authorization and control.

2. There shall be free circulation of French troops on the Haiphong-Soson road. Moreover, it is to be understood that the roads connecting various French garrisons are to be cleared of obstacles or breaks which may have been made therein.

I should appreciate a prompt reply.

Please accept, Mr. Minister, the assurance of my very high consideration.

(Signed): Morlière

I have the honor to acknowledge receipt of your letter dated November 28, 1946. As the French proposal is of a very important nature, I suggest to you that we agree to form a joint commission to discuss the question.

Please accept, Sir, the assurance of my very high consideration.

(Signed): Vo Nguyen Giap

I have the honor to acknowledge receipt of your letter of today and to inform you that the measures stipulated in my letter of the morning of November 28 are the result of the very precise instructions which have been sent to me. They are not, therefore, subject to examination by the joint commission which you contemplate, and the constitution of which I consider unnecessary, unless its sole purpose is to fix the terms and conditions of execution thereof.

Please accept, Mr. Minister, the assurance of my very high consideration.

(Signed): Morlière

I have the honor to acknowledge receipt of your letter of the afternoon of November 28.

As the conditions of the French High Command, laid down in that letter of the morning (sic) of November 28, affect our sovereignty, I propose to you again that, in the interest of Franco-Viet Nam cooperation, you reconsider the question and that you inform the French High Command at Saigon of my suggestions.

Please accept, Sir, the assurance of my very high consideration.

(Signed): Vo Nguyen Giap

I have the honor to acknowledge receipt of your letter of November 29, 1946.

In accordance with the desire which you expressed, I have transmitted by telegram the contents thereof to the French High Command at Saigon, which I had also kept informed of the proposal expressed in your letter of November 28, 1946.

But I confirm to you that the measures contemplated in my letter of the morning of November 28 are perfectly well-known to the French High Command at Saigon, and have received its full approval.

Moreover, I state explicitly to you, as I had already done in the course of our conversation, that these military measures in no way prejudice any Franco-Viet Nam commercial and customs agreements which are to govern the port of Haiphong later.

Please accept, Mr. Minister, the assurance of my very high consideration.

(Signed): Morlière

37. TELEGRAM FROM ACTING SECRETARY ACHESON TO DIVISION CHIEF MOFFAT IN SAIGON, DECEMBER 5, 1946

Despite his anxiety at the French intention to reestablish control by military force, Acheson instructed State Department Chief of the Division of Southeast Asian Affairs Abbot Low Moffat, who was visiting Hanoi, that he was to tell Ho Chi Minh that he would have to give up the DRV insistence on a referendum in Cochinchina and accept a "compromise" on its status. Acheson indicated that the United States was interested in finding Vietnamese groups to support as an alternative to Ho's government, because of its alleged Moscow connections.

Assume you will see Ho in Hanoi and offer following summary our present thinking as guide.

Keep in mind Ho's clear record as agent international communism, absence evidence recantation Moscow affiliations, confused political situation France and support Ho receiving French Communist Party. Least desirable eventuality would be establishment Communist-dominated, Moscow-oriented state Indochina in view DEPT, which most interested INFO strength non-communist elements Vietnam. Report fully, repeating or requesting DEPT repeat Paris.

Recent occurrences Tonkin cause deep concern. Consider March 6 accord and *modus vivendi* as result peaceful negotiation provide basis settlement outstanding questions between France and Vietnam and impose responsibility both sides not prejudice future, particularly forthcoming Fontainebleau Conference, by resort force. Unsettled situation such as pertains certain to offer provocations both sides, but for this reason conciliatory patient attitude especially necessary. Intransigence either side and disposition exploit incidents can only retard economic rehabilitation Indochina and cause indefinite postponement conditions cooperation France and Vietnam which both agree essential.

If Ho takes stand non-implementation promise by French of Cochinchina referendum relieves Vietnam responsibility compliance with agreements, you might if you consider advisable raise question whether he believes referendum after such long disorder could produce worthwhile result and whether he considers compromise on status Cochinchina could possibly be reached through negotiation.

May say American people have welcomed attainments Indochinese in efforts realize praiseworthy aspiration greater autonomy in framework democratic institutions and it would be regrettable should this interest and sympathy be imperilled by any tendency Vietnam administration force issues by intransigence and violence.

May inform Ho Caffery discussing situation French similar frankness. For your INFO, Baudet in DEC 3 conversation stated 1) no question reconquest Indochina as such would be counter French public opinion and probably beyond French military resources, 2) French will continue base policy March 6 accord and *modus*

SOURCE: *U.S.-Vietnam Relations*, Book 8, pp. 85–86.

vivendi and make every effort apply them through negotiation Vietnam, 3) French would resort forceful measures only on restricted scale in case flagrant violation agreements Vietnam, 4) d'Argenlieu's usefulness impaired by outspoken dislike Vietnam officials and replacement perhaps desirable, 5) French Communists embarrassed in pose as guardian French international interests by barrage telegraphic appeals from Vietnam. Caffery will express gratification this statement French policy with observation implementation such policy should go far obviate any danger that 1) Vietnamese irreconcilables and extremists might be in position make capital of situation 2) Vietnamese might be turned irrevocably against West and toward ideologies and affiliations hostile democracies which could result perpetual foment Indochina with consequences all Southeast Asia.

Avoid impression US Govt making formal intervention this juncture. Publicity any kind would be unfortunate.

Paris be guided foregoing.

38. LETTER FROM MOFFAT IN HANOI TO THE STATE DEPARTMENT, DECEMBER 1946 [Extracts]

Moffat called on Ho Chi Minh in Hanoi at the height of the tension between the Vietnamese and the French. Ho and Deputy Foreign Minister Hoang Minh Giam did their best to get the United States to help Vietnam preserve its independence, even going so far as to hold out the prospect of an American naval base at Cam Ranh Bay—ironically the site of the largest U.S. base complex during the second Indochina War. But Moffat made it clear that Vietnam would have to have French approval for any diplomatic relationship with the United States.

At 5:00, after a siesta, we went again to the Presidency. Giam met us in the hall and led us upstairs to Ho Chi Minh's room, where he lay in a large bed with a black muffler around his neck. Although he had no fever, he was obviously weak and his voice was often very feeble. He spoke of his friendship and admiration for the United States and the Americans he had known and worked with in the jungle, etc., and how they had treated the Annamese as equals. He spoke of his desire to build up Vietnam in collaboration with the French so that his people might be better off, and to that end they wanted independence to seek friends among other countries as well as France and to secure the capital needed to develop their country, which France was now too poor to give them. He said he knew that the United States did not like communism, but that that was not his aim. If he could secure their independence that was enough for his life time. "Perhaps fifty years from now the United States will be communist; and then the Vietnam can be also or "then

SOURCE: *The United States and Vietnam: 1944–1947*, Staff Study, Committee on Foreign Relations, U.S. Senate, April 3, 1972 (Washington: Government Printing Office, 1972), Appendix II, pp. 41–42.

they will not object if the Vietnam is also." He spoke in English, but I am not sure of his exact words. The intent, at any rate, was a smiling, and friendly "Don't worry"—which coincides with the able French views (not the popular view) that the group in charge of Vietnam are at this stage nationalists first, utilizing their party techniques and discipline to the end; that an effective nationalist state is a prerequisite to any attempt at developing a communist state—which objective must for the time being be secondary. He also stressed his desire for peace, but made it clear that he also felt that the Vietnam could not surrender to France with respect to the new order to withdraw from the environs of Haiphong. I confined my remarks to expressing a hope for a peaceful settlement and my very genuine pleasure at meeting him (as well, of course, as the reason for my trip throughout SEA).

At 5:00 Giam had an official tea for me at the Presidency. Madame Saincanny [sic] was there. Morliere, Lami and a few other French. I met some of the other Vietnamese officials, some businessmen and doctors and admired some rather lovely lacquer pictures which is a Tonkinese specialty. Giam asked if he could talk with me privately and that he had a present for me from Ho Chi Minh and wanted to ask some questions; so I left at 6:00 and went with Jim [James O'Sullivan, U.S. vice consul in Hanoi] to the Consulate where Giam joined us presently. There he presented me with an autographed photograph and a piece of "mountain brocade" inscribed to Ho. (The purpose, of course, to show that the hill people also back Ho. The Tonkinese never live above the 25 meter level, occupy the Delta, but *not* the mountains). Then he started to explain how Vietnam wanted free ports, and the right to trade freely; to get foreign capital where they would; they wanted American capital, commerce; they hoped an American airline would use Hanoi; an American shipline use Haiphong regularly, etc. In short, he kept reiterating they did not always want to be "compressed" by the French. I interrupted finally to explain that under the March 6 Agreement, their status in many respects is unsettled— "subject to future French-Vietnam negotiations"—such as foreign affairs (for which reason we do not recognize and have relations with the Vietnam Government) and finance, etc. (for which reason, until agreement is reached, we assume in such matters French laws still obtain). He demurred on this last—said the customs question was the cause of the Haiphong incident—and passed on). He then stated Vietnam had no navy and had no intention of being warlike, but would be glad to cooperate with the U.S. in developing Cam Ranh Bay as a naval base, that it was a very important location between Singapore and Hong Kong and opposite the P.I. I replied I knew nothing of the military plans of my Government, but doubted if we would be interested in such a base. (Cam Ranh Bay, as you know, is in South Annam and is presently controlled by the French). I explained that I was sure that the U.S. would want to have trade and commerce with Vietnam; mentioned the proposed route approved by CAB which includes Hanoi: but stated before there could be any direct relations, the Vietnamese and French would have to agree on the respective powers of the two governments. Giam also stated the Vietnam desire for an economic federation of Indochina; a customs union and free trade between the three states; and federal collection of customs so that the revenues could be fairly distributed to the states. But, he stated, the Vietnam was strongly opposed to any political power in the federation. I have perhaps given his remarks more coherence than they had. The impression I received was one of extreme naivety.

39. TELEGRAM FROM HO CHI MINH
TO PREMIER BLUM, DECEMBER 15, 1946

*On December 13, a Conference of Party Zonal Chiefs was convened in Ha
Dong, and the Central Committee's assessment was that "French reactionaries in
the colony are trying to push into war," but said the Party had to "struggle for the
possibility of peace," even while "preparing urgently to carry on all-people,
all-sided long-term warfare." (Quoted in* Lich Su Quan Doi Nhan Viet Nam
[History of the Viet Nam People's Army], *(Hanoi: Quan Doi Nhan Dan, 1974), p.
249.)*

*Two days later Ho sent a telegram to Blum proposing a series of steps the two
sides could take to return to the previous accords and begin "definitive negotiations." But the message was held by French authorities in Saigon until December
26—a deliberate sabotage of any move toward negotiations by the Blum government. See Philippe Devillers,* Histoire du Vietnam de 1940 à 1952 *(Paris: Editions
du Seuil), p. 351.*

Occasion your election Presidency French Government,

To show our confidence in you and in people France,

To show our sincere desire fraternal cooperation with French people,

To prove that our only aspiration is independence and territorial integrity of
Viet Nam within French Union,

To prove our ardent desire to settle peacefully serious incidents which at
present steep our country in blood,

To prove that we have always been prepared to apply loyally agreements
signed by our two Governments,

To dispel atmosphere of hostility, reestablish atmosphere of confidence and
friendship, and effectively prepare definitive negotiations,

I have the honor to make to you the following concrete proposals:

a) On the Viet Nam side:

1) To invite the evacuated Viet Nam population to return to the cities.

2) To take all necessary measures to assure the return to the cities of the
economic life disturbed by the present state of hostility.

3) To put an end to the measures of self-protection taken by the inhabitants of the cities.

4) To assure the return to normalcy of the Hanoi-Langson thoroughfare.

b) On the French side:

1) Return of the French and Viet Nam troops to the positions held before
November 20, 1946 at Haiphong and Langson, and withdrawal of the reinforcements recently sent to Tourane, contrary to the agreements.

2) To cease the so-called mopping-up operations and campaigns of repression in Cochin-China and North Annam.

c) On both sides:

1) To start working immediately the agencies contemplated for the ap-

SOURCE: Enclosure to Despatch 366 from Bangkok, April 24, 1947

plication of the *Modus-Vivendi*, a part of the Commission at Hanoi, another at Saigon, as the country resort of DALAT offers us no conveniences for work.

2) To put an end to all unfriendly propaganda in French and Viet Nam radio-broadcasts and press.

Awaiting the honor of your reply, I beg you to accept the expression of my very high consideration.

40. GIAP'S ORDER FOR NATIONWIDE RESISTANCE, DECEMBER 19, 1946

On December 16, the Party Central Committee's Current Affairs Committee sent a message to its Province Party organs in the South making it clear that a nationwide resistance war would have to be fought. On December 17, there was a massacre of dozens of civilians by French troops in Hanoi, who also continued unilaterally to destroy barricades. The following day the Executive Committee of the Party Central Committee began meeting in special session and decided to mobilize the population for resistance. For the next two days, fundamental problems of resistance war were discussed.

The French continued to push for a showdown with Vietnam. On December 18, while the Vietnamese leaders were secretly discussing plans for resistance, the French occupied the Ministries of Finance and Communications in Hanoi. On the evening of December 19, General Morlière brought matters to a head by demanding the disarming of Vietnamese militia in Hanoi. That night, the Indochinese Communist Party Central Committee met and decided to begin the resistance war. At 9:00 p.m. December 19, the orders for armed struggle were issued over Vo Nguyen Giap's signature.

Order for Nationwide Resistance

Officers of the National Guard, Commanders of units and members of the self-defense militia and self-defense forces,

At 8 o'clock tonight, December 19, 1946, the French troops have provoked hostilities in the capital of the Democratic Republic of Vietnam.

The Fatherland is in danger!
The hour of combat has come!

In accordance with the order of Chairman Ho and the Government, as Minister of National Defense, I order all soldiers of the National Guard and Self-defense militia in the Center, South and North to:

Stand up in unison,
Dash into battle,
Destroy the invaders and save the country,

Sacrifice to the last drop of blood in the struggle for the Independence and Unification of the Fatherland.

SOURCE: Giap, *Orders of the Day*, pp. 19–20. [Translation by the editor.]

The resistance will be long and extremely hard, but the just cause is on our side, and we will definitely be victorious.

Annihilate the French colonialists!
Long live independence and unified Vietnam!
Long live the victory of the resistance!
Resolve to fight!

41. TELEGRAM FROM CONSUL REED IN SAIGON TO BYRNES, DECEMBER 24, 1946

While the French disclaimed any intention of imposing a settlement by force, in a conversation with the U.S. consul in Saigon, Admiral d'Argenlieu, French High Commissioner for Indochina, confirmed that the French would no longer deal with Ho's government and would seek to detach Annam as well as Cochinchina from Tonkin, making them independent states in the French-sponsored Indochinese Federation.

Unprovoked premeditated attack by Vietnam, with atrocities against innocent civilians, at time when French Govt sending representative discuss association accords and plan future French-Vietnam relations, leaves French free hand to deal with situation, especially as Vietnam Govt has fled and effectively no such govt. So said High Commissioner in conversation yesterday prior arrival Moutet. He stated French do not plan exploit situation and there is, first, no intention reconquer FIC, and, second, no intention return former colonial system—enough troops will be sent restore order and assure opportunity all persons carry on peaceful pursuits. He admitted many mistakes made in past due those persons reluctant give up prewar life and policy in FIC and said mistakes will be made in future but France holds intention aid honest and meritorious aspirations native peoples (but commented difficult to treat with persons whose aim is destruction as recent events have shown to be aim of Ho and his govt) and France desired chiefly promote their economic interests. French prepared deal with any govt in which can place confidence.

He stressed federation plan is only possible solution, giving peoples of FIC measure of autonomy of which they are now capable, but not excluding possibility of larger independence when peoples are capable thereof. He felt majority natives will welcome removal Ho regime which established and maintained by terroristic methods and in no sense democratic—also felt that with fear reprisals removed, Annam would prefer be state apart from Tonkin confederation, thus being composed of same five states as formed FIC in past. Expressed satisfaction he now had backing French Govt (with certain notable exceptions) and declared his policy vindicated especially his distrust Ho and his associates but made one remark that indicated he might not be here long. He mentioned return General Leclerc, expected here shortly, but I have reason believe High Commissioner not particularly pleased. Factually, situation in north improving and he hoped all under control within 15 days—expressed grave concern fate of French at Vinh from which no news since French surrendered.

SOURCE: *Foreign Relations of the United States (Washington, D.C.: GPO, 1971)* 1946 Vol. VIII, pp. 78–79.

In comment [by me?] French have one more chance impress natives their desire deal fairly with them and to give them advantages both economic and social withheld in past, and if French fail to take advantage this opportunity and institute repressive high handed measures (policy of force) of past no settlement of situation can be expected foreseeable future and period guerilla warfare will follow. [Apparent garble] however presupposes willingness Vietnam act with reasonableness and doubt whether French will treat with Ho in view of "treacherous" attack on civilians as well as military. Perhaps mediation third party only solution.

Please repeat Paris, London.

1947

42. TELEGRAM FROM SECRETARY OF STATE GEORGE C. MARSHALL TO CAFFERY, FEBRUARY 3, 1947

The first policy statement by the State Department under the new secretary of state, George C. Marshall, reflected two contradictory aspects of the American attitude toward Indochina: on one hand, the United States wanted France restored to its position as a world power, which meant its restoration as the imperialist power in Indochina; on the other hand, it feared that France did not recognize that colonialism in the nineteenth-century sense was outmoded. Despite doubts about French policy in Indochina, Marshall accepted the idea that French colonialism was preferable to a Communist revolution in Vietnam and offered no alternative to the French policy of using force to maintain control.

There is reason for increasing concern over situation as it is developing in Indochina and for that reason I feel you might well take early occasion to have frank talk with Ramadier or Bidault or both somewhat along lines conversations you have already had with Blum, but at this time going in fact beyond position you took in those talks. We have only very friendliest feelings toward France and we are anxious in every way we can to support France in her fight to regain her economic, political and military strength and to restore herself as in fact one of major powers of world. In spite any misunderstanding which might have arisen in minds French in regard to our position concerning Indochina they must appreciate that we have fully recognized France's sovereign position in that area and we do not wish to have it appear that we are in any way endeavoring undermine that position, and French should know it is our desire to be helpful and we stand ready assist any appropriate way we can find solution for Indochinese problem. At same time we

SOURCE: Foreign Relations of the United States, 1947, (Washington, D.C.: GPO, 1972), Vol. VI, pp. 67–68.

cannot shut our eyes to fact that there are two sides this problem and that our reports indicate both a lack French understanding of other side (more in Saigon than in Paris) and continued resistance dangerously outmoded colonial outlook and methods in area. Furthermore, there is no escape from fact that trend of times is to effect that colonial empires in XIX Century sense are rapidly becoming thing of past. Action felt in India and Burma and Dutch in Indonesia are outstanding examples this trend, and French themselves took cognizance of it both in new Constitution and in their agreements with Vietnam. On other hand we do not lose sight fact that Ho Chi Minh has direct Communist connection and it should be obvious that we are not interested in seeing colonial empire administrations supplanted by philosophy and political organizations emanating from and controlled by Kremlin. Fact does remain, however, that a situation does exist in Indochina which can no longer be considered, if it ever was considered, to be of a local character. If that situation continues deteriorate some country in direct interest is very likely to bring matter before Security Council under Chapter 11 of Charter. We have no intention taking such action ourselves at this time, but French will surely appreciate that we do have a vital interest in political and economic well being this area. If some country should bring matter before Security Council we would find it difficult to oppose an investigation Indochinese problem unless negotiations between parties were going on. It might be added that it would not in our estimation be in France's long-range interest to use her veto position to keep matter from coming before Council. Frankly we have no solution of problem to suggest. It is basically matter for two parties to work out themselves and from your reports and those from Indochina we are led to feel that both parties have endeavored to keep door open to some sort of settlement. We appreciate fact that Vietnam started present fighting in Indochina on December 19 and that this action has made it more difficult for French to adopt a position of generosity and conciliation. Nevertheless we hope that French will find it possible to be more than generous in trying to find a solution.

43. DRV ACCOUNT OF HO CHI MINH–PAUL MUS MEETING, MAY 12, 1947

To counteract French propaganda that his government was dominated by anti-French extremists, as well as to appeal to those French officials who wanted a peace settlement, Ho Chi Minh asked for an immediate cease-fire. And the following month, the newly nominated foreign minister, Hoang Minh Giam, offered again to negotiate a peaceful settlement of the conflict. In response to Hoang Minh Giam's appeal, High Commissioner Emile Bollaert dispatched Professor Paul Mus, a former political adviser to General LeClerc, Commander of French Forces in the Far East in 1945, to present France's nonnegotiable demands. This Vietnamese account of the French position presented by Mus is confirmed by Mus

SOURCE: Translation of a Vietnamese-language document distributed by the DRV, in Airgram from U.S. Consul O'Sullivan in Hanoi to the secretary of state, June 20, 1947, 851G.00/6-2047, Diplomatic Papers, National Archives.

*himself, although he adds two further conditions for peace: surrender of all hos-
tages and of all non-Vietnamese personnel serving with Viet Minh forces. See Paul
Mus,* Viet-Nam: Sociologie d'une Guerre *(Paris: Editions du Seuil, 1952), p. 315.*

President HO and Minister of Foreign Affairs GIAM met with a representative
of High Commissioner BOLLAERT in a place not far from Hanoi.

This meeting was most cordial for the representative of the High Commissioner is an old acquaintance of President HO and Minister GIAM.

When the discussion began on the question of the cessation of hostilities, the
representative of M. BOLLAERT proposed the following conditions:

1) The Vietnam Government will abstain from all reprisals against pro-French
people upon the cessation of hostilities.

2) The Vietnamese troops will surrender all their arms and munitions to
France.

3) The French troops have the right to circulate and occupy freely throughout
the territory of Vietnam. Vietnamese troops will assemble in spots designated by
the French Army.

President HO replied to the first condition: After the last worldwide hostilities,
if France took action against Frenchmen who delivered France to Germany, we
ought to punish Vietnamese who have decided to deliver our country to a foreign
nation. However, we can promise leniency toward these individuals.

To the other conditions, President HO replied:

High Commissioner BOLLAERT is a French democrat and also a patriot. I
ask you if High Commissioner BOLLAERT has recognized the act by which the
Pétain Government delivered arms and munitions to the German Army, permitted
German troops freedom of action in French territory and obliged French troops to
assemble in determined positions? Is this an armistice?

At this point in the conversation, the representative of M. BOLLAERT said:
In these circumstances, we have nothing more to say to you.

The diplomatic interview thus ended.

President HO then asked the French representative: You certainly know the
history of Vietnam

Yes, I have made several studies of it.

In that case, you recall the feats of our ancestors. TRAN HUNG DAO who
fought for five years against the Mongol armies and LE LOI who resisted for ten
years against the Chinese armies. Well, at the present time, we can resist five
years, ten years and more. Our compatriots are firmly decided to unite and to obey
the government's orders to resist until independence and unification are obtained.

44. TELEGRAM FROM MARSHALL TO CAFFERY IN PARIS, MAY 13, 1947

*In a telegram revealing the main lines of American thinking not only about
Vietnam but about South Asia as a whole, Marshall warned France on one hand,
that efforts to maintain colonial control in Vietnam would bolster the Communists
through the area and jeopardize the tenuous position of the Western powers in the*

SOURCE: *Foreign Relations,* 1947, Vol. VI, pp. 95–97.

region. But he asserted, on the other hand, that, without the guiding hand of the western powers, Vietnam and other countries might band together and turn hostile to the West, whether under Communist or militant nationalist leadership. The telegram thus adumbrated the idea of a Franco-Vietnamese arrangement that at the same time offered formal independence or autonomy and maintained a dominant French influence over the country.

We becoming increasingly concerned by slow progress toward settlement Indochina dispute. We fully appreciate French are making effort reach satisfactory settlement and hope visit Commissioner Bollaert to Indochina will produce concrete results. The following considerations, however, are submitted for your use any conversations you may have with French authorities at appropriate time this subject. We recognize it might not be desirable make such approach to newly constituted government in first days its reorganization, but nevertheless feel early appropriate opportunity might be found inform French Gov of our concern in this matter.

Key our position is our awareness that in respect developments affecting position Western democratic powers in southern Asia, we essentially in same boat as French, also as British and Dutch. We cannot conceive setbacks to long-range interests France which would not also be setbacks our own. Conversely we should regard close association France and members French Union as not only to advantage peoples concerned, but indirectly our own.

In our view, southern Asia in critical phase its history with seven new nations in process achieving or struggling independence or autonomy. These nations include quarter inhabitants world and their future course, owing sheer weight populations, resources they command, and strategic location, will be momentous factor world stability. Following relaxation European controls, internal racial, religious, and national differences could plunge new nations into violent discord, or already apparent anti-Western Pan-Asiatic tendencies could become dominant political force, or Communists could capture control. We consider as best safeguard against these eventualities a continued close association between newly-autonomous peoples and powers which have long been responsible their welfare. In particular we recognize Vietnamese will for indefinite period require French material and technical assistance and enlightened political guidance which can be provided only by nation steeped like France in democratic tradition and confirmed in respect human liberties and worth individual.

We equally convinced, however, such association must be voluntary to be lasting and achieve results, and that protraction present situation Indochina can only destroy basis voluntary cooperation, leave legacy permanent bitterness, and irrevocably alienate Vietnamese from France and those values represented by France and other Western democracies.

While fully appreciating difficulties French position this conflict, we feel there is danger in any arrangement which might provide Vietnamese opportunity compare unfavorably their own position and that of other peoples southern Asia who have made tremendous strides toward autonomy since war.

While we are still ready and willing to do anything we can which might be considered helpful, French will understand we not attempting come forward with any solution our own or intervene in situation. However, they will also understand we inescapably concerned with situation Far East generally, upon which developments Indochina likely have profound effect.

Plain fact is that Western democratic system is on defensive in almost all emergent nations southern Asia and, because identified by peoples these nations with what they have considered former denial their rights, is particularly vulnerable to attacks by demagogic leaders political movements of either ultra-nationalist or Communist nature which promise redress and revenge past so-called wrongs and inequalities. Signs development anti-Western Asiatic consciousness already multiplying, of which Inter-Asian CONF an example. Unanimity support for Vietnamese among other Asiatic countries very striking, even leading to moves Burma, India, and Malaya send volunteer forces their assistance. Vietnam cause proving rallying-cry for all anti-Western forces and playing in hands Communists all areas. We fear continuation conflict may jeopardize position all Western democratic powers in southern Asia and lead to very eventualities of which we most apprehensive.

We confident French fully aware dangers inherent in situation and therefore venture express renewed hope they will be most generous attempt find early solution which, by recognizing legitimate desires Vietnamese, will restore peace and deprive anti-democratic forces of powerful weapon.

For your INFO, evidence that French Communists are being directed accelerate their agitation French colonies even extent lose much popular support France (URTEL 1719 Apr 25) may be indication Kremlin prepared sacrifice temporary gains with 40 million French to long range colonial strategy with 600 million dependent people, which lends great urgency foregoing views. French position Indochina dispute since DEC 19, which based on Vietnam initiative attack, seems DEPT dangerously one-sided in ignoring Debès attack Haiphong NOV 23 and understandable Vietnam contention that stand had be made some point view steady French encroachments after MAR 6 on authority and territory Vietnam (e.g., establishment Cochinchinese REP, occupation southern Annam and Moi Plateau, and Dalat plan French-dominated Federation to which Vietnam would be subservient). DEPT much concerned lest French efforts find QUOTE true representatives Vietnam UNQUOTE with whom negotiate result creation impotent puppet GOVT along lines Cochinchina regime, or that restoration Baodai may be attempted, implying democracies reduced resort monarchy as weapon against Communism. You may refer these further views if nature your conversations French appears warrant.

Saigon and Hanoi should be guided by this TEL in any conversation Bollaert.

45. AIRGRAM FROM REED TO ACHESON, JUNE 14, 1947 [Extract]

In the most complete analysis of French political policy in Indochina under High Commissioner Bollaert's regime, the consul in Saigon noted that most Vietnamese regarded Ho Chi Minh's government as the only legitimate government of Vietnam and would look upon any French-approved alternative as a puppet regime. But he concluded that the Vietnamese were incapable of governing themselves "without Occidental check or control" and that there would have to be a compromise between Vietnamese and French interests in Indochina.

SOURCE: 851G.00/6-1447, Diplomatic Papers, National Archives.

From the beginning, in great contrast to the non-committal austerity of Admiral d'Argenlieu, Mr. Bollaert radiated an atmosphere of confidence and optimism, although many in his entourage were definitely pessimistic. This optimism was good psychology as it tended to impress upon people that the situation was not hopeless and that there was a solution to the complex political problem. His declaration at Dalat on May 8 that he hoped that the vacant seats at the Economic Conference would soon be filled was definitely an olive branch to the abstaining Vietnamese. His speech at Hanoi on May 15 was a presentation of the most liberal policy that the French had so far formulated. To the great majority it appeared that the High Commissioner was sincere in his endeavor to put an end to the intercine war of the past 20 months and to arrive at a mutually acceptable formula for the future. His optimism must have been shaken at times and he must have wondered whether there was any solution short of military reconquest or complete capitulation—the attack on the convoy to Mythe in which some 40 persons were killed, the ever spreading wave of terrorism in the south, and the devastation of the north, were undoubtedly causes of just concern. One may well ask, however, whether or not Mr. Bollaert's optimism and fine speeches were entirely sincere. Thus, it is alleged that the French themselves were to blame for the failure to arrive at an armistice, as reputedly proposed by Ho Chi Minh in a letter forwarded by Mr. AESCHLIMAN of the International Red Cross to the French authorities, because the harsh terms they offered amounted to virtually a demand for the abject surrender of the Viet Minh forces. Moreover, it was well within the bounds of reason that the French hoped that Ho Chi Minh would meet with an "unfortunate" accident, which would solve the question to treat or not to treat with him. But if the French did not want to consider Ho Chi Minh as the representative of the Annamites how could they, the French, justify their dickering with Bao Dai? It is hard to believe that as sagacious a person as the High Commissioner appeared to be could believe that an obviously French created regime, around the person of Bao Dai, would succeed or that the millions of Asiatics now clamoring for independence would accept such a regime at its face value.

What plan if any the High Commissioner has taken back to France is of course not known. Logically, however, any plan likely to succeed will represent a great concession on the part of France and the unquestionable sacrifice of many of her interests. France has already jettisoned the idea of a Federation of the five entities making up the French Indochina of the past, France may well be prepared to throw overboard the Provisional Government of the Republic of Cochinchina, and France appears to be willing to accept a Vietnam Federation so long as both French and native rights are protected and not to be the spoil of an admittedly totalitarian regime. What security France can exact for such protection in the future is difficult to say. France, if Mr. Bollaert's declaration is to be given credence, will refuse to deal with any one faction. On the other hand Ho Chi Minh has always said he is not fighting the French but only the colonialists, and he has given some indication of willingness to make concessions in his acknowledgement of the right of each of the three Kys to have local autonomy. How far communist-trained Ho Chi Minh is to be trusted is problematic and his concession of local autonomy may be merely a blind. Unfortunately, the majority of natives stoutly maintain that Ho Chi Minh is the man, *and the only one*, who represents them and they will oppose the putting forward of any other candidate as the creation of but another puppet and the erecting of a smoke screen for France's real intentions. While the natives are tired of fighting and are apprehensive of the destruction and famine that impend for the future there is still a determined nucleus who are prepared to wage a bitter and ruthless warfare if the greater part of their claims is not met. To reconcile these differences will be difficult, but for the future of Indochina, for the stability of Southeast Asia, for the good of the whole Far East, and for the prestige of western democracy, whatever plan is adopted must be put into operation without great loss of time.

From a purely practical point of view too great concessions on the part of France might be very disastrous, if such concessions give the natives virtually a free hand. Many observers doubt whether they are capable of running an independent state and point to the fact that the Philippines after 40 odd years of benevolent tutelage, in which the advantages of education and instruction were available to all, are still not a model of good government. How much less chance would the Annamites have of making a success? The majority of these observers opine that without Occidental check or control the result would be chaos—and in that chaos either the Soviet or the Chinese would find their opportunity. The former would be able to establish their ideology in the very heart of teeming Southeast Asia, with millions of people to indoctrinate and to prepare for the ultimate struggle with the western democracies. The latter would be able to realize their age-old desire to dominate if not to take over this part of the Far East, a desire which is even now manifest. To many observers, the Chinese danger is the greater, even if not imminent because of China's preoccupation with her own political problems. Be that as it may, something must be done to eradicate the distrust and almost contempt of the French for the natives, and to eradicate the distrust and hatred of the natives for the French; something must be done to bring home to the French the fact that times have changed and that the natives have a right to more than a semblance of independence, and to bring home to the natives that the French have a legitimate interest and place in Indochina. Mr. Bollaert must have learned that the above are imperative and that they are the stones in the foundation of peace in Indochina.

The High Commissioner has now gathered the necessary data and it is the task of the French Government to supply and apply the answer. While that Government may continue to procrastinate in the hopes of wearing down the native opposition, I believe that that Government will be led to accept a Federated Republic of Vietnam, in which each of the three Kys will have autonomy, freely associated with the French Union. And Ho Chi Minh, if he is really the nationalist and patriot that he claims to be, must accept that his totalitarian government and Tonkin cannot speak for all Annamites.

46. TELEGRAM FROM MARSHALL TO REED, JULY 17, 1947

By mid-1947, the U.S. State Department was taking seriously the possibility that the French would be forced to accept a unified Vietnam under Ho's government. This telegram from Marshall reveals the department's toying with the idea of

SOURCE: *Foreign Relations*, 1947, Vol. VI, pp. 117–118.

a "national communism" in Vietnam and the possibility that the United States might be able to live with it.

Request your and Hanoi's appraisal implications relation US objectives stable Southeast Asia friendly to democratic West in event French should be forced deal present Vietnam Govt and this Govt should eventually emerge as controlling power three Annamese provinces. Refer particularly the following:

1. Whether influence Communists in present coalition Govt and behind-scenes Communists like Dang Xuan Khu and Ha Ba Cang would be sufficient put Vietnam in Soviet camp.

2. Position Ho respect above. Whether your opinion evidence increasing opposition to Ho by militants tends substantiate repeated reports his abandonment Party line and to corroborate reported letter to Chiang Kai Shek in which Ho excused past Communists connection on grounds nowhere else turn, and stated only interest now independence his country. (Impression here Ho publicly attempting walk chalked line between nationalism and Communism effort retain backing both forces.)

3. Whether intellectuals backing Vietnam realize what Communism means as international political force distinct its economic aspects and whether nationalists among them feel they can cope in future with Communist leaders Vietnam.

4. Whether, with removal solidifying effect French pressure, coherent Govt likely be extended over Vietnam representing real interests Annamese and allowing reasonably free political expression or whether coalition would break in factions which would settle differences by terrorism and armed force, resulting chronic disorders or eventual police state under one-party rule.

5. Sensitivity Vietnamese to US opinion and importance this fact or future orientation Vietnam Govt. While French Communists exploit every show of US interest developments Indochina to warn of US intervention, Vietnamese apparently welcome this interest.

6. Effect on Laotians and Cambodians should Soviet-oriented Vietnam emerge Dept fully realizes paucity solid info on which base appraisal.

47. TELEGRAMS FROM VICE-CONSUL JAMES L. O'SULLIVAN IN HANOI AND REED IN SAIGON TO MARSHALL, JULY 21 AND 24, 1947

In their responses to Secretary Marshall's query on the implications of a Communist-controlled Vietnam, both O'Sullivan and Reed indicated that it would not necessarily be subservient to the Soviet Union and that the United States could play a role there. Both predicted chaos and a "police state" in Vietnam unless Western authority was maintained over the country.

SOURCE: *Foreign Relations*, 1947, Vol. VI, pp. 121–126.

Reference Department's telegram 66, July 17. Department's assumptions do not make clear how much French influence it expects would remain event French are forced directly with Ho Chi Minh. But assuming French will deal with Ho only in last extremity and their control would tend become negligible thereafter:

1. Influence Communists in present government would not be sufficient to put Viet Nam squarely in Soviet camp although there would be pull in that direction. Agreement with French which would satisfy nationalism of Viet Namese people would probably lead to decrease in under-cover activities of characters such as Ha Ba Cang and Dang Xuan Khu and Tongbo members who would tend to emerge from shadows. Geographic isolation Indochina from Russia and realization by Ho Chi Minh of United States power based in Philippines would be sufficient to prevent him or any government formed here from entering whole-heartedly Soviet camp.

2. Until further information available, I am very skeptical regarding apparent opposition of militants to Ho. However, Ho's very great reluctance to admit that he is Nguyen Ai Quoc or to show any connection whatsoever with Russia is indicative of his realization that he must deal with West. Ho wrote 25 years ago that national revolution must precede Communist revolution in Indochina and it is obvious his first concern is get rid of French here. He is trying to obtain aid wherever he can and will tend be oriented toward source from whence assistance comes.

3. Have impression that intellectuals backing Viet Nam do not realize what is meaning Communism as international force and that they really would not care if it was thoroughly explained to them. They have been driven to Communism by French colonial policy here and they consider that nothing can be any worse. Hate for French blinds them to many things and makes them accept others they do not like. Intellectuals backing Vietnam government hate French so much that any future without French is attractive.

4. Removal French pressure would unquestionably have effect of causing present government in first instance to break into factions which would then for time tend develop into more or less full-blown party movements as those understood in Indochina. There probably then would be demand use armed force to some extent as country has widely distributed arms, has held exactly one general election in last 80 years, has no democratic tradition (outside of villages) which would enable it withstand strain political differences. There unquestionably would be danger police state under one-party rule which danger would have to be combatted by whatever French influence might remain and by United States through propaganda, student exchange, etc.

5. Viet Namese people here still regard United States as promised land and earthly paradise. American flag is still best protection available. Viet Namese are exceeding sensitive to United States opinion and unquestionably would accept United States advice and/or advisers and would be more than willing to have United States intervene if such intervention were directed toward satisfaction their political and economic needs.

6. Should Soviet oriented Viet Nam emerge, Cambodia and Laos would probably be subjected to considerable pressure to overthrow present regimes there. Independent Viet Nam, whether Soviet oriented or not, and absence of protecting power such as France, could be expected to resume encroachment upon Mekong

delta which was interrupted by French occupation in 1860. Viet Namese migration to southern plains has gone on for ten centuries and probably will continue.

Independent Viet Nam, not oriented toward Soviet, would probably leave Laos to its own devices.

In effect, there are dangers in French dealing with Viet Nam Government. There are dangers equally as great in French dealing with series of puppets in continuing effort to establish, despite all statements to contrary, something which strongly resembles *status quo* of before war.

Problem was and remains primarily nationalist problem in overpopulated area with illiterate populace which has no democratic traditions on national level largely because colonial power gave populace no opportunity express itself politically. With middle-class small, intellectuals who are generally ineffective, and Catholics who are split, best possibility of retaining some stability and preventing development of police state seems to be retention some degree French or international control to act as arbiter between parties.

Communist problem here results from fact French have allowed Communist group to seize and monopolize fight for felt necessity of people and Communist problem will remain without hope solution as long as this necessity is not satisfied elsewhere.

O'Sullivan

Have given considerable thought Deptel 122, July 17, and feel if French compelled treat with present Vietnam Govt their position in French Indo China will be definitely weakened, also if this govt emerges as controlling power in three Kys gradual deterioration of ties with democratic West may be expected. Unquestionably aid from western democracies, especially US, will be welcomed at first but query whether this Govt and in fact any native govt not subject to check or control will not develop a definitely oriental orientation and will not become a prey for non-democratic influences. Such a govt without considerable economic and moral support will not be strong enough to resist the impact of a concerted move by either the Communists or the Chinese for both of whom this part of Asia is indeed a happy hunting ground, fertile field for the inculcation of anti-western sentiment, and expansion. However, it appears improbable that solution situation can be found without treating with present Vietnam Govt but as noted above and hereafter to treat with that Govt alone is a danger but there is equal danger in treating only with puppets. If French cannot reconcile all political elements or if they try to retain any large degree control, denying independence in regard which both present Vietnam Govt and Nationalist Front elements are united, only solution may be neutral intervention to establish a Vietnam state satisfactory to majority Annamites and to exercise control to see the state is run on democratic and equitable lines. If present Vietnam Govt is honestly nationalistic, it should welcome such solution but am reasonably sure French, particularly French Communists, will view such suggestion with alarm.

Replying *ad seriatim*.

1. While tendency is toward Soviet camp as result Communist orientation Vietnam leaders, do not believe Vietnam will come out openly on side of Soviets until ground is prepared; present Soviet policy toward Vietnam appears to be one

of remote control rather than open support and such policy will probably be pursued until time is ripe for avowal Soviet affiliation; in meantime Ho is straddling the fence and hopes to win support of west on platform dedicated to fulfillment nationalist aspirations.

2. As I have reported, very possible so-called militant opposition to Ho as being too moderate is only a blind; there is no proof he has renounced his Communist training but it is reasonably certain his indoctrination will be soft pedalled until independence is won and the French are out; a wily opportunist, Ho will take any aid coming his way to gain his ends without disclosing ultimate intentions.

3. Most Annamite intellectuals do not realize what communism means except that it symbolized revolution, nor do they care; as their conflict with French is basically revolutionary, they will accept communism or any other 'is[m]" as a means to the end.

. . . Pure nationalists among these intellectuals want independence and the future can take care of itself; average Annamite not good Communist prospect but strong leaders of aggressive minority can easily bring about evolution Communist state.

4. Removal French pressure and absence Western democracy control will result in chaos as factional fighting with accompanying terrorism will ensue; great bulk of population not prepared for self-government and destinies of country would be in hands of few, those now strongly suspeced of Communist leanings; unless active steps were taken, through economic and political pressure, there would be little possibility preventing and combatting resultant police state.

5. American opinion still highly valued by all Annamites, including present Vietnam Government, and American aid is definitely desired to any other; however, if American advice and action run counter to what they think is full sum their desiderata, US might not be so popular; this difference must be noted—present Vietnam Government welcomes American aid in gaining independence, getting rid of present Vietnam Government and Communists; if firmly applied, American pressure can be the strongest influence in the country but there can be no temporizing.

6. Strong Vietnam state whether or not Soviet oriented will bring pressure on Laos and Cambodia and definite political and economic encroachments are to be expected; unless full protection given those countries, they would be forced into orbit Buddhist countries to the west and there would follow indefinite period political readjustment and dispute.

While Communist danger exists, it is future one and only when Vietnam Government is firmly established and in position disregard opinion and aid Western democracies will such government align itself with Soviet satellites—events elsewhere may make such alignment only far distant possibility. French overstress this danger. Present dangers are (1) French terms will be such as to prevent any peaceful solution and (2) if Annamites turned loose, only way combatting resultant economic and political chaos will be totalitarian police state, with ruthless suppression opposition. Both alternatives are alarming. Also must not overlook Chinese ambitions in this area which are only inactive because of China's internal situation.

                                                                                                                    Reed

48. STUDY ON THE VIETNAMESE
RESISTANCE BY TRUONG CHINH,
SEPTEMBER 1947 [Extracts]

From March until August 1947, the Party newspaper Su That *(Truth) published a series of eleven installments on the political line and strategy of the anti-French resistance war by Party theoretician Truong Chinh. In September the articles were published together as a book. In these excerpts Truong Chinh discusses how Vietnam could achieve a favorable balance of forces against a physically stronger foe. The analysis is notable for its realistic attitude toward the difficulties the resistance might face—including possible intervention by a "third country" on the French side. It also established the party's policy toward winning over other governments and peoples: to take it with utmost seriousness but not to count on it as a "panacea."*

We have described our strong and weak points, and the strong and weak points of the enemy. But this exposition does not exhaust the question of victory or defeat in the war.

We should not be content with comparing the potentialities and problems, the strengths and weaknesses of the two sides, and slip into complacency because of our advantages. The attitude of groundless optimism robs us of clear vision, makes us short-sighted, passive, and without the will to make progress.

In the history of war, there have been countries which met with fewer difficulties and had fewer weaknesses than the enemy, but which failed. On the other hand, there have been countries which met with more difficulties and had more weaknesses than the enemy, but which triumphed. Why should this be so? Because the country which had the advantage of its enemy did not try hard enough, underestimated its enemy and lacked skill. On the other hand, the country whose situation was disadvantageous made strenuous efforts, "knew itself and knew the enemy," and triumphed because it had skillful leadership. The author of "Kim Van Kieu" when he wrote: "The will of man triumphs over fate," was thinking of the talent and subjective efforts of man, which may exercise a great influence on objective conditions. Of course, if we look at this question closely, we can see that this influence is more or less powerful depending on the favourable or unfavourable objective material conditions.

When our people struggle, when our leadership is skillful we can take advantage of the favourable conditions of time and situation to turn "difficulties" into "advantages," "weaknesses" into "strengths," and there is nothing strange in this at all! Moreover, war itself is a great movement. Difficulties for the belligerents created by the war ("strengths" or "weaknesses" depending on the side), cannot remain unchanged. They change according to the development of the war. The side which is skillful and makes great efforts will be able to cause these changes to be of advantage to itself, and harmful to the enemy. On the other hand, if this side lacks

SOURCE: *Truong Chinh, The Resistance Will Win* (Hanoi: Foreign Languages Publishing House, 1947), Chapters X–XIII, pp. 94–101.

vigilance, is foolish, passive or cowardly, these changes will become advantageous to enemy and harmful to it.

Moreover, we should ask ourselves: If we have more strong points than the enemy, then why do we remain on the defensive and go on retreating? Why, looking at our situation in general, do we still remain in a passive position, and have not yet won the initiative? In our opinion, it is because most of the enemy's weaknesses are moral ones, and most of his strong points are material ones. As for us, our weaknesses are for the most part material, and our strong points moral. War is a struggle between two forces from both moral and material viewpoints. Material conditions are quite necessary to victory—even a temporary victory—in any military action, whether in war, or in an armed uprising.

That is why, to check the advance of the enemy, to defeat him, we should strive to diminish our material weaknesses, increase our moral strength, and at the same time reduce the material strong points of the enemy and aggravate his moral weaknesses.

*   *   *

We uphold a just cause against barbarism, employ sincerity against perfidy. Therefore, we shall certainly win the sympathy of the French people, of personalities in other countries, of small nations, particularly Asian people and the peoples of the French colonies. Furthermore, we might request the Soviet Union to raise the problem of Viet Nam before the United Nations Organisation and demand that France negotiate with Viet Nam. We should take full advantage of the contradictions between France and other countries to make propaganda against the French crimes against our people, against foreign residents and the adherents of various religions; and documents proving our humanitarian behaviour towards French prisoners of war, our correct policies in regard to all religious people and foreign residents. Propaganda with foreign countries must be undertaken by a responsible organ, and by a number of specialized cadres, in order to avoid negligence and a happy-go-lucky manner of working. We should also send abroad cultural delegates or National Assembly deputies to make propaganda. We should get rid of the tendency to consider propaganda with foreign countries as a completely auxiliary task and thus neglect it; or to consider it as a "panacea," or, in other words, to rely upon others without making any attempt to develop our own resources, or to make our own efforts.

Such are the things to be done to minimize our weaknesses and diminish the enemy's strong points. To develop our strong points and accentuate the enemy's weaknesses, there is no other way than to carry out the following fundamental tasks: to unite the entire people, mobilize the whole country, wage a long resistance, make skillful propaganda with the enemy and have a good foreign policy.

However, if we know how to direct our subjective efforts to turning his disadvantages against the enemy, is the enemy so stupid as not to aim our own disadvantages at our heads in return? The enemy is more perfidious and cunning than we think.

In the course of the resistance war, some disadvantages may come our way, created by efforts made by the enemy, by our own errors, or by circumstances unforeseen either by us or the enemy. For instance: natural calamities, or famine might occur, there might be intervention by a third country which would first help the French colonialists to fight us and then oust them; again, the loss of a number of our cadres and outstanding men could have a considerable effect on the leadership of the resistance; or grave errors by our officers could lead to serious losses . . .

Such things may happen. The duty of our leading organization is to foresee such eventualities and take all necessary preventive measures. But when something has happened that we were unable to prevent, we should remain calm, hold out, and deal with the situation. If we stick closely to the people, we will never be defeated.

1948

49. DEPARTMENT OF STATE POLICY STATEMENT ON INDOCHINA, SEPTEMBER 27, 1948 [Extracts]

The State Department's first full-length policy statement on Indochina again ruled out military reconquest but also rejected French military withdrawal, on the ground that there would be "chaos and terroristic activities." Since the United States could support neither conquest nor withdrawal, it was left in an essentially passive position of accepting a French policy with which it could not agree.

A. Objectives

The immediate objective of US policy in Indochina is to assist in a solution of the present impasse which will be mutually satisfactory to the French and the Vietnamese peoples, which will result in the termination of the present hostilities, and which will be within the framework of US security.

Our long-term objectives are: (1) to eliminate so far as possible Communist influence in Indochina and to see installed a self-governing nationalist state which will be friendly to the US and which, commensurate with the capacity of the peoples involved, will be patterned upon our conception of a democratic state as opposed to the totalitarian state which would evolve inevitably from Communist domination; (2) to foster the association of the peoples of Indochina with the western powers, particularly with France with whose customs, language and laws they are familiar, to the end that those peoples will prefer freely to cooperate with the western powers culturally, economically and politically; (3) to raise the standard of living so that the peoples of Indochina will be less receptive to totalitarian influences and will have an incentive to work productively and thus contribute to a better balanced world economy; and (4) to prevent undue Chinese penetration and subsequent influence in Indochina so that the peoples of Indochina will not be hampered in their natural developments by the pressure of an alien people and alien interests.

SOURCE: *U.S.-Vietnam Relations*, Book 8, pp. 144–148.

B. Policy Issues

To attain our immediate objective, we should continue to press the French to accommodate the basic aspirations of the Vietnamese: (1) unity of Cochinchina, Annam, and Tonkin, (2) complete internal autonomy, and (3) the right to choose freely regarding participation in the French Union. We have recognized French sovereignty over Indochina but have maintained that such recognition does not imply any commitment on our part to assist France to exert its authority over the Indochinese peoples. Since V-J day, the majority people of the area, the Vietnamese, have stubbornly resisted the reestablishment of French authority, a struggle in which we have tried to maintain insofar as possible a position of non-support of either party.

While the nationalist movement in Vietnam (Cochinchina, Annam, and Tonkin) is strong, and though the great majority of the Vietnamese are not fundamentally Communist, the most active element in the resistance of the local peoples to the French has been a Communist group headed by Ho Chi Minh. This group has successfully extended its influence to include practically all armed forces now fighting the French, thus in effect capturing control of the nationalist movement.

The French on two occasions during 1946 attempted to resolve the problem by negotiation with the government established and dominated by Ho Chi Minh. The general agreements reached were not, however, successfully implemented and widescale fighting subsequently broke out. Since early in 1947, the French have employed about 115,000 troops in Indochina, with little result, since the country-side except in Laos and Cambodia remains under the firm control of the Ho Chi Minh government. A series of French-established puppet governments have tended to enhance the prestige of Ho's government and to call into question, on the part of the Vietnamese, the sincerity of French intentions to accord an independent status to Vietnam.

1. Political

We have regarded these hostilities in a colonial area as detrimental not only to our own long-term interests which require as a minimum a stable Southeast Asia but also detrimental to the interest of France, since the hatred engendered by continuing hostilities may render impossible peaceful collaboration and cooperation of the French and the Vietnamese peoples. This hatred of the Vietnamese people toward the French is keeping alive anti-western feeling among oriental peoples, to the advantage of the USSR and the detriment of the US.

We have not urged the French to negotiate with Ho Chi Minh, even though he probably is now supported by a considerable majority of the Vietnamese people, because of his record as a Communist and the Communist background of many of the influential figures in and about his government.

Postwar French governments have never understood, or have chosen to under-estimate, the strength of the nationalist movement with which they must deal in Indochina. It remains possible that the nationalist movement can be subverted from Communist control but this will require granting to a non-Communist group of nationalists at least the same concessions demanded by Ho Chi Minh. The failure of

French governments to deal successfully with the Indochinese question has been due, in large measure, to the overwhelming internal issues facing France and the French Union, and to foreign policy considerations in Europe. These factors have combined with the slim parliamentary majorities of postwar governments in France to militate against the bold moves necessary to divert allegiance of the Vietnamese nationalists to non-Communist leadership.

In accord with our policy of regarding with favor the efforts of dependent peoples to attain their legitimate political aspirations, we have been anxious to see the French accord to the Vietnamese the largest possible degree of political and economic independence consistent with legitimate French interests. We have therefore declined to permit the export to the French in Indochina of arms and munitions for the prosecution of the war against the Vietnamese. This policy has been limited in its effect as we have allowed the free export of arms to France, such exports thereby being available for re-shipment to Indochina or for releasing stocks from reserves to be forwarded to Indochina.

D. Policy Evaluation

The objectives of US policy towards Indochina have not been realized. Three years after the termination of war a friendly ally, France, is fighting a desperate and apparently losing struggle in Indochina. The economic drain of this warfare on French recovery, while difficult to estimate, is unquestionably large. The Communist control in the nationalist movement has been increased during this period. US influence in Indochina and Southeast Asia has suffered as a result.

The objectives of US policy can only be attained by such French action as will satisfy the nationalist aspirations of the peoples of Indochina. We have repeatedly pointed out to the French the desirability of their giving such satisfaction and thus terminating the present open conflict. Our greatest difficulty in talking with the French and in stressing what should and what should not be done has been our inability to suggest any practicable solution of the Indochina problem, as we are all too well aware of the unpleasant fact that Communist Ho Chi Minh is the strongest and perhaps the ablest figure in Indochina and that any suggested solution which excluded him is an expedient of uncertain outcome. We are naturally hesitant to press the French too strongly or to become deeply involved so long as we are not in a position to suggest a solution or until we are prepared to accept the onus of intervention. The above considerations are further complicated by the fact that we have an immediate interest in maintaining in power a friendly French Government, to assist in the furtherance of our aims in Europe. This immediate and vital interest has in consequence taken precedence over active steps looking toward the realization of our objectives in Indochina.

We are prepared, however, to support the French in every way possible in the establishment of a truly nationalist government in Indochina which, by giving satisfaction to the aspirations of the peoples of Indochina, will serve as a rallying point for the nationalists and will weaken the Communist elements. By such support and by active participation in a peaceful and constructive solution in Indochina we stand to regain influence and prestige.

Some solution must be found which will strike a balance between the aspirations of the peoples of Indochina and the interests of the French. Solution by French military reconquest of Indochina is not desirable. Neither would the complete withdrawal of the French from Indochina effect a solution. The first alternative would delay indefinitely the attainment of our objectives, as we would share inevitably in the hatred engendered by an attempted military reconquest and the denial of aspirations for self-government. The second solution would be equally unfortunate as in all likelihood Indochina would then be taken over by the militant Communist group. At best, there might follow a transition period, marked by chaos and terroristic activities, creating a political vacuum into which the Chinese inevitably would be drawn or would push. The absence of stabilization in China will continue to have an important influence upon the objective of a permanent and peaceable solution in Indochina.

We have not been particularly successful in our information and education program in orienting the Vietnamese toward the western democracies and the US. The program has been hampered by the failure of the French to understand that such informational activities as we conduct in Indochina are not inimical to their own long-term interests and by administrative and financial considerations which have prevented the development to the maximum extent of contacts with the Vietnamese. An increased effort should be made to explain democratic institutions, especially American institutions and American policy, to the Indochinese by direct personal contact, by the distribution of information about the US, and the encouraging of educational exchange.

1949

50. TELEGRAM FROM SECRETARY OF STATE DEAN ACHESON TO THE EMBASSY IN FRANCE, FEBRUARY 25, 1949

Reviewing the French record of the previous three years, the new Secretary of State, Dean Acheson, instructed Paris that the United States would not commit itself to support French efforts to bring back ex-Emperor Bao Dai as head of a Vietnamese government until it proved successful in terms of popular support.

SOURCE: *Foreign Relations of the United States, 1949* (Washington, D.C.: GPO, 1975), Vol. VII, pp. 8–9.

Urtel 718, Feb 18. Dept despite reported progress Fr-Bao Dai negots queries whether Fr are really making such concessions as to (1) induce Bao Dai return Indochina (2) give him best opportunity succeed even if he returns there. For months, even though Commie successes [in] China should have induced Fr make outstanding effort, negots have dragged, with Fr unable or unwilling put question status Cochinchina before Fr Assembly. Foregoing connection Dept fully realizes polit difficulties present Fr Govt putting this question before Assembly but Dept equally aware that over past three years Fr have shown no impressively sincere intention or desire make concessions which seem necessary solve Indochina question. Present formula solving status Cochinchina may have virtue but in Dept's thinking it may be but another device to obtain delay and unless proof is adduced to offset record of past three years Dept is now far from inclined give public approval any arrangements with Bao Dai. This disinclination springs from Dept's considered belief it would be unwise give public support to any arrangements for Indochina concluded by Fr unless that arrangement embodies means clearly sufficient insure its success or until it achieves substantial measure of success. Thus even though Bao Dai induced return Indochina DD Dept views failure Fr Govt take decisive action, at very least re status Cochinchina, as seriously weakening possibility ex-Emperor will obtain support any appreciable portion population. Without such support Bao Dai cannot hope, even though supported by Fr arms as he must necessarily be, wean away militant and organized followers of Ho Chi Minh.

Dept believes therefore, it should not now be committed in any way to approval Fr action vis-a-vis Bao Dai and must reserve aforementioned public expression until Fr have provided Bao Dai with means to succeed and he has demonstrated ability use successfully such means to obtain support appreciable portion Vietnamese population. This connection, Emb may recall doubts expressed in several Fr quarters re Bao Dai's capacities and abilities when negots were first undertaken with him two years ago. Accordingly Emb should make clear to FonOff that for these reasons US not prepared give public indication its approval until, in Dept's opinion, conditions noted above fulfilled.

At same time Emb may state while US remains willing reconsider its ECA Indochinese policy such reconsideration must await developments.

Sent Paris as 598. Rptd Saigon as 15.

Emb should note particularly with respect to first part para 1 that above tel was drafted before receipt embtel 771 Feb. 24, 4 p.m.

51. TELEGRAM FROM ACHESON TO THE CONSULATE GENERAL IN SAIGON, MAY 10, 1949

On March 8, 1949 Bao Dai concluded the "Elysée Agreement" with the French, under which he would return as Head of State of Vietnam. Acheson, while expressing a cautious attitude toward recognition of Bao Dai, introduced the idea

SOURCE: *Foreign Relations,* 1949, Vol. VII, pp. 23–25.

*that support by non-Communist Asian governments would help remove from the
Bao Dai regime the appearance of a U.S.-French-British "gambit."*

Assumption urtel 141 Dept desires success Baodai experiment entirely correct. Since appears be no other alternative to estab Commie pattern Vietnam, Dept
considers no effort shld be spared by Fr, other Western powers, and nonCommie
Asian nations to assure experiment best chance succeeding.

At proper time and under proper circumstances Dept will be prepared do its
part by extending recognition Baodai Govt and by exploring possibility of comply-
ing with any request by such Govt for US arms and econ assistance. Must be
understood however aid program this nature wld require Congressional approval.
Since US cld however scarcely afford backing govt which wld have color and be
likely suffer fate of puppet regime, it must first be clear Fr will offer all necessary
concessions to make Baodai solution attractive to nationalists. This is step of which
Fr themselves must see urgent necessity view possibly short time remaining before
Commie successes Chi are felt Indochina. Moreover, Baodai Govt must through
own efforts demonstrate capacity organize and conduct affairs wisely so as to
ensure maximum opportunity obtaining requisite popular support inasmuch as govt
created Indochina analogous Kuomintang wld be foredoomed failure.

Assuming essential Fr concessions are forthcoming, best chance success Baodai
wld appear lie in persuading Vietnamese nationalists (1) their patriotic aims may be
realized promptly through Fr-Baodai agreement (2) Baodai govt will be truly representative even to extent including outstanding non-Commie leaders now supporting
Ho and (3) Baodai solution probably only means safeguarding Vietnam from aggressive designs Commie Chi. While attainment these objectives depends initially
upon attitude Fr and Baodai circle, Dept believes more will ultimately be required.
Best hope might lie in active demonstration of interest in and support of Baodai
solution by other non-Commie Asian govts. Appeal such solution to Vietnam
nationalists wld presumably be far greater if it had appeared sponsored by free Asian
nations animated by interest self-determination Asian peoples and their own self-
preservation in face immed Commie menace rather than if it had appearance gambit
engineer by Fr, US and UK as part strategy of West-East conflict.

Dept giving closest consideration to means whereby US might assist attainment these ends.

From above, you will see Dept thinking closely parallels your own. Dept
agrees when time comes Baodai must certainly be fully warned of danger yielding
to any temptation include Commies his govt and this connection again believes
other Asian govts cld serve most useful purpose since India, Siam, Philippines, and
Indonesians (both Repubs and Federalists) are fully alive growing Commie threat
Asia.

Re last para urtel 141 "reliability Baodai solution" was error. Deptel 70 shld
have read "viability" meaning able live.

While Dept continues believe it wld be premature and unwise for you make
special point (such as trip Dalat) see Baodai, there no objection your talking
informally with polit personalities close to him with whom you have doubtless
already made contact in normal course carrying out your functions. In such talks
you might well as suggested urtel 141 take occasion cite examples futility collaboration Commies and grave danger such course.

52. TELEGRAM FROM ACHESON TO THE CONSULATE IN HANOI, MAY 20, 1949

In response to some pro-French Vietnamese suspicions that the United States might not be opposed to participation by Viet Minh leadership in a future govern-ment, Acheson pictured Vietnam as losing its independence either to Russia or China if the anti-Communists did not prevail, dismissing the idea of a "national communist" state as only a "theoretical possibility." He indicated the American preference for an all-out effort against the Communists under the most favorable circumstances–i.e., while French troops were still in Vietnam.

Reur informative tel 36: In talks Xuan and reps his govt you may take fol line as representing consensus informed Americans:

In light Ho's known background, no other assumption possible but that he outright Commie so long as (1) he fails unequivocally repudiate Moscow connec-tions and Commie doctrine and (2) remains personally singled out for praise by internatl Commie press and receives its support. Moreover, US not impressed by nationalist character red flag with yellow stars. Question whether Ho as much nationalist as Commie is irrelevant. All Stalinists in colonial areas are nationalists. With achievement natl aims (i.e., independence) their objective necessarily be-comes subordination state to Commie purposes and ruthless extermination not only opposition groups but all elements suspected even slightest deviation. On basis examples eastern Eur it must be assumed such wld be goal Ho and men his stamp if included Baodai Govt. To include them in order achieve reconciliation opposing polit elements and "national unity" wld merely postpone settlement issue whether Vietnam to be independent nation or Commie satellite until circumstances probably even less favorable nationalists than now. It must of course be conceded theoretical possibility exists estab National Communist state on pattern Yugoslavia in any area beyond reach Soviet army. However, US attitude cld take acct such possibility only if every other possible avenue closed to preservation area from Kremlin control. Moreover, while Vietnam out of reach Soviet army it will doubtless be by no means out of reach Chi Commie hatchet men and armed forces.

Fol is for urinfo and such reference as you deem judicious:

Dept naturally considers only Fr can through concessions to nationalist move-ment lay basis for solution Indochina problem. As suggested Deptel 83 to Saigon, if nationalists find concessions Mar 8 agreements inadequate, much may depend upon willingness Fr put agreements in most favorable possible context by empha-sizing expectations rapid evolution Vietnam beyond status envisaged those agree-ments. Provided Fr display realistic and generous attitude, most important part remainder immed program—viz, winning support nationalists away from Commie leadership—must devolve upon Baodai and Xuan group seconded by other South Asian govts who stand in most immed danger from Commie conquest Indochina and who by full polit and propaganda support Baodai solution might more that anyone else be able to deprive Ho of talking-points in event he continues demand armed resistance Baodai regardless circumstances (which appears certain in light vitriolic tone current Vietminh broadcasts on Baodai which give no recognition any

Source: *Foreign Relations*, 1949, Vol. VII, pp. 29–30.

Fr concessions to nationalist demands). Even with conditions for US support Baodai realized it futile expect US be able assist effectively this initial task beyond stressing requirements situation in talks South Asian govts and providing materials evidencing realities of Communism through USIS for distribution as you and Congen Saigon consider desirable in conjunction with Baodai efforts arouse compatriots to Commie menace. Experience Chi has shown no amt US mil and econ aid can save govt, even if recognized by all other powers and possessed full opportunity achieve natl aims, unless it can rally support people against Commies by affording representation all important natl groups, manifesting devotion to natl as opposed to personal or Party interests, and demonstrating real leadership.

Re Viet opinion reports Saigon's 145 that US abandonment Nationalist China presents unfavorable augury for non-Commie regime Vietnam, there no objection emphasizing to persons with this view that Nationalist China came to present pass through deficiency above qualities and lack will to fight, not because US "wrote it off."

Re Xuan query whether US wld propose Vietnam for membership UN shld Fr renege, you sld avoid discussion this matter, at most if pressed state circumstances at moment will of course determine US action. For urinfo only it unlikely US cld even vote for Vietnam membership US if as it appears now Fr wld remain in control Vietnam fon relations.

53. STATE DEPARTMENT REPORT FOR THE NATIONAL SECURITY COUNCIL (NSC), "U.S. POLICY TOWARD SOUTHEAST ASIA," (NSC 51), JULY 1, 1949 [Extracts]

A comprehensive view of American policy toward Southeast Asia concluded that the problem of "militant nationalism" could not be solved by full support for the French and Dutch nor by full support for the nationalists. It accurately predicted a new conflict once French power was removed from Vietnam, in which the United States, "working through a screen of anti-Communist Asiatics," would try to defeat the Communists.

57. The Indochinese situation is in an advanced stage of deterioration. The communists are dominant in the nationalist movement. They achieved this position by assuming the most aggressive role in resistance to French imperialism. This meant that all activist nationalist elements, including large numbers of non-communists, rallied around them to form a popular front known as the Viet Minh. The communists have maintained this dominance thanks to the constant military pressure exerted by the French, the effect of which has been to keep most nationalist elements pressed into reliance on the communists.

58. After an initial show of conciliation, French policy in Indochina was to reconquer and no nonsense. But it has simply not been in the realm of practicability

SOURCE: Document declassified by the National Security Council, April 7, 1973.

for France to crush the Viet Minh by military means. The French military effort has therefore dwindled to footling punitive campaigns which have been and are a drain on the strength of France itself. As we do not contribute ERP [European Recovery Program] aid directly to Indochina, the charges are passed on to us in Europe. The falseness of our position was last year made evident when, at great effort and with special Presidential sanction, we provided partial equipment for three French divisions in Germany while about 100,000 French troops with American equipment were and still are being squandered in Indochina on a mission which can be justified only in terms of Gallic mystique.

59. As the French came to comprehend that military measures were a delusion, they resorted to political maneuvers with native collaborators hoping to create a puppet regime which would, with French help, dispose of the Viet Minh and allow France to retain its paramountcy. But the French have been so niggardly in those negotiations that they have thus far failed to create an effective puppet regime capable of drawing nationalist elements away from the Viet Minh. Current negotiations with the ex-Emperor, Bao Dai, appear thus far to be of this description.

60. A constructive solution of the Indochinese impasse depends on the French yielding their claims to sovereignty to a native regime. Only if that is done will the false issue of French imperialism, which cements communists and non-communists in unity, be dissolved. A French withdrawal would permit the elementary indigenous forces in Indochina to come into full play. The basis conflict would be between nationalism and Stalinism. Nationalist elements would thereupon tend to gravitate away from the present Viet Minh popular front and coalesce in a nationalist anti-Stalinist organization. The strong anti-Chinese sentiments, now submerged by the issue of French imperialism, would likewise be released and act as a force resistant to Chinese Communist influence.

61. The French claim to sovereignty over Indochina could be yielded either to a regime composed of present collaborators of the French or to the Viet Minh. Provided that it is clear-cut and expeditious, a transfer to the former is of course preferable because the non-communist elements in Indochina would thereby be given an advantageous start. A withdrawl in favor of the Viet Minh would obviously be less desirable. It is debatable, however, whether it is more or less desirable than the Stalinist blind alley down which French policy is now blundering.

62. Whichever course were followed, civil war would sooner or later probably eventuate. With the dissolution of the present artificial situation, the new alignments would naturally be precipitated and come into conflict. Resistance to Soviet and Chinese communist influence would then for the first time possess deep and extensive roots in the Indochinese scene. But this new conflict, for foreign anti-communists, including ourselves, would be only a point of departure. It would then be necessary for us, working through a screen of anti-communist Asiatics, to ensure, however long it takes, the triumph of Indochinese nationalism over Red imperialism.

*   *   *

76. We should accept the fact that the crucial immediate issue in Southeast Asia—that of militant nationalism in Indonesia and Indochina—cannot be resolved by any of the following policies on our part: (1) full support of Dutch and French imperialism, (2) unlimited support of militant nationalism, or (3) evasion of the

problem. Because the key to the solution of this issue lies primarily with the Netherlands and France, we should as a matter of urgent importance endeavor to induce the Dutch and French to adapt their policies to the realities of the current situation in Southeast Asia, as set forth in this paper. Our first step should be, in conjunction with the British, to set forth to the Dutch and French in candor, detail, and with great gravity our interpretation of the situation in and intentions with regard to SEA. We should make a major effort to persuade them to join us and the states mentioned in the following paragraph in a constructive overall approach to the region as a whole.

* * *

84. Because we are powerless to bring about a constructive solution of the explosive Indochinese situation through unilateral action, the determination of our future policy toward Indochina should await the outcome of the demarche recommended in paragraph 76 and the earliest feasible consultation with India and the Philippines.

54. MEMORANDUM OF CONVERSATION AMONG ACHESON, FRENCH FOREIGN MINISTER ROBERT SCHUMAN AND BRITISH FOREIGN MINISTER ERNEST BEVIN, SEPTEMBER 17, 1949 [Extract]

In the conversation between the American secretary of state and French foreign minister on the subject of Indochina, Acheson backed away from the position taken by the department earlier in the year of pressing for the unfettered independence for Vietnam and committed the United States to help get Asian countries to recognize the Bao Dai Government.

Mr. Schuman then talked about Indochina. He said the Bao Dai government was not quite complete but it was satisfactory. The government was not yet fully established but it would be and it was the only way for a permanent solution. There is no love lost between the Chinese and the Indochinese. The Indochinese are afraid of China. Some of Ho's men, if there was a threat of invasion from China, might go over to Bao Dai. If the Southeast Asian countries recognize the Bao Dai government, its prestige would be increased. Perhaps the United Kingdom and the United States could help the French with Southeast Asia. The agreement with the Bao Dai government would be ratified by the French Parliament soon. Siam perhaps could be encouraged to recognize, by a word from the United States or the United Kingdom, the Bao Dai government. Bevin asked when the French Parliament would ratify the agreement. Schuman replied that Parliament meets on October 18 and should ratify it in a few weeks after that—perhaps in November. Bevin remarked that France has to ratify the agreement before anyone else can help.

SOURCE: *Foreign Relations,* 1949, Vol. III, pp. 86–89.

The Secretary said that if the French ratify the March 8 Agreement and transfer dealings with Bao Dai to the Foreign Office, we could help with the Philippines and Siam. The Southeast Asian countries should take the first steps, otherwise recognition by the United Kingdom and the United States in advance of other countries would make the Bao Dai government look like a Western "front." Congress may take up the question of Point Four Program after the Military Assistance Pact. Perhaps we can arrange technical assistance and Export-Import Bank funds.

55. MEMORANDUM BY RAYMOND B. FOSDICK (CONSULTANT TO THE SECRETARY OF STATE ON FAR EASTERN POLICY) FOR AMBASSADOR AT LARGE PHILIP JESSUP, NOVEMBER 4, 1949

While the State Department drifted closer to recognition of the Bao Dai regime on the grounds that there was "no alternative," opinion in the department was not unanimous. Calling the Elysée Agreements "a kind of semi-colonialism," Raymond Fosdick, an adviser for the Far East, called for acceptance of the Ho Chi Minh government.

In his memorandum of November 1 on Indochina, Mr. Yost argues that "a further major advance of communism will be considered as, and will in fact be, a defeat for the United States, whether or not we are directly involved." He therefore recommends, among other steps, support of the Bao Dai government (after the March 8 agreements are ratified) economic assistance to Bao Dai, etc.

It seems to me this point of view fails to take into consideration the possible, and I think the probable consequences of such a decision. In grasping one horn of the dilemma, it ignores the other. My belief is that the Bao Dai regime is doomed. The compromises which the French are so reluctantly making cannot possibly save it. The Indochinese are pressing toward complete nationalism and nothing is going to stop them. They see all too clearly that France is offering them a kind of semi-colonialism; and to think that they will be content to settle for less than Indonesia has gained from the Dutch or India from the British is to underestimate the power of the forces that are sweeping Asia today.

What kind of independence is France offering the Indochinese today in the March 8th agreements?

(1) The foreign policy of Indochina is to be under the final control of France.

(2) French military bases are to be established and the Indochinese Army in time of war is to be under French direction.

(3) France is to be in charge of the so-called General Services:
    (a) Control of immigration
    (b) Communications
    (c) Industrial development of Indochina

SOURCE: Document declassified by Department of State, July 21, 1975.

(4) Customs receipts are to be divided between France and Indochina in accordance with a formula to be agreed upon.

(5) Extraterritorial courts for French citizens are to be continued.

This shabby business is a mockery of all the professions we have made in the Indonesian case. It probably represents an improvement over the brutal colonialism of earlier years, but it is now too late in the history of the world to try to settle for the price of this cheap substitute. For the United States to support France in this attempt will cost us our standing and prestige in all of Southeast Asia. A lot of that prestige went down the drain with Chiang Kai-shek; the rest of it will go down with the Bao Dai regime if we support it. Ambassador Stuart calls our relationship to this regime "shameful" and I am inclined to agree with him.

Ev Case argued yesterday that it is too late to do anything else except support Bao Dai. I disagree. It is never too late to change a mistaken policy, particularly when the policy involves the kind of damage that our adherence to the Generalissimo brought us. Why get our fingers burned twice?

Ho Chi Minh as an alternative is decidedly unpleasant, but as was pointed out at our meeting with FE [Far Eastern Bureau] yesterday, there may be unpredictable and unseen factors in this situation which in the end will be more favorable to us than now seems probable. The fundamental antipathy of the Indochinese to China is one of the factors. Faced with a dilemma like this the best possible course is to wait for the breaks. Certainly we should not play our cards in such a way that once again, as in China, we seem to be allied with reaction. Whether the French like it or not, independence is coming to Indochina. Why, therefore, do we tie ourselves to the tail of their battered kite?

1950

56. TELEGRAM FROM ACHESON TO THE EMBASSY IN THE UNITED KINGDOM, JANUARY 30, 1950

In deciding to recognize the Bao Dai government de jure, *Acheson conceded, the United States would reduce its ability to get France to yield control over diplomacy and armed forces.*

Re Lond's 479, rptd Paris 137, Jan 27. Fol comments on recognition Viet Nam shld be passed to Brit:

SOURCE: *Foreign Relations of the United States,* 1950 (Washington, D.C.: GPO, 1976) Vol. VI, pp. 703–704.

As Dept understands it the purpose of according recognition to Bao Dai is to give him stature in the eyes of non-communist nationalist elements in Viet Nam and thus increase his following. This being the case recognition, if accorded by U.K. or ourselves, wld appear most effective if given without any strings attached, i.e. the *de facto* step contemplated by Brit as a bargaining point with the Fr in order obtain further concessions. Dept has come to view that the Fr have for the moment gone as far as they can in according independence. This does not mean of course that either we, the Brit or the Fr shld not continue to view the Mar 8 Agreements as an evolutionary step in the independence of Viet Nam.

We are of course aware of fact that the UK does not have unanimous support of the commonwealth re recognition and that no formula re Viet Nam cld be found at Colombo acceptable to all participants. We nevertheless believe that a straightforward recognition without the qualification of *de facto*, or for that matter *de jure*, wld best serve our and UK interests and this viewpoint shld be pressed upon the commonwealth govts. In this connection, it shld be borne in mind that simultaneous recognition will have to be accorded to Laos and Cambodia, whose govts fulfill the requirements for the *"de jure"* status. The Mao Tse Tung govt on the other hand appears indeed to be a *"de facto"* form of govt altho it was simply "recognized" without qualifications.

Along the lines above Dept is of opinion that merely to give the UK ConGen in Saigon the "courtesy of rank of minister" is a skittish and timorous approach to problem of according diplomatic recognition to Viet Nam which wld tend in large measure to negate the benefits of such recognition. Dept considering making ConGen Saigon a diplomatic agent accredited to all 3 govts with personal rank of minister if this appears indicated.

57. PAPER ON MILITARY AID FOR INDOCHINA BY A WORKING GROUP IN THE DEPARTMENT OF STATE, FEBRUARY 1, 1950 [Extract]

In January, a working group had been formed consisting of representatives of the Office of Western European Affairs, the Office of Philippine and Southeast Asian Affairs, and the Mutual Defense Assistance Program, to prepare a paper on possible U.S. military aid to the French for Indochina. The paper reflected the atmosphere of crisis and confrontation with Communism then prevailing in Washington: it failed to examine the dangers of involvement in the Indochina War along with the perceived dangers of the defeat of the French there and expressed optimism about French military prospects, in stark contrast to the internal assessment before the decision on recognition had been made.

I. The Problem

Should the United States provide military aid in Indochina and, if so, how much and in what way.

SOURCE: *Foreign Relations*, 1950, Vol. VI, pp. 711–715.

II. Assumption

A. There will not be an effective split between the USSR and Communist China within the next three years.

B. The USSR will not declare war on any Southeast Asian country within the next three years.

C. Communist China will not declare war on any Southeast Asian country within the next three years.

D. The USSR will endeavor to bring about the fall of Southeast Asian governments which are opposed to Communism by using all devices short of war, making use of Communist China and indigenous communists in this endeavor.

*   *   *

8. Ho Chi Minh, a Moscow-trained Communist, controls the Viet Minh movement which is in conflict with the government of Bao Dai for control of Vietnam. Ho actually exercises control of varying degree over more than two-thirds of Vietnam territory and his "government" maintains agents in Thailand, Burma and India. This communist "government" has been recognized by Communist China and the USSR.

9. Most Indochinese, both the supporters of Bao Dai and those of Ho Chi Minh, regard independence from the French as their primary objective. Protection from Chinese Communist imperialism has been considered, up to now, a secondary issue.

10. Unavoidably, the United States is, together with France, committed in Indochina. That is, failure of the French Bao Dai "experiment" would mean the communization of Indochina. It is Bao Dai (or a similar anti-Communist successor); there is no other alternative. The choice confronting the United States is to support the French in Indochina or face the extension of Communism over the remainder of the continental area of Southeast Asia and, possibly, farther westward. We then would be obliged to make staggering investments in those areas and in that part of Southeast Asia remaining outside Communist domination or withdraw to a much-contracted Pacific line. It would seem a case of "Penny wise, Pound foolish" to deny support to the French in Indochina.

11. The US plans on extending recognition to the newly-created states of Vietnam, Laos and Cambodia, following French legislative action which is expected in early February 1950.

12. Another approach to the problem is to apply the practical test of probability of success. In the present case we know from the complex circumstances involved that the French are going to make literally every possible effort to prevent the victory of Communism in Indochina. Briefly, then, we would be backing a determined protagonist in this venture. Added to this is the fact that French military leaders such as General Cherrière are soberly confident that, in the absence of an invasion in mass from Red China, they (the French) can be successful in their support of the anti-Communist governments in Indochina.

13. Still another approach to the problem is to recall that the United States has undertaken to provide substantial aid to France in Europe. Failure to support French

policy in Indochina would have the effect of contributing toward the defeat of our aims in Europe.

V. Conclusions

A. Significant developments have taken place in Indochina since the Mutual Defense Assistance Act of 1949 was drawn up, these changes warranting a reexamination of the question of military aid.

B. The whole of Southeast Asia is in danger of falling under Communist domination.

C. The countries and areas of Southeast Asia are not at present in a position to form a regional organization of self-defense nor are they capable of defending themselves against militarily aggressive Communism, without the aid of great powers. Despite their lack of military strength, however, there is a will on the part of the legal governments of Indochina toward nationalism and a will to resist whatever aims at destroying that nationalism.

D. The French native and colonial troops presently in Indochina are engaged in military operations aimed at denying the expansion southward of Communism from Red China and of destroying its power in Indochina.

E. In the critical areas of Indochina France needs aid in its support of the legally-constituted anti-Communist states.

VI. Recommendations

1. The United States should furnish military aid in support of the anti-Communist nationalist governments of Indochina, this aid to be tailored to meet deficiencies toward which the United States can make a unique contribution, not including United States troops.

2. This aid should be financed out of funds made available by Section 303 of the Mutual Defense Assistance Act of 1949.

58. PAMPHLET BY GIAP ON SHIFTING TO THE GENERAL COUNTEROFFENSIVE, FEBRUARY 1950 [Extract]

On February 2, 1950, the ICP's Third National Conference, which had begun twelve days earlier, concluded that the time had come to "complete preparations to switch over to the stage of general counteroffensive." The year 1950 was seen as

---

SOURCE: Vo Nguyen Giap, *Nhiem Vu Quan Su Truoc Mat Chuyen Sang Tong Phan Cong* [Immediate military tasks for switching to the general counteroffensive] (Ha Dong: Resistance and Administrative Committee of Ha Dong Province, 1950). Original document in Vietnamese language collection, South Asia Section, Library of Congress. [Translation by the editor.]

one of transition to the final stage of the war. The analysis of the third stage of the war, written by General Giap after this conference, is the most detailed and comprehensive account of his strategic thinking available from the first Indochina War. It is a careful and prescient analysis that predicts the expanded role of the U.S. in the war and the possibility of the third stage being prolonged and comprising several periods. The document also reveals that Giap's primary worries were the weakness of his army's material base and the French ability to exploit the Indochina-wide scope of the war.

1950 is a year of a strategic change of direction, when our revolutionary war shifts to the third phase, the phase of the general counteroffensive.

What is the strategy, and what are the concrete strategic objectives of the third phase? What is the general line of the third phase? Those are the problems we must understand clearly in order to guide the war to victory.

Counteroffensive Strategy

Our strategy during the third phase is a counteroffensive strategy, while the strategy of the enemy is a strategy of withdrawal. We counterattack until complete victory, until we have swept the enemy's troops from Indochina soil and reconquered the whole territory.

Looking generally at the counteroffensive throughout the entire phase of counterattack until final victory, we call the third phase the phase of General counteroffensive. The General counteroffensive means just this, and not that our counteroffensive will be carried out everywhere on battlefields from South to North, from Vietnam to Laos and Cambodia. Furthermore, it does not mean that the counteroffensive will occur in one swift moment everywhere, or will succeed easily at once like the August general uprising. On the contrary, because of objective and subjective conditions, our general counteroffensive may be prolonged and may be carried out in waves, prevailing on each battlefield until the enemy has finally lost, and we have won complete victory.

Our strategic objectives during the third phase are:

1) Annihilate the enemy's manpower.
2) Reconquer the entire territory.
3) Destroy the will of the French colonialists to resist.

The objective of annihilating the enemy's manpower is correct from a strategic standpoint. In the first phase, we wore the enemy's troops down gradually, and in the second phase, we continued to wear their troops down gradually. All combat, whether war of attrition or war of annihilation throughout the three phases, is aimed at one final objective: the annihilation of all the enemy's manpower.

With regard to territory, our strategic objective is to reconquer the entire territory of Indochina, the territory of all three countries, Vietnam, Cambodia and Laos, from the Nam quan gate to the Ca mau cape, from Dong hai shore to the banks of the Mekong and the Dangrek mountain range.

We must also destroy the invaders' will to resist, because that is the objective of the whole war. Moreover, France is far from Indochina, but the Indochina War for France is a colonial war, taking only one part of French forces; we cannot attack the colonialists right in the heart of their own country; if their will to resist is not yet destroyed, the war could still continue.

The above three objectives are closely related to each other. But the main objective is to annihilate the enemy's manpower.

$$*\quad*\quad*$$

Mobile Warfare Is Primary, Guerrilla Warfare Is Secondary, Positional Warfare Is Auxiliary

During the third phase, in order to achieve the strategic objectives mentioned above, based on the characteristics we have analyzed, what forms of combat tactics will we apply?

Our fundamental line regarding this aspect is:

Mobile warfare is primary;
Guerrilla warfare is secondary;
War of position is auxiliary.

Mobile warfare is the primary tactic, first of all because mobile warfare can exploit to the utmost the spiritual element to defeat the invader, and because in the general counteroffensive phase, our army must advance to besiege and destroy the enemy's power.

Based on the change in the form of the war on the battlefield, mobile warfare will have an ever-increasing importance. Confronted with the progress of our force generally, in regard to the degree of concentration, the technical level, and combat effectiveness, the enemy's deployment and manner of using his troops will change. The enemy will reinforce his positions, and reinforce his intervention units and reserve units. In the mission of defending positions, intervention units at the subsector and sector level will become more important. In the mission of defending the whole battlefield, the enemy advances to the use of large mobile troops and strong reserve forces. Therefore the tactic of destroying the enemy's positions must be linked with the tactic of destroying his intervention units. And, if we want mobile warfare to progress, our troops must be built up to take care of positions and advance to big battles of encirclement, while at the same time advancing to encircling and destroying strong mobile troop units in order take care of interventionary units.

Mobile warfare on the Indochina battlefield will still emphasize the guerrilla element during a rather long period, because of conditions of equipment and supply, and because of conditions of concentration. And soon there will be a positional war element, because of the enemy's manner of defensive deployment. Mobile warfare will usually be carried out within a narrow framework, because of the conditions of the battlefield, because of the way in which the enemy uses his troops, and because of our conditions of equipment and concentration.

Guerrilla warfare is secondary, but still has a very important position. That is because guerrilla warfare is a form of combat which employs high combat morale and is appropriate to the conditions of inferior equipment and technology.

$$*\quad*\quad*$$

How Will the General
Counteroffensive Phase Evolve?

How will the third phase begin and how will it evolve?

Does the third phase begin with a fundamental battle, a decisive battle, or not? Not necessarily.

It is possible that the third phase will open with a fundamental battle which will unbalance the relation of forces, just as the second phase began with the Viet-Bac battle.

But it is also possible that the second phase will pass into the third phase through a very long period, during which there are a number of big battles; a number of campaigns accumulate, creating a change in the relation of forces. In those circumstances, the third phase will also begin with a big battle, but that big battle itself will not necessarily have a fundamental character. This is because of the nature of the war between France and us, because of the French method of dispersed deployment, because strategic geographical position is not only having one important point on the Indochinese battlefield, and because of the conditions of our army.

*   *   *

Will the third phase be drawn out or will it be cut short?

Due to the above-mentioned characteristics, due to favorable conditions and unfavorable conditions, the third phase of the Indochinese revolutionary war could be cut short and, on the contrary, could be prolonged.

It could be cut short because of our absolute superiority in morale. Due to that superiority, on our side there could be unprecedented advances by our army, unprecedented sacrifices of the entire people, resistance high tides and uprisings in the occupied zone; our forces and the general mobilization of manpower, material means, and possibly international help could increase very rapidly. Also due to the above-mentioned superiority, major disintegration could take place in the ranks of the enemy's troops, or anti-war actions by French soldiers; the situation in France could also encounter many disorders due to defeat in Indochina and the anti-war movement; or due to campaigns for independence by the colonies. The French could also commit major errors in their strategic conduct of the war.

But the third phase could also be prolonged:

a) Because our material power is weak, and many phases are required to overcome that weakpoint;

b) Because the enemy can exploit the Indochinese terrain to prolong the war, continuing the fight in the South after he is defeated in the North;

c) Because the U.S., and Britain will intervene actively, to give assistance to France.

If the third phase is prolonged, our struggle will become fierce. In regard to the form of combat, the war will gradually lose the character of ordinary colonial wars, with one side having very strong military forces and one side very weak. The regular form of combat will develop very highly, perhaps there will be mobile warfare on a rather large scale, and the possibility of positional warfare will increase. Our army will need to become modern in order to dominate the battlefield and destroy completely the enemy's power.

In the event that the third phase is prolonged, the Southern battlefield will meet many new difficulties. Therefore, in our strategic conduct of the war, we must pay special attention to the strategic geographical conditions of the Indochinese theater, overcome the disadvantages that those conditions create for us, and prevent the enemy from exploiting advantages they create for him. When aiming to make one battlefield the main battlefield, the increase of forces on other battlefields should not be forgotten. When concentrating forces to destroy the enemy in the North, do not let them have time to consolidate their bases and prepare to prolong the war in the South.

In reality whether the third phase will be cut short or prolonged will be determined by our own guidance and efforts. That guidance must be clearsighted, flexible, realistic, exploiting all possibilities, strong, bold, and timely. Those efforts must be extraordinary and continuous, not only when switching over to the general counteroffensive but throughout the entire counteroffensive phase until complete victory.

59. ARTICLE BY TRUONG CHINH ON THE DIPLOMATIC RECOGNITION OF THE DRV, FEBRUARY 18, 1950

The diplomatic recognition of the DRV by the Soviet Union and its allies opened a new phase of the Vietnamese revolution. This article, written immediately after the Party's Third National Conference, presented for the first time the new international line of the Vietnamese revolution. A major feature of the Party's foreign policy was to present itself as being the "advance post" of the "democratic and socialist system" in the struggle against imperialism—the mirror image of the one used by the Bao Dai regime to emphasize its importance to the United States.

The fact that the Soviet Union and the people's democracies have just officially recognized the Ho Chi Minh Government has stirred up world opinion as well as opinion in the country.

It is an important political victory for the Democratic Republic of Viet-nam, for the Vietnamese people who are waging resistance war, and at the same time a big defeat for the French colonialist aggressors.

The Soviet Union and people's democracies recognized the Ho Chi Minh Government before the U.S.-British imperialists and their camp recognized the puppet Bao Dai, showing that, with regard to democratic world, the Ho Chi Minh Government is the sole legal government, the true representative of the Vietnamese people. The Bao Dai puppets are a gang of lackeys, for the French colonialists and

SOURCE: Su That, February 18, 1950, reprinted in Truong Chinh, *The Vietnamese People's National Democratic Revolution*, Vol. II, pp. 238–242. [Translation by the editor.]

U.S. imperialists. The French policy of setting up and supporting the puppet government is not only regarded by the Vietnamese people with contempt but severely condemned by the democratic and progressive forces in the world.

For more than four years, the Vietnamese nation has struggled to gain freedom, independence for itself, while protecting world peace. The French colonialists invade Vietnam and destroy world peace. At the present time, the right of the Vietnamese nation to exist and the interest of world peace are closely related to each other.

The resistance of the Vietnamese people is supported by the forces of peace and democracy in the world. The fact that the Soviet Union, China and other people's democracies have recognized the Government of the Democratic Republic of Viet-nam cannot be isolates; the Vietnamese people have many friends, have big friends such as the Soviet people, the Chinese people, etc. The Democratic Republic of Viet-nam is part of the democratic and socialist system stretching from Central Europe to Southeast Asia. Viet-nam naturally stands on the side of democracy and against imperialism. As the advance post on the line of defense against imperialism in Southeast Asia, Viet-nam is now the focal point of conflict between the democratic and anti-democratic forces in the world. The Vietnamese-French war not only reveals the highest degree of contradiction between the Vietnamese people and French colonialism. It is one part of the struggle between the two camps: the democratic anti-imperialist camp and the anti-democratic imperialist camp after the second world war.

The fact that the Soviet Union and the people's democracies recognize the Government of the Democratic Republic of Viet-nam shows clearly that the Vietnamese problem is an international problem. While the world imperialists recognize the puppet Bao Dai, provide further money and arms to French colonialism and Bao Dai to attack the Vietnamese people, the Soviet Union and the people's democracies officially recognize and establish diplomatic relations with the Government of the Democratic Republic of Vietnam. The forces of peace and democracy in the world wanted to gain time to support and assist the resistance of the Vietnamese people before U.S. imperialism intervenes directly in the Vietnamese problem, turning Viet-nam and Indochina into a colony and strategic base of the U.S.

The great diplomatic victory which the Government of the Democratic Republic of Viet-nam has just achieved is the result of more than four years of sacrifice and heroic struggle of the army and people of Viet-nam, the result of the correct line and policy of the Government of the Democratic Republic of Viet-nam led by Chairman Ho. It strengthens the position of the Democratic Republic of Viet-nam in the international arena, increasing the influence of the Vietnamese people. Thanks to this diplomatic victory, the friendship between the Vietnamese people and the people of socialist and democratic countries in the world is warmer, and the assistance of friendly countries for the Vietnamese people's resistance and national construction is increased. The Vietnamese people will have further favorable conditions to study the experiences of the people of friendly countries.

At the same time, the recent diplomatic victory also places on the shoulders of the Vietnamese people further heavy responsibilities. The Vietnamese army and people must understand that they have the responsibility to liberate completely their own Fatherland from the yoke of imperialism, but also have the responsibility to contribute their efforts to breaking up the plan of war preparations of world imperialism, led by the U.S.

60. TELEGRAM FROM ACHESON TO U.S. AMBASSADOR DAVID BRUCE IN FRANCE, MARCH 4, 1950

Aware that channelling military assistance to France would be another symbol of Vietnam's lack of independence, Acheson sought to find a formula that would permit Bao Dai to be the "publicized" recipient while in fact giving the aid to France. The Embassy in France agreed to the Acheson suggestion two days later.

In connection with possible military assistance to be given to Indochina Dept is interested in knowing your views on Fr plans regarding the manner and extent of participation by Bao Dai in this aid. Bao Dai's extravagant requests as presented in his memo to Jessup (which we are assuming has not been seen by the Fr) indicate that he may soon raise the question. The granting of arms to Bao Dai raises question about Fr supervision. In order to build up his political position in Vietnam the Dept considers it important that some formula be found to make Bao Dai appear to be the overt recipient of such aid. This may, of course, involve more of a concession than the Fr are prepared to make at this time, but may, from US viewpoint, be necessary. Dept may wish to ask you to discuss with Fr an approach by us to Bao Dai along the fol lines:

1) That his ideas for equipping Vietnamese army, militia, air force and navy, as set forth in his memo to Jessup seem beyond the realm of practical possibility.

2) That for long time to come he will have to look primarily to Fr for supplies of arms, training and military assistance in general.

3) It is up to him as much as it is to Fr to establish a *modus vivendi* re this question which will enable him to receive from them adequate support to pacify the country without jeopardizing his own position as the chief of an independent Viet Nam.

4) We are considering making a contribution to the joint Fr-Vietnamese war effort in the area. However, in view of urgency of their joint need for assistance it will, for purely practical reasons, be necessary to extend material assistance to them thru the Fr., but preserving Bao Dai as publicized recipient.

5) Since the appearance of it being a joint Franco-Vietnamese operation is of great importance politically we are likewise suggesting to the Fr that they associate him in their request for an arms program for Indochina.

SOURCE: *Foreign Relations*, 1950, Vol. VI., p. 749.

Emb's comments urgently requested. No action should be taken with Fr on above without further instructions.

Rptd Saigon as 122 for info only.

61. ARTICLE BY TRUONG CHINH ON THE GENERAL COUNTEROFFENSIVE, JULY 1950 [Extracts]

During the spring and summer of 1950, Party leaders were troubled by signs that both overoptimism and doubts were appearing in the ranks of the people and the Party itself. In an article aimed at correcting these "deviationist" tendencies, Truong Chinh said that the final phase might be prolonged and warned against assuming that the opposition to the war within France would be a decisive factor in the outcome of the war.

In the political report and military report at the Third National Conference, the Central Committee explained about the general counteroffensive. Here I only summarize the Central Committee's judgment and emphasize points which have been wrongly understood and must be corrected.

From the standpoint of space, the general counteroffensive is a strong counteroffensive on the main battlefield, while on other battlefields we hold back the enemy. Holding back here means counterattacking to a certain degree with the objective of annihilating and wearing down the enemy in order to disperse the enemy's forces and holding on to the enemy. We concentrate our forces to master the main battlefield, then gradually master the other battlefields, until the enemy's forces have been swept from Indochina. There could also be times when there are sufficient conditions to master two or three battlefields at once, but the main thing is to dominate the primary battlefield.

From the standpoint of time, the general counteroffensive is a counteroffensive throughout an entire strategic phase. That phase may be divided into many periods. In each period, we open one or several big or small campaigns, aimed at achieving the final objective of the resistance war, which is to drive the enemy army from the country.

Thus, given the present relation of forces between the enemy and us, the general counteroffensive is not a counteroffensive on all battlefields at once, nor is it fighting a single, swift battle to decide victory or defeat, which is over in five or ten days. The counteroffensive is a process of fierce and decisive struggle; victories and defeats may follow one another, but defeat is the smaller part, and victory is the primary one; defeat is temporary, but victory is decisive.

The general counteroffensive in the present resistance war is the completion of

SOURCE: "Hoan Thanh Nhiem Vu Chuan Bi, Chuyen Manh Sang Tong Phan Cong," [Complete the task of preparation, switch strongly to the general counteroffensive], *Tap chi Cong san* [Communist Review], no. 1, July, 1950, in Truong Chinh, *The Vietnamese People's National Democratic Revolution*, Vol. II, pp. 250–265. [Translation by the editor.]

the task of liberating the nation which the August General Uprising (1945) began. The general counteroffensive and the August General Uprising are closely linked. But we should not compare the general counteroffensive with the General Uprising of August and conclude that the general counteroffensive is as easy as the General Uprising of August. We should not understand them in a mechanical matter because of the word "General." Historical phenomena never fit together in the same manner. The conditions are different each time. The situation of the French colonialists now is different from that of the Japanese before. In August 1945, we attacked the Japanese little, but we scored a big victory, because Japan had been defeated by the whole democratic front which had the Soviet Union leading it, while Japan's allies, Nazi Germany and Italy, had been overthrown. Therefore we acknowledge having seized the government in a relatively easy manner. On the contrary, today we must shoulder the responsibility for defeating French colonialism in our country, while it is aided by U.S. imperialism, but is not (or not yet) having to cope with many battlefields outside Indochina.

At present French colonialism is being actively aided by American and British imperialism, so we must still contend with the ememy, and in the future our counteroffensive phase may be prolonged. Every time the French colonialists exhaust their strength, U.S. imperialism injects them with another dose of medicine to restore it, making them healthy again for a period of time until they lose their strength once more. Of course, the illness is critical and difficult to treat, so the medicine can only put off the hour of death and not save the patient's life. But we must make the enemy lose more than they can replace (remembering that the amount replaced is comprised of the efforts of the French colonialism in part and of U.S.-British assistance to France in part). To put it another way, we must fight until the enemy cannot increase assistance and cannot replace losses fast enough, for only then will they be prepared to surrender at last.

We have friendly socialist countries and people's democracies supporting and helping us. But to be victorious, above all else, we must make our own efforts. Our efforts are primary, while help from abroad is very important, but only adds further to those efforts. Therefore, we cannot depend on the aid from abroad. We must use that assistance well and turn it into our own material strength. Remember that friendly countries do not bring troops to fight in place of us, and those countries are not the "omnipotent" talisman of a sorcerer.

The anti-war movement of the French people and political change which could take place in France will have a big influence on our resistance war. But we must correctly assess the struggle of the French people for nation, democracy, and peace, and have absolutely no illusions. Our assessment of the influence that political change in France will have on us depends on the nature of that change. If there is a change in a progressive direction, bringing the pro-peace faction into power, obviously it will be favorable for us. But if it is a change in the reactionary direction, then obviously, it will not only be unfavorable but will be harmful. There could also be a time when a change having a reactionary character pushes the French people to rise up and oppose it, and at that time, we must consider how the French people react to decide. However we ought not and cannot expect a complete disintegration of French expeditionary force as happened to the Japanese army in August 1945. The disintegration of the French army, if it occurs, will be caused by the victory of the Vietnamese resistance war and nothing else.

62. TELEGRAM FROM CHAIRMAN OF
THE JOINT SURVEY MISSION
JOHN F. MELBY TO RUSK,
AUGUST 7, 1950 [Extract]

In a pessimistic report to the Far Eastern Division of the State Department, a Joint Survey Mission led by John F. Melby reverted to the American view of the 1945–1948 period—that a military solution to the problem of Indochina was probably impossible and that the only answer was a French promise of complete independence some years in the future, as the United States had done in the Philippines.

In summary then there is good reason to believe that proper application of sufficient military force, plus goading the French into a more offensive spirit, can hold the lid on the Indochinese kettle for the predictable, if relatively limited, future. It will not however solve the long-range problem. Neither can the French do it on their present promises or without a radical change of heart and approach. If American interests can be served by the short-range approach then the rest need not concern us. This must be determined with relationship to over-all world situation, prospects, and time factors. If however the longer alley is important, then Franco-Vietnamese behavior in that alley, to borrow from the Churchillian analogy of the gorilla in the jungle, is a matter of the gravest concern.

If the latter be the case and the foregoing analysis valid, a satisfactory solution can only be found when the French have been persuaded to sweeter reasonableness and the Vietnamese firmly led by the hand through the growing pains of adolescence. Recent Korean precedent may be suggestive. I could propose consideration of following: French undertaking for Vietnam independence within specified period of 5, 10, 20, or 30 years with certain special compensations for French such as are found in Philippines-American arrangements.

French would undertake to guarantee inviolability Indochina border. Vietnam national army would be rapidly created to assure responsibility internal situation and as this progressed French forces would withdraw to border areas or where unnecessary depart. Civil administration would increasingly be Vietnam responsibility. All such agreements would have UN public guarantee and such supervision as necessary. Assumably [*sic*] US would as usual pay most of bills. If US can bring its Korean responsibilities within UN framework, there is little solid reason why French cannot do same for Indochina.

Ever recognizing that this form is hardly likely to provoke dancing in the streets of Paris, it may well be that this or something similar is only real prospect for salvaging anything and French must be coerced into realizing it and behaving accordingly. If Vietnam has determined on complete independence as all evidence suggests, it probably cannot get it for a long time in face of French opposition, but it can create the kind of uproar which will constitute a continuing drain on French strength and in end benefit only Communists. Coincidentally, American identification with French in such eventuality will further weaken American influence in

SOURCE: *Foreign Relations,* 1950, Vol. VI, pp. 845–848.

Asia. Historically no ruling group has ever remained more or less indefinitely in power in face of active or even passive resistance from the governed, or without ruining itself in the process. There is no convincing evidence Nationalism in Indochina proposes to be an exception.

63. APPEAL BY GIAP AT THE BEGINNING OF THE FRONTIER CAMPAIGN, SEPTEMBER 16, 1950 [Extracts]

In June 1950, the ICP Central Committee decided on a major campaign to attack French forces in the Chinese border region, in order to open communications with China further and broaden the Viet-Bac base area. At the end of July, it was decided to broaden the purpose of the campaign to include the liberation of a section of the border from Cao Bang to That Khe. The preparations for the offensive were extensive, involving the shifting of one-third to one-half of all local cadres to civilian labor tasks. On the day the campaign began, Giap explained its significance and exhorted his troops.

All command echelons and fighters of the National Protection Army, local troops, and guerrilla-militia!

In accordance with the order of Chairman Ho, the Cao-Lang campaign has begun.

This campaign is our first major campaign.

If we win this battle, we will not only destroy the enemy's power, open communications routes, and broaden our base areas, but also make the enemy's morale decline, break up by their Autumn-Winter plan, influence directly the Northwest and the midlands, create conditions to open a new situation in the North, and create further confidence and encouragement for the people and army in the entire country.

If we win this battle, it will mean winning a big battle at a time when our army is switching from guerrilla attacks to mobile warfare attacks and attacks against defense construction, accumulating many rich experiences, creating fine traditions, and establishing good bases for the development of our strength later on.

* * *

We must:

Resolutely annihilate the enemy's manpower.

Assault cadres, set an example of completing your mission, raise the spirit of unity, coordinate the common effort to destroy the enemy's army. All cadres and fighters must thoroughly obey orders, struggle heroically, assault fearlessly, strive to compete in the recording of accomplishments, and win total victory for the campaign.

On the Cao-Lang battlefield, our army is concentrating its forces, and will be

SOURCE: Giap, *Orders of the Day*, pp. 101–103. [Translation by the editor.]

fully equipped: the level of its tactics and technology are improved, the spirit of killing the invader is very ardent, and we are supported by the entire people and the great masses in the rear areas with all their hearts.

Chairman Ho has appealed to us to compete in killing the invader and recording accomplishments.

In order to respond to Chairman Ho's appeal and continue the tradition of Bac-son, Cao-bang, and of the Cao-Bac-Lang combat zone, all command echelons and fighters, fearlessly advance!

We will definitely win!

We are determined to defeat the enemy!

64. TELEGRAM FROM ACHESON TO BRUCE, NOVEMBER 11, 1950

The British Ambassador in Paris suggested a démarche *urging on the French government a pledge to give up all controls over the Associated States. Acheson made it clear that the United States was still concerned about the impact of such a statement on the morale of French troops in Indochina, without whom the war would be lost to the Viet Minh. Pressure on the French to make such a statement, Acheson told Bruce, should only come after the political and military situation was more favorable. The Pau Conference mentioned in the text brought together representatives of France, Vietnam, Laos and Cambodia in June 1950 to discuss the organs that would take over various administrative functions from France in Indochina.*

Dept has followed developments concerning suggestion that UK Amb Paris inform Fr Govt that "they make formal statement of intention release control Indochina without, however, mentioning time limit" with interest (Lond's tel 2234, Oct 18).

We had agreed fully with reasoning behind Harvey's request that he use discretion as to timing approach to Schuman and that it be delayed at least until end Pau Conference. As matter has and will, undoubtedly, continue to be discussed with Fr by Malcolm McDonald Dept now considering suggestion to Brit Govt that their *démarche* to Fr through McDonald or Harvey be coordinated not joined with similar one on our part. Do not believe joint *démarche* advisable as traditional Fr suspicion UK FR might lead them resent Brit action. Joining Brit might thus reduce effectiveness our approach.

Informing approach to Fr we do not wish to overlook consideration that morale of troops fighting in Indochina is of prime importance and that, therefore, Fr Govt should not be urged to make any statement concerning further relinquishment Fr controls except under most favorable conditions. Dept would include among factors which might constitute "favorable conditions" (re: Embtel 2436, Nov 3): (1) demonstration renewed Fr mil potential in form absence further deterioration, (2) visible proof of formation National Armies beyond present paper steps which

SOURCE: *Foreign Relations*, 1950, Vol. VI, pp. 920–921.

are excellent beginning, (3) further evidence Bao Dai's intention and ability assume active leadership his govt, still waited.

Moreover, Dept agrees that considerations morale troops Indochina and public opinion Fr in face expenditures lives and money will make it necessary that statement be not so extreme as to remove whatever stake for Fr in Indochina is sufficient to assure their continued acceptance of "primary responsibility" to extent of proceeding with present program. Dept eager in this matter, as in others relating to Indochina, to strengthen ties Fr Union and maximize protection Fr economic interests Indochina.

Nevertheless Dept is increasingly of conviction that further evolutionary statement is required to consolidate gains which development National Armies, support Franco-Vietnamese mil potential and enhancement Bao Dai Govt's authority either as result decisions Pau Conference or, possibly, as we hope, through his own revitalization. We are also obviously concerned to see that every means to increase effectiveness of use our own considerable financial and military aid be brought to bear. This would include as a minimum, official declaration by Fr at highest level (Auriol or Schuman) on present and future intentions regarding Indochina, as they have been stated to us by various high officials including Schuman, Moch and Letourneau, on several recent occasions.

Points outlined in Embtel 2436, Nov 3, Para two, are those which we consider should be included. Without attempting suggest actual form we would view something along lines of Letourneau's statements at Saigon press conference (Saigon 657, Oct 24) and Embassys suggestions in reftel as basic text to build on.

Today's Paris press despatches report McDonald will continue discussions re Indochina with Fr officials during coming week. We would welcome invitation Emb officer participate but as approach shld not be joint realize this might be impossible. Emb shld continue exchange views with McDonald and Fr separately, informing former of our thoughts on concurrent Anglo-U.S. approach to Fr and latter of our agreement with Brit views as expressed to Bruce by McDonald.

London note and, after consultation Paris, inform ForOff our views and general concurrence theirs as expressed McDonald; sound out possibilities similar approach Fr.

65. MEMORANDUM BY DEPUTY DIRECTOR OF THE MUTUAL DEFENSE ASSISTANCE PROGRAM JOHN OHLY TO ACHESON, NOVEMBER 20, 1950 [Extracts]

As French forces suffered repeated defeats in the north, the pressures on the United States to become full partners in the Indochina War mounted rapidly. The director of the military assistance program asked Acheson to name a special task force under the National Security Council to reassess U.S. policy in Indochina before plunging further into the conflict. Noting reports from military observers

SOURCE: *Foreign Relations*, 1950, Vol. VI, pp. 925–930.

which cast grave doubts on the ability of the French Union forces to defeat the Viet Minh, he emphasized that the United States could not afford to supply the sums required to support the anti-Communist forces in Indochina and at the same time meet its other global defense commitments, including, of course, the Korean War.

I. This memorandum is designed to stress the urgent necessity for an immediate, thorough and realistic re-examination of our policy with respect to Indochina. From the standpoint of the Mutual Defense Assistance Program, such a re-examination is imperative, because the continuance of the present policy of substantial aid may, without achieving its intended purpose, make impossible the fulfillment of mutual defense objectives elsewhere in the world. Such a re-examination may well lead to a reaffirmation of this policy without significant change, but in my opinion, and in the light of the considerations set forth below, it would be the height of folly to pursue such policy further in the absence of a far more searching analysis than has heretofore been made of its possibilities of success and its global consequences. Even if the need for such an approach was not urgent before (and I believe it was), it has certainly been made so by the direct Chinese Communist intervention in Korea which (1) places large additional operating demands upon the limited materiel resources available for both U.S. requirements and *all* foreign military assistance programs and (2) indicates that the Kremlin may be prepared to accept the risks inherent in the actual commitment of Chinese troops to assist Ho Chi Minh, a step which would, as subsequently indicated, completely transform the character of the military problem in Indochina.

*   *   *

IV. Recommendations

I strongly recommend that before any further substantial commitments of equipment, prestige or forces are made in Indochina, the kind of assessment suggested in the preceding pages be undertaken. I suggest that this be done by a special task force under the auspices of the National Security Council, because it is so urgent that it cannot and should not be pursued through slower channels. We have reached a point where the United States, because of limitations in resources, can no longer simultaneously pursue all of its objectives in all parts of the world and must realistically face the fact that certain objectives, even though they may be extremely valuable and important ones, may have to be abandoned if others of even greater value and importance are to be attained. The situation is not unlike that which faced the United States in the early days of the last war, when a choice had to be made between pursuing the offensive in either the West or the East and not in both places at once.

As an after thought, and by way of additional caveat, I would like to point out that the demands on the U.S. for Indochina are increasing almost daily and that, sometimes imperceptibly, by one step after another, we are gradually increasing our stake in the outcome of the struggle there. We are, moreover, slowly (and not too slowly) getting ourselves into a position where our responsibilities tend to supplant rather than complement those of the French, and where failures are attributed to us as though we were the primary party at fault and in interest. We may be on the road to being a scapegoat, and we are certainly dangerously close to the point of being so deeply committed that we may find ourselves completely committed even to direct intervention. These situations, unfortunately, have a way of snowballing.

1951

66. MEMORANDUM BY THE JOINT CHIEFS OF STAFF TO SECRETARY OF DEFENSE GEORGE C. MARSHALL, JANUARY 10, 1951

Asked by Secretary of Defense Marshall for their view on the French proposal for tripartite military talks on Indochina, the Joint Chiefs reiterated their view that the United States should stay out of Indochina militarily, even in the event of a Chinese Communist invasion.

Subject: Proposed Military Talks Regarding Defense of Indochina.

1. This memorandum is in response to your memorandum of 21 December 1950 dealing with the matter of proposed military talks regarding defense of Indochina.

2. In view of the present United States military position in the Far East, the Joint Chiefs of Staff believe the following to be basic:

   a. The United States should not permit its military forces to become engaged in French Indochina at this time, and

   b. In the Event of a communist invasion of Indochina, therefore, the United States should under current circumstances limit its support of the French there to an acceleration and expansion of the present military assistance program, together with taking other appropriate action to deny Indochina to communism, short of the actual employment of military forces.

   In light of the above, and in view of the considerations expressed in their memorandum to you of 8 December 1950, the Joint Chiefs of Staff feel, from the strictly military point of view, that no additional military staff talks are desirable at this time.

3. On the other hand, the Joint Chiefs of Staff recognize that the political considerations raised in your memorandum of 21 December 1950 may be regarded as overriding. Under such circumstances, the Joint Chiefs of Staff would not interpose further objection to the holding of additional tripartite military staff talks at this time. Any such talks, however, would be restricted in scope by the Joint

SOURCE: *Foreign Relations*, 1951, Vol. VI, pp. 347–348.

Chiefs of Staff and would not be permitted to deal with matters of strategy affecting United States global policies and plans.

4. In the event of a global war, the major United States measures in support of the French in Indochina would of necessity also be limited to the acceleration and expansion of the present military assistance program as feasible, and, operationally, to matters connected with convoy, routing, and protection of shipping. If the decision is made to hold the proposed additional military talks involving military operational commanders, it would be appropriate, therefore, that the chief United States military representative should be an officer designated by the Commander in Chief, Pacific (CINCPAC), and that he should be assisted by General Brink.

67. TELEGRAM FROM ACHESON TO THE LEGATION IN SAIGON, JANUARY 30, 1951

In a summary of the talks between President Truman and French Premier René Pleven in Washington on January 30, Acheson reported Pleven as wary of French Commander Jean de Lattre de Tassigny's request for reinforcements and needing assurances of sufficient United States financial assistance for the creating of national armies in order to justify further French commitments. Pleven was also reported as raising the possibility of negotiations with the DRV for the first time since the start of the war.

The fol is rough summary of Truman-Pleven discussions of yesterday as they pertain to IC:

Pleven presented his position as fols:

1) Events in the Far East make it necessary for the Western Powers to coordinate economically, militarily and politically and procedure for permanent consultation between US, Brit and Fr shld be established. It might include the establishment of a permanent tripartite body for this purpose.

2) As far as IC is concerned three hypotheses shld be considered:

a. The present situation of fighting an internal rebellion which Fr is and has faced for the last five years. With a reinforced VM Fr can only foresee heavier and heavier losses. The only possible daylight in matter lies in the planned development of Viet natl army. Immed question to be faced is whether Gen de Lattre's demands for reinforcement shld be met or declined in the realization that similar demands may be expected regularly hereafter and cannot be met. The fact that Fr present effort entailed a comparable drain on her contribution to the defense of Western Europe is also pertinent. Amt of US aid to be anticipated is dominant consideration in arriving at decision in matter. Formation of four Vietnamese divisions during 1951 under study. Wld involve a cost of 58 billion francs, 25 billion of which cannot be covered in the contemplated contributions from both Fr and Vietnamese budgets. Particular mention was made of the furnishing of an aircraft carrier. Recommended that this and other technical questions shld be studied by Fr-US mil experts.

SOURCE: *Foreign Relations, of the United States,* 1951 (Washington, D.C.:GPO, 1977), Vol. VI. Pt. 1, pp. 368–369.

b. The second possibility is that which wld be created by an overt Chi Commie attack. Before the Fr can make any decision of action to be taken in this eventuality they must ask for further clarification of the US position vis-a-vis aid in both men and material. Fr Govt wld also appreciate infor concerning anticipated US aid in the event of a forced evacuation.

The Fr invite us to consider the effect of the loss of Tonkin or of all IC on the rest of SEA (polit, econ and mil). A study of this matter might be considered by the group suggested in para one.

c. The third possibility is that which wld be created if peace negotiations were undertaken. While Fr observe that it is impossible to calculate if such possibility exists they believe consideration must be given to it "especially in the light of the recent reverses suffered by the VM."

Although detailed minutes are not available fol is a brief summary of our replies to various questions:

Although we are not prepared to consider question of tripartite SEA command as suggested by Fr we are prepared under certain specific and limiting conditions to adhere to our agreement to take part in high level tripartite mil conversations as agreed at the Sep FonMin Conf. We are prepared to appoint man from Admiral Radford's staff to represent us.

We assured Fr that our aid program to IC will be carried out as presently planned, barring unforeseen developments. We are prepared to give the Fr more detailed info on the way our aid program works and specific consideration being given to IC in overall picture. We have told the Fr we are not prepared to commit ground forces but wld, dependent on circumstances applicable at time, supply logistic support in the event of a forced evacuation.

Re the 25 billion franc deficit in sum required for natl armies (Fr state only 33 billion of 58 required can be covered by Fr and Viet budgets combined). The Fr made us a formal request for additional aid of 70 million dollars. We have given them no assurance in that regard and are now engaged in detailed studies at specialists level concerning matter. For your info it is very unlikely that this Govt will engage itself to finance the budgetary deficit of another govt but we hope to devise some other method to assure that necessary funds for the development of the natl armies be forthcoming.

Although we did not accede to the Fr request for another air-craft carrier, Gen Marshall informed Pleven that the present restrictions on the use of the Langley wld be removed, thus apparently making Langley available to Fr for use in Far Eastern waters if they so choose. We assured the Fr that the effect of the loss of Tonkin or of all of IC to rest of SEA is constantly under study by this govt.

We had no comment concerning third hypothesis.

The 58 billion franc figure for the formation of the natl armies is based on armies of 51 battalions. Of this sum it is estimated that the Fr budget cld only make a 15½ billion franc contribution and the Viet one of 17 billion as a maximum (40% of estimated total receipts). The deficit is thus 25½ billion francs or roughly $70 million. Of this sum approximately ⅔ wld be required for payroll and ⅓ for equipment and goods payable in francs and piasters. Eventually natl armies wld consist of four Vietnamese divisions of 34 battalions plus five Cambodian and two Laotian battalions. Fr have stated it will be impossible for them to furnish any equipment for battalions still to be formed and they count on the US for that.

68. REPORT BY ACHESON TO THE NSC ON CONVERSATIONS BETWEEN PRESIDENT TRUMAN AND FRENCH PRIME MINISTER RENÉ PLEVEN, FEBRUARY 23, 1951 [Extract]

During two days of meetings with President Truman in Washington, January 29–30, 1951, French Prime Minister René Pleven lobbied unsuccessfully for more formal coordination of policies among the three Western powers in the Far East and for United States financial support to cover the budgetary deficits of the Associated States. The substance of the discussion, as reported by Acheson, suggested a common feeling that Indochina might have to be abandoned in the event of Chinese intervention, and an American fear of becoming militarily overcommitted there. The passages in quotation marks were taken from the published final communiqué of January 30.

Far East

4a. 'The President and the Prime Minister found themselves in complete agreement as to the necessity of resisting aggression and assisting the free nations of the Far East in their efforts to maintain their security and assure their independence.' The U.S. and France should not over-commit themselves militarily in the Far East and thereby endanger the situation in Europe.

b. 'The President and the Prime Minister agreed that continuous contact should be maintained between the interested nations on these problems.' The Prime Minister's suggestion to create a U.S., U.K., French consultative body to coordinate the three governments' Asiatic policies was not accepted by the President, who preferred to rely on existing mechanisms.

c. 'The situation in Korea was discussed and they concurred that every effort must be exerted to bring about an honorable solution there. Until that end can be accomplished, resistance by United Nations forces to aggression must continue. Both France and the United States will support action directed toward deterring aggression and toward preventing the spread of hostilities beyond Korea.'

d. With regard to Indochina, 'the Prime Minister declared that France was determined to do its utmost to continue' its efforts to resist 'the Communist onslaught in order to maintain the security and independence of the Associated States, Viet Nam, Cambodia, and Laos.'

e. It was desirable to build up the native Indochinese forces as rapidly as possible. We held out no hope for the provision of U.S. budgetary assistance for the National Army in Indochina. We cannot become directly involved in local budgetary deficits of other countries.

f. 'The President informed the Prime Minister that United States aid for the French Union forces and for the National Armies of the Associated States will continue, and that the increased quantities of material to be delivered under the program authorized for the current fiscal year will be expedited.' Additional mea-

---

SOURCE: *Foreign Relations,* 1951, Vol. VI, p. 367.

sures for U.S. aircraft carrier *Langley* in the Mediterranean in view of our inability
to provide another U.S. carrier for service in Indochina; and (2) an agreement to
study the possibility of reallocating funds now available in an effort to provide
equipment for four Vietnamese divisions.

g. The President said that the United States was agreeable to U.S., U.K.,
French military consultations on Indochinese matters.

h. · In the event of a Chinese Communist attack on Indochina, the U.S. desires
to assist in the evacuation of French forces if such action becomes necessary. The
extent of the aid would be limited by other demands on our forces, such as Korea,
which exist at the time any request for assistance is made.

69. NSC STAFF STUDY ON OBJECTIVES, POLICIES AND COURSES OF ACTION IN ASIA (ANNEX TO NSC 48/4), MAY 17, 1951 [Extract]

*The NSC staff analysis underlined the point that the United States was not free
to devote maximum resources to its policy objectives in Asia, but had to constantly
weigh them against the requirements of its European commitments. It concluded
that the United States could not guarantee the denial of Southwest Asia to Communism.*

Problem

1. To determine United States national objectives, policies, and courses of
action with respect to Asia.

United States Long-Range National Objectives in Asia

2. The long-range national security objectives of the United States with respect to Asia are:

a. Development by the nations and peoples of Asia, through self-help
and mutual aid, of stable and self-sustaining non-communist governments,
oriented toward the United States, acting in accordance with the purposes and
principles of the United Nations Charter, and having the will and ability to
maintain internal security and prevent communist aggression.

b. Elimination of the preponderant power and influence of the USSR in
Asia or its reduction to such a degree that the Soviet Union will not be capable
of threatening from that area the security of the United States or its friends, or
the peace, national independence and stability of the Asiatic nations.

c. Development of power relationships in Asia which will make it impossible for any nation or alliance to threaten the security of the United States
from that area.

SOURCE: *U.S.-Vietnam Relations*, Book 8, pp. 438–445.

d. In so far as practicable, securing for the United States and the rest of the free world, and denying to the communist world, the availability through mutually advantageous arrangements, of the material resources of the Asian area.

Analysis of the Situation

3. United States objectives, policies, and courses of action in Asia should be designed to contribute toward the global objectives of strengthening the free world vis-a-vis the Soviet orbit, and should be determined with due regard to the relation of United States capabilities and commitments throughout the world. However, in view of the communist resort to armed force in Asia, United States action in that area must be based on the recognition that the most immediate threats to United States security are currently presented in that area.

4. Current Soviet tactics appear to concentrate on bringing the mainland of Eastern Asia and eventually Japan and the other principal off-shore islands in the Western Pacific under Soviet control, primarily through Soviet exploitation of the resources of communist China. The attainment of this objective on the mainland of Eastern Asia would substantially enhance the global position of the USSR at the expense of the United States, by securing the eastern flank of the USSR and permitting the USSR to concentrate its offensive power in other areas, particularly in Europe. Soviet control of the off-shore islands in the Western Pacific, including Japan, would present an unacceptable threat to the security of the United States.

5. Asia is of strategic importance to the United States.

a. The strategic significance of Asia arises from its resources, geography, and the political and military force which it could generate. The population of the area is about 1,250,000,000. The demonstrated military capacity of the North Korean and Chinese armies requires a reevaluation of the threat to the free world which the masses of Asia would constitute if they fell under Soviet Communist domination.

b. The resources of Asia contribute greatly to United States security by helping to meet its need for critical materials and they would be of great assistance in time of war if they remained available. At least until stockpiling levels are met, this phase of the area's importance to the United States will continue. Further, the development of events which might lead to the exhaustion of such stockpiles would magnify the importance of this source of supply. The area produces practically all the world's natural rubber, nearly 5% of the oil, 60% of the tin, the major part of various important tropical products, and strategic materials such as manganese, jute, and atomic materials. Japan's potential in heavy industry is roughly equal to 50% of the Soviet Union's present production. Therefore, it is important to U.S. security interests that U.S. military and economic assistance programs be developed in such a manner as to maximize that availability of the material resources of the Asian area to the United States and the free world.

c. Control by an enemy of the Asiatic mainland would deny to us the use of the most direct sea and air routes between Australia and the Middle East and between the United States and India. Such control would produce disastrous moral and psychological effects in border areas such as the Middle East and a critical effect in Western Europe.

6. The fact of Soviet power and communist aggression in Asia establishes the context within which the policies of the United States must operate.

    a. The problem of China is the central problem which faces the United States in Asia. A solution to this problem, through a change in the regime in control of mainland China, would facilitate the achievement of United States objectives throughout Asia. Therefore, United States policies and course of action in Asia should be determined in the light of their effect upon the solution of the central problem, that of China.

*   *   *

Strengthening of Southeast Asia

41. It is important to the United States that the mainland states of Southeast Asia remain under non-communist control and continue to improve their internal conditions. These states are valuable to the free world because of their strategic position, abundant natural resources, including strategic materials in short supply in the United States, and their large population. Moreover, these states, if adequately developed and organized, could serve to protect and contribute to the economic progress and military defense of the Pacific off-shore islands from Japan to New Zealand. Communist control of both China and Southeast Asia would place Japan in a dangerously vulnerable position and therefore seriously affect the entire security position of the United States in the Pacific. The fall of the mainland states would result in changing the status of the off-shore island chain from supporting bases to front line positions. Further, it would tend to isolate these base areas from each other, requiring a review of our entire strategic deployment of forces. Communist domination of the area would alleviate considerably the food problem of China and make available to the USSR considerable quantities of strategically important materials.

42. In the absence of overt Chinese Communist aggression in Southeast Asia, the general problems facing the United States in this area are: the real threat of Chinese Communist invasion and subversion, the political instability and weak leadership of the non-communist governments, the low standards of living and underdeveloped resources of the peoples of the area, the prevailing prejudice against colonialism and Western "interference" and the insensitivity to the danger of communist imperialism. Further acts of communist aggression in Southeast Asia can be expected to stimulate resistance on the part of countries which have thus far failed to take a positive stand.

43. Therefore, the general objectives of the United States in Southeast Asia are: (1) to contribute to the will and ability of all countries in the region to resist communism from within and without, and (b) to aid in the political, economic and social advancement of the area. For this purpose, the United States has developed support programs to strengthen the governments' administrative and military capabilities, to improve living standards, to encourage pro-Western alignments, and to stave off communist intervention.

44. Chinese Communist conquest of Indochina, Thailand and Burma, by military force and internal subversion, would seriously threaten the critical security interests of the United States. However, in the event of overt Chinese aggression, it is not now in the over-all security interests of the United States to commit any United States armed forces to the defense of the mainland states of Southeast Asia.

Therefore, the United States cannot guarantee the denial of Southeast Asia to communism. The United States should continue its present support programs to strengthen the will and ability to resist the Chinese Communists, to render Communist military operations as costly as possible, and to gain time for the United States and its allies to build up the defenses of the off-shore chain and weaken communist power at its source.

70. TELEGRAM FROM SPECIAL FAR EAST REPRESENTATIVE ECA, R. ALLEN GRIFFIN TO RICHARD M. BISSELL, JR., ACTING ADMINISTRATOR, ECONOMIC COOPERATION ADMINISTRATION, NOVEMBER 1951

After a visit to Indochina, R. Allen Griffin, who had been the chief of the first official U.S. Mission to Southeast Asia on economic assistance, presented a radically different view of the French-created State of Vietnam. The primary weakness of the Tran Van Huu government, he argued, was that it had no program for, and no interest in, improving the lives of the poverty-stricken peasant population. He called the Saigon regime "a relic of the past as much as French colonialism," but called for more active U.S. involvement in creating a more responsive Vietnamese government, rather than disengagement from it.

613. Dept pass ECA. To Bissell from Griffin.

1. US econ aid program Viet basically on right track for US objectives and should be contd as orig conceived. Those objectives remain sound and practical if new govt is to be supported in policies necessary to build loyalty and appreciation among population. However, I believe it is necessary for US clearly to realize the greatest impediment to success of US program and attainment objectives is nature of present Huu Govt, its lack of vitality and public leadership, its lack of enthusiasm for progressive progress that wld improve the gen welfare of peasants.

2. We are dealing with able land owners—mandarin type—functionaire govt. Its weakness is not that it is subordinate in many way to Fr but that it is in no sense the servant of the people. It has no grass roots. It therefore has no appeal whatsoever to the masses. It evokes no popular support because nature of its leaders tends to an attitude that this wld be a "concession." This govt might reluctantly try to mollify public opinion, but it does not consist of men who wld lead public opinion. Therefore though France-Vietnam Armed Forces may cont to win small engagements for ltd objectives, no real progress is being made in winning war, which depends equally on polit solution.

3. It has been perhaps error in judgment in believing essential struggle has been between the constricting polit influence and pressure of Fr—which undoubtedly still exists and patriotic effort of Viets to win increasing degree of independence. Perhaps the essential struggle is one not undertaken which is to get grass roots ability, conviction and patriotism on behalf of people of Viet into govt. So-call

SOURCE: *Foreign Relations,* 1951, Vol. VI, pp. 548–550.

independence Huu Govt represents means nothing to masses. It simply means a change of functionaires, not a change of social direction, not a drive to advance lot of the people. Revolution will continue and Ho Chi-minh will remain popular hero, so long as "independence" leaders with Fr support are simply native mandarins who are succeeding foreign mandarins. The period of mandarin and functionaire govt in Asia is over. The present type of govt in Viet is a relic of the past as much as Fr colonialism.

4. I believe this predicament is now fully realized by Fr. There is little doubt of fact they know they are fighting war that cannot be won without a polit solution, and the polit solution depends at least as much upon the relationship of Govt of Viet with masses of people of Viet as upon the relationship with Fr on subj of independence. The issue in Viet, in my mind, is more than nationalism and Francophobia. It is old Asian issue that destroyed the Kuomintang in Chi, Communist opportunity to exploit insecurity, and hunger and wretchedness of masses of people to whom their govt has failed to make an effective appeal. The Huu Govt makes no such appeal. Its heart is not in that kind of appeal. If it talked land reform it wld never be believed. It is my opinion that Fr are now fully awake to this predicament. They realize that their interests are not being served by a Viet Govt that not only has no appeal to masses but that has no program and perhaps only doubtful sympathy for masses. Such condition will not help the Fr to extricate themselves from the milit burden. Nor will it help US to lessen the load of increasing costs the Fr require us to share. It is my opinion that we shld consider this problem jointly with the Fr, to the end that a govt with some grass roots instincts, intentions and social purpose may result.

5. It may be pointed out that US is now engaged in massive milit assistance in Indochina and an econ program of great potential social and polit impact. Fr are insisting on an even greater Amer participation in Fr costs of defending this semi-independent state. US has paid for right to exercise stronger voice in determination of policies. Fr failure to achieve satis polit results out of compliant, obedient landowners nonreform Cabinet may now make possible a practical and farsighted program for improving polit situation, which in itself awaits improvement of social outlook Viet Govt, a condition now obvious to Fr. I believe Fr are ready for that. If we fail to secure their collaboration for setting up a govt fitted for its job by something better than obedience to Fr, then one day we will discover that the Fr in disgust and discouragement will abandon their attempt to defend this flank of sea.

6. I have discussed this outlook with Heath but did not have time to draft cable before leaving Saigon.

71. TELEGRAM FROM MINISTER DONALD R. HEATH IN SAIGON TO ACHESON, DECEMBER 9, 1951 [Extract]

In response to Griffin's analysis of the Huu government, U.S. Minister in Saigon Donald R. Heath noted that there were no leaders with popular support who would be willing to serve the French-sponsored regime.

SOURCE: *Foreign Relations*, 1951, Vol. VI, pp. 558–559.

1156. Re Singapore tels 618 and 621, Nov 30.

1. As Dept aware, I have for some time been concerned re inadequacies Huu Govt and I welcome Griffin corroborations. I am also pleased register my concurrence with his finding that present STEM [Special Technical and Economic Mission] programs fundamentally sound in this trying situation.

2. I am not sure, however, when Griffin speaks of govt with grass roots he means Cabinet nominated by present methods but including agrarian and popular leaders or whether he has in mind govt clothed with some popular mandate based on development forms of popular consultation. As to former, I doubt that much can be done at this time outside possible Catholic participation and acceptance of post by Tri, even this wld be limited advance since Catholics are minority sometimes suspected of too much western orientation and Tri, in entering govt, wld have to swallow disgrace and suppression his Dai Viet backers, who altho in sense "grass roots" have Asiatic fascistic, exotic, secret society aspects.

3. Fact is that no leaders with "grass roots" support presently known who wld join govt constituted on basis existing Franco-Viet relations and if there were such persons, doubtful if Fr wld accept them or that they wld be proof against Asiatic neutralism or Viet Minh infiltration. Fr know this which accounts for their quandary about replacement for Huu.

72. TELEGRAM FROM BRUCE TO ACHESON, DECEMBER 26, 1951 [Extract]

Bruce warned that French policy in Indochina was rapidly reaching the point where a fundamental reexamination would be unavoidable, and that the United States might be asked both to step up its assistance dramatically and make certain defense commitments with regard to Indochina. The alternative, he said, would probably be overwhelming sentiment in France for withdrawal.

14. We may soon be presented with a definite either/or situation: Either we increase our present aid to Indochina to a very considerable extent and make certain definite commitments as to what we will do in the event of a Chi invasion, or the Fr will be compelled to re-examine their entire policy in the area.

15. The issue is not entirely or even primarily whether the Fr will continue their effort at the now existing level. The present level will not be high enough if, even without an actual invasion, the Chi further step up their assistance to the VM. The Fr are becoming increasingly sensitive to the possibility of a sitn in which the Fr govt might be confronted either with the necessity for rapid withdrawal or a military disaster. In the circumstances we must decide whether we wish to go much further than we have heretofore in the direction of a multilateral approach to the problem.

16. If we agree in principle to a multilateral approach, it wld seem that we must immed engage in tripartite conversations, not only at the mil but also at the polit level. Amongst other considerations, we might, for instance, wish to reach a

SOURCE: *Foreign Relations*, 1951, Vol. VI, pp. 573–578.

tripartite decision as to the accuracy of present Fr estimates of the mil and polit sitn, and the wisdom of existing plans to deal with them.

17. To conclude, I believe that the snowball has started to form, and public sentiment for withdrawal, in the absence of adoption of some course of action envisaging either internationalization of Indochina problem or Fr receipt of massive additional aid, will gain steadily and perhaps at accelerated rate. It wld be incorrect to assume that Fr Govt is trying merely to horse trade or bargain with US. It is responding slowly and unwillingly to pressures far stronger than party positions. Consequently, Emb recommends that US reexamine problem in the light of these changing circumstances prior to a final precipitation of these mixed elements in order avoid risk of a sitn threatening the security of all SEA and entailing grave polit and mil repercussions elsewhere.

1952

73. NSC STAFF STUDY, "U.S. OBJECTIVES AND COURSES OF ACTION WITH RESPECT TO COMMUNIST AGGRESSION IN SOUTHEAST ASIA," FEBRUARY 13, 1952 [Extract]

A senior staff study annexed to NSC 124 rejected any negotiated settlement by the French with the Communists that would involve withdrawal of French forces, given the weakness of the French-sponsored governments and the "dubious attitudes of the population even in areas under French control." It recommended that the United States oppose any French move to withdraw and consider measures it could take, along with other nations, to prevent Communist victory. In the event of a Chinese intervention, either overt or covert, it called for "appropriate military actions against Communist China," under UN auspices if possible, but as part of a collective international action in any case.

20. The military situation in Indochina continues to be one of stalemate. Increased U.S. aid to the Franco-Vietnamese forces has been an essential factor in enabling them to withstand recent communist attacks. However, Chinese aid to the Viet Minh in the form of logistic support, training, and technical advisors is increasing at least at a comparable rate. The prospect is for a continuation of the present stalemate in the absence of intervention by important forces other than those presently engaged.

21. While it is unlikely under the present circumstances that the French will suffer a military defeat in Indochina, there is a distinct possibility that the French

SOURCE: Document declassified by National Security Council, March 3, 1976.

Government will soon conclude that France cannot continue indefinitely to carry the burden of her total military commitments. From the French point of view, the possible means of lessening the present burden include: (1) a settlement with the communists in Indochina; (2) an agreement to internationalize the action in Indochina; (3) reduction of the NATO obligations of France.

22. A settlement based on a military armistice would be more complicated in Indochina than in the case of Korea. Much of Indochina is not firmly under the control of either side, but subject to occasional forays from both. Areas controlled by the opposing sides are interspersed, and lines of contact are fluid. Because of the weakness of the native governments, the dubious attitudes of the population even in areas under French control, and the certainty of continued communist pressure, it is highly probable that any settlement based on a withdrawal of French forces would be tantamount to handing over Indochina to communism. The United States should therefore continue to oppose any negotiated settlement with the Viet Minh.

23. In the event that information and circumstances point to the conclusion that France is no longer prepared to carry the burden in Indochina, or if France presses for a sharing of the responsibility for Indochina, whether in the UN or directly with the U.S. Government, the United States should oppose a French withdrawal and consult with the French and British concerning further measures to be taken to safeguard the area from communist domination. In anticipation of these possibilities, the United States should urgently re-examine the situation with a view to determining:

a. Whether U.S. participation in an international undertaking would be warranted.

b. The general nature of the contributions which the United States, with other friendly governments, might be prepared to make.

24. A cessation of hostilities in Korea would greatly increase the logistical capability of the Chinese Communists to support military operations in Indochina. A Korean peace would have an even more decisive effect in increasing Chinese air capabilities in that area. Recent intelligence reports indicate increased Chinese Communist military activity in the Indochinese border area. If the Chinese Communists directly intervene with large forces over and above those introduced as individuals or in small units, the French would probably be driven back to a beachhead around Haiphong. The French should be able to hold this beachhead for only a limited time at best in the absence of timely and substantial outside support.

25. In view of the world-wide reaction to overt aggression in Korea, Communist China may prefer to repeat in Indochina the method of "volunteer" intervention. Inasmuch as the French do not control the border between China and Indochina nor large areas north of Hanoi, it may be difficult to detect the extent of preparation for such intervention. It is important to U.S. security interests to maintain the closest possible consultation with the French Government on the buildup of Chinese Communist intervention in Indochina. The Government of France has agreed to consult with the United States before it requests UN or other international action to oppose Chinese Communist aggression in Indochina in order that the two countries may jointly evaluate the extent of Chinese Communist intervention.

26. If it is thus determined that Chinese Communist forces (including volunteers) have overtly intervened in the conflict in Indochina, or are covertly participating to such an extent as to jeopardize retention of the Tonkin Delta by the French

forces, the United States should support the French to the greatest extent possible preferably under the auspices of the UN. It is by no means certain that an appropriate UN resolution could be obtained. Favorable action in the UN would depend upon a change in the attitude of those governments which view the present regime in Indochina as a continuation of French colonialism. A new communist aggression might bring about a reassessment of the situation on the part of these governments and an increased recognition of the danger. Accordingly, it is believed that a UN resolution to oppose the aggression could be passed in the General Assembly by a small margin.

27. Even if it is not possible to obtain a UN resolution in such a case, the United States should seek the maximum possible international support for and participation in any international collective action in support of France and the Associated States. The United States should take appropriate military action against Communist China as part of a UN collective action or in conjunction with France and the United Kingdom and other friendly governments. However, in the absence of such support, it is highly unlikely that the United States would act unilaterally. It is probably however, that the United States would find some support and token participation at least from the United Kingdom and other Commonwealth countries.

28. The U.S. forces which would be committed, and the manner of their employment, as well as the military equipment which could be furnished to bolster the French Union forces, would be dependent upon certain factors which cannot now be predicted with accuracy. These include the extent of progress in U.S. rearmament, whether or not hostilities in Korea were continuing, and strategic developments in other parts of the world. It would be desirable to avoid the use of major U.S. ground forces in Indochina. Other effective means of opposing the aggression would include naval, air and logistical support of the French Union forces, naval blockade of Communist China, and attacks by land and carrier-based aircraft on military targets in Communist China. The latter could be effective against the long, tenuous, and vulnerable supply lines by which Chinese operations in Indochina would have to be supported. In the event of a forced evacuation, US. forces might provide cover and assistance. United Kingdom participation in these measures might well result in the seizure of Hong Kong by the Chinese Communists.

29. It is recognized that the commitment of U.S. military forces against Communist China would: (a) increase the risk of general hostilities in the Far East, including Soviet participation under cover of the existing Sino-Soviet agreements; (b) involve U.S. military forces in another Asiatic peripheral action, thus detracting from U.S. capabilities to conduct a global war in the near future; (c) arouse public opposition to "another Korea"; and (d) imply willingness to use U.S. military forces in other critical areas subject to communist aggression. Nevertheless, by failing to take action, the United States would permit the communists to obtain, at little or no cost, a victory of major world consequence.

30. Informed public opinion might support use of U.S. forces in Indochina regardless of sentiment against "another Korea" on the basis that: (a) Indochina is of far greater strategic importance than Korea: (b) the confirmation of UN willingness to oppose aggression with force, demonstrated at such a high cost in Korea, might be nullified by the failure to commit UN forces in Indochina; and (c) a

second instance of aggression by the Chinese Communists would justify measures not subject to the limitations imposed upon the UN action in Korea.

31. The military action contemplated herein would constitute, in effect, a war against Communist China which would be limited only as to its objectives, but would not be subject to any geographic limitations. Employment of U.S. forces in a *de facto* war with a formal declaration would raise questions which would make it desirable to consult with key members of both parties in Congress in order to obtain their prior concurrence in the courses of action contemplated.

1953

74. REPORT BY HO CHI MINH TO THE FOURTH CONFERENCE OF THE PARTY CENTRAL COMMITTEE, JANUARY 25–30, 1953 [Extract]

The Central Committee's Fourth Conference concentrated on two major problems: putting an effective rent reduction program into effect to lay the groundwork for land reform, and setting the military line for 1953. Ho Chi Minh presented a report to the conference reviewing the course of the war in 1952 and the situation in 1953. He warned that the war would become even harder and more complex, because the United States and France would step up their efforts, hoping to "occupy our country and make it a military base to attack China." Regarding military policy, he presented ten principles to guide the strategy of the resistance.

1. Avoid strong points and attack weak points in order to disperse the enemy's forces, destroy the enemy's manpower and widen the free zone.

That is our strategic line at present.

2. Main force troops on the Northern battlefield must use fluid mobile warfare, in order to annihilate the enemy's manpower bit by bit and weaken the enemy and must coordinate it with attacks on fortified positions, one by one in order to take important points and small towns where the enemy has gaps or is weak. We do this in order to achieve the objectives of fighting where we are sure of victory, and of broadening the free zone. At the same time, we may use positional warfare to draw the enemy's forces to us in order to attack them, disperse the enemy's forces, confuse the enemy's plans and create conditions for mobile warfare.

3. The battlefield in the enemy's rear must broaden guerrilla warfare in order to annihilate and wear down small parts of the enemy; in order to resist enemy sweeps, protect the lives and property of the people, harass, sabotage, and domi-

SOURCE: Committee to Research Army History, Political Directorate, Vietnam People's Army, *Lich Su Quan Doi Nhan Dan Viet Nam* [History of the Vietnam People's Army] (Hanoi: Quan Doi Nhan Dan, 1974), pp. 511–513. [Translation by the editor.]

nate the enemy; propagandize and educate the masses in those zones, reduce the pool of recruitment for puppet troops, widen our guerrilla zones and guerrilla base areas, and establish and strengthen resistance bases in the enemy's rear.

4. Besides increasing main force troops and building local troops, the free zone, and rather large guerrilla bases, we must build guerrilla militia organizations not detached from production. Those guerrilla militia organizations not only can take responsibility for repression of counterrevolutionaries, maintain security in the villages, protect the interests of the masses, struggle with the enemy and coordinate combat with main force troops, but also can be used for replacements for main force troops.

5. Regarding the military guidance we must combine the forms of struggle mentioned above in a flexible, shrewd manner. That would be profitable, on one hand, for the main force troops who can find many opportunities to annihilate the enemy; and on the other hand, it can help guerrillas operate and help our guerrilla bases in the enemy's rear develop and be consolidated.

6. In the guidance of the forms of struggle mentioned above, we must realize clearly the long-term character of resistance war. Therefore, we must pay much attention to maintaining the firm combat strength of the army, not allowing it to be worn down or too tired. At the same time we must ask the troops to accept difficulty and hardship, to be resolute and fearless and to emulate in killing the enemy and recording feats of arms. Those two things are not in conflict but are united with each other.

7. We must strengthen political work, always raising the political level and class consciousness of our troops; we must insure the implementation of the policy of the Party and Government; we must thoroughly maintain self-conscious discipline regarding the military and political aspect. Thus we must strengthen the leadership of the Party in the army and must achieve democracy in the army.

8. We must strengthen military work, first of all always regarding training troops as important. We must strive to bring up cadres, forge their thinking, and raise the level of political consciousness as well as the tactical and technical level of the cadres. That is the most important point in various kinds of work.

We must strengthen the work of the General Staff and of the Supply Directorate. Only if the work of the General Staff is strengthened can we raise the tactics and technique of the troops. Only if the work of the Supply Directorate is strengthened can we insure sufficient supplies to the war and raise the combat strength of the troops.

But we must resolutely resist the erroneous tendency for agencies to become swollen.

9. We must have a common plan for the building and reinforcement of the army. Besides mobilizing youth in the free zone to join the army, we must pay much attention to winning over and reforming puppet troops who have surrendered to us in order to reinforce our troops. In organizing new troops, we must use completely new cadres and new officers, but must use the method of taking old troops and making them the foundation for broadening new troops. At the same time, we must not deplete guerrilla troops in order to provide replacements for main force troops.

10. We must strengthen and improve gradually the equipment of our troops, especially the manufacture of artillery.

75. VO NGUYEN GIAP'S TET LETTER, JANUARY 1953 [Extract]

The resistance army's Northwest Campaign, beginning in September and last-ing until the end of the year, succeeded in liberating some 28,000 square miles of territory, including the Dienbienphu valley, and some 250,000 people, while inflict-ing heavy losses on French troops. In his Tet letter, Giap discussed the victories of the previous year and looked ahead to the strategic requirements for 1953. The main emphasis in his analysis was on the necessity for land reform, which had just been decided by the Party Central Committee at its Fourth Conference.

Today, the first day of Tet, while we are all welcoming the new year together with the people, welcoming our new task and happily reading the Tet greetings from Chairman Ho, we review the great victories during the past year: the Spring victory at Hoa-binh, the fall-winter victory in the Northwest, and the victory throughout the year in the enemy's rear area in the Northern plain. In the center and South, the guerrilla warfare held firm and on the An-khe front we are winning a big victory.

In one year of struggle, we have annihilated 65,000 of the enemy's manpower. That is a big accomplishment compared with the year before.

Those victories show the clearsighted leadership of the Party, the Govern-ment, and Chairman Ho.

Those victories show the big results of the political retraining and the progress of our army on all aspects: ideology, strategic guidance, and tactics technology.

These victories show the spirit of heroic sacrifice, the determination to strug-gle to complete our army's mission, and our people's spirit of determination to serve the frontlines, particularly the brother and sister civilian laborers on all battlefields.

Those victories show the firm faith of our army and people in the leadership of the Party, Government, and Chairman Ho, and their confidence that the longterm and difficult resistance war will definitely win.

Those victories have caused the enemy to meet many difficulties and forced them to disperse the main forces in order to cope with us, made them even more passive than they were before, and further our consolidated posture of holding the initiative on the Northern battlefields.

The glorious victories of our army and people mentioned above mesh with the victories of the Korean People's Army and the Chinese volunteer army struggling to annihilate the American imperialist aggressors and their gang of lackies, with the victories of the Asian and Pacific Peace Conference, of the Conference of World's People struggling to protect peace in Vienna and increase further the forces of the front of world peace and democracy lead by the Soviet Union.

In the new year, we are happy to receive these new tasks:

1. We must continue our political retraining, and strengthen political retrain-ing in the military.

2. We must raise our determination, establish a style of energetically annihi-lating the enemy, heroically struggle and annihilate still more of the enemy's manpower.

SOURCE: Giap, *Orders of the Day*, pp. 177–180.

3. We must actively execute the policy of the Party and Government, and especially participate in the approaching great mobilization of the peasants. This year, the Party Central Committee, the Government, and Chairman Ho have decided to launch the mobilization of peasants to thoroughly reduce rents, carry out reduction of debts, and distribute communal land and the land of French colonialists and Vietnamese traitors to the peasants. The main thing is to reduce rents, aiming at satisfying initially the just demand of the peasants for land and winning political preeminence for the peasants.

The Central Committee of the Party, the Government, and Chairman Ho have decided on this because the peasants are the main force of the revolution and the resistance, and because serving their real interests and gaining political preeminence for the peasants in the countryside means strengthening the primary forces of the people, and increasing the power of the resistance.

As cadres and fighters of the People's Army, an army whose composition includes an absolute majority of peasants, we must recognize clearly the importance and the great function of mobilizing the peasants. We must actively participate in the task of mobilizing the peasants, not only to take back the rights for the people in the rear area but to take back rights for ourselves as well. We must actively study and carry out the policy of the Party and Government, and endeavor to forge further the class standpoint, the mass concept and the sense of serving the people.

Going to the frontlines, you heroically kill the invader; returning to the rear area, you actively participate in and support the struggle of the peasants—that is the task and honor of each cadre and fighter in the army.

In the new year, our task is very heavy but also very glorious. Under the leadership of the Party, Government, and Chairman Ho, having confidence in the strong forces of the laboring people and in the support of the front of world peace and democracy led by the Soviet Union, we will definitely succeed in political retraining, fight heroically, annihilate a great part of the enemy's manpower, win back and protect the people, develop guerrilla warfare strongly, and take the resistance war to complete victory.

76. TELEGRAM FROM SECRETARY OF STATE JOHN FOSTER DULLES TO AMBASSADOR C. DOUGLAS DILLON IN PARIS, MARCH 19, 1953

The new secretary of state, John Foster Dulles, instructed his ambassador in Paris, C. Douglas Dillon, to inform the French government that the United States believed a plan for destroying the "principal regular enemy forces" within approximately two years was "essential." He indicated that the United States would have to be able to assure Congress that French plans were sound in order to obtain the necessary financial support for them. Thus, the United States was about to enter a new phase of involvement in the strategic conduct of the war.

Recent Paris working-level discussions added substantially to our factual background on Indochina. Please express to Foreign Minister my appreciation for

SOURCE: *U.S.-Vietnam Relations*, Book 9, pp. 15–16.

cooperation all concerned. Also take early opportunity discuss informally on my behalf with Mayer or Bidault forthcoming conversations along following general lines:

QTE Secretary Acheson in December 1952 and I last month have discussed with our French colleagues the Indochina situation. On both occasions we received indications French Government was planning to request US GOVT to increase already considerable share of financial burden of the struggle which it is now bearing. I assume that when Mayer, Bidault and Letourneau come to Washington they will furnish further particulars regarding French Government's plans and resulting requirements. It may be helpful to them in formulating their position to express to them informally some of considerations involved not only in matter of additional aid but also in continuation American assistance at present substantial level. Considerations are:

First, Government and people of US are fully aware of importance to free world of war being waged in Indochina by armies of France and Associated States. They appreciate sacrifices which have been and are being made and degree to which Communist plans have been thwarted by magnificent defense carried out in Indochina against Communist aggression.

Second, we envisage Indochina situation with real sense of urgency. We believe continued military stalemate will produce most undesirable political consequences in Indochina, France and U.S. Therefore, we heartily agree that considerable increased effort having as its aim liquidation principal regular enemy forces within period of, say, twenty-four months is essential. We obviously do not wish share Franco-Vietnamese responsibility for conduct operations. However, if interested Departments this Government are to urge Congress to make necessary appropriations for Indochina for FY 54, those Departments must be convinced that necessarily top secret strategic plans for Indochina are sound and can be and will be aggressively and energetically prosecuted.

Third, I share concern frequently expressed in French circles regarding adequacy of the financial contribution to prosecution of war derived from residents of the Associated States including French businessmen. While I welcome increased Vietnamese Government contribution recently made, I believe there is ground for thoroughgoing re-examination this problem into which balance of payment and rate of exchange considerations enter and which of course is of interest to us in its bearing upon the need for U.S. aid.

Fourth, I look forward to opportunity talking with my French colleagues on question of free world policy in Far East as whole and particularly the policies which we should adopt in order to discourage further Chinese Communist aggression. I hope to reach agreement that speedy defeat of Viet Minh forces in Indochina would deter rather than provoke Chinese Communist aggression in Tonkin since it would be a clear indication of our joint determination to meet force with effective force.

Fifth, I should appreciate receiving any views which my French friends may care to convey regarding relations between the U.S. and the Associated States of Indochina and particularly regarding participation by latter in discussions of military and economic policy and in reception of U.S. aid. END QUOTE

Please handle on strictly oral basis and let me have reaction. The specified points are designed to be exploratory; I would welcome any ideas French may wish to convey on these or other topics prior to our conversation.

77. TELEGRAM FROM SECRETARY DULLES TO AMBASSADOR DILLON, MARCH 26, 1953 [Extract]

In discussions with French Premier René Mayer and Minister of overseas France Jean Letourneau, President Eisenhower emphasized the need to convince both Americans and the people of the Associated States that the latter were fighting for their own independence. Mayer assured him that Franco-Vietnamese plans were aimed at reducing the revolutionary forces to a "negligible factor" within two years.

Concerning Indochina President expressed full American sympathy for valiant French struggle as part of over-all fight against Communist aggression.

He recognized this struggle not just another colonial war but advised French to make this very clear as many Americans still under misapprehension. President expressed great American interest in French program leading to solution of Indochina problem making clear that he was not talking in terms of a complete victory. However requests for further American assistance could not be considered without full knowledge of French political and military plans permitting US Government to see why its assistance was required and how it would be used. President expressed great interest in measures being taken by French to obtain greatest possible support by local populations through convincing them they were fighting their own war for their own independence.

Re Indochina Mayer started by referring to NAC Resolution December 1952 re QTE continuing aid UNQTE from NATO Governments. He said French political and military plans would be communicated to us later during the talks. Meanwhile he stressed his full agreement with President that the task was two-fold: militarily, Associated States Armies had to be developed for victory and for internal pacification. Politically it was necessary to develop popular basis for national government to protect them from eventual take-over by Vietminh forces. While expressing the greatest interest in Gen Clark's report following visit to Indochina Mayer was careful to point out differences between Korea and Indochina.

Le Tourneau said that details of recent Dalat agreements would be given to us later but that in meanwhile he can say that these will permit presentation of a Franco-Vietnamese plan which should lead within two years to reduction of Vietminh to a negligible factor in Indochina if no material increase in Chinese or Soviet aid in meanwhile. LeTourneau expressed confidence that popular support for local governments was increasing day by day, pointing to success of January elections in Vietnam, to fact that much more officer material is now available for National Armies and that all enlisted men needed under present financial limitations were available on volunteer basis. Finally he expressed confidence that local populations supported local governments more vigorously now that Vietminh was clearly recognized as the agent not only of Communism but also of traditional Chinese enemy.

SOURCE: *U.S.-Vietnam Relations,* Book 9, pp. 17–18.

78. MEMORANDUM BY ASSISTANT SECRETARY OF STATE FOR CONGRESSIONAL RELATIONS DOUGLAS MACARTHUR II, APRIL 27, 1953

Dulles reported to Eisenhower that the French desperately needed C-119 transport planes to cope with the new military threat posed by the loss of Samnua Province. The French wanted U.S. Air Force personnel to fly them, but Dulles suggested that civilian pilots in Formosa be used to fly them instead. The reference was to personnel of Civil Air Transport (CAT), a company that had been acquired by the Central Intelligence Agency to carry out air operations in the Far East. The loan of six planes was approved by the Joint Chiefs, and they were flown by CIA-controlled CAT pilots.

At a meeting with the President at the White House this afternoon for the purpose of briefing the President on the recent NATO Paris meeting and bilateral talks with the British and the French, the President asked Secretary Dulles what the French views were on the situation in Laos.

The Secretary replied that the French were very gravely concerned about the situation there. He said that when he had met with Prime Minister René Mayer last evening just prior to departure from Paris, M. Mayer had stated that the French needed more urgently the loan of some C-119 aircraft to help them get tanks and heavy equipment into Laos to assist in its defense. Having such equipment might mean the difference between holding and losing Laos. M. Mayer had envisaged U.S. Air Force personnel operating the aircraft during the period of the loan.

The Secretary said to the President that such a procedure would mean the sending of U.S. personnel on combat missions in Indochina. This, obviously, was a decision which would have repercussions and would raise many problems. However, there was an alternative, which would be to loan the French the C-119's, which he understood the Department of Defense was willing to do, and have civilian pilots fly them. Following his return to Washington this morning, the Secretary had made inquiry and had ascertained that there were pilots in Formosa who were not members of the U.S. armed forces and who might well be able to carry out these missions. This possibility was being explored on an urgent basis to see whether it would not be possible to have the aircraft loaned and the above-mentioned personnel in Formosa operate them.

79. REPORT BY LT. GEN. JOHN W. O'DANIEL TO JOINT CHIEFS OF STAFF ON U.S. JOINT MILITARY MISSION TO INDOCHINA, JULY 14, 1953 [Extracts]

General O'Daniel's report on the U.S. military mission shows that what later became known as the "Navarre Plan" owed more to O'Daniel's ideas than to

SOURCE: *U.S.-Vietnam Relations*, Book 9, p. 38.
SOURCE: *U.S.-Vietnam Relations*, Book 9, pp 69–79, 85–86.

those of the French command in Indochina. O'Daniel got the French to organize
three new divisions from northern Indochina as an offensive striking force to wrest
the initiative from the "Viet Minh" immediately. He believed the French Union
forces would "accomplish the decisive defeat of the Viet Minh" by 1955, given the
reorganization which he proposed.

1. The attached Report of the U.S. Joint Military Mission to Indochina is
submitted as directed by paragraph 10 of the "Terms of Reference for the Chief of
the U.S. Military Mission to Indochina."
2. In summarizing the subject report I wish to emphasize the following:
    a. General Navarre, Commander-in-Chief, French Forces, Far East, sub-
mitted to me in writing a new aggressive concept for the conduct of operations
in Indochina which, in brief, calls for (a) taking the initiative immediately
with local offensives, emphasizing guerrilla warfare, (b) initiating an offensive (utilizing the equivalent of three (3) divisions) in Tonkin by 15 September
1953, (c) recovering a maximum number of units from areas not directly
involved in the war, (d) reorganizing battalions into regiments and regiments
into divisions, with necessary support units and (e) developing the Armies of
the Associated States and giving them greater leadership responsibility in the
conduct of operations.
    b. General Gambiez, Chief of Staff to General Navarre, presented a
discussion of operations to take place during the balance of the current rainy
season. These operations include four (4) offensive operations outside the
Tonkin perimeter aimed at destroying enemy personnel and existent enemy
supply dumps, a clearing operation in North Annam, and an offensive operation in South Annam aimed at linking the Phan Tiet beachhead with Plateau
forces and thus permanently severing the principal enemy supply line to Co-
chin China. These operations are to be followed by a large-scale offensive in
Tonkin on or about 15 September 1953.
    c. General Navarre agreed to establish a French MAAG [Military Assis-
tance Advisory Group] organization to supervise all training of the military
forces of the Associated States and to include three (3) U.S. officers. This will
provide an excellent opportunity for indirect U.S. participation in the training
of indigenous forces and for exercising follow up action on matters already
agreed upon with the French and the Associated States.
    d. General Navarre agreed to cooperate wholeheartedly in (1) providing
the U.S. with increased intelligence and (2) the stationing of one or two
military attaches in Hanoi for this purpose.
    e. General Navarre agreed to keep the Chief, MAAG, Indochina in-
formed of French plans and stated that he will invite MAAG officers to attend
all operations.
    f. General Lauzin, Commander-in-Chief, French Air Force, Indochina
agreed to (1) the removal of the six (6) C-119's from Indochina, (2) request
C-119's in the future on a temporary basis only, (3 or 4 days) to support
airborne operations requiring the simultaneous drop of forces in excess of two
battalions, (3) step-up pilot and mechanic training and (4) organize a Vietnamese
National Air Force.
    g. Admiral Auboyneau agreed to a reorganization of French Naval forces
to include a Joint Amphibious Command for the purpose of (1) attaining

increased amphibious effectiveness and (2) delegating increased responsibility to Vietnamese leaders and units.

    h. Once the French became convinced of the soundness of our initial proposals they became increasingly receptive to our subsequent recommendations.

    i. As evidence of French sincerity in carrying out actions designed to improve the status of anti-communist military forces in Indochina, General Navarre and other French officers repeatedly invited me to return in a few months "to witness the progress we will have made."
3. I recommend that the Joint Chiefs of Staff:

    a. Note the contents of the attached report and take appropriate action where required.

    b. Propose to the Secretary of Defense that he recommend to the Secretary of State the sending of a small group of qualified experts to Indochina to study the desirability of the U.S. assisting in the development of Associated States small industry capable of producing certain military items or military-support items such as small arms, batteries or recap tires.

    c. Approve an increase in artillery units in the force basis for Indochina if MAAG and Department of the Army screening indicates such increase is necessary for a balance of forces in the new divisional organization.

    d. Approve my return to Indochina in 3 or 4 months for a follow-up of the mission's activities, and

    e. Insure that the Chief, MAAG, Indochina, receives copies of the approved report for his guidance and that he be instructed to take follow-up action where appropriate.
4. I recommend that the Chiefs of the individual Services approve necessary personnel augmentations of the MAAG, Indochina to allow for three (3) U.S. officers (one from each Service) for attachment to the French Training Command, and that the Chief of Staff, U.S. Army assign two (2) additional U.S. Assistant Army Attaches to be used for collecting combat intelligence in conjunction with the French G-2 in the Hanoi area.

80. EDITORIAL IN NHAN DAN, AUGUST 16–20, 1953 [Extracts]

When the Korean armistice was signed on July 27, 1953, the Soviet Union began immediately to cite it as a model for bringing peace to Indochina. Chinese Communist broadcasts echoed the same theme. But the Vietnamese media remained silent, indicating serious differences with its socialist allies on the question of war and peace in Indochina. When the Vietnamese Party did comment on the relationship between the Korean armistice and Indochina nearly three weeks later, it clearly rejected a settlement in which it would give up its aim of an independent, unified Vietnam, calling instead for a step-up in the resistance war.

SOURCE: *The Vietnamese People's Sacred Resistance War* Vol. IV, 96–99. *Cuoc Khang Chien Than Thanh cua Nhan Dan Viet-Nam* [The Vietnamese People's Sacred Resistance War] (Hanoi: Nah Xuat Ban Su That, 1960) [Translation by the editor.]

Recently, the French imperialists keep propagandizing about resolving the Vietnamese-Cambodian-Laotian war peacefully. In fact, neither the U.S. interventionists or the French colonialists really want peace. They have not yet been beaten, not yet hurt to the point that they cannot continue the war. On the contrary, they still hope to defeat us and are preparing to step up their aggressive war. Therefore they talk peace mainly to deceive the French people and world opinion, and to dampen our people's fighting spirit, hoping to attract shaky elements in our ranks.

At present, in France, leaving aside the French Communist Party, the French bourgeois parties and French ruling circles are divided into several groups regarding their attitude toward the war in Vietnam-Cambodia-Laos.

The pro-war faction is the faction of French reactionaries. In this faction there are those who want to continue the war with the help of the U.S. but who don't want to relinquish control of Vietnam-Cambodia-Laos to the U.S. That is the faction which is now in power in the French government. In addition, there are groups who support internationalizing the war, meaning that they want the U.S. and other imperialist countries to send troops to Vietnam-Cambodia-Laos to join France in its aggression.

Another faction wants to end immediately a war harmful to France, but still wants to maintain the interests of French imperialism in Vietnam-Cambodia-Laos. At present this faction has no ruling position in French government circles.

Thus at present only the French Communist Party and French working people have a true pro-peace standpoint. The more strongly we attack, the more our resistance is victorious, the more the world peace movement is on the rise, the stronger, broader and more victorious will be the struggle of the French Communist Party and the French people for their genuine peace standpoint.

* * *

Our viewpoint on the problem of peace in Vietnam is: only when the resistance is stronger, destroying much more of the manpower of the enemy and the puppets and making it impossible for them to carry on the war of aggression, will real peace return to Vietnam. We have long recognized that our resistance is for national independence and the defense of world peace. So, only when the Vietnamese people have independence and national unification will there be complete and genuine peace in Vietnam. The independence, unification and peace of the Vietnamese people must be won by the Vietnamese people themselves, who must have no illusions about peace, and must not rely on anyone else.

81. TELEGRAM FROM DULLES TO DILLON, SEPTEMBER 9, 1953 [Extract]

Dulles instructed Dillon to advise the French government that the United States had approved additional aid for Indochina, provided that France give a series of assurances on its political and military policies. Dillon was to begin working on language for a French note embodying the assurances.

SOURCE: *U.S.-Vietnam Relations*, Book 9, pp. 150–152.

1. Subject to our receiving necessary assurances from French, NSC today approved additional aid proposed for Indochina based on substance DEPTEL 827, with Presidential approval expected tomorrow. Comments URTELS 939, 940, 941 fully taken into account in presentation to NSC.

2. On most confidential basis you should therefore now informally advise Laniel and Bidault above action and indicate assurances desired are to effect that French Government is determined:

    a. but promptly into effect program of action set forth its memorandum Sept 1;

    b. carry this program forward vigorously with object of eliminating regular enemy forces in Indochina;

    c. continue pursue policy of perfecting independence of Associated States in conformity with July 3 declaration;

    d. facilitate exchange information with American military authorities and take into account their views in developing and carrying out French military plans Indochina;

    e. assure that no basic or permanent alteration of plans and programs for NATO forces will be made as result of additional effort Indochina;

    f. provide appropriate info to US Govt of amount of expenditures for military program set forth in memo of Sept 1.

3. We would expect these assurances be embodied in note which US in reply would acknowledge. US reply would go on to make clear that:

    a. appropriately established financial requirements for military program as indicated in Sept 1 memo from French Govt, not rpt not to exceed $385 million or its equivalent in Calendar Year 1954, will be met by US Govt (see para 8 below);

    b. amount of $385 million or its equivalent in francs or piasters is deemed to satisfy in full request made by French memo of Sept 1;

    c. no further financial assistance may be expected for Calendar Year 1954;

    d. US Govt retains right to terminate this additional assistance should for any reason French Govt plan as outlined in memo of Sept 1 prove incapable of execution or should other unforeseen circumstances arise which negate the understandings arrived at between the two govts.

4. You should immediately begin informally to work out language with French covering paragraph 2 above. (We will cable soonest new draft of US reply.) It should be made crystal clear to French that final US Govt agreement will be given only when satisfactory language for exchange notes has been obtained.

82. REPLIES BY HO CHI MINH TO THE SWEDISH NEWSPAPER *EXPRESSEN*, NOVEMBER 26, 1953

In an interview with a Swedish newsman, Ho Chi Minh indicated a Vietnamese readiness to negotiate an armistice with France, provided that France showed

SOURCE: Ho Chi Minh, *Selected Writings*, pp. 153–154.

"sincere respect for the genuine independence of Viet Nam." Ho's answer also reflected the Vietnamese conclusion that contradictions between American and French interests had grown acute and were an important factor in French politics and policy. The interview represented the opening of a new "diplomatic front" in the Indochina struggle.

QUESTION: *The debate in the French National Assembly has shown that a great number of French politicians are for a peaceful settlement of the conflict in Viet Nam through direct negotiations with the Vietnamese Government. This is spreading among the French people. Is it welcomed by yourself and your Government?*

ANSWER: The war in Viet Nam was launched by the French Government. The Vietnamese people were obliged to take up arms and have heroically struggled for nearly eight years now against the aggressors, to safeguard their independence and their right to live in freedom and peace. If the French colonialists continue their aggressive war, the Vietnamese people are determined to carry on their patriotic resistance until final victory. However, if the French Government have drawn a lesson from the war they have been waging these last few years and want to negotiate an armistice in Viet Nam and solve the Viet Nam problem by peaceful means, the people and Government of the Democratic Republic of Viet Nam are ready to meet this desire.

QUESTION: *Will a ceasefire or an armistice be possible?*

ANSWER: An armistice can take place in Viet Nam, provided that the French Government ends its war of aggression in Viet Nam. The basis for such an armistice is that the French Government should show sincere respect for the genuine independence of Viet Nam.

QUESTION: *Would you agree to mediation by a neutral country for a meeting between you and representatives of the High Command of the other side? May Sweden offer such a mediation?*

ANSWER: If some neutral countries try to help bring a speedy end to the hostilities in Viet Nam by means of negotiations, such an effort will be welcomed. However, the negotiation for an armistice essentially concerns the Government of the Democratic Republic of Viet Nam and the French Government.

QUESTION: *In your opinion, is there any other way to end the hostilities?*

ANWER: The war in Viet Nam has brought havoc to the Vietnamese people and at the same time has caused much suffering to the French people. That is why the French people have been struggling for an end to this war.

I have constantly shown my sympathy and esteem for the French people and the French peace fighters. At present not only is the independence of Viet Nam seriously encroached upon but the independence of France itself is also gravely threatened. On the one hand, the US imperialists are pressing the French colonialists to continue and expand the aggressive war in Viet Nam, hoping thus to weaken France more and more and eventually replacing it in Indochina; on the other, they oblige France to ratify the European defence treaty, which means the revival of German militarism.

Therefore, the struggle of the French people for independence, democracy and peace and for an end to the war in Viet Nam, constitutes one of the important factors of a peaceful settlement of the Viet Nam question.

83. REPORT BY HO CHI MINH TO THE NATIONAL ASSEMBLY, DECEMBER 1, 1953 [Extracts]

In December 1953, the National Assembly of the DRV met for the first time since the resistance war began, primarily to pass land reform legislation. Land reform was the most important and most difficult political decision regarding domestic matters that the Communist leadership had made. Undertaking an agrarian revolution, with the social upheaval that implied, in the midst of the resistance war was a gamble that the renewed enthusiasm of the poor and landless peasant majority for the resistance would more than compensate for the time and energy spent by cadres in conflict, not only in the villages but within the ranks of army and government, which were staffed to a great extent by relatives of landowners.

Our slogan during the war of resistance is "All for the front, all for victory!" The more the war of resistance develops, the more manpower and wealth it requires. Our peasants have contributed the greatest part of this manpower and wealth to the resistance. We must liberate them from the feudal yoke and foster their strength in order fully to mobilize this huge force for the resistance and win victory.

The key victor for the resistance lies in consolidating and enlarging the National United Front, consolidating the worker-peasant alliance and the people's power, strengthening and developing the Army, consolidating the Party and strengthening its leadership in all respects. Only by mobilizing the masses for land reform can we carry out these tasks in favourable conditions.

The enemy actively seeks to use Vietnamese to fight Vietnamese and to feed war with war. They are doing their utmost to deceive, divide and exploit our people. Land reform will exert an influence on our peasant compatriots in the enemy's rear areas and will encourage them to struggle even more vigorously against him in order to liberate themselves, and to give even more enthusiastic support to the democratic Government of the Resistance; at the same time it will have an impact on the puppet armed forces and cause their disintegration because the absolute majority of the puppet soldiers are peasants in enemy-occupied areas.

The overwhelming majority of our people are peasants.

Over these last years, it is thanks to their forces that the war of resistance has been going on successfully. It is also thanks to the peasant forces that it will gain complete victory and our country will be successfully rebuilt.

Our peasants account for almost 90 percent of the population but they own only 30 per cent of the arable land; they have to work hard all the year round and suffer poverty all their lives.

The feudal landlord class accounts for less than 5 per cent of the population but they and the colonialists occupy about 70 per cent of the arable land and live in clover. This situation is most unjust. Because of it our country has been invaded and our people are backward and poor. During the years of resistance, the Government has decreed the reduction of land rent, the refunding of excess land rent and the temporary distribution of land belonging to the French and the Vietnamese

SOURCE: Ho Chi Minh, *Selected Writings*, pp. 163–168.

traitors and that of communal land to the peasants in the free areas. But the key problem remains unsolved: the peasant masses have no land or lack land. This affects the forces of the resistance and the production work of the peasants.

Only by carrying out land reform, giving land to the tillers, liberating the productive forces in the countryside from the yoke of the feudal landlord class can we do away with poverty and backwardness ad strongly mobilize the huge forces of the peasants in order to develop production and push the war of resistance forward to complete victory.

The goal set for land reform is to wipe out the feudal system of land owner-ship, distribute land to the tillers, liberate the productive forces in the countryside, develop production and push forward the war of resistance.

The general line and policy is to rely entirely on the landless and poor peas-ants, closely unite with the middle peasants, enter into alliance with the rich peasants, wipe out feudal exploitation step by step and with discrimination, de-velop production, and push forward the war of resistance.

To meet the requirements of the resistance and the National United Front, which consist in satisfying the land demands of the peasants while consolidating and developing the National United Front in the interests of the resistance and production, in the course of land reform we must apply different kinds of treatment to the landlords according to their individual political attitudes. This means that depending on individual cases we shall order confiscation or requisition with or without compensation, but not wholesale confiscation or wholesale requisition without compensation.

The *guiding principle for land reform* is boldly to mobilize the peasants, rely on the masses, correctly follow the mass line, organize, educate and lead the peasants to struggle according to plan, step by step, with good discipline and under close leadership.

The dispersion of land by landlords after the promulgation of the land rent reduction decree (July 14, 1949) is illegal (except for particular cases mentioned in the circular issued by the Prime Minister's Office on June 1, 1953).

The land confiscated or requisitioned with or without compensation is to be definitively allotted to the peasants who have no or not enough land. These peasants will have the right of ownership over the land thus distributed.

The *guiding principle for land distribution* is to take the village as unit, to allot land in priority to those who have been tilling it, to take into consideration the area, quality and location of the land, so as to give a fair share to everyone; especial consideration must be given to the peasants who have previously tilled the land to be distributed. As for the diehard elements bent on sabotaging land reform, the traitors, reactionaries, and local despots, those among them who are sentenced to 5 years' imprisonment and more will not receive any land.

*   *   *

In the *military field*, our peasant compatriots will joint the resistance even more enthusiastically, hence it will be easier to build up the army and recruit voluntary civilian manpower. Our soldiers, with their minds at peace about their families, will fight even more resolutely.

In the *political field*, political and economic power in the countryside will be in the hands of the peasants, the people's democratic dictatorship will be truly carried into effect, the worker-peasant alliance will be consolidated, the National United Front will include more than 90 per cent of the people in the countryside and will become prodigiously great and strong.

In the *economic field,* liberated from feudal landlordism, the peasants will enthusiastically carry out production and practise thrift, their purchasing power will increase, industry and commerce will develop and the national economy as a whole will expand.

Thanks to the development of production, the livelihood of the peasants, workers, soldiers and cadres will be improved more rapidly.

In the *cultural and social field,* the large majority of the people, now having enough food and clothing, will study even harder, in accordance with the saying: "One must have enough to eat before one could practise the good doctrine." Good customs and habits will develop. The experience drawn from localities where mass mobilization has been launched shows that our compatriots are very fond of study and that there are good opportunities for the intellectuals to serve the people.

As said above, land reform is an immense, complex and hard class struggle. It is all the more complex and all the harder because we are conducting a war of resistance. But it is precisely because we want to push the resistance forward to victory that we must be determined to make land reform a success.

84. EDITORIAL IN NHAN DAN ON HO CHI MINH'S REPLY TO EXPRESSEN, DECEMBER 6–10, 1953 [Extracts]

The day after Ho's interview with Expressen, *the Party Central Executive Committee issued a circular explaining the interview by saying that the "flag of peace" had to be in the DRV's hands, but warning against the "illusion that peace will come quickly or easily." Some days later* Nhan Dan *carried an editorial that followed closely the lines of the circular. It signalled the DRV's readiness to begin the process of peace negotiations while continuing the military struggle, asserting that Vietnam would be negotiating from a position of strength rather than weakness as claimed by the French.*

The Vietnamese traitors and puppets are worried and confused. They are bewildered and worried because of the Voice of Chairman Ho is the voice of justice, the strong and sincere voice of heroic people determined to protect their independence and freedom to live in peace. They follow each other in distorting the truth, trying to misrepresent the meaning of Chairman Ho's answers in order to deceive the Vietnamese people, the French people and the people of the world.

They fabricate the story that they want peace but we don't want peace. The truth is our people and government always advocate peace in order to construct a truly independent Viet-nam. This was true before now and will be true in the future. The truth is that French colonialists provoked atrocious war on our soil seven or eight years ago, and it is precisely for independence and peace that our army and

SOURCE: *The Vietnamese People's Sacred Resistance War,* Vol. IV, pp. 150–152.

people are determined to wage resistance war. If the French Government now sincerely respects our country's right to true independence and wishes to negotiate with us in order to end the war, we are prepared to talk. That is clear.

*   *   *

If the French colonialists blindly refuse to see that truth, are still stubborn and follow the orders of U.S. imperialism to continue their war of aggression in Viet-nam, the Vietnamese people, under the leadership of Chairman Ho and the Demo-cratic Republic of Viet-nam are determined to resist until complete victory. The patriotic war of the Vietnamese people has the sympathy of the French people and the people of the world, and though it must be long-term and hard, it will definitely win.

The Vietnamese people know from their own experience that independence and peace are a protracted, hard struggle.

The Vietnamese people resolutely refuse to have any illusion that peace is easy. The previous experience of the Korean people demonstrates that.

Independence, unification have not yet been completely achieved; the Viet-namese people are always vigilant, determined to resist, and ready to smash every military and political scheme of the enemy.

1954

85. REPORT BY GIAP TO SENIOR FIELD COMMANDERS ON THE DIENBIENPHU CAMPAIGN, JANUARY 14, 1954 [Extract]

In December 1953, the Political Bureau decided to launch the biggest cam-paign of the war to annihilate the French garrison at Dienbienphu. In his presenta-tion to the field commanders for the campaign in January, Giap surveyed Vietnam People's Army victories on other fronts and explained how they had forced Navarre to disperse his mobile forces—a major strategic objective of the resistance. Then he discussed the objective and significance of the Dienbienphu campaign.

Two main objectives:

1. To annihilate an important part of enemy forces.
2. To liberate the whole of the Northwest.

This campaign has a great significance:

SOURCE: "Contribution to the History of Dien Bien Phu," *Vietnamese Studies* (Hanoi), no. 3, March 1965, pp. 50–52.

a) It will be the greatest positional battle in the annals of our army. Hitherto, we have attacked fortified positions only with forces numbering up to one or two regiments; now we are throwing into action several divisions; we have never before co-ordinated infantry and artillery action on a large scale; we have succeeded only in capturing positions defended by one or two companies, one battalion at most. This time we shall have to coordinate the action of several branches of the army on a large scale and to annihilate an entrenched camp defended by 13 battalions.

Our victory will mark a big leap forward in the growth of our army, which will have an enormous influence on the future military situation.

b) By annihilating such an important part of enemy forces, by liberating such a wide area, we shall foil the Navarre plan, which is the French and American imperialists' plan for the extension of the war, and shall create conditions for destroying enemy forces on all fronts.

What does this mean, to foil the Navarre plan?

The enemy is seeking to concentrate mobile forces in the delta: we compel him to scatter them in mountain regions where they will be destroyed piecemeal.

He is seeking to increase the size of the puppet army and to bring reinforcements from France: we shall annihilate an important part of his forces to aggravate his manpower crisis beyond retrieve.

He is seeking to pacify the Northern plans and various theatres of operations in the South: our victory at Dien Bien Phu will make it possible for our forces to intensify their action on those various fronts thus creating conditions for the annihilation of important enemy forces and foiling his plans for pacification.

The enemy is seeking to wrest back the initiative; our victory will drive him further to the defensive and will consolidate our offensive situation.

c) From the political point of view, this battle will have a very great influence. On the internal plane, it will consolidate our rear, and *ensure the success of the land reform.* By winning a victory, the People's Army, which is fighting imperialism by force of arms, will make an effective and glorious complement to the mighty battle being waged in the rear by millions of peasants against feudalism.

This battle is taking place at a time when French imperialism is meeting with numerous difficulties in Vietnam, Laos and Cambodia, when the French people's struggle for an end to the war is increasing and when the struggle of the world's peoples for the defence of peace and an end to the war in Vietnam has reached unequalled designs and will be *an important contribution of our army to the defence of world peace.*

86. APPEAL BY GIAP TO ALL CADRES AND FIGHTERS, UNITS, AND SERVICES, ON BEGINNING THE DIENBIENPHU CAMPAIGN, MARCH 1954 [Extract]

After three months of preparation, during which the Party leadership suspended work on land reform in order to concentrate all human resources on

SOURCE: Giap, *Orders of the Day*, pp. 202–204.

material support for the campaign, Giap was ready to begin the attack on Dien-
bienphu. In a message to those who would be participating in the campaign, Giap
said it would deal a death blow to the Navarre plan and contribute to the pressure
on France to negotiate a peace settlement.

All cadres and fighters!

The Dienbienphu campaign is about to begin.

This is the largest scale positional campaign in the history of our Army up to the present.

During the past three months, from the time the enemy forces parachuted into Diebienphu, our army has surrounded and confined their main force in there, creating conditions for continuously defeating the enemy on all battlefields in the entire country.

Today Lai-chau was liberated, the Nam-hu River defense line of the invaders was broken, and there is no shadow of an invader in Phong Saly. Dienbienphu has become a collection of important points completely isolated, standing alone in the middle of our broad rear area.

Today, the time has come for our main forces to begin the attack on Dienbienphu.

If we are victorious at Dienbienphu, we will annihilate a very important part of the invaders' manpower, liberate the entire Northwest territory, widen and consolidate the broad rear area of our resistance war, and help to insure that the land reform achieves success.

If we are victorious at Dienbienphu, our heroic People's Army will take a stride forward, and our resistance war will achieve a very important victory.

If we are victorious at Dienbienphu, we will smash the Navarre plan, which has already been heavily defeated. The victorious Dienbienphu campaign will have a resounding influence both within and outside the country; it will be a worthy contribution to the world peace movement demanding an end to the war in Vietnam-Cambodia-Laos, especially at a time when the French Government is being defeated continuously and has begun to have to talk of negotiating in order to peacefully resolve the problem of the war in Indochina.

87. MEMORANDUM BY THE JOINT CHIEFS OF STAFF FOR SECRETARY OF DEFENSE CHARLES E. WILSON, MARCH 12, 1954

In mid-February 1954, the U.S., Britain, France and the Soviet Union agreed
that Indochina would be discussed at the Geneva Conference to open in late April.
Confronting directly for the first time the likelihood that any negotiated settle-
ment would involve a coalition government, partition, or elections, the Joint Chiefs
recommended that the United States disassociate itself from any settlement that would
not insure the "future political and territorial integrity of Indochina." For the
first time, they urged that the United States maintain "freedom of action" to
continue the war without the French.

SOURCE: *U.S.-Vietnam Relations*, Book 9, pp. 266–270.

1. This memorandum is in response to your memorandum dated 5 March 1954, subject as above.

2. In their consideration of this problem, the Joint Chiefs of Staff have reviewed UNITED STATES OBJECTIVES AND COURSES OF ACTION WITH RESPECT TO SOUTHEAST ASIA (NSC 5405), in the light of developments since that policy was approved on 16 January 1954, and they are of the opinion that, from the military point of view, the statement of policy set forth therein remains entirely valid. The Joint Chiefs of Staff reaffirm their views concerning the strategic importance of Indochina to the security interests of the United States and the Free World in general, as reflected in NSC 5405. They are firmly of the belief that the loss of Indochina to the Communists would constitute a political and military setback of the most serious consequences.

3. With respect to the possible course of action enumerated in paragraph 2 of your memorandum, the Joint Chiefs of Staff submit the following views:

a. Maintenance of the status quo. In the absence of a very substantial improvement in the French Union military situation, which could best be accomplished by the aggressive prosecution of military operations, it is highly improbable that Communist agreement could be obtained to a negotiated settlement which would be consistent with basic United States objectives in Southeast Asia. Therefore, continuation of the fighting with the objective of seeking a military victory appears as the only alternative to acceptance of a compromise settlement based upon one or more of the possible other courses of action upon which the views of the Joint Chiefs of Staff have been specifically requested in your memorandum.

b. Imposition of a cease-fire. The acceptance of a cease-fire in advance of a satisfactory settlement would, in all probability, lead to a political stalemate attended by a concurrent and irretrievable deterioration of the Franco-Vietnamese military position. (See paragraph 27 of NSC 5405).

c. Establishment of a coalition government. The acceptance of a settlement based upon the establishment of a coalition government in one or more of the Associated States would open the way for the ultimate seizure of control by the Communists under conditions which might preclude timely and effective external assistance in the prevention of such seizure. (See subparagraph 26 *b* of NSC 5405.)

d. Partition of the country. The acceptance of a partitioning of one or more of the Associated States would represent at least a partial victory for the Viet Minh, and would constitute recognition of a Communist territorial expansion achieved through force of arms. Any partition acceptable to the Communists would in all likelihood include the Tonkin Delta area which is acknowledged to be the keystone of the defense of mainland Southeast Asia, since in friendly hands it cuts off the most favorable routes for any massive southward advance towards central and southern Indochina and Thailand. (See paragraph 4 of NSC 5405.) A partitioning involving Vietnam and Laos in the vicinity of the 16th Parallel, as has been suggested (See State cable from London, No. 3802, dated 4 March 1954), would cede to Communist control approximately half of Indochina, its people and its resources, for exploitation in the interests of further Communist aggression; specifically, it would extend the Communist dominated area to the borders of Thailand, thereby enhancing the opportunities for Communist infiltration and eventual subversion of that country. Any cession of Indochinese territory to the Communists would constitute a retrogressive step in the Containment Policy, and would invite similar Communist tactics against other countries of Southeast Asia.

e. Self-determination through free elections. Such factors as the prevalence of illiteracy, the lack of suitable educational media, and the absence of adequate communications in the outlying areas would render the holding of a truly representative plebiscite of doubtful feasibility. The Communists, by virtue of their superior capability in the field of propaganda, could readily pervert the issue as being a choice between national independence and French Colonial rule. Furthermore, it would be militarily infeasible to prevent widespread intimidation of voters by Communist partisans. While it is obviously impossible to make a dependable forecast as to the outcome of a free election, current intelligence leads the Joint Chiefs of Staff to the belief that a settlement based upon free elections would be attended by almost certain loss of the Associated States to Communist control.

4. The Joint Chiefs of Staff are of the opinion that any negotiated settlement which would involve substantial concessions to the Communists on the part of the Governments of France and the Associated States, such as in *c* and *d* above, would be generally regarded by Asian peoples as a Communist victory, and would cast widespread doubt on the ability of anti-Communist forces ultimately to stem the tide of Communist control in the Far East. Any such settlement would, in all probability, lead to the loss of Indochina to the Communists and deal a damaging blow to the national will of other countries of the Far East to oppose Communism.

5. Should Indochina be lost to the Communists, and in the absence of immediate and effective counteraction on the part of the Western Powers which would of necessity be on a much greater scale than that which could be decisive in Indochina, the conquest of the remainder of Southeast Asia would inevitably follow. Thereafter, longer term results involving the gravest threats to fundamental United States security interests in the Far East and even to the stability and security of Europe could be expected to ensue. (See paragraph 1 of NSC 5405.)

6. Orientation of Japan toward the West is the keystone of United States policy in the Far East. In the judgment of the Joint Chiefs of Staff, the loss of Southeast Asia to Communism would, through economic and political pressures, drive Japan into an accommodation with the Communist Bloc. The communization of Japan would be the probable ultimate result.

7. The rice, tin, rubber, and oil of Southeast Asia and the industrial capacity of Japan are the essential elements which Red China needs to build a monolithic military structure far more formidable than that of Japan prior to World War II. If this complex of military power is permitted to develop to its full potential, it would ultimately control the entire Western and Southwestern Pacific region and would threaten South Asia and the Middle East.

8. Both the United States and France have invested heavily of their resources toward the winning of the struggle in Indochina. Since 1950 the United States has contributed in excess of 1.6 billion dollars in providing logistic support. France is reported to have expended, during the period 1946–1953, the equivalent of some 4.2 billion dollars. This investment, in addition to the heavy casualties sustained by the French and Vietnamese, will have been fruitless for the anti-Communist cause, and indeed may rebound in part to the immediate benefit of the enemy, if control of a portion of Indochina should now be ceded to the Communists. While the addi-

tional commitment of resources required to achieve decisive results in Indochina might be considerable, nevertheless this additional effort would be far less than that which would be required to stem the tide of Communist advance once it had gained momentum in its progress into Southeast Asia.

9. If, despite all United States efforts to the contrary, the French Government elects to accept a negotiated settlement which, in the opinion of the United States, would fail to provide reasonably adequate assurance of the future political and territorial integrity of Indochina, it is considered that the United States should decline to associate itself with such a settlement, thereby preserving freedom of action to pursue directly with the governments of the Associated States and with other allies (notably the United Kingdom) ways and means of continuing the struggle against the Viet Minh in Indochina without participation of the French. The advantages of so doing would, from the military point of view, outweigh the advantage of maintaining political unity of action with the French in regard to Indochina.

10. It is recommended that the foregoing views be conveyed to the Department of State for consideration in connection with the formulation of a United States position on the Indochina problem for the forthcoming Conference and for any conversation with the governments of the United Kingdom, France, and, if deemed advisable, with the governments of the Associated States preliminary to the conference. In this connection, attention is particularly requested to paragraphs 25 and 26 of NSC 5405; it is considered to be of the utmost importance that the French Government be urged not to abandon the aggressive prosecution of military operations until a satisfactory settlement has been achieved.

11. It is further recommended that, in order to be prepared for possible contingencies which might arise incident to the Geneva Conference, the National Security Council considers now the extent to which the United States would be willing to commit its resources in support of the Associated States in the effort to prevent the loss of Indochina to the Communists either:

    a. In concert with the French; or

    b. In the event the French elect to withdraw, in concert with other allies, or, if necessary, unilaterally.

12. In order to assure ample opportunity for the Joint Chiefs of Staff to present their views on these matters, it is requested that the Military Services be represented on the Department of Defense working team which, in coordination with the Department of State, will consider all U.S. position papers pertaining to the Geneva discussions on Indochina.

88. ADDRESS BY DULLES, NEW YORK CITY, MARCH 29, 1954 [Extract]

With the French garrison at Dienbienphu under siege and the possibility of a major Communist military victory looming, Admiral Arthur Radford, Chairman of the Joint Chiefs of Staff, unsuccessfully pressed French General Ely to accept a direct U.S. role in training Vietnamese troops. He expressed grave fears that the

SOURCE: Department of State *Bulletin*, April 12, 1954, pp. 539–540.

French would not be able to hold Indochina and suggested to Ely that the U.S. carry out bombing raids at Dienbienphu from bases in Manila.

Radford's suggestion for American air intervention at Dienbienphu was being seriously considered by the Eisenhower Administration during the last days of March. But it was clear that such an intervention would require congressional approval and therefore acceptance by the American public. Dulles used the occasion of a speech at the Overseas Press Club in New York to indicate that the situation might require U.S. military intervention, regardless of whether Chinese troops intervened in the conflict. The phrase he used, ''united action,'' suggested that the United States wanted other nations to join in action to save Indochina.

Southeast Asia is the so-called "rice bowl" which helps to feel the densely populated region that extends from India to Japan. It is rich in many raw materials, such as tin, oil, rubber, and iron ore. It offers industrial Japan potentially important markets and sources of raw materials.

The area has great strategic value. Southeast Asia is astride the most direct and best-developed sea and air routes between the Pacific and South Asia. It has major naval and air bases. Communist control of Southeast Asia would carry a grave threat to the Philippines, Australia, and New Zealand, with whom we have treaties of mutual assistance. The entire Western Pacific area, including the so-called "offshore island chain," would be strategically endangered.

President Eisenhower appraised the situation last Wednesday [March 24] when he said that the area is of "transcendent importance."

The United States has shown in many ways its sympathy for the gallant struggle being waged in Indochina by French forces and those of the Associated States. Congress has enabled us to provide material aid to the established governments and their peoples. Also, our diplomacy has sought to deter Communist China from open aggression in that area.

President Eisenhower, in his address of April 16, 1953, explained that a Korean armistice would be a fraud if it merely released aggressive armies for attack elsewhere. I said last September that if Red China sent its own army into Indochina, that would result in grave consequences which might not be confined to Indochina.

Recent statements have been designed to impress upon potential aggressors that aggression might lead to action at places and by means of free-world choosing, so that aggression would cost more than it could gain.

The Chinese Communists have, in fact, avoided the direct use of their own Red armies in open aggression against Indochina. They have, however, largely stepped up their support of the aggression in that area. Indeed, they promote that aggression by all means short of open invasion.

Under all circumstances it seems desirable to clarify further the Untied States position.

Under the conditions of today, the imposition on Southeast Asia of the political system of Communist Russia and its Chinese Communist ally, by whatever means, would be a grave threat to the whole free community. The United States feels that that possibility should not be passively accepted but should be met by united action. This might involve serious risks. But these risks are far less than those that will face us a few years from now if we dare not be resolute today.

The free nations want peace. However, peace is not had merely by wanting it.

Peace has to be worked for and planned for. Sometimes it is necessary to take risks to win peace just as it is necessary in war to take risks to win victory. The chances for peace are usually bettered by letting a potential aggressor know in advance where his aggression could lead him.

I hope that these statements which I make here tonight will serve the cause of peace.

89. TELEGRAM FROM DILLON TO DULLES, APRIL 4, 1954

French Premier Laniel and Foreign Minister Bidault, bolstered by Admiral Radford's support for U.S. bombing strikes around Dienbienphu, made an official request to Dillon for carrier aircraft support late in the evening of April 4. They argued that this U.S. effort could prevent the loss of Dienbienphu and presented new evidence of Chinese military personnel in Tonkin.

URGENT. I was called at 11 o'clock Sunday night and asked to come immediately to Matignon where a restricted Cabinet meeting was in progress.

On arrival Bidault received me in Laniel's office and was joined in a few minutes by Laniel. They said that immediate armed intervention of US carrier aircraft at Dien Bien Phu is now necessary to save the situation.

Navarre reports situation there now in state of precarious equilibrium and that both sides are doing best to reinforce—Viet Minh are bringing up last available reinforcements which will way outnumber any reinforcing French can do by parachute drops. Renewal of assault by reinforced Viet Minh probable by middle or end of week. Without help by then fate of Dien Bien Phu will probably be sealed.

Ely brought back report from Washington that Radford gave him his personal (repeat personal) assurance that if situation at Dien Bien Phu required US naval air support he would do his best to obtain such help from US Government. Because of this information from Radford as reported by Ely, French Government now asking for US carrier aircraft support at Dien Bien Phu. Navarre feels that a relatively minor US effort could turn the tide but naturally hopes for as much help as possible.

French report Chinese intervention in Indochina already fully established as follows:

First. Fourteen technical advisors at Giap headquarters plus numerous others at division level. All under command of Chinese Communist General Ly Chen-hou who is stationed at Giap headquarters.

Second. Special telephone lines installed maintained and operated by Chinese personnel.

Third. Forty 37 mm. anti-aircraft guns radar-controlled at Dien Bien Phu. These guns operated by Chinese and evidently are from Korea. These AA guns are now shooting through clouds to bring down French aircraft.

Fourth. One thousand supply trucks of which 500 have arrived since 1 March, all driven by Chinese army personnel.

SOURCE: *U.S.-Vietnam Relations*, Book 9, pp. 296–297.

Fifth. Substantial material help in guns, shells, etc., as is well known.

Bidault said that French Chief of Air Staff wishes US be informed that US air intervention at Dien Bien Phu could lead to Chinese Communist air attack on delta airfields. Nevertheless, government was making request for aid.

Bidault closed by saying that for good or evil the fate of Southeast Asia now rested on Dien Bien Phu. He said that Geneva would be won or lost depending on outcome at Dien Bien Phu. This was reason for French request for this very serious action on our part.

He then emphasized necessity for speed in view of renewed attack which is expected before end of week. He thanked US for prompt action on airlift for French paratroops. He then said that he had received Dulles' proposal for Southeast Asian coalition, and that he would answer as soon as possible later in week as restricted Cabinet session not competent to make this decision.

New Subject. I passed on Norstad's concern that news of airlift (DEPTEL 3470, April 3) might leak as planes assembled, Pleven was called into room. He expressed extreme concern as any leak would lead to earlier Viet Minh attack. He said at all costs operation must be camouflaged as training exercise until troops have arrived. He is preparing them as rapidly as possible and they will be ready to leave in a week. Bidault and Laniel pressed him to hurry up departure date of troops and he said he would do his utmost.

90. TELEGRAM FROM DULLES TO DILLON, APRIL 5, 1954

At a meeting at the White House on April 3, congressional leaders informed Dulles that they could not approve of U.S. air strikes at Dienbienphu unless there was a coalition of nations behind the intervention and unless the French accelerated process of granting independence to the Associated States and promised to continue the war with their own ground troops. The following day, Eisenhower, in a meeting with Dulles and Radford, decided that the United States would intervene only if those three conditions were met. Dulles instructed Dillon to inform the French of the decision.

As I personally explained to Ely in presence of Radford, it is not (rpt not) possible for US to commit belligerent acts in Indochina without full political understanding with France and the other countries. In addition, Congressional action would be required. After conference at highest level, I must confirm this position. US is doing everything possible as indicated my 5175 to prepare public, Congressional and Constitutional basis for united action in Indochina. However, such action is impossible except on coalition basis with active British Commonwealth participation. Meanwhile US prepared, as has been demonstrated, to do everything short of belligerency.

FYI US cannot and will not be put in position of alone salvaging British Commonwealth interests in Malaya, Australia and New Zealand. This matter now under discussion with UK at highest level.

SOURCE: *U.S.-Vietnam Relations,* Book 9, pp. 359.

91. NSC PLANNING BOARD REPORT ON NSC ACTION NO. 1074-A, APRIL 5, 1954 [Extract]

The first substantive discussion of U.S. military intervention in Indochina presented three possible scenarios: (1) intervention by the United States with French cooperation; (2) by the United States and a regional grouping with French cooperation; (3) without the French. The report conceded that, despite U.S. statements to the contrary, the French effort was viewed by many as "essentially colonial or imperialist in character" and said the United States should try to modify that view, if intervention in conjunction with the French was contemplated.

Problem

1. To analyze the extent to which, and the circumstances and conditions under which, the United States would be willing to commit its resources in support of the effort to prevent the loss of Indochina to the Communists, in concert with the French or in concert with others or, if necessary, unilaterally.

Issues Involved

2. The answer to this problem involves four issues:
   a. Will Indochina be lost to the Communists unless the United States commits combat resources in some form?
   b. What are the risks, requirements and consequences of alternative forms of U. S. military intervention?
   c. Should the United States adopt one of these forms of intervention rather than allow Indochina to be lost to the Communists and if so which alternative should it choose?
   d. When and under what circumstances should this decision be taken and carried into effect?

Prospect of Loss of Indochina

3. The first issue turns on whether the French Union can and will prevent the loss of Indochina and what further actions, if any, the United States can take to bolster or assist the French effort. Some of these questions were covered by the Report of the Special Committee of March 17, 1954. Others are matters of continuous intelligence estimates. At the present time there is clearly a possibility that a trend in the direction of the loss of Indochina to Communist control may become irreversible over the next year in the absence of greater U. S. participation. There is not, however, any certainty that the French have as yet reached the point of being willing to accept a settlement which is unacceptable to U.S. interests or to cease their military efforts. Moreover, regardless of the outcome of the fight at Dienbienphu, there is no indication that a military decision in Indochina is imminent. It is clear that the United States should undertake a maximum diplomatic effort to cause the French and Associated States to continue the fight to a successful conclusion.

SOURCE: *U.S.-Vietnam Relations*, Book 9, pp. 298–305.

Risks, Requirements, and Consequences of U.S. Intervention

4. The attached Annex addresses itself to the second issue: The risks, requirements and consequences of certain alternative forms of U.S. military intervention. In order to permit analysis of military requirements and allied and hostile reactions, this annex assumes that there will be either: (1) a French and Associated States invitation to the United States to participate militarily; or (2) an Associated States invitation to the United States after a French decision to withdraw, and French willingness to cooperate in phasing out French forces as U.S. forces are phased in. If neither of these assumptions proved valid the feasibility of U.S. intervention would be vitiated. If the French, having decided on withdrawal and a negotiated settlement, should oppose U.S. intervention and should carry the Associated States with them in such opposition, U.S. intervention in Indochina would in effect be precluded. If, after a French decision to withdraw, the Associated States should appeal for U.S. military assistance but the French decided not to cooperate in the phasing in of U.S. forces, a successful U.S. intervention would be very difficult.

Desirability and Form of U.S. Intervention

5. The third issue is whether the United States should intervene with combat forces rather than allow Indochina to be lost to the Communists, and which alternative it should select?

   a. U.S. commitment of combat forces would involve strain on the basic western coalition, increased risk of war with China and of general war, high costs in U.S. manpower and money, and possible adverse domestic political repercussions. Moreover, the United States would be undertaking a commitment which it would have to carry through to victory. In whatever form it might intervene, the U.S. would have to take steps at the outset to guard against the risks inherent in intervention. On the other hand, under the principles laid down in NSC 5405, it is essential to U.S. security that Indochina should not fall under Communist control.

   b. Of the alternative courses of action described in the Annex, Course A or B has these advantages over Course C. Neither Course A or B depends on the initial use of U.S. ground forces. For this reason alone, they obviously would be much more acceptable to the American public. For the same reason, they would initially create a less serious drain on existing U.S. military forces. But either Course A or B may turn out to be ineffective without the eventual commitment of U.S. ground forces.

   c. A political obstacle to Course A or Course B lies in the fact that the present French effort is considered by many in Southeast Asia and other parts of the world as essentially colonial or imperialist in character. If the United States joined its combat forces in the Indochina conflict, it would be most important to attempt to counteract or modify the present view of this struggle. This would also be essential in order to mobilize maximum support for the war within Indochina.

   d. An advantage of Course B over Course A lies in the association of the Asian States in the enterprise which would help to counteract the tendency to view Indochina as a colonial action. There would be advantages in Course B also in that U.S. opinion would be more favorable if the other free nations and the Asian nations were also taking part and bearing their fair share of the burden.

e. As between UN and regional support it appears that regional grouping would be preferable to UN action, on the ground that UN support would be far more difficult to get and less likely to remain solid until the desired objective was reached.

6. In order to make feasible any regional grouping, it will be essential for the United States to define more clearly its own objectives with respect to any such action. In particular, it would be important to make perfectly clear that this action is not intended as a first step of action to destroy or overthrow Communist China. If the other members of a potential regional grouping thought that we had such a broad objective, they would doubtless be hesitant to join in it. The Western powers would not want to increase the risks of general war which would, in their opinion, flow from any such broad purpose. The Asian countries would be equally reluctant to engage in any such broad activity. Both groups would doubtless want to make very clear that we object essentially to the expansionist tendencies of Communist China and that, if those ceased, we would not go further in attempting to carry on military activities in the Far East. Furthermore, to attract the participation of Asian States in a regional grouping, the United States would undoubtedly have to undertake lasting commitments for their defense.

Timing and Circumstances of Decision to Intervene with U.S. Combat Forces

7. The timing of the disclosure or implementation of any U.S. decision to intervene in Indochina would be of particular importance.

a. In the absence of serious military deterioration in Indochina, it is unlikely that France will agree to the arrangements envisaged in Alternatives A, B, or C in light of the hopes widely held in France and elsewhere that an acceptable settlement can be achieved.

b. On the other hand, inaction until after exhaustive discussions at Geneva, without any indication of U.S. intentions, would tend to increase the French government and people settling, or accepting the inevitability of settling, on unacceptable terms. Hints of possible U.S. participation would tend to fortify French firmness, but might also tend to induce the Communists to put forward more acceptable terms.

c. On balance, it appears that the United States should now reach a decision whether or not to intervene with combat forces, if that is necessary to save Indochina from Communist control, and, tentatively, the form and conditions of any such intervention. The timing for communication to the French of such decision, or for its implementation, should be decided in the light of future developments.

8. If the United States should now decide to intervene at some stage, the United States should now take these steps:

a. Obtain Congressional approval of intervention.

b. Initiate planning of the military and mobilization measures to enable intervention.

c. Make publicized U.S. military moves designed to make the necessary U.S. air and naval forces readily available for use on short notice.

d. Make maximum diplomatic efforts to make it clear, as rapidly as possible, that no acceptable settlement can be reached in the absence of far greater Communist concessions than are now envisaged.

e. Explore with major U.S. allies—notably the UK, Australia, and New Zealand, and with as many Asian nations as possible, such as Thailand and the Philippines, and possibly Nationalist China, the Republic of Korea, and Burma—the formation of a regional grouping.

f. Exert maximum diplomatic efforts with France and the Associated States designed to (1) bring about full agreement between them, if possible prior to Geneva, on the future status of the Associated States; (2) prepare them to invite U.S. and if possible group participation in Indochina, if necessary.

92. DRAFT REPORT BY THE PRESIDENT'S SPECIAL COMMITTEE; SOUTHEAST ASIA—PART II, APRIL 5, 1954 [Extract]

Reaffirming the position taken in previous policy papers that the United States should accept "nothing short of a military victory" in Indochina, the President's Special Committee urged "all possible political and economic pressure on France" to insure that the French continued the war.

IV. Conclusions

A. The Special Committee considers that these factors reinforce the necessity of assuring that Indo-China remain in the non-Communist bloc, and believes that defeat of the Viet Minh in Indo-China is essential if the spread of Communist influence in Southeast Asia is to be halted.

B. Regardless of the outcome of military operations in Indo-China and without compromising in any way the overwhelming strategic importance of the Associated States to the Western position in the area, the U.S. should take all affirmative and practical steps, with or without its European allies, to provide tangible evidence of Western strength and determination to defeat Communism; to demonstrate that ultimate victory will be won by the free world; and to secure the affirmative association of Southeast Asian states with these purposes.

C. That for these purposes the Western position in Indo-China must be maintained and improved by a military victory.

D. That without compromise to C, above, the U.S. should in all prudence reinforce the remainder of Southeast Asia, including the land areas of Malaya, Burma, Thailand, Indonesia, and the Philippines.

V. Recommended Courses of Action

A. The Special Committee wishes to reaffirm the following recommendations which are made in NSC 5405, the Special Committee Report concerning military operations in Indo-China, and the position paper of the Special Committee, con-

SOURCE: *U.S.-Vietnam Relations,* Book 9, pp. 346–358.

curred in by the Department of Defense, concerning U.S. courses of action and policies with respect to the Geneva Conference:

(1) It be U.S. policy to accept nothing short of a military victory in Indo-China.

(2) It be the U.S. position to obtain French support of this position; and that failing this, the U.S. actively oppose any negotiated settlement in Indo-China at Geneva.

(3) It be the U.S. position in event of failure of (2) above to initiate immediate steps with the governments of the Associated States aimed toward the continuation of the war in Indo-China, to include active U.S. participation and without French support should that be necessary.

(4) Regardless of whether or not the U.S. is successful in obtaining French support for the active U.S. participation called for in (3) above, every effort should be made to undertake this active participation in concern with other interested nations.

B. The Special Committee also considers that all possible political and economic pressure on France must be exerted as the obvious initial course of action to reinforce the French will to continue operations in Indo-China. The Special Committee recognizes that this course of action will jeopardize the existing French Cabinet, may be unpopular among the French public, and may be considered as endangering present U.S. policy with respect to EDC [European Defense Community]. The Committee nevertheless considers that the free world strategic position, not only in Southeast Asia but in Europe and the Middle East as well, is such as to require the most extraordinary efforts to prevent Communist domination of Southeast Asia. The Committee considers that firm and resolute action now in this regard may well be the key to a solution of the entire problem posed by France in the free world community of nations.

93. ARMY POSITION ON NSC ACTION NO. 1074-A, APRIL 1954

The U.S. Army, in an unsigned paper on the NSC Staff analysis of scenarios under which the United States might intervene militarily, pointed out several military facts omitted from the analysis: that air and naval forces alone would not assure victory, and that the equivalent of twelve American divisions would be required if the French were to withdraw and the Chinese intervened.

1. There are important military disadvantages to intervention in Indochina under the assumptions set forth in NSC Action No. 1074-a.

2. A military victory in Indochina cannot be assured by U.S. intervention with air and naval forces alone.

3. The use of atomic weapons in Indochina would not reduce the number of ground forces required to achieve a military victory in Indochina.

4. It is estimated that seven U.S. divisions or their equivalent, with appropriate naval and air support, would be required to win a victory in Indochina if the French withdraw and the Chinese Communists do not intervene. However, U.S.

SOURCE: *U.S.-Vietnam Relations*, Book 9, p. 332.

military intervention must take into consideration the capability of the Chinese Communists to intervene.

5. It is estimated that the equivalent of 12 U.S. divisions would be required to win a victory in Indochina if the French withdraw and the Chinese Communists intervene.

6. The equivalent of 7 U.S. divisions would be required to win a victory in Indochina if the French remain and the Chinese Communists intervene.

7. Requirements for air and naval support for ground force operations are:

    a. Five hundred fighter-bomber sorties per day exclusive of interdiction and counter-air operations.

    b. An airlift capability of a one division drop.

    c. A division amphibious lift.

8. One U.S. airborne regimental combat team can be placed in Indochina in 5 days, one additional division in 24 days, and the remaining divisions in the following 120 days. This could be accomplished partially by reducing U.S. ground strength in the Far East with the remaining units coming from the general reserve in the United States. Consequently, the U.S. ability to meet its NATO commitment would be seriously affected for a considerable period. The time required to place a total of 12 divisions in Indochina would depend upon the industrial and personnel mobilization measures taken by the government.

94. MEMORANDUM FROM WILSON TO THE SERVICE SECRETARIES AND THE JOINT CHIEFS OF STAFF, APRIL 15, 1954

At the National Security Council meeting of April 6, Eisenhower expressed the view that if a regional grouping could be organized congressional authorization for U.S. military intervention should be sought. In the meantime, it was agreed that contingency planning for intervention in Indochina should start.

1. At its meeting on 6 April 1954, the National Security Council agreed on the following, which has been subsequently approved by the President (NSC Action No. 1086-*a, b* and *c*):

    a. Noted and discussed the reference report and postponed decision on the recommendation in paragraph 7-*c* thereof, but agreed that military and mobilization planning to be prepared for this contingency should be promptly initiated.

    b. Agreed that the United States should direct its efforts prior to the Geneva Conference toward:

        (1) Organizing a regional grouping, including initially the U.S., the U.K., France and the Associated States, Australia, New Zealand, Thailand, and the Philippines, for the defense of Southeast Asia against Communist efforts by any means to gain control of the countries in this area.

        (2) Gaining British support for U.S. objectives in the Far East, in order to strengthen U.S. policies in the area.

        (3) Pressing the French to accelerate the program for the independence of the Associated States.

SOURCE: *U.S.-Vietnam Relations*, Book 9, pp. 382–383.

c. Noted the President's view that, if agreement for the organization of the above-mentioned regional grouping could be achieved, Congressional authorization for U.S. participation therein should then be requested.

2. The action set forth in paragraph 1-*a* above has been referred to the Secretary of Defense and the Director, Office of Defense Mobilization for appropriate implementation and was discussed at the Armed Forces Policy Council on 15 April 1954. The action in paragraph 1-*b* was referred to the Secretary of State.

3. It is requested that the Joint Chiefs of Staff promptly prepare the military plans involved under paragraph 1-*a* above. It is further requested that the Joint Chiefs of Staff, in close collaboration, under existing arrangements, with the Secretaries of the Military Departments and the Assistant Secretaries of Defense (Supply and Logistics), (Manpower and Personnel) and (Comptroller), promptly develop the supply, manpower and other requirements arising from these military plans which might affect production, manpower and budgetary planning by the Department of Defense and the Office of Defense Mobilization. This military planning and the development of requirements should cover not only specific intervention in Indochina, but also any augmentations in forces or supplies required to permit the United States to maintain at present levels its present defense commitments and to be prudently prepared to face possible increased risks of (1) Chinese Communist intervention and (2) general war.

4. It is further requested that the Joint Chiefs of Staff report to my office on the above by 10 May 1954. If it has not been possible to complete the planning by that date, a progress report on 10 May 1054 is requested.

5. The Assistant Secretaries of Defense (Supply and Logistics) and (Manpower and Personnel) will collaborate with the Office of Defense Mobilization, as appropriate, in the preparation of production and manpower plans based upon and required to implement the military plans.

6. Because of the security sensitivity of this planning, appropriate security precautions will be taken by all concerned.

95. MINUTES OF MEETING BETWEEN PRESIDENT EISENHOWER, DULLES, AND ROBERT CUTLER, SPECIAL ASSISTANT TO THE PRESIDENT, MAY 7, 1954

Informed of the position of the military members of the NSC Planning Board that the United States should not support the Bidault proposal for a cease-fire but should propose to France in "internationalization" of the war, in which the United States would become an equal partner in it, Eisenhower indicated he would want the conditions of such "internationalization" to include a regional coalition and an invitation from the indigenous governments of Indochina.

At a meeting in the President's office this morning with Dulles, three topics were discussed:

1. Whether the President should approve paragraph 1*b* of the tentative Record of Action of the 5/6/54 NSC Meeting, which covers the proposed answer to the

SOURCE: *U.S.-Vietnam Relations*, Book 9, pp. 436–438.

Eden proposal. The Secretary of State thought the text was correct. Wilson and Radford preferred the draft message to Smith for Eden prepared yesterday by MacArthur and Captain Anderson, and cleared by the JCA, which included in the Five Power Staff Agency Thailand and the Philippines. Radford thinks that the Agency (which has hitherto been not disclosed in SEA) has really completed its military planning; that if it is enlarged by top level personnel, its actions will be necessarily open to the world; that therefore some Southeast Asian countries should be included in it, and he fears Eden's proposal as an intended delaying action.

The President approved the text of paragraph 1*b*, but suggested that Smith's reply to Eden's proposal should make clear the following:

1. Five Power Staff Agency, alone or with other nations, is not to the United States a satisfactory substitute for a broad political coalition which will include the Southeast Asian countries which are to be defended.

2. Five Power Staff Agency examination is acceptable to see how these nations can give military aid to the Southeast Asian countries in their cooperative defense effort.

3. The United States will not agree to a "white man's party" to determine the problems of the Southeast Asian nations.

I was instructed to advise Wilson and Radford of the above, and have done so.

2. The President went over the draft of the speech which Dulles is going to make tonight, making quite a few suggestions and changes in text. He thought additionally the speech should include some easy to understand slogans, such as "The US will never start a war," "The US will not go to war without Congressional authority," "The US, as always, is trying to organize cooperative efforts to sustain the peace."

3. With reference to the cease-fire proposal transmitted by Bidault to the French Cabinet, I read the following, as views principally of military members of the Planning Board, expressed in their yesterday afternoon meeting:

1. US should not support the Bidault proposal.

2. Reasons for this position:

a. The mere proposal of the cease-fire at the Geneva Conference would destroy the will to fight of French forces and make fence-sitters jump to Vietminh side.

b. The Communists would evade covertly cease-fire controls.

3. The US should (as a last act to save IndoChina) propose to France that if the following 5 conditions are met, the US will go to Congress for authority to intervene with combat forces:

a. grant of genuine freedom for Associated States

b. US take major responsibility for training indigenous forces

c. US share responsibility for military planning

d. French forces to stay in the fight and no requirement of replacement by US forces.

(*e*. Action under UN auspices?)

This offer to be made known simultaneously to the other members of the proposed regional grouping (UK, Australia, NZ, Thailand, Associated States, Philippines) in order to enlist their participation.

I then summarized possible objections to making the above proposal to the French:

   a. No French Government is now competent to act in a lasting way.

   b. There is no indication France wants to "internationalize" the conflict.

   c. The US proposal would be made without the prior assurance of a regional grouping of SEA States, a precondition of Congress; although this point might be added as another condition to the proposal.

   d. US would be "bailing out colonial France" in the eyes of the world.

   e. US cannot undertake *alone* to save every situation of trouble.

I concluded that some PB members felt that it had never been made clear to the French that the US was willing to ask for Congressional authority, if certain fundamental preconditions were met; that these matters had only been hinted at, and that the record of history should be clear as to the US position. Dulles was interested to know the President's views, because he is talking with Ambassador Bonnet this afternoon. He indicated that he would mention these matters to Bonnet, perhaps making a more broad hint than heretofore. He would not circulate any formal paper to Bonnet, or to anyone else.

The President referred to the proposition advanced by Governor Stassen at the April 29 Council Meeting as not having been thoroughly thought out. He said that he had been trying to get France to "internationalize" matters for a long time, and they are not willing to do so. If it were though advisable at this time to point out to the French the essential preconditions to the US asking for Congressional authority to intervene, then it should also be made clear to the French as an additional precondition that the US would never intervene alone, that there must be an invitation by the indigenous people, and that there must be some kind of regional and collective action.

I understand that Dulles will decide the extent to which he cares to follow this line with Ambassador Bonnet. This disucssion may afford Dulles guidance in replying to Smith's request about a US alternative to support the Bidault proposal, but there really was no decision as to the US attitude toward the cease-fire proposal itself.

96. FRENCH PEACE PROPOSAL PRESENTED BY FOREIGN MINISTER GEORGES BIDAULT TO THE GENEVA CONFERENCE, MAY 8, 1954

The French proposal for peace in Indochina, as presented by Foreign Minister Bidault, called for concentration of all forces in certain areas, with international supervision, and provided for no political settlement in conjunction with a cease-fire.

I. Viet Nam

1. All regular units to be assembled in assembly areas to be defined by the Conference on the basis of proposals by the Commanders-in-Chief.

SOURCE: Great Britain, Parliament, Papers by Command, *Documents Relating to the Discussion of Korea and Indo-China at the Geneva Conference, April 27-June 1954* (London: Her Majesty's Stationery Office, Cmd. 9186, 1954), pp. 107–111.

2. All elements not belonging either to the army or to the policy forces to be disarmed.

3. All prisoners of war and civil internees to be released immediately.

4. Execution of the above provisions to be supervised by international commissions.

5. Hostilities to cease as soon as the agreement is signed.

The assembly of troops and disarmament of forces as above provided to begin no later than *x* days (the number to be fixed by the Conference) after the signature of the agreement.

II. Cambodia and Laos

1. All regular and irregular Vietminh forces which have entered the country to be evacuated.

2. All elements which do not belong either to the army or to the police forces to be disarmed.

3. All prisoners of war and civil internees to be released immediately.

4. Execution of the above provisions to be supervised by international commissions.

III. These agreements shall be guaranteed by the States participating in the Geneva Conference. In the event of any violation thereof there shall be an immediate consultation between the guarantor States for the purpose of taking appropriate measures either individually or collectively.

97. PEACE PROPOSAL BY DRV PRESENTED BY DELEGATION CHIEF PHAM VAM DONG TO THE GENEVA CONFERENCE, MAY 10, 1954 [Extract]

The DRV delegation proposed a cease-fire, the immediate regroupment of French forces (referred to as "dislocation" in the translation) in Vietnam, withdrawal of all foreign forces from all three countries within an agreed period, and free elections in all three countries to be supervised by local commissions. The reference to "all foreign troops" in the proposal was meant to include Vietnamese troops serving in Laos and Cambodia. The Vietnamese proposal also specified that reprisal against those engaged on either side during the war would be prohibited— something the French proposal had not mentioned.

Restoration of Peace in Indo-China

1. Recognition by France of the sovereignty and independence of Viet-Nam over the entire territory of the country, and recognition of the sovereignty and independence of Khmer and Pathet Lao.

2. Agreement to withdraw all foreign troops from Viet-Nam, Khmer and Pathet Lao within time limits to be agreed upon by the belligerents. Pending

SOURCE: *New Times* (Moscow), May 15, 1954, Supplement, pp. 7–13.

withdrawal of the foreign forces, agreement shall be reached as to the dislocation of French forces in Viet-Nam, particular attention being paid to limiting the number of dislocation areas to a minimum. It shall be provided that the French forces may not interfere in the affairs of the local administration in the areas of their dislocation.

3. The holding of free general elections in Viet-Nam, Khmer and Pathet Lao. The convening of consultative conferences of representatives of the governments of the two sides in Viet-Nam, Khmer and Pathet Lao respectively, for the purpose of preparing and conducting, with guarantees of freedom of activity for patriotic parties, groups and public organizations, the free general elections with a view to establishing a single government in each country. All outside interference shall be precluded. Local commissions shall be set up to supervise the preparation and conduct of the elections.

Pending the establishment of a single government in each of the aforementioned countries, the governments of the two sides shall respectively administer the areas which are under their control after the settlement prescribed by the armistice agreement.

4. Declaration by the delegation of the Democratic Republic of Viet-Nam that the government of the D.R.V. is prepared to examine the question of entering the French Union on a voluntary basis, and the conditions of such entry. Similar declarations to be made by the governments of Khmer and Pathet Lao.

5. Recognition by the Democratic Republic of Viet-Nam, and by Khmer and Pathet Lao, that France has cultural and economic interests in these countries.

Following the formation of single governments in Viet-Nam, Khmer and Pathet Lao, the economic and cultural relations of these countries with France shall be subject to settlement in accordance with the principle of equality and respect for reciprocal interests. Pending the formation of single governments in the three countries, Indo-China's economic and cultural relations with France shall temporarily remain as at present. However, in areas where communication and commercial relations have been disrupted, they may be re-established by mutual agreement.

The citizens of each side shall enjoy privileged status, to be determined later, in respect of domicile, movement and business activity in the territory of the other side.

6. Each side undertakes not to persecute persons who collaborated with the other side during the war.

7. Mutual exchange of war prisoners.

8. Implementation of the measures enumerated in points 1-7 shall be preceded by a cease-fire in Indo-China in accordance with agreements concluded between France and each of the three countries, which shall contain the following provisions.

a) A complete and simultaneous cease-fire throughout the territory of Indo-China by all the armed forces of the belligerents—land, naval and air. With a view to consolidating the armistice, the two sides shall, in each of the three Indo-Chinese countries, delimit the areas under their control, and shall not hinder the passage of troops of the other side through their territory in the course of this delimitation.

b) No new land, naval or air units or personnel, or weapons and ammunition of any description, shall be dispatched to Indo-China.

c) Supervision of the armistice agreement and the appointment for this purpose of mixed commissions of representatives of the two side in each of the three countries.

98. MEMORANDUM BY CHAIRMAN OF THE JOINT CHIEFS OF STAFF ADMIRAL ARTHUR RADFORD FOR WILSON, MAY 20, 1954

Radford gave Wilson the position of the Joint Chiefs of Staff on issues to be negotiated with France in regard to U.S. participation in the fighting. He indicated that the Joint Chiefs assumed the use of atomic weapons "whenever it is to our military advantage" and would urge bombing of supply lines in China.

1. In recent discussions between the French and the Department of State relating to U.S. military intervention in Indo-china, the U.S. Government specified certain conditions which would have to obtain if U.S. military intervention were to be undertaken. Among these conditions were:

   a. That France would undertake not to withdraw its forces from Indo-china during period of united action so that forces from U.S. principally air and sea and others would be supplementary and not in substitution;

   b. That agreement would have to be reached on training of native troops and on command structure for united action.

2. On the assumption that United States armed forces intervene in the conflict in Indochina, the Joint Chiefs of Staff have agreed that a Department of Defense position should be formulated as to the size and composition of U.S. force contributions to be made and the command structure to be established. In formulating these views the Joint Chiefs of Staff have been guided by several factors, among which are:

   a. The limited availability of U.S. forces for military action in Indochina.

   b. The current numerical advantage of the French Union forces over the enemy, i.e., approximately 5 to 3.

   c. The undesirability of basing large numbers of U.S. forces in Indochina.

   d. The primary need of an expanded and intensified training program as being the current greatest need.

   e. The lack of required facilities for superimposing U.S. Air Force forces on existing facilities in Indochina.

   f. The implications of a reaction by the Chinese Communists in the event of U.S. participation.

   g. Atomic weapons will be used whenever it is to our military advantage.

3. The Joint Chiefs of Staff consider that the basic principle underlying any command structure for operations in Indochina which is acceptable to the United States must enable the U.S. to influence future strategy in Indochina. In addition, they believe that some new means to furnish the military guidance which heretofore has come from Paris must be found. A possible solution for over-all strategic guidance is a Military Representatives Committee with membership from those nations contributing the principal forces of the coalition with a steering or standing

SOURCE: *U.S.-Vietnam Relations*, Book 9, pp. 477–479.

group along the lines of NATO. This group would be served by a staff organized along the lines of the U.S. Joint Staff composed primarily of U.S. and French officers.

4. Although the Allied Commander in Chief in Indochina should be French, there must be a U.S. Deputy with sufficient staff assistance to provide liaison with the French and coordinate U.S. activities with the over-all operations. CINCPAC would exercise command over all U.S. forces based in Indochina and other forces assigned to him for operations in Indochina. In addition, a U.S. Air Advisor would be provided the French Commander in Chief for the purpose of advising him concerning the air effort.

5. The Joint Chiefs of Staff believe that the best military course for eventual victory in Indochina is the development of effective native armed forces. Thus far the French have been unsuccessful in their efforts to develop such forces. A firm commitment by the French and firm requests from the respective government of the Associated States for the training and development of native forces by the United States should be a prerequisite of U.S. participation. It is estimated that an augmentation of MAAG Indochina on the order of 2250, with an appropriate logistic support force, would be required to initiate this program. The size of this force and security arrangements therefore will be determined in light of recommendations requested from CINCPAC and Chief, MAAG Indochina.

6. The Joint Chiefs of Staff recommend that U.S. participation be limited primarily to Naval and Air Forces. The composition of these forces should be on the order of the following:

   a. Naval Forces. A fast carrier Task Force and supporting forces as necessary in accordance with developments in the situation.

   b. Air Forces. U.S. Air Force units operating from present bases outside Indochina as may be required. The order of magnitude of this effort cannot now be estimated since it will depend on developments in the situation.

7. The Joint Chiefs of Staff note that the principal sources of Viet Minh military supply lie outside Indochina. The destruction or neutralization of those outside sources supporting the Viet Minh would materially reduce the French military problems in Indochina.

8. The Joint Chiefs of Staff believe that committing to the Indochina conflict Naval forces in excess of the above or basing substantial air forces therein will involve maldeployment of forces and reduced readiness to meet probable Chinese Communist reaction elsewhere in the Far East. From the point of view of the United States, with reference to the Far East as a whole, Indochina is devoid of decisive military objectives and the allocation of more than token U.S. armed forces to that area would be a serious diversion of limited U.S. capabilities.

99. TREATY OF INDEPENDENCE OF THE STATE OF VIETNAM, JUNE 4, 1954

The treaty by which France was to have given Vietnam its final and complete independence was signed by the premiers of the two states in the midst of the

SOURCE: France, *Direction de la Documentation, Articles et Documents, No. 067* (June 15, 1954), *"Textes du Jour,"* p. 1 [Translation by Gail Theisen.]

Geneva Conference. Under the treaty of independence Vietnam was responsible for international obligations undertaken by France on its behalf. However, the agreement was only initialed and not signed, nor was it ever ratified by either government. As a result, France remained legally responsible for the implementation of the agreement, despite the fact that the State of Vietnam was treated as a fully independent state.

Article I:

France recognizes Vietnam as a fully independent and sovereign state and invested of all powers recognized by international law.

Article II:

Vietnam is substituted for France in all laws and obligations resulting from international treaties of conventions contracted by France on behalf of or in the name of the State of Vietnam or all other treaties or conventions concluded by France in the name of French Indochina to the measure in which these acts concerned Vietnam.

Article III:

France pledges to transfer to the Vietnamese government the powers and public services still guaranteed by [France] on Vietnamese territory.

Article IV:

The present treaty, which will enter into force on the date of its signing, abrogates (all) previous acts and provisions contrary to it. The instruments of ratification of the present treaty will be exchanged as of its approval by qualified representatives of France and Vietnam.

100. TELEGRAM FROM DULLES TO DILLON, JUNE 14, 1954

Dulles confirmed that the deterioration in Indochina was such as to make US military intervention unlikely and blamed it on French and British indecision.

It is true that there is less disposition now than two months or one month ago to intervene in Indochina militarily. This is the inevitable result of the steady deterioration in Indochina which makes the problem of intervention and pacification more and more difficult. When united defense was first broached, the strength and morale of French and Vietnam forces were such that it seemed that the situation could be held without any great pouring-in of U.S. ground forces. Now all the evidence is that the morale of the Vietnamese Government, armed forces and civilians has deteriorated gravely; the French are forced to contemplate a fall-back which would leave virtually the entire Tonkin Delta population in hostile hands and the Saigon area is faced with political disintegration.

SOURCE: *U.S.-Vietnam Relations*, Book 9, pp. 559–560.

What has happened has been what was forecast as for example by my Embassy Paris 4117 TEDUL 78 of May 17. I there pointed out that probably the French did not really want intervention but wanted to have the possibility as a card to play at Geneva. I pointed out that the Geneva game would doubtless be a long game and that it could not be assumed that at the end the present U.S. position regarding intervention would necessarily exist after the Communists had succeeded in dragging out Geneva by winning military successes in Indochina. This telegram of mine will bear rereading. That point of view has been frequently repeated in subsequent cables.

I deeply regret any sense of bitterness on Bidault's part, but I do not see that he is justified in considering unreasonable the adaptation of U.S. views to events and the consequences of prolonged French and U.K. indecision.

I do not yet wholly exclude possibility U.S. intervention on terms outlined PARIS 402 TEDUL 54. UK it seems is now more disposed to see movement in this direction but apparently the French are less than ever disposed to internationalizing the war.

101. TELEGRAM FROM UNDERSECRETARY OF STATE WALTER BEDELL SMITH, HEAD OF THE U.S. DELEGATION IN GENEVA, TO DULLES, JUNE 17, 1954

In conversation with Eden, Chou En-lai indicated that regroupment areas would have to be established in Laos, but not in Cambodia, and that the Vietnamese would withdraw their volunteers from the two countries as part of a general withdrawal of foreign forces. Chou's proposal was ultimately accepted as the basis for the settlement in both countries.

Dennis Allen (UK) gave Johnson this morning additional details on conversation with Chou En-lai. Chou stated that in *case Cambodia resistance forces were small and all that was necessary was a political settlement by the present royal government with them "which could easily be obtained." In case of Laos, resistance forces were larger, and it would be necessary recognize this fact by formation of regrouping areas along the border with Vietnam and China.* The task of both States was twofold: The removal of foreign forces and dealing with the problem of domestic resistance movements. The military staff should get down to this task.

In reply to Eden's query as to whether it would not (repeat not) be difficult obtain Viet Minh admission Viet Minh forces were in Laos and Cambodia, Chou stated it would "not (repeat not) be difficult" to get Viet Minh to agree to withdrawal all foreign forces. Chou made no (repeat no) direct reply to Eden's reference to French-Laotian treaty on French bases in Laos. Eden expressed personal view that *Chou wants settlement, but has some doubt with regard to degree of control he exercises over Viet Minh.*

SOURCE: *U.S.-Vietnam Relations,* Book 9, pp. 574–575.

In long talk with *Bidault* this morning (first direct contact with Chinese and French) Chou substantially repeated what he told Eden yesterday (in conversation with Bidault, Chou referred to Viet Minh forces in Cambodia and Laos as "volunteers"). Bidault had also seen Molotov this morning and reported that both Molotov and Chou are obviously greatly concerned over any break-up Indochina conference in pattern of Korean conference as well as of lowering level conference below level of Foreign Ministers. Bidault said they clearly want to keep the conference going. *Bidault and I agree (Eden did not (repeat not) comment) that it was very important we do nothing dispel Chou's worries over US bases in Laos and Cambodia.*

I also expressed personal opinion that important Laos and Cambodia move ahead as quickly as and as vigorously as possible with appeal to UN. Eden and Bidault agreed, Eden adding that important Vietnam not (repeat not) get mixed up with Laos and Cambodia cases UN.

Chauvel showed me handwritten note from Ely, in his political capacity, urging against attempting hold any enclave in delta and recommending straight partition formula. I could not (repeat not) resist expressing contempt for such an easy "selling-out" of last remaining foothold in north and said we could under no (repeat no) circumstances publicly associate ourselves with such a solution.

102. TELEGRAM FROM SMITH TO DULLES, JUNE 18, 1954

The U.S. delegation informed the French at Geneva that the surrender of all enclaves in the North would force the United States to disassociate itself publicly from the settlement, but pledged support to the French effort to get the best settlement possible. The French defended the partition solution as more enforceable then the "leopard spot" alternative.

Johnson saw Chauvel this morning and discussed with him conference situation in light TEDUL 211. Johnson stated seemed to us that such fundamental questions as composition, voting procedures and authority or international control commission would be dealt with in conference rather than by committee. If conference reached decision on fundamental principles, working out of details could be done by committee of experts of principally interested parties in same pattern as present Franco-Viet Minh military conversations.

Chauvel said this would be agreeable except that question of authority, which he termed "relationship between international commission and joint committees" could be dealt with by technical committee, thus implying France not (repeat not) prepared to maintain principle of subordination joint committees to international commission. As French have already circulated proposal contained SECTO 460 through secretariat, it was agreed we would make suggestion along foregoing lines at today's restricted meeting. Chauvel said they did not (repeat not) yet have any further indication as to what attitude Chinese would take on French proposal entirely clear from conversation with Chauvel that his main interest is in keeping

SOURCE: *U.S.-Vietnam Relations*, Book 9, pp. 578–579.

some conference activity of nine going and that if regardless of level representation we prepared continue some conference meetings would probably meet French point of view. Appears French proposal made on assumption that there would be complete recess of conference with departure of Smith and Eden.

Chauvel made reference to his conversation with Smith yesterday (DULTE 193—last paragraph), making inquiry as to exactly what we had in mind. Johnson in reply read to him paragraphs 5, 6 and 7 basic instructions (TOSEC 138) stating that French willingness surrender even minimum enclave in north of Haiphong would so clearly contravene the principles which the US considered essential as to require our public dissociation with such a solution. In reply to Chauvel's questions, Johnson made it clear we were speaking only of public disassociation from such a settlement. The US had in the past and of course would continue working with and supporting France in every possible way and wherever we could. Chauvel indicated full understanding our position. He said they had come to conclusion that what he termed any "leopard spot" solution was entirely impracticable and unenforceable. From standpoint of future it would be much better to retain a reasonably defensible line in Vietnam behind which there would be no (repeat no) enclaves of Viet Minh and do all possible behind that line to build up effective Vietnamese Government and defense. They had no (repeat no) intention of "any immediate surrender of Haiphong" which in any event must remain under their control for a considerable period for purely military reasons to effect evacuation of French Union Forces from the north. However, if, as appeared likely, choice was giving Viet Minh an enclave in south in exchange for French enclave in Haiphong, they thought it preferable to give up Haiphong. He said no (repeat no) French parliament would approve conditions which the US had laid down for its intervention, and French had no (repeat no) choice but made the best deal they could, obtaining as strong position as possible in south. Chauvel understood fully we would probably not (repeat not) be able to publicly associate ourselves with such a solution, but he hoped that when it came time to put it to the Vietnamese the US would consider it possible very discreetly to let the Vietnamese know that we considered it best that could be obtained under the circumstances and our public disassociation would not (repeat not) operate so as to encourage Vietnamese opposition. Johnson replied he did not (repeat not) see how it would be possible for us to do this, and in any event he would of course have to see what the solution was. Chauvel said that such a solution as partition should come as no (repeat no) surprise to the Vietnamese as Buu Loc had sometime ago indicated to Dejean. There had been conversations between Vietnamese and Viet Minh in which Viet Minh had made it clear that only two alternatives were coalition government or partition. Chauvel said Ngo Dinh and Diem are very unrealistic, unreasonable, and would probably prove to be "difficulte".

Chauvel said the line French had in mind had been made available to US defense representatives at some five-power talks, but was vague about time and place. He referred to it as "line of the chalk cliffs", which he said was defensible position running from the sea across Vietnam and Laos to the Mekong. Understand this is a line roughly 19 parallel running from vicinity of Dong Haoi to Thakhek. Replying to query, Chauvel said French Union Forces removed from the north would be deployed along that line.

Chauvel said all indications were Mendès-France would succeed in forming government next day or two and would probably himself assume Foreign Minister post. Said he had been in touch with Mendès-France and had sent emissary to Paris this morning to brief him on situation in Geneva. Chauvel said was anxious to show complete continuity of French effort here in Geneva and hoped there could be another restricted meeting tomorrow. Chauvel said, "Underground military talks" last night had been completely unproductive, Viet Minh obviously taking strong line in view of French Government situation.

103. REPORT BY HO CHI MINH TO THE SIXTH PLENUM OF THE PARTY CENTRAL COMMITTEE, JULY 15, 1954

Even before the agreement was reached at Geneva, the Vietnam Workers' Party changed its strategic line from concentrating on resisting the French to win final victory to compromise with the French in order to ward off U.S. direct intervention in the war. Ho's report indicated that the Party leadership was counting heavily on contradictions between the French and the Americans to bring about reunification of the country through elections.

The Vietnamese, Cambodian and Lao peoples are united and their resistance grows ever more vigorous. Our guerilla forces in South, Central and North Viet Nam, not only have stood firm but have grown ever stronger. From the Border Campaign to the Hoa Binh, Tay Bac and other campaigns, our regular forces have recorded repeated successes. These victories plus the major one at Dien Bien Phu have brought about an important change in the situation. The fiasco of the Navarre plan has led to the collapse of the Laniel-Bidault cabinet and the shrinking of French-occupied zones.

We owe our successes to the correct policy of our Party and Government, the heroism of our armed forces and people, and the support of the fraternal countries and the world's people. Our successes also belong to the world movement for peace and democracy.

Besides military successes, initial ones have also been scored on the antifeudal front. The former have had a good effect on the mobilization of the masses to implement our land policy and the latter, on our struggle against imperialism. Our successes inspire our people and the peoples of the world and reinforce our diplomatic position at Geneva; they have compelled our enemy to enter into talks with us. Compared with what Bollaert put forward in 1947, France's attitude at present has noticeably changed. Thus, since the start of the resistance, our posture has grown stronger and the enemy's weaker. But we should bear in mind that this should be understood in a relative, not absolute, sense. We must guard against subjectiveness and not underrate our enemy. Our successes have awakened the American imperialists. After the Dien Bien Phu campaign, the latter's intentions and plan for intervention have also undergone changes aimed at protracting and internationalizing the Indochina war, sabotaging the Geneva Conference, and oust-

SOURCE: Ho Chi Minh, *Selected Writings*, pp. 172–173.

ing the French by every means, in order to occupy Viet Nam, Cambodia and Laos, enslave the peoples of these countries and create further tension in the world.

Therefore, the *US imperialists* not only are the enemy of the world's people but are becoming the *main and direct enemy of the Vietnamese, Cambodian and Lao peoples*.

These changes in the world and domestic situation have led to the Geneva Conference. This Conference has further exacerbated the contradictions between the imperialist countries, with France willing to negotiate, Britain wavering, and the United States bent on sabotaging the talks. The Americans have grown ever more isolated.

* * *

The new situation has set new tasks, new guidelines and new tactics. Over nearly nine years of resistance, under the leadership of our Party and Government, our people and army have overcome difficulties, fought heroically, and won glorious victories. Our forces have made headway in all respects. Thanks to the correct policy of our Party and Government, we have recorded good achievements.

At present the situation has changed; so have our tasks and consequently so should our policy and slogans. Up to now we have concentrated our efforts on wiping out the forces of the French imperialist aggressors. But now the French are having talks with us while the American imperialists are becoming our main and direct enemy; so our spearhead must be directed at the latter. Until peace is restored, we shall keep fighting the French; but the brunt of our attack and that of the world's peoples should be focused on the United States. US policy is to expand and internationalize the Indochina war. Ours is to struggle for peace and oppose the US war policy. For some nine years now, our Party has made clear its programme: Complete independence for Viet Nam, Cambodia and Laos, which must be freed from the French yoke; to refuse to recognize the French Union, drive out all French troops from Indochina, destroy the puppet administrations and armed forces, confiscate all properties of the imperialists and the traitors, launch a drive for the reduction of land rents and interest rates as a step towards agrarian reform, bring democracy to the whole nation, and carry our war of resistance through to final victory. This programme has won many successes. It is a correct one.

However, in the new situation we cannot maintain the old programme. Our previous motto was "Resistance to the end". At present, we must put forward a new one: "Peace, Unity, Independence, Democracy". We must take firm hold of the banner of peace to oppose the US imperialists' policy of direct interference in, and prolongation and expansion of, the war in Indochina. Our policy must change in consequence: formerly we confiscated the French imperialists' properties; now, as negotiations are going on, we may, in accordance with the principle of equality and mutual benefit, allow French economic and cultural interests to be preserved in Indochina. Negotiations entail reasonable mutual concessions. Formerly we said we would drive out and wipe out all French aggressive forces; now, in the talks held, we have demanded and the French have accepted, that a date be set for the withdrawal of their troops. In the past, our aim was to wipe out the puppet administration and army with a view to national reunification; now we practise a policy of leniency and seek reunification of the country through nationwide elections.

Peace calls for an end to the war; and to end the war one must agree on a cease-fire. A cease-fire requires regrouping zones, that is, enemy troops should be regrouped in a zone with a view to their gradual withdrawal, and ours in another. We must secure a vast area where we would have ample means for building, consolidating and developing our forces so as to exert influence over other regions and thereby advance towards reunification. The setting up of regrouping zones does not mean partition of the country; it is a temporary measure leading to reunification. Owing to the delimitation and exchange of zones, some previously free areas will be temporarily occupied by the enemy; their inhabitants will be dissatisfied; some people might fall prey to discouragement and to enemy deception. We should make it clear to our compatriots that the trials they are going to endure for the sake of the interests of the whole country, for the sake of our long-range interests, will be a cause for glory and will earn them the gratitude of the whole nation. We should keep everyone free from pessimism and negativism and urge all to continue a vigorous struggle for the complete withdrawal of French forces and for independence.

To set up regrouping zones as a step towards peace, to hold nationwide elections to achieve national reunification, such is our policy. The aims of our war of resistance and independence, unity, democracy and peace. The very restoration of peace is aimed at serving the cause of reunification, independence and democracy. The new situation requires a new policy for securing new successes.

At any juncture, peace or war, we must firmly hold the initiative, show foresight and be in full readiness.

To secure peace is not an easy task; it is a long, hard and complex struggle; with advantageous conditions but also with difficulties. The advantageous conditions: the friendly countries support us, so do the world's people; our people are full of spirit and confidence in our Party and Government, under whose wise leadership they will certainly unite and struggle in peace as in war. The difficulties: the United States is trying its hardest to sabotage the restoration of peace in Indochina, the partisans of peace in France have not completely freed themselves from American influence.

104. TELEGRAM FROM SMITH TO DULLES, JULY 17, 1954

Mendès-France, Eden, and Molotov were unable to make any progress on the key issues of setting a date for Vietnamese elections and the demarcation line for the zones of administration in Vietnam. Mendès-France finally suggested that the two issues would be linked, with each side making a concession on one of them. Although there was no immediate response, it was apparently on this basis that the DRV was induced to make a further concession on the partition line in return for setting a specific date for the elections.

Following account of Mendès-France-Eden-Molotov meeting last night is based on report of this meeting to Foreign Office made available to Johnson by Caccia.

SOURCE: *U.S.-Vietnam Relations*, Book 9, pp. 648–650.

This telegram expands upon and supersedes preliminary account transmitted in first three paragraphs SECTO 630 (repeated information Paris 76, Saigon 48).

At Eden's suggestion, French enumerated documents before conference:

(A) Armistice agreements to be signed by local commanders-in-chief. French have prepared drafts for Vietnam and Laos and Cambodians draft for Cambodia. Viet Minh delegation preparing counter draft for Vietnam.

(B) Control arrangements. French have circulated papers for Vietnam, Laos, and Cambodia.

(C) Political arrangements. After having seen military documents, certain delegations might make unilateral statements. For example, Laos and Cambodia are preparing statements on their willingness to limit their armed forces. Conference as whole would then agree upon common statement taking note of military agreements and unilateral declarations. French have circulated draft of such statement. Soviets have prepared counter draft and French second redraft.

French explained that if conference did not (repeat not) have time to agree on all details of armistice, it might approve only parts providing for cessation of hostilities and first stage of regroupment. Remaining aspects of agreements could be covered by statement of general principles for guidance of experts who would work out details after conference had dispersed.

It was agreed that British, French, and Soviet experts would meet July 17 to consider various drafts.

At Eden's suggestion, Mendès-France summarized main outstanding problems as (A) demarcation line for Vietnam; (B) elections; and (C) control arrangements. Concerning demarcation line, he said French had proposed line near 18th parallel whereas Viet Minh proposed 16th parallel. On elections in Vietnam, he said question was whether to fix firm date now (repeat now) (Soviets had proposed June 1955) or whether, as French proposed, to settle now (repeat now) only manner in which date would be set. Elections in Laos and Cambodia already provided for in constitutions for August and September 1955, respectively. On control, he said main questions were: Whether there should be one commission or three, composition, voting, execution of commissions' recommendations, and freedom of movement for inspection teams.

Molotov added to outstanding issues: (D) time required for regrouping (French have proposed 380 days and Soviets 6 months); and (E) prevention of importation of new arms and military personnel subject to certain exceptions for Laos and Cambodia, prohibition of foreign military bases, and prohibition of military alliances by three states.

Eden added (F) question of regroupment areas for resistance forces in Laos.

Discussion then turned to substantive issues:

(A) *Elections in Vietnam*. Molotov said conference should fix date for elections. He conceded more flexible formula might be found than firm date of June 1955 previously proposed by Soviets and suggested agreement merely that elections be held during 1955 with precise date to be fixed by Vietnamese and Viet Minh authorities.

Mendès-France argued that it would be prudent to fix date as early as the end of 1955. He suggested two ways of providing necessary flexibility in arrangements: Date for elections might be fixed after completion of regrouping; or exact date might be fixed now (repeat now) and international control commission be given authority to advance date if necessary.

Eden supported Mendès-France on need for flexibility and suggested that two parts of Vietnam fix date after completion of regrouping. Mendès-France agreed to consider this suggestion, but Molotov continued to urge elections during 1955.

(B) *Demarcation line.* Molotov argued that in moving from 13th to 16th parallel, Viet Minh had made substantial concession which called for proper response from French. Mendès-France disagreed, arguing that Viet Minh would be giving up much less in Annam than they would be getting in Tonkin. He said that Pham Van Dong had admitted that line on 16th parallel would require special arrangements for Tourane, Bue, on route No. 9 leading into Laos. Mendès-France stated that necessity for such special arrangements showed how unnatural demarcation line at 16th parallel would be. He said that there was no (repeat no) chance of persuading French Government to accept line which excluded either Hue or route No. 9. Eden supported Mendès-France.

Molotov suggested that discussion move to question of control arrangements. Mendès-France replied might be better to postpone such discussion. He observed that questions of elections and demarcation line had been discussed together and might be linked in sense that conceivably one party might yield on one question and another party on other.

105. FINAL DECLARATION OF THE GENEVA CONFERENCE ON THE PROBLEM OF RESTORING PEACE IN INDOCHINA, JULY 1954

1.—The Conference takes note of the Agreements ending hostilities in Cambodia, Laos, and Viet-Nam and organizing international control and the supervision of the execution of the provisions of these agreements.

2.—The Conference expresses satisfaction at the ending of hostilities in Cambodia, Laos and Viet-Nam; the Conference expresses its conviction that the execution of the provisions set out in the present Declaration and in the Agreements on the cessation of hostilities will permit Cambodia, Laos and Viet-Nam henceforth to play their part, in full independence and sovereignty, in the peaceful community of nations.

3.—The Conference takes note of the declarations made by the Governments of Cambodia and of Laos of their intention to adopt measures permitting all citizens to take their place in the national community, in particular by participating in the next general elections, which, in conformity with the constitution of each of these countries, shall take place in the course of the year 1955, by secret ballot and in conditions of respect for fundamental freedoms.

4.—The Conference takes note of the clauses in the Agreement on the cessation of hostilities in Viet-Nam prohibiting the introduction into Viet-Nam of foreign troops and military personnel as well as all kinds of arms and munitions. The

SOURCE: Democratic Republic of Viet-nam Ministry of Foreign Affairs, Press and Information Department, *Documents Related to the Implementation of the Geneva Agreements Concerning Viet-nam* (Hanoi: 1956), pp. 181–183. Hereafter cited as *Documents Related to the Implementation of the Geneva Agreements.*

Conference also takes note of the declarations made by the Governments of Cambodia and Laos of their resolution not to request foreign aid, whether in war material, in personnel or in instructors except for the purpose of the effective defence of their territory and, in the case of Laos, to the extent defined by the Agreements on the cessation of hostilities in Laos.

5.—The Conference takes note of the clauses in the Agreement on the cessation of hostilities in Viet-nam to the effect that no military base under the control of a foreign State may be established in the regrouping zones of the two parties, the latter having the obligation to see that the zones allotted to them shall not constitute part of any military alliance and shall not be utilized for the resumption of hostilities or in the service of an aggressive policy. The Conference also takes note of the declarations of the Governments of Cambodia and Laos to the effect that they will not join in any agreement with other States if this agreement includes the obligation to participate in a military alliance not in conformity with the principles of the Charter of the United Nations or, in the case of Laos, with the principles of the Agreement on the cessation of hostilities in Laos or, so long as their security is not threatened, the obligation to establish bases on Cambodian or Laotian territory for the military forces of foreign powers.

6.—The Conference recognizes that the essential purpose of the Agreement relating to Viet-nam is to settle military questions with a view to ending hostilities and that the military demarcation line is provisional and should not in any way be interpreted as constituting a political or territorial boundary. The Conference expresses its conviction that the execution of the provisions set out in the present Declaration and in the Agreement on the cessation of hostilities creates the necessary basis for the achievement in the near future of a political settlement in Viet-nam.

7.—The Conference declares that, so far as Viet-nam is concerned, the settlement of political problems, effected on the basis of respect for principles of independence, unity and territorial integrity, shall permit the Vietnamese people to enjoy the fundamental freedoms, guaranteed by democratic institutions established as a result of free general elections by secret ballot. In order to ensure that sufficient progress in the restoration of peace has been made and that all the necessary conditions obtain for free expression of the national will, general elections shall be held in July 1956, under the supervision of an international commission composed of representatives of the Member States of the International Supervisory Commission, referred to in the Agreement on the cessation of hostilities. Consultations will be held on this subject between the competent representative authorities of the two zones from 20 July, 1955 onwards.

8.—The provisions of the Agreements on the cessation of hostilities intended to ensure the protection of individuals and of property must be most strictly applied and must, in particular, allow everyone in Viet-nam to decide freely in which zone he wishes to live.

9.—The competent representative authorities of the Northern and Southern zones of Viet-nam, as well as the authorities of Laos and Cambodia, must not permit any individual or collective reprisals against persons who have collaborated in any way with one of the parties during the war, or against members of such persons' families.

10.—The Conference takes note of the declaration of the Government of the French Republic to the effect that it is ready to withdraw its troops from the territory of Cambodia, Laos and Viet-nam, at the request of the governments concerned and within periods which shall be fixed by agreement between the parties except in the cases where, by agreement between the two parties, a certain number of French troops shall remain at specified points and for a specified time.

11.—The Conference takes note of the declaration of the French Government to the effect that for the settlement of all the problems connected with the re-establishment and consolidation of peace in Cambodia, Laos and Vietnam, the French Government will proceed from the principle of respect for the independence and sovereignty, unity and territorial integrity of Cambodia, Laos and Viet-nam.

12.—In their relations with Cambodia, Laos and Viet-nam, each member of the Geneva Conference undertakes to respect the sovereignty, the independence, the unity and the territorial integrity of the above-mentioned States, and to refrain from any interference in their internal affairs.

13.—The members of the Conference agree to consult one another on any question which may be referred to them by the International Supervisory Commission, in order to study such measures as may prove necessary to ensure that the Agreements on the cessation of hostilities in Cambodia, Laos and Viet-nam are respected.

106. DECLARATION BY SMITH TO THE GENEVA CONFERENCE, JULY 21, 1954

The official U.S. response to the political provisions of the final declaration was to express explicit reservations on the provision for elections by July 1956. Smith said that only United Nations supervision of elections would be acceptable to the United States.

The Government of the United States being resolved to devote its efforts to the strengthening of peace in accordance with the principles and purposes of the United Nations.

Takes note of the Agreements concluded at Geneva on July 20 and 21, 1954 between the *(a)* Franco-Laotian Command and the Command of the People's Army of Viet-Nam; *(b)* The Royal Khmer Army Command and the Command of the People's Army of Viet-Nam; *(c)* Franco-Viet-Namese Command and the Command of the People's Army of Viet-Nam, and of paragraphs 1 to 12 inclusive of the Declaration presented to the Geneva Conference on July 21, 1954.

Declares with regard to the aforesaid Agreements and paragraphs (i) it will refrain from the threat or the use of force to disturb them, in accordance with Article 2 (4) of the Charter of the United Nations dealing with the obligation of Members to refrain in their international relations from the threat or use of force; and (ii) it would view any renewal of the aggression in violation of the aforesaid agreements with grave concern and as seriously threatening international peace and security.

In connection with this statement in the Declaration concerning free elections

SOURCE: *Documents relating to British involvement in the Indochina Conflict*, p. 86

in Viet-Nam, my Government wishes to make clear its position which it has expressed in a Declaration made in Washington June 19, 1954, as follows: "In the case of nations now divided against their will, we shall continue to seek to achieve unity through free elections, supervised by the United Nations to ensure that they are conducted fairly."

With respect to the statement made by the Representative of the State of Viet-Nam, the United States reiterates its traditional position that peoples are entitled to determine their own future and that it will not join in any arrangement which would hinder this. Nothing in its declaration just made is intended to or does indicate any departure from this traditional position.

We share the hope that the agreement will permit Cambodia, Laos and Viet-Nam to play their part in full independence and sovereignty, in the peaceful community of nations, and will enable the peoples of that area to determine their own future.

107. NATIONAL INTELLIGENCE ESTIMATE 63-5-54 ON THE POST-GENEVA OUTLOOK IN INDOCHINA, AUGUST 3, 1954 [Extract]

The intelligence community predicted in its first assessment after the Geneva Agreements that the DRV would probably increase its attractiveness to the Vietnamese population and would "almost certainly win" the scheduled elections if it did not "prejudice its political prospects." The intelligence estimate also noted the difficulty the new government of Premier Ngo Dinh Diem would have in dealing with Viet Minh cadres in the South, because of armistice provisions guaranteeing them against reprisals.

23. *Outlook in South Vietnam.* We believe that the Viet Minh will seek to retain sizeable military and political assets in South Vietnam. Although the agreements provide for the removal to the north of all Viet Minh forces, many of the regular and irregular Viet Minh soldiers now in the south are natives of the area, and large numbers of them will probably cache their arms and remain in South Vietnam. In addition, Viet Minh administrative cadres have been in firm control of several large areas in central and south Vietnam for several years. These cadres will probably remain in place. French and Vietnamese efforts to deal with "stay-behind" military and administrative units and personnel will be greatly hampered by armistice provisions guaranteeing the security of pre-armistice dissidents from reprisals.

24. The severe problem of establishing and maintaining security in South Vietnam will probably be increased by certain provisions of the Geneva agreements which prohibit the import of arms and military equipment, except as replacements, and the introduction of additional foreign military personnel, the establishment of new military bases, and military alliances. These provisions limit the development of a Vietnamese national army to such numbers as may be equipped by stocks evacuated from Tonkin, plus stocks now held in Saigon. However, in the last

SOURCE: *U.S.-Vietnam Relations*, Book 10, pp. 692–698. [Extract]

analysis, Vietnamese security will be determined by the degree of French protection and assistance in the development of a national army, the energy with which the Vietnamese themselves attack the problem, and by the will of the non-Communist powers to provide South Vietnam with effective guarantees.

25. In addition to the activities of stay-behind military and administrative groups, the Viet Minh will make a major effort to discredit any South Vietnam administration, and to exacerbate French-Vietnamese relations, and appeal to the feeling for national unification which will almost certainly continue strong among the South Vietnamese population. The Communist goal will be to cause the collapse of any non-Communist efforts to stabilize the situation in South Vietnam, and thus to leave North Vietnam the only visible foundation on which to re-establish Vietnamese unity. French and anti-Communist Vietnamese efforts to counter the Viet Minh unit appeal and Communist subversive activities will be complicated at the outset by the strong resentment of Vietnamese nationalists over the partitioning of Vietnam and the abandoning of Tonkin to Communist control. It may be difficult to convince many Vietnamese troops, political leaders, and administrative personnel in Tonkin to go south, let alone to assist actively in the development of an effective administration in South Vietnam.

26. Developments in South Vietnam will also depend in large part on French courses of action. Prospects for stability in South Vietnam would be considerably enhanced if the French acted swiftly to insure Vietnam full independence and to encourage strong nationalist leadership. If this were done, anti-French nationalist activity might be lessened. With French military and economic assistance—backed by US aid—the Vietnamese could proceed to develop gradually an effective security force, local government organization, and a long-range program for economic and social reform. Nevertheless, it will be very difficult for the French to furnish the degree of assistance which will be required without at the same time reviving anti-French feeling to the point of endangering the whole effort.

27. On the basis of the evidence we have at this early date, however, we believe that a favorable development of the situation in South Vietnam is unlikely. Unless Mendès-Frances is able to overcome the force of French traditional interests and emotions which have in the past governed the implementation of policy in Indochina, we do not believe there will be the dramatic transformation in French policy necessary to win the active loyalty and support of the local population for a South Vietnam Government. At the present time, it appears more likely that the situation will deteriorate in South Vietnam and that the withdrawal from Tonkin will involve recriminations, distrust, and possibly violence. There will be delays in the development of effective administration in the south; the French military will probably be forced to retain a large measure of control for reasons of "security"; and efforts by French colonial interests to develop a puppet Cochin-China state will persist. It is even possible that at some point during the next two years the South Vietnam Government could be taken over by elements that would seek unification with the Viet Minh in the North even at the expense of Communist domination. Even if "If the scheduled national elections are held in July 1956, and if the Viet Minh does not prejudice its political prospects, the Viet Minh will almost certainly win."

28. In the interim, Viet Minh propaganda will find ample opportunities to influence Vietnamese attitudes. Within a year, Viet Minh stay-behind units will

probably be active politically, and possibly involved in open guerrilla fighting. In these circumstances, the French will probably be able to maintain their "presence" in South Vietnam through mid-1956, but this influence will probably become increasingly restricted to major cities and the perimeters of military installations and bases. The French might be willing to resolve this situation by an arrangement with the Communists which seemed to offer a chance of saving some remnant of the French economic and cultural position in Vietnam. Such an arrangement might include an agreement to hold early elections, even with the virtual certainty of Viet Minh victory. Only if such an arrangement proved impossible, and the situation deteriorated to the point of hopelessness, would the French withdraw completely from the country.

108. NSC 5492/2, "REVIEW OF U.S. POLICY IN THE FAR EAST," AUGUST 20, 1954 [Extracts]

The NSC viewed the results of the Geneva settlement as a loss in prestige for the United States and as giving the Communists an "advance salient" for pressures against non-Communist states in Southeast Asia. The first post-Geneva statement of policy called for negotiating a Southeast Asia collective security treaty and urged "covert operations on a large and effective scale" to maintain non-Communist governments in Indochina and make Communist control of North Vietnam more difficult.

Preface

Consequences of the Geneva Conference

Communist successes in Indochina, culminating in the agreement reached at the Geneva Conference, have produced the following significant consequences which jeopardize the security interests of the U.S. in the Far East and increase Communist strength there:

a. Regardless of the fate of South Vietnam, Laos and Cambodia, the Communists have secured possession of an advance salient in Vietnam from which military and non-military pressures can be mounted against adjacent and more remote non-Communist areas.

b. The loss of prestige in Asia suffered by the U.S. as a backer of the French and the Bao Dai Government will raise further doubts in Asia concerning U.S. leadership and the ability of the U.S. to check the further expansion of Communism in Asia. Furthermore, U.S. prestige will inescapably be associated with subsequent developments in Southeast Asia.

c. By adopting an appearance of moderation at Geneva and taking credit for the cessation of hostilities in Indochina, the Communists will be in a better position

SOURCE: *U.S.-Vietnam Relations*, Book 10, pp. 731–733, 736–737.

to exploit their political strategy of imputing to the United States motives of extremism, belligerency, and opposition to coexistence seeking thereby to alienate the U.S. from its allies. The Communists thus have a basis for sharply accentuating their "peace propaganda" and "peace program" in Asia in an attempt to allay fears of Communist expansionist policy and to establish closer relations with the nations of free Asia.

d. The Communists have increased their military and political prestige in Asia and their capacity for expanding Communist influence by exploiting political and economic weakness and instability in the countries of free Asia without resort to armed attack.

e. The loss of Southeast Asia would imperil retention of Japan as a key element in the off-shore island chain.

Courses of Action

I. Communist China

1. Reduce the power of Communist China in Asia even at the risk of, but without deliberately provoking, war:

a. (1) React with force, if necessary and advantageous, to expansion and subversion recognizable as such, supported and supplied by Communist China.

(2) React with immediate, positive, armed force against any belligerent move by Communist China.

b. Increase efforts to develop the political economic and military strength of non-Communist Asian countries, including the progressive development of the military strength of Japan to the point where she can provide for her own national defense, and, in time, contribute to the collective defense of the Far East.

c. Maintain political and economic pressures against Communist China, including the existing embargo and support for Chinese Nationalist harassing actions.

d. Support for the Chinese National Government on Formosa as the Government of China and the representative of China in all UN agencies.

e. Create internal division in the Chinese Communist regime and impair Sino-Soviet relations by all feasible overt and covert means.

* * *

IV. Southeast Asia

7. *General.* The U.S. must protect its position and restore its prestige in the Far East by a new initiative in Southeast Asia, where the situation must be stabilized as soon as possible to prevent further losses to Communism through (1) creeping expansion and subversion, or (2) overt aggression.

8. *Security Treaty.* Negotiate a Southeast Asia security treaty with the UK, Australia, New Zealand, France, the Philippines, Thailand and, as appropriate, other free South and Southeast Asian countries willing to participate, which would:

a. Commit each member to treat an armed attack on the agreed area (including Laos, Cambodia and South Vietnam) as dangerous to its own peace, safety and vital interests, and to act promptly to meet the common danger in accordance with its own constitutional processes.

b. Provide so far as possible a legal basis to the President to order attack on Communist China in the event it commits such armed aggression which endangers the peace, safety and vital interests of the United States.

c. Ensure that, in such event, other nations would be obligated in accordance with the treaty to support such U.S. action.

d. Not limit U.S. freedom to use nuclear weapons, or involve a U.S. commitment for local defense or for stationing U.S. forces in Southeast Asia.

The U.S. would continue to provide a limited military assistance and training missions, wherever possible, to the states of Southeast Asia in order to bolster their will to fight, to stabilize legal governments, and to assist them in controlling subversion.

9. *Action in the Event of Local Subversion*. If requested by a legitimate local government which requires assistance to defeat local Communist subversion or rebellion not constituting armed attack, the U.S. should view such a situation so gravely that, in addition to giving all possible covert and overt support within Executive Branch authority, the President should at once consider requesting Congressional authority to take appropriate action, which might if necessary and feasible include the use of U.S. military forces either locally or against the external source of such subversion or rebellion (including) Communist China if determined to be the source).

10. *Indochina: Political and Covert Action*.

a. Make every possible effort, not openly inconsistent with the U.S. position as to the armistice, to maintain and support friendly non-Communist governments in Cambodia and Laos, to maintain a friendly non-Communist South Vietnam, and to prevent a Communist victory through all-Vietnam elections.

b. Urge that the French promptly recognize and deal with Cambodia, Laos and free Vietnam as independent sovereign nations.

c. Strengthen U.S. representation and deal directly, wherever advantageous to the U.S., with the governments of Cambodia, Laos, and free Vietnam.

d. Working through the French only insofar as necessary, assist Cambodia, Laos and free Vietnam to maintain (1) military forces necessary for internal security and (2) economic conditions conducive to the maintenance and strength of non-Communist regimes and comparing favorably with those in adjacent Communist areas.

e. Aid emigration from North Vietnam and resettlement of peoples unwilling to remain under Communist rule.

f. Exploit available means to prevent North Vietnam from becoming permanently incorporated in the Soviet block, using as feasible and desirable consular relations and non-strategic trade.

h. Conduct covert operations on a large and effective scale in support of the foregoing policies.

1955

109. DECLARATION OF THE DRV ON NORMAL RELATIONS BETWEEN NORTHERN AND SOUTHERN ZONES, FEBRUARY 4, 1955

At a time when it was increasingly clear that Diem would not enter into discussions with the DRV on elections, Hanoi made a major political-diplomatic move aimed at exploiting nationalist sentiments in the South: it announced its willingness to enter into economic, cultural, and social exchanges between the two zones. It presented such North-South relations as creating the basis for the "political settlement" provided in the Geneva Conference's Final Declaration. The Diem government did not respond to the initiative.

Following the appeal made by President Ho-Chi-Minh on New Year's Day, the Council of Ministers of the Democratic Republic of Viet-nam has, in its session early in February 1955, considered the question of restoring normal relations between North and South Viet-nam on either side of the provisional military demarcation line. The Council holds that:

1—Viet-nam is a unified country from the North to the South. The political, economic, cultural, social and sentimental relations and the solidarity of the Vietnamese people are indivisible. During the eight to nine years of the patriotic war, the Vietnamese people from the North to the South have heroically fought to restore peace and struggled together to build up the Fatherland. That is why, after the implementation of the armistice and pending the general elections to bring about the reunification of the country, the re-establishment of normal relations between the Northern and Southern zones fully conforms to the earnest aspiration of the various strata of the population in the two zones and is indispensable for the restoration of a normal and prosperous life of the Vietnamese people throughout the country;

2—The restoration of normal relations between the two zones is in complete conformity with the spirit of the Geneva Armistice Agreement.

The first sentence of the Agreement on the cessation of hostilities in Vietnam stipulates that the demarcation line, on either side of which the forces of the two parties shall be regrouped after their withdrawal, is only provisional.

The Final Declaration of the Geneva Conference clearly mentioned that: "The military demarcation line should not in any way be interpreted as constituting a political or territorial boundary".

The restoration of relations between the two zones does not infringe upon the administrative control of each side. On the contrary, it will provide the authorities of both sides with good opportunity for mutual understanding, thereby creating

SOURCE: *Documents Related to the Implementation of the Geneva Agreements,* pp. 33–35.

"the necessary basis for the achievement of a political settlement in Viet-nam," as stipulated in the Final Declaration of the Geneva Conference.

Due to the above-mentioned reasons the Government of the Democratic Republic of Viet-nam declares that:

1—Responding to the earnest desire of the Vietnamese people and in conformity with the spirit of the Geneva Armistice Agreement, the Government of the Democratic Republic of Viet-nam is disposed to grant all facilities to the people in the Northern and Southern zones on either side of the provisional military demarcation line in sending mail, moving, carrying out business or enterprises from one zone to the other, and in exchanging cultural, artistic, scientific, technical, sporting and other activities. The Government of the Democratic Republic of Viet-nam fully encourages and helps the population in the two zones in all economic, cultural and social exchanges advantageous for the restoration of normal life of the people,

2—The Government of the Democratic Republic of Viet-nam hopes that the authorities in South Viet-nam will agree to the restoration of normal relations between the Northern and Southern zones with a view to bringing about solutions favourable for the entire people.

110. TELEGRAM FROM DULLES TO THE EMBASSY IN SAIGON, APRIL 6, 1955 [Extract]

In the only document which reveals his private thinking on the subject of the Geneva elections in Vietnam after the accords, Dulles instructed the Embassy that the general U.S. approach would be to insist on agreement on "safeguards" for free elections as a precondition to discussion of any other issues connected with the elections. He indicated that the "safeguards" to be demanded would be such that the Communists would be expected to reject them. The Saigon Embassy was instructed to sound out Diem to see if he would go along with the approach.

FYI. We have been working on problem of elections in Viet-Nam, in great detail over last several weeks. NSC has asked Department submit policy for consideration by mid-April and we sure that elections will be discussed during proposed U.S-French talks Washington April 20. The British have offered give use their views on elections prior these talks.

We feel best solution is for us be in position inform French British our views prior talks and believe it best we can put such forward as support of policy of Free Viet-Nam rather than as unilateral U.S. recommendations.

Our proposal is based on Eden's plan put forward at Berlin-Conference for all German elections and has already been approved by France for use Germany and rejected by the Communists. The basic principle is that Free Viet-Nam will insist to the Viet Minh that unless agreement is first reached by the latter's acceptance of the safeguards spelled out, that no repeat no further discussions are possible regarding the type of elections, the issues to be voted on or any other factors.

SOURCE: *U.S.-Vietnam Relations*, Book 10, pp. 892–893.

After we have Diem's general acceptance we can proceed inform UK and France of this plan which we think only formula which ensures both satisfactory response to Geneva Agreement and at same time plan which is unassailable in intent but probably unacceptable to Communists because of provisions for strict compliance to ensure genuinely free elections. END FYI.

You should speak to Diem privately regarding elections, without showing him formula outlined next telegram. We are not now attempting secure his approval as such to our position but to assure he understands our viewpoint and accepts it to degree we can proceed with French British on broad assumption Free Viet-Nam's position similar our own.

Believe best way accomplish this is to remind him of his foreign ministers conversations with Secretary on this subject and to continue that in specific cases of elections in Korea and Germany Free World has stood firm on issue of guarantees of genuine free elections, supervised by body having authority guarantee elements free elections PAREN outlined last paragraph following telegram UNPAREN. In each case Communists have refused accept these safeguards which we think basic and fundamental. We believe unless such guarantees previously agreed upon would be dangerous for Free Viet-Nam be drawn into further discussions of other issues of election. Ask Diem of we can assume our thinking is alike on this point.

Since time exceedingly important, hope we can have affirmative answer soonest.

111. TELEGRAM FROM DULLES TO SPECIAL REPRESENTATIVE GENERAL J. LAWTON COLLINS IN SAIGON, APRIL 9, 1955

After five months in Saigon as President Eisenhower's personal representative, Gen. J. Lawton Collins had come to the conclusion that Ngo Dinh Diem lacked executive and leadership ability. As Diem began attacking the private army of the Binh Xuyen, which had controlled both organized crime and the national police under Bao Dai, Collins recommended that the U.S. replace Diem with one of two other figures popular with the Americans in Saigon, as desired by the French. Dulles responded that he and Eisenhower were inclined to continue supporting Diem, explaining that they saw no better alternative and that replacing him would mean that U.S. influence in South Vietnam would be weakened in relation to that of the French.

Have this morning discussed situation with highest authority. We are disposed to back whatever your final decision is but before you actually finalize we want to be sure you have weighed all of the factors which concern us here.

We feel that what has happened does not reveal anything new about Diem but rather a basic and dangerous misunderstanding as between France and the U.S.

We have always known the qualities which Diem possesses and those which

SOURCE: *U.S.-Vietnam Relations*, Book 10, pp. 907–909.

he lacks. Nevertheless our two countries agreed to support him in default of anyone possessing better qualifications. The only alternatives now suggested are the same persons who were regarded as unacceptable substitutes some months ago.

What has happened is that whereas the United States has been proceeding on the assumption that Diem would be backed as against any who might challenge him assuming that he had the capability, apparently the French have given their support only on the assumption that the Binh Xuyen would also be supported on an autonomous authority and that when they challenged Diem he would not be allowed to use force to assert his authority over it.

We can appreciate the reluctance of the French to see force used but if it cannot be used then what is the point of our supporting at great cost the national army which I thought it had been agreed was primarily to be an army for domestic security rather than an army to fight external aggression.

U.S. recognizes the Cao Dai and even the Hoa Hao are genuine sects with cultural religious and political roots which cannot be forcibly torn up without grave consequences which should be avoided but we do not believe that any central government can exist as more than a figurehead if it does not have control over the national police and if this control is farmed out to a gang which exploits its privileges to protect vice on a vastly profitable scale and which exists by virtue of the backing of the self-exiled Bao Dai and the French.

We cannot see that replacement of Diem by any persons you mentioned will of itself correct this situation and indeed we have had the impression that Quat was less acceptable to the sects than is Diem.

There are two other factors to be borne in mind.

One is that it is widely known that Diem has so far existed by reason of U.S. support despite French reluctance. If, however, when the showdown comes the French view prevails then that will gravely weaken our influence for the future both in Vietnam and elsewhere. Removal of Diem under these circumstances may well be interpreted in Vietnam and Asia as example of U.S. paying lip service to nationalist cause and then forsaking true nationalist leader when QUOTE colonial interests UNQUOTE put enough pressure on us. The French constantly assert that the U.S. has a primary responsibility in this part of the world but it is difficult to have responsibility without authority. In essence, will not the ouster of Diem on the present conditions mean that from now on we will be merely paying the bill and the French will be calling the tune. Any successor of Diem will clearly know where the real authority lies.

The second factor is that there will be very strong opposition in the Congress to supporting the situation in Indochina generally and Vietnam in particular if Diem is replaced under existing circumstances. We do not say that this opposition may not in the last instance be overcome, particularly if you personally can make a case before the Congressional committees but Mansfield who is looked upon with great respect by his colleagues with reference to this matter, is adamantly opposed to abandonment of Diem under present conditions. I wonder whether there is not some intermediate solution between the present extremes now discussed and that Diem can be allowed to regain his damaged prestige by an assertion of authority over the Binh Xuyen and at the same time other elements be brought into the government under conditions which will assure a real delegation of authority.

I feel that as with most Orientals Diem must be highly suspicious of what is going on about him and that this suspicion exaggerates his natural disposition to be secretive and untrustful. If he ever really felt that the French and ourselves were solidly behind him might he not really broaden his government? We must I think have some sympathy for his precidament as he is constantly called QUOTE the Diem experiment UNQUOTE.

In conclusion I want to reaffirm the very great confidence which we all have in you and in your judgment. You have done and are doing a wonderful job in the face of tremendous difficulties.

Your 4448 has just arrived in Department but is not yet decoded. We will comment on it in subsequent telegram.

112. NSC 5519, DRAFT STATEMENT AND NSC STAFF STUDY ON U.S. POLICY ON ALL-VIETNAM ELECTIONS, MAY 17, 1955 [Extracts]

In an analysis and draft policy statement, the NSC staff observed that the Communists would have the advantage in the elections to be held in 1956 but urged that the Diem government be encouraged to agree to preliminary consultations. Primary considerations in this position were the belief that rejecting elections would be extremely unpopular in South Vietnam, the fear that it would conflict with U.S. policy elsewhere in the world, and the French-British commitment to the elections.

General Considerations

1. It is U.S. policy to maintain a friendly non-Communist Free Vietnam; to assist Free Vietnam to maintain (a) military forces necessary for internal security, and (b) economic conditions conducive to the maintenance of the strength of the non-Communist regime; and to prevent a Communist victory through all-Vietnam elections.

2. Free Vietnamese strength is essential to any effective approach to the election problem. If Free Vietnam is to cope adequately with national elections it will have to be strong enough to deter or defeat Vietminh insurrections in its territory, to impose and sustain order in its territory, and to win a free election limited to its own zone and held under its own auspices and control. Otherwise, the Vietminh can take over through internal insurrections or the Government of Free Vietnam will be so weak that it will find it difficult even to give lip service to the idea of national unification through elections, or to insist on adequate conditions for free elections.

3. U.S. policy toward all-Vietnam elections should be predicated on the assumption that there is a possibility of assisting Free Vietnam to achieve the degree of strength described above. If it becomes clear that Free Vietnam cannot achieve such strength, U.S. policy toward Free Vietnam should be reviewed.

SOURCE: Document declassified by the National Security Council, May 11, 1977.

4. U.S. policy must also protect against a Communist take-over of Free Vietnam, even if the Communists were able to win elections under safeguards in North Vietnam. On the other hand, U.S. policy should be prepared to take advantage of the unlikely possibility that North Vietnam might be freed through elections.

Courses of Action

5. Continue to encourage the Government of Free Vietnam to proceed with the consultations about elections called for in July 1955 by the Geneva Agreements.

6. Provide the Government of Free Vietnam with information and advice about Communist positions and tactics with regard to elections elsewhere, e.g., Greece, Germany, Austria and Korea.

7. Assist the Government of Free Vietnam to make it clear that any failure to secure free elections is the fault of the Communists.

8. Encourage the Government of Free Vietnam:

a. To lay stress on the necessity of compliance with the stipulation of the Geneva Agreements that "all the necessary conditions obtain for free expression of the national will" before all-Vietnam elections can take place. For this purpose the Government of Free Vietnam should insist in the first instance on adequate guarantees of freedom of elections* and adequate supervisory powers in a Supervisory Commission.

b. To adopt positions with respect to the objectives and details of elections which: (1) will avoid terms which would be likely to result in a Communist take-over of Free Vietnam; and (2) to the degree feasible, will maintain a position generally consistent with that adopted by the Free World in other areas such as Korea and Germany.

9. Seek British and French support for the foregoing courses of action.

10. If pursuit of the above policy should result in a renewal of hostilities by the Communists, the U.S., in the light of the general circumstances then prevailing, should be prepared to oppose any Communist attack with U.S. armed forces, if necessary and feasible—consulting the Congress in advance if the emergency permits—preferably in concert with the Manila Pact allies of the U.S., but if necessary alone.

The Problem

Difficulties Involved in Elections

4. The Communists would hold certain advantages in all Vietnam elections, particularly if such elections were not held under conditions of complete freedom and rigorous supervision: (a) Communist popular appeal derived from long identification with the struggle for independence; (b) the greater organizational capacity of the Communists to influence elections through propaganda, control, and coercion; (c) the continuing difficulties of the Free Vietnam Government in consolidating its political control in its own zone and moving ahead with programs of popular appeal.

*For examples of such guarantees, see para. 8 of the attached Staff Study.

Problems Involved in Avoiding the Elections

5. Despite these Communist advantages, there are a number of factors which have led the U.S. to encourage Free Vietnam to agree to the preliminary consultations stipulated in the Geneva Agreements in order to determine whether the conditions of free elections and international supervision can be met.

   a. Free Vietnam has already suffered in its contest with the Communists from the fact that the Communists have been able, largely because of the French position in Vietnam, to pre-empt for themselves identification with the slogan of national independence. Actions by Free Vietnam which were clearly directed towards avoiding elections would be seized on by the Communists to demonstrate that Free Vietnam was opposed to unification. To allow the Communists to pose as the sole champions of national unification would greatly increase the problems of Free Vietnam in securing popular support.

   b. The over-all United States position in the world would be harmed by U.S. identification with a policy which appeared to be directed towards avoidance of elections. World public opinion, and for that matter domestic U.S. opinion, would have difficulty in understanding why the U.S. should oppose in Vietnam the democratic procedures which the U.S. has advocated for Korea, Austria and Germany.

   c. It is clear that both the French and the British believe themselves committed as signatories of the Geneva Agreements to a program of encouraging the holding of elections. In addition, the French fear that failure to hold elections would provoke a resumption of hostilities by the Vietminh in which France would be directly and involuntarily involved due to the probable presence of at least large numbers of the French Expeditionary Corps through 1955 and the first half of 1956.

*   *   *

Free Vietnam Position in Election Negotiations

7. It will be advantageous to the U.S. if Free Vietnam, in negotiating on elections with the Communists, adopts a position which: (a) will avoid terms which would be likely to result in a Communist takeover of Free Vietnam; (b) will, to the degree feasible, maintain a position generally consistent with that adopted by the Free World in other areas such as Korea and Germany.

8. In negotiating for conditions of genuine freedom for the holding of elections, Free Vietnam can serve both these objectives by insisting on provisions such as those already supported by the Western Powers at Berlin: Agreement on safeguards to assure conditions of genuine freedom before, after, and during elections; full powers for any Supervisory Commission to act to ensure free elections and to guarantee against prior coercion or subsequent reprisal; adequate guarantees for, among other things, freedom of movement, freedom of presentation of candidates, immunity of candidates, freedom from arbitrary arrest or victimization, freedom of association and political meetings, freedom of expression for all, freedom of press, radio, and free circulation of newspapers, secrecy of vote, security of polling stations and ballot boxes. The Communists would find it most difficult to accept such conditions or to allow their implementation if accepted. Accordingly, it would be useful for the Free Vietnamese to center their position on securing agreement to

conditions for free elections prior to discussion of the forms and objectives of the elections.

9. If the negotiations extend to the subjects of the forms and objectives of elections it will be more difficult for Free Vietnam to adopt positions which clearly protect the interests of Free Vietnam and at the same time are completely consistent with Free World positions on Germany or Korea. Free Vietnam is probably slightly less populous than North Vietnam (although there has been a substantial refugee movement to the South and there are no firm population statistics), so that representation proportionate to population, which we have insisted on in other areas, would be less advantageous in Vietnam than would be equal representation from the two zones. Limitation of the functions of any elected body solely to drafting of a constitution would be clearly desirable in the case of Vietnam, while in other areas we are considering bodies which may have additional functions. It would be advantageous for the Free Vietnam Government to reserve the power to accept or reject any constitution that might be agreed upon in an elected constituent assembly. Such a position is probably not desirable in the other areas. In general, however, it should be possible to devise positions with regard to the details and objectives of elections which would safeguard the non-Communist position of Free Vietnam without violating important principles on which the U.S. is standing elsewhere. Insistence on limiting the powers of any elected body to drafting a constitution, or insisting on a census prior to agreeing to number of representatives, would not, for example, weaken the U.S. position with respect to either German or Korean elections.

113. JOINT COMMUNIQUE ISSUED BY THE GOVERNMENTS OF THE SOVIET UNION AND THE DRV, MOSCOW, JULY 18, 1955 [Extract]

After talks with Soviet Premier Nikita Krushchev and other Soviet leaders, Ho obtained Soviet agreement on the necessity for "signatories" to the agreement to "take necessary measures to realize them." But there was no accusation against the United States for obstructing the consultations on elections, as there had been in an earlier Chinese-Vietnamese communiqué. And the criticism of SEATO was both milder in wording and further down in the communique than its Chinese-Vietnamese counterpart. These were indications that the Soviets were refusing to take as strong a position on the issue as the Vietnamese desired.

The USSR and the DRV Governments unanimously confirmed their readiness to seek unswervingly a strict implementation of the Geneva Agreements on Indochina. Both Governments attach special importance to the fulfillment of the conditions of the Geneva Agreements regarding Vietnam, proceeding from the precept that peace in Indochina can be consolidated only after the unification of Vietnam on the basis of the respect for its sovereignty, independence, unity, and territorial integrity—as laid down in the Geneva Agreements.

SOURCE: *Moscow, Soviet Home Service,* July 18, 1955. Translated by the Foreign Broadcast Information Service, July 19, 1955, pp. CC1–CC4.

Both Governments noted with satisfaction stated the successful completion of the regrouping of troops envisaged by the Geneva Agreements, and the realization of other military conditions of the Geneva Agreements regarding Vietnam, which have been achieved as a result of the joint effort of the states in question.

They recognized that the success in fulfilling the Geneva Agreements is a considerable contribution to the cause of consolidation of peace and security in Indochina and the whole world.

They noted the fruitful work of the International Supervision and Control Committees for Vietnam, Laos, and Cambodia consisting of representatives of India, Poland, and Canada and headed by a representative of India. They expressed the hope that these committees will successfully complete their mission in the work of achieving a political settlement according to the Geneva Agreements.

Both Governments unanimously emphasized the importance of conducting consultations, within the time limit provided for in the Geneva Agreements between competent representatives of the Democratic Republic of Vietnam and South Vietnam on questions connected with the preparations for the general elections in July 1956 for the purpose of uniting Vietnam.

The Governments of the Soviet Union and the Democratic Republic of Vietnam think that the states signatories of the Geneva Agreements as well as all states which have a place in the carrying out of the Geneva Agreements should take the necessary measures to realize them. Both Governments have noted with satisfaction the great and positive significance of the Afro-Asian Conference at Bandung, where an especially fruitful role was played by the Chinese People's Republic and the Republic of India. This conference was a graphic example of successful cooperation in the interests of peace between countries with different political, social, and economic systems.

In the course of the negotiations it was stated that in their relations both Governments followed the principles of mutual regard for sovereignty and territorial integrity, nonaggression and noninterference in internal affairs, equality and mutual benefit, and peaceful coexistence. It was also noted with satisfaction that the above principles were being more and more widely accepted and applied by various states as a basis of extensive and fruitful international collaboration. Both Governments believe that friendly relations between the DRV and other Asian countries based on these principles will contribute to the establishment and widening of the zone of peace in Southeast Asia, and thus to the cause of consolidating peace throughout the world.

The Governments of the USSR and the DRV are determined in their condemnation of attempts to include South Vietnam, Laos, and Cambodia in the sphere of operations of the aggressive military bloc in Southeast Asia—SEATO—which is contrary to the Geneva Agreements. They also draw attention to the incompatibility with the Geneva Agreement of these attempts on the part of some foreign powers to interfere in internal affairs of South Vietnam, Cambodia, and Laos, and of attempts to enforce on these countries agreements of a military nature. Both governments believe that the settlement of international political problems is at present entirely dependent on the readiness of interested states to achieve agreement among them on the basis of regard for the just interests of either side.

The Governments of the Soviet Union and the DRV noted with satisfaction the growing activity of peoples aimed at the safeguarding of peace which has already led to certain relaxation of tension in international relations. This has found expression specifically in the fact of the convocation of the conference of the heads of the Government of the Four Powers.

Both Governments expressed the hope that the great powers will continue their efforts for the regulation of controversial questions by means of negotiations, which undoubtedly will foster the establishment of an atmosphere of mutual trust and the strengthening of universal peace.

114. NIE 63-1-55, "PROBABLE DEVELOPMENTS IN NORTH VIETNAM TO JULY 1956," JULY 19, 1955 [Extract]

The intelligence community guessed that Vietnamese Communists would be willing to accept "neutral" supervision of all-Vietnamese elections, though not "complex and elaborate safeguards and guarantees," but did not rule out reactivation of guerrilla activities in the South should the Diem government refuse to agree on an election plan or consolidate its strength.

The Problem

To analyze the present strengths and weaknesses of North Vietnam and to estimate probable future developments and trends to July 1956.

Conclusions

1. The immediate concern of the "Democratic Republic of Vietnam" (DRV) is to consolidate its control in the area north of the 17th Parallel and to gain control of South Vietnam. *(Para. 14)*

2. We believe that the DRV will experience no great difficulty in maintaining effective control of North Vietnam during the period of this estimate and will probably retain a considerable measure of prestige and general acceptance. However, passive resistance and discontent resulting from harsh control measures and poor economic conditions may increase toward the end of the period. If the situation in the South does not deteriorate, the nationalist appeal of Ho Chi Minh and the DRV will probably be reduced throughout Vietnam. *(Para. 23)*

3. The DRV is confronted by serious economic problems of which the current rice shortage is the most critical. Its present export potential falls far short of providing sufficient funds to pay for necessary imports. However, the Sino-Soviet Bloc will almost certainly provide sufficient economic and technical assistance to meet minimum requirements for stability and control. With such assistance the DRV will probably make gradual progress in gaining control of the economy and in rehabilitating transportation, irrigation, and industrial facilities. *(Paras. 24-30)*

4. Since the Geneva Conference, the strength of the DRV regular army has been increased substantially by drawing on regional forces to form new units and by the receipt of new and heavier military equipment from Communist China. DRV forces are capable of defeating all military forces, including the French, now located in South Vietnam, Laos, and Cambodia. *(Paras. 31-35)*

SOURCE: *U.S.-Vietnam Relations*, Book 10, pp. 994–996.

5. The present DRV tactic with respect to South Vietnam is to pose as the champion of Vietnamese independence and unification, and as the defender of the provisions of the Geneva Agreement. The DRV probably still believes that it could emerge from free nationwide elections with control of all Vietnam. It will attempt to appear reasonable in any negotiations concerning procedures for elections. While the Communists almost certainly would not agree to complex and eleborate safe-guards and guarantees, they probably would agree to some form of "neutral" (but not UN) supervision. They would probably estimate that such election controls would work to their advantage in the South and, as manipulated, would not ad-versely affect their position in the North. *(Paras, 44-45)*

6. In the meantime, the DRV will continue its efforts, through subversion, intimidation, and propaganda, to weaken the Diem government, and to bring to power in the South men prepared to accept a coalition with the DRV. *(Para. 46)*

7. The Communists in their propaganda have revealed sensitivity to the impli-cation of the Manila Pact which incorporated Vietnam, Cambodia, and Laos in its area of protection. We believe that concern for Western, and particularly US reactions, together with general considerations arising from over-all Bloc policy, will prevent the DRV from openly invading the South during the period of this estimate. Similarly, the resumption of widespread guerrilla activities appears un-likely prior to the election deadline, unless the DRV should come to the con-clusion that South Vietnam can be won only by force. Such a conclusion would become more likely should the Diem government persist in refusing to enter the election discussions, should election discussions not proceed favorably for the DRV, or should the Diem government succeed, with US assistance, in consolidat-ing its strength to the point of becoming a nationalist alternative to the Ho regime. Moreover, if during the period of this estimate little progress is made towards relaxing tension, Peiping and Moscow might permit the DRV greater freedom of action. Should the DRV decide to use force short of open invasion, it would probably attempt to undermine the Saigon government by initiating a campaign of sabotage and terror, seeking to formation of a new government more amenable to demands for a national coalition. These tactics are likely to include the activation of DRV guerrilla units now in South Vietnam and their reinforcement by the infiltration in small units of regulars from the North. *(Para. 47)*

115. MESSAGE FROM HO CHI MINH AND FOREIGN MINISTER PHAM VAN DONG TO RVN CHIEF OF STATE BAO DAI AND PRIME MINISTER NGO DINH DIEM JULY 19, 1955 [Extract]

One day before the date for the beginning of consultations on elections under the Geneva Agreement, the DRV, in a letter to Diem from Ho and Pham Van Dong, proposed that the South Vietnamese government nominate its representative for those consultations. But the deadline passed without any response from Saigon.

SOURCE: *Documents Related to the Implementation of the Geneva Agreement*, pp. 41–44.

The holding on schedule of the consultative conference by the competent authorities of the North and the South is of great importance, and has a bearing not only on the prospect of the unity of our country but also on the loyal implementation of the Geneva Agreements, and the consolidation of peace in Indo-China and in the world.

Following the June 6, 1955 declaration by the Government of the Democratic Republic of Viet-nam, Sai-gon Radio on July 16, 1955, made known the "position of the Government of the State of Viet-nam on the problem of general elections for the unification of the national territory". The statement mentioned general elections and reunification but did not touch upon a very important and most realistic issue, that of the meeting of the competent representative authorities of the two zones, of the holding of the consultative conference on the question of general elections and reunification, as provided for by the Geneva Agreements. Moreover there were in the statement things which are untrue and which would not help to create a favourable climate for the convening of the consultative conference.

Our compatriots from the South to the North, irrespective of classes, creeds and political affiliations have deeply at heart the reunification of the country, and are looking forward to the early convening of the consultative conference and to its good outcome. All the countries responsible for the guarantee of the implementation of the Geneva Agreements and in general all the peace-loving countries in the world are anxious to see that the consultative conference will be held and yield good results and that the reunification of our country will be achieved.

The Government of the Democratic Republic of Viet-nam proposes that you appoint your representatives and that they and ours hold the consultative conference from July 20, 1955 onwards, as provided for by the Geneva Agreements, at a place agreeable to both sides, on the Vietnamese territory, in order to discuss the problem of reunification of our country by means of free general elections all over Viet-nam.

116. REPORT OF U.S. CENTRAL INTELLIGENCE AGENCY COVERT OPERATIONS TEAM IN VIETNAM, MID-1955 [Extracts]

While the Geneva Conference was meeting in the spring of 1954, the United States was sending Col. Edward G. Lansdale to Saigon to head a CIA covert operations mission under the title "Saigon Military Mission," (SMM). Lansdale's team engaged in psychological warfare, paramilitary operations, and sabotage. The extracts of the report of the team's operations, presumably written by Lansdale himself, show how the CIA tried to sow fear and division within the "Vietminh" zones through rumors and documents disguised to appear of Communist origin. The "Binh" mentioned in the text was the top Vietnamese agent working for SMM.

SOURCE: *The Pentagon Papers as Published by the New York Times* (New York: Bantam Books, 1971), pp. 53–66. Hereafter cited as *The Pentagon Papers*.

Towards the end of the month, it was learned that the largest printing establishment in the north intended to remain in Hanoi and do business with the Vietminh.
An attempt was made by SMM to destroy the modern presses, but Vietminh
security agents already had moved into the plant and frustrated the attempt. This
operation was under a Vietnamese patriot whom we shall call Trieu; his case officer
was Capt. Arundel. Earlier in the month they had engineered a black psywar strike
in Hanoi: leaflets signed by the Vietminh instructing Tonkinese on how to behave
for the Vietminh takeover of the Hanoi region in early October, including items
about property, money reform, and a three-day holiday of workers upon takeover.
The day following the distribution of these leaflets, refugee registration tripled. Two
days later Vietminh currency was worth half the value prior to the leaflets. The
Vietminh took to the radio to denounce the leaflets; the leaflets were so authentic in
appearance that even most of the rank and file Vietminh were sure that the radio
denunciations were a French trick.

The Hanoi psywar strike had other consequences. Binh had enlisted a high
police official of Hanoi as part of his team, to effect the release from jail of any
team members if arrested. The official at the last moment decided to assist in the
leaflet distribution personally. Police officers spotted him, chased his vehicle through
the empty Hanoi streets of early morning, finally opened fire on him and caught
him. He was the only member of the group caught. He was held in prison as a
Vietminh agent.

*   *   *

Hanoi was evacuated on 9 October. The northern SMM team left with the last
French troops, disturbed by what they had seen of the grim efficiency of the
Vietminh in their takeover, the contrast between the silent march of the victorious
Vietminh troops in their tennis shoes and the clanking armor of the well-equipped
French whose Western tactics and equipment had failed against the Communist
military-political-economic campaign.

The northern team had spent the last days of Hanoi in contaminating the oil
supply of the bus company for a gradual wreckage of engines in the buses, in taking
the first actions for delayed sabotage of the railroad (which required teamwork with
a CIA special technical team in Japan who performed their part brilliantly), and in
writing detailed notes of potential targets for future paramilitary operations (U.S.
adherence to the Geneva Agreement prevented SMM from carrying out the active
sabotage it desired to do against the power plant, water facilities, harbor, and
bridge). The team had a bad moment when contaminating the oil. They had to work
quickly at night, in an enclosed storage room. Fumes from the contaminant came
close to knocking them out. Dizzy and weak-kneed, they masked their faces with
handkerchiefs and completed the job.

Meanwhile, Polish and Russian ships had arrived in the south to transport
southern Vietminh to Tonkin under the Geneva Agreement. This offered the opportunity for another black psywar strike. A leaflet was developed by Binh with the
help of Capt. Arundel, attributed to the Vietminh Resistance Committee. Among
other items, it reassured the Vietminh they would be kept safe below decks from
imperialist air and submarine attacks, and requested that warm clothing be brought;

the warm clothing item would be coupled with a verbal rumor campaign that Vietminh were being sent into China as railroad laborers.

SMM had been busily developing G-5 of the Vietnamese Army for such psywar efforts. Under Arundel's direction, the First Armed Propaganda Company printed the leaflets and distributed them, by soldiers in civilian clothes who penetrated into southern Vietminh zones on foot. (Distribution in Camau was made while columnist Joseph Alsop was on his visit there which led to his sensational, gloomy articles later; our soldier "Vietminh" failed in an attempt to get the leaflet into Alsop's hands in Camau; Alsop was never told this story). Intelligence reports and other later reports revealed that village and delegation committees complained about "deportation" to the north, after distribution of the leaflet. . . .

*   *   *

The patriot we've named Trieu Dinh had been working on an almanac for popular sale, particularly in the northern cities and towns we could still reach. Noted Vietnamese astrologers were hired to write predictions about coming disasters to certain Vietminh leaders and undertakings, and to predict unity in the south. The work was carried out under the direction of Lt. Phillips, based on our concept of the use of astrology for psywar in Southeast Asia. Copies of the almanac were shipped by air to Haiphong and then smuggled into Vietminh territory.

Dinh also had produced a Thomas Paine type series of essays on Vietnamese patriotism against the Communist Vietminh, under the guidance of Capt. Arundel. These essays were circulated among influential groups in Vietnam, earned front-page editorials in the leading daily newspaper in Saigon. Circulation increased with the publication of these essays. The publisher is known to SMM as The Dragon Lady and is a fine Vietnamese girl who has been the mistress of an anti-American French civilian. Despite anti-American remarks by her boy friend, we had helped her keep her paper from being closed by the government . . . and she found it profitable to heed our advice on the editorial content of her paper.

Arms and equipment for the Binh paramilitary team were being cached in the north in areas still free from the Vietminh. Personnel movements were covered by the flow of refugees. Haiphong was reminiscent of our own pioneer days as it was swamped with people whom it couldn't shelter. Living space and food were at a premium, nervous tension grew. It was a wild time for our northern team.

First supplies for the Hao paramilitary group started to arrive in Saigon. These shipments and the earlier ones for the Binh group were part of an efficient and effective air smuggling effort by the 581st [word illegible] Wing, U.S. Air Force, to support SMM, with help by CIA and Air Force personnel in both Okinawa and the Philippines. SMM officers frequently did coolie labor in manhandling tons of cargo, at times working through the night . . . All . . . officers pitched in to help, as part of our "blood, sweat and tears". . . .

By 31 January, all operational equipment of the Binh paramilitary group had been trans-shipped to Haiphong from Saigon, mostly with the help of CAT, and the northern SMM team had it cached in operational sites. Security measures were tightened at the Haiphong airport and plans for bringing in the Hao equipment were changed from the air route to sea. Task Force 98, now 98.7 under command of Captain Frank, again was asked to give a helping hand and did so. . . .

. . . Major Conein had briefed the members of the Binh paramilitary team and started them infiltrating into the north as individuals. The infiltration was carried out in careful stages over a 30 day period, a successful operation. The Binhs became normal citizens, carrying out every day civil pursuits, on the surface.

We had smuggled into Vietnam about eight and a half tons of supplies for the Hao paramilitary group. They included fourteen agent radios, 300 carbines, 90,000 rounds of carbine ammunition, 50 pistols, 10,000 rounds of pistol ammunition, and 300 pounds of explosives. Two and a half tons were delivered to the Hao agents in Tonkin, while the remainder was cached along the Red River by SMM, with the help of the Navy. . . .

117. DECLARATION OF THE GOVERNMENT OF THE STATE OF VIETNAM ON REUNIFICATION, AUGUST 9, 1955

Instead of answering the DRV's July 19 note requesting the convening of the consultative conference on general elections called for in the Geneva Agreement, the Diem government issued a statement repeating that it was not bound by the agreement. The South Vietnamese note made it clear that there could be no negotiations of any kind with the North as long as the Communist regime remained in power.

In the last July 1955 broadcast, the Vietnamese national Government has made it clear its position towards the problem of territorial unity.

The Government does not consider itself bound in any respect by the Geneva Agreements which it did not sign.

Once more, the Government reasserts that in any circumstance, it places national interests above all, being resolved to achieve at all cost the obvious aim it is pursuing and eventually to achieve national unity, peace and freedom.

The Viet-Minh leaders have had a note dated July 19 transmitted to the Government, in which they asked for the convening of a consultative conference on general elections. This is just a propaganda move aimed at making the people believe that they are the champions of our territorial unity. Everyone still remembers that last year at Geneva, the Vietnamese Communists boisterously advocated the partition of our territory and asked for an economically self-sufficient area whereas the delegation of the State of Viet-nam proposed an armistice without any partition, not even provisional, with a view to safeguarding the sacred rights of the Vietnamese national and territorial unity, national independence and individual freedom. As the Vietnamese delegation states, the Vietnamese Government then stood for the fulfillment of national aspirations by the means which have been given back to Viet-nam by the French solemn recognition of the independence and sovereignty of Viet-nam, as a legal, independent state.

SOURCE: *Documents Related to the Implementation of the Geneva Agreements*, pp. 98–99.

The policy of the Government remains unchanged. Confronted with the partition of the country, which is contrary to the will of the entire people, the Government will see to it that everybody throughout the country may live free from fear, and completely free from all totalitarian oppression. As a champion of justice, of genuine democracy, the Government always holds that the principles of free general election is a peaceful and democratic means only if, first of all, the freedom to live and freedom of vote is sufficiently guaranteed.

In this connection, nothing constructive can be contemplated in the present situation in the North where, under the rule of the Vietnamese Communists, the citizens do not enjoy democratic freedoms and fundamental human rights.

118. MEMORANDUM FOR THE SECRETARY OF DEFENSE BY THE JOINT CHIEFS OF STAFF, SEPTEMBER 9, 1955 [Extract]

Having signed the Manila Pact and organized the Southeast Asia Treaty Organization primarily to deter a further Communist move in Indochina, the U.S. government continued to take seriously the possibility of U.S. forces intervening directly in Vietnam. The Joint Chiefs, asked to determine the requirements not only for repulsing a Viet Minh attack but for taking control of North Vietnam, recommended that, if the United States intended to take over North Vietnam, it should do so with atomic weapons. Without them, they suggested, such an operation might be more costly than would be justified.

10. In the early stages, Vietminh aggression would probably be characterized by a fluid situation with dispersed clashes between opposing forces. In such operations, the opportunities for employing atomic weapons would not justify significant reductions in early force requirements. During later stages, however, suitable targets could be expected to develop as a result of friendly efforts to force concentrations or particularly if the Chinese Communists should intervene overtly. Use of atomic weapons should result in a considerable reduction in friendly casualties and in more rapid cessation of hostilities. In any event, no prohibitions should be imposed on the use of atomic weapons, or on other military operations, to the extent of precluding effective military reaction as the situation develops. The Joint Chiefs of Staff consider that if atomic weapons were not used, greater forces than the U.S. would be justified in providing would probably be needed.

11. The Joint Chiefs of Staff reiterate the view expressed in their memorandum, dated 11 February 1955, subject: "Concept and Plans for the Implementation, if necessary, of Article IV, 1, of the Manila Pact," that the United States cannot guarantee the territorial integrity of any member nation (of the Manila Pact), but at most can help secure the independence of those countries whose peoples desire it and who are willing to undertake the responsibilities of self government. This appears to be particularly applicable to protected, non-member countries.

12. The foregoing is a rough estimate of the requirements. A more definitive

SOURCE: Document declassified by the Joint Chiefs of Staff, November 10, 1976.

answer cannot be made until the Commander in Chief, Pacific, provides a plan which he is presently developing.

13. The Chairman, Joint Chiefs of Staff, did not participate in the action of the Joint Chiefs of Staff outline in this memorandum.

1956

119. MESSAGE FROM THE TWO CO-CHAIRMEN OF THE GENEVA CONFERENCE TO THE GOVERNMENTS OF THE DEMOCRATIC REPUBLIC OF VIETNAM AND THE REPUBLIC OF VIETNAM, MAY 8, 1956.

The crucial negotiations on the implementation of the Geneva election provision were held between Soviet Deputy Foreign Minister Andrei Gromyko and British Minister of State Lord Reading in late April and early May, 1956. The message which was hammered out by the two sides represented a compromise falling far short of what the DRV hoped to get: a call for another Geneva Conference on Indochina. In return for a specific request for views from the Saigon and Hanoi governments on when consultations could be held, the Soviets did not insist on such a conference.

Acting with the authority of the Governments of the United Kingdom and the Soviet Union, the Minister of State for Foreign Affairs of Great Britain, Lord Reading, and the First Deputy Foreign Minister of the Union of Soviet Socialist Republics, Mr. A. A. Gromyko, have met in London, as representatives of the two Co-Chairmen of the Geneva Conference on Indo-China, and have made a thorough examination of the problems relating to the fulfilment of the Geneva Agreements in Vietnam. They have also exchanged views on the proposal to convene a further conference of Members of the original Geneva Conference and of the Supervisory Powers to discuss these problems.

2. In the course of these talks they expressed their concern about the present situation in relation to the fulfilment of the Geneva Agreements in Vietnam, where the implementation of the political provisions of the Geneva Agreements has not yet begun. In particular, consultations have not taken place about the preparation and holding of free, nation-wide elections in Vietnam under the supervision of an

SOURCE: Great Britain, Foreign Office, *Vietnam and the Geneva Agreements, Documents Concerning the Discussions Between Representatives of Her Majesty's Government and the Government of the Union of Soviet Socialist Republics Held in London in April and May 1956* (Vietnam No. 2 [1956]. London, Cmd. 9763), pp. 10–11.

International Commission with a view to the reestablishment of the national unity of Vietnam. There is thus at present a threat to the fulfilment of this important provision of the Geneva Agreements, although both sides in Vietnam have accepted the principle of national reunification by means of free general elections.

3. Pending the holding of free general elections for the reunification of Vietnam, the two Co-Chairman attach great importance to the maintenance of the cease-fire under the continued supervision of the International Commission for Vietnam. They recognise that the dissolution of the French Union High Command has increased the difficulties of the International Supervisory Commission in Vietnam in carrying out the functions specified in the Geneva Agreements, which are the basis for the Commission's activities, and that these difficulties must be overcome. The Co-Chairmen are confident that the authorities in both parts of Vietnam will show effective co-operation and that these difficulties will in practice be removed.

4. Prompted by their desire to strengthen peace in Indo-China on the basis of the principles and provisions of the Geneva Agreements, the Co-Chairmen strongly urge the authorities of the Democratic Republic of Vietnam and those of the Republic of Vietnam to make every effort to implement the Geneva Agreements on Vietnam, to prevent any future violation of the military provisions and principles embodied in the Final Declaration of the Geneva Conference. To this end the authorities of both parts of Vietnam are invited to transmit to the Co-Chairmen as soon as possible, either jointly or separately their views about the time required for the opening of consultations on the organisation of nation-wide elections in Vietnam and the time required for the holding of elections as a means of achieving the unification of Vietnam.

5. Having noted with appreciation the valuable work performed by the International Supervisory Commission for Vietnam, the Co-Chairmen strongly urge the authorities in both parts of Vietnam to give the Commission all possible assistance in future in the exercise of their functions as defined by the Geneva Agreements on Vietnam.

6. The Co-Chairmen will continue to consult together about the situation in Vietnam and, if necessary in the light of that situation, they will also discuss the measures which should be taken to ensure the fulfilment of the Geneva Agreements on Vietnam, including the proposal to convene a new conference of the Members of the original Geneva Conference and of the States represented in the International Commissions in Indo-China.

120. NIE 63-56, JULY 17, 1956 [Extract]

On the eve of the second anniversary of the Geneva Accords, the intelligence community predicted that Hanoi would refrain from using force in the South, primarily because Soviet and Chinese policy would not support such a move. The estimate pointed to the Soviet bloc's failure to demand strict implementation of the electoral provision of the accord as a factor bolstering the status quo. It thus reflected Washington's feeling that Moscow was implicitly recognizing South Vietnam as being in the American sphere of influence. "ICC" in the text refers to the

SOURCE: *U.S.-Vietnam Relations*, Book 10, pp. 1073–1079.

International Control Commission, comprising India, Poland and Canada, which was created by the Geneva Conference to supervise the implementation of the Geneva Agreement.''GVN'' (Government of Vietnam) refers to Diem's Republic of Vietnam.

IV. The Outlook in Vietnam

Probable Communist Courses of Action Toward South Vietnam

64. The DRV probably estimates that its chances for securing control of South Vietnam by means short of open attack or large-scale guerrilla action supported from the North will gradually diminish with the passage of time. As indicated by Soviet and Chinese Communist performance in the past several months, the DRV probably cannot expect strong support from the Bloc for the "strict implementation" of the Geneva Agreements. The lack of strong Bloc pressure strengthens international acceptance of the status quo in Vietnam and increases confidence in the future in South Vietnam. Although the DRV may still believe that it could obtain control of all Vietnam through ICC supervised nationwide elections, Vietnamese Communist leaders are probably increasingly doubtful on this point because of their own internal difficulties and the growing nationalist stature of Diem. The DRV probably also believes that its covert assets in South Vietnam will gradually decline if the Diem government is permitted to concentrate on internal security and economic problems free of external harassment.

65. Despite the declining prospects for the "peaceful" take-over of South Vietnam, we believe that the USSR and Communist China will almost certainly continue unwilling to support open DRV military action against South Vietnam during the period of this estimate. They are probably unwilling to risk the chance of US or SEATO intervention which would make it difficult to limit the conflict to Vietnam, and probably believe that overt DRV military action would seriously undercut the worldwide effort of the Bloc to win friends and supporters. Although the DRV retains the capability to launch an independent military action against South Vietnam, the chances of such action in the absence of assured Bloc support appear to be extremely small.

66. The only remaining course of action holding out some promise for the early achievement of Communist control in South Vietnam appears to be the development of large scale guerrilla warfare in the south. In recent weeks a number of reports from sources of untested reliability have indicated that the Communists may have started preparations in both South Vietnam and in the north to begin guerrilla action. DRV allegations of Vietnamese violations of the demilitarized zone along the 17th parallel and Communist claims of US-Diem plans to violate the Armistice could be propaganda cover for the initiation of guerrilla action against the south.

67. However, the possible indications of armed action appear inconsistent with the DRV's insistence on the continued functioning of the ICC—which is in a position to make at least limited observations of DRV activities. Moreover, guerrilla action in South Vietnam, if it were to be sustained and not to result simply in the identification and gradual elimination of Communist cadres, would require large scale support from the north. This would involve some risk of detection by the ICC and of intervention by the US and possibly SEATO. It would also tend to prejudice

current Communist maneuvers elsewhere in Asia. For these reasons, we believe that the DRV will refrain from instituting large scale guerrilla action within South Vietnam during the period of this estimate. Communist capabilities for guerrilla warfare in South Vietnam will exist for some time, however, and the chances of their being employed would probably increase in the event of any substantial deterioration in the domestic situation in South Vietnam—such as might conceivably occur on the death of Diem. The chances of Communist guerrilla warfare would also be increased by deterioration of the international aspects of the situation, such as a withdrawal of the ICC under circumstances which would permit the Communists to place the blame for this event on the GVN.

121. NSC 5612/1: STATEMENT OF POLICY ON U.S. POLICY IN MAINLAND SOUTHEAST ASIA, SEPTEMBER 5, 1956 [Extracts]

A codification of U.S. policy objectives with regard to mainland Southeast Asia called for a "rollback" policy toward North Vietnam, aimed at eventual reunification of the country under "anti-Communist leadership."

Viet Nam

54. Assist Free Viet Nam to develop a strong, stable and constitutional government to enable Free Viet Nam to assert an increasingly attractive contrast to conditions in the present Communist zone.

55. Work toward the weakening of the Communists in peaceful reunification of a free and independent Viet Nam under anti-Communist leadership.

56. Support the position of the Government of Free Viet Nam that all-Viet Nam elections may take place only after it is satisfied that genuinely free elections can be held throughout both zones of Viet Nam.

57. Assist Free Viet Nam to build up indigenous armed forces, including independent logistical and administrative services, which will be capable of assuring internal security and of providing limited initial resistance to attack by the Viet Minh.

58. Encourage Vietnamese military planning for defense against external aggression along lines consistent with U.S. planning concepts based upon approved U.S. policy, and discreetly manifest in other ways U.S. interest in assisting Free Viet Nam, in accordance with the SEATO Treaty, to defend itself against external aggression.

*   *   *

VI. Supplementary Statement of Policy on The Special Situation in North Viet Nam

65. Treat the Viet Minh as not constituting a legitimate government, and discourage other non-Communist states from developing or maintaining relations with the Viet Minh regime.

SOURCE: Document declassified by National Security Council, September 19, 1977.

66. Prevent the Viet Minh from expanding their political influence and territorial control in Free Viet Nam and Southeast Asia.

67. Deter the Viet Minh from attacking or subverting Free Viet Nam or Laos.

68. Probe weaknesses of the Viet Minh and exploit them internally and internationally whenever possible.

69. Exploit nationalist sentiment within North Viet Nam as a means of weakening and disrupting Sino-Soviet domination.

70. Assist the Government of Viet Nam to undertake programs of political, economic and psychological warfare against Viet Minh Communists.

71. Apply, as necessary to achieve U.S. objectives, restrictions on U.S. exports and shipping and on foreign assets similar to those already in effect for Communist China and North Korea.

122. INTERNAL STUDY DOCUMENT BY SECRETARY OF THE LAO DONG PARTY COMMITTEE FOR THE SOUTH LE DUAN: "THE PATH OF REVOLUTION IN THE SOUTH," NOVEMBER 1956 [Extracts]

Despite the passage of the July 21, 1956, date for general election without any progress toward a political settlement, the Lao Dong Party leadership reaffirmed the line of "peaceful political struggle" in a document written by the secretary of the Party Committee for the South, Le Duan, in 1956 and probably approved at the 11th Central Committee Plenum in December 1956. The document emphasized the conclusion of the Soviet Party's Twentieth Congress in February 1956 that revolutionary movements in many countries could "develop peacefully." It suggested that the revolutionary movement in South Vietnam could also develop peacefully, even though the Diem regime had a strong military-police apparatus, because Diem's regime was so weak politically. It argued that the peaceful line was necessary because the population of the South was so ardent in its desire for peace, and was possible because the U.S. and Diem would not be able to identify and repress the Communists who led the revolutionary movement in the South. Le Duan's essay would serve as the guideline for the Party's Southern policy for the next three years.

The situation forces bellicose states such as the U.S. and Britain to recognize that if they adventurously start a world war, they themselves will be the first to be destroyed, and thus the movement to demand peace in those imperialist countries is also developing strongly.

Recently, in the U.S. Presidential election, the present Republican administration, in order to buy the people's esteem, put forward the slogan "Peace and

---

SOURCE: *"Duong Loi Cach Mang Mien Nam"* [The path of revolution in the south]. Communist Party document captured in Long An Province, South Vietnam, in 1957. Document No. 1002 in the collection of Communist Documents assembled by Jeffrey Race and deposited with the Center for Research Libraries, Chicago, pp. 1–2, 5–9. [Translation by the editor.]

Prosperity," which showed that even the people of an imperialist warlike country like the U.S. want peace.

The general situation shows us that the forces of peace and democracy in the world have tipped the balance toward the camp of peace and democracy. Therefore we can conclude that the world at present can maintain long-term peace.

On the other hand, however, we can also conclude that as long as the capitalist economy survives, it will always scheme to provoke war, and there will still remain the danger of war.

Based on the above world situation, the Twentieth Congress of the Communist Party of the Soviet Union produced two important judgments:

1. All conflicts in the world at present can be resolved by means of peaceful negotiations.

2. The revolutionary movement in many countries at present can develop peacefully. Naturally in the countries in which the ruling class has a powerful military-police apparatus and is using fascist policies to repress the movement, the revolutionary parties in those countries must look clearly at their concrete situation to have the appropriate methods of struggle.

Based on the general situation and that judgment, we conclude that, if all conflicts can be resolved by means of peaceful negotiations, peace can be achieved.

Because the interest and aspiration of peaceful reunification of our country are the common interest and aspiration of all the people of the Northern and Southern zones, the people of the two zones do not have any reason to provoke war, nor to prolong the division of the country. On the contrary the people of the two zones are more and more determined to oppose the U.S.-Diem scheme of division and war provocation in order to create favorable conditions for negotiations between the two zones for peaceful unification of the country.

The present situation of division is created solely by the arbitrary U.S.-Diem regime, so the fundamental problem is how to smash the U.S.-Diem scheme of division and war-provocation.

As observed above, if they want to oppose the U.S-Diem regime, there is no other path for the people of the South but the path of revolution.

What, then, is the line and struggle method of the revolutionary movement in the South?

If the world situation can maintain peace due to a change in the relationship of forces in the world in favor of the camp of peace and democracy, the revolutionary movement can develop following a peaceful line, and the revolutionary movement in the South can also develop following a peaceful line.

First of all, we must determine what it means for a revolutionary movement to struggle according to a peaceful line.

A revolutionary movement struggling according to a peaceful line takes the political forces of the people as the base rather than using people's armed forces to struggle with the existing government to achieve their revolutionary objective.

A revolutionary movement struggling according to a peaceful line is also different from a reformist movement in that a reformist movement relies fundamentally on the law and the constitution to struggle, while a revolutionary movement relies on the revolutionary political forces of the masses as the base. And another difference is that a revolutionary movement struggles for revolutionary objectives, while a reformist movement struggles for reformist goals.

With an imperialist, feudalist, dictatorial, fascist government like the U.S.-Diem, is it possible for a peaceful political struggle line to achieve its objective?

We must recognize that all accomplishments in every country are due to the people. That is a definite law: it cannot be otherwise. Therefore the line of the revolutionary movement must be in accord with the inclinations and aspirations of the people. Only in that way can a revolutionary movement be mobilized and succeed.

The ardent aspiration of the Southern people is to maintain peace and achieve national unification. We must clearly recognize this longing for peace: the revolutionary movement in the South can mobilize and advance to success on the basis of grasping the flag of peace, in harmony with popular feelings. On the contrary, U.S.-Diem is using fascist violence to provoke war, contrary to the will of the people and therefore must certainly be defeated.

Can the U.S.-Diem regime, by using a clumsy policy of fascist violence, create a strong force to oppose and destroy the revolutionary movement?

Definitely not, because the U.S.-Diem regime has no political strength in the country worth mentioning to rely on. On the contrary, nearly all strata of the people oppose them. Therefore the U.S.-Diem government is not a strong government. It is only a vile and brutal government. Its vile and brutal character means that it not only has no mass base in the country but is on the way to being isolated internationally. Its cruelty definitely cannot shake the revolutionary movement, and it cannot survive for long.

The proof is that in the past two years, everywhere in the countryside, the sound of the gunfire of U.S.-Diem repression never ceased; not a day went by when they did not kill patriots. But the revolutionary spirit is still firm, and the revolutionary base of the people still has not been shaken.

Once the entire people have become determined to protect the revolution, there is no cruel force that can shake it.

But why has the revolutionary movement not yet developed strongly?

This is also due to certain objective and subjective factors. Objectively, we see that, after nine years of waging strong armed struggle, the people's movement generally speaking now has a temporarily peaceful character which is a factor in the change of the movement from violent forms of struggle to peaceful forms. It has the correct character of rebuilding in order to advance later.

With the cruel repression and exploitation of the U.S.-Diem, the people's revolutionary movement definitely will rise up. The people of the South have known the blood and fire of nine years of resistance war, but the cruelty of the U.S.-Diem cannot extinguish the struggle spirit of the people.

On the other hand, subjectively, we must admit that a large number of cadres, those have responsibility for guiding the revolutionary movement, because of the change in the method of struggle and the work situation from public to secret, have not yet firmly grasped the political line of the party, have not yet firmly grasped the method of political struggle, and have not yet followed correctly the mass line, and therefore have greatly reduced the movement's possibilities for development.

At present, therefore, the political struggle movement has not yet developed equally among the people, and a primary reason is that a number of cadres and masses are not yet aware that the strength of political forces of the people can defeat the cruelty, oppression and exploitation of the U.S.-Diem, and therefore they have a half-way attitude and don't believe in the strength of their political forces.

We must admit that any revolutionary movement has times when it falls and times when it rises; any revolutionary movement has times which are favorable for development and times which are unfavorable. The basic thing is that the cadres must see clearly the character of the movement's development in order to lead the mass struggle to the correct degree, and find a way for the vast determined masses to participate in the movement. If they are determined to struggle from the bottom to the top, no force can resist the determination of the great masses.

In the past two years, the political struggle movement in the countryside and in the cities, either by one form or another, has shown that the masses have much capacity for political struggle with the U.S.-Diem. In those struggles, if we grasp more firmly the struggle line and method, the movement can develop further, to the advantage of the revolution. The cruel policy of U.S.-Diem clearly cannot break the movement, or the people's will to struggle.

There are those who think that the U.S.-Diem's use of violence is now aimed fundamentally at killing the leaders of the revolutionary movement in order to destroy the Communist Party, and that if the Communist Party is worn away to the point that it doesn't have the capacity to lead the revolution, the political struggle movement of the masses cannot develop.

This judgment is incorrect. Those who lead the revolutionary movement are determined to mingle with the masses, to protect and serve the interests of the masses and to pursue correctly the mass line. Between the masses and Communists there is no distinction any more. So how can the U.S.-Diem destroy the leaders of the revolutionary movement, since they cannot destroy the masses? Therefore they cannot annihilate the cadres leading the mass movement.

In fact more than twenty years ago, the French imperialists were determined to destroy the Communists in order to destroy the revolutionary movement for national liberation, but the movement triumphed. It wasn't the Communists but the French imperialists themselves and their feudal lackeys who were destroyed on our soil.

Now twenty years later, U.S.-Diem are determined to destroy the Communists in the South, but the movement is still firm, and Communists are still determined to fulfill their duty. And the revolutionary movement will definitely advance and destroy the imperialist, feudalist government. U.S-Diem will be destroyed, just as the French imperialists and their feudal lackeys were destroyed.

We believe that: the peaceful line is appropriate not only to the general situation in the world but also to the situation within the country, both nation-wide and in the South. We believe that the will for peace and the peace forces of the people throughout the country have smashed the U.S.-Diem schemes of war provocation and division.

We believe that the will for peace and Southern people's democratic and peace forces will defeat the cruel, dictatorial and fascist policy of U.S.-Diem and will advance to smash the imperialist, feudalist U.S.-Diem government. Using love and righteousness to triumph over force is a tradition of the Vietnamese nation. The aspiration for peace is an aspiration of the world's people in general and in our own country, including the people of the South, so our struggle line cannot be separated from the peaceful line.

Only the peaceful struggle line can create strong political forces in order to defeat the scheme of war provocation and the cruel policy of U.S.-Diem.

We are determined to carry out our line correctly, and later the development of the situation will permit us to do so.

Imperialism and feudalism are on the road to disappearance.

The victory belongs to our people's glorious task of unification and independence, to our glorious Communism. . . . We believe that we will definitely be victorious.

1957

123. ARTICLE BY TRAN VAN GIAU
ON HANOI RADIO,
NOVEMBER 23, 1957 [Extract]

In 1956 and 1957, there were signs of growing discontent among both Communist Party members and former resistance fighters in the South. Hounded by Diem's security agents and unable to resist by armed force, many of them agitated for a change in the Party's line of "peaceful political struggle" in the South. Some took matters into their own hands and assassinated police officials and other representatives of the Diem government. (See Jeffrey Race, "The Origins of the Second Indochina War," Asian Survey, May 1950, p. 381; "Crimp Document," in U.S. Department of State, Captured Documents and Interrogation Reports, Washington, D.C., 1968.) The Party leadership was concerned enough about the pressure building in the South in favor of armed struggle that it had the former Chairman of the Committee of the South during the early days of the resistance to the French, Tran Van Giau, lecture Southerners on the dangers of premature and armed uprising. On the occasion of the 1940 Cochinchinese uprising, which had started without the approval of the Party Central Committee and was brutally suppressed by the French, Giau told his Southern compatriots who were eager to enter the phase of armed struggle that the contemporary situation paralleled that of 1940. The message was clear: armed struggle would have to wait for more propitious conditions.

Revolution is an art. The question is not the acquiring of a good reputation for the revolutionist; the question is the success of the revolution. Thus a revolt must be caused by an extraordinarily powerful force. Revolutionary uprisings must be rationally and fundamentally organized. Revolutionary uprisings must be guided scientifically.

We Easterners used to say: "We can kill a chicken with a knife used to cut areca nuts; but we cannot cut an areca nut with a knife used to kill chickens." As far

---

SOURCE: Hanoi, Voice of Vietnam, in Vietnamese to South Vietnam, November 23, 1957. Foreign Broadcast Information Service, Far East, December 2, 1957, pp. EEE5-EEE6.

as the problem we are discussing is concerned, this saying means that the method of organizing and leading an uprising during a colonialist period must be suitable to the organization and resistance of the enemy who is not unfamiliar with the science of domination. Moreover, this enemy has a powerful concentrated and rapid repressive machinery. Thus if an uprising is raised when the revolutionary force is not powerful enough or when the powerful revolutionary force is not well organized, correctly led, and closely united, this uprising cannot succeed. It cannot escape certain failure, and an abortive uprising will exert a bad influence, especially upon the revolutionary force itself.

To make a revolution means to lead the masses, not to follow them. Toward the end of 1940, many Vietnamese soldiers were led to the front to fight against the Siamese. Of course, they did not wish to die to defend the pockets of French colonialists. They preferred to die in Saigon in the struggle against the French colonialists than to die in Cambodian forests and mountains in a struggle for a bad cause.

Faced with this situation, the Saigon party chapter ordered an early uprising—before thousands of these compatriots were sent to the front—instead of guiding them to resort to suitable forms of antiwar resistance. Such antiwar struggles could have stimulated the patriotism of other soldiers throughout the country and that of their Cambodian and Laotian counterparts, could have pushed forward the antiFrench movement of the compatriots throughout the country and especially, could have created favorable conditions for the coming general uprising. To succeed, a revolution needs soldiers, but first, it needs the workers' and peasants' support.

Here we can draw a fundamental lesson: The skillfulness of the vanguard party does not consist in mobilizing and pushing forward a movement, but under definite circumstances, it consists in correctly—for the future of the movement—guiding it, that is, the party must steer it. If it is too windy, the captain must trim his sails so that the ship will not be upset. On a hillside, a driver must slow the speed of his car. In other words, one must contain oneself before a temporarily powerful enemy. All these are aimed at husbanding our strength and developing it in view of the final battle, the life or death struggle.

1958

124. LETTER FROM PHAM VAN DONG TO NGO DINH DIEM, MARCH 7, 1958 [Extract]

Beginning in 1957, North Vietnam made a series of public proposals to the Diem government for exchanges in the economic and cultural fields, as well as for reductions in military forces by both sides. In mid-1957, Pham Van Dong ini-

SOURCE: Hanoi, Vietnam News Agency, in English Morse to Southeast Asia, March 9, 1958, in Foreign Broadcast Information Service, Far East, March 10, 1958, pp. EEE1-EEE4.

tiated a series of letters to President Ngo Dinh Diem proposing discussions between the two zones on these matters. The letters, which blamed the impasse between the zones as well as the situation in the South on the United States, were extremely conciliatory toward Diem, but they were never answered.

The American policy of military reinforcement, together with economic grasp and political control, constitutes a very great danger to peace, an obstacle to the reunification of our country, and a cause of tension in Vietnam and in Southeast Asia. This American intervention is causing the gradual deterioration of the economy of South Vietnam which has been thrown into a deadlock, and is creating ever increasing difficulties in the daily life of the various strata of the population, in cities as well as in the countryside.

In my note of July 18, 1957, to the South Vietnam authorities, I pointed out that the American policy of intervention in the military, political, and economic fields was threatening peace in Vietnam and in Southeast Asia, seriously infringing upon the independence and sovereignty and injuring the national feelings of our compatriots in South Vietnam and impeding the reunification of the fatherland. Today the forces of peace are stronger than ever. The peace-loving peoples in the world are strengthening their unity and intensifying their struggle against war and for the preservation of peace. Fully conscious of the dangers created by the American policy of war and intervention, all our people from north to south demand that an end be put to any American interference in South Vietnam, that American military personnel be withdrawn from South Vietnam, that the expansion and building of military bases be stopped, and that South Vietnam not be enticed to participate in any manner whatsoever in a military alliance, in conformity with the spirit and letter of the Geneva agreements.

Our people's aspirations for peace and unity enjoy the sympathy and support of peace and justice-loving people the world over. The recent Cairo conference voiced the strong determination of hundreds of millions of Asian and African people to unite and struggle for national independence and world peace against the policy of intervention and war of the American imperialists.

The DRV Government has reduced its army by 80,000 men and cut its 1957 national defense budget.

To show our desire for peace and our earnest desire for the reunification of the country, in opposition to the American war policy, to insure peace and ease the people's contribution, a bilateral reduction of armed forces in the present situation would, in our opinion, be of great significance. To build up a prosperous economy as evidence of the independence and sovereignty of the country, and to improve the living standards of the people we reaffirm once again the necessity to restore and develop normal relations, initially to reestablish economic relations, between the two zones.

Consequently, on behalf of the DRV Government, I propose an early meeting of the competent authorities of the two zones to discuss the question of bilateral reduction of armed forces and find ways and means to promote trade exchanges between the two zones.

The above-mentioned practical measures will create favorable conditions for a rapprochement and mutual understanding between the two sides, thus paving the way for the consultative conference and free general elections with a view to reunifying the country.

We are firmly convinced that these proposals will be warmly welcomed by all our people and approved by the patriots in the South Vietnam administration and army.

We hope that, in the supreme interests of the fatherland, for the sake of the legitimate aspirations of all strata of the population in both zones, and for the sake of world peace, the South Vietnam authorities will make the necessary efforts and put forward constructive views concerning our above-mentioned proposals.

Hoping to receive an early reply from the govenment of the Republic of Vietnam, I ask you, sir, to accept the assurances of my high consideration.

125. LAO DONG PARTY DIRECTIVE FOR THE SOUTH: "SITUATION AND TASKS FOR 1959," LATE 1958 [Extracts]

1958 was the most difficult postwar year for the revolution in the South. The repression by the Diem government of Party bases was heavier and more successful than in previous years, according to the Party's own assessment. The pressure within the Party for a change of line to protect the political assets still remaining in the South was growing stronger. Nevertheless, the Party leadership was not yet ready by the end of 1958 to overhaul its Southern policy. Its annual directive for the South, analyzing the Party's missions for 1959, conceded that the losses to Diem's repression were "significant" and heavier than in previous years, and forecast more of the same in the future. But it argued that the Party Section in the South was not only surviving but was still developing, and that the tasks of the Party were still the same: to continue demanding living rights and democratic rights as well as establishment of normal relations between the two zones. The document notes that the severity of repression had caused some party members to carry out "individual assassination" and to begin working for armed struggle and "general uprising— tendencies which were condemned as deviations.

3) Because the enemy is determined to strengthen the apparatus of repression and war provocation by increasing its forces and its reactionary character in a number of villages and to use that apparatus to attack us, and because the people's movement under the leadership of our Party is not yet strong enough to hold back their bloody hand, during the past period, the enemy has caused heavier losses for our Party and people's movement than in previous years. They have carried out their schemes to a relatively greater degree, especially in plundering sweeps, despite the fact that the struggle movement of the people opposing them is more advanced than in previous years.

4) However, the deeper it goes into its country-stealing and country-selling scheme, the more difficulties and obstacles U.S-Vietnam meets every day, and the more it is impaled on the life and death contradictions between it and the people and on their own internal contradictions.

* * *

SOURCE: "Tinh Hinh va Nhiem Vu 59" document captured in July 1959. Number 1025 in Race Collection. [Translation by the editor.]

7) The Path and line of struggle of the Party in the South has been relatively understood from the top to the bottom. Liaison has been relatively healthy and improved. Party cells have been consolidated in a relatively well-rounded manner, and there is more of a spirit of secrecy. The quality and quantity of the Party action has been strengthened, the organization of the Party section is relatively more stable and solid. Because of that, despite the enemy's cruel terror and repression (which has caused the Party a significant number of losses) our Party section still survives, is strengthened and developing, and is leading the masses' struggle on to many accomplishments.

—That is a fundamental defeat for the enemy. It is an accomplishment, and a fundamental strongpoint of our Party section.

—However, our advance is only a first step. We have been guilty of many deficiencies and mistakes, and we must do everything to correct them in order to have enough strength to lead the struggle movement of the masses to develop with each passing day.

—A considerable number of Party members do not yet truly understand and believe in the political struggle line of the Party, have not yet firmly held the line of longterm, difficult, but definitely victorious struggle of the South; do not yet believe in the forces of the masses; have not yet earnestly paid attention to the life, the needs and the aspirations of the masses, and have not yet relied completely on the masses and led the masses to struggle to fight the enemy.

—The widespread, dominant ideological error in the Party section is: a rightist desire for peace, due to assessing the enemy too highly and ourselves too low, and due to standpoints whose preparation has not been thorough. It is shown in the struggle movement every day in the tendency toward reformism, not daring to mobilize the masses to struggle or going over to individual assassination, punishing traitors in a disorderly manner, expecting armed uprising or attacking the enemy carelessly, and lacking determination to overcome difficulties and hardships in their work. There is also leftist deviation, of devoting all the forces to armed struggle and general uprising (Tay Ninh).

* * *

II. Tasks for 59 (Three immediate tasks)

We have analyzed the comparison of forces between us and the enemy during the recent period and at present. In the next period, how will the comparison of forces develop?

The U.S.-Diem government losses in the comparison of forces in the world and in the country will change more unfavorably for them every day (this will be discussed when we study it).

That situation creates contradictions between the U.S.-Diem government and people's strata in the South which are constantly deepening, creating favorable conditions for the revolutionary struggle movement to become stronger and broader every day and to cause the internal contradictions of the enemy, created by the dictatorial, fascist, family-ruled U.S. colony to further increase every day. Given their natural decline, U.S.-Diem will definitely step up their country-stealing and country-selling policies which were described above.

Having no further doubts, U.S.-Diem will do everything possible to terrorize, repress the masses' movement and our Party section more violently, hoping to save their situation of isolation and decline.

Therefore, they will still create many difficulties for us, and they will be able to achieve a certain part of their schemes. Our Party section must see ahead and try to overcome them in order to guide the mass movement steadily forward to hinder the enemy.

Based on the above situation between the enemy and ourselves now and the changes about to take place, we can see that the three immediate tasks of the Party put forward by the District conference from 1957 to now are fundamentally still appropriate. The tasks have not changed, but the forms and the level of the struggle movement in the near future must be broader, stronger, and more decisive.

1960

126. ARTICLE IN A LAO DONG PARTY INTERNAL JOURNAL IN THE SOUTH, FEBRUARY 1960 [Extracts]

Although the Party leadership had decided in January 1959 to authorize the use of armed force in the South, the policy was still far from being one of overthrowing the Saigon government by waging guerrilla warfare, as was assumed in Washington. The new policy, which began to reach the local level in late 1959, permitted the use of armed forces only in support of political struggle and not for the purpose of militarily defeating Saigon. As this article in an internal Party organ in the South made clear, armed struggle under the new line was very different from guerrilla warfare, much less the mobile warfare of the anti-French resistance. The policy was based on the idea that the Diem regime could ultimately be toppled by political means, through a "general uprising" which would avoid the necessity for full-scale war. Indeed, the Party was ready, as indicated in this article, to take advantage of whatever possibility existed to negotiate an agreement with Diem on the proposals previously made by the DRV.

The above situation puts before the entire Party and people the task of actively preparing in all spheres for the general uprising to seize political power. That is the only correct way; there is no other way. But the general uprising to seize political power is a path which must be prepared for a long time, for which we must accumulate our forces, preserve them, consolidate and develop them, create the

SOURCE: "Muc Tieu Phan Dau cua Toan Dang va Toan Dan ta Hien Nay" [The Struggle objective of the entire party and people at present], *Hoc Tap* (South Viet-nam), No. 1 February 1960 and No. 2, May 25, 1960. Document No. 1038 in the Race Collection [Translation by the editor].

opportune moment and seize it well to act, and determinedly avoid being either premature or passive, waiting for something to happen.

How must we conceive the path of general uprising to seize political power?

The path of general uprising to seize political power is the path of long-term political struggle combined with armed struggle. Because purely political struggle or purely armed struggle are equally incapable of achieving the objective and line of general uprising to seize political power. Therefore political struggle must be combined with armed struggle. Political struggle and armed struggle must advance side by side. But political struggle must still be fundamental and primary. Armed struggle is aimed at serving the political struggle, at guiding the political struggle movement of the masses forward, helping the struggle movement of the workers and the poor strata in the cities, and the struggle movement of the peasants and other strata and classes. At the same time, it aims chiefly at building the political forces of the working class peasants and poor urban strata to become political forces making the enemy weaker everyday and making him suffer defeats and becoming decisive political forces during the general uprising to seize political power.

During the process of preparing to advance according to the objective and line of general uprising to seize political power, what possibilities could develop which we must see in order to know how to use them and to guard against them?

The process of advancing to achieve the objective and line of general uprising to seize political power is a process taking political struggle as primary, and is a process of political, economic, and cultural struggle combined with armed struggle. So the political forces and power of the Party and the masses will rise and the power of the enemy will diminish with each day. In that process, the situation becomes complex, and two possibilities may develop as follows:

First: a peaceful possibility could develop. Although this possibility is small, our party does not reject it but must know how to use it. The strength of the struggle of the people could force U.S.-Diem into circumstances in which they are forced to carry out a number of conditions in our government's diplomatic note, acquiescing in economic, cultural, and postal exchanges and travel, etc. We must know how to use that possibility, and must not cause the masses to stray from the objective and line of the general uprising to seize political power.

Second: the possibility of long-term armed struggle could also develop if our leadership and guidance leans in the direction of arms and defending a base area but not stretching out, not paying attention to helping the political struggle movement in the cities and the countryside rise and not building the political forces of the workers, poor urban strata, peasants and other classes. In those circumstances, we cannot have a strong political force in order to make the enemy weak and make him suffer defeats and cannot be determined to seize political power when there is an opportune moment for the general uprising.

But on the other hand, the possibility of long-term armed struggle could develop due to the bellicose, insane nature of American imperialism. If it were to jump in and intervene directly with military force, the situation would finally become a long-term struggle between our people and imperialism. But the final victory would be ours. However, we must also assess correctly the possibility of intervention by the U.S. imperialists, which is very limited at present.

We must see all the above mentioned possibilities, in order to conduct the revolutionary struggle correctly toward the objective and line we have fixed, in order to use to the correct degree the possibility of peace and also in order to vigilantly prepare to take the initiative and deal with the enemy.

The situation in the world and in the country changes daily to the advantage of the revolution and unfavorably for the enemy. There are many opportunities, as well as many difficulties. But under the leadership of the party, we must be more determined, overcome difficulties, correct weaknesses and mistakes and develop strong points to make every effort to correctly execute the direction, line and policy of the party. In this way we will definitely change the situation for the better, obstruct and push the enemy's schemes back step by step, and advance to overturning the entire U.S.-Diem scheme and structure in order to complete the revolutionary task before us.

*   *   *

How must we conceive of the armed struggle?

The concept of armed struggle at present is in accordance with the line of general uprising to seize political power and not armed struggle as during the period of resistance war in which we took the countryside to surround the cities and finally liberated cities. Armed struggle at the present time is not guerrilla war, nor is it protracted interzonal warfare, fighting for a liberated area and to establish a government as during the resistance period.

Armed struggle at the present time means the whole people armed for self-defense and propaganda. If we wish to achieve the objective of the whole people armed and propagandizing, we must rely on the political forces of the masses, rely on the organized masses and on that basis arm the masses, with the main factor being arms for the people. The people must get their own arms, in order to defend themselves, oppose and annihilate puppet personnel, militia, security agents, spies, and cruel and stubborn landlords in order to protect their rights and their homes, preserve the country and keep their own land. They must not passively sit and wait but must stand up and liberate themselves. But on the other hand, the people must also have armed self-defense units in order to join with the people and help them destroy the stubborn and cruel group within the government and army of U.S.-Diem and, with the forces of the entire people, make the U.S-Diem army disintegrate in terms of morale and organization.

The task and requirement of armed self-defense activity is to serve the interests of the political struggle. But on the other hand, the political struggle also has the significance and objective of guarding and pushing forward the armed struggle. But the main task and requirement of the armed struggle is to serve the political struggle, to build, assemble, organize and develop the political forces of workers, peasants, and other classes. On the other hand, the armed struggle must also aim at destroying security agents, spies, militia, puppet officials, cruel and stubborn landlords, reducing the influence of the enemy, causing the enemy to shrink, clearing out and destroying concentration centers of the enemy, raising high the political influence of the Party and masses, and maintaining the long-term legal position of the masses.

To a certain degree and in a certain number of localities, our armed forces must also oppose the mop-up and terror operations of the enemy and when necessary thrust deep to fight battles and carry out armed propaganda to affect the morale of the enemy in order to advance the political struggle of the masses in the rural area and the cities, creating favorable conditions to promote more strongly the building, assembling and organizing of the political forces of the masses.

The line of operation of the armed forces is that they must assemble and disperse quickly, be lively, secret, quick, hide and not show off, not make the enemy vigilant, take precautions against commandoes, avoid attrition, know how to consolidate and develop the armed forces in accordance with the possibilities of each locality, and avoid negligence.

Speaking generally, only when we have built the political forces and led the political struggle movement of the working class and urban poor and the political struggle movement of the peasants in the rural area with the vast majority of the population can we protect, strengthen, and develop the armed forces and push the armed struggle movement forward. On the contrary, only by pushing armed force and coordinating it correctly can we conduct the political struggle movement forward.

127. TELEGRAM FROM AMBASSADOR ELDRIDGE DURBROW IN SAIGON TO SECRETARY OF STATE CHRISTIAN A. HERTER, MARCH 7, 1960

By the beginning of 1960, the deterioration of security in South Vietnam had convinced U.S. and South Vietnamese officials that the "Viet Cong", as the Communist-led foes of Diem were now called, were going to mount a general guerrilla war against the Diem regime. The Embassy's first assessment of the problem put most of the emphasis on the "signs of considerable dissatisfaction and silent opposition" to the government because of coercion, involuntary labor, extortion, and corruption, among other government practices. The Embassy's effort to explain why the armed struggle had begun ranged from Chinese pressures to the Communist failure to disrupt the August 1959 National Assembly election, but failed to mention pressures from Party members and resistance fighters to respond to the Diemist repression against them.

Enclosed is a special report prepared by a Country Team study group on the current internal security situation in Viet-Nam. A summary of this report and an analysis of the main factors in Viet-Nam's current serious internal security problem are given below:

Situation. Internal security, which improved greatly since the nip and tuck period from 1954–56 but which nevertheless has been a steady concern of the GVN over the past few years, has again become its No. 1 problem as a result of intensification of Viet Cong guerrilla and terrorist activities, weaknesses apparent in the GVN security forces and the growth of apathy and considerable dissatisfaction among the rural populace. The situation has grown progressively more disturbing since shortly after the National Assembly elections at the end of August 1959, despite the fact that President DIEM was claiming, up to the end of December, that internal security was continuing to improve. The monthly rate of assassinations

SOURCE: *U.S.-Vietnam Relations*, Book 10, pp. 1254–1257.

rose substantially starting in September, and other signs of increasingly aggressive VC tactics such as ambushes of GVN security forces began to appear about the same time. The full impact of the seriousness of the present situation was brought home by a series of VC incidents in late January and February, particularly an attack on an ARVN regimental post near Tay Ninh, other smaller and less dramatic attacks on security posts elsewhere in the southwest and serious VC depredations in Kien Hoa Province.

President Diem and other GVN officials are now showing a reassuring awareness of the gravity of the situation. They have not permitted themselves to become panic-stricken, and there is no reason to become alarmist if prompt steps are taken to correct the situation.

VC Intentions and Potential. Indications are growing that the VC are mounting a special campaign aimed at undermining the Diem Government. According to CAS [Controlled American Source, a term used for the Central Intelligence Agency] sources, VC armed cadre strength has increased to about 3,000 in the southwest, double the number in September. VC groups now operate in larger strength, and their tactics have changed from attacks on individuals to rather frequent and daring attacks on GVN security forces. A recent CAS report has indicated a VC intention to press general guerrilla warfare in South Viet-Nam in 1960, and indicates the VC are convinced they can mount a coup d'état this year. President Diem also told me in late February about the capture of a VC document indicating their intention to step up aggressive attacks all over the country, including Saigon, beginning in the second quarter.

These signs indicate that aggressively worded statements emanating from the DRV in 1959 may accurately reflect DRV intentions. In May 1959 the central committee of the Lao'Dong Party passed a resolution stating that the struggle for reunification of Viet-Nam should be carried out by all "appropriate means". Subsequently in conversations with Western officials, Prime Minister Phan Van Dong made statements to the effect that "We will be in Saigon tomorrow" and "We will drive the Americans into the sea".

It is not completely clear why the DRV has chosen this particular time to mount an intensified guerrilla campaign in South Viet-Nam. Several hypotheses have been put forward. The campaign may be part of general Chicom strategy to increase pressure on non-communist countries all along the southern rim of the Asian communist bloc. Several GVN officials, including President Diem, have said that the present DRV tactics may be related to the forthcoming East-West summit meeting, but they do not seem to be clear as to just what this relationship might be. Diem and others have also expressed the view that the DRV is aiming at disruption of the GVN's economic, social and security programs, many of which have been making steady progress while others, like the agroville program, threaten to weaken the VC position if carried out successfully. The DRV may also have been embittered by its failure to interfere successfully with the GVN National Assembly elections last August and resolved, as a result of this failure, to intensify activities in the South.

.GVN Security and Political Weaknesses. At the same time that the DRV guerrilla potential has increased in the South, weaknesses have become more appar-

ent in the GVN security forces. GVN leaders have in recent weeks stressed the need for more anti-guerrilla training of ARVN. The desirability of centralized command in insecure areas and a centralized intelligence service has also become more evident. The need for a capable, well-equipped, well-trained, centrally-controlled Civil Guard is even more keenly felt than previously.

Likewise, at the same time, signs of general apathy and considerable dissatisfaction which the VC can play upon have become more evident among the people in rural areas. Fear among the peasants engendered by sustained VC terrorist activities against which the GVN has not succeeded in protecting them is combined with resentment of the GVN because of the methods which are all too often employed by local officials. Coercion rather than suasion are often used by these officials in carrying out the programs decided upon in Saigon. There is a tendency to disregard the desires and feelings of the peasantry by, for instance, taking them away from their harvests to perform community work. The new agroville program requiring large numbers of "volunteer" laborers has accentuated this trend. Improper actions by local officials such as torture, extortion and corruption, many of which have been reported in the press, have also contributed to peasant dissatisfaction. Favoritism and fear of officials and members of the semi-covert Can Lao Party have likewise contributed to this situation.

Diem cannot be completely absolved of blame for this unsatisfactory situation in the rural areas. Considerable evidence has existed that he has not in the past kept himself properly informed of what is going on. Officials have tended to tell him what he wants to hear, largely because of fear of removal if they indicate that mistakes have been made or reply that projects which he is pushing should not be carried out as rapidly as he desires.

GVN Counteractions. Developments during the last month or so have, however, awakened Diem and other officials to the gravity of the present internal security and political situation. As already indicated, they are now emphasizing the need for increased anti-guerrilla training of the security forces. Diem also has indicated that he is establishing a special commando force with "volunteers" from ARVN, the Civil Guard and reservists who had guerrilla experience during the Indochina war. Diem has also stated that the new commander of the Fifth Military Region (the area of greatest insecurity) has been given full powers over all the security forces in that area, thus recognizing the need for centralized command rather than fragmentation of authority among the province chiefs.

Diem has also indicated that he is replacing local officials who are incompetent or have abused their power. He is placing renewed emphasis with these officials on the necessity of winning the confidence of the people and explaining to them the reasons for the government's programs. He has also indicated that he has ordered a slowdown in the construction of agrovilles, apparently in recognition of the indications that the people were being driven too hard to carry out this new program.

The Embassy's views on these countermeasures of the GVN as well as on certain other actions which should be taken have been expressed in a separate dispatch. As the situation develops, the Embassy expects to make additional recommendations.

128. LETTER FROM THE PARTY COMMITTEE FOR SOUTH VIETNAM TO PARTY CHAPTERS, MARCH 28, 1960 [Extracts]

When province, district and village Party officials in the South began to apply the new line of the Party, they tended to view it as an authorization for ridding themselves of the local Diem government organs and openly seizing power in the villages. A letter from the regional Party Committee after the first few months of implementation of the new line indicated that Party leaders were unhappy with what had developed. It complained that local Party organs were "getting into rash adventures," which it defined as any activities which resulted in "destroying the legal status of the population" vis-à-vis the Diem government. The Committee had to explain that the revolutionary movement had "not yet reached the period of direct overthrow of the American-Diem government," and reminded the Party branches that armed force was to be used only as an auxiliary to political struggle.

Dear comrades!

There have been new developments in the general situation in the South which are very favorable to us. Our [central] Party Headquarters have approved the principle of "strongly pushing the political struggle forward, and combining it to the right degree with armed propaganda activities" in order to obtain good results.

In this letter, the Committee of the South, along with you, will review the past and present situation, and discuss with you the direction and method to increase our successes and correct our errors in order to push the movement one step forward.

I. *In the past, we have scored a number of achievements right at the beginning.*

Compared with the previous period of time, the people's struggle movement in some areas [to implement] the vital slogans relating to democracy and their livelihood—such as opposition to forced labor, exploitation, agrovilles, seizure of land and terrorism, opposition to the enemy's forcing the people to join reactionary organizations—in the two months at the end of 1959 and the first month of 1960, has developed more strongly than before.

In many areas in the countryside the people have destroyed the tight grip of the enemy and obtained definite successes with regard to democracy and other vital economic rights and interests.

In a number of areas where, in the past, the movement either did not exist or was very weak, many struggles have taken place, some of which were quite fierce.

In some instances, the Party Headquarters succeeded in gathering large numbers of people—sometimes in the thousands—to take part in such struggles.

In the cities and on rubber plantations, the movement has also begun to step up—especially the movement of the high school and university students in Saigon, and that of the workers in the rubber plantations in Eastern Nam Bo.

These achievements, scored right at the beginning, were due to the fact that

SOURCE: Captured Party document. Race Collection Document No. 1044. Translated by Mai Van Elliott.

we had implemented correctly the resolutions and directives of Central and the Resolution of the Fourth Nam Bo Conference (October 1959), and also to our comrades' unceasing efforts, enthusiasm and determination to carry out their tasks; ever since they studied the Resolution of the Fourth Nam Bo Conference, and once the struggle spirit within the Party Headquarters began to develop strongly, these comrades—through their own initiatives—have solved many of the difficulties of the past and successfully implemented the policies of the Party. Even though these are only successes achieved in the first phase, they form a favorable foundation for our Party Headquarters to march forward and fulfill their responsibilities toward the Party and toward the people.

*   *   *

II. *However, in the past, a number of our Party Headquarters have committed a number of errors, some of which are very serious.*

Along with the achievements scored in the first phase, mentioned above, a number of Party Headquarters have committed errors, some of which are critical.

With regard to the implementation [of policies], the most critical error concerns the self-defense armed forces in a number of areas which did not implement correctly the lines of the Party, whose attacks spilled on to targets that were not the most vital, and which have punished a number of elements that we do not, as yet, have to punish. They have also warned and threatened village officials and spies in an indiscriminate manner.

In a number of areas, the leading organs have gone as far as getting into rash adventures: dissolving [local] administrative machinery, guiding the people to tear up their ID Cards, pushing a number to commit provocative actions, such as taking over posts, setting fire to village offices, cutting down trees, digging up roads, setting up obstacles, etc.—generally speaking, thereby destroying the legal status of the people [vis-à-vis the enemy government].

There are areas where orders were issued forbidding boats and cars to pass through, forbidding rice mills belonging to the capitalists to operate, forcing the people to mill their own rice, etc., thus hindering the work of the people.

From the point of view of organization, a number of Party Headquarters failed to see that the general situation is very favorable for the consolidation and expansion of the Party at the grass root level, of the Labor Youth Group and of the people's movement; they have not come up with any plans to further their mission and to consolidate and build up the organization at the grass root level in an urgent manner. On the contrary, many Party and Labor Youth members in many grass root organizations who had been operating clandestinely before, rushed out to operate openly and thus seriously exposed themselves. At present, many Party Headquarters concentrated too heavily on conducting meetings and developing the Party Chapters in an open manner—they have either neglected or have not given proper consideration to the task of consolidating and developing the Party Chapters in a secret manner.

With regard to the policy concerning the front, a number of our comrades have failed to implement the policy and strategy of the Party correctly. In some areas, the term "traitors" was given too broad a definition and made to include even those who, to make a living, have had to work for the enemy. In some areas, no distinction was made in the treatment of the landlords, and all the landlords were lumped together as direct enemies of the revolution, without due regard to their political stand, and without distinguishing cruel landlords from other landlords.

With regard to the enemy soldiers, these comrades did not pay enough attention to propagandizing them about our policy—instead they relied too much on threats, and thereby frightened these soldiers. These comrades have failed to see the need for us to win the sympathy of these soldiers, to isolate the reactionaries, sow dissension to a high degree within the ranks of the government of the South, and direct [our strength] against the Americans and Diem. To the point that, in the areas where former local officials, spies and reactionaries—frightened by the present situation—went looking for our comrades to beg forgiveness, our comrades and the people either were indifferent and did not try to win them over to our side, or drove them away.

At present, generally speaking many areas are concentrating too heavily on building up and organizing armed self-defense, and on directing armed activities, and are neglecting the task of pushing ahead and leading the political struggle movement of the people.

The errors and shortcomings mentioned above had led to the following unfavorable situation:

The masses are enthusiastic, but since they do not understand clearly the policy of the Party, they think that the time has come to launch the insurrection, and they therefore have become impatient and extremely adventurous. In a number of areas, the people have stopped all their work, and seem to be waiting.

At the same time, a number of people are still worried and wonder what the situation will be like. They are particularly afraid that the enemy will take revenge and terrorize them. This is why a number of people have moved to the market areas or withdrawn deep into our base areas.

The reactionaries within the government have toned down a bit, but generally speaking the soldiers, local officials and civil servants do not understand our policy yet, and therefore are confused and frightened. In this state of mind, they are easily deceived by the plots and schemes of the enemy.

This situation has somewhat diminished the favorable effect [of the situation] for the movement, and created difficulties for a number of Party Headquarters.

*   *   *

At present, we are in contention with the enemy, and we have not yet reached the stage of direct revolution, that is to say, we have not yet reached the period of direct overthrow of the American-Diem government in order to put government in the hands of the people. In this period of contention, we should do our utmost to build up, preserve, and expand our grass root organizations. Generally speaking, we should maintain the people's movement under legal cover. We cannot as yet wipe out the enemy government machinery; we can only chip it and damage it, etc. We are doing our utmost to push our struggle movement strongly forward to evolve from the contention phase to the direct revolution phase. In order to do so, we need time.

If we disregard the balance of forces, if we are impatient and want to proceed immediately to general insurrection, then we will commit a foolhardy and adventurous error which can lead to premature violence and will lead us to a very dangerous and vulnerable position.

What should we do to cope with such a situation?

1)—First of all, we should reaffirm that in the present phase, we do not advocate disbanding the local officials or stamping out the local government machinery. At present, the main thing is to damage the local government machinery (that is to say, to prevent it from implementing successfully the policy of the enemy, to crush the power and prestige of the local officials, to restrict their capacity to oppress the people, eliminate tyrannical elements from the local government machinery, and try to win over the uncommitted elements), to "chip" the local machinery (that is to say, to damage it, to make it short of personnel so that it cannot cover the entire village, so that it has enough personnel to cover only a few hamlets in the village or to staff a few branches within the local administration only).

However, in the areas where there are no local officials left—either because we have disbanded the local officials or because these officials themselves have fled elsewhere—*we do not advocate calling them back to the villages, or asking the district and province officials to re-establish a government machinery there*. Our requirement is to struggle and have a contention with the enemy.

129. CABLEGRAM FROM DURBROW TO HERTER, DECEMBER 24, 1960 [Extract]

In October 1960, U.S. Ambassador Durbrow, viewing the threat to the Diem regime as "quite serious," got State Department approval for presenting Diem with a memorandum urging political and administrative reforms. On November 11, younger army officers staged a coup against Diem that nearly succeeded. Diem and Nhu were deeply suspicious of the United States because it had supported a peaceful settlement. In another meeting with Durbrow about proposed reforms, Diem was more openly hostile to the thrust of the U.S. suggestions. Durbrow reported his impression that Diem was still thinking of using force as the primary means of saving his regime.

On a few occasions he let me talk, I urged he adopt reforms soonest since it essential to win further support of the people if Viet Cong menace is to be overcome, but he gave me no indication of reforms he may adopt. Before leaving I again expressed hope that he would accept our suggestion that he announce all liberalizing programs at one time in order to make best impact. Diem replied he would think about this but made no commitment.

Comments. We have heard that Nhu, Thuan and others have been running into resistance when urging Diem to adopt worthwhile reforms. I also received impression he very reluctant to adopt reforms and is still basically thinking in terms of force to save the day, hence his insistence several times that we approve force level increase and his action raising Civil Guard ceiling by 10,000. While I still believe it absolutely essential he adopt more liberal programs, it is not certain from his attitude and remarks that he will take effective action in these matters, although I learned later he has agreed to engage the services of a public relations expert suggested by CAS to make a survey GVN foreign public relations needs.

SOURCE: *U.S.-Vietnam Relations*, Book 10, pp. 1348–1351.

130. MANIFESTO OF THE SOUTH VIET NAM NATIONAL FRONT FOR LIBERATION, DECEMBER 1960 [Extract]

The National Liberation Front of South Vietnam, established in December 1960 in accordance with the Party's policy announced at the Third Party Congress, was aimed primarily at attracting those social and political elements not already aligned with the revolution in the South: intellectuals, businessmen, notables, students, and personnel of the Saigon army. As its moderate manifesto suggests, it represented a vehicle for an alliance between the revolutionaries and more conservative opponents of the Diem regime.

*   *   *

At present, our people are urgently demanding an end to the cruel dictatorial rule; they are demanding independence and democracy, enough food and clothing, and peaceful reunification of the country.

To meet the aspirations of our compatriots, the *South Viet Nam National Front for Liberation* came into being, pledging itself to shoulder the historic task of liberating our people from the present yoke of slavery.

The *South Viet Nam National Front for Liberation* undertakes to unite all sections of the people, all social classes, nationalities, political parties, organizations, religious communities and patriotic personalities, without distinction of their political tendencies, in order to struggle for the overthrow of the rule of the US imperialists and their stooges—the Ngo Dinh Diem clique—and for the realization of independence, democracy, peace and neutrality pending the peaceful reunification of the fatherland.

The *South Viet Nam National Front for Liberation* calls on the entire people to unite and heroically rise up as one man to fight along the line of a program of action summarized as follows:

1. To overthrow the disguised colonial regime of the US imperialists and the dictatorial Ngo Dinh Diem administration—lackey of the United States—, and to form a national democratic coalition administration.

2. To bring into being a broad and progressive democracy, promulgate freedom of expression, of the press, of belief, of assembly, of association, of movement and other democratic freedoms. To grant general amnesty to all political detainees, dissolve all concentration camps dubbed "prosperity zones" and "resettlement centres", abolish the fascist 10-59 law and other anti-democratic laws.

3. To abolish the economic monopoly of the United States and its henchmen, to protect home-made products, encourage home industry and trade, expand agriculture and build an independent and sovereign economy. To provide jobs for the unemployed, increase wages for workers, armymen and office employees. To

SOURCE: *Vietnamese Studies* (Hanoi), No. 23 "South Vietnam From the N.F.L. to the Provisional Revolutionary Government," pp. 247–254.

abolish arbitrary fines and apply an equitable and rational tax system. To help those who have gone South to return to their native places if they so desire, and to provide jobs for those among them who want to remain in the South.

4. To carry out land rent reduction, guarantee the peasants' right to till present plots of land, redistribute communal land and advance toward land reform.

1961

131. MESSAGE FROM THE JOINT CHIEFS OF STAFF TO COMMANDER IN CHIEF, PACIFIC FORCES, ADMIRAL HARRY D. FELT, APRIL 26, 1961

In the opening months of the presidency of John F. Kennedy the United States was preoccupied with Laos, where the United States-supported regime was suffering serious military reverses at the hands of a neutralist-Communist coalition. Despite the signs that the Laotian crisis was moving to the conference table, Kennedy met with the National Security Council on April 26 to discuss the question of sending troops to Laos. Later that night the Joint Chiefs of Staff informed Admiral Felt, Commander of Pacific Forces, that the U.S.-backed Royal Lao Government (RLG) might request intevention by SEATO if a cease-fire was not quickly achieved. The message ordered him to prepare for possible bombing in North Vietnam and China if that became necessary in the event of a SEATO intervention. One paragraph of this document remains classified by the Joint Chiefs.

1. Situation in Laos has become exceedingly grave. USG is conferring with British and French Governments now, initially to obtain their ideas on what should now be done and to support a possible RLG request to UN for an immediate cease fire. British and French Governments may subsequently be requested to sympathetically support a request from RLG for intervention by SEATO within 48 hours if an effective cease fire is not quickly obtained. JCS approve prepositioning moves directed in your 262130Z.

2. CINCPAC is directed to: *officially deleted.*

3. In view of Red Chinese threat, be prepared to stop Red Chinese intervention, including strikes on intermediate bases in North Vietnam and, if necessary, strikes on bases in Red China which support their operations against Laos.

4. Unified and specified commanders, other than CINCPAC, are not expected to raise DEFCONS by virtue of this message. It is important that every effort be taken to avoid public discussion.

SOURCE: Document declassified by Department of Defense, April 21, 1978.

132. REPORT OF THE GILPATRICK TASK FORCE, APRIL 27, 1961 [Extract]

Kennedy requested an appraisal of the Communist insurgency in South Vietnam and recommendations for actions to counter it, to be delivered within a week. The report of the interagency task force, headed by Under Secretary of Defense Roswell Gilpatric recommended a modest increase in the American military advisory mission and financial support for the two-hundred-thousand-man increase in the South Vietnamese army and for the Civil Guard and Self-Defense Corps. More important, however, as an indication of the mood within the bureaucracy, was the report's suggestion that there was a Communist "master plan" to "take over all of Southeast Asia," and its call for the United States to indicate to both friends and foes that it intended to "win" the "countersurgency" war in South Vietnam.

After meeting in Hanoi on 13 May 1959, the Central Committee of the North Vietnamese Communist Party publicly announced its intention "to smash" the government of President Diem. Following this decision, the Viet Cong have significantly increased their program of infiltration, subversion, sabotage and assassination designed to achieve this end.

At the North Vietnamese Communist Party Congress in September 1960, the earlier declaration of underground war by the Party's Control Committee was reaffirmed. This action by the Party Congress took place only a month after Kong Le's coup in Laos. Scarcely two months later there was a military uprising in Saigon. The turmoil created throughout the area by this rapid succession of events provides an ideal environment for the Communist "master plan" to take over all of Southeast Asia.

Since that time, the internal security situation in South Vietnam has become critical. What amounts to a state of active guerrilla warfare now exists throughout the country. The number of Viet Cong hard-core Communists has increased from 4400 in early 1960 to an estimated 12,000 today. The number of violent incidents per month now averages 650. Casualties on both sides totaled more than 4500 during the first three months of this year. Fifty-eight percent of the country is under some degree of Communist control, ranging from harassment and night raids to almost complete administrative jurisdiction in the Communist "secure areas."

The Viet Cong over the past two years have succeeded in stepping up the pace and intensity of their attacks to the point where South Vietnam is nearing the decisive phase in its battle for survival. If the situation continues to deteriorate, the Communists will be able to press on to their strategic goal of establishing a rival "National Liberation Front" government in one of these "secure areas" thereby plunging the nation into open civil war. They have publicly announced that they will "take over the country before the end of 1961."

This situation is thus critical, but is not hopeless. The Vietnamese Government, with American aid, has increased its capabilities to fight its attackers, and provides a base upon which the necessary additional effort can be founded to defeat the Communist attack. Should the Communist effort increase, either directly or as a result of a collapse of Laos, additional measures beyond those proposed herein would be necessary.

SOURCE: *United States*–Vietnam Relations, Book 2, IV. B. 1, pp. 25–27.

In short, the situation in South Vietnam has reached the point where, at least for the time being, primary emphasis should be placed on providing a solution to the internal security problem.

The US Objective: To create a viable and increasingly democratic society in South Vietnam and to prevent Communist domination of the country.

Concept of Operations: To initiate on an accelerated basis, a series of mutually supporting actions of a military, political economic, psychological and covert character designed to achieve this objective. In so doing, it is intended to use, and where appropriate extend, expedite or build upon the existing US and Government of Vietnam (GVN) programs already underway in South Vietnam. There is neither the time available nor any sound justification for "starting from scratch." Rather the need is to focus the US effort in South Vietnam on the immediate internal security problem; to infuse it with a sense of urgency and a dedication to the overall US objective; to achieve, through cooperative inter-departmental support both in the field and in Washington, the operational flexibility needed to apply the available US assets in a manner best calculated to achieve our objective in Vietnam; and, finally, to impress on our friends, the Vietnamese, and on our foes, the Viet Cong, that come what may, the US intends to *win* this battle.

133. MEMORANDUM OF CONVERSATION INVOLVING SECRETARY OF STATE DEAN RUSK, SECRETARY OF DEFENSE ROBERT MCNAMARA, THE JOINT CHIEFS OF STAFF AND OTHER OFFICIALS, APRIL 29, 1961 [Extracts]

On April 29, the issue of sending American troops to Laos was still the subject of high-level discussions. Key policy-makers from State, Defense, and the Joint Chiefs met in an atmosphere of acute crisis. There was general agreement among the officials that if the United States did not intervene in Laos, it would certainly have to fight in either Thailand or South Vietnam, or attack North Vietnam. Defense Secretary McNamara appeared to prefer to take a stand in Thailand and South Vietnam rather than in Laos, but Rusk was worried that the loss of Laos would cause irreparable damage to the U.S. reputation for power. Air Force Chief of Staff Curtis Le May urged that the United States go to war with China "soon" because China would have nuclear weapons in a year or two.

The Attorney General asked where would be the the the best place to stand and fight in Southesast Asia, where to draw the line. Mr. McNamara said he thought we would take a stand in Thailand and South Vietnam. The Attorney General asked whether we would save any of Laos, but the major question was whether we would stand up and fight.

Admiral Burke said that we could hold Tourane, and General Le May observed that we could use our air power back as far as necessary, letting the enemy have all of the countryside but that the PL [Pathet Lao] could be stopped by air power.

SOURCE: *U.S.-Vietnam Relations, Book II*, pp. 62–66.

Mr. McNamara said that we would have to attack the DRV if we gave up Laos.

The Secretary suggested that the part of Laos from the 17th Parallel across to the Mekong might be easier to hold than the entire country.

General Decker thought that there was no good place to fight in Southeast Asia but we must hold as much as we can of Vietnam, Cambodia and Laos. At this point the Secretary said we had missed having government troops who were willing to fight.

Mr. Steeves pointed out that we had always argued that we would not give up Laos and that it was on the pleas of our military that we had supported Phoumi; that we had reiterated in the press and to the public what Laos meant to us. If this problem is unsolvable then the problem of Vietnam would be unsolvable. If we decided that this was untenable then we were writing the first chapter in the defeat of Southeast Asia. Mr. McNamara said the situation was not as bad five weeks ago as it was now.

Admiral Burke pointed out that each time you give ground it is harder to stand next time. If we give up Laos we would have to put US forces into Vietnam and Thailand. We would have to throw enough in to win—perhaps the "works". It would be easier to hold now than later. The thing to do was to land now and hold as much as we can and make clear that we were not going to be pushed out of Southeast Asia. We were fighting for the rest of Asia.

Mr. McNamara wondered whether more Viet Cong would necessarily enter South Vietnam if Laos went down the drain. He mentioned that some 12,000 Viet Cong had entered South Vietnam under present conditions and that the Communists held the area south of the 17th Parallel to a depth of twenty-five miles with a supposedly friendly government in South Vietnam. (Several of those present questioned the accuracy of the figure of 12,000.)

Turning to the question of the morale of the Southeast Asians, the Secretary recalled that the Thai Foreign Minister had told him during the recent SEATO conference that Thailand was like a "golden bell" which had to be protected from outside. The Secretary said he was not sure the Foreign Minister was wrong. He added that he was less worried about escalation than he was about infectious slackness. He said he would not give a cent for what the Persians would think of us if we did not defend Laos.

General Decker thought that we should have stood last August and wondered what would happen if we got "licked". The Secretary suggested that Thai and US troops might be placed together in Vientiane and, if they could not hold, be removed by helicopter. Even if they were defeated they would be defeated together and this would be better than sitting back and doing nothing. General Decker said we cannot win a conventional war in Southeast Asia; if we go in, we should go in to win, and that means bombing Hanoi, China, and maybe even using nuclear bombs. He pointed out that all the advantage we have in heavy equipment would be lost in the difficult terrain of Laos where we would be at the mercy of the guerrillas. The Secretary pointed out that this fact was also true at the time of the Bangkok Resolution but that we had gone ahead with the resolution anyway and had issued statements indicating that we would back up our words with deeds. Mr. McNamara repeated that the situation is now worse than it was five weeks ago. Mr. Steeves pointed out that the same problems existed in South Vietnam, but Admiral Burke thought that South Vietnam could be more easily controlled.

General Decker then suggested that troops be moved into Thailand and South Vietnam to see whether such action would not produce a ceasefire. General Decker said then we would be ready to go ahead.

Mr. Kennedy said we would look sillier than we do now if we got troops in there and then backed down. He reiterated the question whether we are ready to go the distance.

The Secretary said that we would want to get the United Nations "mixed up" in this.

Mr. Bohlen said he saw no need for a fixation on the possibility of a reaction by the Chinese Communists. He said we had no evidence that they want to face the brink of nuclear war. He said that he was more concerned about the objectives we would seek if we took military action.

There followed a discussion about the possibility of the restoring the kingdom of Champassak where Boun Oum relinquished the throne and where he is popular. It was thought that Sihanouk would support a partition of Laos. General Decker thought that if a cease-fire could be effected now it would be possible to secure southern Laos.

General Le May did not believe that it would be possible to get a cease-fire without military action. He admitted that he did not know what US policy is in Laos. He knew what the President had said but he also pointed out that the military had been unable to back up the President's statements. He then enumerated a number of possibilities: 1) do nothing and lose Laos; 2) use B-26's and slow up the enemy; 3) use more sophisticated bombers and stop supplies and then perhaps Phoumi's forces could be brought up to where they could fight; 4) implement Plan 5, backing up troops with air. General Le May did not think the Chinese would escalate but believed on the contrary that a cease-fire would then be brought about. He added that he believed we should go to work on China itself and let Chiang take Hainan Island. He thought Chiang had a good air force.

*   *   *

Mr. Bowles said he thought the main question to be faced was the fact that we were going to have to fight the Chinese anyway in 2, 3, 5 or 10 years and that it was just a question of where, when and how. He thought that a major war would be difficult to avoid. General Le May said that, in that case, we should fight soon since the Chinese would have nuclear weapons within one or two years.

Mr. McNamara said that the situation was worsening by the hour and that if we were going to commit ourselves, then we must do so sooner rather than later.

The Secretary then adjourned the meeting saying he would like to consider the matter further.

134. NSC ACTION NO. 2417, MAY 1, 1961

Although pressure from the National Security bureaucracy was evidently building for some commitment of American troops in Southeast Asia as a show of strength, President Kennedy resisted it. At a National Security Council meeting on

SOURCE: Document declassified by National Security Council, September 30, 1977.

*May 1, he refused to make any decisions on troop deployments until the negotia-
tions between Laotian parties made it clear whether or not there would be a
cease-fire. On May 3, a cease-fire became effective in Laos, and the pressure for
American steps to save Laos eased considerably.*

    a. Discussed the current situation in Laos and agreed that no final decisions as
to U.S. courses of action with respect to that situation should be taken at this
meeting, pending further developments in the cease-fire negotiations.
    b. Noted that the President would be prepared under certain conditions to
deploy U.S. forces in Thailand.
    c. Agreed that the Joint Chiefs of Staff should prepare, for presentation at a
meeting of the National Security Council to be held on Tuesday, May 2, 1961, at
4:00 p.m., an appreciation of the military implications of various measures that
might be taken in Laos, Thailand, and other countries of Southeast Asia.

135. TELEGRAM FROM AMBASSADOR FREDERICK E. NOLTING, JR., IN SAIGON TO RUSK, MAY 16, 1961

    *Anticipating that the United States would be required by the decision already
made by the Kennedy Administration to increase military equipment and training
personnel beyond what the International Control Commission would agree was
consistent with the Geneva Agreement, Ambassador Nolting recommended that the
United States not attempt to justify each increase as consistent with the Geneva
Agreement. He urged instead that it renounce Articles 16 and 17 of the Agreement,
which restricted the dispatch of troops and arms to Vietnam to "rotation" and
replacement, citing the failure of international controls to prevent Communist
violations of the agreement. Acting on Nolting's advice, the State Department
informed close allies that it would increase its training personnel in South Vietnam
beyond the Geneva limit, charging North Vietnam violations of the Geneva Agreement.*

    1. Indications are that additional military equipment and training personnel
required to accomplish aims and objectives generally agreed upon in VP Johnson's
talks with President Diem and other GVN officials will be such as to exceed likely
limits to which ICC can realistically be expected to agree.
    We therefore think it important that this question be discussed promptly and
frankly by both GVN and US with Canadians, British and perhaps French making it
clear that we cannot permit Geneva accord restrictions on quantities and types of
equipment and on numbers of personnel to hamper effective action for defense of
Vietnam against Communist threat. Canadian ICC delegation here has already
asked Embassy for frank discussion of press reports suggesting US proposing send
troops SVN, increase size of MAAG and take other actions which imply serious
violations of Geneva accord. We have told Canadians that we will talk to them in
near future.

SOURCE: Document declassifed by Department of State, December 3, 1974.

To approach this problem piecemeal by attempting to make explanations for each increment in order demonstrate adherence to Geneva accord will only weaken our case when time comes to exceed outside limit of ICC acceptance. We may in fact have reached such limit on personnel since members of Canadian delegation have privately warned that any request for increase in MAAG ceiling likely be doomed to eventual negative response after long hassle which would only benefit Communist propaganda.

We also believe it undesirable to adopt approach that we shall say nothing about further personnel and equipment increases unless asked. It would in any case with respect to equipment be only very short time before ICC, in view its control over entry all shipments into SVN, would begin ask for explanations and Communist propaganda attacks would follow. Thus we would find ourselves on defensive rather than taking psychological offensive with respect our actions.

Therefore strongly believe we should make decision now in conjunction with GVN A) to take public position that in fighting Communist threat to GVN we will no longer observe our self-imposed adherence to restrictions in articles 16 and 17 of Geneva accord and B) talk with our allies in order obtain prior tacit support or at least non-objection to such action. Such action would not only demonstrate our determination support GVN in all-out effort against Communist threat but also shore up morale our friends SEA and strengthen our position vis-á-vis Communists at 14-nation conference by showing that in absence effective international control estimable restrain Communist US prepared take such actions as it deems necessary to preserve independence free nations like Laos and Vietnam. Also believe limiting action to articles 16 and 17 would permit ICC continue function on limited basis in Vietnam and thus retain such deterrent value against open DRV aggression as ICC may be able provide.

2. After consultation with GVN and allies we would envisage GVN sending letter to ICC along following lines; (A) GVN although not signatory to Geneva accord has voluntarily complied fully with both letter and spirit and given fullest possible cooperation to assure ICC success maintaining peace; (B) ICC, in part because of construction [obstruction] of DRV, unable to fulfill this task; specifically, it has failed take action to control subversion and infiltration into SVN of DRV agents and forces, investigate Kontum attack, stop Soviet airlift through Hanoi and Haiphong, detect control either introduction foreign military personnel or importation of war material into DRV and prevent creation military bases in and near demilitarized zone and in Laos as bases for aggression against SVN (Saigon's G-467); (C) in this situation, given threat to peace not only in Vietnam but also throughout SEA as result DRV aggressiveness which ICC unable control, GVN required take certain actions in interest of self-defense against threat of Communist aggression and has requested US to assist it in this endeavor; (D) it should be clearly understood that in face present threat to its very existence, GVN can no longer enforce vis-a-vis DRV, where such limitations restrict GVN in taking defensive action to counter threat to its own security and peace of SEA.

We believe GVN letter should be made public and US should give full support to GVN position in official public statement and seek similar statements from our allies.

3. If Department agrees to above, request prompt authorization discuss subject with GVN and recommend Department subsequently take up with Canadians, British and perhaps French as suggested above. Highly desirable we reach common

US-GVN position quickly in order be able meet desire Canadian ICC delegation for early talks.

136. TELEGRAM FROM NOLTING TO RUSK, JUNE 21, 1961 [Extract]

The commissioner of the Canadian delegation to the International Control Commission urged against the U.S. plan to renounce Articles 16 and 17 on the ground that the DRV would also declare itself not bound by the agreement. Instead he suggested that the United States introduce men and materiel covertly and claim credits based on French shipments out of the country, which were not controlled by the ICC.

1. Canadian ICC Commissioner Woodsworth and senior military advisor Brigadier Allan called on Cunningham and me June 20. They stated delegation had received brief and purposely general instruction to discuss with us increased US programs of assistance to Vietnam and ICC organizations. I stated that US had taken decision that greater US contribution required to keep Vietnam from falling into Communist hands; it appeared that actions required implement this decision would likely run counter to Article 16 and 17 of Geneva accord and Embassy had recommended to Washington that after consultation with other governments concerned GVN-US publicly denounce Article 16 and 17. I noted that following discussions with GVN, Finnish and Canadians Washington had decided postpone talking to Indians and GVN had postponed action vis-à-vis ICC denouncing Article 16 and 17. I added that it seemed to me there following 3 possible alternatives for handling ICC problem: (1) Meet issue squarely by denunciation Article 16 and 17; (2) bring men and materiel "in the back door"; or (3) maintain present procedures of full notification, et cetera with practical certainty GVN and US would come under heavy attack in ICC to benefit Communist propaganda.

2. Woodsworth emphasized full Canadian agreement with US increased support for GVN and desire to be helpful. Noting this as far as he instructed to go officially, he and Allan wished present following unofficial and personal views (please protect):

(A) To meet problem head on as we proposing would make position of ICC untenable, lead DRV denounce other articles of Geneva accord and be beginning of end of ICC Vietnam. Canadians therefore wish avoid any action which obviously contrary to ICC and Canadian delegation terms of reference, but otherwise want to be helpful.

(B) Various techniques could be used to avoid US actions coming to attention ICC and resulting citations for violation of Geneva accord. Additional MAAG personnel could be introduced: (1) As civilians and arrive on civilian aircraft; (2) on unscheduled military flights synchronized to arrive and depart again when ICC teams not at airport; and/or (3) into area where ICC teams do not operate. ICC control only effective regarding observed arrivals and departures, and once in country new arrivals would be helded [melded?] with

---

SOURCE: Document declassified by Department of State, March 25, 1975.

present MAAG personnel and ICC has no check of total number in country. Re materiel—introduction could be made at ports not controlled by ICC, e.g. river ports on Mekong, or infrequent uncontrolled coastal areas. Once in country materiel not distinguishable from that already here, or, in case types for which there no precedent, materiel could be positioned in areas where ICC teams do not operate. In many cases where quantity of credits for items represents major problem items could be notified and reference made to [two words garbled] claims for credit based on French outshipments which since not controlled out by ICC not included on ICC war materiel register. This would permit Canadians stall question for year or more. At worst ICC could only order re-export of equipment. In response to my question, Woodsworth stated that combination of open and covert introduction could be used.

137. NATIONAL SECURITY ACTION MEMORANDUM NO. 80, AUGUST 29, 1961

As the Geneva Conference wrestled with the problem of a neutralized Laos, fighting continued in the mountains of Eastern Laos between the Pathet Lao and U.S.-controlled Meo tribesmen. Kennedy approved efforts to get Souvanna Phouma, the "neutralist" Prince, one of the three Laotian factions to the Conference, to agree to proposals for a Laotian settlement worked out by the United States and France. The proposals included provisions for strong international controls that would impinge on the sovereignty of the tripartite Laotian government and were being opposed by the Communist delegations at Geneva. The reference in McGeorge Bundy's memorandum to a U.S. offer of support of Souvanna if he accepted the proposals was an indication of a major change in U.S. policy from the Eisenhower Administration, which had considered Souvanna pro-Communist for his acceptance of Soviet, North Vietnamese, and Pathet Lao help in fighting the U.S.-supported right-wing forces after December 1960. The Bundy memorandum also reveals moves by Kennedy to increase covert American and Thai advisory personnel working with the anti-Communist forces in Laos and to increase the number of Meo tribesmen continuing the fight behind the lines of the Pathet Lao.

The President approved the following actions:

1. An intensification of the diplomatic effort to achieve agreement to the Paris proposals on the part of Souvanna, especially by direct conversations between Ambassador Harriman and Souvanna, with an emphasis not only upon the interlocking importance of the Paris proposals, but also upon U.S. support of Souvanna in the event that he accepts the Paris plan.

2. Authorization to undertake conversations with SEATO allies both bilaterally and with the SEATO Council, exploring the possibility of an enlargement of the concept of SEATO Plan 5. It must be understood that this exploration was in the nature of contingency planning and did not represent a flat commitment of the United States to participate in such an enlarged enterprise.

3. An immediate increase in mobile training teams in Laos to include advisers

SOURCE: *U.S.-Vietnam Relations, Book 11*, pp. 247–248.

down to the level of the company, to a total U.S. strength in this area of 500, together with an attempt to get Thai agreement to supply an equal amount of Thais for the same purpose.

4. An immediate increase of 2,000 in the number of Meos being supported to bring the total to a level of 11,000.

5. Authorization for photo-reconnaissance by Thai or sanitized aircraft over all of Laos.

It is assumed that these actions will be carried out under the general direction of the Southeast Asia Task Force under the direction of Deputy Under Secretary Johnson.

138. RESOLUTION OF AN ENLARGED CONFERENCE OF THE CENTRAL OFFICE FOR SOUTH VIETNAM (COSVN), OCTOBER 1961 [Extracts]

In October 1961, the headquarters of the Lao Dong Party leadership in the South, the Central Office for South Vietnam (COSVN), which used the code name "R" in its internal documents, convened an enlarged conference on the new situation in the struggle against Diem. The conference resolution, which was distributed for study throughout the Party and armed forces in the South, observed that a "revolutionary high-tide" had appeared in the South, characterized by what the leadership called "partial uprising"–a situation distinguished from the "general uprising" that would bring down the regime–and guerrilla warfare, which was still distinguished from "complete war" as in the anti-French resistance. The Party was still interested in preserving the "legal position" of the people in the populated areas in order to avoid bringing massive military repression and also to minimize the possibilities of American intervention. Military struggle was now placed on a par with political struggle rather than being subordinated to it as it had been at the beginning of 1961, and was considered primary in the little-populated mountainous region. As for the possibility of direct U.S. military intervention, the resolution did not rule it out but cited several factors that would tend to limit it–primarily fear of counteraction by the Soviet Union and China.

However, in the process of leading the revolution we must take precautions against another possibility: the possibility of total war as in the time of the resistance war. This possibility can develop in two circumstances: either because U.S. imperialism has new schemes which make it impossible for the political struggle of the masses to advance, or because our Party has strayed from the path leading to the general uprising in its leadership.

As for the possibility that we could not advance toward the general uprising because of a new scheme by U.S. imperialism, which we must take into account

SOURCE: "Nghi Quyet Hoi Nghi R (mo rong). Thang 10/61" [Resolution of the R Conference (enlarged). October 61]. Captured party document, Combined Documents Exploitation Center log number 1706/KTTL/69 [Translation by the editor.]

despite the restrictions on it, because, as mentioned above, the nature of U.S. imperialism is aggressive and stubborn and because there have been circumstances which have shown they also dare to carry out reckless actions: the South is for imperialism an advanced outpost in the Southeast Asia region, one of the bastions of imperialism in its attack on the socialist camp. In order to guard against this circumstance, we must always maintain high vigilance and prepare our thinking in the Party and among the people, and try to establish real strength, not regarding lightly the building of armed strength, and simultaneously prepare for the general uprising and be ready to take the initiative in any eventuality, while following the situation closely and seeking by all means to control it.

In order to avoid going down the road to complete war as during the resistance war, because of our leadership straying from the correct direction, we must follow the movement closely and correct in time deviations in the implementation of the line and policy of the Party. These deviations can occur on various fronts: either seeing only political struggle, and not seeing fully the function of armed struggle, or only seeing the role of armed struggle in line with the previous experience during the resistance war period and thus regarding political struggle lightly and causing political struggle to be restricted, or not actively pushing the revolutionary move-ment in the three basic zones, the mountains and forest, the rural areas of the plains, and cities, so that they rise together and are closely combined with one another.

* * *

II. The Character of the Present Period, and Our Tasks and Line of Action

1) The development of the situation shows that the Southern revolution has entered a high tide with characteristics and possibilities of development which the Central Committee has judged as follows:

" . . . The period of temporary stabilization of the U.S.-Diem regime has passed and the period of continuous crisis and serious decline has begun."

" . . . The forms of limited guerrilla war and partial uprisings have appeared, the period of prolonged political crisis has begun; those forms of active guerrilla warfare have opened a revolutionary high tide and develop more strongly everyday. Through that process, the enemy's forces and government will continue to disintegrate, the revolutionary forces will be rapidly built and developed and forms of revolutionary government will appear in localities everywhere. A general all-sided crisis of the U.S.-Diem regime will appear, and a general offensive and general uprising of the people will break out, overthrow the U.S.-Diem regime and liberate the South. Also during that process, the enemy will experience increasingly deep internal contradictions and the revolutionary movement will rise higher every-day. Coups or military revolts could occur, in which the revolution must seize the opportune moment in order to turn it into a situation favorable to the revolution. At the same time, the possibility of armed intervention by bringing troops of U.S. imperialism and its lackeys into the South by whatever forms and in whatever scope is also a complex problem which we must follow and find ways to limit, guard against and be prepared to cope with in a timely fashion.

Clearly the high tide situation has not yet entered into the general offensive and uprising but only opens a period of partial uprising and partial offensive and expands more and more to hasten the process of the enemy's disintegration, develop our forces, and fundamentally change the relationship of forces between the enemy and ourselves; that is the process of creating ripe conditions for a general offensive and general uprising.

That is a process of striving determinedly to mobilize the entire Party and people to develop every revolutionary capability, overcome every difficulty, urgently expand the movement, develop its strength, correct our weak points, exploit the enemy's weak points, and advance to gaining absolute superiority over the enemy.

The process does not yet give us the advantage because the enemy still have strong military forces, and still makes many new efforts to oppose the revolution with great ferocity, so we must assess all the complex difficulties during the process of fierce struggle on the line of march to the complete overthrow of the enemy's government.

2) Based on the characteristics and possibilities for development of the present revolutionary period, the Central Committee has presented the following tasks and line of action:

"The immediate revolutionary task in the South is to endeavor to rapidly build up our forces in both political and military aspects, concentrate the vast revolutionary forces in the National Liberation Front, launch a powerful political struggle movement of the masses, actively annihilate the enemy's manpower, preserve and develop our forces, make the enemy's government and forces fall apart on an ever broadening scale; advance to become master of the mountain and jungle, win the whole lowlands and strive to build bases and push the political struggle in the cities, create conditions and grasp every opportune movement to overthrow the U.S.-Diem government and liberate the South.

Promote the political struggle further while pushing armed struggle up till it is equal with political struggle, attack the enemy in both political and military aspects. . . . Depending on the relationship of forces between the enemy and ourselves, and depending on the concrete situation in each region, put forward appropriate lines for action and forms of struggle, taking military struggle as primary in the mountainous region, with the task of annihilating the enemy's manpower in order to expand our base areas and build our forces. In the plains region political and military struggle can be on the same level, and depending on the concrete situation in each place in the plans, aim at striking a balance between the two forms of struggle, and in the degree of wearing down and annihilating the enemy's manpower. In the cities, take political struggle as primary, including both legal and illegal forms."

139. MEMORANDUM FROM THE JOINT CHIEFS OF STAFF TO MCNAMARA (JCSM-716-61), OCTOBER 9, 1961 [Extract]

In early October, Presidential adviser Walt W. Rostow drafted a plan to put a SEATO force of some 25,000 men into Vietnam along the South Vietnamese border

SOURCE: Document declassified by the Joint Chiefs of Staff, January 8, 1975.

to stop infiltration. The paper was submitted to the Joint Chiefs on October 5, and a few days later, they wrote to McNamara criticizing the plan as militarily unfeasible. The Joint Chiefs took the opportunity to push once more for their favorite plan for intervention, SEATO Plan 5/61, which would have concentrated U.S. military forces in Laos. Since it was clear that the Kennedy Administration had chosen not to intervene in force in Laos, however, they offered an alternative plan for putting SEATO forces in South Vietnam.

1. Reference is made to the memorandum by the Deputy Secretary of Defense, dated 5 October 1961, subject as above. The Joint Chiefs of Staff have considered the proposed concept for the use of SEATO forces in South Vietnam and the suggested two principal military possibilities for its implementation.

2. It is their opinion that the use of SEATO forces at the greatest possible number of entry points along the whole South Vietnam border, but excluding that part of the 17th parallel now held by the South Vietnamese Army itself, is not feasible for the following reasons:

    a. SEATO forces will be deployed over a border of several hundred miles and will be attacked piecemeal or by-passed at the Viet Cong's own choice.

    b. It may reduce but cannot stop infiltration of Viet Cong Personnel and material.

    c. It deploys SEATO forces in the weakest defense points should DRV or CHICOM forces intervene.

    d. It compounds the problems of communications and logistical support.

3. Further, the alternative possibility of using SEATO forces to cover solely the 17th parallel, although considered feasible to a limited extent, is militarily unsound in view of the following considerations:

    a. The 17th parallel is not a main avenue of approach being used by the Viet Cong.

    b. North Vietnam may interpret such SEATO action as preparation for aggression against them, thus promoting the possibility of communist harassment and destruction of friendly combat and logistic forces concentrated near the parallel, if not escalation.

4. As stated in your memorandum, the proposed concept set forth must be analyzed in the total context of the defense of Southeast Asia. Any concept which deals with the defense of Southeast Asia that does not include all or a substantial portion of Laos is, from a military standpoint, unsound. To concede the majority of northern and central Laos would leave three quarters of the border of Thailand exposed and thus invite an expansion of communist military action. To concede southern Laos would open the flanks of both Thailand and South Vietnam as well as expose Cambodia. Any attempt to combat insurgency in South Vietnam, while holding areas in Laos essential to the defense of Thailand, would require an effort on the part of the United States alone on the order of magnitude of at least three divisions plus supporting units. This would require an additional two divisions from the United States.

5. What is needed is not the spreading out of our forces throughout Southeast Asia but rather a concentrated effort in Laos where a firm stand can be taken saving all or substantially all of Laos which would, at the same time, protect Thailand and protect the borders of South Vietnam.

6. The over-all objective could best be served by the implementation of SEATO Plan 5/61, or a variation thereof, now. This would accomplish the objective of personnel and material in support of the Viet Cong thus freeing Vietnamese forces to conduct more effective offensive operations in South Vietnam. In addition, this action would stem further communist gains in Laos and, at the same time, give concrete evidence of US determination to stand firm against further communist advances world-wide.

7. If implementation of SEATO Plan 5, or a variation thereof, is considered a politically unacceptable course of action at this time, there is provided herewith a possible limited interim course of action. This course of action, covered in the Appendices hereto, could provide a degree of assistance to the Government of South Vietnam to regain control of its own territory, and could free certain South Vietnamese forces for offensive actions against the Viet Cong. While the Joint Chiefs of Staff agree that implementation of this limited course of action would not provide for the defense of Thailand or Laos, nor contribute substantially or permanently to solution of the over-all problem of defense of Southeast Asia, they consider the Plan preferable to either of the two military possibilities described in referenced memorandum.

Political Objectives

1. To enable the Government of South Vietnam to regain full control of its own territory and to eliminate the Viet Cong threat.

2. To defend Thailand and South Vietnam, holding Laos or areas thereof to the extent required as being essential to the defense of Thailand and South Vietnam.

Military Objectives

1. To assist by the use of SEATO forces in securing the borders of South Vietnam to the maximum extent possible against the infiltration of personnel and material in support of the Viet Cong.

2. To assist the Government of South Vietnam to regain full control of its own territory and to eliminate the Viet Cong threat by freeing South Vietnam forces for offensive action against the Viet Cong.

3. To defend Thailand and South Vietnam, holding Laos or areas thereof essential to such defense.

Assumptions

1. Forces available will be the British Commonwealth Brigade, Pakistan, Philippine, and US forces and limited amount of Thai forces.

2. The United States will provide for stationing in Thailand one US brigade Task Force Team as suggested to Foreign Minister Thanat by Deputy Undersecretary of State Johnson.

3. South Vietnamese forces released by SEATO forces will conduct effective offensive operations against the Viet Cong.

4. Maximum possible use of SEATO forces will be made to establish an effective communications network in as wide an area as possible and to serve as a means for introducing new techniques into the South Vietnamese Army.

Concept of Operations

1. SEATO ground and air forces will deploy to South Vietnam to assist in protecting the South Vietnam-Laos border, exclusive of that part of the 17th parallel now held in force by I Corps of the South Vietnamese Army (I Corps Tactical Area), southward to the Cambodian border.

2. SEATO ground forces of approximately one division strength (11,000) initially will deploy to the high plateau region of the Pleiku area. Securing this region with SEATO forces will free South Vietnamese forces to conduct effective offensive operations elsewhere. Further deployments to assist in interrupting the flow of personnel and material in support of the Viet Cong into South Vietnam will be at the discretion of the SEATO Field Force Commander in light of the existing tactical situation. The SEATO force will further assist South Vietnamese forces by the provision of air, communications and logistic support.

3. The additional command and control communications—electronics requirements for the support of this concept are set forth in Appendix B to Enclosure B.

Command Arrangements

- Command arrangements for this concept would be as now provided for in SEATO Plan 5/61 except that the United States would have the responsibilities of the Appointed Nation. In addition, coordination between the SEATO forces and the Government of South Vietnam would be required.

Force Involvement

1. The forces involved in support of this concept would include those forces now committed to support SEATO Plan 5/61 less both the Thai commitment and the US commitment to the Central Reserve. This force would be composed of approximately 9600 combat forces, of which about 500 would be US. Headquarters units, air component, logistic and other support units would total about 13,200. This would provide a total force of about 22,800.

140. CABLEGRAM FROM GENERAL MAXWELL TAYLOR, IN BAGUIO, THE PHILIPPINES, TO KENNEDY, NOVEMBER 1, 1961

Following his extended visit to South Vietnam, Kennedy's military advisor, Gen. Maxwell Taylor viewed the conflict primarily in global terms, as a manifestation of Communist global strategy rather than as the result of indigenous Vietnamese forces and decisions. He urged that the United States seize the opportunity afforded by the floods in the Mekong Delta to send a military task force to South Vietnam, primarily as a symbolic show of U.S. presence in the country. Other recommendations included the insertion of American officials into the South Vietnamese government, not as advisers but as actual administrators.

SOURCE: U.S.-Vietnam Relations, *Book 11,* pp. 331–336.

1. Transmitted herewith are a summary of the fundamental conclusions of my group and my personal recommendations in response to the letter of the President to me dated 13 October 1961. At our meeting next Friday I hope to be allowed to explain the thinking which lies behind them. At that time I shall transmit our entire report which will provide detailed support for the recommendations and will serve as a working paper for the interested departments and agencies.

2. It is concluded that:

a. Communist strategy aims to gain control of Southeast Asia by methods of subversion and guerrilla war which by-pass conventional U.S. and indigenous strength on the ground. The interim Communist goal—en route to total takeover—appears to be a neutral Southeast Asia, detached from U.S. protection. This strategy is well on the way to success in Vietnam.

b. In Vietnam (and Southeast Asia) there is a double crisis in confidence: doubt that the U.S. is determined to save Southeast Asia; doubt that Diem's methods can frustrate and defeat Communist purposes and methods. The Vietnamese (and Southeast Asians) will undoubtedly draw rightly or wrongly—definitve conclusions in coming weeks and months concerning the probable outcome and will adjust their behavior accordingly. What the U.S. does or fails to do will be decisive to the end result.

c. Aside from the morale factor, the Vietnamese Government is caught in interlocking circles of bad tactics and bad administrative arrangements which pin their forces on the defensive in ways which permit a relatively small Viet-Cong force (about one tenth the size of the GVN regulars) to create conditions of frustration and terror certain to lead to a political crisis, if a positive turning point is not soon achieved. The following recommendations are designed to achieve that favorable turn, to avoid further deterioration in the situation in South Vietnam, and eventually to contain and eliminate the threat to its independence.

3. It is recommended:

General

a. That upon request from the Government of Vietnam (GVN) to come to its aid in resisting the increasing aggressions of the Viet-Cong and in repairing the ravages of the Delta flood which, in combination, threaten the lives of its citizens and the security of the country, the U.S. Government offer to join the GVN in a massive joint effort as a part of a total mobilization of GVN resources to cope with both the Viet-Cong (VC) and the ravages of the flood. The U.S. representatives will participate actively in this effort, particularly in the fields of government administration, military plans and operations, intelligence, and flood relief, going beyond the advisory role which they have observed in the past.

Specific

b. That in support of the foregoing broad commitment to a joint effort with Diem, the following specific measures be undertaken:

(1) The U.S. Government will be prepared to provide individual

administrators for insertion into the governmental machinery of South Vietnam in types and numbers to be worked out with President Diem.

(2) A joint effort will be made to improve the military-political intelligence system beginning at the provincial level and extending upward through the government and armed forces to the Central Intelligence Organization.

(3) The U.S. Government will engage in a joint survey of the conditions in the provinces to assess the social, political, intelligence, and military factors bearing on the prosecution of the counter-insurgency in order to reach a common estimate of these factors and a common determination of how to deal with them. As this survey will consume time, it should not hold back the immediate actions which are clearly needed regardless of its outcome.

(4) A joint effort will be made to free the Army for mobile, offensive operations. This effort will be based upon improving the training and equipping of the Civil Guard and the Self-Defense Corps, relieving the regular Army of static missions, raising the level of the mobility of Army forces by the provision of considerably more helicopters and light aviation, and organizing a Border Ranger Force for a long-term campaign on the Laotian border against the Viet-Cong infiltrators. The U.S. Government will support this effort with equipment and with military units and personnel to do those tasks which the Armed Forces of Vietnam cannot perform in time. Such tasks include air reconnaissance and photography, airlift (beyond the present capacity of SVN forces), special intelligence, and air-support techniques.

(5) The U.S. Government will assist the GVN in effecting surveillance and control over the coastal waters and inland waterways, furnishing such advisors, operating personnel and small craft as may be necessary for quick and effective operations.

(6) The MAAG, Vietnam, will be reorganized and increased in size as may be necessary by the implementation of these recommendations.

(7) The U.S. Government will offer to introduce into South Vietnam a military Task Force to operate under U.S. control for the following purposes:

(a) Provide a U.S. military presence capable of raising national morale and of showing to Southeast Asia the seriousness of the U.S. intent to resist a Communist take-over.

(b) Conduct such logistical operations as in support of military and flood relief operations.

(c) Conduct such combat operations as are necessary for self-defense and for the security of the area in which they are stationed.

(d) Provide an emergency reserve to back up the Armed Forces of the GVN in the case of a heightened military crisis.

(e) Act as an advance party of such additional forces as may be introduced if CINCPAC or SEATO contingency plans are invoked.

(8) The U.S. Government will review its economic aid program to take into account the needs of flood relief and to give priority to those projects in support of the expanded counter-insurgency program.

141. CABLEGRAM FROM RUSK IN JAPAN TO THE DEPARTMENT OF STATE, NOVEMBER 1, 1961

The first reaction from a top policy maker to Taylor's recommendation was a cablegram from Rusk, then in Japan, questioning whether U.S. troops would make the difference if Diem did not carry out reforms desired by the United States. Rusk already foresaw the possibility that the U.S. role in South Vietnam would become one of "de facto direction" of Vietnamese affairs.

Since General Taylor may give first full report prior my return, believe special attention should be given to critical question whether Diem is prepared take necessary measures to give us something worth supporting. If Diem unwilling trust military commanders to get job done and take steps to consolidate non-Communist elements into serious national effort, difficult to see how relative handful American troops can have decisive influence. While attaching greatest possible importance to security in Southeast Asia, I would be reluctant see US make major additional commitment American prestige to a losing horse. Suggest Department carefully review all measures we expect from Diem if our assistance forces US to assume de facto direction Vietnamese affairs.

142. MEMORANDUM FOR THE PRESIDENT BY MCNAMARA, NOVEMBER 8, 1961

McNamara, supported by the Joint Chiefs, warned Kennedy that the limited commitment recommended by Taylor had to be seen as only the beginning of what might be a long conflict involving North Vietnam and China directly. He favored accompanying that initial commitment of troops with a warning to Hanoi that North Vietnam would be punished by the United States for continued support of the Viet Cong. Based on military contingency plans drawn up in 1959, he assured Kennedy that at most about 205,000 American troops would be required, even to deal with overt intervention by Hanoi and Peking.

The basic issue framed by the Taylor Report is whether the U.S. shall:

    a. Commit itself to the clear objective of preventing the fall of South Vietnam to Communism, and

    b. Support this commitment by necessary immediate military actions and preparations for possible later actions.

SOURCE: *The Pentagon Papers, The Defense Department History of United States Decision-making on Vietnam: The Senator Gravel Edition* (Boston: Beacon Press, 1971) Vol II, p. 105. Hereafter cited as *The Pentagon Papers: Gravel Edition.*
SOURCE: U.S.-Vietnam Relations, *Book 11*, pp. 343–344.

The Joint Chiefs, Mr. Gilpatric, and I have reach the following conclusions:

1. The fall of South Vietnam to Communism would lead to the fairly rapid extension of Communist control, or complete accommodation to Communism, in the rest of mainland Southeast Asia and in Indonesia. The strategic implications worldwide, particularly in the Orient, would be extremely serious.

2. The chances are against, probably sharply against, preventing that fall by any measures short of the introduction of U.S. forces on a substantial scale. We accept General Taylor's judgment that the various measures proposed by him short of this are useful but will not in themselves do the job of restoring confidence and setting Diem on the way to winning his fight.

3. The introduction of a U.S. force of the magnitude of an initial 8,000 men in a flood relief context will be of great help to Diem. However, it will not convince the other side (whether the shots are called from Moscow, Peiping or Hanoi) that we mean business. Moreover, it probably will not tip the scales decisively. We would be almost certain to get increasingly mired down in an inconclusive struggle.

4. The other side can be convinced we mean business only if we accompany the initial force introduction by a clear commitment to the full objective stated above, accompanied by a warning through some channel to Hanoi that continued support of the Viet Cong will lead to punitive retaliation against North Vietnam.

5. If we act in this way, the ultimate possible extent of our military commitment must be faced. The struggle may be prolonged and Hanoi and Peiping may intervene overtly. In view of the logistic difficulties faced by the other side, I believe we can assume that the maximum U.S. forces required on the ground in Southeast Asia will not exceed 6 divisions, or about 205,000 men, (CINCPAC Plan 32-59, Phase IV). Our military posture is, or, with the addition of more National Guard or regular Army divisions, can be made, adequate to furnish these forces without serious interference with our present Berlin plans.

6. To accept the stated objective is of course a most serious decision. Military force is not the only element of what must be a most carefully coordinated set of actions. Success will depend on factors many of which are not within our control—notably the conduct of Diem himself and other leaders in the area. Laos will remain a major problem. The domestic political implications of accepting the objective are also grave, although it is our feeling that the country will respond better to a firm initial position than to courses of action that lead us in only gradually, and that in the meantime are sure to involve casualties. The over-all effect on Moscow and Peiping will need careful weighing and may well be mixed; however, permitting South Vietnam to fall can only strengthen and encourage them greatly.

7. In sum:

    a. We do not believe major units of U.S. forces should be introduced in South Vietnam unless we are willing to make an affirmative decision on the issue stated at the start of this memorandum.

    b. We are inclined to recommend that we do commit the U.S. to the clear objective of preventing the fall of South Vietnam to Communism and that we support this commitment by the necessary military actions.

    c. If such a commitment is agreed upon, we support the recommendations of General Taylor as the first steps toward its fulfillment.

143. TELEGRAM FROM RUSK TO NOLTING, NOVEMBER 15, 1961

Nolting was informed that Kennedy had decided against sending American troops to South Vietnam. A major consideration in the decision was the fear that the introduction of U.S. forces might wreck the chances for a Laotian settlement, which it was hoped would prevent the use of Laos for transit from North to South Vietnam.

This telegram is the first of a series pertaining to the decisions of the USG arising from the Taylor Report. For your background only, it sets forth the general philosophy upon which your instructions to follow are based. The review by the USG of General Taylor's report has resulted in the following basic decisions:

1. It must be essentially a GVN task to contain and reduce the threat represented by the VC at their present level of capability. This means organizing to go on to the offensive. As indicated in para 1 g. your instructions, we are prepared to contemplate further supplemental assistance after joint assessment establishes the needs and possibilities of US aid more precisely.

2. No amount of such supplemental US assistance can be a substitute [to] the GVN taking those measures necessary to permit them to assure the offensive against the VC and to strengthen the administrative and political base of the Government.

3. We do not propose to introduce into the GVN US combat troops now, but we do propose a phase of intense public and diplomatic activity designed to focus on the infiltration of men from the North. We shall decide what course of action we shall take later should infiltration not be radically reduced.

4. With respect to the flood, we have decided that our best course is to treat this as primarily a civil problem and we believe that the occasion should be used within the framework of the GVN flood plan. [*Officially deleted.*] We are prepared to put maximum pressure on the FAO to plan an important role in flood reconstruction effort. [Word missing] US military aid in the flood area is not excluded.

5. Diplomatically our position is that, in view of the violations which will be documented in the Jorden report, and the strong references to DRV attacks against SVN contained in President Diem's letter to President Kennedy, we need not confirm to the World and the Communists that the Geneva Accords are thus making the Communist job easier. The GVN should be advised to counter these inevitable charges, not by admitting transgression but by leveling charges against the DRV and insisting that if there is an investigation of charges against the GVN there be equally an investigation of longstanding GVN charges against the DRV. We appreciate that this approach will make the ICC task extremely difficult, but we shall explain our position to the Canadians and Indians to their [support].

6. You should bear in mind that a crucial element in US Government's willingness [to] move forward is concrete demonstration by Diem that he is now prepared to work in an orderly way with his subordinates and broaden the political base of his regime.

7. In general, also, whole package should be presented as the first stage in a

---

SOURCE: Document declassified by Department of State (no date shown).

partnership in which US is prepared to do more as joint study of the facts and GVN performance makes increased US assistance possible and productive.

8. Notwithstanding some recent deterioration of negotiating prospects both in Geneva and Laos, there remains possibility that Laotian settlement can be reached holding out some prospect of attainment our minimum objective of independent Laos, on basis neutral coalition government (albeit weak and unsatisfactory one) headed by Souvanna Phouma. Prospective agreement would include provision that Lao not be used as transit area or as base for interference in affairs of other countries such as South Vietnam. Therefore we must constantly keep in mind what impact our actions in Vietnam may have on the prospects for an acceptable Lao settlement.

9. Introduction of US or SEATO forces into South Vietnam before Laotian settlement reached might wreck chances for such agreement, lead to breakup of Geneva Conference, and breach of Laotian cease-fire by Communists with resumption hostilities.

10. The decision whether to introduce major US combat forces into GVN would have to be taken in light of GVN effort, including the support it has secured from the people, Laotian situation, Berlin crisis, readiness of allies for sharply increased tensions with Sino-Soviet bloc and enormous responsibilities which would have to be borne by US in event of escalation in Southeast Asia or other areas.

11. We hope that the measures outlined in your instructions to follow will galvanize and supplement GVN effort, making decision on use US combat forces unnecessary, and thus no need for decision which would in effect shift primary responsibility for defense of South Vietnam from GVN to USG.

12. In making far-reaching decisions for greatly increased scale of assistance for defense of Vietnam, we are fully cognizant of extent to which these decisions if implemented through Diem's acceptance, will sharply increase commitment our prestige in struggle to save that Republic.

13. Very strictly for your own information, you should know that the Department of Defense has been instructed to prepare plans for the use of US combat forces in South Vietnam under the various contingencies that can be foreseen, including stepped-up infiltration from the North as well as organized Communist military intervention into South Vietnam. However, you should be entirely clear that it must be the objective of our policy to do all possible to accomplish our purpose with respect to GVN without the use of US combat forces.

144. NATIONAL SECURITY ACTION MEMORANDUM NO. 111 BY WHITE HOUSE SPECIAL ASSISTANT FOR NATIONAL SECURITY AFFAIRS MCGEORGE BUNDY, NOVEMBER 22, 1961

Kennedy authorized Ambassador Nolting to tell Diem that the United States would step up assistance, increase its advisors, collaborate with Saigon in the

SOURCE: Document declassified by the National Security Council, September 8, 1976.

direction in the war effort, and provide American military personnel for the war effort. The decision conveyed to Diem in this document included a direct combat role for U.S. personnel, for the "instruction in and execution of air-ground support techniques" meant that American pilots would be carrying out bombing missions with Vietnamese personnel at their side. The decision included new demands on Diem for political and administrative reforms as his part in the "sharply increased joint effort."

The President has authorized the Secretary of State to instruct our Ambassador to Vietnam to inform President Diem as follows:

1. The U.S. Government is prepared to join the Vietnam Government in a sharply increased joint effort to avoid a further deterioration in the situation in South Vietnam.

2. This joint effort requires undertakings by both Governments as outlined below:

a. On its part the U.S. would immediately undertake the following actions in support of the GVN:

(1) Provide increased air lift to the GVN forces, including helicopters, light aviation, and transport aircraft, manned to the extent necessary by United States uniformed personnel and under United States operational control.

(2) Provide such additional equipment and United States uniformed personnel as may be necessary for air reconnaissance, photography, instruction in and execution of air-ground support techniques, and for special intelligence.

(3) Provide the GVN with small craft, including such United States uniformed advisers and operating personnel as may be necessary for operations in effecting surveillance and control over coastal waters and inland waterways.

(4) Provide expedited training and equipping of the civil guard and the self-defense corps with the objective of relieving the regular Army of static missions and freeing it for mobile offensive operations.

(5) Provide such personnel and equipment as may be necessary to improve the military-political intelligence system beginning at the provincial level and extending upward through the Government and the armed forces to the Central Intelligence Organization.

(6) Provide such new terms of reference, reorganization and additional personnel for United States military assistance in the operational collaboration with the GVN and operational direction of U.S. forces and to carry out the other increased responsibilities which accrue to the U.S. military authorities under these recommendations.

(7) Provide such increased economic aid as may be required to permit the GVN to pursue a vigorous flood relief and rehabilitation program, to supply material in support of the security efforts, and to give priority to projects in support of this expanded counter-insurgency program. (This could include increases in military pay, a full supply of a wide range of materials such as food, medical supplies, transportation

equipment, communications equipment, and any other items where material help could assist the GVN in winning the war against the Viet Cong.)

(8) Encourage and support (including financial support) a request by the GVN to the FAO [Food, and Agricultural Organization] or any other appropriate international organization for multilateral assistance in the relief and rehabilitation of the flood area.

(9) Provide individual administrators and advisers for the Governmental machinery of South Vietnam in types and numbers to be agreed upon by the two Governments.

(10) Provide personnel for a joint survey with the GVN of conditions in each of the provinces to assess the social, political, intelligence, and military factors bearing on the prosecution of the counter-insurgency program in order to reach a common estimate of these factors and a common determination of how to deal with them.

b. On its part, the GVN would initiate the following actions:

(1) Prompt and appropriate legislative and administrative action to put the nation on a wartime footing to mobilize its entire resources. (This would include a decentralization and broadening of the Government so as to realize the full potential of all non-Communist elements in the country willing to contribute to the common struggle.)

(2) The vitalization of appropriate Governmental wartime agencies with adequate authority to perform their functions effectively.

(3) Overhaul of the military establishment and command structure so as to create an effective military organization for the prosecution of the war and assure a mobile offensive capability for the Army.

145. TELEGRAM FROM NOLTING TO RUSK, NOVEMBER 25, 1961

Diem parried Kennedy's demands for political-administrative changes by arguing that his acceptance of such demands would make him appear to be subordinate to the United States and therefore "play into the Communists' hands." Nolting suggested that the United States give up any hope for political reforms and concentrate on "efficiency" in its negotiations with Diem. In December Nolting was informed that the United States would not insist on influencing GVN decisions in return for the new U.S. military involvement in South Vietnam.

I saw President Diem this morning on question of Vietnamese newspaper article reported Reftel, and subsequent article also same line in this morning's issue of same paper (Thoi Bao). I told him that I had not come to push him on response to our proposals of November 17, although I hoped he would soon be in position to give me his views. I wished specifically to bring to his attention two articles appearing in one Vietnamese newspaper which were untrue in their implication and

SOURCE: Document declassified by Department of State, August 8, 1975.

obviously damaging to our joint enterprise. Our one hour's conversation was inconclusive, but rather revealing.

Diem said he had just read the articles in question. They did reflect, in his opinion, the latent feelings of most Vietnamese (and, he added most Asians) concerning fancied or real conditions attached to Western aid. He went on to say that, because of this fact he had not told anyone except Thuan, Ngo Dinh Nhu and Vu Van Mau the content of our proposals of last week. He said he feared the reaction even among his own Cabinet members. I said I thought he misjudged their sentiments. Diem went on to say that newspaper articles in question were not inspired by government and could not have been based on knowledge or US proposals (except that obtained from US press), but that they expressed a point of view which he felt would be widespread if our proposals were known. He speculated that articles in part reaction to US press (mentioned in particular Rose's story in Time and Elegant's story in Newsweek), which he said indicated that US would have to "take charge" if Vietnam were to be saved. He mentioned in this connection, and read from, an article in Hong Kong Observer of November 8. I said I would not argue the point of whether or not Vietnamese articles in question were [word garbled], but that I wished to point out frankly that line taken in them had certain clear resemblances to what I had understood to be Mr. Ngo Dinh Nhu's views expressed in recent conversation with correspondent of Christian Science Monitor. Beyond that, I wanted to make point that our difficult and complex problem of establishing a more effective joint partnership to win the war here could only be complicated, and perhaps be made impossible, by a continuation of emotional, incorrect, and damaging line in newspapers. Diem concurred in this, but insisted that misrepresentations of his government in our own press could not but provoke nationalistic rejoinders from newspapers in Vietnam. He did not offer, nor did I press him, to issue any countervailing release; but I believe our conversation may help dampen down this foolish and dangerous business.

Throughout this discussion, Diem continued to make references to the quid pro quo aspects of our proposals, claiming that they played right into the hands of the Communists. He argued that we are pressing him to give a monopoly on nationalism to the Communists. I told him that this was the exact opposite of our aim; that we were not seeking quid pro quo as such, but were definitely seeking a structure of government in Vietnam, under his leadership, which could bear the weight of increased US assistance and could channel that assistance effectively; and that we were definitely seeking a basis in US and world opinion to enable US to support his government even more heavily. He promised next week to sit down and systematically go over our proposals point by point and to give his considered reaction. I said it would be helpful if he could give his response in due course in written form for clarity and precision. Throughout, Diem stressed that any attempt to "broaden the government" and to "make it more popular" was putting the cart before the horse. Giving security to the people, he said, is the first essential of regaining popular support; it is Communist terror and propaganda which is destroying Vietnamese support of their government; the will exists but can only be demonstrated when the people are free to express it; no additions of "dissidents" to his government would alter this fact. Moreover, he had many independents in the government already, and had had for many years. He cited educators, doctors, and others in this regard.

Without prejudging outcome these negotiations, I think we should be [doing?]

some [hard?] thinking whether we should not put major stress on efficiency in GVN rather than on more nebulous concept of "political reform". I think we can get a certain measure of improvement in GVN efficiency, which may open up possibility of political liberalization and broadening of political base, with all deliberate speed.

146. DRAFT MEMORANDUM BY ASSISTANT SECRETARY OF DEFENSE WILLIAM P. BUNDY, NOVEMBER 1961 [Extracts]

The Defense Department's William Bundy, who had already advocated sending American combat troops to South Vietnam, considered it probable that the United States would have to take over the war from the South Vietnamese and possible that it would have to go to war with China if it intervened militarily. Bundy assumed that U.S. "punishment" of North Vietnam and/or China would include at least the threat to use nuclear weapons.

The range of possible outcomes:

"Good" Scenarios

Scenario A: Diem takes heart and also takes the measures needed to improve efficiency, with only the 8000 man force and US specialist help. Hanoi heeds our warning and lays low, so that control is reasserted in South Vietnam. (Laos is a big question mark here and in other Scenarios.)

Scenario B: The struggle continues to go against Diem, and his own efforts at improvement are feeble. Thus, the US moves into the driver's seat and eventually brings the situation under control, using forces on the scale of 25,000–75,000. Hanoi and Peiping do not intervene directly, and we do not attack Hanoi.

Scenario C: As the struggle becomes prolonged, the US strikes at Hanoi (or Hanoi and Peiping intervene overtly). The US wins the resulting conflict, i.e., obtains at least a restoration of the status quo, after inflicting such punishment on Hanoi and/or Peiping that further aggressive moves are forestalled for a long time to come.

"Bad" Scenarios

Scenario X: The US decides not to put in the 8000 men, or later forces, and Diem is gradually overcome.

Scenario Y: The US puts in the 8000 men, but when Diem fails to improve his performance pulls out and lets him be overcome.

Scenario Z: Moscow comes to the aid of Hanoi and Peiping, supplying all necessary equipment (including a limited supply of air-deliverable nuclear weapons to retaliate in kind against US use) so that the outcome is a stalemate in which great destruction is wreaked on the whole area.

* * *

SOURCE: Document declassified by Department of Defense, May 28, 1975.

Of these, only A is truly a good outcome from all long-term standpoints—it stiffens us generally vis-à-vis the Bloc, holds the area (save perhaps Laos, does not discomfit us unduly in the neutral world, excellent for domestic US will and drive. Only trouble is—it's unlikely! *However,* it is still so much better than any other that it is worth accepting some added degree of difficulty in achieving B and C to give A every chance to happen.

The choice between B and C is a hard one. Despite all our warnings and Jorden Reports, our case of aggression against Hanoi will not convince neutrals of its accuracy and justice, or major allies of its wisdom and practicality. On the other hand, B is a road that has almost no end in sight. The US is poorly cast as a permanent protecting power, but the local capabilities would be so low at the end of such a struggle that we would almost have to assume that role. There is a very considerable chance that under continuing US protection, South Vietnam and the area as a whole would become a wasting asset and an eyesore that would greatly hamper all our relations worldwide. On the whole, the short-term onus attached to C may be preferable. However, as we play the hand toward C (especially if we use Moscow as the channel to Hanoi) we may well raise the chances of Moscow acting to bring on Z.

On the "bad" side, X and Z are clearly nightmares. Though X means loss of the area for a long time to come, it is probably better in the long run than Z. The chances of the Soviets acting to bring about Z do not appear great in the short run, but we must certainly try to keep those chances low (e.g., by making our dealings with Moscow private).

Y is also a nightmare. It loses the area. Moreover, vis-à-vis the Bloc it would be worse than X, since they would take it as an almost final proof that we would not stand up. It might have some compensating gains in the neutral world, at least in the short run. But on the whole it seems the worst possible outcome.

The basic strategic issues are:

a. How long to give A a chance?
b. Whether B is preferable to the weighted odds of C vs. Z?

1962

147. EDITORIAL IN *NHAN DAN* ON THE GENEVA AGREEMENT ON LAOS, JULY 24, 1962 [Extract]

On July 23, 1962, the Geneva Agreement was signed guaranteeing the neutrality of Laos, under a tripartite coalition government. The North Vietnamese portrayed the Agreement as a model for resolving other problems, evidently refer-

SOURCE: Hanoi Radio, Vietnam News Agency, in English to Europe and Asia, July 24, 1962, in Foreign Broadcast Information Service (FBIS) Far East, July 25, 1962, pp. JJJ8–9.

*ring to the conflict in South Vietnam–the one remaining conflict in which Hanoi
had the most interest. Nhan Dan noted also that the agreement showed how the
"forces of peace"–meaning the socialist countries, led by the Soviet Union–could
"effectively oppose the local wars started by the imperialists". This was North
Vietnam's answer to the Soviet argument that armed struggle against U.S.-supported
regimes was likely to turn into a conflagration involving nuclear weapons.*

The victory of the Laotian people and the success of the Geneva conference on
Laos are a very significant lesson: However small, a nation which is united and
determined to rise up in arms to struggle, and which enjoys warm support from the
socialist countries and freedom and peace-loving people of the world, can certainly
defeat the imperialist aggressors including their most frenzied ringleaders—the
U.S. imperialists. That the U.S. imperialists were compelled to sign the Geneva
agreement on Laos was a heavy failure for their policy of aggression there.

The success of the Geneva conference [word indistinct] also testifies to an
important truth in the present world situation in which the forces of peace are
becoming definitely stronger than the forces of war. The forces of peace can
effectively oppose the local wars started by the imperialists, and stamp out the
hotbeds of such wars,' as was stated by the conference of representatives of communist and workers parties held in Moscow in November 1960.

The peaceful settlement of the Laotian problem has a good bearing upon the
situation in southeast Asia and the world, and it contributes to easing world tension.
It also proves that many other problems can be solved by peaceful negotiations
provided the independence, freedom, and peace-loving forces are united in struggle
against the imperialist aggressors and warmongers. The success of the peaceful
settlement of the Laotian issue is also a success of the socialist forces and other
forces in southeast Asia and the world, which have persistently struggled inside and
outside the Geneva conference for over a year with the aim of settling peacefully
the Laotian problem, on the basis of ending U.S. intervention and respecting Laos'
independence and freedom.

148. MEMORANDUM BY ASSISTANT SECRETARY OF STATE ROGER HILSMAN, "THE SITUATION AND SHORT-TERM PROSPECTS IN SOUTH VIETNAM," DECEMBER 3, 1962 [Extract]

*Examining the short-term prospects in South Vietnam, Assistant Secretary of
State for Far Eastern Affairs Roger Hilsman noted that a significant worsening of
the internal security situation would increase the chance of a coup against Diem,
particularly by military leaders. In a remarkably accurate conclusion, Hilsman
anticipated the advance U.S. notice of the coup and the consequent administrative
disruption causing severe setbacks to the pacification effort.*

SOURCE: *U.S. Vietnam Relations*, Book 12, pp. 520–521.

D. Political Situation

The stability of the government during the next year will continue to depend principally on Diem's handling of the internal security situation. If Diem can demonstrate a continuing improvement in security conditions, he should be able to alleviate concern and boost morale within his bureaucracy and military establishment. However, if the fight against the Viet Cong goes badly, if the Viet Cong launches a series of successful and dramatic military operations, or if South Vietnamese army casualties increase appreciably over a protracted period, the chances of a coup attempt against Diem could increase substantially. Moreover, the possibility of a coup attempt at any time cannot be excluded. Many officials and oppositionists feel that, despite the government's military victories and improved military capabilities and initiative, the GVN is not winning the war principally because of Diem's virtual one-man rule and his failure to follow through with the political and economic measures necessary to gain the support of the peasants.

It is more difficult now than at any time since the crisis in South Vietnam began in late 1959 to estimate reliably the elements that would be most likely to precipitate a coup attempt, the prospects for the success of a coup attempt, or the effects of such an attempt on internal stability and on the counterinsurgency effort itself. During the past year or so, the Viet Cong presumably has improved its ability to initiate a coup and might attempt to do so. However, the Viet Cong probably would not be able to carry out a successful coup, and the odds that it could gain control of a successful coup, although somewhat better than last year, appear to be less than even.

The coup most likely to succeed would be one with non-Communist leadership and support, principally involving South Vietnamese military elements and civilian officials and perhaps some oppositionists outside the government. The abortive coup attempt in November 1960 and the palace bombing in February 1962 have undoubtedly demonstrated to coup plotters the necessity for better preparation and broader participation by the military. Any future non-Communist coup group probably would not be as deficient in this respect and its leaders, unlike the leaders of 1960 coup attempt, can be expected to be better prepared to execute their plan quickly. Although the possibility of a Kong Le-type coup, i.e., a coup led by a junior and relatively unknown officer, cannot be completely discounted, it is more likely that the coup leadership would include some middle and top echelon military officials. While their role is by no means certain, a major polarization of the GVN military leadership into coup and anti-coup groups does not appear likely. Most of them would probably elect to remain uncommitted at the outset of the coup, as they apparently did in November 1960, and would then give their tacit or active support to whatever side appeared to have the best chance of winning. Under these circumstances, a military coup appears to have a better than even chance of succeeding.

Diem's removal—whether by a military coup, assassination, or death from accidental or natural causes—would probably considerably strengthen the power of the military. The odds appear about even between a government led by a military junta or by Vice President Tho, with the army, in the latter case, playing a major if not the predominant role behind the scenes. On the one hand, the military might conclude that a military-led government would be better able to maintain national unity and internal political cohesion and, more importantly, to conduct a determined and effective campaign against the Viet Cong. On the other hand, they might conclude that Tho, who apparently has been on good terms with some of the present top military leaders, would not disagree with their views on the manner of conducting the fight against the Communists and this his constitutional succession would legalize the change in government and possibly avert a serious power struggle. (Although Diem's brothers, Nhu and Can, would probably also be removed by a coup, if Diem left the scene for other reasons his brothers might attempt to retain real political power.) In any event, a government led by the military, by Tho, or by any other civilian approved by the military would probably maintain South Vietnam's pro-US orientation.

If there is a serious disruption of government leadership as a result of a military coup or as a result of Diem's death, any momentum the government's counterinsurgency efforts had achieved would probably be halted and possibly reversed, at least for a time. Moreover, the confusion and suspicion attending the disruption would provide the Viet Cong guerrillas an opportunity to strengthen their position in the countryside and attack some installations in large force, but they would probably fail if they attempted to seize control of the government.

Under most of the foreseeable circumstances involving a coup, the role of the US could be extremely important. Although this is by no means certain, US military and intelligence officials might well have advance notice of an impending coup and might be able to restrain the coup plotters from precipitous action. Even if unable to restrain such action, however, US officials might have greater success in averting widespread fighting and a serious power struggle which would lead to excessive bloodshed and weaken the front against the Viet Cong. The US could also be helpful in achieving agreement among the coup leaders as to who should lead the government in restoring the momentum of the government's counterinsurgency effort.

149. REPORT TO THE PRESIDENT ON SOUTHEAST ASIA-VIETNAM BY SENATOR MIKE MANSFIELD, DECEMBER 18, 1962 [Extract]

After a visit to Southeast Asia, Senator Mike Mansfield, an early and influential supporter of Ngo Dinh Diem, warned President Kennedy that the U.S. was in danger of being sucked into full-scale war against the Communist guerrillas and of setting up "some form of neocolonial rule" in South Vietnam. He noted that little thought had been given to the possibility of a serious worsening of the situation and advised the President to begin to think in terms of a diplomatic solution that would minimize U.S. involvement on the mainland of Southeast Asia.

Even assuming that aid over a prolonged period would be available, the question still remains as to the capacity of the present Saigon government to carry out the task of social engineering. Ngo Dinh Diem remains a dedicated, sincere, hardworking, incorruptible and patriotic leader. But he is older and the problems

SOURCE: *Two Reports on Viet Nam and Southeast Asia to the President of the U.S. by Senator Mike Mansfield*, U.S. Congress, Senate, Committee on Foreign Relations, 93rd Cong., 1st Session, April 1973.

which confront him are more complex than those which he faced when he pitted his genuine nationalism against, first, the French and Bao Dai and then against the sects with such effectiveness. The energizing role, which he played in the past appears to be passing to other members of his family, particularly Ngo Dinh Nhu. The latter is a person of great energy and intellect who is fascinated by the operations of political power and has consummate eagerness and ability in organizing and manipulating it. But it is Ngo Dinh Diem, not Ngo Dinh Nhu, who has such popular mandate to exercise power as there is in South Vietnam. In a situation of this kind there is a great danger of the corruption of unbridled power. This has implications far beyond the persistent reports and rumors of fiscal and similar irregularities which are, in any event, undocumented. More important is its effect on the organization of the machinery for carrying out the new concepts. The difficulties in Vietnam are not likely to be overcome by a handful of paid retainers and sycophants. The success of the new approach in Vietnam presupposes a great contribution of initiative and self-sacrifice from a substantial body of Vietnamese with capacities for leadership at all levels. Whether that contribution can be obtained remains to be seen. For in the last analysis it depends upon a diffusion of political power, essentially in a democratic pattern. The trends in the political life of Vietnam have not been until now in that direction despite lip service to the theory of developing democratic and popular institutions "from the bottom up" through the strategic hamlet program.

To summarize, our policies and activities are designed to meet an existing set of internal problems in south Vietnam. North Vietnam infiltrates some supplies and cadres into the south; together with the Vietnamese we are trying to shut off this flow. The Vietcong has had the offensive in guerrilla warfare in the countryside; we are attempting to aid the Vietnamese military in putting them on the defensive with the hope of eventually reducing them at least to ineffectiveness. Finally, the Vietnamese peasants have sustained the Vietcong guerrillas out of fear, indifference or blandishment and we are helping the Vietnamese in an effort to win the peasants away by offering them the security and other benefits which may be provided in the strategic hamlets.

That, in brief, is the present situation. As noted, there is optimism that success will be achieved quickly. My own view is that the problems can be made to yield to present remedies, *provided* the problems and their magnitude do not change significantly and *provided* that the remedies are pursued by both Vietnamese and Americans (and particularly the former) with great vigor and self-dedication.

Certainly, if these remedies do not work, it is difficult to conceive of alternatives, with the possible exception of a truly massive commitment of American military personnel and other resources—in short going to war fully ourselves against the guerrillas—and the establishment of some form of neocolonial rule in south Vietnam. That is an alternative which I most emphatically do not recommend. On the contrary, it seems to me most essential that we make crystal clear to the Vietnamese government and to our own people that while we will go to great lengths to help, the primary responsibility rests with the Vietnamese. Our role is and must remain secondary in present circumstances. It is their country, their future which is most at stake, not ours.

To ignore that reality will not only be immensely costly in terms of American lives and resources but it may also draw us inexorably into some variation of the unenviable position in Vietnam which was formerly occupied by the French. We are not, of course, at that point at this time. But the great increase in American military commitment this year has tended to point us in that general direction and we may well begin to slide rapidly toward it if any of the present remedies begin to falter in practice.

As indicated, our planning appears to be predicated on the assumption that existing internal problems in South Vietnam will remain about the same and can be overcome by greater effort and better techniques. But what if the problems do not remain the same? To all outward appearances, little if any thought has been given in Saigon at least, to the possibilities of a change in the nature of the problems themselves. Nevertheless, they are very real possibilities and the initiative for instituting change rests in enemy hands largely because of the weakness of the Saigon government. The range of possible change includes a step-up in the infiltration of cadres and supplies by land or sea. It includes the use of part or all of the regular armed forces of North Vietnam, reported to be about 300,000 strong, under Vo Nguyen Giap. It includes, in the last analysis, the possibility of a major increase in any of many possible forms of Chinese Communist support for the Vietcong.

None of these possibilities may materialize. It would be folly, however, not to recognize their existence and to have as much clarification in advance of what our response to them will be if they do.

This sort of anticipatory thinking cannot be undertaken with respect to the situation in Vietnam alone. The problem there can be grasped, it seems to me, only as we have clearly in mind our interests with respect to all of Southeast Asia. If it is essential in our own interests to maintain a quasi-permanent position of power on the Asian mainland as against the Chinese then we must be prepared to continue to pay the present cost in Vietnam indefinitely and to meet any escalation on the other side with at least a commensurate escalation of commitment of our own. This can go very far, indeed, in terms of lives and resources. Yet if it is essential to our interests then we would have no choice.

But if on the other hand it is, at best, only desirable rather than essential that a position of power be maintained on the mainland, then other courses are indicated. We would, then, properly view such improvement as may be obtained by the new approach in Vietnam primarily in terms of what it might contribute to strengthening our diplomatic hand in the Southeast Asian region. And we would use that hand as vigorously as possible and in every way possible not to deepen our costly involvement on the Asian mainland but to lighten it.

1963

150. TELEGRAM FROM NOLTING TO RUSK, APRIL 6, 1963

Although tensions between the United States and President Diem would flare over Diem's handling of the Buddhist crisis in May 1963, the first serious clash

SOURCE: Document declassified by Department of State, June 9, 1978.

between the two governments came over Diem's rejection of the U.S. plan to expand and deepen its advisory effort in South Vietnam, as creating the impression of a U.S. "protectorate." Nolting proposed reducing U.S. support for Diem's military budget if necessary to "convince Diem that we mean business." The retaliatory move proved unnecessary, as Diem withdrew his formal objection. But his suspicions of American motives remained.

In assessing Diem's rejection of our proposal for counterinsurgency fund, most significant point is that grounds advanced for rejection approach repudiation of concept of expanded and deepened U.S. advisory effort, civil and military. This concept was fundamental element our agreement with GVN in December 1961 on greatly stepped up U.S. assistance effort. Progress made since that date would not have occurred, in our view, without massive advisory effort, nor do we believe it can be maintained if drastic reduction made at this stage in number of advisors, particularly in provinces and with smaller military formations—which are precisely areas where Diem seems to find most difficulty. We would not deny that some advisors may, on occasion, have acted in way to cause complaint or that their number and zeal have reached point where, to those who want to see it that way, there are similarities with a "protectorate" situation. Point is we don't think GVN can win without U.S. advisors in roughly present density for the next year at least.

We also gravely doubt that momentum of strategic hamlet program can be maintained and, especially, gains already made consolidated without piastre fund of roughly size we have proposed and procedures for its use as effective as those we have had for purchased piastres. Although Diem says GVN will make necessary funds available, he is probably thinking of much smaller sum than we are (very likely the 400 million piastres already earmarked by GVN vs 1300 million in our proposal) and it is clear that he is not thinking of procedures which would give us satisfactory voice in use of GVN funds. (He probably wants to revert to former unsatisfactory GVN procedures). In short, we conclude that unless we can get something comparable to what we have proposed, there is grave risk that strategic hamlet program will founder. Without successful strategic hamlet program, it will take longer to get insurgency under control.

If this is correct evaluation of significance of Diem's position, we see no viable alternative to taking action (or possibly series of actions) designed to convince Diem that we mean business—not withstanding grave risk that such action (A) will not move Diem but on contrary lead to retaliatory action and descending spiral our relations and (B) might light coup fuse,. (We continue have no grounds to believe that coup would bring to power a government more likely to win the war than Diem. On contrary, we think a coup, either accomplished or abortive, would weaken chances of preserving independence of SVN.)

Unless tactical move prescribed at end this message bears fruit, first action we would recommend is to inform GVN that we are revising counterpart support to GVN military budget downward by, say, 1.3 billion piastres (from 7.5 billion) and are tentatively earmarking this sum for support to strategic hamlet program. This would be very serious matter for GVN but action not irreversible if Diem comes around and would not involve dislocations inherent in cancelling orders for hamlet materials, for example. Moreover, it is in any case going to be necessary, to reduce counterpart allocation to military budget (if joint fund is not approved), simply in order to provide funds to carry on minimum existing economic projects and for USOM [United States Operations Mission] operating expenses.

In informing Diem of above, we would at same time offer (A) to review advisor situation with view to seeing what reduction can be made and (B) to replace any advisor who abuses his position or undermines GVN authority. Finally, as earnest our firm intention to phase out special military assistance, would give him detailed briefing on 3-year comprehensive plan (request authority to do this).

Before taking step of informing Diem of reduced support for military budget; believe it advisable for tactical reasons to ask him to give me written response our proposal for counterinsurgency fund, to include reasons for rejection. This move would provide time for him to reflect on consequences his decision and for members his government to work on him if they are disposed to do so. I might also use this period for further talks with Diem and others in course of which I might draw on arguments in immediately preceding paragraph. Meanwhile, we would quietly hold up approval of military budget support level and any new allocations of funds.

151. ARTICLE BY LAO DONG PARTY POLITICAL BUREAU MEMBER NGUYEN CHI THANH, JULY 1963 [Extract]

In the context of the Soviet Union's argument that armed struggle should be avoided because of the danger of world war, Nguyen Chi Thanh, later the commander of all Communist forces in the South, asserted Hanoi's view that the United States was not invincible and should not be feared.

Although ultimate conclusions cannot yet be reached insofar as the struggle is still going on in south Viet Nam, we may however put forth the following views:

1. The U.S. imperialists are not invincible. Compared with imperialists of other countries, they are mightier, but compared with the revolutionary forces and the forces of the people of the world, they are not at all strong. If the proletarian revolution and people of the world resolutely struggle against U.S. imperialism, they can surely repel it step by step and narrow down its domain.

We do not have any illusions about the United States. We do not underestimate our opponent—the strong and cunning U.S. imperialism. But we are not afraid of the United States. The strategic concept thoroughly pervades the revolutionary line of south Viet Nam and is the fundamental factor determining the success of the revolution. If, on the contrary, one is afraid of the United States and thinks that to offend it would court failure, and that firm opposition to U.S. imperialism would touch off a nuclear war, then the only course left would be to compromise with and surrender to U.S. imperialism.

2. A powerful north Viet Nam will be a decisive factor in the social development of our entire country. But this does not mean that simply because the north is

SOURCE: Nguyen Chi Thanh, *Who Will Win in South Viet Nam?* (Peking: Foreign Language Press, 1963), pp. 8–9.

strong, the revolutionary movement in the south will automatically succeed. The powerful north Viet Nam and the revolutionary movement of the south Vietnamese people are mutually complementary and must be closely coordinated; the building of the north itself cannot replace the resolution of the inherent social contradictions of south Viet Nam. Adhering to this correct view, we have avoided opportunistic mistakes. If, on the contrary, we had feared the United States and had no faith in the success of our struggles against it, we would have called on the people in south Viet Nam to "wait" and "coexist peacefully" with the U.S.-Diem clique, and committed an irreparable error. We have correctly handled the relations between north and south Viet Nam. This is a Marxist-Leninist strategic concept which is in conformity with the latest experience in the world developments and those in our own country.

152. TELEGRAM FROM ACTING SECRETARY OF STATE GEORGE BALL TO AMBASSADOR HENRY CABOT LODGE, AUGUST 24, 1963

After General Tran Van Don blamed a violent attack against Buddhist pagodas on police and special forces believed loyal to Diem's brother, Ngo Dinh Nhu, Harriman and Hilsman in the State Department and White House Assistant Michael Forrestal immediately called for action to rid the GVN of the influence of Nhu and his wife, and, if necessary, of Diem. In a telegram drafted in Rusk's absence, the State Department ordered Lodge to let military leaders know that the United States could not continue to support the GVN unless the Nhus were removed.

It is now clear that whether military proposed martial law or whether Nhu tricked them into it, Nhu took advantage of its imposition to smash pagodas with policy and Tung's Special Forces loyal to him, thus placing onus on military in eyes of world and Vietnamese people. Also clear that Nhu has maneuvered himself into commanding position.

US Government cannot tolerate situation in which power lies in Nhu's hands. Diem must be given chance to rid himself of Nhu and his coterie and replace them with best military and political personalities available.

If, in spite of all of your efforts, Diem remains obdurate and refuses, then we must face the possibility that Diem himself cannot be preserved.

We now believe immediate action must be taken to prevent Nhu from consolidating his position further. Therefore, unless you in consultation with Harkins perceive overriding objections you are authorized to proceed along following lines:

(1) First, we must press on appropriate levels of GVN following line:

(a) USG cannot accept actions against Buddhists taken by Nhu and his collaborators under cover martial law.

SOURCE: Document declassified by Department of State, November 27, 1974.

(b) Prompt dramatic actions redress situation must be taken, including repeal of decree 10, release of arrested monks, nuns, etc.

(2) We must at same time also tell key military leaders that US would find it impossible to continue support GVN militarily and economically unless above steps are taken immediately which we recognize requires removal of the Nhus from the scene. We wish give Diem reasonable opportunity to remove Nhus, but if he remains obdurate, then we are prepared to accept the obvious implication that we can no longer support Diem. You may also tell appropriate military commanders we will give them direct support in any interim period of breakdown central government mechanism.

(3) We recognize the necessity of removing taint on military for pagoda raids and placing blame squarely on Nhu. You are authorized to have such statements made in Saigon as you consider desirable to achieve this objective. We are prepared to take same line here and to have Voice of America [VOA] make statement along lines contained in next numbered telegram whenever you give the word, preferably as soon as possible.

Concurrently with above, Ambassador and country team should urgently examine all possible alternative leadership and make detailed plans as to how we might bring about Diem's replacement if this should become necessary.

Assume you will consult with General Harkins re any precautions necessary protect American personnel during crisis period.

You will understand that we cannot from Washington give you detailed instructions as to how this operation should proceed, but you will also know we will back you to the hilt on actions you take to achieve our objectives.

Needless to say we have held knowledge of this telegram to minimum essential people and assume you will take similar precautions to prevent premature leaks.

153. TELEGRAM FROM RUSK TO LODGE AND COMMANDER, U.S. MILITARY ASSISTANCE COMMAND, VIETNAM (MACV) GEN. PAUL HARKINS, AUGUST 29, 1963

The Kennedy Administration moved a step further toward stimulating a coup against Diem and Nhu when General Paul Harkins, Commander of the Military Assistant Command Vietnam, was authorized to establish liaison with potential coup planners in order to review their plans. Lodge was also given authority to announce the suspension of aid to Diem at a time of his own choosing.

1. Highest level meeting noon today reviewed your 375 and reaffirmed basic course. Specific decisions follow:

2. In response to your recommendation, General Harkins is hereby authorized to repeat to such Generals as you indicate the messages previously transmitted by

---

SOURCE: Document declassified by Department of State, November 29, 1974.

CAS officers. He should stress that the USG supports the movement to eliminate the Nhus from the government, but that before arriving at specific understandings with the Generals, General Harkins must know who are involved, resources available to them and overall plan for coup. The USG will support a coup which has good chance of succeeding but plans no direct involvement of U.S. Armed Forces. Harkins should state that he is prepared to establish liaison with the coup planners and to review plans, but will not engage directly in joint coup planning.

3. Question of last approach to Diem remains undecided and separate personal message from Secretary to you develops our concerns and asks your comment.

4. On movement of U.S. forces, we do not expect to make any announcement or leak at present and believe that any later decision to publicize such movements should be closely connected to developing events on your side. We cannot of course prevent unauthorized disclosures or speculation, but we will in any event knock down any reports of evacuation.

5. You are hereby authorized to announce suspension of aid through [to?] Diem Government at a time and under conditions of your choice. In deciding upon use of this authority, you should consider importance of timing and managing announcement so as to minimize appearance of collusion with Generals, and also to minimize danger of unpredictable and disruptive reaction by existing government. We also assume that you will not in fact use this authority unless you think it essential, and we see it as possible that Harkins' approach and increasing process of cooperation may provide assurance Generals desire. Our own view is that it will be best to hold this authority for use in close conjunction with coup, and not for present encouragement of Generals, but decision is yours.

154. MEMORANDUM FOR THE RECORD OF MEETING AT THE STATE DEPARTMENT, AUGUST 31, 1963

After the coup plotters suspended their planning, realizing they did not yet have sufficient military forces under their control, those who had been more skeptical about a move against Diem took the initiative, as the mood in the administration became more cautious. The old argument about whether the war could be won with Diem surfaced again. To bolster the case for continuation of the existing policy line, Hilsman also presented evidence that Nhu was secretly trying to make a deal with the North.

1. Secretary Rusk stated that, in his judgment, we were back to where we were about Wednesday of last week, and this causes him to go back to the original problem and ask what in the situation led us to think well of a coup. Ruling out hatred of the Nhus, he said, there would appear to be three things:

a. The things that the Nhus had done or supported, which tended to upset the GVN internally.

SOURCE: *The Pentagon Papers*, pp. 202–205.

b. The things that they had done what had an adverse external effect.

c. The great pressures of U.S. public opinion.

2. Mr. Rusk then asked if we should not pick up Ambassador Lodge's suggestion in his message of today (Saigon 391) and determine what steps are required to re-gird solidarity in South Vietnam—such as improvement in conditions concerning students and Buddhists and the possible departure of Madame Nhu. He said that we should determine what additional measures are needed to improve the international situation—such as problems affecting Cambodia—and to improve the Vietnamese position wherein U.S. public opinion is concerned. He then said that he is reluctant to start off by saying now that Nhu has to go; that it is unrealistic.

3. Mr. McNamara stated that he favored the above proposals of the Secretary of State, with one additional step—that is to establish quickly and firmly our line of communication between Lodge, Harkins and the GVN. He pointed out that at the moment our channels of communication are essentially broken and that they should be reinstituted at all costs.

4. Mr. Rusk added that we must do our best not to permit Diem to decapitate his military command in light of its obviously adverse effect on the prosecution of the war. At this point he asked if anyone present had any doubt in his mind but that the coup was off.

5. Mr. Kattenburg said that he had some remaining doubt; that we have not yet sent the generals a strong enough message; that the VOA statement regarding the withdrawal of aid was most important, but that we repudiated it too soon. He stated further that the group should take note of the fact that General Harkins did not carry out his instructions with respect to communication with the generals. Mr. Rusk interrupted Kattenburg to state that, to the contrary, he believed Harkins' conduct was exactly correct in light of the initial response which he received from General Khiem (they were referring to Harkins' report in MACV 1583).

6. Mr. Hilsman commented that, in his view, the generals are not now going to move unless they are pressed by a revolt from below. In this connect Ambassador Nolting warned that in the uncoordinated Vietnamese structure anything can happen, and that while an organized successful coup is out, there might be small flurries by irresponsible dissidents at any time.

7. Mr. Hilsman undertook to present four basic factors which bear directly on the problem confronting the U.S. now. They are, in his view:

a. The mood of the people, particularly the middle level officers, non-commissioned officers and middle level bureaucrats, who are most restive. Mr. McNamara interrupted to state that he had seen no evidence of this and General Taylor commented that he had seen none either, but would like to see such evidence as Hilsman could produce. Mr. Kattenburg commented that the middle level officers and bureaucrats are uniformly critical of the government, to which Mr. McNamara commented that if this indeed be the fact we should know about it.

b. The second basic factor, as outlined by Hilsman, was what effect will be felt on our programs elsewhere in Asia if we acquiesce to a strong Nhu-dominated government. In this connection, he reported that there is a Korean study now underway on just how much repression the United States will tolerate before pulling out her aid. Mr. McNamara stated that he had not seen this study and would be anxious to have it.

c. The third basic factor is Mr. Nhu, his personality and his policy. Hilsman recalled that Nhu has once already launched an effort aimed at withdrawal of our province advisors and stated that he is sure he is in conversation with the French. He gave, as supporting evidence, the content of an intercepted message, which Mr. Bundy asked to see. Ambassador Nolting expressed the opinion that Nhu will not make a deal with Ho Chi Minh on Ho's terms.

d. The fourth point is the matter of U.S. and world opinion, Hilsman stated that this problem was moving to a political and diplomatic plane. Part of the problem, he said, is the press, which concludes incorrectly that we have the ability to change the things in Vietnam of which they are critical. To this Mr. Murrow added that this problem of press condemnation is now worldwide.

8. Mr. Kattenburg stated that as recently as last Thursday it was the belief of Ambassador Lodge that, if we undertake to live with this repressive regime, with its bayonets at every street corner and its transparent negotiations with puppet bonzes, we are going to be thrown out of the country in six months. He stated that at this juncture it would be better for us to make the decision to get out honorably. He went on to say that, having been acquainted with Diem for ten years, he was deeply disappointed in him, saying that he will not separate from his brother. It was Kattenburg's view that Diem will get very little support from the military and, as time goes on, he will get less and less support and the country will go steadily down hill.

9. General Taylor asked what Kattenburg meant when he said that we would be forced out of Vietnam within six months. Kattenburg replied that in from six months to a year, as the people see we are losing the war, they will gradually go to the other side and we will be obliged to leave. Ambassador Nolting expressed general disagreement with Mr. Kattenburg. He said that the unfavorable activity which motivated Kattenburg's remarks was confined to the city and, while city support of Diem is doubtless less now, it is not greatly so. He said that it is improper to overlook the fact that we have done a tremendous job toward winning the Vietnam war, working with this same imperfect, annoying government.

10. Mr. Kattenburg added that there is one new factor—the population, which was in high hopes of expelling the Nhus after the VOA announcement regarding cessation of aid; now, under the heel of Nhu's military repression, they would quickly lose heart.

11. Secretary Rusk commented that Kattenburg's recital was largely speculative; that it would be far better for us to start on the firm basis of two things—that we will not pull out of Vietnam until the war is won, and that we will not run a coup. Mr. McNamara expressed agreement with this view.

12. Mr. Rusk then said that we should present questions to Lodge which fall within these parameters. He added that he believes we have good proof that we have been winning the war, particularly the contrast between the first six months of 1962 and the first six months of 1963. He then asked the Vice President if he had any contribution to make.

13. The Vice President stated that he agreed with Secretary Rusk's conclusions completely; that he had great reservations himself with respect to a coup, particularly so because he had never really seen a genuine alternative to Diem. He

stated that from both a practical and political viewpoint, it would be a disaster to pull out; that we should stop playing cops and robbers and get back to talking straight to the GVN, and that we should once again go about winning the war. He stated that after our communications with them are genuinely reestablished, it may be necessary for someone to talk rough to them—perhaps General Taylor. He said further that he had been greatly impressed with Ambassador Nolting's views and agreed with Mr. McNamara's conclusions.

14. General Taylor raised the question of whether we should change the disposition of the forces which had been set in motion as a result of the crisis. It was agreed that there should be no change in the existing disposition for the time being.

155. MEMORANDUM TO RUSK FROM HILSMAN, SEPTEMBER 16, 1963

Hilsman outlined two possible lines of policy toward Diem, one acquiescing in the status quo, the other taking a tough posture. He argued against a "reconciliation track" on the ground that Nhu had already decided to reduce the American presence and possibly strike a deal with Hanoi for a "neutralist" South Vietnam.

Attached are two cables—one on the "Reconciliation Track" and one on the "Pressures and Persuasion Track."

I think it is important to note that these are true alternatives—i.e., the "Reconciliation Track" is not the same as Phase I of the "Pressures and Persuasion Track." The difference is in public posture. Phase I of the "Pressures and Persuasion Track" continues to maintain a public posture of disapproval of the GVN's policies of repression. The "Reconciliation Track" requires a public posture of acquiescence in what the GVN has recently done, and even some effort by the US to put these recent actions in as good a light as we possibly can.

If this distinction, which is a real one, is preserved, then it seems to me clear that it will *not* be possible to switch from the "Reconciliation Track" to a "Pressures and Persuasion Track" if the former does not work—except in the event that Diem and Nhu provide us with another dramatic of act of repression as an excuse. On the other hand, it *will* be possible to switch from a "Pressures and Persuasion Track" to a "Reconciliation Track" at any time during Phases I and II of the "Pressures and Persuasion Track," although probably not after we had entered Phases III and IV.

My own judgment is that the "Reconciliation Track" will not work. I think that Nhu has already decided on an adventure. I think he feels that the progress already made in the war and the US materiel on hand gives him freedom to launch on a course that has a minimum and a maximum goal. The minimum goal would be sharply to reduce the American presence in those key positions which have political significance in the provinces and the strategic hamlet program and to avoid any meaningful concessions that would go against his Mandarin, "personalist" vision of the future of Viet-Nam. The maximum goal, I would think, would be a deal with

---

SOURCE: Document declassified by authority of the president, February 14, 1968.

North Vietnam for a truce in the war, a complete removal of the US presence, and a "neutralist" or "Titoist" but still separate South Viet-Nam.

At the same time, I would give Phases I and II of the "Pressures and Persuasion Track" only a fair chance of success, and I think that Phases III and IV will create a situation over which we would have little if any control, at least if they were launched in the immediate future.

Thus, I would recommend adopting as our initial course Phases I and II of the "Pressures and Persuasion Track," testing and probing as we go along and being ready to switch to "Reconciliation" at any moment that it becomes necessary, using the decision to switch as a means of getting at least nominal concessions in order to save as much of our face as possible.

I make this recommendation with the caveat that we do not have sufficient information to make a final and complete judgment on either of the two key issues—where Nhu will lead Viet-Nam if he remains in power and whether or not enough people will continue to fight the Viet Cong to bring victory.

The trouble is the necessary information for a final judgment on these two key issues is simply not available. Nor is anyone likely to acquire it before we must make a fundamental decision. This is not an unfamiliar dilemma in the making of foreign policy. At such a time governments perforce operate on informed hunch, hoping only that the hunch they use is the best one available.

But I also think that at such a time governments must not even attempt to make final judgments or to take irreversible actions, but to proceed by incremental steps. It is for this reason that I would reject both "Reconciliation" and Phases III and IV—at least at this time.

156. MEMORANDUM BY CHESTER COOPER FOR CIA DIRECTOR JOHN MCCONE, SEPTEMBER 19, 1963 [Extract]

After a column by Joseph Alsop suggesting that Diem and Nhu had explored a possible rapprochement with the North, CIA official Chester Cooper assessed the likelihood of Diem making a deal with the Communists at "less than even" but indicated that the matter required "close attention" by U.S. intelligence.

Subject: Possible Rapprochement Between North and South Vietnam

1. *Summary.* The information, rumors and interviews on which Joseph Alsop's article in the 18 September *Washington Post* was based are but the most recent signs that the GVN, the DRV, and the French may have been engaged of late in exploring the possibilities of some kind of North-South rapprochement. It is highly unlikely that any such explorations seriously concern imminent reunification, since Hanoi's frequently stated conditions for unification would entail the capitulation of the GVN and the handing over of South Vietnam to the Communist North. We

SOURCE: Document declassified by the Central Intelligence Agency, November 14, 1978.

consider chances less than even that the GVN is now seriously interested in a form of rapprochement of lesser import than reunification—e.g., *de facto cease-fire, formal cease-fire,* or a variant of *neutralization.* Ngo family actions in this realm merit continuing close attention. A variety of motives could induce (or may have already induced) the Ngo's to explore the possibilities of rapprochement with Hanoi: (a) a desire to develop their own "sanction" to counter threats of US aid cuts and provide the GVN some maneuverability in face of US pressures; (b) a general interest in maximizing available options during a crisis period (e.g., one in which they might find themselves losing the military support necessary to prevent total defeat); and (c) a new willingness to listen to long-standing French arguments or overtures. We would expect such exploratory activity to subside if US-GVN relations or the course of the war against the Viet Cong should improve—and, conversely, to increase if either of these should further deteriorate.

157. REPORT OF THE MCNAMARA-TAYLOR MISSION TO SOUTH VIETNAM, OCTOBER 2, 1963 [Extract]

McNamara and Taylor returned from their visit to South Vietnam with the conclusion that the war effort had made "great progress" since the beginning of 1962, but that it was doubtful that Diem and Nhu had sufficient support from the urban elite to win the war. They called for a program of selected pressures on Diem through withholding of aid funds and a public posture of disapproval of Diem's repression.

I. Conclusions and Recommendations

A. Conclusions.

1. The military campaign has made great progress and continues to progress.

2. There are serious political tensions in Saigon (and perhaps elsewhere in South Vietnam) where the Diem-Nhu government is becoming increasingly unpopular.

3. There is no solid evidence of the possibility of a successful coup, although assassination of Diem or Nhu is always a possibility.

4. Although some, and perhaps an increasing number, of GVN military officers are becoming hostile to the government and at least for the near future they will continue to perform their military duties.

5. Further repressive actions by Diem and Nhu could change the present favorable military trends. On the other hand, a return to more moderate methods of control and administration, unlikely though it may be, would substantially mitigate the political crisis.

6. It is not clear that pressures exerted by the U.S. will move Diem and Nhu toward moderation. Indeed, pressures may increase their obduracy. But unless such pressures are exerted, they are almost certain to continue past patterns of behavior.

SOURCE: *U.S.-Vietnam Relations,* Book 12, pp. 554–573.

B. Recommendations.

We recommend that:

1. General Harkins review with Diem the military changes necessary to complete the military campaign in the Northern and Central areas (I, II, and III Corps) by the end of 1954, and in the Delta (IV Corps) by the end of 1965. This review would consider the need for such changes as:

    a. A further shift of military emphasis and strength to the Delta (IV Corps).

    b. A increase in the military tempo in all corps areas, so that all combat troops are in the field an average of 20 days out of 30 and static missions are ended.

    c. Emphasis on "clear and hold operations" instead of terrain sweeps which have little permanent value.

    d. The expansion of personnel in combat units to full authorized strength.

    e. The training and arming of hamlet militia at an accelerated rate, especially in the Delta.

    f. A consolidation of the strategic hamlet program, especially in the Delta, and action to insure that future strategic hamlets are not built until they can be protected, and until civic action programs can be introduced.

2. A program be established to train Vietnamese so that essential functions now performed by U.S. military personnel can be carried out by Vietnamese by the end of 1965. It should be possible to withdraw the bulk of U.S. personnel by that time.

3. In accordance with the program to train progressively Vietnamese to take over military functions, the Defense Department should announce in the very near future presently prepared plans to withdraw 1000 U.S. military personnel by the end of 1963. This action should be explained in low key as an initial step in a long-term program to replace U.S. personnel with trained Vietnamese without impairment of the war effort.

4. The following actions be taken to impress upon Diem our disapproval of his political program.

    a. Continue to withhold commitment of funds in the commodity import program, but avoid a formal announcement. The potential significance of the withholding of commitments for the 1964 military budget should be brought home to the top military officers in working level contacts between USOM and MACV and the Joint General Staff; up to now we have stated $95 million may be used by the Vietnamese as a planning level for the commodity import program for 1964. Henceforth we could make clear that this is uncertain both because of lack of final appropriation action by the Congress *and* because of executive policy.

    b. Suspend approval of the pending AID [Agency for International Development] loans for the Saigon-Cholon Waterworks and Saigon Electric Power Project. We should state clearly that we are doing so as a matter of policy.

    c. Advise Diem that MAP [Military Assistance Program] and CIA support for designated units, now under Colonel Tung's control (mostly held in or near the Saigon area for political reasons) will be cut off unless these units are promptly assigned, to the full authority of the Joint General Staff and transferred to the field.

d. Maintain the present purely "correct" relations with the top GVN, and specifically between the Ambassador and Diem. Contact between General Harkins and Diem and Defense Secretary Thuan on military matters should not, however, be suspended, as this remains an important channel of advice. USOM and USIA should also seek to maintain contacts where these are needed to push forward programs in support of the effort in the field, while taking care not to cut across the basic picture of U.S. disapproval and uncertainty of U.S. aid intentions. We should work with the Diem government but not support it.[1]

As we pursue these courses of action, the situation must be closely watched to see what steps Diem is taking to reduce repressive practices and to improve the effectiveness of the military effort. We should set no fixed criteria, but recognize that we would have to decide in 2–4 months whether to move to more drastic action or try to carry on with Diem even if he had not taken significant steps.

5. At this time, no initiative should be taken to encourage actively a change in government. Our policy should be to seek urgently to identify and build contacts with an alternative leadership if and when it appears.

6. The following statement be approved as current U.S. policy toward South Vietnam and constitute the substance of the government position to be presented both in Congressional testimony and in public statements.

a. The security of South Vietnam remains vital to United States security. For this reason, we adhere to the overriding objective of denying this country to Communism and of suppressing the Viet Cong insurgency as promptly as possible. (By suppressing the insurgency we mean reducing it to proportions manageable by the national security forces of the GVN, unassisted by the presence of U.S. military forces.) We believe the U.S. part of the task can be completed by the end of 1965, the terminal date which we are taking as the time objective of our counterinsurgency programs.

b. The military program in Vietnam has made progress and is sound in principle.

c. The political situation in Vietnam remains deeply serious. It has not yet significantly affected the military effort, but could do so at some time in the future. If the result is a GVN ineffective in the conduct of the war, the U.S. will review its attitude toward support for the government. Although we are deeply concerned by repressive practices, effective performance in the conduct of the war should be the determining factor in our relations with the GVN.

d. The U.S. has expressed its disapproval of certain actions of the Diem-Nhu regime and will do so again if required. Our policy is to seek to bring about the abandonment of repression because of its effect on the popular will to resist. Our means consist of expressions of disapproval and the withholding of support from GVN activities that are not clearly contributing to the war effort. We will use these means as required to assure an effective military program.

---

[1]Mr. Colby [William Colby, Deputy Director of Plans, Central Intelligence Agency] believes that the official "correct" relationships should be supplemented by selected and restricted unofficial and personal relationships with individuals in the GVN, approved by the Ambassador, where persuasion could be fruitful without derogation of the official U.S. posture.

158. CABLEGRAM FROM THE WHITE HOUSE TO LODGE ON CIA CHANNEL, OCTOBER 5, 1963

After General Duong Van Minh told a CIA contact on October 5 that army generals believed a coup was necessary to win the war and asked for assurances that the United States would not thwart a coup plan, Kennedy ordered that the United States no longer actively try to promote a coup but that it build up contacts with potential coup planners for the purpose of "surveillance and readiness."

In conjunction with decisions and recommendations in separate EPTEL, President today approved recommendation that no initiative should now be taken to give any active covert encouragement to a coup. There should, however, be urgent covert effort with closest security, under broad guidance of Ambassador to identify and build contacts with possible alternative leadership as and when it appears. Essential that this effort be totally secure and fully deniable and separated entirely from normal political analysis and reporting and other activities of country team. We repeat that this effort is not repeat not to be aimed at active promotion of coup but only at surveillance and readiness. In order to provide plausibility to denial suggest you and no one else in Embassy issue these instructions orally to Acting Station Chief and hold him responsible to you alone for making appropriate contacts and reporting to you alone.

All reports to Washington on this subject should be on this channel.

159. CABLEGRAM FROM CIA STATION CHIEF JOHN RICHARDSON TO CIA DIRECTOR MCCONE, OCTOBER 5, 1963

The CIA station chief in Saigon indicated that he recommended to Lodge that the United States not "irrevocably" oppose Minh's plans to assassinate Diem's brothers, apparently the subject of discussions.

1. [*Officially deleted.*]
2. I have recommended to Ambassador Lodge that:

A. That we proceed with these conversations with Gen. Minh.

B. We do not set ourselves irrevocably against the assassination plot, since the other two alternatives mean either a bloodbath in Saigon or a protracted struggle which could rip the army and the country asunder.

160. CABLEGRAM FROM MCCONE TO LODGE, OCTOBER 6, 1963

The CIA director, after talking with Kennedy, added to the previous instruction that the United States not actively seek the overthrow of Diem the assurance

SOURCE: *The Pentagon Papers*, pp. 215–216.

SOURCE: Document declassified by CIA (no date shown).

SOURCE: *U.S. Involvement in the Overthrow of Diem, 1963*, A Staff Study, Committee on Foreign Relations, U.S. Senate, Study No. 3, July 20, 1972, Appendix 23, p. 57.

*that it would not "thwart" a coup. He also asked Lodge to have the CIA contact
General Minh to seek more information on the coup plans, in order to evaluate
their chances of success.*

1. Believe CAP 63560 gives general guidance requested, REFTEL. We have
following additional general thoughts which have been discussed with President.
While we do not wish to stimulate coup, we also do not wish to leave impression
that U.S. would thwart a change of government or deny economic and military
assistance to a new regime if it appeared capable of increasing effectiveness of
military effort, ensuring popular support to win war and improving working relations with U.S. We would like to be informed on what is being contemplated but
we should avoid being drawn into reviewing or advising on operational plans or any
other act which might tend to identify U.S. too closely with change in government.
We would, however, welcome information which would help us assess character of
any alternate leadership.

2. With reference to specific problem of General Minh you should seriously
consider having contact take position that in present state his knowledge he is
unable present Minh's case to responsible policy officials with any degree of
seriousness. In order to get responsible officials even to consider Minh's problem,
contact would have to have detailed information clearly indicating that Minh's
plans offer a high prospect of success. At present contact sees no such prospect in
the information so far provided.

3. You should also consider with Acting Station Chief whether it would be
desirable in order to preserve security and deniability in this as well as similar
approaches to others whether appropriate arrangements could be made for follow-up
contacts by individuals brought in especially from outside Vietnam. As we indicated in CAP 63560 we are most concerned about security problem and we are
confining knowledge these sensitive matters in Washington to extremely limited
group, high officials in White House, State, Defense and CIA with whom this
message cleared.

161. CABLEGRAM FROM
MCGEORGE BUNDY TO LODGE,
OCTOBER 30, 1963 [Extract]

*With the coup plans ready to be put into effect, the White House began to
develop cold feet about possible failure. Bundy emphasized that the U.S. attitude
could decisively affect the decisions of the coup group and expressed the desire of
the President to be assured of a clearly favorable balance of forces for any coup
attempt.*

2. Believe our attitude to coup group can still have decisive effect on its
decisions. We believe that what we say to coup group can produce delay of coup
and that betrayal of coup plans to Diem is not repeat not our only way of stopping
coup. We therefore need urgently your combined assessment with Harkins and

SOURCE: *U.S. Involvement in the Overthrow of Diem, 1963*, pp. 65–67.

CAS (including their separate comments if they desire). We concerned that our line-up of forces in Saigon (being cabled in next message) indicates approximately equal balance of forces, with substantial possibility serious and prolonged fighting or even defeat. Either of these could be serious or even disastrous for U.S. interests, so that we must have assurance balance of forces clearly favorable.

3. With your assessment in hand, we might feel that we should convey message to Don, whether or not he gives 4 or 48 hours notice that would (A) continue explicit hands-off policy, (B) positively encourage coup, or (C) discourage.

4. In any case, believe Conein should find earliest opportunity express to Don that we do not find presently revealed plans give clear prospect of quick results. This conversation should call attention important Saigon units still apparently loyal to Diem and raise serious issue as to what means coup group has to deal with them.

162. CABLEGRAM FROM LODGE TO RUSK, OCTOBER 30, 1963 [Extract]

Lodge discounted the possibility that any expression of U.S. doubt would stop the coup plan from being implemented. Any effort to discourage a coup at that late date would give up any future chance for a change of government, he argued. Therefore, he recommended against expressing any sign of doubt to the coup planners.

1. We must, of course, get best possible estimate of chance of coup's success and this estimate must color our thinking, but do not think we have the power to delay or discourage a coup. Don has made it clear many times that this is a Vietnamese affair. It is theoretically possible for us to turn over the information which has been given to us in confidence to Diem and this would undoubtedly stop the coup and would make traitors out of us. For practical purposes therefore I would say that we have very little influence on what is essentially a Vietnamese affair. In addition, this would place the heads of the Generals, their civilian supporters, and lower military officers on the spot, thereby sacrificing a significant portion of the civilian and military leadership needed to carry the war against the VC to its successful conclusion. After our efforts not to discourage a coup and this change of heart, we would foreclose any possibility of change of the GVN for the better. Diem/Nhu have displayed no intentions to date of a desire to change the traditional methods of control through police action or take any repeat any actions which would undermine the power position of solidarity of the Ngo family. This, despite our heavy pressures directed DEPTEL 534. If our attempt to thwart this coup were successful, which we doubt, it is our firm estimate that younger officers, small groups of military, would then engage in an abortive action creating chaos ideally suited to VC objectives.

2. While we will attempt a combined assessment in a following message, time has not yet permitted substantive examination of this matter with General Harkins. My general view is that the U.S. is trying to bring this medieval country

SOURCE: *U.S. Involvement in the Overthrow of Diem, 1963*, pp. 70–72.

into the 20th Century and that we have made considerable progress in military and economic ways but to gain victory we must also bring them into the 20th Century politically and that can only be done by either a thoroughgoing change in the behavior of the present government, or by another government. The Viet Cong problem is partly military but it is also partly psychological and political.

163. CABLEGRAM FROM MCGEORGE BUNDY TO LODGE, OCTOBER 30, 1963 [Extract]

Responding to Lodge's cable, Bundy disagreed with his assessment of U.S. power to delay or discourage a coup, and ordered him to exercise his own judgment on the chances of success or failure of the coup and to do everything possible to stop it if his judgment was negative. Once a coup began, he directed, it was in U.S. interest to have it succeed. On November 1, Diem was overthrown and killed, along with his brother Nhu, in a coup.

1. Our reading your thoughtful 2063 leads us to believe a significant difference of shading may exist on one crucial point (see next para.) and on one or two lesser matters easily clarified.

2. We do not accept as a basis for U.S. policy that we have no power to delay or discourage a coup. In your paragraph 12 you say that if you were convinced that the coup was going to fail you would of course do everything you could do to stop it. We believe that on this same basis you should take action to persuade coup leaders to stop or delay any operation which, in your best judgment, does not clearly give high prospect of success. We have not considered any betrayal of generals to Diem, and our 79109 explicitly rejects that course. We recognize the danger of appearing hostile to generals, but we believe that our own position should be on as firm ground as possible, hence we cannot limit ourselves to proposition implied in your message that only conviction of certain failure justifies intervention. We believe that your standard for intervention should be that stated above.

3. Therefore, if you should conclude that there is not clearly a high prospect of success, you should communicate this doubt to generals in a way calculated to persuade them to desist at least until chances are better. In such a communication you should use the weight of U.S. best advice and explicitly reject any implication that we oppose the effort of the generals because of preference for present regime. We recognize need to bear in mind generals' interpretation of U.S. role in 1960 coup attempt, and your agent should maintain clear distinction between strong and honest advice given as a friend and any opposition to their objectives.

4. We continue to be deeply interested in up-to-the-minute assessment of prospects and are sending this before reply to our CAS 79126. We want continuous exchange latest assessments on this topic.

5. To clarify our intent, paragraph 7 of our 79109 is rescinded and we restate our desires as follows:

SOURCE: *U.S. Involvement in the Overthrow of Diem, 1963*, pp. 72–73.

a. While you are in Saigon you will be Chief of Country Team in all circumstances and our only instruction is that we are sure it will help to have Harkins fully informed at all stages and to use advice from both him and Smith in framing guidance for coup contacts and assessment. We continue to be concerned that neither Conein nor any other reporting source is getting the clarity we would like with respect to alignment of forces and level of determination among generals.

b. When you leave Saigon and before there is a coup, Truehart will be Chief of the Country Team. Our only modification of existing procedures is that in the circumstance we wish all instruction to Conein to be conducted in immediate consultation with Harkins and Smith so that all three know what is sold in Conein. Any disagreement among the three on such instruction should be reported to Washington and held for our resolution, when time permits.

c. If you have left and a coup occurs, we believe that emergency situation requires, pending your return, that direction of country team be vested in most senior officer with experience of military decisions, and the officer in our view is Harkins. We do *not* intend that this switch in final responsibility should be publicized in any way, and Harkins will of course be guided in basic posture by our instructions, which follow in paragraph 6. We do not believe that this switch will have the effect suggested in your paragraph 8.

6. This paragraph contains our present standing instructions for U.S. posture in the event of a coup.

a. U.S. authorities will reject appeals for direct intervention from either side, and U.S.-controlled aircraft and other resources will not be committed between the battle lines or in support of either side, without authorization from Washington.

b. In event of indecisive contest, U.S. authorities may in their discretion agree to perform any acts agreeable to both sides, such as removal of key personalities or relay of information. In such actions, however, U.S. authorities will strenuously avoid appearance of pressure on either side. It is not in the interest of USG to be or appear to be either instrument of existing government or instrument of coup.

c. In the event of imminent or actual failure of coup, U.S. authorities may afford asylum in their discretion to those to whom there is any express or implied obligation of this sort. We believe however that in such a case it would be in our interest and probably in interest of those seeking asylum that they seek protection of other Embassies in addition to our own. This point should be made strongly if need arises.

d. But once a coup under responsible leadership has begun, and within these restrictions, it is in the interest of the U.S. Government that it should succeed.

7. We have your message about return to Washington and we suggest that all public comment be kept as low-key and quiet as possible, and we also urge that if possible you keep open the exact time of your departure. We are strongly sensitive to great disadvantage of having you out of Saigon if this should turn out to be a week of decision, and if it can be avoided we would prefer not to see you pinned to a fixed hour of departure now.

164. RESOLUTION OF THE NINTH CONFERENCE OF THE LAO DONG PARTY CENTRAL COMMITTEE, DECEMBER 1963 [Extract]

In the aftermath of the overthrow of Diem, the Party Central Committee convened its Ninth Plenum in December to discuss its strategy in South Vietnam. It directed a major effort to build up revolutionary military forces in the South to tip the balance of forces in its favor. While seizing opportunities to win victories in a relatively short time, the Southern Party apparatus was ordered to be prepared as well for a protracted struggle, with transitional phases. The secret resolution, which was later captured in military operations by U.S.-South Vietnamese forces, reaffirmed the policy of the Party that the war was to be confined within South Vietnam, meaning that the North would not overtly participate in it.

We must and have the capability to check and defeat the enemy in his "special war." This capability will increase if we are determined to fight the U.S. imperialists and their henchmen, if we have a clever strategem, and know how to exploit the contradictions in the enemy's internal organizations, contradictions between the U.S. imperialists and the other imperialists, especially the French imperialists, contradictions between the U.S. and their henchmen in South Viet-Nam and the bourgeois ruling clique in Southeast Asia. In this way, we can cause difficulties for the U.S. in using the aggressive force of the Southeast Asia bloc to escalate the war in South Viet-Nam. Additionally, we must develop the movement against the U.S. aggressors, and gain the support of the people of the world (especially those of the socialist countries, and countries in Asia, Africa, and Latin America) for the South Viet-Nam Revolution. This Revolution is conducted on three fronts: the political, military and diplomatic fronts; the diplomatic front is designed to isolate the enemy in the international arena and gain the backing of the entire world.

However, we must always be vigilant and prepared to cope with the U.S. if she takes the risk of turning the war in South Viet-Nam into a limited war. The possibility that a limited war in South Viet-Nam would turn into a world war is almost nonexistent because the purpose and significance of this war cannot generate conditions leading to a world war.

In the framework of the "special war," there are two possibilities:

—First, the Americans would carry on the war at the present or slightly higher level.

—Second, the Americans would intensify the war by bringing in troops many times larger [than the present number] or both American troops and troops from the Southeast Asian aggressive bloc will intervene in the war.

If the U.S. takes a stronger part in the Viet-Nam war but still uses the troops of the satellite countries to play the main role, this war is still considered a "special

SOURCE: Viet-Nam Documents and Research Notes (U.S. Embassy, Saigon), Document No. 96, July 1971.

war." If they use their own troops as the main force and deploy the armed forces of the Southeast Asia aggressive bloc into Viet-Nam, the Viet-Nam war will no longer be a "special war" but a limited war, although it is going on within South Viet-Nam. This may occur in the following cases:

—First, faced with their numerous difficulties in South Viet-Nam, the U.S. imperialists believe that they will be successful if they fight more violently.

—Second, the U.S. believes that the North will not strongly react.

—Third, if they believe their increased involvement in the war in South Viet-Nam will not raise a strong opposition from the people of the U.S. and the world.

However, the above are only remote possibilities because the U.S. cannot evaluate all the disastrous consequences she might bear if she wages the war on a larger scale. She realizes that if she is bogged down in a large-scale and protracted war, she will be thrown into a very passive position in the world. However, the above possibilities may become more probable if the revolutionary movement in South Viet-Nam is not strong enough.

Through our subjective efforts, let us strive to deal with the first eventuality; at the same time, let us also positively prepare to defeat the enemy should the second eventuality materialize.

We have sufficient conditions to quickly change the balance of forces in our favor. And whether the U.S. maintains its combat strength at the present level or increases it, she must still use her henchmen's army as a main force. However, this army becomes weaker day by day due to the serious decline of its quality, the demoralization of its troops and the disgust of the latter for the Americans and their lackeys. These are the factors that cause the collapse of Americans' and their lackeys' troops. No U.S. financial assistance or weapons can prevent this collapse.

As for us, we become more confident in the victory of our armed forces. Our technical and tactical skills are improved and our fighting spirit is heightened. The people in South Viet-Nam have stood up against the imperialists for almost 20 years, so they have a high political enlightenment. At the present time, the more they fight, the bigger victories they win, the revolutionary movement has created favorable conditions for building up the armed forces. If we properly guide the political and military struggle and the force building program, our military force will grow up rapidly. To create a basic change in the balance of forces between the enemy and us is within our grasp. In the days ahead, our force will be increasingly developed, whereas the enemy will certainly encounter a great deal of difficulties and he will be demoralized. His weaknesses are obvious nad have increased after his defeat at Ap Bac, especially after the overthrow of Diem's regime. A strong development of the Revolution will cause many more troubles for the enemy and bring about a quicker disorganization of his armed forces and government. *The Revolution in SVN will inevitably evolve into a General Offensive and Uprising to achieve the complete victory*.

If the U.S. imperialists send more troops to Viet-Nam to save the situation after suffering a series of failures, *the Revolution in Viet-Nam will meet more difficulties, the struggle will be stronger and harder but it will certainly succeed in attaining the final victory*. With 800,000 well trained troops, the French imperialists could not defeat the 12 million courageous Algerians and finally had to give independence and freedom to them. For the same reason, the U.S. imperialists cannot win over 14 million Vietnamese people in the South who have taken arms to fight the imperialists for almost 20 years, and who, with all the compatriots throughout the country, have defeated the hundreds of thousands of troops of the French expeditionary force. Now the South Vietnamese people show themselves capable of beating the enemy in any situation. They certainly have the determination, talents, strength and patience to crush any U.S. imperialists' schemes and plans, and finally to force them to withdraw from Viet-Nam as the French imperialists did.

There is the possibility that the South Viet-Nam Revolution must go through a transitional period which entails complex forms and methods of struggling before it attains the final victory. The reunification of the country must be carried out step by step. In the present national democratic revolutionary phase in South Viet-Nam, *we must strive to attain victory step by step and gradually push back the enemy before reaching the General Offensive and Uprising to win complete victory.* However, we may pass through a transitional period before we attain complete victory. In any case, we must encourage the entire Party, people, and army to attain the maximum victory, and we should not have a hesitating attitude or to pause at the transitional period. If we are highly determined to win and prepared to face any situation, the final victory will certainly be in the hands of our people.

165. MEMORANDUM FOR THE PRESIDENT FROM MCNAMARA, DECEMBER 21, 1963

After another visit to South Vietnam, McNamara reported that the situation was deteriorating so fast that it would lead to neutralization and possibly Communist victory within two to three months unless it was reversed. He informed Johnson that proposals for sabotage and psychological operations against the North would be presented to him for consideration within a matter of days.

In accordance with your request this morning, this is a summary of my conclusions after my visit to Vietnam on December 19-20.

1. *Summary.* The situation is very disturbing. Current trends, unless reversed in the next 2-3 months, will lead to neutralization at best and more likely to a Communist-controlled state.

2. *The new government* is the greatest source of concern. It is indecisive and drifting. Although Minh states that he, rather than the Committee of Generals, is making decisions, it is not clear that this is actually so. In any event, neither he nor the Committee are experienced in political administration and so far they show little talent for it. There is no clear concept on how to re-shape or conduct the strategic hamlet program; the Province Chiefs, most of whom are new and inexperienced, are receiving little or no direction; military operations, too, are not being effectively directed because the generals are so preoccupied with essentially political affairs. A specific example of the present situation is that General Dinh is spending little or no time commanding III Corps, which is in the vital zone around Saigon

SOURCE: Document from the Lyndon Baines Johnson Library.

and needs full-time direction. I made these points as strongly as possible to Minh, Don, Kim, and Tho.

3. *The Country Team* is the second major weakness. It lacks leadership, has been poorly informed, and is not working to a common plan. A recent example of confusion has been conflicting USOM and military recommendations both to the Government of Vietnam and to Washington on the size of the military budget. Above all, Lodge has virtually no official contact with Harkins. Lodge sends in reports with major military implications without showing them to Harkins, and does not show Harkins important incoming traffic.

[*Officially deleted.*]

Lodge's newly-designated deputy, David Nes, was with us and seems a highly competent team player. I have stated the situation frankly to him and he has said he would do all he could to constitute what would in effect be an executive committee operating below the level of the Ambassador.

As to the grave reporting weakness, both Defense and CIA must take major steps to improve this. John McCone and I have discussed it and are acting vigorously in our respective spheres.

4. *Viet Cong progress* has been great during the period since the coup, with my best guess being that the situation has in fact been deteriorating in the countryside since July to a far greater extent than we realized because of our undue dependence on distorted Vietnamese reporting. The Viet Cong now control very high proportions of the people in certain key provinces, particularly those directly south and west of Saigon. The Strategic Hamlet Program was seriously overextended in these provinces, and the Viet Cong have been able to destroy many hamlets, while others have been abandoned or in some cases betrayed or pillaged by the government's own Self Defense Corps. In these key provinces, the Viet Cong have destroyed almost all major roads, and are collecting taxes at will.

As remedial measures, we must get the government to re-allocate its military forces so that its effective strength in these provinces is essentially doubled. We also need to have major increases in both military and USOM staffs, to sizes that will give us a reliable, independent U.S. appraisal of the status of operations. Thirdly, realistic pacification plans must be prepared, allocating adequate time to secure the remaining government-controlled areas and work out from there.

This gloomy picture prevails predominantly in the provinces around the capital and in the Delta. Action to accomplish each of these objectives was started while we were in Saigon. The situation in the northern and central areas is considerably better, and does not seem to have deteriorated substantially in recent months. General Harkins still hopes these areas may be made reasonably secure by the latter half of next year.

In the gloomy southern picture, an exception to the trend of Viet Cong success may be provided by the possible adherence to the government of the Cao Dai and Hoa Hao sects, which total three million people and control key areas along the Cambodian border. The Hoa Hao have already made some sort of agreement, and the Cao Dai are expected to do so at the end of this month. However, it is not clear that their influence will be more than neutralized by these agreements, or that they will in fact really pitch in on the government's side.

5. *Infiltration* of men and equipment from North Vietnam continues using (a) land corridors through Laos and Cambodia; (b) the Mekong River waterways from

Cambodia; (c) some possible entry from the sea and the tip of the Delta. The best guess is that 1000-1500 Viet Cong cadres entered South Vietnam from Laos in the first nine months of 1963. The Mekong route (and also the possible sea entry) is apparently used for heavier weapons and ammunition and raw materials which have been turning up in increasing numbers in the south and of which we have captured a few shipments.

To counter this infiltration, we reviewed in Saigon various plans providing for cross-border operations into Laos. On the scale proposed, I am quite clear that these would not be politically acceptable or even militarily effective. Our first need would be immediate [*officially deleted*] mapping of the whole Laos and Cambodian border, and this we are preparing on an urgent basis.

[*Officially deleted.*]

As to the waterways, the military plans presented in Saigon were unsatisfactory, and a special naval team is being sent at once from Honolulu to determine what more can be done. The whole waterway system is so vast, however, that effective policing may be impossible.

In general, the infiltration problem, while serious and annoying, is a lower priority than the key problems discussed earlier. However, we should do what we can to reduce it.

166. MEMORANDUM FOR THE RECORD BY MCNAMARA, DECEMBER 21, 1963 [Extract]

McNamara's summary of the discussions held in South Vietnam concluded that the Military Revolutionary Committee (MRC) governing South Vietnam after the coup had not proven its ability to reverse the unfavorable trends of previous months. He cited political conflicts within the military leadership in expressing doubts about its political stability.

The military government may be an improvement over the Diem-Nhu regime, but this is not as yet established and the future of the war remains in doubt.

The Viet Cong are receiving substantial support from North Vietnam and possibly elsewhere, and this support can be increased. Stopping this by sealing the borders, the extensive waterways, and the long coast line is difficult, if not impossible.

The VC appeal to the people of South Vietnam on political grounds has been effective, gained recruits for their armed forces, and neutralized resistance.

The ability of the GVN to reverse this trend remains to be proven. Much depends on the ability of the MRC to deploy their forces and pursue the conflict in a manner which will ensure the security of the people and provide them desired freedom, privileges, and some tangible benefits.

The lack of an outstanding individual to lead and absence of administrative experience within the MRC are ominous indicators.

SOURCE: Document declassified by Department of Defense, April 15, 1975.

The political stability of the new government under the MRC is subject to serious doubt. Conflicts of ambition, jealousy, differences of opinion over policy matters are all possible, could develop serious schisms, precipitate further dissensions and coup attempts all of which will affect the war effort against the VC.

Overcoming the VC movement by the GVN is formidable and difficult, but not impossible. The problems can be intensified by continuing increased support from NVN and political failures by the MRC. Hence, in my judgment, there are more reasons to doubt the future of the effort under present programs and moderate extensions to existing programs (i.e., harassing sabotage against NVN, border crossings, etc.;) than there are reasons to be optimistic about the future of our cause in South Vietnam.

1964

167. JOINT CHIEFS OF STAFF MEMORANDUM, JCSM-46-64, JANUARY 22, 1964

The Joint Chiefs pressed once more for "bolder actions which may embody greater risks" in Southeast Asia. They called for a series of steps, beginning with getting the South Vietnamese government to turn over direction of the war to the American Commander of MACV, and giving him control over all U.S. programs in Vietnam as well. They also wanted the United States to commit its forces "as necessary" in actions against North Vietnam.

1. National Security Action Memorandum No. 273 makes clear the resolve of the President to ensure victory over the externally directed and supported communist insurgency in South Vietnam. In order to achieve that victory, the Joint Chiefs of Staff are of the opinion that the United States must be prepared to put aside many of the self-imposed restrictions which now limit our efforts, and to undertake bolder actions which may embody greater risks.

2. The Joint Chiefs of Staff are increasingly mindful that our fortunes in South Vietnam are an accurate barometer of our fortunes in all of Southeast Asia. It is our view that if the US program succeeds in South Vietnam it will go far toward stabilizing the total Southeast Asia situation. Conversely, a loss of South Vietnam to the communists will presage an early erosion of the remainder of our position in that subcontinent.

3. Laos, existing on a most fragile foundation now, would not be able to endure the establishment of a communist—or pseudo neutralist—state on its eastern flank. Thailand, less strong today than a month ago by virtue of the loss of

SOURCE: *The Pentagon Papers*, pp. 496–499.

Prime Minister Sarit, would probably be unable to withstand the pressures of infiltration from the north should Laos collapse to the communists in its turn. Cambodia apparently has estimated that our prospects in South Vietnam are not promising and, encouraged by the actions of the French, appears already to be seeking an accommodation with the communists. Should we actually suffer defeat in South Vietnam, there is little reason to believe that Cambodia would maintain even a pretense of neutrality.

4. In a broader sense, the failure of our program in South Vietnam would have heavy influence on the judgments of Burma, India, Indonesia, Malaysia, Japan, Taiwan, the Republic of Korea, and the Republic of the Philippines with respect to US durability, resolution, and trustworthiness. Finally, this being the first real test of our determination to defeat the communist wars of national liberation formula, it is not unreasonable to conclude that there would be a corresponding unfavorable effect upon our image in Africa and in Latin America.

5. All of this underscores the pivotal position now occupied in South Vietnam in our world-wide confrontation with the communists and the essentiality that the conflict there be brought to a favorable end as soon as possible. However, it would be unrealistic to believe that a complete suppression of the insurgency can take place in one or even two years. The British effort in Malaya is a recent example of a counterinsurgency effort which required approximately ten years before the bulk of the rural population was brought completely under control of the government, the police were able to maintain order, and the armed forces were able to eliminate the guerrilla strongholds.

6. The Joint Chiefs of Staff are convinced that, in keeping with the guidance in NSAM 273, the United States must make plain to the enemy our determination to see the Vietnam campaign through to a favorable conclusion. To do this, we must prepare for whatever level of activity may be required and, being prepared, must then proceed to take actions as necessary to achieve our purposes surely and promptly.

7. Our considerations, furthermore, cannot be confined entirely to South Vietnam. Our experience in the war thus far leads us to conclude that, in this respect, we are not now giving sufficient attention to the broader area problems of Southeast Asia. The Joint Chiefs of Staff believe that our position in Cambodia, our attitude toward Laos, our action in Thailand, and our great effort in South Vietnam do not comprise a compatible and integrated US policy for Southeast Asia. US objectives in Southeast Asia cannot be achieved by either economic, political, or military measures alone. All three fields must be integrated into a single, broad US program for Southeast Asia. The measures recommended in this memorandum are a partial contribution to such a program.

8. Currently we and the South Vietnamese are fighting the war on the enemy's terms. He has determined the locale, the timing, and the tactics of the battle while our actions are essentially reactive. One reason for this is the fact that we have obliged ourselves to labor under self-imposed restrictions with respect to impeding external aid to the Viet Cong. These restrictions include keeping the war within the boundaries of South Vietnam, avoiding the direct use of US combat forces, and limiting US direction of the campaign to rendering advice to the Government of Vietnam. These restrictions, while they may make our international position more readily defensible, all tend to make the task in Vietnam more complex, time

consuming, and in the end, more costly. In addition to complicating our own problem, these self-imposed restrictions may well now be conveying signals of irresolution to our enemies—encouraging them to higher levels of vigor and greater risks. A reversal of attitude and the adoption of a more aggressive program would enhance greatly our ability to control the degree to which escalation will occur. It appears probable that the economic and agricultural disappointments suffered by Communist China, plus the current rift with the Soviets, could cause the communists to think twice about undertaking a large-scale military adventure in Southeast Asia.

9. In adverting to actions outside of South Vietnam, the Joint Chiefs of Staff are aware that the focus of the counterinsurgency battle lies in South Vietnam itself, and that the war must certainly be fought and won primarily in the minds of the Vietnamese people. At the same time, the aid now coming to the Viet Cong from outside the country in men, resources, advice, and direction is sufficiently great in the aggregate to be significant—both as help and as encouragement to the Viet Cong. It is our conviction that if support of the insurgency from outside South Vietnam in terms of operational direction, personnel, and material were stopped completely, the character of the war in South Vietnam would be substantially and favorably altered. Because of this conviction, we are wholly in favor of executing the covert actions against North Vietnam which you have recently proposed to the President. We believe, however, that it would be idle to conclude that these efforts will have a decisive effect on the communist determination to support the insurgency; and it is our view that we must therefore be prepared fully to undertake a much higher level of activity, not only for its beneficial tactical effect, but to make plain our resolution, both to our friends and to our enemies.

10. Accordingly, the Joint Chiefs of Staff consider that the United States must make ready to conduct increasingly bolder actions in Southeast Asia; specifically as to Vietnam:

a. Assign to the US military commander responsibilities for the total US program in Vietnam.

b. Induce the Government of Vietnam to turn over to the United States military commander, temporarily, the actual tactical direction of the war.

c. Charge the United States military commander with complete responsibility for conduct of the program against North Vietnam.

d. Overfly Laos and Cambodia to whatever extent is necessary for acquisition of operational intelligence.

e. Induce the Government of Vietnam to conduct overt ground operations in Laos of sufficient scope to impede the flow of personnel and material southward.

f. Arm, equip, advise, and support the Government of Vietnam in its conduct of aerial bombing of critical targets in North Vietnam and in mining the sea approaches to that country.

g. Advise and support the Government of Vietnam in its conduct of large-scale commando raids against critical targets in North Vietnam.

h. Conduct aerial bombing of key North Vietnam targets, using US resources under Vietnamese cover, and with the Vietnamese openingly assuming responsibility for the actions.

j. Commit additional US forces, as necessary, in support of the combat action within South Vietnam.

11. It is our conviction that any or all of the foregoing actions may be required to enhance our position in Southeast Asia. The past few months have disclosed that considérably higher levels of effort are demanded of us if US objectives are to be attained.

12. The governmental reorganization which followed the coup d'état in Saigon should be completed very soon, giving basis for concluding just how strong the Vietnamese Government is going to be and how much of the load they will be able to bear themselves. Additionally, the five-month dry season, which is just now beginning, will afford the Vietnamese an opportunity to exhibit their ability to reverse the unfavorable situation in the critical Mekong Delta. The Joint Chiefs of Staff will follow these important developments closely and will recommend to you progressively the execution of such of the above actions as are considered militarily required, providing, in each case, their detailed assessment of the risks involved.

13. The Joint Chiefs of Staff consider that the strategic importance of Vietnam and of Southeast Asia warrants preparations for the actions above and recommend that the substance of this memorandum be discussed with the Secretary of State.

168. DRAFT MEMORANDUM FOR THE PRESIDENT BY ASSISTANT SECRETARY OF DEFENSE WILLIAM P. BUNDY, MARCH 1, 1964 [Extract]

In the earliest elaboration of the case for striking against the North, William P. Bundy urged beginning with a blockade of the Port of Haiphong–an action he said would challenge the sovereignty of North Vietnam–and then bombing targets in the North. He discounted any serious Communist reaction to such a move. Bundy proposed a congressional resolution along the lines of the Quemoy-Matsu resolution of 1958 that would authorize military action in advance.

VI. U.S. Military Action Against North Vietnam: Objectives, Elements, Pros and Cons, Chances of Success

A. Basic to this course of action is that it is a military course of action only in support of a political *objective,* and requiring consideration at every stage of political factors and working in parallel on a political track. We would expressly *not* be trying to conquer North Vietnam, or even to overthrow its Communist regime although of course we would welcome that result if it ever came as a by-product. Rather, we are aiming to do three things: (a) get North Vietnam to stop, or at least sharply cut down, its supply of key items to the Viet Cong; (b) stiffen the Khanh government, completely assure it of our determination, and discourage moves toward neutralism in South Vietnam; (c) show all of Southeast Asia, including Sukarno, that we will take strong measures to prevent the spread of Communism specifically, and the grab of territory generally, in the area. And all three of these

SOURCE: Document declassified by Department of State, April 10, 1975.

objectives are equally important; particularly, we must never lose sight of the second, for if we lose out on this front we shall be defending an empty shell and would virtually have to stop except as we could then relate our actions to a delaying action in Laos and to holding Thailand.

B. Justification and Expressed Rationale

We must have at the outset the strongest possible factual document to support the charge not only that the Viet Cong are controlled and supplied in key items from the North but that the pace of supply has been increased so that stronger action by us is now required. The first part is an old story, and the fact that the Viet Cong *do* have a lot of appeal in South Vietnam and *do* rely heavily on captured U.S. weapons has left the impression even in some U.S. circles that the North Vietnam role is actually marginal at best and that the conflict is "just a civil war." We badly need a new twist and a much stronger one, and if we have to blow some sensitive sources to get it, or even use a degree of overemphasis, we probably must do so. We may get good hard evidence that the pace has stepped up, and if we do this would be vital.

We also should consider going back in time to show much more clearly than we have ever done how the North Vietnamese planned the whole show over a long period, planted or returned cadres, etc. Although we have made noises on this in the past, we simply have not made a firm case. Again, disclosure of sensitive sources may be required; at this stage, we can afford a lot of compromise and should not be squeamish about this unless the results on future operations would really be vital.

Assuming such a document can be drafted, we then want to use it—perhaps through a Presidential statement—to make clear just what our objective is, and what it is not. As was done in the Cuba crisis of 1962, such a statement should be held for anxious impact until we have decided what we want to do and are ready to do it. Even at this point, the security problem becomes obvious and points to the immediate creation of a tight inner circle of planners. The Washington miracle of the Cuba crisis *must* be repeated, in far more difficult circumstances.

On the diplomatic front, the Cuba crisis again applies. The odds on our getting any benefit from outright consultation, apart from general continuing soundings, appear sharply against. Almost certainly, we would want to *inform* key allies at the last possible minute, but this we should plan to do. The variant scripts will not be easy.

C. Best Action Possibilities

These need more study, but preliminary analysis is that the best way to start might be through a blockade of Haiphong—not because the short-term effect would be major, even in POL, [Petroleum, Oil and Lubricants] but because this is a recognized military action that hits at the sovereignty of North Vietnam and almost inevitably means we would go further.

The next steps—which we should foreshadow at the outset—would be to hit by air attack at: (a) the key rail lines to Communist China; (b) the key road nets to Laos and South Vietnam; (c) camps (which we can now identify) used for training cadres for South Vietnam; (d) key industrial complexes, notably the limited number of power stations and the few showcase industrial plants. We should probably make clear we do *not* intend, at least at the outset, to attack Hanoi and Haiphong except on a pinpoint basis under the above heading (d). It is not people we are after, but the will of the government and its capacity to act and to receive help in acting.

D. Probable Communist Reactions

This needs a careful intelligence judgment. Preliminary views are that:

(1) *Hanoi* would pull all the propaganda stops (trying to make us aggressors, etc.), and aim its blasts particularly at the South ("this has now become wholly a white man's war—you will be destroyed in retaliation just to preserve an American puppet government"). Increased anti-American terrorism in the South is possible, but they may well be doing this now as hard as they can.

More seriously, we do not think they would cut off the supply to the South, but equally it is unlikely that they would pour major forces across the borders of Laos and South Vietnam.

Rather they would probably look for relief, at least for some time, to put pressure on the U.S. from other countries, to desist and to agree to neutralization. They would also hammer in the South.

As for air action, this would depend on their receiving aircraft from the Communist Chinese. It seems doubtful that they would ask for this, or would seek to launch air reprisals either against U.S. forces or against Hue or Saigon from North Vietnamese territory.

(2) *Communist China* would probably not regard the U.S. action—clearly stated to be limited and punitive—as a direct threat to its borders. They would recognize that, if successful, it would be a serious set-back to Communist advance and their view of the need for aggressive Communist action. Nonetheless, this stake would not be so great as to draw them into large-scale troop or air involvement; the latter would leave them open to immediate sharp reprisals by us.

Thus, again, maximum use of pressures to get the U.S. to negotiate seems the most likely response, plus all the propaganda stops.

(3) The *Soviets* would be bound to oppose us strenuously for the record, and to join in the cry for negotiation. But they would almost certainly not play a serious "rocket" note or make any actual military moves—even if we made limited specific reprisals against Communist China for some military move.

On the other hand, the Soviets might well watch the world outcry carefully to see if it offered them the chance for some action elsewhere. We do not think this would mean Berlin or some really vital U.S. interest. It might mean a play in Africa, or in relation to Cuba.

In summary, the danger of drastic early Communist military action is less likely than the problems of fighting off pressures for negotiation and, of course, the serious and constant danger that the South would fall apart under our feet. In relation to the latter, firm U.S. action would have an initial tonic effect, *but* once it became clear that the war was still going on in the South—as it would be—a reverse wave might well set in. The Viet Cong would be doing everything to see that it did, and to point a picture of wholesale destruction for the sake of white domination.

E. Congressional and World Problems.

The military actions proposed would normally require a declaration of war under the Constitution. But this seems a blunt instrument carrying heavy domestic overtones and above all not suited to the picture of punitive and selective action only.

The opposite alternative of no resort at all to the Congress also seems unsatisfactory. We have no armed attack as in Korea and no sudden change of events as in Cuba.

The best answer seems to be a resolution along the lines of the Offshore Islands Resolution. That resolution took several days to pass, however, and this time we have doubtful friends in key quarters on the Hill. To ask for a resolution and not act at all would give all too much time for world pressures to build up. Perhaps the best, though not a perfect, answer is to start the blockade at once, but await the resolution for other actions.

As to world reaction, there would undoubtedly be widespread protests even including parts of NATO, and certainly including the bulk of the Afro-Asian countries. However, as the Offshore Islands crisis showed, and Lebanon, the *eventual* world reaction would depend on the result we achieved. A lot of people would criticize us first, and cheer us (behind their hands perhaps) later, *if* it came out right.

The specific immediate problem is, of course, the UN. We could probably avoid a Security Council resolution that condemned us alone—if we had our evidence really ready—but we would certainly be faced with one that called on both us and the North Vietnamese to stop, at which point it would be clear whether or not we did, and not at all clear whether the North Vietnamese had. (Indeed, with the war in the South going on, they could probably make a strong noise that it wasn't their doing at all!) If we took the course of vetoing such a resolution in the Security Council, the issue would speedily move to the General Assembly, and we would almost certainly be outvoted there. In any case, the sum total would be tremendous pressure to stop and negotiate.

F. The Interplay of Action and Negotiation.

Part of our initial statement must be our negotiating position, and we should probably say in so many words that we are ready at any time to negotiate an end to North Vietnamese intervention and for an independent South Vietnam free to accept outside help, but *not* prepared to negotiate at all on any other basis.

The odds are then heavy that our position would be accepted by many nations on their own behalf, but we would have great difficulty in getting them to agree that it had to be accepted in *advance* by the Communist nations. The British, as Co-Chairmen of the 1954 Geneva Conference on Indochina, would be crucial. Despite all the pressures we would bring to bear, British public opinion would virtually compel this or any other British governments join in a conference call. Thus, we would have at least a preliminary negotiation on our hands from the start.

Yet we obviously cannot fall into the Korean position of 1951–53, and must maintain a measured tempo of action until we either have our result in practice or have it through negotiation.

169. MEMORANDUM FOR THE PRESIDENT BY MCNAMARA, MARCH 16, 1964 [Extracts]

McNamara found on his visit to South Vietnam that the Communist movement controlled or predominantly influenced 40 percent of the territory, that large segments of the population were indifferent to the outcome, and that another coup was possible. He dismissed American withdrawal or negotiations as equivalent to Communist takeover, recommended against overt attacks against the North, and concluded that putting the nation on a war footing improving the military, police, and paramilitary forces of the GVN and providing additional equipment could bring significant improvement in four to six months. McNamara used Bundy's March 1 draft as the basis for the discussion of policy options. These recommendations were accepted by President Johnson as official United States policy.

III. The Present Situation in South Vietnam

The key elements in the present situation are as follows:

A. The military tools and concepts of the GVN/US effort are generally sound and adequate.[1] Substantially more can be done in the effective employment of military forces and in the economic and civic action areas. These improvements may require some selective increases in the U.S. presence, but it does not appear likely that major equipment replacement and additions in U.S. personnel are indicated under current policy.

B. The U.S. policy of reducing existing personnel where South Vietnamese are in a position to assume the functions is still sound. Its application will not lead to any major reductions in the near future, but adherence to this policy as such has a sound effect in portraying to the U.S. and the world that we continue to regard the war as a conflict the South Vietnamese must win and take ultimate responsibility for. Substantial reductions in the numbers of U.S. military training personnel should be possible before the end of 1965. However, the U.S. should continue to reiterate that it will provide all the assistance and advice required to do the job regardless of how long it takes.

C. The situation has unquestionably been growing worse, at least since September:

> 1. In terms of government control of the countryside, about 40% of the territory is under Viet Cong control or predominant influence. In 22 of the 43 provinces, the Viet Cong control 50% or more of the land area, including 80% of Phuoc Tuy; 90% of Binh Duong; 75% of Hau Nghia; 90% of Long An; 90% of Kien Tuong; 90% of Dinh Tuong; 90% of Kien Hoa; and 85% of An Xuyen.

SOURCE: *The Pentagon Papers*, pp. 499–510.

[1]Mr. McCone emphasizes that the GVN/US program can never be considered completely satisfactory so long as it permits the Viet Cong a sanctuary in Cambodia and a continuing uninterrupted and unmolested source of supply and reinforcement from NVN through Laos.

2. Large groups of the population are now showing signs of apathy and indifference, and there are some signs of frustration within the U.S. contingent:

a. The ARVN and paramilitary desertion rates, and particularly the latter, are high and increasing.

b. Draft dodging is high while the Viet Cong are recruiting energetically and effectively.

c. The morale of the hamlet militia and of the Self Defense Corps, on which the security of the hamlets depends, is poor and falling.

3. In the last 90 days the weakening of the government's position has been particularly noticeable. For example:

a. In Quang Nam province, in the I Corps, the militia in 17 hamlets turned in their weapons.

b. In Binh Duong province (III Corps) the hamlet militia were disarmed because of suspected disloyalty.

c. In Binh Dinh province, in the II Corps, 75 hamlets were severely damaged by the Viet Cong (in contrast, during the twelve months ending June 30, 1963, attacks on strategic hamlets were few and none was overrun).

d. In Quang Ngai province, at the northern edge of the II Corps, there were 413 strategic hamlets under government's control a year ago. Of that number, 335 have been damaged to varying degrees or fallen into disrepair, and only 275 remain under government control.

e. Security throughout the IV Corps has deteriorated badly. The Viet Cong control virtually all facets of peasant life in the southernmost provinces and the government troops there are reduced to defending the administrative centers. Except in An Giang province (dominated by the Hua Hoa religious sect) armed escort is required for almost all movement in both the southern and northern areas of the IV Corps.

4. The political control structure extending from Saigon down into the hamlets disappeared following the November coup. Of the 41 incumbent province chiefs on November 1, 35 have been replaced (nine provinces had three province chiefs in three months; one province had four). Scores of lesser officials were replaced. Almost all major military commands have changed hands twice since the November coup. The faith of the peasants has been shaken by the disruption in experienced leadership and the loss of physical security. In many areas, power vacuums have developed causing confusion among the people and a rising rate of rural disorders.

5. North Vietnamese support, always significant, has been increasing:

a. Communications between Hanoi and the Viet Cong (see classified annex).

b. Since July 1, 1963, the following items of equipment, not previously encountered in South Vietnam, have been captured from the Viet Cong:

Chicom 75 mm. recoilless rifles.

Chicom heavy machine guns.

U.S. .50 caliber heavy machine guns on Chicom mounts.

In addition, it is clear that the Viet Cong are using Chinese 90 mm rocket launchers and mortars.

c. The Viet Cong are importing large quantities of munitions and chemicals for the production of explosives: Approximately 50,000 pounds of explosive-producing chemicals destined for the Viet Cong have been intercepted in the 12 months ending March 1964. On December 24, five tons of ammunition, of which one and one-half tons were 75 mm recoilless rifle ammunition, was captured at the Dinh Tuong Viet Cong arsenal. Ninety percent was of Chicom manufacture.

D. The greatest weakness in the present situation is the uncertain viability of the Khanh government. Khanh himself is a very able man within his experience, but he does not yet have wide political appeal and his control of the Army itself is uncertain (he has the serious problem of the jailed generals). After two coups, as was mentioned above, there has been a sharp drop in morale and organization, and Khanh has not yet been able to build these up satisfactorily. There is a constant threat of assassination or of another coup, which would drop morale and organization nearly to zero.[2] Whether or not French nationals are actively encouraging such a coup, de Gaulle's position and the continuing pessimism and anti-Americanism of the French community in South Vietnam provide constant fuel to neutralist sentiment and the coup possibility. If a coup is set underway, the odds of our detecting and preventing it in the tactical sense are not high.

E. On the positive side, we have found many reasons for encouragement in the performance of the Khanh government to date. Although its top layer is thin, it is highly responsive to U.S. advice, and with a good grasp of the basic elements of rooting out the Viet Cong. Opposition groups are fragmentary, and Khanh has brought in at least token representation from many key groups hitherto left out. He is keenly aware of the danger of assassination or coup and is taking resourceful steps to minimize these risks. All told, these evidences of energy, comprehension, and decision add up to a sufficiently strong chance of Khanh's really taking hold in the next few months for us to devote all possible energy and resources to his support.

170. TELEGRAM FROM PRESIDENT LYNDON B. JOHNSON TO LODGE, MARCH 17, 1964 [Extract]

Johnson informed Lodge that he had already agreed to South Vietnamese "cross-border penetrations" into Laos, to be worked out by RVN Premier Nguyen Khanh and the right-wing Laotian military chief, Phoumi Nosovan. Phoumi and Khanh met secretly at Dalat on March 13, 1964, to reach agreement on military cooperation between the Lao and Vietnamese military, including South Vietnamese operations in Laos and the training of right-wing Laotian troops and officers in South Vietnam.

---

[2]Mr. McCone does not believe the dangers of another coup (except as a result of a possible assassination) at this time are as serious as he believes this paragraph implies.

SOURCE: Document from the Lyndon Johnson Library.

4. Specifically with respect to the comments in your 1757 your wholehearted support of first eleven recommendations covers our most important efforts which are still in South Vietnam. On your additional comments, I have reached the following conclusions:

(1) I think additional actions against Laos and Cambodia should be intensively examined. We have agreed that cross-border ground penetrations should be initiated into Laos along any lines which can be worked out by Khanh and Phoumi with Souvanna's endorsement, and I will authorize low-level reconnaissance there wherever the present high-level flights indicate that such reconnaissance may be needed.

The questions of further U.S. participation and of air and ground strikes against Laos raise tough diplomatic issues and I have asked Rusk and McNamara to concern a further recommendation. My first thought is that it is important to seek support from Souvanna Phouma and to build a stronger case before we take action which might have only limited military effect and could trigger wider Communist action in Laos.

On Cambodia we find ourselves hard put to keep abreast of the rapid changes Sihanouk introduces into the scene. Our impression is that bilateral GVN-RKG talks may now be in progress and State has sent you some thoughts on those prospects. However, in the event of further deterioration, I would expect to authorize hot pursuit.

On overt high- or low-level reconnaissance over North Vietnam, we are not ready to make a decision now. I have asked that political and diplomatic preparations be made to lay a basis for such reconnaissance if it seems necessary or desirable after a few weeks, for military or political reasons, or both.

(2) As I read your comments on John McCone's points, the main items are those discussed above on Laos and Cambodia. We agree that Mekong traffic is a trump card, and State has already sent you a message on this question.

We agree that large-scale Chinese Nationalist incursion would be a mistake, but high quality advisers are different matter and we will send further thoughts on that.

(3) I have ordered a review of your paper of October 30. My own inclination is to favor such pressures, short of overt military action.

(4) Like you, I reserve judgment on such overt U.S. measures against North Vietnam. Question of direct retaliation for attacks on Americans is more complex. As I understand it from McNamara mission, these attacks are not an immediate present threat, but you are authorized to prepare contingency recommendation for specific tit-for-tat actions in the event attacks on Americans are renewed.

171. TELEGRAM FROM JOHNSON TO LODGE, MARCH 20, 1964

Explaining why direct military pressures against the North were being delayed, Johnson revealed that the United States expected a "showdown" between

SOURCE: *The Pentagon Papers: Gravel Edition*, Vol. III, p. 511.

the Russian and Chinese Communist parties, which would make it easier to attack the North. Johnson also responded to Lodge's call for diplomatic efforts to persuade French President de Gaulle to retract his call for a neutralization agreement by declaring that there was "nothing more important" than to "stop neutralist talk."

1. We have studied your 1776 and I am asking State to have Bill Bundy make sure that you get out latest planning documents on ways of applying pressure and power against the North. I understand that some of this was discussed with you by McNamara mission in Saigon, but as plans are refined it would be helpful to have your detailed comments. As we agreed in our previous messages to each other, judgment is reserved for the present on overt military action in view of the consensus from Saigon conversations of McNamara mission with General Khanh and you on judgment that movement against the North at the present would be premature. We have share General Khanh's judgment that the immediate and essential task is to strengthen the southern base. For this reason our planning for action against the North is on a contingency basis at present, and immediate problem in this area is to develop the strongest possible military and political base for possible later action. There is additional international reason for avoiding immediate overt action in that we expect a showdown between the Chinese and Soviet Communist parties soon and action against the North will be more practicable after than before a showdown. But if at any time you feel that more immediate action is urgent, I count on you to let me know specifically the reasons for such action, together with your recommendations for its size and shape.

2. On dealing with deGaulle, I continue to think it may be valuable for you to go to Paris after Bohlen has made his first try. (State is sending you draft instruction to Bohlen, which I have not yet reviewed, for your comment.) *It ought to be possible to explain in Saigon that your mission is precisely for the purpose of knocking down the idea of neutralization wherever it rears its ugly head, and on this point I think that nothing is more important than to stop neutralist talk wherever we can by whatever means we can.* I have made this point myself to Mansfield and Lippmann and I expect to use every public opportunity to restate our position firmly. You may want to convey our concern on this point to General Khanh and get his ideas on the best possible joint program to stop such talk in Saigon, in Washington, and in Paris. I imagine that you have kept General Khanh abreast of our efforts in Paris. After we see the results of the Bohlen approach you might wish to sound him out on Paris visit by you.

172. MEMORANDUM FROM VIETNAM DESK OFFICER JOSEPH A. MENDENHALL TO U. ALEXIS JOHNSON, JUNE 1, 1964

On a visit to Ottawa on April 30, Rusk had gotten Canadian government agreement to send J. Blair Seaborn, Canada's chief representative on the Interna-

---

SOURCE: *U.S.-Vietnam Relations, VI.C.1, "Settlement of the Conflict, History of Contacts, Negotiations, 1965–1966."* (An unpublished volume declassified by the Department of Defense, March 10, 1975), pp. 17–21.

tional Control Commission, to Hanoi to act as an interlocutor for the United States with North Vietnam. In instructions for Seaborn, drafted by William Sullivan, Chairman of an Interagency Vietnam Committee, he was told to convey the American threat of air and naval attack against the North unless Hanoi agreed to stop the war in the South. He was also instructed to offer economic advantages to the North, diplomatic recognition and phased reduction of U.S. forces to the level permitted by the Geneva Accords. The paper further indicated that the war had to stop within one week of the conversation in Hanoi, or the United States would initiate retaliatory actions "immediately." According to a telegram from Rusk to Lodge on June 7, Seaborn was given a condensed version of this draft.

I am enclosing a copy of the "Outline of Subjects for Mr. Seaborn" which Bill Sullivan prepared prior to departure for Honolulu. He gave a copy of this general paper of instructions to Mr. Robinson, Minister-Counselor of the Canadian Embassy, on May 30.

At your request I have prepared and am enclosing a draft of a further outline in specific terms of the message which we would expect the Canadian interlocutor to get across in Hanoi. This further outline is based on the assumptions that (a) a U.S. decision has been taken to act against North Viet-Nam and (b) we plan to use "carrots" as well as a "stick" on Hanoi. I believe that we would probably not wish to hand this further outline to the Canadian Government pending the initial soundings of the Canadian interlocutor in Hanoi pursuant to Mr. Sullivan original set of instructions.

Enclosures:

1. Outline of Subjects for Mr. Seaborn.
2. Further Outline for Mr. Seaborn.

Outline of Subjects for Mr. Seaborn

1. The President wishes Hanoi to understand that he is fundamentally a man of peace. However, he does not intend to let the North Vietnamese take over all of Southeast Asia. He wishes to have a highly confidential, responsible interlocutor who will deliver this message to the authorities in Hanoi and report back their reaction.

2. The messages which may be transmitted through this channel would involve an indication of the limitations both upon US ambitions in Southeast Asia and upon US patience with Communist provocation. The interlocutor or his Government need not agree with not associate themselves with the messages that are passed. The only requirement is that there be faithful transmittal of the messages in each direction.

3. Mr. Seaborn should arrive in Hanoi as soon as possible and establish his credentials as a political personality who can and will deal with senior representatives of the Hanoi regime.

4. Mr. Seaborn should also, by listening to the arguments and observing the attitudes of the North Vietnamese, form an evaluation of their mental outlook. He should be particularly alert to (a) differences with respect to the Sino-Soviet split, (b) frustration or war weariness, (c) indications of North Vietnamese desire for contacts with the West, (d) evidences of cliques or factions in the Party or Government, and (e) evidence of differences between the political and the military.

5. Mr. Seaborn should explore the nature and the prevalence of Chinese Communist influence in North Viet Nam; and perhaps through direct discussions with the Soviet representatives, evaluate the nature and influence of the Soviets.

6. Mr. Seaborn should stress to appropriate North Vietnamese officials that US policy is to see to it that North Viet Nam contains itself and its ambitions within the territory allocated to its administration by the 1954 Geneva Agreements. He should stress that US policy in South Viet Nam is to preserve the integrity of that state's territory against guerrilla subversion.

7. He should state that the US does not seek military bases in the area and that the US is not seeking to overthrow the Communist regime in Hanoi.

8. He should stipulate that the US is fully aware of the degree to which Hanoi controls and directs the guerrilla action in South Viet Nam and that the US holds Hanoi directly responsible for that action. He should similarly indicate US awareness of North Vietnamese control over the Pathet Lao movement in Laos and the degree of North Vietnamese involvement in that country. He should specifically indicate US awareness of North Vietnamese violations of Laotian territory along the infiltration route into South Viet Nam.

9. Mr. Seaborn should point out that the nature of US commitment in South Viet Nam is not confined to the territorial issue in question. He should make it clear that the US considers the confrontation with North Vietnamese subversive guerrilla action as part of the general Free World confrontation with this type of violent subversion in other lesser developed countries. Therefore, the US stake in resisting a North Vietnamese victory in South Viet Nam has a significance of world-wide proportions.

10. Mr. Seaborn can point to the many examples of US policy in tolerance of peaceful coexistence with Communist regimes, such as Yugoslavia, Poland, etc. He can hint at the economic and other benefits which have accrued to those countries because their policy of Communism has confined itself to the development of their own national territories and has not sought to expand into other areas.

11. Mr. Seaborn can couple this statement with the frank acknowledgement that US public and official patience with North Vietnamese aggression is growing extremely thin.

12. Insofar as Mr. Seaborn considers it might be educational he could review the relative military strengths of the US, North Viet Nam, and the available resources of Communist China in Southeast Asia.

13. In sum, the purpose of Mr. Seaborn's mission in North Viet Nam would be as an interlocutor with both active and passive functions. On the passive side, he should report either observations or direct communications concerning North Vietnamese attitude toward extrication from or escalation of military activities. On the active side, he should establish his credentials with the North Vietnamese as an authoritative channel of communications with the US. In each of these functions it would be hoped that Mr. Seaborn would assume the posture that the decision as to the future course of events in Southeast Asia rests squarely with Hanoi.

Further Outline for Mr. Seaborn

1. The U.S. objective is to maintain the independence and territorial integrity of South Viet-Nam. This means that the South Vietnamese Government in Saigon

must be able to exercise its authority throughout the territory south of the 17th Parallel without encountering armed resistance directed and supported by Hanoi.

2. We know that Hanoi can stop the war in South Viet-Nam if it will do so. The virtually complete cease-fires which have obtained at Tet time for the past two years demonstrate the ability of Hanoi to control all Viet Cong operations in South Viet-Nam if it has the will to do so.

3. In order to stop the war in South Viet-Nam the United States is prepared to follow alternative courses of action with respect to North Viet-Nam.

(a) Unless Hanoi stops the war within a specified time period (i.e., ceases all attacks, acts of terror, sabotage or armed propaganda or other armed resistance to government authority by the VC), the United States will initiate action by air and naval means against North Viet-Nam until Hanoi does agree to stop the war.

(b) If Hanoi will agree to stop the war, the United States will take the following step:

(1) Undertake to obtain the agreement of Saigon to a resumption of trade between North Viet-Nam and South Viet-Nam, which would be helpful to North Viet-Nam in view of the complementarity of the two zones of Viet-Nam and the food difficulties now suffered by North Viet-Nam.

(2) Initiate a program of foodstuffs assistance to North Viet-Nam either on a relief grant basis under Title II of Public Law 480 or on a sales for local currency basis under Title I PL-480 (as in Poland and Yugoslavia).

(3) Remove U.S. foreign assets controls from the assets of North Viet-Nam and reduce controls on U.S. trade with North Viet-Nam to the level now applicable to the USSR (i.e., strategic items only).

(4) Recognize North Viet-Nam diplomatically and, if Hanoi is interested, undertake an exchange of diplomatic representatives.

(5) Remove U.S. forces from South Viet-Nam on a phased basis, winding up with a reduction to the level of 350 military advisors or trainers as permitted under the Geneva Accords. (This was the number of U.S. military personnel in Viet-Nam when the Geneva Accords were signed in 1954).

4. If Hanoi stops resistance in South Viet-Nam, the United States and South Vietnamese Governments will permit Hanoi to withdraw any Viet Cong personnel whom it may wish from South Viet-Nam. The Government of South Viet-Nam will also make a clear public announcement of full amnesty for all rebels who discontinue armed resistance to the authority of the Government.

5. If Hanoi agrees to cease resistance, the order from Hanoi to the Viet Cong units and personnel can be issued, if Hanoi prefers, either publicly or confidentially through the communications channels from Hanoi to the Viet Cong. The test the U.S. will apply will be whether or not all armed resistance to the authority of the Government at Saigon actually stops.

6. Timetable for these actions:

(a) All hostilities must cease within one week of the approach to the authorities at Hanoi. If they have not stopped within that time, the U.S. will immediately initiate air and naval action against North Viet-Nam.

(b) If agreement is reached between the U.S. and North Viet-Nam on the cessation of resistance in South Viet-Nam, the cessation of hostilities will be preceded by a general GVN amnesty announcement.

(c) If the DRV desires to repatriate Viet Cong from South Viet-Nam, this can be done over whatever period the DRV desires.

(d) If the DRV desires to announce an agreement publicly with the United States, the entire package of measures on both sides can be announced within three days of the complete cessation of hostilities. If the DRV does not desire a public announcement of its agreement to have the Viet Cong cease resistance, then the United States measures of concession to North Viet-Nam can be announced only over a phased period starting one week from the complete cessation of hostilities. Announcement of all steps taken by the U.S. as concessions to North Viet-Nam would be completed by three months from the cessation of hostilities.

(e) U.S. forces would be removed from South Viet-Nam on a phased basis over a period of one year from the data of cessation of resistance to the Government of South Viet-Nam. At the end of one year U.S. military personnel would be down to the 350 permitted by the Geneva Accords.

173. TELEGRAM FROM BALL TO PRESIDENT JOHNSON AND RUSK, JUNE 5, 1964 [Extract]

In a conversation with Under Secretary of State George Ball, French President Charles de Gaulle said he did not believe that the United States could win in Vietnam and proposed a "diplomatic operation" as an alternative to a major war. Ball rejected the idea of a peace conference and said the United States could not negotiate until it had increased Vietnamese "will to resist" or reduced North Vietnam's "subversive efforts."

General de Gaulle said he had listened with great attention to what Mr. Ball had said. There was little surprising in it since he had suspected for some time the difficulties of the situation. The US has taken on itself alone the responsibilities which the French had borne in the past.

He said he agreed that South Vietnam was the main problem, with Laos and Cambodia as accessory problems. He referred to our hope that we can bring about a suppression of the insurgency by supplying Vietnam with arms, credits, military advice, etc. I take note, said General De Gaulle, of your hope but I cannot agree with it. I do not believe that you can win in this situation even though you have more aircraft, cannons, and arms of various kinds.

The problem was primarily a political and psychological problem. He was not referring merely to General Khanh but to the people. To them the US was a very big foreign power. "I do not mean that all of the Vietnamese are against you but they regard the US as a foreign power and a very powerful foreign power."

SOURCE: Document from the Lyndon Baines Johnson Library.

The more the US becomes involved in the actual conduct of military operations the more the Vietnamese will turn against us, as will others in Southeast Asia.

He said he understood the immense difficulties which the US faced. The US has the possibility and the means of going to war. We could destroy [word missing] on the Chinese mainland and even American [word garbled] if we desired. But what would happen when the war began? What would be its consequences? He côuld not say.

In 1900, at the time of the Boxer Rebellion, it had been very easy. The only problem was that of frightening the Empress. Now continents were involved.

War was, of course, a possibility which the US could envisage. General MacArthur had thought it was a good idea. However, he said, the French would never resume war in Asia. He had told this to President Kennedy. The French consider that Southeast Asia is a "rotten" territory in which to fight. Even if the US were involved France would not get into a war in Asia, as an ally or otherwise.

If the US did not make war we still appeared to think that by reinforcing the existing situation we could strengthen the Vietnamese and win the current struggle. He did not agree with this. The United States might maintain the struggle in this manner for an extended period of time. But we could not bring the affair to an end. Once we realized this, i.e., that we could not put an end to the situation, we might come to the conclusion that we would have to make peace. This would mean peace with China and others in the area.

He said he noticed that we thought that China was like Russia in 1917—intransient, warlike, and expansive. He did not know whether this was true or not. Personally he doubted it. He thought if possible that China would see the advantage to itself, at least for a few years, in a passive posture. He did not mean that this would last forever but it might for a few years. China needs rest, it needs help, it needs commerce and technical assistance from other countries. The Russians had been in a different position. Russia had had an intelligentsia, an army, and agriculture. China has none of these things. In any event, the French thought that we should try to see what China was up to. He then asked for Mr. Ball's comments.

Mr. Ball said if we were now to undertake diplomatic efforts with Peking or Hanoi this would threaten the collapse of the existing resistance in South Vietnam. General De Gaulle had said—and he agreed—that the problem was more political and psychological than military. Our task was to help the South Vietnamese create a govt in which the people would have confidence, and to which they would feel allegiance. But if we began, or attempted to begin, negotiations of the type that General De Gaulle was speaking about, the result might be a general failure of the will to resist.

Either we must increase the Vietnamese will to resist or we must reduce the subversive efforts of the North. To negotiate before either of these objectives was achieved would destroy the only basis on which we can hope to build in the future. Moreover we said now reason to believe that an agreement made with the communists would be carried out. We remembered the agreement of 1962 for the neutralization of Laos, and the attitude of Hanoi and Peking towards it.

De Gaulle said that if a diplomatic operation were undertaken by the US alone, it would, of course, not succeed. What he had in mind was a vast diplomatic operation which would include the participation of France, India, China, Japan, and other countries. This would provide the Vietnamese people—and he was not speaking of General Khanh—with a sense of support and assurance for the future. He doubted that even Ho Chi Minh could continue to kill South Vietnamese while taking part in a conference. World opinion would make it impossible.

He repeated, however, such a diplomatic effort could not be done by the Americans. A large conference had been attempted in 1954 and although the talks had taken a very long time he felt that this in itself was not a bad thing. If a world conference of the type he was thinking of could be put into operation it would change the state of mind of the Vietnamese people and produce a détente. This would render it very difficult for Ho Chi Minh to keep on with his activities. If such a diplomatic operation were undertaken a resulting détente would bring about a new political situation. This, however, was not possible under conditions of civil war. Mr. Ball said the situation in South Vietnam presented problems of exceptional difficulty. If we were dealing with conventional warfare—with regular armies drawn up in opposing formations—it would be possible to agree to a ceasefire and police it. But in South Vietnam there were scattered groups of guerrillas. Many only came out at night. It would be extremely difficult to police any ceasefire. Moreover, it was not realistic to assume that the insurgents would be willing to lose momentum and thus would be willing to accept a ceasefire. Ho Chi Minh would probably argue with contrived innocence that he had no connection with what was going on in Vietnam. At the same time he would covertly maintain the subversive action. There was enormous danger that a conference would play into the hands of the communists who would exploit it covertly and dishonestly. Thereafter it might well be impossible to infuse any vitality into a Vietnamese Govt. We would be reluctant to take such a risk.

De Gaulle replied "all policy involves risks. If it is a policy that does not involve risks there is no choice of policy." He thought a conference of Europeans, Asians and US would produce a very powerful impact of the Vietnamese people and succeed in changing the whole situation, at least for a certain period of time. The present situation, he said, would not result in anything. France has had experience which proved it.

174. MEMORANDUM ON THE SOUTHEAST ASIA SITUATION BY ASSISTANT SECRETARY OF STATE FOR FAR EASTERN AFFAIRS WILLIAM BUNDY, JUNE 12, 1964 [Extract]

In preparation for a major interagency meeting on recommendations to the president regarding the issue of a congressional resolution, William Bundy reviewed the case for a congressional resolution. He defined the primary problem as demonstrating American "firmness" to Souvanna Phouma in Laos and to the

---

SOURCE: Document declassified by Department of State, August 1978.

South Vietnamese. No military move that was then contemplated would serve as a sufficiently clear signal to Hanoi, he concluded. So the most effective action for the administration would be a congressional resolution that could be passed without divisive debate but would support "any action required."

6. In sum, there are military moves that we can take that would contribute to a continuing impression of firmness as we try to keep the Laos negotiations moving and to preserve our options concerning Viet-Nam. *But* it is at least doubtful that any combination of the moves listed above would in fact do the trick. [deleted] Finally, we must never lose sight of the fact that the situation in South Viet-Nam—*without* necessarily any dramatic event—could deteriorate to the point where we had to consider at least beginning stronger actions to the north in order to put greater pressure on Hanoi and lift morale in South Viet-Nam.

7. For all of these reasons there is a very strong argument for a continuing demonstration of US firmness and for complete flexibility in the hands of the Executive in the coming political months. The action that most commends itself for this purpose is an immediate Congressional Resolution, subject to the following conditions:

a. A formula must be devised, in consultation with the Congressional leadership, that would ensure rapid passage without amended and divisive debate. The draft resolution must support any action required but must at the same time place maximum stress on our peaceful objectives and our willingness to accept eventual negotiated solutions, so that we might hope to have the full support of the school of thought headed by Senator Mansfield and Senator Aiken and leave ourselves with die-hard opposition only from Senator Morse and his very few cohorts.

b. Timing must be considered. Because of proximity on either side to the Republican convention, July appears very difficult. Early August is likewise difficult because the Congress will probably be rushing to complete other measures and adjourn before the Democratic convention. We thus conclude that the only feasible time for presentation would be shortly following the conclusion of the Civil Rights debate, i.e. during the week of June 22. In addition to being virtually inevitable from a political standpoint, this timing does fit very well with the probable date of the convening of [deleted] consultations and with the time when our existing and planned signals to Hanoi may begin to taper off.

It may be argued that a Congressional Resolution under present circumstances faces the serious difficulty that there is no drastic change in the situation to point to. The opposing argument is that we might well not have such a *drastic* change even later in the summer and yet conclude—[deleted] that we had to act.

c. The line of argument to be followed in presenting the resolution requires careful thought. A separate memorandum deals with the suggested theme of presentation and with basic questions that would be raised and the line of answer that would be followed. From this theme, and these questions and answers, appropriate Presidential messages, testimony by Secretaries Rusk and McNamara, special presentations to the Congress (e.g. of the evidence concerning North Vietnamese involvement), and other necessary elements would be drawn.

8. Conclusion

It is recommended that the President urgently review with the Congressional leadership a resolution along the lines covered in the accompanying folder.

175. NOTES BY CANADIAN ICC REPRESENTATIVE BLAIR SEABORN ON MEETING WITH PHAM VAN DONG, JUNE 18, 1964

Responding to Seaborn's presentation of the American warnings, Pham Van Dong outlined the DRV terms for a settlement, said the revolutionaries would finally win, and indicated that his government would not "provoke" the United States.

President Ho Chi Minh has explained what we mean by a just solution. First it requires an American withdrawal from Indochina. Secondly it means that the affairs of the South must be arranged by the people of the South. It must provide for the participation of the Liberation Front. No other group represents the broad wishes of the people. The programme of the Front is the best one possible. There must be peace and neutrality for South Vietnam, neutrality in the Cambodian manner. Thirdly, a just solution means re-unification of the country. This is a "drame, [as in original document] national, fundamental". But we want peaceful unification, without military pressures. We want negotiation 'round a table. There must be sincere satisfaction with the arrangement for it to be viable. We are in no hurry. We are willing to talk but we shall wait till SVN is ready. We are a divided people, without even personal links across the dividing line.

The United States must show good will, but it is not easy for the USA to do so. Meanwhile the war intensifies. USA aid may increase in all areas, not only for the SVN army but in terms of USA army personnel as well. I suffer to see the war go on, develop, intensify. Yet our people are determined to struggle. It is impossible, quite impossible (excuse me for saying this) for you Westerners to understand the force of the people's will to resist and to continue. The struggle of the people exceeds the imagination. It has astonished us too.

Since the fall of the Ngo brothers, it has been a "cascade". The prospect for the USA and its friends in SVN is *"sans issu."* Reinforcing the Khanh army doesn't count. The people have had enough. The SVN mercenaries have sacrificed themselves without honour. The Americans are not lovers, for they commit atrocities. How can the people suffer such exactions and terror?

Let me stress, insofar as the internal situation in SVN is concerned, the

SOURCE: *United States-Vietnam Relations*, VI.C.I., pp. 28–29.

realistic nature of the Liberation Front's programme. It is impossible to have a representative government which excludes the Front. The idea of a government of national coalition *"fait boule de niege"* in the South. The Laos pattern of 1962 should serve as a guide for SVN.

To return to Vietnam, it is a question of a *"guerre à outrance"* which the USA won't win in any event, or neutrality. He had not (as I had suggested) referred to neutrality as a first step only. Whether SVN would continue neutral would depend upon the people of SVN. He did not prejudge the issue.

176. TELEGRAM FROM AMBASSADOR MAXWELL TAYLOR TO RUSK, JULY 25, 1964 [Extract]

Ambassador Maxwell Taylor suggested that Nguyen Khanh's public threat to "March North" could become a serious problem in American-GVN relations, resulting either in a rash action by hotheads in the GVN or in frustration and a lurch toward a neutralist settlement. He proposed offering to enter into joint planning with the GVN on attacking the North, without any commitment in advance, to take the steam out of the movement. The State Department approved Taylor's suggestion while expressing the suspicion that Khanh might try to publicize the joint planning for his own political purposes.

The GVN public campaign for "Marching North" (reported EMBTEL 201) may take several courses. In the face of U.S. coolness and absence of evidence of real grassroots support outside certain military quarters, it may die down for a while although it is hardly likely to disappear completely. On the other hand, the proponents of a "Quick Solution" may be able to keep it alive indefinitely as an active issue, in which case it is likely to foment an increasing amount of dissatisfaction with the U.S. (assuming that we continue to give it no support) to the serious detriment of our working relations with the GVN and hence of the ultimate chances of .success of the in-country pacification program. In such a case, Vietnamese leaders in and out of government, unable to find a vent to their frustration in "Marching North" may seek other panaceas in various forms of negotiation formulas. General Khanh may find in the situation an excuse or a requirement to resign.

Finally, this "March North" fever can get out of hand in an act of rashness—one maverick pilot taking off for Hanoi with a load of bombs—which could touch off an extension of hostilities at a time and in a form most disadvantageous to U.S. interests.

Faced with these unattractive possibilities, we propose a course of action designed to do several things.

We would try to avoid head-on collision with the GVN which unqualified U.S. opposition to the "March North" campaign would entail. We could do this by expressing a willingness to engage in joint contingency planning for various forms of extended action against GVN [sic]. Such planning would not only provide an

SOURCE: *The Pentagon Papers*, pp. 283–289.

outlet for the martial head of steam now dangerously compressed but would force the generals to look at the hard facts of life which lie behind the neon lights of the "March North" slogans. This planning would also gain time badly needed to stabilize this government and could provide a useful basis for military action if adjudged in our interest at some future time. Finally, it would also afford U.S. an opportunity, for the first time, to have a frank discussion with GVN leaders concerning the political objectives which they would envisage as the purposes inherent in military action against the DRV. . . .

It would be important, however, in initiating such a line of action that we make a clear record that we are not repeat not assuming any commitment to supplement such plans. . . .

177. TELEGRAM FROM THE VIETNAM PEOPLE'S ARMY (VPA) TO THE INTERNATIONAL CONTROL COMMISSION, JULY 31, 1964

On the night of July 30–31, South Vietnamese naval forces using American "swiftboats" carried out an amphibious commando raid on Hon Me and Hon Nieu islands off the North Vietnamese coast, while bombarding the islands, as part of the covert U.S. "OPLAN 34." The DRV reacted immediately and publicly, accusing the United States and South Vietnam of an "extremely serious" violation of the Geneva Agreements—without mentioning the landings by commandos. It was in the context of this raid that the U.S.S. Maddox, later revealed to be carrying out electronic surveillance along the Chinese and North Vietnamese coasts, was intercepted by North Vietnamese patrol boats on August 2 only twenty-eight miles from the coast. The North Vietnamese boats, which the Pentagon's own account suggests mistook the Maddox for a South Vietnamese vessel escorting the boats that carried out the earlier attacks, closed in on the Maddox and launched a torpedo at the ship, whereupon U.S. planes from the Ticonderoga destroyed one of the North Vietnamese ships and damaged the other two.

At 2340 hours on 30 July, the Americans and their henchmen in South Vietnam sent two warships to bombard Hon Ngu Island off Qua Hoi Hoi, Nghe An Province. This island is four kilometers from the coast. At the same time, another warship was sent to bombard Hon Me island off Ba Lang, Thanh Hoa Province. This island is 12 kilometers from the coast.

These acts of the Americans and the southern administration constitute a gross violation of the sovereignty and territorial integrity of the DRV, an extremely serious violation of the 1954 Geneva agreements on Vietnam, and a shameless provocation toward North Vietnam. Obviously, these are not individual acts, but are part of the premeditated common plan of the Americans and their henchmen to

SOURCE: Broadcast on Hanoi radio in Vietnamese to South Vietnam, August 1, 1964. Translated in Foreign Broadcast Information Service, Far East, August 3, 1964, pp. JJJ2.

carry out schemes to intensify the provocative and destructive acts against the DRV while striving to step up their aggressive war in South Vietnam.

The VPA strongly protests the above-mentioned bombardments of these two islands by the warships of the Americans and their henchmen and urges the ICC to adopt effective measures to force the Americans and the southern administration to stop immediately their extremely dangerous and provocative acts and to respect and properly implement the 1954 Geneva agreements on Vietnam.

178. ORDER FROM ADMIRAL THOMAS H. MOORER, COMMANDER IN CHIEF, PACIFIC FLEET, TO ALL SUBORDINATE UNITS, AUGUST 2, 1964

Immediately following the Maddox *incident, the Joint Chiefs of Staff, with presidential approval, ordered that the* Maddox *patrol, code-named "DeSoto Patrols," be resumed as soon as possible. The order to the Seventh Fleet called for two destroyers to run to within three nautical miles of the North Vietnamese coast and four nautical miles of the offshore islands during the day and retire eastward at night. The new patrol plans would increase the prospect of conflict with the DRV naval forces patrolling the coastline. Admiral Moorer's order suggested that the United States was eager to test the North Vietnamese by asserting the "right of freedom of the seas" right up to the DRV's doorstep.*

1. In view *Maddox* incident, consider it our best interest that we assert right of freedom of the seas and resume Golf of Tonkin patrol earliest.

2. For COMSEVENTHFLT [Commander, Seventh Fleet] UNODIR [unless otherwise directed] conduct patrol with two destroyers, resuming ASAP [as soon as possible]. When ready, proceed to Point Charlie arriving first day, thence patrol northward toward Point Delta during daylight hours. Retire to the east during hours of darkness. On second day proceed to Point Delta thence patrol south toward Point Charlie retiring to night as before. On third day proceed to Point Lima and patrol toward Point Mike, retiring to east at night. On fourth day proceed to Point Mike and patrol toward Point November, retiring night. On fifth day return to [Point] November and retire to south through Points Oscar and Papa and terminate patrol. CPA [closest point of approach] to North Vietnamese coast 8NM [nautical miles]. CPA to North Vietnamese islands 4NM. Above points as specified.

179. TELEGRAM FROM RUSK TO TAYLOR, AUGUST 3, 1964

After resuming the DeSoto Patrols near the North Vietnamese coast, the operational commander for the two destroyers reported to Admiral Moorer that

SOURCE: *Congressional Record*, February 29, 1968, p. 4694.
SOURCE: Document from the Lyndon Baines Johnson Library.

information from "various sources" indicated that that the DRV considered the patrol to be "directly involved with 34-A ops" and thus considered the American ships "as enemies because of these ops. . . ." Whether or not this report was passed on to the highest levels of the Johnson Administration, Secretary Rusk told Taylor that same day that Hanoi was "rattled" by the South Vietnamese attacks on its coast, indicating that the administration understood that the Maddox incident was directly connected with the 34-A operations, contrary to later denials by Secretary McNamara in testimony before Congress.

We have been very sensitive here to the considerations you raise reftel. We would hope that part of the problem has been met by President's public statement today, which you have already received. We have asked JCS to insure that you receive copies of the implementing orders to the appropriate commanders through military channels.

Suggestions made in B, C and D reftel are currently being considered in context OPLAN 34A. Significant additions have been made to list of targets for marine operations and these will be transmitted to you shortly.

We believe that present OPLAN 34A activities are beginning to rattle Hanoi, and MADDOX incident is directly related to their effort to resist these activities. We have no intention yielding to pressure.

In your discretion you may pass these thoughts along to Gen. Khanh. You may also reiterate to him, but only if you believe it appropriate, our concern that actions against the North be limited for the present to the OPLAN 34A type. We do not believe that SVN is yet in a position to mount larger actions so long as the security situation in the near vicinity of Saigon remains precarious. We are impressed with the fact that a battalion-sized attack could have occurred within 4 miles of Saigon without any advance warning.

We would welcome your further comments on Saigon reaction to today's announcement, as well as your continuing assessment of the political temperature there.

180. MESSAGE FROM MOORER TO MADDOX COMMANDER CAPTAIN HERRICK, AUGUST 3, 1964

Knowing that another South Vietnam raid on the North Vietnamese coast was set for the night of August 3–4, Commander Herrick of the Maddox proposed that the DeSoto Patrol be terminated. But Admiral Moorer rejected termination and recommended that the patrol schedule be altered to "avoid interference with 34-A Ops." But he indicated that they were still linked with the raids by suggesting that by remaining far enough northward the patrol might draw North Vietnamese patrol boats away from the area where the raids would take place.

SOURCE: *Congressional Record*, February 29, 1968, p. 4694.

1. Termination of DeSoto patrol after two days of patrol ops [operations] subsequent to *Maddox* incident does not in my view adequately demonstrate United States resolve to assert our legitimate rights in these international waters.

2. Accordingly, recommend following adjustments in remainder of patrol schedule . . . in order to accommodate COMUSMACV [Commander, United States Military Assistance Command Vietnam] request that patrol ships remain north of LAT [latitude] 19-10 north until [deleted time] to avoid intereference with 34-A Ops. 4 August patrol from Point Delta to Charlie remain north of 19-10 North.

The above patrol will (a) clearly demonstrate our determination to continue these operations; (b) possibly draw NVN [North Vietnamese Navy] PGMs [patrol boats] to northward away from area of 34-A Ops; (c) eliminate DeSoto patrol interference with 34-A Ops.

181. LETTER FROM SOVIET PREMIER NIKITA KHRUSHCHEV TO PRESIDENT JOHNSON, AUGUST 5, 1964

South Vietnamese patrol boats attacked military targets on the North Vietnamese mainland around midnight of August 3–4. Nearly a day later, North Vietnamese torpedo boats closed in the Maddox *and the* Turner Joy *sixty-five miles from the shore. Although no damage was done to either American boat, and the attacking boats were driven off, President Johnson announced thirteen hours later that the United States was launching air attacks against bases in North Vietnam. In a private message to Johnson on the crisis, Soviet Premier Khrushchev was cautious in substance and mild in tone, calling on the United States to show "composure and restraint" in order to remove the tension in the Gulf of Tonkin. It not only failed to threaten a Soviet response of any kind—pointedly mentioning the possibility of a response from "the other side"—but refrained even from endorsing the DRV version of events in the area. But Khrushchev tried to play on the United States fear of Chinese influence in Hanoi, suggesting that Washington might be playing into Peking's hands.*

I deem it necessary to personally inform you about the concern that we feel in connection with the events unfolding in the Gulf of Tonkin.

From the very outset I want to mention that we know about these events solely from those statements which have been made these days in Washington, from the published orders to the American armed forces, from the reports of the news agencies and also from the statement, just published by the spokesman of the High Command of the Vietnamese People's Army concerning the incident on August 2 in the Gulf of Tonkin. We do not have other information as yet. One thing is undisputable, however,—the situation there has sharply deteriorated and military conflicts are taking place near the coast of the Democratic Republic of Vietnam and the Chinese People's Republic, in which warships of the U.S. Navy are participating as

SOURCE: Document from the Lyndon Baines Johnson Library.

well as military planes based on American aircraft carriers. Also obvious is the seriousness of these developments—indeed, it is impossible to rule out that they may mushroom into such proportions and turn in such a way that it will be difficult to say where they will stop.

We do not know exactly now just what has happened there. But even irrespective of this the fact remains that the warships of the U.S. Navy have entered the Gulf which cuts deeply into the territories of the DRV and the CPR, and that it is from these ships that fire was opened and aircraft are being launched which according to the latest reports, are making strikes against objectives on the territory of the DRV. Suffice it to look at the map to convince oneself that except the DRV and the CPR [China] there are no other states the territories of which adjoin the Gulf of Tonkin and that, consequently, the very fact of introduction of American warships in that Gulf under any circumstances cannot be viewed in any other way but as a military demonstration, as a challenge to the states whose shores are washed by that Gulf.

With all frankness I must say that if these actions of American warships and air forces pursue the aim of strengthening somehow the position of the corrupt and rotten South Vietnamese regime which exists—and this is not secret to anyone—only because of the foreign support, then such actions will not achieve the given aim. But to increase the danger of a serious military conflict—they can.

A question arises before me: have not clouds been deliberately darkened around the developments in the Gulf of Tonkin? Is not the influence felt here by those quarters and persons who do not conceal their desire to inflame the passions, to pour oil on the flame and to whose militant frame of mind one should regard with great caution and restraint? But if this influence is indeed real and if it has an ear, then another, more serious question arises—where the present developments can lead to?

It would be unnecessary to speak in detail now about the enormous responsibility which our two powers bear, you personally as President of the United States and I as Chairman of the U.S.S.R. Council of Ministers, in keeping the peace, in ensuring that dangerous events whichever area of the globe they begin with, would not become first elements in the chain of ever more critical and maybe irreversible events. I believe that you should agree with this. And if this is so, then at this moment it is most important to draw from this necessary practical conclusions and proceeding from this lofty responsibility to look at the circumstances around the developments in the Gulf of Tonkin with maximum objectivity and to again and again weigh possible consequences.

I would not like here to give play to feelings although this, in all appearance, is justified by the situation. Because of lack of reliable information I confine myself 'to expressing those thoughts which follow from the main and undeniable fact, namely, that the warships and air forces of the United States have taken military actions in the Gulf of Tonkin area.

I want to emphasize that no one has asked the Soviet Government to address you in connection with the developments near the coast of the DRV and the CPR. If there appears a threat to peace, I am deeply convinced that we should not wait for requests or appeals from anybody but must act so as to remove that threat without delay.

I would like to hope that on your part there will be shown necessary composure and restraint in order to remove the military tension and stop defiant actions of the American armed forces in the Gulf of Tonkin area which may lead to an appropriate response from the other side.

182. LETTER FROM JOHNSON TO KHRUSHCHEV, AUGUST 5, 1964

Johnson responded to the Soviet premier's letter by trying to widen the rift between Moscow and Hanoi still further, pointing to possible cooperation between North Vietnam and China, and asking Khrushchev to restrain the Asian Communist states in the future.

I share the concern expressed in your message of August fifth concerning the incidents in the Gulf of Tonkin.

I also fully share your view of the heavy responsibility which we both bear for keeping the peace and for preventing incidents anywhere in the world from starting a chain of dangerous and irreversible developments. It was for this reason that we took only the minimum defensive action in response to the first attack upon the American destroyer in the Gulf of Tonkin. I think you can understand that the second deliberate attack—on which there is complete and incontrovertible evidence—could not be allowed to pass without reply. Our action was carefully measured to fit the circumstances, and we have no wish at all to see this matter go further. We have, of course, made appropriate deployments in the area as we are uncertain of the purpose of these flagrant attacks on our ships on the high seas. We do not know, for example, whether they were instigated by Peiping or made by the North Vietnamese in an effort to draw Peiping into the area. I have made it clear, publicly, that we ourselves do not wish an escalation of this situation.

183. THE GULF OF TONKIN RESOLUTION, AUGUST 7, 1964

Three days after the second incident in the Tonkin Gulf, the Administration submitted a Joint Resolution to Congress which approved in advance the president's taking "all necessary steps" to assist South Vietnam or any other member or protocol state of the Southeast Asia Treaty Organization. It was approved unanimously by the House and by a vote of 88 to 2 in the Senate.

To Promote the Maintenance of International Peace and Security in Southeast Asia.

Whereas naval units of the Communist regime in Vietnam, in violation of the principles of the Charter of the United Nations and of international law, have

SOURCE: Document from the Lyndon Baines Johnson Library.
SOURCE: Department of State *Bulletin*, August 24, 1964.

deliberately and repeatedly attacked United States naval vessels lawfully present in international waters, and have thereby created a serious threat to international peace; and

Whereas these attacks are part of a deliberate and systematic campaign of aggression that the Communist regime in North Vietnam has been waging against its neighbors and the nations joined with them in the collective defense of their freedom; and

Whereas the United States is assisting the peoples of southeast Asia to protect their freedom and has no territorial, military or political ambitions in that area, but desires only that these peoples should be left in peace to work out their own destinies in their own way: Now, therefore, be it

Resolved by the Senate and House of Representatives of the United States of America in Congress assembled.

That the Congress approves and supports the determination of the President, as Commander in Chief, to take all necessary measures to repel any armed attack against the forces of the United States and to prevent further aggression.

SEC.2. The United States regards as vital to its national interest and to world peace the maintenance of international peace and security in southeast Asia. Consonant with the Constitution of the United States and the Charter of the United Nations and in accordance with its obligations under the Southeast Asia Collective Defense Treaty, the United States is, therefore, prepared, as the President determines, to take all necessary steps, including the use of armed force, to assist any member or protocol state of the Southeast Asia Collective Defense Treaty requesting assistance in defense of its freedom.

SEC. 3. This resolution shall expire when the President shall determine that the peace and security of the area is reasonably assured by international conditions created by action of the United Nations or otherwise, except that it may be terminated earlier by concurrent resolution of the Congress.

184. INTELLIGENCE ASSESSMENT ON THE SITUATION IN VIETNAM BY A NATIONAL SECURITY COUNCIL WORKING GROUP ON VIETNAM, NOVEMBER 13, 1964 [Extract]

A working group made up of representatives of the CIA, Defense Intelligence Agency, and the State Department's Bureau of Intelligence and Research submitted a joint assessment that concluded that sanctions against the North, would change the situation in the South only if they affected the will of the DRV to contribute to the war effort in the South. The panel suggested that the threat of destruction of the DRV industrial sector and its transport and communications system would probably not bring the country to its knees and that Hanoi would be prepared to endure it.

SOURCE: Document from the Lyndon Baines Johnson Library.

8. The nature of the war in Vietnam is such that US ability to compel the DRV to end or reduce the VC insurrection rests much more upon the effect of US sanctions on the will of DRV leadership to sustain and enlarge that insurrection, than upon the effect of sanctions on the capabilities of the DRV to do so. Increased US pressures on the DRV would be effective only if they persuaded Hanoi that the price of maintaining the insurrection in the South at a high level would be too great and that it would be preferable to reduce its aid to the VC and direct at least a temporary reduction of VC activity. A respite so gained would provide an opportunity for the US/GVN to strengthen the military and civil machinery for combatting and controlling the VC insurgency. Even so, lasting success would depend upon a substantial improvement in the energy and effectiveness of the GVN government and pacification machinery.

*   *   *

10. *Hanoi's comprehension of US intentions.*

a. The course of actions the Communists have pursued in South Vietnam over the past few years implies a fundamental estimate on their part that the difficulties facing the US are so great that US will and ability to maintain resistance in that area can be gradually eroded—without running high risks that the US would wreak heavy destruction on the DRV or Communist China. Hanoi's immediate estimate is probably that the passing of the US election gives Washington greater policy flexibility with respect both to new military actions against the DRV and/or new diplomatic initiatives.

b. Initiation of new levels of military pressure against the DRV with the declared aim of getting Hanoi to stop its support of the VC in the South and the PL in Laos would confront Hanoi's leaders with a basic question. Is the US determined to continue escalating its pressures to achieve its announced objectives regardless of the danger of war with Communist China and regardless of the international pressures that could be brought to bear against it, or is the US escalation essentially a limited attempt to improve the US negotiating position? They would also have to decide whether US aims were indeed limited. Their decision on these questions would be affected by the extent and nature of the US escalation, the character of the US communication of its intentions, and their reading of domestic US and international reactions to the inauguration of US attacks on the North. In any event, comprehension of the other's intentions would almost certainly be difficult on both sides, and especially so as the scale of hostilities mounted.

11. *DRV ability and willingness to sustain damage.*

We have many indications that the Hanoi leadership is acutely and nervously aware of the extent to which North Vietnam's transportation system and industrial plant is vulnerable to attack. On the other hand, North Vietnam's economy is overwhelmingly agricultural and, to a large extent, decentralized in a myriad of more or less economically self-sufficient villages. Interdiction of imports and extensive destruction of transportation facilities and industrial plants would cripple DRV industry. These actions would also seriously restrict DRV military capabilities, and would degrade, though to a lesser extent, Hanoi's capabilities to support guerrilla warfare in South Vietnam and Laos. We do not believe that such actions would have a crucial effect on the daily lives of the overwhelming majority of the North Vietnamese population. We do not believe that attacks on industrial targets would so greatly exacerbate current economic difficulties as to create unmanageable control problems. It is reasonable to infer that the DRV leaders have a psychological investment in the work of reconstruction they have accomplished over the last decade. Nevertheless, they would probably be willing to suffer some damage to the country in the course of a test of wills with the US over the course of events in South Vietnam.

12. *DRV appraisal of the value and hazards of Chinese communist rescue.*

Strong US pressures on North Vietnam would pose painful questions for the DRV leadership and doubtless occasion sharp debates within the upper echelons of the hierarchy. We believe, however, that Hanoi would refrain as long as possible from requesting such Chinese assistance as might endanger DRV independence: for example, large-scale ground force "volunteer" intervention. This hesitancy would of course be overcome if DRV leaders considered the existence of their regime to be at stake.

13. *DRV judgment of the weight to attach to world pressures against the US.*

Hanoi probably believes that considerable international pressure would develop against a US policy of expanding the war to the North and that this might impel the US to an international conference on Vietnam. With both open and covert USSR and Communist Chinese propaganda and political action support, Hanoi would endeavor to intensify such free world sentiments—probably overestimating their impact on the US. Hanoi would probably be confident that in any case—while this game was being played or while an international conference was being held—the VC and Pathet Lao could continue to undermine non-Communist authority in South Vietnam and Laos.

185. TELEGRAM FROM RUSK TO U.S. EMBASSIES IN LONDON, CANBERRA, AND WELLINGTON, DECEMBER 4, 1964

Summarizing policy decisions made after weeks of high-level discussions about bombing the North, William Bundy informed friendly diplomats that the United States would intensify jet strikes on infiltration routes in Laos and launch reprisals against any "dramatic" Communist action in the South. But sustained attacks on the North were ruled out for the time being because of the "fragile" political situation in the South. Bundy also mentioned to Australian and New Zealand ambassadors the possibility of deploying division-size U.S. forces in South Vietnam to "preempt" a North Vietnamese response to American military actions.

A. In talks with Peck and Stewart (UK) on December 3 and with Waller and Laking jointly on December 4, Bundy explained general decisions made here during Taylor's discussions along following lines:

1. We deeply concerned about fragility internal GVN situation. Huong

---

SOURCE: Document from the Lyndon Baines Johnson Library.

[Premier Tran Van Huong] himself has guts and his areas of inexperience are partially supplied by Deputy PM Vien [Dr. Nguyen Luu Vien] and on military side by Khanh, who appears be cooperating reasonably well although not as fully as we would wish. Thus, GVN as whole does have some promise settling down and slowly improving its performance if rpt if it can deal with major Buddhist threat now building up. On security side, armed forces have held together well and such factors as recruitment showing improvement. Nonetheless, situation is still slowly deteriorating although little likelihood really major VC military successes at least in next two months or so.

2. USG believes this fragile situation makes any dramatic action unwise for this reason alone but that it does require some additional elements that would tend to lift SVN morale and would also convey slightly stronger signal to Hanoi. USG therefore proposes immediate program including two new elements: (a) intensified US "armed reconnaissance" strikes against infiltration routes in Laos; (b) reprisals against any dramatic VC action in south such as Bien Hoa attack, preferably with reprisal occasion involving GVN and not solely US elements. Reprisal targets would be carefully selected, probably infiltration installations, between 17th and 19th parallels. Actions in Laos would necessarily require Souvanna's concurrence.

3. Time table for above calls for Taylor consultations with GVN on his return to obtain agreement series GVN actions in return for above program and additional US undertakings, support forces increases, economic measures, etc. (These will be worked out in Saigon and announced there.) Sullivan will thereafter talk to Souvanna about 10 December and Martin will concurrently brief Thai rather fully. Laos air actions would be initiated about 15 December if RLG has concurred.

4. Para 2 program now worked out only for initial 30-day period. May then be continued or we may at some time move onward into program of gradually increased pressures through air attacks on DRV with GVN forces playing major role at least at outset. This second phase not rpt not yet decided but clearly preferred to any alternative of more sharp and dramatic military action. Crucial determinants will be whether GVN settles down and whether Hanoi shows any signs of responding to Para 2 program designed to impress them with our determination and to foreshadow possible future actions.

B. Following this briefing, Bundy went on to say prospect possible more serious decisions made it more than ever vital have increased third country contributions. Suggested UK increases numbers of police advisors, Australia consider 200-man augmentation combat advisors, and GNZ likewise seek to increase its contribution markedly. Indicated President had deep personal concern this aspect, would discuss this with Wilson, and would send personal messages to Menzies and Holycake early next week.

C. In response to presentation [*Officially deleted*]

1. [*Officially deleted*]

2. Waller and Laking likewise raised question re negotiations and Commie reactions. They further asked about scale Lao operations to which we responded exact program being worked out and would in any case depend on RLG acceptance.

D. To Waller and Laking only we mentioned that planning for possible second phase had considered possibility introducing division-size ground forces into northern SVN to pre-empt any ground reaction by DRV. We said such a force would be much more effective if it included at least small units from GOA and GNZ. They responded that Malaysia commitments increasingly onerous but that they would pass suggestion on for comment.

E. Above is for information Ambassador Powell and Charges only at this time. Ambassador Bruce being brief here. You will be further instructed, but may discuss above with senior officials if they raise with you. We stressed vital importance avoiding press leaks that go beyond formal statements here or possibly later in Saigon.

1965

186. LAO DONG PARTY CENTRAL COMMITTEE DIRECTIVE ON THE REORIENTATION CAMPAIGN FOR SPRING 1965, JANUARY 2, 1965 [Extract]

Preparing for an offensive against the Saigon regime that would increase the risk of American bombing and possibly even invasion of the North, the Party began to prepare its membership for those eventualities through this directive on ideological reorientation.

In sum, our people in the South are in the posture of continuous offensive while the enemy is in the passive posture of reacting. The comparison of forces between the enemy and us in the South is changing in our favor.

In order to push forward that process of change and to win even bigger victories for the Southern revolution, the people of our entire country must make big efforts. At present the role of the Northern revolution with regard to the Southern revolution is not only to make sure that the Northern people fulfill the task of constructing socialism in order to motivate their Southern compatriots, but to do whatever can be done to help the Southern revolution, to be side by side with the Southern compatriots in their struggle against American imperialism and its lackeys, and to rapidly win complete victory.

We must always remember that: U.S. imperialism and the lackey clique, although in a declining position which they cannot escape, nevertheless have many poisonous schemes and actions to oppose the people of our country as well as to oppose the Lao and Khmer peoples. U.S. imperialism is in a dilemma: if they withdraw from South Vietnam they would lose face, but if they attack further they will suffer ignominious defeat. In order to get out of this dead end, they are thinking of several things: First is to push even more strongly "special war" in the South,

SOURCE: *"Chi Thi Ve Cuoc Van Dong Chinh Huan Mua Xuan Nam 1965"* [*Directive on the reorientation campaign for Spring 1965*], No. 83 CT/TW. Document no. 912 in the Douglas Pike Collection, pp. 16–18. [Translation by the editor.]

while stepping up their prevocations and sabotage of the North on a broader scale and attacking and occupying the liberated zone of Lao patriotic forces, while trying to destroy the national independence, peace, neutrality and territorial integrity of Cambodia. Second is to turn "special war" in South Vietnam into limited war with the more direct participation of American troops and of the troops of a number of satellite states of the U.S. Third is to attack the North, broadening the war to our entire country. Fourth is to try to secure a strong military position so that, if they are forced by the situation, they could obtain some political solution to resolve the problem of the South.

At present, U.S. imperialism is actively carrying out the first scheme, hoping to save the situation, while preparing to bring South Korean troops into the South, that is, preparing to carry out the second scheme.

We must be prepared to be able to cope with all four of the above possibilities, to smash any schemes and actions of the enemy. The Northern people must not only actively assist the Southern revolution and be prepared to smash schemes to provoke and sabotage or carry out aggression in order to defend the North, but must also actively support the just struggle of the Lao and Khmer peoples, etc.

187. LETTER FROM VICE-PRESIDENT OF THE CENTRAL COMMITTEE OF THE NATIONAL LIBERATION FRONT HUYNH TAN PHAT TO GEN. NGUYEN KHANH, COMMANDER IN CHIEF OF THE ARMED FORCES OF THE REPUBLIC OF VIETNAM, JANUARY 28, 1965

A coup by military leaders against the Huong government on January 27 brought back to the center of power Nguyen Khanh, who had denounced U.S. interference in South Vietnamese politics in late December and was sharply at odds with Taylor. On January 28, National Liberation Front (NLF) Vice-President Huynh Tan Phat addressed a letter to Khanh praising his struggle for independence from the United States and offered to join with him in an effort to "save our homeland."

> National Liberation Front of South Vietnam,
> South Vietnam, January 28, 1965.
>
> To: General Nguyen-Khanh
> Commander-in-Chief of the Armed Forces of the
> Republic of South Vietnam.

Dear General Khanh,

Replying to a number of your ideas, I previously had occasion to write you a long letter in which I clearly set forth our point of view, and also informed you that

SOURCE: Mimeographed text of English translation distributed by Nguyen Khanh on January 26, 1975.

we were prepared to offer you our friendly cooperation and join with all who manifested these same desires and aspirations.

I heartily approve of your determined declaration against American intervention and I congratulate you for having made it. You stated quite clearly, in fact, that "the USA must let South Vietnam settle the problem of South Vietnam!" In your recent press-conference, your attitude was equally clear: "For national sovereignty and against foreign intervention in South Vietnam's domestic affairs."

"You have now committed yourself, as well as your friends, to pursuing the struggle for peace and independence from American intervention. You are, so to speak, the first in the South Vietnamese administration to choose a new, more advanced orientation, one that is more independent of the United States of America. The road you have taken will be a difficult one and the pitfalls will be many. But with your ardent patriotism, your indomitable spirit in the face of imperialist, colonialist oppression, your determination to oppose any kind of intervention by outsiders, you will undoubtedly receive the support of the people. And as you pursue this goal, you may rest assured that you also have our support, as we stated in our last letter.

We are convinced, given our common determination to serve our people and our country, valiantly to combat for national sovereignty and independence, and against foreign intervention, that whatever our differences of political opinion, we can join together and coordinate our efforts to accomplish our supreme mission, which is, to save our homeland.

Signed: Huynh-Tan-Phat, Vice-President
Central Committee, FNL/SVN

188. TELEGRAM FROM TAYLOR TO RUSK, JANUARY 29, 1965 [Extract]

Taylor, who reported only two days earlier that Khanh had reached an agreement with the Buddhist leadership to bring down Huong and suggested that Khanh might see himself as the "Sihanouk" of South Vietnam, now warned that the possibility of negotiations "does constitute real danger which we must work to counter." On February 17, Khanh was ousted in a coup by extreme right-wing Catholic officers.

It is of course too soon to evaluate with any certainty move of Armed Forces Council yesterday in withdrawing confidence from Suu-Huong government and in charging Gen. Khanh with responsibility for resolving present political crisis. Not yet known are Khanh's real intentions, nature of new government which will emerge, and future reactions of major g oups (including Buddhist Institute leadership).

Nevertheless, some analysis can be made with reasonable degree of assurance. There is sufficient evidence to conclude that overthrow of Prime Minister Huong's government by Armed Forces Council was made possible by understandings reached between Khanh and Buddhist Institute leadership. This new victory for Institute

SOURCE: Document from the Lyndon Baines Johnson Library.

leadership places it in position of increased prestige and influence in country. Most disquieting is possibility that Buddhist victory could create an atmosphere conducive to pressures for a "negotiated settlement." Such negotiations may not rpt not be active objective of Buddhist leadership, but could come about as result of continuing Buddhist agitation. Prospect of negotiations, therefore, is probably not immediate one, as there are important factors militating against it premarily militarily [sic] opposition, but it does constitute real danger which we must work to counter.

Buddhist Institute-Khanh understandings thus represent merger of two elements adverse to US interests. However, certain variables make this combination precarious one. Khanh no doubt hopes to share with Buddhist leaders dominant position of power and influence and to use this position to his own advantage. We are inclined to believe, however, based on past experience, that it will be Buddhist leaders who will use Khanh. Moreover, latter's performance since he assumed power last January 30 has created deep divisions and discord within armed forces and, although Armed Forces Council's action of yesterday boosts Khanh's prestige and power, it was arrived at after much wrangling and debate. There is little doubt that some officers who have supported Khanh's latest bid did so unhappily, and that others did so hoping to place Khanh in exposed position from which he can be toppled at opportune moment (VNAF Commander Ky and I Corps Commander Thi seem to be men to watch in this latter connection). In addition, there are increasing number of reports that many combat officers in field who are becoming fed to teeth with wrangling and politicking of generals in Saigon and who place large measure of blame for this on Khanh's maneuvering. At same time it must be cautioned that any opposition to Khanh within military is likely to remain latent, and that bulk of senior officers are likely overtly to support Khanh, unless and until they feel their own future are clearly jeopardized by Khanh's actions. This not now case. It should also be noted that if Khanh were suddenly removed from scene, his departure could lead to another round of power struggles within military among Young Turk officers. Many military officers oppose Buddhist leadership's tactics of creating civil disorders and are suspicious of their long-term objectives, which should serve to brake any slippery slide toward negotiations with Communists, and also could provide spark for move against Khanh if many officers became convinced of his decision to cast lot with Buddhist leadership. However, case with which anti-American feelings were whipped up in last few days suggests that further drift toward negotiation with Vietnamese brothers could be advanced cloaked under label of nationalism and independence from foreign dominance.

189. MEMORANDUM BY TAYLOR, FEBRUARY 2, 1965 [Extract]

Looking back on six months in Saigon, Taylor noted his past insistence that some degree of GVN stability and performance should be a condition for direct attacks on the North. ("Phase Two Operations"). Now, he concluded, the most the United States could ask from the GVN was that it "exist" and "be able to ask for U.S. help."

SOURCE: Document from the Lyndon Baines Johnson Library.

In considering military action against the DRV, the Mission has often commented on the necessity for some minimal government in SVN precedent to opening the air operation we call Phase II. Until the end of 1964, I had hopes that U.S. agreement to Phase II operations might be used as a carrot to incite GVN leaders to better efforts in the governmental field but that hope has been disappointed. In the case of the generals, their desire to punish the DRV has always been less than their pleasure in playing politics—although in their defense it must be admitted that only Khanh and a few others were aware of the relation between stable government and Phase II.

With repeated disappointments in the government, the Mission cables to Washington show a progressive lowering of the standards of governmental performance considered a prerequisite for Phase II. At various times the desired performance included the ability to provide leadership to the people, to maintain law and order in urban centers, to make operational plans and effect their execution by loyal military and police forces, to keep the in-country base secure from any VC/DRV reaction to Phase II and, following strikes against the DRV, to exploit their success in carrying out a national pacification plan. The latter point was often emphasized since it was clear that air attacks against the DRV would not in themselves eliminate the VC problem in SVN.

By January, the Mission view of the requirements for government had been tempered by the sad experiences of the preceding months and a growing realization that we would probably never have in the foreseeable future a stable government as we use the term in the U.S. and Europe. The rock-bottom criterion was expressed in Embtel 2116 (January 11) which asks only for a government to exist and to have the strength of voice able to ask for U.S. help.

It is our present belief that this criterion is the right one to apply to a GVN provided the Armed Forces are behind it. In the unusual situation here, it is the Armed Forces who carry out most of the functions associated with stable government. They are the ultimate source of law and order; they execute the military aspects of pacification and through the Province Chiefs direct many of the non-military aspects as well. They secure the home base and would contain any VC/DRV reaction.

190. MEMORANDUM FOR THE PRESIDENT FROM MCGEORGE BUNDY, FEBRUARY 7, 1965

Within hours after a Communist attack on the U.S. military advisers' compound at Pleiku killed nine and wounded seventy-six, U.S. Embassy officials were getting the concurrence of acting Prime Minister Nguyen Xuan Oanh for reprisal attacks on North Vietnam. The day before the Pleiku attack, McGeorge Bundy had urged the adoption of a policy of "sustained reprisal." His memorandum made it clear that the primary hope for the policy was that it would allow the United States to "speak in Vietnam on many topics and in many ways, with growing force and effectiveness." Specifically, he indicated that the United States could expect a "con-

---

SOURCE: Document from the Lyndon Baines Johnson Library.

trolling'' role in joint military planning and more bargaining power on GVN operations generally.

Annex A—A Policy of Sustained Reprisal

I. Introductory

We believe that the best available way of increasing our chance of success in Vietnam is the development and execution of a policy of *sustained reprisal* against North Vietnam—a policy in which air and naval action against the North is justified by and related to the whole Viet Cong campaign of violence and terror in the South.

While we believe that the risks of such a policy are acceptable, we emphasize that its costs are real. It implies significant U.S. air losses even if no full air war is joined, and it seems likely that it would eventually require an extensive and costly effort against the whole air defense system of North Vietnam. U.S. casualties would be higher—and more visible to American feelings—than those sustained in the struggle in South Vietnam.

Yet measured against the costs of defeat in Vietnam, this program seems cheap. And even if it fails to turn the tide—as it may—the value of the effort seems to us to exceed its cost.

II. Outline of the Policy

1. In partnership with the Government of Vietnam, we should develop and exercise the option to retaliate against *any* VC act of violence to persons or property.

2. In practice, we may wish at the outset to relate our reprisals to those acts of relatively high visibility such as the Pleiku incident. Later, we might retaliate against the assassination of a province chief, but not necessarily the murder of a hamlet official; we might retaliate against a grenade thrown into a crowded cafe in Saigon, but not necessarily to a shot fired into a small shop in the countryside.

3. Once a program of reprisals is clearly underway, it should not be necessary to connect each specific act against North Vietnam to a particular outrage in the South. It should be possible, for example, to publish weekly lists of outrages in the South and to have it clearly understood that these outrages are the cause of such action against the North as may be occurring in the current period. Such a more generalized pattern of reprisal would remove much of the difficulty involved in finding precisely matching targets in response to specific atrocities. Even in such a more general pattern, however, it would be important it insure that the general level of reprisal action remained in close correspondence with the level of outrages in the South. We must keep it clear at every stage both to Hanoi and to the world, that our reprisals will be reduced or stopped when outrages in the South are reduced or stopped—and that we are *not* attempting to destroy or conquer North Vietnam.

4. In the early stages of such a course, we should take the appropriate occasion to make clear our firm intent to undertake reprisals on any further acts, major or minor, that appear to us and the GVN as indicating Hanoi's support. We would announce that our two governments have been patient and forebearing in the hope that Hanoi would come to its senses without the necessity of our having to take

further action; but the outrages continue and now we must react against those who are responsible; we will not provoke; we will not use our force indiscriminately; but we can no longer sit by in the face of repeated acts of terror and violence for which the DRV is responsible.

5. Having once made this announcement, we should execute our reprisal policy with as low a level of public noise as possible. It is to our interest that our acts should be seen—but we do not wish to boast about them in ways that make it hard for Hanoi to shift its ground. We should instead direct maximum attention to the continuing acts of violence which are the cause of our continuing reprisals.

6. This reprisal policy should begin at a low level. Its level of force and pressure should be increased only gradually—and as indicated about it should be decreased if VC terror visibly decreases. The object would not be to "win" an air war against Hanoi, but rather to influence the course of the struggle in the South.

7. At the same time it should be recognized that in order to maintain the power of reprisal without risk of excessive loss, an "air war" may in fact be necessary. We should therefore be ready to develop a separate justification for energetic flak suppression and if necessary for the destruction of Communist air power. The essence of such an explanation should be that these actions are intended solely to insure the effectiveness of a policy of reprisal, and in no sense represent any intent to wage offensive war against the North. These distinctions should not be difficult to develop.

8. It remains quite possible, however, that this reprisal policy would get us quickly into the level of military activity contemplated in the so-called Phase II of our December planning. It may even get us beyond this level with both Hanoi and Peiping, if there is Communist counter-action. We and the GVN should also be prepared for a spurt of VC terrorism, especially in urban areas, that would dwarf anything yet experienced. These are the risks of any action. They should be carefully reviewed—but we believe them to be acceptable.

9. We are convinced that the political values of reprisal require a *continuous* operation. Episodic responses geared on a one-for-one basis to "spectacular" outrages would lack the persuasive force of sustained pressure. More important still, they would leave it open to the Communists to avoid reprisals entirely by giving up only a small element of their own program. The Gulf of Tonkin affair produced a sharp upturn in morale in South Vietnam. When it remained an isolated episode, however, there was a severe relapse. It is the great merit of the proposed scheme that to stop it the Communists would have to stop enough of their activity in the South to permit the probable success of a determined pacification effort.

III. Expected Effect of Sustained Reprisal Policy

1. We emphasize that our primary target in advocating a reprisal policy is the improvement of the situation in *South* Vietnam. Action against the North is usually urged as a means of affecting the will of Hanoi to direct and support the VC. We consider this an important but longer-range purpose. The immediate and critical targets are in the South—in the minds of the South Vietnamese and in the minds of the Viet Cong cadres.

2. Predictions of the effect of any given course of action upon the states of mind of people are difficult. It seems very clear that if the United States and the

Government of Vietnam join in a policy of reprisal, there will be a sharp immediate increase in optimism in the South, among nearly all articulate groups. The Mission believes—and our own conversations confirm—that in all sectors of Vietnamese opinion there is a strong belief that the United States could do much more if it would, and that they are suspicious of our failure to use more of our obviously enormous power. At least in the short run, the reaction to reprisal policy would be very favorable.

3. This favorable reaction should offer opportunity for increased American influence in pressing for a more effective government—at least in the short run. Joint reprisals would imply military planning in which the American role would necessarily be controlling, and this new relation should add to our bargaining power in other military efforts—and conceivably on a wider plane as well if a more stable government is formed. We have the whip hand in reprisals as we do not in other fields.

4. The Vietnamese increase in hope could well increase the readiness of Vietnamese factions themselves to join together in forming a more effective government.

5. We think it plausible that effective and sustained reprisals, even in a low key, would have a substantial depressing effect upon the morale of Viet Cong cadres in South Vietnam. This is the strong opinion of CIA Saigon. It is based upon reliable reports of the initial Viet Cong reaction to the Gulf of Tonkin episode, and also upon the solid general assessment that the determination of Hanoi and the apparent timidity of the mighty United States are both major items in Viet Cong confidence.

6. The long-run effect of reprisals in the South is far less clear, it may be that like other stimulants, the value of this one would decline over time. Indeed the risk of this result is large enough so that we ourselves believe that a very major effort all along the line should be made in South Vietnam to take full advantage of the immediate stimulus of reprisal policy in its early stages. Our object should be to use this new policy to effect a visible upward turn in pacification, in governmental effectiveness, in operations against the Viet Cong, and in the whole U.S./GVN relationship. It is changes in these areas that can have enduring long-term effects.

7. While emphasizing the importance of reprisals in the South, we do not exclude the impact on Hanoi. We believe, indeed, that it is of great importance that the level of reprisal be adjusted rapidly and visibly to both upward and downward shifts in the level of Viet Cong offenses. We want to keep before Hanoi the carrot of our desisting as well as the stick of continued pressure. We also need to conduct the application of the force so that there is always a prospect of worse to come.

8. We cannot assert that a policy of sustained reprisal will succeed in changing the course of the contest in Vietnam. It may fail, and we cannot estimate the odds of success with any accuracy—they may be somewhere between 25% and 75%. What we can say is that even if it fails, the policy will be worth it. At a minimum it will drop down the charge that we did not do all that we could have done, and this charge will be important in many countries, including our own. Beyond that, a reprisal policy—to the extent that it demonstrates U.S. willingness to employ this new norm in counter-insurgency—will set a higher price for the future upon all adventures of guerrilla warfare, and it should therefore somewhat increase our ability to deter such adventures. We must recognize, however, that that ability will be gravely weakened if there is failure for any reason in Vietnam.

IV. Present Action Recommendations

1. This general recommendation was developed in intensive discussions in the days just before the attacks on Pleiku. These attacks and our reaction to them have created an ideal opportunity for the prompt development and execution of sustained reprisals. Conversely, if no such policy is now developed, we face the grave danger that Pleiku, like the Gulf of Tonkin, may be a short-run stimulant and a long-term depressant. We therefore recommend that the necessary preparations be made for continuing reprisals. The major necessary steps to be taken appear to us to be the following:

(1) We should complete the evacuation of dependents.

(2) We should quietly start the necessary westward deployments of back-up contingency forces.

(3) We should develop and refine a running catalogue of Viet Cong offenses which can be published regularly and relate clearly to our own reprisals. Such a catalogue should perhaps build on the foundation of an initial White Paper.

(4) We should initiate joint planning with the GVN on both the civil and military level. Specifically, we should give a clear and strong signal to those now forming a government that we will be ready for this policy when they are.

(5) We should develop the necessary public and diplomatic statements to accompany the initiation and continuation of this program.

(6) We should insure that a reprisal program is matched by renewed public commitment to our family of programs in the South, so that the central importance of the southern struggle may never be neglected.

(7) We should plan quiet diplomatic communication of the precise meaning of what we are and are not doing, to Hanoi, to Peking and to Moscow.

(8) We should be prepared to defend and to justify this new policy by concentrating attention in every forum upon its cause—the aggression in the South.

(9) We should accept discussion on these terms in any form, but we should *not* now accept the idea of negotiations of any sort except on the basis of a stand down of Viet Cong violence. A program of sustained reprisal, with its direct link to Hanoi's continuing aggressive actions in the South, will not involve us in nearly the level of international recrimination which would be precipitated by a go-North program which was not so connected. For this reason the international pressures for negotiation should be quite manageable.

191. JOINT STATEMENT OF SOVIET PREMIER KOSYGIN AND PHAM VAN DONG, HANOI, FEBRUARY 10, 1965 [Extract]

The post-Khrushchev leadership in the Soviet Union sharply reversed Khrushchev's policy of disengagement from the Vietnamese armed struggle and moved

SOURCE: *Izvestia*, February 12, 1965. Translated in *Current Digest of the Soviet Press*, Vol. XVII, No. 6, (1965), pp. 9–11.

toward closer relations with Hanoi. In November 1964, Pham Van Dong traveled to Moscow and apparently succeeded in obtaining increased economic and military assistance. And Premier Alexei N. Kosygin led a high-level Soviet delegation to Hanoi early in February for the purpose of demonstrating firm Soviet political support for Hanoi in the face of growing U.S. military pressures. The joint communiqué at the end of the Kosygin visit showed that the Soviets had accepted the Vietnamese argument, previously rejected by Khrushchev, that the armed struggle in South Vietnam was a "contribution to the defense of peace."

The delegation of the Soviet Union emphasized that the Democratic Republic of Vietnam, the outpost of the socialist camp in Southeast Asia, is playing an important role in the struggle against American imperialism and is making its contribution to the defense of peace in Asia and throughout the world.

The governments of the U.S.S.R. and the D.R.V. have examined the situation that has arisen as a result of the unceasing provocations and acts of outright aggression by the U.S.A. against the Democratic Republic of Vietnam. Both governments resolutely condemn the aggressive actions of the U.S.A. on Aug. 5, 1964, and especially the barbaric attacks by American aircraft on D.R.V. territory on Feb. 7 and Feb. 8, 1965, in the area of the cities of Donghoi and Vinhlinh as incompatible with both international law and the 1954 Geneva agreements. These highly dangerous actions are at the same time provocations against the whole socialist camp and against all mankind standing for peace, freedom and justice.

The U.S.S.R. government reaffirmed that, adhering to the principles of socialist internationalism, it will not remain indifferent to ensuring the security of a fraternal socialist country and will give the D.R.V. the necessary aid and support. The governments of the two countries reached an understanding on the steps that will be taken to strengthen the defense capacity of the D.R.V. and agreed to hold regular consultations on the above-mentioned questions.

The two sides were unanimous on the fact that for more than ten years now the U.S. government has been breaking the 1954 Geneva agreements on Vietnam, trying to prevent the unification of the country and to turn South Vietnam into a new type of colony and a U.S. military base. It has illegally sent to South Vietnam tens of thousands of its own soldiers and officers and a large quantity of arms and is waging an inhuman and cruel "special war" against the population of South Vietnam. The people of South Vietnam have been forced to wage an armed struggle for their liberation in this highly dangerous situation.

The Soviet Union fully supports the just, heroic struggle by the population of South Vietnam for independence, democracy, peace and neutrality, which they are waging under the leadership of the National Front of Liberation of South Vietnam.

192. TELEGRAM FROM RUSK TO TAYLOR, FEBRUARY 13, 1965

Johnson decided on February 13 to give the go-ahead for the program of "sustained reprisals" outlined by Bundy a few days earlier, to be limited for the

SOURCE: *The Pentagon Papers*, pp. 428–429.

time being to DRV targets below the nineteenth parallel. The policy was to be announced publicly, along with a declaration of U.S. willingness to enter into "talks," to focus on Hanoi's ending of its "aggression."

The President today approved the following program for immediate future actions in follow-up decisions he reported to you in Deptel 1653. (The First FLAMING DART reprisal decision.)

1. We will intensify by all available means the program of pacification within SVN.

2. We will execute a program of measured and limited air action jointly with GVN against selected military targets in DRV, remaining south of 19th parallel until further notice.

FYI. Our current expectation is that these attacks might come about once or twice a week and involve two or three targets on each day of operation. END FYI.

3. We will announce this policy of measured action in general terms and at the same time, we will go to UN Security Council to make clear case that aggressor is Hanoi. We will also make it plain that we are ready and eager for 'talks' to bring aggression to an end.

4. We believe that this 3-part program must be concerted with SVN, and we currently expect to announce it by Presidential statement directly after next authorized air action. We believe this action should take place as early as possible next week.

5. You are accordingly instructed to seek immediate GVN agreement on this program. You are authorized to emphasize our conviction that announcement of readiness to talk is stronger diplomatic position than awaiting inevitable summons to Security Council by third parties. We would hope to have appropriate GVN concurrence by Monday (Feb. 14th) if possible here.

In presenting above to GVN, you should draw fully, as you see fit, on following arguments:

a. We are determined to continue with military actions regardless of Security Council deliberations and any 'talks' or negotiations when (words illegible). (Beginning of sentence illegible) that they cease (words illegible) and also the activity they are directing in the south.

b. We consider the UN Security Council initiative, following another strike, essential if we are to avoid being faced with really damaging initiatives by the USSR or perhaps by such powers as India, France, or even the UN.

c. At an early point in the UN Security Council initiative, we would expect to see calls for the DRV to appear in the UN. If they failed to appear, as in August, this will make doubly clear that it is they who are refusing to desist, and our position in pursuing military actions against the DRV would be strengthened. For some reason we would now hope GVN itself would appear at UN and work closely with U.S.

d. With or without Hanoi, we have every expectation that any 'talks' that may result from our Security Council initiative would in fact go on for many weeks or perhaps months and would above all focus constantly on the cessation of Hanoi's aggression as the precondition to any cessation of military action against the DRV. We further anticipate that any detailed discussions about any possible eventual form of agreement returning to the essentials of the 1954ʻ Accords would be postponed and would be subordinated to the central issue. . . .

193. SNIE 10-3/1-65: "COMMUNIST REACTIONS TO POSSIBLE U.S. COURSES OF ACTION AGAINST NORTH VIETNAM, FEBRUARY 18, 1965 [Extract]

In a supplement to an earlier estimate on the subject, the intelligence community estimated that North Vietnam would seek a respite from sustained U.S. bombing by reducing the level of the war in the South but not by meeting U.S. demands of abandonment of the insurgency. A step-up in the tempo of the war was also indicated as a possibility, but a DRV invasion of the South was discounted as unlikely. The possibility of a commitment of DRV troops on a relatively small scale and clandestinely, which was the option the DRV was then pursuing, was not examined.

Reactions to a Declared and Sustained US Program of Bombing in the North

7. Over the past decade the DRV has invested much time, effort, and capital in the development of industry, transportation, and relatively modern military facilities. They will not lightly sacrifice these hard-won gains. Yet a threat by the US to mount sustained attacks on these assets would probably be greeted in Hanoi with mixed feelings of trepidation and skepticism. At the start, the Communists would not be convinced that the US intended really to follow through with this program. They would almost certainly apply a range of pressures in an endeavor to make the US desist. They would maintain strenuous diplomatic and propaganda efforts to organize international influence against the US policy. They would probably threaten dire consequences to US interests in the area. Chinese Communists threats would be more insistent, and Chinese Communist forces would probably be deployed in more threatening postures. Viet Cong attacks would probably continue, though not necessarily at a steady pace.

8. If despite these pressures, the US vigorously continued in its attacks and damaged some important economic or military assets, the DRV leaders would have to reach a decision. They almost certainly believe that, while the US could destroy much in their country by air attacks, these alone would not cause their regime to collapse or prevent them from continuing to support the insurgency in the South. And they may believe that their international political position would improve if they became the object of sustained air attack from the US. Accordingly, they might decide to intensify the struggle, accepting the destructive consequences in the North in the expectation of early victory in the South.

9. It seems to us somewhat more likely however that they would decide to make some effort to secure a respite from US air attack, especially if the US had indicated that such a respite would follow a sharp reduction of Viet Cong

---

SOURCE: Document declassified by CIA, November 4, 1975.

activity.[1] We do not know how far they would go in concessions, whether the US would accept what might be offered, or what the international situation might be at such a time. We think it extremely unlikely, however, that Hanoi would concede so far to US demands that it would entail abandoning its support of the insurgency in the South or giving up its intention of unifying Vietnam under Communist control.

10. The Chinese Communists would almost certainly be willing to support the DRV in even the more militant course of action outlined in paragraph 8. We have set forth in SNIE 10-3-65 (paragraphs 16-18, with State Department footnotes of dissent) the use the Chinese would be likely to make of their own forces.

Possible, but Unlikely Reactions

11. Instead of temporarily easing off or intensifying present levels of pressure, the Communist leaders might actually engage in actions which would change the scale and nature of the war. These would be much more dangerous and aggressive courses and, although they seem to us unlikely in the light of logic and prudence, they are possibilities which cannot be ignored:

a. They might launch a large-scale DRV invasion of South Vietnam and/or Laos. We think it unlikely that they would do this in response to bombings of North Vietnam. They would feel that at best this drastic policy would only accelerate victories in Laos and Vietnam which they are confident they will win before very long through less costly tactics. Such an invasion would virtually require a greater involvement of the Chinese in Vietnam, which is in itself distasteful to the North Vietnamese. The Communists would recognize that to launch such an invasion would be to invite further major destruction upon the DRV and perhaps upon China.[2]

b. We think it unlikely that the Chinese or DRV would respond to US air raids by air attacks on US aircraft carriers or South Vietnamese airfields. To do so would invite counterattacks on the vulnerable Communist bases and start the escalation of an air war, a form of hostilities most disadvantageous

---

[1]The Director of Intelligence and Research, Department of State, believes this course of action less likely than that described in paragraph 8. He considers that Hanoi would feel that any benefits to be gained by such a respite would be more than offset by a loss of momentum at a time when victory appeared near, by a loss of face with the VC, and by the consequent bolstering of US/CVN morale. Hanoi would have in mind that concessions under such circumstances might only invite the US to resume strikes upon any renewal of Viet Cong military activity.

Moreover, the assumed vigorous US attacks on major targets could easily coincide with the probable use over the DRV of Chinese air defense from Chinese bases. If so, US responses would either have been to acknowledge the privileged sanctuary of Chinese bases or to strike the bases in hot pursuit, thus inviting further Chinese military responses. Hanoi's persistence would be reinforced either way.

[2]The Director of Intelligence and Research, Department of State, believes that paragraph 11a is applicable only in the initial stages of bombings in North Vietnam, well below the Hanoi-Haiphong target complex. Once US attacks destroy major industrial and military targets in this complex, however, Hanoi will have substantially lost its hostage and suffered the maximum damage it could anticipate from the air. In this case the DRV, having suffered the destruction of its major military facilities and the industrial sector of its economy, would probably carry on the fight and proceed to send its own armed forces on a large scale to Laos and South Vietnam. Hanoi might assume that the US would be unwilling to undertake a major ground war, or that if it was, it could ultimately be defeated by the methods which were successful against the French.

Furthermore, if the DRV should persist in this fashion, Peiping would probably introduce limited numbers of Chinese Communist ground forces into the DRV as "volunteers," both to prepare for further escalation and to make clear Peiping's commitment to assist the North Vietnamese.

to the North Vietnamese and Chinese. A sneak attack on a carrier by an unidentifiable Chinese submarine is a more difficult possibility to weigh, but we are inclined to think the chance is slim; the risks would be fairly high and Chinese confidence in the ability of their inexperienced submarine force to pull it off is probably low.

c. We also think it unlikely that the Chinese Communists would start another major crisis elsewhere on the periphery of China. Faced with the possibility of a full scale war in Southeast Asia, Peiping would want to have the greatest possible strength focused there. Chinese propaganda has, indeed, said that America's "meager force" in Asia is spread thinly over a "long arc from South Korea to Indochina," and that if the conflict were expanded, the "time, place, and scale of the war would be beyond US control." However, we think this is no more than a general warning of the dangers of expanding the war. Peiping is likely, however, to continue talking of war "over a vast front" and perhaps even to stir up alarms elsewhere to keep US power dispersed and deter the US in Southeast Asia. The Chinese Communists might, for example, increase the apparent military threat in Korea, bombard the offshore islands in order to raise tensions in the Taiwan area, or perhaps make threatening moves on the borders of India.

194. LAO DONG PARTY STUDY DOCUMENT FOR POLITICAL REORIENTATION, MARCH 5, 1965 [Extract]

Warning its members that the situation in the South might go through "complex changes" in 1965, the Vietnamese Party suggested that the struggle there would probably be long and drawn out. But the analysis minimized the possibility of the United States sending troops to the South on a massive scale or attacking the North.

Entering 1965, we can see clearly that the special war of the U.S. in the South is on a dead end course, the puppet government [one line illegible] is extremely wobbly, the central puppet government is not stable, internal contradictions are becoming very bitter, and its authority has greatly declined. From the top down the puppet government is in confusion and shaken and is suffering serious disintegration at the base. The enemy's troops are being annihilated and cannot be replaced fast enough; its morale has fallen seriously. Its pool for military replacements is much reduced. This shows us that through 1965 we can win a much bigger victory than in 1964 if we are determined to make every effort to develop our armed and political forces more rapidly, further gain the initiative in the cities, further consolidate the liberated zone, and fight to wear down and annihilate the enemy more strongly with more big battles, making the enemy's main forces disintegrate.

Now, due to the fact that we are not yet strong enough to defeat the enemy but

SOURCE: *Tinh Hinh Moi, Nheim Vu Moi*, [New situation, new tasks]. Training Committee of South Vietnam, 1965. Document No. 921 in the Pike Collection, pp. 8–11. [Translated by the editor.]

have accumulated real strength, U.S. imperialism sees that it cannot win but has not yet accepted defeat.

U.S. imperialism is discussing the following options:

1. *Widening the war to the North and attacking Southern China*. When thinking about this idea, they see all the more danger, because they will come up against the socialist camp, with China and its 700 million people who now have the atomic bomb. They also know that they don't have enough troops and that they would not be supported by Britain, France, Germany, and Japan. This possibility is therefore very slight but the enemy has thought about it, so we must also be highly vigilant and be prepared for any possible adventurism.

2. *Send U.S. troops to South Vietnam to become the primary force to fight us*. This possibility is also small because they would have to make enormous expenditures in money and material, but would still not be certain of victory, and if they were defeated, they would lose even more face. As for us, if they send U.S. troops, there will be new difficulties and complexities but we will be determined to fight protractedly and, finally, victory will be ours.

3. Besides the above two options, they are discussing a great deal a third option which is to maintain special war as at present but to increase it one step. In order to carry out this option, U.S. imperialism is striving mightily to create a position of strength militarily and trying to stabilize the political situation in the cities. They try to achieve these two objectives in order to continue to defeat us militarily while at the same time preparing for a political solution on the basis of their position of strength and in accord with their cunning plan.

In the near future, the enemy may carry out bolder military actions in the South and step up provocations against the North.

We must point out the enemy's schemes in order not to become subjective and to increase our vigilance. But at the same time we must also see that the enemy has met many difficulties in his special war, and therefore many possibilities favorable to the revolution have appeared.

We are on the road to victory but not yet strong enough to finish off the enemy. The enemy has encountered defeat and extreme difficulty. However, the enemy still has many schemes and much strength to cope with us. The situation in the South at present is still going through complex changes. Therefore: our task at present is: to win time, exploiting the opportune moment on the basis of the longterm revolutionary standpoint, fight protractedly, our entire party, army and people unite as one mind, concentrate our forces and determinedly fight the enemy, rapidly build our forces, make 1965 a turning point in the comparison of forces favorable to us, and make it the basis for dashing to win a decisive victory.

195. TELEGRAM FROM TAYLOR TO RUSK, MARCH 18, 1965

Addressing the issue of sending large-scale U.S. combat forces to South Vietnam, first raised by Army Chief of Staff General Harold Johnson after his trip

---

SOURCE: *The Pentagon Papers*, pp. 445–447.

to South Vietnam earlier in March, Taylor doubted that it would raise the over-all level of (Army of the Republic of Vietnam) ARVN performance and pointed out serious disadvantages, including the appearance of having assumed the role of "alien colonizer and conquerer." He called for further study before any recommendation would be made.

General Westmoreland has just sought my concurrence in his recommendation for the landing of the Third BLT of the 9th MEB at Phu Bai for the purpose of protecting the 8th RRU and the air strip there. He intends to move helicopters from Da Nang to the strip and thereby reduce field congestion to Da Nang. Because of the military advantages of thus rounding out the MEB, I have no reluctance in agreeing to the merit of his recommendation which, of course, should receive the concurrence of the GVN after that of Washington.

This proposal for introducing the BLT is a reminder of the strong likelihood of additional requests for increases in U.S. ground combat forces in SVN. Such requests may come from the U.S. side, from the GVN side or from both. All of us here are keenly aware of the GVN trained military manpower shortage which will exist throughout 1965 and which probably can be rectified only in part by an accelerated mobilization. We will soon have to decide whether to try to get by with inadequate indigenous forces or to supplement them with Third Country troops, largely if not exclusively U.S. This matter was discussed with General Johnson during his recent visit who no doubt has raised it following his return to Washington. This message examines the pros and cons of such an action—specifically defined as the introduction of a U.S. division (appropriately modified) into SVN.

The purpose of introducing a division would be primarily to relieve the present shortage of ARVN units either by replacing ARVN in the defense of key installations or by engaging in active operations against the VC in conjunction with ARVN. Such a reinforcement would allow a strengthening of military efforts in the I and II Corps areas where the situation is deteriorating and would give a boost to GVN morale, military and civilian. Likewise, it should end any talk of a possible U.S. withdrawal and convince Hanoi of the depth of our resolve to see this thing through to a successful conclusion. This statement of the purpose of introducing a U.S. division is, in effect, a tabulation of the arguments in favor of so doing. However, there are counter arguments on the other side of the case. The introduction of a U.S. division obviously increases U.S. involvement in the counterinsurgency, exposes greater forces and invites greater losses. It will raise sensitive command questions with our GVN allies and may encourage them to an attitude of "let the United States do it." It will increase our vulnerability to Communist propaganda and Third Country criticism as we appear to assume the old French role of alien colonizer and conqueror. Finally, there is considerable doubt that the number of GVN forces which our action would relieve would have any great significance in reducing the manpower gap.

It is possible [sic] to reach a conclusion with regard to the overall merit of this action without first examining in some detail the possible missions which could be assigned a U.S. division. There are two obvious possibilities: the first, the assignment of the division to one or more of the provinces of the high plateau where the climate is good, the terrain relatively open, and the Montagard population more readily distinguishable from the alien Viet Cong. Here, our forces could utilize their mobility and firepower effectively and make an important contribution in cutting off the growing infiltration into and through this area. For the most part, the Montagnards are friendly to the U.S. and our forces would thus be operating in a relatively friendly environment.

On the other hand, such a mission in the highlands would place our forces in an area with highly exposed lines of communication leading to the coast. Their location in this area would create serious logistic problems because of the difficulty of the movement of land transport through areas infested by the Viet Cong. There would be problems both of reinforcement and of withdrawal because of this precariousness of land communications. Finally, the GVN may question the introduction of sizeable U.S. forces into the Montagnard area where we have often been accused of favoring the Montagnards over the Vietnamese and of encouraging Montagnard separatism.

The other role which has been suggested for U.S. ground forces is the occupation and defense of key enclaves along the coast such as Quang Ngai, Qui Nhon, Tuy Hoa and Nah Trang. Such a disposition would have the advantage of placing our forces in areas of easy access and egress with minimum logistic problems associated with supply and maintenance. The presence of our troops would assure the defense of these important key areas and would relieve some GVN forces for employment elsewhere. The troops would not be called upon to engage in counter-insurgency operation except in their own local defense and hence would be exposed to minimum losses.

On the other hand, they would be engaged in a rather inglorious static defensive mission unappealing to them and unimpressive in the eyes of the Vietnamese. Operating in major population areas would maximize the points of contact with Vietnamese and hence maximize the possible points of friction. The division would be badly fragmented to the extent that its command, control and supervision would be awkward.

The foregoing analysis leads me to the following tentative conclusions. First, it is not desirable to introduce a U.S. division into South Vietnam unless there are clear and tangible advantages outweighing the numerous disadvantages, many of which have noted above. One must make a definite determination of the numbers and types of GVN forces relieved by the introduction of the U.S. unit and thus the effect of the increased U.S. presence in closing the manpower gap of 1965. Obviously, our division would make some contribution but it remains to be proved that it will be sufficient to reverse the downward trend and give such a lift to the GVN forces that they would perform better by the stimulation of the U.S. presence rather than worse in a mood of relaxation as passing the Viet Cong burden to the U.S.

If the evidence of the probable effectiveness of this U.S. contribution is convincing, then the matter of mission becomes the primary question. The inland mission in the highlands is clearly the more ambitious and, if well done, will make a greater contribution during the present critical period. On the other hand, it is the more exposed and even permits one to entertain the possibility of a kind of Dien Bien Phu if the coastal provinces should collapse and our forces were cut off from the coast except by air.

The coastal enclave mission is safer, simpler but less impressive and less productive than the inland mission. The contrast of the pros and cons of the two suggests the desirability of reexamining the question to see whether the advantages of the inland disposition could not be combined in some way with the retention of a base coastal area, linked with a position inland. In any case, considerable additional study is required before we are prepared to make a recommendation either for the introduction of a division or for the assignment of its mission. In the meantime, we should be giving much thought both in South Vietnam and in Washington as to the right course of action (if) and when this issue becomes pressing—as it shortly will.

196. NATIONAL SECURITY ACTION MEMORANDUM NO. 328, APRIL 6, 1965

In March the Joint Chiefs proposed that U.S. troops be used in active combat in South Vietnam. On April 6 the president agreed to General Johnson's program of military action in Vietnam, including additional deployment of U.S. troops and a change in their mission to one of active combat. But he insisted that the new policy be portrayed to the public as being "wholly consistent" with past policy.

On Thursday, April 1, the President made the following decisions with respect to Vietnam:

1. Subject to modifications in the light of experience, and to coordination and direction both in Saigon and in Washington, the President approved the 41-point program of non-military actions submitted by Ambassador Taylor in a memorandum dated March 31, 1965.

2. The President gave general approval to the recommendations submitted by Mr. Rowan in his report dated March 16, with the exception that the President withheld approval of any request for supplemental funds at this time—it is his decision that this program is to be energetically supported by all agencies and departments and by the reprogramming of available funds as necessary within USIA.

3. The President approved the urgent exploration of the 12 suggestions for covert and other actions submitted by the Director of Central Intelligence under date of March 31.

4. The President repeated his earlier approval of the 21-point program of military actions submitted by General Harold K. Johnson under date of March 14 and re-emphasized his desire that aircraft and helicopter reinforcements under this program be accelerated.

5. The President approved an 18–20,000 man increase in U.S. military support forces to fill out existing units and supply needed logistic personnel.

6. The President approved the deployment of two additional Marine Battalions and one Marine Air Squadron and associated headquarters and support elements.

7. The President approved a change of mission for all Marine Battalions deployed to Vietnam to permit their more active use under conditions to be established and approved by the Secretary of Defense in consultation with the Secretary of State.

8. The President approved the urgent exploration, with the Korean, Austra-

SOURCE: *The Pentagon Papers*, pp. 442–443.

lian, and New Zealand Governments, of the possibility of rapid deployment of significant combat elements from their armed forces in parallel with the additional Marine deployment approved in paragraph 6.

9. Subject to continuing review, the President approved the following general framework of continuing action against North Vietnam and Laos:

We should continue roughly the present slowly ascending tempo of ROLLING THUNDER operations, being prepared to add strikes in response to a higher rate of VC operations, or conceivably to slow the pace in the unlikely event VC slacked off sharply for what appeared to be more than a temporary operational lull.

The target systems should continue to avoid the effective GCI range of MIGs. We should continue to vary the types of targets, stepping up attacks on lines of communication in the near future, and possibly moving in a few weeks to attacks on the rail lines north and northeast of Hanoi.

Leaflet operations should be expanded to obtain maximum practicable psychological effect on the North Vietnamese population.

Blockade or aerial mining of North Vietnamese ports need further study and should be considered for future operations. It would have major political complications, especially in relation to the Soviets and other third countries, but also offers many advantages.

Air operations in Laos, particularly route blocking operations in the Panhandle area, should be stepped up to the maximum remunerative rate.

10. Ambassador Taylor will promptly seek the reactions of the South Vietnamese Government to appropriate sections of this program and their approval as necessary, and in the event of disapproval or difficulty at that end, these decisions will be appropriately reconsidered. In any event, no action into Vietnam under paragraphs 6 and 7 above should take place without GVN approval or further Presidential authorization.

11. The President desires that with respect to the actions in paragraphs 5 through 7, premature publicity be avoided by all possible precautions. The actions themselves should be taken as rapidly as practicable, but in ways that should minimize any appearance of sudden changes in policy, and official statements on these troop movements will be made only with the direct approval of the Secretary of Defense, in consultation with the Secretary of State. The President's desire is that these movements and changes should be understood as being gradual and wholly consistent with existing policy.

197. MEMORANDUM FOR THE PRESIDENT BY MCNAMARA, APRIL 21, 1965 [Extract]

Meeting in Honolulu, key military and civilian officials from Washington met with Westmoreland and Sharp to talk about military strategy. They agreed that it could take up to two years to "demonstrate VC failure" in South Vietnam. The shared assumption was that "denying victory" to the Communists would break their will, leading to a favorable political solution.

SOURCE: Document from the Lyndon Baines Johnson Library.

Mr. William Bundy, Mr. McNaughton and I met with Ambassador Taylor, General Wheeler, Admiral Sharp and General Westmoreland in Honolulu on Tuesday, April 20. Following is my report of that meeting:

1. None of them expects the DRV/VC to capitulate, or come to a position acceptable to us, in less than six months. This is because they believe that a settlement will come as much or more from VC failure in the South as from DRV pain in the North, and that it will take more than six months, perhaps a yyar or two, to demonstrate VC failure in the South.

2. With respect to strikes against the North, they all agree that the present tempo is about right, that sufficient increasing pressure is provided by repetition and continuation. All of them envisioned a strike program continuing at least six months, perhaps a year or more, avoiding the Hanoi-Haiphong-Phuc Yen areas during that period. There might be fewer fixed targets, or more restrikes, or more armed reconnaissance missions. Ambassador Taylor stated what appeared to be a shared view, that it is important not to "kill the hostage" by destroying the North Vietnamese assets inside the "Hanoi do-nut." They all believe that the strike program is essential to our campaign—both psychologically and physically—but that it cannot be expected to do the job alone. They all considered it very important that strikes against the North be continued during any talks.

3. None of them sees a dramatic improvement in the South in the immediate future. Their strategy for "victory," over time, is to break the will of the DRV/VC by denying them victory. Ambassador Taylor put it in terms of a demonstration of Communist impotence, which will lead eventually to a political solution. They see slow improvement in the South, but all emphasized the critical importance of holding on and avoiding—for psychological and morale reasons—a spectacular defeat of GVN or US forces. And they all suspect that the recent VC lull is but the quiet before a storm.

4. To bolster the GVN forces while they are building up, they all recommend the following deployments in addition to the 2,000 Koreans and 33,500 US troops already in-country (including the 4 Marine battalions at Danang-Hue):

1 US Army brigade (3 btn) at Bien Hoa/Vung Tau	4,000	closing 1 May
3 US Marine air sqs + 3 btns at Chu Lai	6,200	closing 5 May
1 Australian btn at Vun Tau	1,250	closing 21 May
1 US Army brigade (3 btn) at Qui Nhon/Nha Trang	4,000	closing 15 Jn.
1 Korean RCT (3 btn) at Quang Ngai	4,000	closing 15 Jn.
Augmentation of various existing forces	11,00	already approv.
Logistics troops for previously approved force level	7,000	already approv.
Logistics troops for above enclaves and possible 3 divisions	16,000	not yet approv.
TOTAL: US 13 btns	82,000	
ROK & ANZAC 4 btns	7,250	

5. Possible later deployments, not recommended now, include a US Air-Mobile division (9 btns–15,800) to Pleiku/Kontum, and I Corps HQ (1,200) to Nha Trang; and even later, the remainder of the Korean division (6 btns—14,500) to Quang Ngai, and the remainder of the Marine Expeditionary Force (3 btns—24,800) to Danang.

198. MESSAGE FROM JOHNSON TO TAYLOR, MAY 10, 1965

Johnson planned a brief pause in the air attacks on North Vietnam, explaining to Taylor that it was a device for building U.S. and foreign support for stronger military measures.

I have learned from Bob McNamara that nearly all ROLLING THUNDER operations for this week can be completed by Wednesday noon, Washington time. This fact and the days of Buddha's birthday seem to me to provide an excellent opportunity for a pause in air attacks which might go into next week and which I could use to good effect with world opinion.

My plan is not to announce this brief pause but simply to call it privately to the attention of Moscow and Hanoi as soon as possible and tell them that we shall be watching closely to see whether they respond in any way. My current plan is to report publicly after the pause ends on what we have done.

Could you see Quat [Prime Minister Phan Huy Quat] right away on Tuesday and see if you can persuade him to concur in this plan. I would like to associate him with me in this decision if possible, but I would accept a simple concurrence or even willingness not to oppose my decision. In general, I think it important that he and I should get together in such matters, but I have no desire to embarrass him if it is politically difficult for him to join actively in a pause over Buddha's birthday.

[Words illegible] noted your [words illegible] but do you yet have your appreciation of the political effect in Saigon of acting around Buddha's birthday. From my point of view it is a great advantage to use Buddha's birthday to mask the first days of the pause here, if it is at all possible in political terms for Quat. I assume we could undertake to enlist the Archbishop and the Nuncio in calming the Catholics.

You should understand that my purpose in this plan is to begin to clear a path either toward restoration of peace or toward increased military action, depending upon the reaction of the Communists. We have amply demonstrated our determination and our commitment in the last two months, and I now wish to gain some flexibility.

I know that this is a hard assignment on short notice, but there is no one who can bring it off better.

I have kept this plan in the tightest possible circle here and wish you to inform no one but Alexis Johnson. After I have your report of Quat's reaction, I will make a final decision and it will be communicated promptly to senior officers concerned.

199. MESSAGE FOR DRV GOVERNMENT FROM U.S. GOVERNMENT ON BOMBING PAUSE, MAY 11, 1965

On the evening of May 11, just before the bombing pause began, Rusk sent a cable to U.S. Ambassador Foy Kohler in Moscow instructing him to convey a

SOURCE: *The Pentagon Papers*, pp. 446–447.
SOURCE: *United States-Vietnam Relations*, VI, C. 1, pp. 114–115.

message to the government of the DRV. The message was not calculated to impress Hanoi with the U.S. interest in negotiations, since it demanded instant response by the DRV on that ground—something that was clearly impossible. Moreover, it did not pledge anything more than a pause of a few days even if there were such a response.

The highest authority in this Government has asked me to inform Hanoi that there will be no air attacks on North Viet-Nam for a period beginning at noon, Washington time, Wednesday, May 12, and running into next week.

In this decision the United States Government has taken account of repeated suggestions from various quarters, including public statements by Hanoi representatives, that there can be no progress toward peace while there are air attacks on North Vietnam. The United States Government remains convinced that the underlying cause of trouble in Southeast Asia is armed action against the people and Government of South Vietnam by forces whose actions can be decisively affected from North Vietnam. The United States will be very watchful to see whether in this period of pause there are significant reductions in such armed actions by such forces. (The United States must emphasize that the road toward the end of armed attacks against the people and Government Vietnam *is the only road which will permit the Government of Vietnam* (and the Government of the United States) to bring a permanent end to their attacks on North Vietnam.) . . .

In taking this action the United States is well aware of the risk that a temporary suspension of these air attacks may be understood as an indication of weakness, and it is therefore necessary for me to point out that if this pause should be misunderstood in this fashion, by any party, it would be necessary to demonstrate more clearly than ever, after the pause ended, that the United States is determined not to accept aggression without reply in Vietnam. Moreover, the United States must point out that the decision to end air attacks for this limited trial period is one which it must be free to reverse if at any time in the coming days there should be actions by the other side in Vietnam which required immediate reply.

But my Government is very hopeful that there will be no such misunderstanding and that this first pause in the air attacks may meet with a response which will permit further and more extended suspension of this form of military action in the expectation of equally constructive actions by the other side in the future.

200. MEMORANDUM FOR THE PRESIDENT FROM BALL, JULY 1, 1965

In the only dissent from the unanimous support by high-level Johnson Administration officials for massive U.S. military intervention in South Vietnam, George Ball recommended a compromise settlement. Ball argued that the United States could avoid a "long-term catastrophe" by accepting some short-term costs.

(1) A Losing War: The South Vietnamese are losing the war to the Viet Cong. No one can assure you that we can beat the Viet Cong or even force them to the

SOURCE: *The Pentagon Papers, Gravel Edition,* IV, pp. 615–617.

conference table on our terms, no matter how many hundred thousand *white, foreign* (U.S.) troops we deploy.

No one has demonstrated that a white ground force of whatever size can win a guerrilla war—which is at the same time a civil war between Asians—in jungle terrain in the midst of a population that refuses cooperation to the white forces (and the South Vietnamese) and thus provides a great intelligence advantage to the other side. Three recent incidents vividly illustrate this point: (a) the sneak attack on the Da Nang Air Base which involved penetration of a defense parameter guarded by 9,000 Marines. This raid was possible only because of the cooperation of the local inhabitants; (b) the B-52 raid that failed to hit the Viet Cong who had obviously been tipped off; (c) the search and destroy mission of the 173rd Air Borne Brigade which spent three days looking for the Viet Cong, suffered 23 casualties, and never made contact with the enemy who had obviously gotten advance word of their assignment.

(2) The Question to Decide: Should we limit our liabilities in South Vietnam and try to find a way out with minimal long-term costs?

The alternative—no matter what we may wish it to be—is almost certainly a protracted war involving an open-ended commitment of U.S. forces, mounting U.S. casualties, no assurance of a satisfactory solution, and a serious danger of escalation at the end of the road.

(3) Need for a Decision Now: So long as our forces are restricted to advising and assisting the South Vietnamese, the struggle will remain a civil war between Asian peoples. Once we deploy substantial numbers of troops in combat it will become a war between the U.S. and a large part of the population of South Vietnam, organized and directed from North Vietnam and backed by the resources of both Moscow and Peiping.

The decision you face now, therefore, is crucial. Once large numbers of U.S. troops are committed to direct combat, they will begin to take heavy casualties in a war they are ill-equipped to fight in a non-cooperative if not downright hostile countryside.

Once we suffer large casualties, we will have started a well-nigh irreversible process. Our involvement will be so great that we cannot—without national humiliation—stop short of achieving our complete objectives. *Of the two possibilities I think humiliation would be more likely than the achievement of our objectives— even after we have paid terrible costs.*

(4) Compromise Solution: Should we commit U.S. manpower and prestige to a terrain so unfavorable as to give a very large advantage to the enemy—or should we seek a compromise settlement which achieves less than our stated objectives and thus cut our losses while we still have the freedom of maneuver to do so.

(5) Costs of a Compromise Solution: The answer involves a judgment as to the cost to the U.S. of such a compromise settlement in terms of our relations with the countries in the area of South Vietnam, the credibility of our commitments, and our prestige around the world. In my judgment, if we act before we commit a substantial U.S. truce [sic] to combat in South Vietnam we can, by accepting some short-term costs, avoid what may well be a long-term catastrophe. I believe we attended [sic] grossly to exaggerate the costs involved in a compromise settlement. An appreciation of probable costs is contained in the attached memorandum.

(6) With the considerations in mind, I strongly urge the following program:
    (a) Military Program

(1) Complete all deployments already announced—15 battalions—but decide not to go beyond a total of 72,000 men represented by this figure.

(2) Restrict the combat role of the American forces to the June 19 announcement, making it clear to General Westmoreland that this announcement is to be strictly construed.

(3) Continue bombing in the North but avoid the Hanoi-Haiphong area and any targets nearer to the Chinese border than those already struck.

(b) Political Program

(1) In any political approaches so far, we have been the prisoners of whatever South Vietnamese government that was momentarily in power. If we are ever to move toward a settlement, it will probably be because the South Vietnamese government pulls the rug out from under us and makes its own deal *or* because we go forward quietly without advance prearrangement with Saigon.

(2) So far we have not given the other side a reason to believe there is *any* flexibility in our negotiating approach. And the other side has been unwilling to accept what *in their terms* is complete capitulation.

(3) Now is the time to start some serious diplomatic feelers looking towards a solution based on some application of a self-determination principle.

(4) I would recommend approaching Hanoi rather than any of the other probable parties, the NLF, ———— or Peiping. Hanoi is the only one that has given any signs of interest in discussion. Peiping has been rigidly opposed. Moscow has recommended that we negotiate with Hanoi. The NLF has been silent.

(5) There are several channels to the North Vietnamese, but I think the best one is through their representative in Paris, Mai van Bo. Initial feelers of Bo should be directed toward a discussion both of the four points we have put forward and the four points put forward by Hanoi as a basis for negotiation. We can accept all but one of Hanoi's four points, and hopefully we should be able to agree on some ground rules for serious negotiations—including no preconditions.

(6) If the initial feelers lead to further secret, exploratory talks, we can inject the concept of self-determination that would permit the Viet Cong some hope of achieving some of their political objectives through local elections or some other device.

(7) The contact on our side should be handled through a nongovernmental cutout (possibly a reliable newspaper man who can be repudiated).

(8) If progress can be made at this level a basis can be laid for a multinational conference. At some point, obviously, the government of South Vietnam will have to be brought on board, but I would postpone this step until after a substantial feeling out of Hanoi.

(7) Before moving to any formal conference we should be prepared to agree once the conference is started:

(a) The U.S. will stand down its bombing of the North

(b) The South Vietnamese will initiate no offensive operations in the South, and

(c) The DRV will stop terrorism and other aggressive action against the South.

(8) The negotiations at the conference should aim at incorporating our understanding with Hanoi in the form of a multinational agreement guaranteed by the U.S., the Soviet Union and possibly other parties, and providing for an international mechanism to supervise its execution.

201. SPEECH BY LAO DONG PARTY SECRETARY LE DUAN TO A CADRE CONFERENCE, JULY 6–8, 1965 [Extracts]

In a talk to a cadre conference on the war situation, Le Duan gave the assessment of the Party leadership of various contingencies, including an invasion of the North by U.S. forces. While recognizing that the United States might commit up to 400,000 troops to the South, he emphasized factors that would make it disadvantageous to do so. He correctly predicted that the United States would not invade the North with its own forces because it would bring China into the war. He also virtually ruled out use of nuclear weapons by the United States, because "Our camp also has the atomic bomb."

We are not only determined to defeat the U.S. but must know how to defeat the U.S. in the manner most appropriate to the relation of forces between the enemy and us during each historical phase. Putting forward the slogan peace and neutrality for the South as well as the five points of the National Liberation Front of South Vietnam and the Four points in our government's declaration read before the National Assembly as bases for the resolution of the Vietnamese problem means that we know how to fight and defeat the Americans most advantageously.

. . . (T)he U.S. is still strong enough to enter into a limited war in Vietnam, by sending not only 200,000–250,000 but 300,000–400,000 troops to South Vietnam. But if it switches to limited war, the U.S. still will have weaknesses which it cannot overcome. The U.S. rear area is very far away, and American soldiers are "soldiers in chains," who cannot fight like the French, cannot stand the weather conditions, and don't know the battlefield but on the contrary have many weaknesses in their opposition to people's war. If the U.S. puts 300,000–400,000 troops into the South, it will have stripped away the face of its neocolonial policy and revealed the face of an old-style colonial invader, contrary to the whole new-style annexation policy of the U.S. in the world at present. Thus, the U.S. will not be able to maintain its power with regard to influential sectors of the United States. If the U.S. itself directly enters the war in the South it will have to fight for a prolonged period with the people's army of the South, with the full assistance of the North and of the Socialist bloc. Fighting for a prolonged period is a weakness of U.S. imperialism. The Southern revolution can fight a protracted war, while the U.S. can't, because American military, economic, and political resources must be distrib-

SOURCE: *Le Duan, Ta Nhat Dinh Thang, Dich Nhat Dinh Thua* [We will certainly win, the enemy will certainly lose] South Vietnam: Tien Phong, 1966, pp. 17–24. [Translation by the editor.]

uted throughout the world. If it is bogged down in one place and can't withdraw, the whole effort will be violently shaken. The U.S. would lose its preeminence in influential sectors at home, create openings for other competing imperialists and lose the American market. Therefore although the U.S. can send 300,000 to 4000,000 troops at once, why must the U.S. do it step by step? Because even if it does send many troops like that, the U.S. would still be hesitant; because that would be a passive policy full of contradictions; because of fear of protracted war, and the even stronger opposition of the American people and the world's people, and even of their allies who would also not support widening the war.

With regard to the North, the U.S. still carries out its war of destruction, primarily by its air force: Besides bombing military targets, bridges and roads to obstruct transport and communications, the U.S. could also indiscriminately bomb economic targets, markets, villages, schools, hospitals, dikes, etc., in order to create confusion and agitation among the people. But the North is determined to fight back at the U.S. invaders in a suitable manner, determined to punish the criminals, day or night, and determined to make them pay the blood debts which they have incurred to our people in both zones. The North will not flinch for a moment before the destructive acts of the U.S., which could grow more insane with every passing day. The North will not count the cost but will use all of its strength to produce and fight, and endeavor to help the South. For a long time, the Americans have boasted of the strength of their air force and navy but during five to six months of directly engaging in combat with the U.S. in the North, we see clearly that the U.S. cannot develop that strength in relation to the South or in relation to the North, but reveals more clearly every day its weak points. We have shot down more than 400 of their airplanes, primarily with rifles, anti-aircraft guns, the high level of our hatred of the aggressors, and the spirit of determination to defeat the U.S. invaders. Therefore, even if the U.S. sends 300,000–400,000 troops into the South, and turns special war into direct war in the South, escalating the war of destruction in the North, they still can't hope to avert defeat, and the people of both North and South will still be determined to fight and determined to win.

If the U.S. is still more adventurous and brings U.S. and puppet troops of all their vassal states to attack the North, broadening it into a direct war in the entire country, the situation will then be different. Then it will not be we alone who fight the U.S. but our entire camp. First the U.S. will not only be doing battle with 17 million people in the North but will also have to battle with hundreds of millions of Chinese people. Attacking the North would mean that the U.S. intends to attack China, because the North and China are two socialist countries linked extremely closely, and the imperialists cannot attack this socialist country without also intending to attack the other. Therefore the two countries would resist together. Could the American imperialists suppress hundreds of millions of people? Certainly they could not. If they reach a stage of desperation, would the U.S. use the atomic bomb? Our camp also has the atomic bomb. The Soviet Union has sufficient atomic strength to oppose any imperialists who wish to use the atomic bomb in order to attack a socialist country and threaten mankind. If U.S. imperialism used the atomic bomb in those circumstances they would be committing suicide. The American people themselves would be the ones to stand up and smash the U.S. government when that government used atomic bombs. Would the U.S. dare to provoke war between the two blocs because of the Vietnam problem? Would it provoke a third world war in order to put an early end to the history of U.S. imperialism and of the entire imperialist system in general? Would other imperialist countries, factions in the U.S., and particularly the American people, agree to the U.S. warmongers throwing them into suicide? Certainly, the U.S. could not carry out their intention, because U.S. imperialism is in a weak position and not in a position of strength.

But the possibility of the broadening the direct war to the North is a possibility to which we must pay utmost attention, because U.S. imperialism could be adventurous. We must be vigilant and prepared to cope with the worst possibility. The best way to cope, and not to let the US broaden the war in the South or in the North is to fight even more strongly and more accurately in the South, and make the puppet military units—the primary mainstay of the U.S.—rapidly fall apart, push military and political struggle forward, and quickly create the opportune moment to advance to complete defeat of U.S. imperialism and its lackeys in the South.

202. MEMORANDUM FOR THE PRESIDENT BY MCNAMARA, JULY 20, 1965 [Extract]

After a conference in Saigon with Westmoreland, Taylor, and the next Ambassador, Henry Cabot Lodge, McNamara expressed the view that a "favorable outcome," which would leave Saigon in control of virtually all of South Vietnam with a disarmed, quiescent Communist movement, would be more likely to come without a negotiated settlement than with one. He called for a large expansion of the American presence to stave off defeat, bringing the U.S. force level up to 175,000 or 200,000 men, and cited the possibility of the DRV sending several divisions into the South to counter the U.S. build-up. On July 28, Johnson announced that U.S. troop strength in South Vietnam would be increased from 75,000 to 125,000.

SUBJECT: Recommendations of additional deployments to Vietnam

1. *Introduction.* Our object in Vietnam is to create conditions for a favorable outcome by demonstrating to the VC/DRV that the odds are against their winning. We want to create these conditions, if possible, without causing the war to expand into one with China or the Soviet Union and in a way which preserves support of the American people and, hopefully, of our allies and friends. The following assessments, made following my trip to Vietnam and Ambassador designate Lodge and General Wheeler and my own aid are addressed to the achievement of that object. My specific recommendations appear in Paragraph 5; they are concurred by Ambassador Taylor, Ambassador designate Lodge, Ambassador Johnson, General Wheeler, Admiral Sharp and General Westmoreland. I have neither asked for nor obtained their concurrence in other portions of the paper.

SOURCE: Document from the Lyndon Baines Johnson Library.

2. *Favorable outcome:* To my view, a "favorable outcome" for purposes of these assessments and recommendations has nine fundamental elements.

    a. VC stop attacks and drastically reduce incidents of terror and sabotage.

    b. DRV reduces infiltration to a trickle, with some reasonably reliable method of our obtaining confirmation of this fact.

    c. US/GVN stop bombing of North Vietnam.

    d. GVN stays independent (hopefully pro-US, but possibly genuinely neutral).

    e. GVN exercising governmental functions over substantially all of South Vietnam.

    f. Communists remain quiescent in Laos and Thailand.

    g. DRV withdraw PAVN forces and other North Vietnamese infiltration (not regroupees) from South Vietnam.

    h. VC/NLF transform from a military to a purely political organization.

    i. US combat forces (not advisors or AID) withdraw.

A favorable outcome could include also arrangements, regarding elections, relations between North and South Vietnam, participation peace-keeping by international forces, membership for North and South Vietnam in the UN, and so on. The nine fundamental elements can evolve with or without an express agreement and, except for what might be negotiated incidental to a cease-fire, are more likely to evolve without an express agreement than with one. We do not need now to address the question whether ultimately we would settle for something less than the nine fundamentals; because deployment of the forces recommended in paragraph 5 is prerequisite to the achievement of *any* acceptable settlement, and a decision can be made later, when bargaining becomes a reality, whether to compromise in any particular.

3. *Estimate of the situation.* The situation in South Vietnam is worse than a year ago (when it was worse than a year before that). After a few months of stalemate, the tempo of the war has quickened. A hard VC push is now on to dismember the nation and to maul the army. The VC main and local forces, reinforced by militia and guerrillas, have the initiative and, with large attacks (some in regimental strength), are hurting ARVN forces badly. The main VC efforts have been in southern I Corps, northern and central II Corps and north of Saigon. The central highlands could well be lost to the National Liberation Front during this monsoon season. Since June 1, the GVN has been forced to abandon six district capitals; only one has been retaken. US combat troop deployments and US/VNAF strikes against the North have put to rest most South Vietnamese fears that the United States will foresake them, and US/VNAF air strikes in-country have probably shaken VC morale somewhat. Yet the government is able to provide security to fewer and fewer people in less and less territory as terrorism increases. Cities and towns are being isolated as fewer and fewer roads and railroads are usable and power and communications lines are cut.

The economy is deteriorating—the war is disrupting rubber production, rice distribution, Dajat vegetable production and the coastal fishing industry, causing the loss of jobs and income, displacement of people and frequent breakdown or suspension of vital means of transportation and communication; foreign exchange earnings have fallen; and severe inflation is threatened.

The odds are less than even that the Ky government will last out the year. Ky is "executive agent" for a directorate of generals. His government is youthful and inexperienced, but dedicated to a "revolutionary" program. His tenure depends upon unity of the armed forces behind him. If the directorate holds together and the downward trend of the war is halted, the religious and regional factions will probably remain quiescent; otherwise there will be political turbulence and possibly uncoordinated efforts to negotiate settlement with the DRV. The Buddhists, Catholics, out-politicians and business communist are "wait-and-seeing;" the VC, while unable alone to generate effective unrest in the cities, can "piggyback" on any anti-government demonstration or cause.

Rural reconstruction (pacification) even in the Hop Tac area around Saigon is making little progress. Gains in IV Corps are being held, but in I and II Corps and adjacent III Corps areas it has lost ground fast since the start of the VC monsoon offensive (300,000 people have been lost to the VC, and tens of thousands of refugees have poured out of these areas).

The Government-to-VC ratio over-all is now only a little better than 3-to-1, and in combat battalions little better than 0.5-to-1. Some ARVN units have been mauled; many are understrength and therefore "conservation." Desertions are at a high rate, and the force build-up has slipped badly. The VC, who are undoubtedly suffering badly too (their losses are very high), now control a South Vietnamese manpower pool of 500,000 to 1 million fighting-age men and reportedly are trying to double their combat strength, largely by forced draft (down to 15-year-olds) in the increasing areas they control. They seem to be able more than to replace their losses.

There are no signs that we have throttled the inflow of supplies for the VC or can throttle the flow while their material needs are as low as they are: indeed more and better weapons have been observed in VC hands, and it is probable that there has been further build-up of North Vietnamese regular units in the I and II Corps areas, with at least three full regiments (all of the 325th Division) there. Nor have our air attacks in North Vietnam produced tangible evidence of willingness on the part of Hanoi to come to the conference table in a reasonable mood. The DRV/VC seem to believe that South Vietnam is on the run and near collapse; they show no signs of settling for less than a complete take-over.

4. *Options open to us.* We must choose among three courses of action with respect to Vietnam all of which involve different probabilities, outcomes and costs:

a. Cut our losses and withdraw under the best conditions that can be arranged—almost certainly conditions humiliating the United States and very damaging to our future effectiveness on the world scene.

b. Continue at about the present level, with the US forces limited to say 75,000 holding on and playing for the breaks—a course of action which, because our position would grow weaker, almost certainly would confront us later with a choice between withdrawal and an emergency expansion of forces, perhaps too late to do any good.

c. Expand promptly and substantially the US military pressure against the Viet Cong in the South and maintain the military pressure against the North Vietnamese in the North while launching a vigorous effort on the political side to lay the groundwork for a favorable outcome by clarifying our objectives and establishing channels of communication. This alternative would stave off defeat in the short run and offer a good chance of producing a favorable settlement in the longer run; at the same time it would imply a commitment to see a fighting war clear through at considerable cost in casualties and material and would make any later decision to withdraw even more difficult and even more costly than would be the case today.

My recommendations in paragraph 5 below are based on the choice of the third alternative (Option c) as the course of action involving the best odds of the best outcome with the most acceptable cost to the United States.

5. *Military recommendations.* There are now 15 US (and 1 Australian) combat battalions in Vietnam; they, together with other combat personnel and non-combat personnel, bring the total US personnel in Vietnam to approximately 75,000.

a. I recommend that the deployment of US ground troops in Vietnam be increased by October to 34 maneuver battalions (or, if the Koreans fail to provide the expected 9 battalions promptly, to 43 battalions). The battalions together with increases in helicopter lift, air squadrons, naval units, air defense, combat support and miscellaneous log support and advisory personnel which I also recommend—would bring the total US personnel in Vietnam to approximately 175,000 (200,000 if we must make up for the Korean failure). It should be understood that the deployment of more men (perhaps 100,000) may be necessary in early 1966, and that the deployment of additional forces thereafter is possible but will depend on developments.

b. I recommend that Congress be requested to authorize the call-up of approximately 235,000 men in the Reserve and National Guard. [Deleted]

The call-up would be for a two-year period; but the intention would be to release them after one year, by which time they could be relieved by regular forces if conditions permitted.

c. I recommend that the regular armed forces be increased by approximately 375,000 men (approximately 250,000 Army, 75,000 Marines, 25,000 Air Force and 25,000 Navy). [Deleted]

The increase would be accomplished by increasing recruitment, increasing the draft and extending tours of duty of men already in the service.

d. I recommend that a supplemental appropriation of approximately $X for FY 1966 be sought from the Congress to cover the first part of the added costs attributable to the build-up in and for the war in Vietnam. A further supplemental appropriation might be required later in the fiscal year.

It should be noted that in mid-1966 the United States would, as a consequence of the above method of handling the build-up, have approximately 600,000 additional men [deleted] as protection against contingencies.

203. EDITORIAL IN CHINESE NEWSPAPERS, *JEN-MIN JIH PAO*, AND *HUNG CHI*, NOVEMBER 11, 1965 [Extract]

The final Chinese response to Soviet proposal that the two Communist powers cooperate in support of the Vietnamese revolutionaries fighting against the United

SOURCE: "Refutation of the New Leaders of the C.P.S.U. on 'United Action,' " *Peking Review,* November 12, 1965, pp. 15–17.

States was a blistering attack on Soviet policy for allegedly collaborating with the United States against the Vietnamese. This editorial reflected the views of Chairman Mao Tse-tung, who had purged opponents of his policies of refusing limited cooperation with the Soviets.

The crux of the matter is that, so far from opposing U.S. imperialism, the new leaders of the C.P.S.U. are allying themselves and collaborating with it to dominate the world. They have thus set themselves in opposition to the united front against U.S. imperialism. If they really opposed U.S. imperialism and did so by actual deed, we would readily take united action with them. But their so-called opposition to U.S. imperialism is only verbal and not genuine. We must tell them the truth: So long as their line of Soviet-U.S. collaboration against world revolution remains unchanged, and so long as they do not abandon their alliance with U.S. imperialism and reaction, we absolutely refuse to take any "united action" with them. We absolutely refuse to serve as a pawn in their secret diplomacy the U.S. imperialism or help them cover up their assistance to U.S. imperialism in suppressing the peoples' revolution in various countries.

The new leaders of the C.P.S.U. never weary of saying that, however serious the differences between them, Communists must take "united action" on the question of Viet Nam at this urgent juncture in the Vietnamese people's struggle against the United States.

Since the new leaders of the C.P.S.U. have destroyed the basis of international proletarian unity, and since they transpose enemies and friends and persist in the line of Soviet-U.S. collaboration for world domination, is it still possible for the Marxist-Leninist parties to take united action with them on the question of Viet Nam?

At a time when the U.S. imperialists are committing rabid aggression against Viet Nam, all Communist Parties and socialist countries should as a matter of course take a unanimous stand and firmly support the Vietnamese people's just struggle to smash this aggression. The point is that the stand taken by the revisionist leadership of the C.P.S.U. on the question of Viet Nam is inseparable from their revisionist programme and line, and is contrary to the principled stand required of a Marxist-Leninist party.

When Khrushchev was in power, the revisionist leadership of the C.P.S.U. openly sided with U.S. imperialism and opposed and undermined the revolutionary struggle of the Vietnamese people against U.S. aggression. They alleged that "any small 'local war' might spark off the conflagration of a world war." Using this absurd argument to frighten and intimidate all peoples engaged in revolutionary armed struggle, they openly refused to support and aid the Vietnamese people in their anti-U.S. struggle. When the struggles of the Vietnamese and the Laotian peoples against U.S. imperialism grew acute, their policy on the question of Indo-China was one of "disengagement." In July 1964, they indicated the desire of the Soviet Government to resign from its post as one of the two co-chairmen of the Geneva conference. Soon afterwards, when the U.S. imperialists engineered the Bac Bo Gulf incident, Khrushchev went so far as to concoct the slander that the incident was provoked by China.

The situation in Viet Nam developed directly contrary to the wishes of the Khrushchev revisionists. The Vietnamese people won victory after victory in their revolutionary anti-U.S. struggle, while the U.S. aggressors grew hard pressed. The new leaders of the C.P.S.U. came to realize that it was no longer advisable to copy Khrushchev's policy of "disengagement" in its totality. So they switched to the policy of involvement, that is, of getting their hand in.

The policy of involvement and the policy of disengagement are essentially the same. Both are products of Khrushchev revisionism and both are designed to meet the needs of U.S. imperialism.

The U.S. imperialists urgently need to extinguish the roaring flames of the Vietnamese people's revolution. And so do the Khrushchev revisionists because they want to carry out their line of Soviet-U.S. collaboration for world domination. When Khrushchev was following the policy of "disengagement," he was acting in close-co-ordination with John F. Kennedy. And now that the new leaders of the C.P.S.U. are following the policy of involvement, they are similarly acting in tacit agreement and close collaboration with Lyndon B. Johnson.

204. REPORT BY MCNAMARA ON VISIT TO VIETNAM, NOVEMBER 30, 1965

After a two-day visit to South Vietnam at the end of November, McNamara forecast an expansion of Communist forces by almost one-third in about one year and said the projected U.S. buildup would not be sufficient to maintain the military initiative. He recommended sending even more troops than planned and gradually intensifying bombing of North Vietnam, even though he could not guarantee success. He also proposed a bombing pause to build public support for later escalation.

. . . the Ky "government of generals" is surviving, but not acquiring wide support or generating actions; pacification is thoroughly stalled, with no guarantee that security anywhere is permanent and no indications that able and willing leadership will emerge in the absence of that permanent security. (Prime Minister Ky estimates that his government controls only 25% of the population today and reports that his pacification chief hopes to increase that to 50% two years from now.)

The dramatic recent changes in the situation are on the military side. They are the increased infiltration from the North and the increased willingness of the Communist forces to stand and fight, even in large-scale engagements. The Ia Drang River Campaign of early November is an example. The Communists appear to have decided to increase their forces in SVN both by heavy recruitment in the South (especially in the Delta) and by infiltration of regular NVN forces from the North. . . . the enemy can be expected to enlarge his present strength of 110 battalion equivalents to more than 150 battalion equivalents by the end of calendar 1966, when hopefully his losses can be made to equal his input.

As for the Communist ability to supply this force, it is estimated that, even taking account of interdiction of routes by air and sea, more than 200 tons of supplies a day can be infiltrated—more than enough, allowing for the extent to which the enemy lives off the land, to support the likely PAVN/VC force at the likely level of operations.

SOURCE: *The Pentagon Papers*, pp. 622–623.

To meet this possible—and in my view likely—Communist buildup, the presently contemplated Phase I forces will not be enough (approx. 220,000 Americans, almost all in place by end of 1965). Bearing in mind the nature of the war, the expected weighted combat force ration of less than 2-to-1 will not be good enough. Nor will the originally contemplated Phase II addition of 28 more US batallions (112,000 men) be enough; the combat force ratio even with 32 new SVNese batallions, would still be little better than 2-to-1 at the end of 1966. The initiative which we have held since August would pass to the enemy; we would fall far short of what we expected to achieve in terms of population control and disruption of enemy bases and lines of communications. Indeed, it is estimated that with the contemplated Phase II addition of 28 US battalions, we would be able only to hold our present geographical positions.

2. We have but two options, it seems to me. One is to go now for a compromise solution (something substantially less than the "favorable outcome" I described in my memo of Nov. 3) and hold further deployments to a minimum. The other is to stick with our stated objectives and with the war, and provide what it takes in men and materiel. If it is decided not to move now toward a compromise, I recommend that the US both send a substantial number of additional troops and very gradually intensify the bombing of NVN. Amb. Lodge, Wheeler, Sharp and Westmoreland concur in this prolonged course of action, although Wheeler and Sharp would intensify the bombing of the North more quickly.

(Recommend up to 74 battalions by end-66: total to approx. 400,000 by end-66. And it should be understood that further deployments (perhaps exceeding 200,000) may be needed in 1967.)

3. Bombing of NVN. . . . over a period of the next six months we gradually enlarge the target system in the northeast (Hanoi-Haiphong) quadrant until, at the end of the period, it includes "controlled" reconnaissance of lines of communication throughout the area, bombing of petroleum storage facilities and power plants, and mining of the harbors. (Left unstruck would be population targets, industrial plants, locks and dams).

4. Pause in bombing NVN. It is my belief that there should be a three- or four-week pause in the program of bombing the North before we either greatly increase our troop deployments to VN or intensify our strikes against the North. (My recommendation for a "pause" is not concurred in by Lodge, Wheeler, or Sharp.) The reasons for this belief are, first, that we must lay a foundation in the mind of the American public and in world opinion for such an enlarged phase of the war and, second, we should give NVN a face-saving chance to stop the aggression. I am not seriously concerned about the risk of alienating the SVNese, misleading Hanoi, or being "trapped" in a pause; if we take reasonable precautions, we can avoid these pitfalls. I am seriously concerned about embarking on a markedly higher level of war in NV without having tried, through a pause, to end the war or at least having made it clear to our people that we did our best to end it.

5. Evaluation. We should be aware that deployments of the kind I have recommended will not guarantee success. US killed-in-action can be expected to reach 1000 a month, and the odds are even that we will be faced in early 1967 with a "no-decision" at an even higher level. My overall evaluation nevertheless, is that the best chance of achieving our stated objectives lies in a pause followed, if it fails, by the deployments mentioned above.

205. AIDE-MEMOIRE FROM U.S. AMBASSADOR HENRY BYROADE IN RANGOON TO DRV CONSUL GENERAL VU HUU BINH, DECEMBER 29, 1965

On December 24, the United States began a bombing pause of indeterminate length. Five days later, U.S. Ambassador to Burma Henry Byroade was informed that the president would defer resumption of the bombing several more days and wanted to inform the DRV of that fact. Byroade was asked to pass an aide-mémoire to the DRV representative in Rangoon. The message asked the DRV to "reciprocate by making a serious contribution to peace," hinting that the pause could be extended for a substantial period.

1. As you are no doubt aware, there has been no bombing in North Viet-Nam since December 24 although some reconnaissance flights have continued. No decision has been made regarding a resumption of bombings and unless there is a major provocation we would hope that the present stand-down, which is in its fifth day, could extend beyond New Year. If your government will now reciprocate by making a serious contribution toward peace, it would obviously have a favorable effect on the possibility of further extending the suspension.

2. I and other members of my Embassy staff stand available at any time to receive any communication you may wish to address to me or to us.

1966

206. MEMORANDUM BY WILLIAM BUNDY FOR RUSK, FEBRUARY 3, 1966 [Extract]

On January 31, after the bombing pause had ended, the DRV responded with an aide-mémoire denouncing positions taken publicly by the United States on peace terms. Trying to interpret Hanoi behavior in relation to the bombing pause and resumption, Bundy speculated that Hanoi may have been concerned that it would appear afraid of the bombing if it responded during the pause.

It seems to me that our response to this approach will take careful thought. As a first step, since Byroade's cables are hard to read together, I have done the

Source: *United States-Vietnam Relations*, VI.C.1, p. 118.
Source: *U.S.-Vietnam Relations*, VI. C.1, p. 139–140.

attached pull-together, which contains the full text of the aide mémoire, and also the points made in the oral conversation. I think this gives us a much better starting point, with numerical headings, for our own reply. (Tab A).

We may know much better, on the basis of Byroade's interim response, whether Hanoi really intended to start a dialogue after the resumption. In the meantime, the present facts appear to indicate that Hanoi may have sent the instructions prior to the resumption, but that it should have been possible to send a last-minute "recall" or "cancel" message if Hanoi had desired. Byroade reports that the DRV interpreter came to him to seek the appointment in the "early afternoon" of January 31, Rangoon time. (Rangoon time is 1½ hours earlier than Saigon time.) This would suggest that the appointment was sought not earlier than 1500 Saigon time, whereas the first bombs had fallen at about 0900 Saigon time. The fact that the aide mémoire was still being typed when Byroade arrived at 1930 Rangoon time would suggest that the instructions must have been freshly received and that there may even have been a preliminary instruction to seek an appointment, followed by the later transmission of the detailed instructions. By 1730 Rangoon time (1900 Saigon time) ten hours had elapsed after the resumption (which we assume was instantaneously reported to Hanoi). We believe that Hanoi's communications to Rangoon may go either by direct commercial cable or by relay through Peiping, using some cryptographic system that is presumably immune to Chicom reading. We are now checking whether NSA [National Security Agency] has any reading on message transmissions of that date, but what stands out is that it would surely have been possible for Hanoi to send a fast commercial cable that need not have said anything more than a short instruction not to carry out prior instructions. In other words, the evidence does add up to a high probability that Hanoi was prepared to go through with the contact notwithstanding the resumption. Indeed, there appears to be a substantial possibility on the timing, that Hanoi even waited till it knew of the resumption before it dispatched the instructions. Paradoxical as it may seem, Hanoi may have been unwilling to open any dialogue during the suspension, lest this appear as a sign of weakness, and fear of our bombing.

207. SNIE 10-1-66, "POSSIBLE EFFECTS OF A PROPOSED U.S. COURSE OF ACTION ON DRV CAPABILITY TO SUPPORT THE INSURGENCY IN SOUTH VIETNAM, FEBRUARY 4, 1966 [Extract]

Responding to pressure from the military for an all-out effort to destroy the North's ability to support the South Vietnamese insurgency, the intelligence community examined the impact of a program of bombing all POL facilities, large military facilities and electric power facilities, interdiction of land routes from China, and closing of all DRV ports. The conclusion was that it would limit the

SOURCE: Document declassified by CIA, April 12, 1976.

expansion of the Communist main force units in the South, but that the DRV could still make a greater effort than it had in 1965.

The Problem

To estimate how DRV capabilities to support the insurgency in the South would be affected by increasing the scope and intensity of the bombing of North Vietnam, and how long it would take for the impact to be felt in the South.

Concept of the Courses of Action

The immediate aims of the bombing would be:

1. To destroy those resources already in North Vietnam that contribute most to support of Communist forces in the South;
2. To block external assistance to the DRV;
3. To harass, disrupt, and impede the movement of men and material through the southern DRV into Laos and South Vietnam.

Course A: The enlarged bombing program would include aerial attacks designed to:

1. Destroy all known POL facilities in the northern DRV;
2. Destroy all large military facilities in the northern DRV, except airfield and SAM sites;
3. Interdict the land LOCs from China and close DRV ports by various means including mining;
4. Put and keep electric power facilities out of action;
5. Carry out armed reconnaissance against land and water LOCs and all identified military facilities. South of the 20th parallel, such reconnaissance would be particularly intensive and carried out day and night.

Course B: The program as above, but without closing DRV ports by mining or otherwise.

Note

This estimate considers only how DRV physical capabilities to support the insurgency in South Vietnam would be affected by certain assumed US bombing attacks on North Vietnam; it does not deal with the possible effect of these attacks on DRV *will* to continue the war.

Conclusions

A. The combined impact of destroying in-country stockpiles, restricting import capabilities, and attacking the southward LOCs would greatly complicate the DRV war effort. The cumulative drain on material resources and human energy would be severe. The postulated bombing and interdiction campaign would harass, disrupt, and impede the movement of men and material into South Vietnam and impose great overall difficulty on the DRV. However, we believe that, with a determined effort, the DRV could still move substantially greater amounts than in 1965.

B. However, the cumulative effect of the campaign would almost certainly set a limit to the expansion of PAVN and VC mainforce units and activities in South Vietnam. There are too many uncertainties to permit an estimate of just where that limit would be set.

C. If the main ports were not closed, supply of DRV needs from the outside would be greatly simplified, and the problem of moving goods within the DRV would be eased.

208. AIDE-MÉMOIRE FROM THE U.S. STATE DEPARTMENT TO THE DRV, DELIVERED TO DRV CONSUL GENERAL VU HUU BINH IN RANGOON, FEBRUARY 16, 1966

In reply to a DRV aide-mémoire of January 31, the United States denied that it considered itself "sole judge" of the conditions under which its troops could stay in South Vietnam, suggesting for the first time that it would withdraw them under a negotiated settlement. The United States defined its position in terms of strict compliance with the military terms of the Geneva Accords but did not mention the political provisions of the Accords. When Byroade was received by the DRV consul general in February 16, he was informed that the DRV would not continue the contact due to the resumption of U.S. bombing.

1. The USG has taken note of the Aide Mémoire delivered to the American Ambassador in Rangoon on January 31, 1966.

2. The USG fully respects the basic rights of the Vietnamese people to peace, independence, sovereignty, unity and territorial integrity, as set forth in the Geneva Accords of 1954. As the USG has repeatedly said, it believes that these Accords, together with the 1962 Accords concerning Laos, are an adequate basis for peace in Southeast Asia or for negotiations looking toward a peaceful settlement.

3. The USG has repeatedly stated and hereby reaffirms that it is prepared t withdraw its forces from South Viet-Nam when peace is restored. The US has never stated that it must be the sole judge of when this condition exists. Plainly, the restoration of peace of the Geneva Accords dealing with the regroupment of opposing forces to their respective areas, and dealing with the obligations that the two zones shall not be utilized for the resumption of hostilities or in the service of an aggressive policy. It is the view of the USG that the DRV, in introducing armed forces, military equipment, and political cadres into South Viet-Nam, has breached the provisions of the Accords, and has thus made necessary the actions undertaken

SOURCE: Telegram from Rusk to Byroade, February 16, 1966, in *U.S.-Vietnam Relations*, VI. C. 1, pp. 143–145.

by the USG in support of the legitimate right of the Republic of Viet-Nam to self-defense. The withdrawal of US forces would be undertaken in the light of the actions taken by the DRV in this regard, and would necessarily be subject also the existence of adequate measures of verification.

The USG seeks no military bases of any kind in South Viet-Nam and has no desire whatever to retain its forces in South Viet-Nam after peace is secured.

4. With respect to the third of the DRV's four points, the US takes note that Chairman Ho Chi Minh in his letter of January 29 described the program of the NLF as seeking "to achieve independence, democracy, peace and neutrality in South Viet-Nam and to advance toward peaceful reunification." If this is all that is intended when it is stated that the affairs of the South Vietnamese be settled "in accordance with the program of the NLF," the third point would not be an obstacle to negotiations.

However, it appears that in referring to the program of the NLF the DRV may contemplate that the NLF arbitrarily be accorded integral participation in a coalition government or be accepted as the "sole genuine representative of the entire South Vietnamese people" prior to, and without regard to, an election. If this is what is meant by the think point, we would consider it in contradiction of the very objections specified above, and quite without warrant in the Geneva Accords of 1954.

It remains the essence of the USG view that the future political structure in South Viet-Nam should be determined by the South Vietnamese people themselves through truly free elections. The USG is categorically prepared to accept the results of elections held in an atmosphere free from force, intimidation or outside interference.

5. In the light of the foregoing and to make clear our understanding of a possible basis for discussions leading to a peaceful settlement, we submit for consideration of the DRV the following:

Point I—The basic rights of the Vietnamese people to peace, independence, sovereignty, unity and territorial integrity are recognized as set forth in the Geneva Accords of 1954. Obtaining compliance with the essential principles in the Accords is an appropriate subject for immediate, international discussions, or negotiations without preconditions. Such discussions or negotiations should consider, among other things, appropriate means, including agreed stages, for the withdrawal of military and quasi-military personnel and weapons introduced into South Viet-Nam or North Viet-Nam from one area to the other or into either area from any other outside source; the dismantling of any military bases in either areas, and the cancellation of any military alliances, that may contravene the Accords; and the regrouping and redeployment of indigenous forces.

Point II—Strict compliance with the military provisions of the Geneva Accords must be achieved in accordance with schedules and appropriate safeguards to be agreed upon in the said discussions or negotiations.

Point III—The internal affairs of South and North Viet-Nam must be settled respectively by the South and North Vietnamese peoples themselves in conformity with the principles of self-determination. Neither shall interfere in the affairs of the other nor shall there by any interference from any outside source.

Point IV—The issue of reunification of Viet-Nam must be decided peacefully, on the basis of free determination by the people of South and North Viet-Nam without outside interference.

209. SUMMARY OF A SPEECH BY CHAIRMAN OF THE LAO DONG PARTY REUNIFICATION DEPARTMENT, GEN. NGUYEN VAN VINH AT A COSVN CONGRESS, APRIL 1966 [Extract]

Explaining the Party's strategy on negotiations, a North Vietnamese general discussed frankly the differences between the Vietnamese and their Soviet and Chinese allies: the Soviets were advising the Vietnamese that the time was ripe for a settlement, while the Chinese were advising them that conditions for a settlement would not be present for years. The Vietnamese Party, he said, would enter into negotiations as soon as the situation was ripe, but would continue to fight in order to force the United States to accept its conditions.

Fighting and Negotiating:

The resolution of the Party's 11th conference clearly stated that in the process of achieving success a situation where fighting and negotiations are conducted simultaneously may arise. At present, the situation is not yet ripe for negotiations. Fighting while negotiating is aimed at opening another front with a view to making the puppet army more disintegrated, stimulating and developing the enemy's internal contradictions and thereby making him more isolated in order to deprive him of the propaganda weapons, isolate him further, and make a number of people who misunderstand the Americans clearly see their nature.

In a war between a powerful country which waged aggression and a weak country, as long as we have not yet acquired adequate strength, a situation where fighting and negotiations are conducted simultaneously does not exist. Fighting continues until the emergence of a situation where both sides are fighting indecisively. Then a situation where fighting and negotiations are conducted simultaneously may emerge. In fighting while negotiating, the side which fights more strongly will compel the adversary to accept its conditions. Considering the comparative balance of forces, the war proceeds through the following stages:

—The fighting stage.
—The stage of fighting while negotiating.
—Negotiations and signing of agreements.

Whether or not the war will resume after the conclusion of agreements depends upon the comparative balance of forces. If we are capable of dominating the

SOURCE: Captured document, in U.S. Department of State, *Working Paper on the North Vietnamese Role in the War in South Viet-nam,* mimeographed, 1968, Annex D, Document No. 303.

adversary, the war will not break out again, and conversely. Therefore, fighting while negotiating also represents a principal step in the evolution of the war. Thus, a situation where fighting and negotiations are conducted simultaneously will un-mistakably emerge. In our anti-French resistance, there were also times when fighting and negotiations were conducted simultaneously. The same situation emerged in China.

At present, there are [different] viewpoints with regard to war and peace.

—The Americans find it necessary to negotiate, but negotiate from a strong position, partly because they have deceitful motives, and partly because the situa-tion has compelled them to negotiate. Yet, they want us to make concessions to them.

—A number of countries want us to enter into negotiations, any form of negotiations—so that a big war does not break out and that the war can be ended—regardless of the interests of Vietnam. Some other countries wonder whether we can defeat the Americans, and if not, [they think] we should enter into negotia-tions. (Most of these countries are nationalist countries in Asia, Africa, and Latin America.) A number of East European socialist countries hold the view that [proper] conditions [for negotiations] do prevail, and are ripe for achieving success. (The Americans would withdraw their troops, and we will continue the struggle to achieve total success.) These socialist countries also pose a number of conditions: cessation of the bombing of the North; gradual withdrawal of U.S. troops from the South.

—China holds the view that conditions for negotiations are not yet ripe, [and will] not [be] until a few years from now, and, even worse, seven years from now. In the meantime, we should continue fighting to bog down the enemy, and should wait until a number of socialist countries acquire adequate conditions for strength-ening their main force troops to launch a strong, all-out, and rapid offensive, using all types of weapons and heeding no borders. What we should do in the South today is to try restraining the enemy and make him bogged down, waiting until China has built strong forces to launch an all-out offensive.

—Our policy: to continue fighting until a certain time when we can fight and negotiate at the same time.

This is also a fighting method: repulsing the enemy step by step, and achieving decisive success.

The Party Central Committee entrusts the Politburo with the task of deciding on the time for negotiations.

210. TELEGRAM FROM RUSK TO LODGE, APRIL 5, 1966

After Danang was taken over by a Buddhist-oriented "struggle movement" against the military directorate, the United States urged Ky to do something to reestablish order in central Vietnam. On April 4, U.S. transport planes flew four

---

SOURCE: Document from the Lyndon Baines Johnson Library.

battalions of Ky's troops to Danang, but local troops continued to support the "struggle movement," and Ky began to back away from a military clash. The following day, Rusk urged Lodge to have the Embassy play a more active role in bringing a solution to the political crisis, suggesting that CIA "assets" could be used to persuade various political groups to support such a solution. Lodge was urged to persuade the militant Buddhists not to press for "unrealistic demands" for quick elections for a national assembly. But on April 6 Premier Nguyen Cao Ky offered elections for a national assembly within six months—a much faster timetable than the Embassy had wanted.

Following suggestions have arisen in high-level discussions today of situation:

1. In general, we believe present circumstances call for USG taking more active role in political discussions in every way possible. Whether or not current GVN effort in Da Nang produces local solution, crisis has clearly come to a head and some political answer must be found as quickly and peacefully as possible. Fact that we have now contributed aircraft for Da Nang effort both gives US some added leverage with GVN and, from public standpoint here and elsewhere, likely to create strong reaction to our acting to support use of force if we are not also working on political solution. We have tried in press handling today to counter latter impression, so far as possible, but we believe attacks along these lines could build up to serious point.

2. To this end, and of course subject to your tactical judgment, we urge substantially more contact with GVN and with opposing and other political elements than has hitherto seemed wise either to you or to us. We believe time has come for maximum use of your own great personal prestige both with GVN and with other key leaders. On Buddhist side, we see the force of objections to your personally seeing Tri Quang, but if Thieu and Ky understood what you were doing believe you could do so to convey message along lines our previous cable and to seek to hasten settlement of issues with or without his agreement. Alternatively, Negroponte could do it more quietly at least to have essential contact with him. In any event, every effort should be made with such Buddhist leaders as Minh to persuade them that present situation represents grave danger of simply handing over country to VC and that they must cease to insist on unrealistic demands.

3. Obviously, key GVN move would be immediate convening of leaders council. We are disheartened by Chieu's statement of difficulty of getting groups to participate, and hope that GVN will place immediate convening of some kind of council ahead of any effort to have its composition absolutely perfect and balanced at outset. (Others could be brought in later). Close contact with GVN might produce ways in which USG assets could be used to persuade key groups that their participation at this time is absolutely vital to preserving government structure. Even if USG Role in this direction becomes well known, we believe it would be entirely defensible and indeed advantageous both in itself and in terms of public opinion here and elsewhere.

4. Another immediate issue is key important of Thi personally and getting prompt solution to his future. Here again question arises whether USG contact and persuasion might be helpful. We know Wilson and others have good tie, and there are other less visible possibilities we are suggesting through CAS channels. Despite

Chieu's denial that any offer of position to Thi was made by him, our own supposition would be that this was objective of Chieu mission and that we need to find out more about what GVN dealings with Thi have been, if not from GVN then from Thi himself. In any case we believe early contact would be useful.

5. Above comments assume present government can survive. Septel contains our thoughts on possible alternatives.

211. TELEGRAM FROM LODGE TO RUSK, JUNE 29, 1966 [Extract]

The Polish ICC Representative, Janusz Lewandowski, returned to Saigon from a visit to Hanoi with a "very specific" North Vietnamese peace offer, which was conveyed to Lodge through Italian Ambassador in Saigon Giovanni D'Orlandi. The proposal was to focus on a "political compromise" to settle the war, rather than on a mutual deescalation. The Polish representative indicated that Hanoi wished to explore Washington's proposals for such a compromise through Moscow rather than directly, suggesting that exchanges had to be kept secret from Peking. This was the beginning of a set of exchanges that were given the code name "Marigold."

9. The Pole began by saying that Hanoi has been deeply disappointed by the proposals made by Ronning which, they are sure, had emanated originally from the United States and not from the Canadians. Ronning had proposed that the U.S. stop the bombing if North Viet-Nam stopped the infiltration, and had talked about the exchange of prisoners' parcels and letters. This had bitterly disappointed North Vietnam. The first point, they had said, would be unconditional surrender, and they could not accept it, but they are open to a "political compromise" settling once and for all the entire Viet-Nam question.

10. When D'Orlandi said that he was skeptical, the Pole said that Hanoi was prepared to go "quite a long way." "It is useless for me to add," said the Pole, "that should there not be any kind of a preliminary agreement, Hanoi will deny flatly ever having made any offer." According to the Pole, the North Vietnamese are "tightly controlled" by the Chinese Communists. The preliminary talks, therefore, should be between Moscow and Washington. When and if proposals should emerge which could be considered as a basis for negotiations, Hanoi would at that time and under those circumstances get into it. The Pole said that Hanoi was afraid of the Chinese Communists who have an interest in dragging on the war for many years. D'Orlandi added that the Pole was evidently "proud of himself" for having brought these proposals about.

11. The proposals are as follows:

A. They insist that the so-called National Liberation Front "take part" in the negotiations. The key word is "take part." According to D'Orlandi, there is "no question of their being the representative; they are not to have any monopoly."

SOURCE: *U.S.-Vietnam Relations*, VI. C. 2, pp. 24–26.

B. There must be suspension of the bombing.

12. These are the two proposals.

13. Then there are other points, which D'Orlandi called "negative ones," which are that (a) Hanoi will not ask for immediate reunification, either by elections or otherwise, of North and South Vietnam; (b) They will not ask for establishment of a "socialist" system in South Viet-Nam; (c) They will not ask South Viet-Nam to change the relationships which it has in the field of foreign affairs; and (d) They will not ask for neutralization. (e) Although they will ask for U.S. withdrawal, they are ready to discuss a "reasonable calendar." (f) Although "we would like someone other than Ky"—to quote the words of Hanoi—they do not want to interfere with the South Vietnamese Government.

* * *

18. The Pole said that his Government would be willing to arrange for D'Orlandi to meet with appropriate Polish spokesmen anywhere—Hong Kong or Singapore. In response to a question by D'Orlandi as to why they had come to him, the Pole said they wanted "an able debater to put the case to President Johnson, and we feel that the Italian Government has the sympathy of the United States Government." Moreover, the Italians have the same interest we have in agreement between Washington and Moscow, and in shutting out Peking.

19. D'Orlandi's impression is that the Poles are desperately seeking a way out on Moscow's instructions. This, he said, may need further exploration. He had the definite impression that now Hanoi "was amenable to common sense" saying "they do not want anything that would not stop the whole war. They want a political settlement, and are prepared to go a long way."

212. TELEGRAM FROM LODGE TO RUSK, NOVEMBER 30, 1966

After the U.S. bombing of oil depots near Hanoi and Haiphong on June 29 and 30, Hanoi was evacuated, and Ho Chi Minh declared negotiations with the United States "out of the question." The Marigold channel was suspended. But in mid-November, Lewandowski attempted to put in summary form a U.S. position on negotiations that would serve as the basis for secret talks, saying his proposal was based on conversations with Prime Minister Pham Van Dong. He urged the United States to contact the North Vietnamese ambassador at once if it accepted the document, suggesting that there were officials who were opposed to talks with the United States.

Lewandowski summarized the ten points to Lodge as follows:

(1) The U.S. is interested in a peaceful solution through negotiations.

(2) Negotiations should not be interpreted as a way to negotiated surrender by those opposing the U.S. in Vietnam. A political negotiation would be aimed at

SOURCE: *U.S.-Vietnam Relations,* VI. C. 4, pp. 73–74.

finding an acceptable solution to all the problems, having in mind that the present status quo in SVN must be changed in order to take into account the interests of the parties presently opposing the policy of the U.S. in South Vietnam.

(3) The U.S. does not desire a permanent or a long-term military presence in SVN.

(4) The U.S. is willing to discuss all problems with respect to the settlement.

(5) The U.S. is willing to accept the participation of "all" in elections and the supervision of these elections by an appropriate international body.

(6) The U.S. believes that reunification should be settled by the Vietnamese themselves after peace and proper representative organs are established in SVN.

(7) The U.S. is prepared to abide by a neutral South Vietnam.

(8) The U.S. is prepared to stop bombing "if this will facilitate such a peaceful solution." In this regard the U.S. is prepared to accept DRV modalities on the cessation and not require the DRV to admit infiltration into SVN.

(9) The U.S. will not agree to "reunification under military pressure."

(10) The U.S. "will not declare now or in the future its acceptance of North Vietnam's 4 or 5 points."

Lewandowski asked if these 10 points were a proper formulation of the U.S. position. Lodge said that they seemed to be in order, but that the matter was of such sensitivity and importance that he would have to refer the points back to Washington for approval. Lodge added, however, that he saw two difficulties right off. First, he suggested changing Point 2 to read "would" instead of "must." Second, he questioned the phraseology in Point—"if this would facilitate such a peaceful solution."

Lewandowski insisted that his statement was a serious proposition based on conversations with the "most respectable government sources in Hanoi." Later Lewandowski admitted that Pham Van Dong was the source and that he had the "Presidium behind him."

Lewandowski stated: "I am authorized to say that if the U.S. are really of the views which I have presented, it would be advisable to confirm them directl by conversation with the North Vietnamese Ambassador in Warsaw."

Lewandowski said that there was a vital need to move quickly because (1) there was a danger of a leak and that secrecy was essential for Hanoi; and (2) that delays would give those "working against a solution" time to "put down the clamps on talks."

213. TELEGRAM FROM RUSK TO LODGE, DECEMBER 2, 1966

Lodge was instructed to tell Lewandowski that the United States was ready to meet with a North Vietnamese representative in Warsaw, but the Lewandowski ten-point document was said to be subject to "important differences of interpretation" on several points.

SOURCE: Document declassified by Department of State, July 18, 1978.

You may tell Lewandowski that we are instructing our Embassy in Warsaw to contact North Vietnamese representative there on December 6. (This date will give time for Hanoi to instruct their Ambassador if they have not already done so.) Embassy Officer will be able to confirm that the ten points outlined by Lewandowski broadly represent our position. Officer will have to say, however, that several specific points are subject to important differences of interpretation. If North Vietnamese Representative is prepared to engage in a discussion we will then arrange to brief appropriate officer in order that he may be able to explain directly our position.

Does your para. Q reporting Lewandowski's statement that Moscow has been informed mean Soviet Government has been advised?

214. TELEGRAM FROM LODGE TO ACTING SECRETARY OF STATE NICHOLAS DE B. KATZENBACH, DECEMBER 9, 1966

On December 2, the same day that Lodge told Lewandowski that the United States was willing to meet the North Vietnamese in Warsaw, U.S. fighter bombers hit targets only five miles from the center of Hanoi. Similar raids were carried out in the Hanoi area on December 4. On December 8, after an earlier warning by the Polish Foreign Minister in Warsaw that Hanoi would have to reconsider the Warsaw contact in light of the new bombing, Lewandowski told D'Orlandi that he believed Hanoi would not enter into direct discussions. In passing on the Lewandowski message to Rusk, D'Orlandi said he thought Lewandowski had personally persuaded Pham Van Dong to overcome objections in the North Vietnamese leadership to the direct contact with the United States.

D'Orlandi asked to see Secretary and Ambassador this evening following dinner party in Secretary's honor. Conversation was as follows:

1. Lewandowski had called urgently on D'Orlandi evening of December 8, on instructions, to express grave concern that U.S. had carried out heavy bombing attacks in Hanoi area on December 2 and December 4, directly following December 1 conversation between Lewandowski and Lodge. Lewandowski conveyed lurid reports from Polish attache Hanoi alleging that December 2 attack had included bombing and machine-gunning within city area and had caused 600 casualties. December 4 attack also described as serious and in Hanoi area. Lewandowski protested to D'Orlandi—urging him to convey message to Lodge and to Secretary if possible—that such attacks could only threaten or destroy possibility of contact in Warsaw. Lewandowski argued that Hanoi could not be expected to enter discussions in face of such escalation. (While whole tenor of message was extremely strong, Lewandowski did not repeat not state that he was actually reporting Hanoi's expressions of view, but rather Warsaw judgment.)

SOURCE: *U.S.-Vietnam Relations*, VI. C. 4, pp. 77–79.

2. D'Orlandi had responded to Lewandowski that no contact had in fact taken place as yet because of apparent refusal of Rapacki to convey firm message, that U.S. had taken forthcoming action in declaring itself ready for discussions and prepared to make contact on December 6, and that it was thus not fair to say possibility of contact destroyed by U.S. action. D'Orlandi went on to say that his hope had been to make contact in any event.

215. TELEGRAM FROM KATZENBACH TO AMBASSADOR JOHN A. GRONOUSKI IN WARSAW, DECEMBER 10, 1966

Still anticipating a possible secret meeting with Hanoi representatives, the State Department informed Ambassador Gronouski that the United States "did not wish to withdraw authorization" for bombing which might be interpreted by the Poles (and the North Vietnamese) as further escalation of the war.

1. Appreciate effective way you have handled Rapacki's arguments. Hope that he will now in fact transmit to Hanoi specific proposal for direct US-NVN meeting or, if he has already done this, will urge Hanoi to agree to meeting. We surmise that Rapacki's involved argumentation and accusations were aimed at getting us to withdraw all reservations and state unequivocally that our position is precisely as Lewandowski told Lodge he had transmitted it to Hanoi. We would be interested in your opinion as to what is the state of the dialogue between the Polish and North Vietnamese Governments.

2. If Poles take up "reservations" point again suggest you follow again your line of argumentation reported Reftel A. It is to be expected that in actual negotiations we and Hanoi would have to "hammer out greater precision" (as Rapacki said himself) on how to implement the points involved and that in this process some differences would be revealed which we would surely be using our best endeavors to resolve—this course takes two to accomplish.

3. We concur in your reserving para 2 of State 98924 from your conversation with Rapacki but urge you to keep it in mind for us if there is further backsliding on part of Poles.

4. FYI only (rpt. FYI only). You should be aware that for the immediate future the bombing pattern will remain unchanged from what it has been over the past several weeks. This may well involve some targets which Rapacki will insist represent further escalation, just as in the past he took to be escalation certain variations in our bombing pattern which in fact represented no real new departures in the pattern as a whole. With foregoing in mind you should avoid giving Poles even any slight indications which they might take to mean that we are escalating or de-escalating at present. Present bombing pattern has been authorized for some time and we do not wish to withdraw this authorization at this time.

5. If direct meeting is arranged you should handle it in accordance with instructions already conveyed in State tels.

SOURCE: Document declassified by Department of State, July 18, 1978.

216. TELEGRAM FROM GRONOUSKI TO KATZENBACH, DECEMBER 15, 1966

Rapacki informed Gronouski that the Warsaw meeting had been delayed because of Lodge's interpretation clause and the U.S. bombing of a Hanoi suburb. On December 13 and 14, U.S. fighter bombers attacked the Yen Vien railroad yard and Van Dien vehicle depot two miles from the Hanoi city limits. Hanoi, Moscow, and Peking news media charged that the U.S. had bombed within the city, reporting damage and casualties in a residential area and the diplomatic area of the city. The State Department denied any bombing within the city. In Warsaw on December 15, Rapacki said this bombing had prompted Hanoi to terminate the contact through Poland. Gronouski, reporting his meeting with Rapacki to State, called for an assurance that the United States would not bomb in the immediate vicinity of Hanoi and Haiphong while trying to get the talks back on the track.

1. I met with Rapacki (Michalowski and Janczewski present) at Poles' request at 1800 Dec 14. (In contrast to previous meetings, Rapacki entered the room unsmiling, and during entire meeting maintained a calm, serious and matter-of-fact attitude)

2. Rapacki said that first he would like to bring some precision with respect to our conversation of yesterday (Warsaw 1458). He said that this conversation took place before Poles were aware of last bombing of Hanoi. He said, "If I had had this news then, our conversation of course would have had different character than it did."

3. Rapacki continued, "Today I must state the following facts. First, that the U.S. had to be conscious of and realize the importance of establishing direct contact with Hanoi." He added, "You have stressed the unique possibility of a peaceful settlement that the Warsaw talks with Hanoi presented." He continued, "We thought so too, ever since we obtained the signal for which the USG had asked for for so long in so many official statements." He added, "In this instance we received more than a signal; we received a direct, positive response from Hanoi about the possibility of talks in Warsaw."

4. Rapacki said that immediately after this direct response was transmitted to the USG the US reserved the possibility of modifying their attitude and, of far greater importance, entered a new stage of escalation.

5. Rapacki continued that the USG was bound to be conscious of the reaction which its conduct would evoke and of the consequences of such action. He added that the Poles have done everything in their power to dispel any illusions, noting that on six occasions in Warsaw and Saigon, "We have warned the USG side in all seriousness and with the greatest emphasis of the consequences of their actions."

6. "Yesterday," Rapacki continued, "The US Air Force engaged in a new and particularly brutal raid on the residential area in Hanoi precisely at the moment when the USG knew that the matter of a Warsaw contact with Hanoi was actively being considered. This," he added, "was the last drop that spilled over the cup. From that moment, in Hanoi and Warsaw, all doubts as to the real intentions of the

SOURCE: *U.S.-Vietnam Relations*, VI. C. 4, pp. 89–91.

USG disappeared, including doubts not only in the present case but with respect to all other instances in the past when the US has advanced positions which it has described as peaceful initatives."

7. Rapacki then said, "We understand therefore and fully share the wish of the Democratic Republic of North Vietnam, which was transmitted to us today, that we terminate all conversations begun months ago in Saigon. The Polish Govt states that the whole responsibility for losing this chance of a peaceful solution to the Vietnam war rests on the USG." He added, "I would like to express more than regrets because of the utilization by the USG of our good will. Once again it becomes clear how difficult it is to believe in your words." He added, "In future only facts can be taken into consideration."

8. I said that I would have no comment except to say that I regretted this turn of events and would immediately convey these observations to Washington.

9. Comment: If Moscow dateline account of latest Hanoi bombing published in Dec 14 Paris edition of New York Times and Herald Tribune, and recounted to me tonight by Rapacki, is true then we are in an incredibly difficult position. I am convinced that if this represents the breakdown of the current peace initiative—and it surely does unless we take decisive and immediate action—then the Soviets, the Poles and the North Vietnamese will have no trouble convincing the leadership in every capital of the world that our stated desire for peace negotiations is insincere. If we treat this turn of events as anything less than a crisis in our world leadership role than I believe we are making a tragic mistake.

10. I am convinced that up till now the Poles, accepting the genuineness of our interest in negotiation, have used whatever influence they have in Hanoi (in all likelihood with Soviet backing) in an effort to initiate US-NVN peace talks. I also am convinced that Rapacki was expressing genuine concern when he warned that the increase in bombing was destroying what appeared to him a good chance that NVN would overcome Chinese influence and engage in Warsaw talks.

11. We have no choice but to take immediate action to try to get discussions back on track. For any chance of success this would require, in my judgment, conveying to Poles that we are willing to accept Rapacki's Dec 13 reasoning (Warsaw 1458) and are prepared now to assure the Poles that we will take care not to create impression of bombing intensification in NVN during the period of delicate negotiations over the holding of Warsaw USG-NVN peace talks. We would also assure the Poles that we do not intend to bomb in the immediate vicinity of Hanoi and Haiphong during this period. We would again express our deep desire for the initiation of talks and ask the Poles to continue their efforts.

217. TELEGRAM FROM KATZENBACH TO GRONOUSKI, DECEMBER 15, 1966 [Extract]

In its response to Rapacki, State expressed its belief that Rapacki was merely trying to get maximum concessions from the United States and its doubt that the North Vietnamese had been seriously involved in Rapacki's communications with

SOURCE: Document declassified by Department of State, July 18, 1978.

*the United States. State instructed Gronouski to remind Rapacki that there was no
understanding with Hanoi involving U.S. bombing and argued that the best chance
of getting the contact with Hanoi was to "maintain and strongly defend our position" on the bombing. But the same day orders went out to CINCPAC to suspend
air strikes against targets hit December 13 and 14 "until further notice." The
United States then offered to create a ten-mile "sanctuary" around Hanoi. But
it was too late. The DRV terminated the "Marigold" exchanges for good on
December 30.*

8. Your further interpretation and discussion contained Warsaw's 1475 is
very much appreciated and I am sure you fully realize that all of us here profoundly
share your concern over the turn events have taken in the last few days. Likewise I
can well imagine that in the atmosphere of Warsaw and without full information
available, particularly concerning the bombing of North Viet-Nam the Polish position may appear to be a strong one, whatever their motivation presenting it as
Rapacki has just done. We want to assure you, however, that on the basis of the
over-all picture as we can see it from Washington, the Polish case, except for some
fairly superficial and transitory matters, is a weak one and we wonder whether they
will try to sell it to world opinion. We still believe that the Poles basically wish to
work for a peaceful settlement and we think it more likely that Rapacki's present
ploy is an opportunistic one, seizing the chance presented by the sensational publicity given to recent bombings in the Hanoi area (undoubtedly fed by the North
Vietnamese) in order to extract one more ounce. As noted above we will be
providing you today with everything we can on the objective facts on bombing as
well as the information on terrorism promised earlier.

9. Rapacki's last representations to you probably brings us to the crisis phase
in our current efforts and we believe we will have the best chance of securing a
resolution in our favor, i.e. by Hanoi's being ready to undertake talks on the basis
worked out with Lewandowski, if we maintain and strongly defend our position
and rebut and reject the line which Rapacki is trying to sell. We are counting on you
in this most challenging assignment.

1967

218. MESSAGE FROM PRESIDENT
JOHNSON TO BRITISH PRIME MINISTER
HAROLD WILSON, FEBRUARY 7, 1967

*During British Prime Minister Harold Wilson's talks with Soviet Premier
Alexei Kosygin in London, President Johnson conveyed directly to Wilson the*

SOURCE: Telegram from Rusk to Ambassador David Bruce and White House Assistant Chester Cooper in London, *U.S.-Vietnam Relations*, VI. C. 3, pp. 61–63.

*American account of the Marigold contact and the American two-phase proposal
for a bomb halt and mutual deescalation. He told Wilson the United States wanted
an "assured stoppage" of infiltration in return for the end of the bombing and
further augmentation of U.S. forces in South Vietnam. The term* assured *turned out
later to have a meaning that was not apparent at the time.*

I am sending these thoughts to you on the question posed as to whether the
U.S. could stop the bombing of North Vietnam in exchange for an indication that
Hanoi would enter into talks without any military acts of de-escalation on their
side.

It is important to recall that the Poles said to us in the first part of December
that Hanoi would be prepared to hold discussions with us on the basis of a Polish
summary of what the Poles understood our position to be. Discussion of mutual
de-escalation, including a cessation of the bombing, would be a part of those talks.
We promptly agreed to such talks but found that Hanoi (so the Poles told us) was
unwilling to proceed with such talks because of certain bombing action which
occurred on 13–14 December. Although we had seen no real move toward talks
before that date, we nevertheless removed that obstacle (if that was the obstacle) by
informing Hanoi that we were refraining from bombing within a radius of 10 nautical
miles of the center of Hanoi—restrictions which have been in effect for more than a
month. We took this action without conditions but did state that we would be
impressed by any corresponding action by Hanoi. This was an important military
move on our part. We have seen neither a corresponding military step on their side
nor a use of existing channels to get on with discussions. In contacts with Hanoi
since December 23 Hanoi has received messages from us but we have not had any
replies from Hanoi on any points of substance. Indeed, the Burchett interview
represents a step backward from Hanoi's position in December if the Poles were
accurately reporting to us.

We have recently informed Hanoi directly that we would be prepared to take
additional military measures of de-escalation similar to the limitation of bombing
within the Hanoi perimeter, on similar terms. We have had no reply to that suggestion.

We are ready and willing to hold discussion with Hanoi through any feasible
process—publicly or privately, directly or indirectly. We are inclined to the view
that better progress could be made if such talks were private and direct.

If we are asked to take military action on our side, we need to know what the
military consequences will be, that is, what military action will be taken by the
other side. We have noted that a suspension of the bombing has been termed by the
other side as unacceptable and that we must accept an unconditional and permanent
cessation of bombing. That makes it all the more necessary to know what military
action Hanoi would take if we in fact stopped the bombing.

We are prepared to take up with Hanoi steps of mutual de-escalation and are
prepared to have the most private preliminary conversations with them on arrangements for serious discussions of a final settlement.

Specifically, we are prepared to and plan, through established channels, to
inform Hanoi that if they will agree to an assured stoppage of infiltration into
South Vietnam, we will stop the bombing of North Vietnam and stop further
augmentation of U.S. forces in South Vietnam. We would welcome your joint
advocacy of this position.

Further, or alternatively, you should know we would recommend to the South Vietnamese military authorities that they discuss with North Vietnamese military authorities a prolongation of the Tet ceasefire.

For your own information, you should be aware of my feeling that, in all of our various contacts with Hanoi, we have had no impression from them as to the substance of the issues which must be resolved as a part of a peaceful settlement. They have received repeated statements from us about our [*illegible*]. They have reiterated their four points and the Liberation Front's five points with varying degree of vagueness as to their status, but they have not replied to our suggestions for a revision of point three of their four points or a readiness to hold preliminary discussions looking toward agreed points as a basis for negotiations.

In sum, I would suggest that you try to separate the political processes of discussion from military action. We will participate fully in any political process including discussions of de-escalation. We are prepared to move immediately on major steps of mutual de-escalation, as indicated above. What we cannot accept is the exchange of guarantee of a safe haven for North Vietnam merely for discussions which thus far have no form or content, during which they could continue to expand their military operations without limit.

I doubt very much that Kosygin expected to resolve this matter on his first evening in London and it would be helpful if you could fully explore just what Kosygin is willing or able to do. If he has counter-proposals to my major suggestion of mutual military de-escalation, we will give them immediate attention.

If Kosygin is seriously worried about China, as he told you he was, we would hope that he would exert himself to help bring peace to Vietnam and allow North Vietnam to participate in the peaceful development of Southeast Asia.

Finally, I would strongly urge that the two co-chairmen not suggest a stoppage of the bombing in exchange merely for talks, but, instead, appeal to Hanoi to consider seriously the reasonable proposals we are putting before them, which would take us not merely into negotiation but a long step towards peace itself.

219. TELEGRAM FROM RUSK TO WHITE HOUSE ASSISTANT CHESTER COOPER, FEBRUARY 9, 1967

Wilson read Kosygin a draft public announcement by the Geneva cochairmen incorporating a version of the U.S. phase A-phase B formula. In response to this draft, Rusk noted that the British had revised the U.S. formula to propose that both sides stop "augmentation of forces" after a bombing halt, and asked that the British text reflect the original U.S. insistence on total cessation of North Vietnamese infiltration—but not of introduction of U.S. troops—into South Vietnam.

1. We understand that at this morning's session Wilson or Brown probed Kosygin whether his remarks on possible role of co-chairmen had any significance and obtained strong impression that they were intended to have. We understand

SOURCE: Document declassified by Department of State, May 3, 1978.

further that, based on this, British went ahead to read orally from draft public announcement along lines para 4, London 6399. In response to Kosygin inquiry, British said this formula did not have USG approval. Kosygin finally asked for British text. Although he did not refer to having USG acceptance of such text, we can only suppose that this was the underlying implication.

2. As we believe we have made clear to you, we have major doubts whether, if Hanoi in fact accepts the deal we have proposed, they will ask to have it nailed down in public through any announcement, and might have additional misgivings about the Soviets doing so in the light of whatever degree of concern they still have about Chicom reactions. We would suppose the latter factor would also operate strongly on the Soviets, since any public announcement would carry the unmistakeable flavor that the Soviets had colluded with the US, through the UK, to put this deal across. In other words, you should impress on the British that while it may be possible to get Hanoi to accept our proposal, it by no means follows that they or the Soviets would wish a public announcement. We are inclined to interpret Soviet response as indicating a desire to see the US proposal spelled out clearly and in writing, which they could then use with Hanoi but in all probability later drawing back on the idea of a public announcement. British should be left in no doubt that, while we are most grateful for their serious considered efforts, they may well have to accept results rather than overt British participation in them.

3. With this evaluation in mind, we have reviewed text in para 4 of London 6399 and note that, like the British oral formula (London 6329, para 5), it speaks only of DRV stopping "augmentation of forces" in South Vietnam. This would leave way open for DRV to continue to send equipment without restrictions and also to send forces in the guise of rotation. Moreover, there would be no restraint whatsoever on political cadre and others who could be described as not technically uniformed "forces." In light of these objections, any specific formula along these lines which the British might put forward would have to be amended along following lines:

QTE.   The two cochairmen will announce immediately that they:
a. Invite the US to assure them that the bombing of North Vietnam will stop:
b. Invite the North Vietnamese to assure the cochairmen that infiltration into South Vietnam will stop, and invite the US to assure the cochairmen that it will stop further augmentation of US forces in South Vietnam. (FYI: These are the operative parts both of our own message to the British (State 132481) and of our message to Hanoi. End FYI).
c. If all the foregoing assurances are promptly received, the two cochairmen will invite members of the 1954 Geneva Conference to reconvene in Geneva on 15 February to work out a settlement of the present conflict. END QTE.

4. British should know further that while we have left subpara c of this text unchanged, recognizing that cochairmen status pertains to Geneva conference grouping, they must be as aware as we that Soviets and even Hanoi may have grave reservations about presence of Communist China at any conference. Moreover, we should leave British in no doubt that we might have to press strongly, if and when any multilateral grouping is convened, for inclusion of other appropriate nations

who were not at Geneva in 1954. We do of course recognize that under present circumstances Chinese might not attend, but nonetheless we suppose Soviets or Hanoi may still be sensitive to their being included in the grouping. With these factors in mind, we wonder whether British might not find some more general language more realistic and more appealing to Soviet, referring perhaps to inviting "appropriate nations." While cochairmen mandate might be strictly construed to permit only reconvening of Geneva Conference, we believe broader interpretation could be sustained that cochairmen have mandate to take any action that could lead to peace and involve discussion of the 1954 and 1962 Geneva Accords as the basis for settlement.

5. Seeing as we do these possibly serious difficulties with a precise formulation of the deal—and doubting, as we do, that Hanoi will wish a really specific public announcement—you should tell British that we ourselves would be much more inclined to have them table the general Phase A/Phase B formula.

6. As foregoing makes clear, we gravely doubt that Soviets really envisage any public announcement or that Hanoi would wish it. The main point is the British should leave Soviets in no doubt of essential elements of our proposal. In fact, we have one final and serious worry that the Soviets and Hanoi might interpret British suggestions of a public announcement as indicating that we ourselves visualize the deal being handled in this public way. You should make clear to the British, and they in turn must make clear to the Soviets, that while the British do understand that either of the above formulations reflect the US position accurately, the US has by no means urged a public statement unless the Soviets can completely ascertain that such a public statement is acceptable to Hanoi. We have always been very sensitive to Hanoi's desire that the stoppage of the bombing be ostensibly unilateral, and this fundamental reason for the whole Phase A/Phase B line of thought would be destroyed by a public statement in the only form in which we could accept it.

220. TELEGRAM FROM RUSK TO LODGE, FEBRUARY 10, 1967 [Extract]

At the afternoon session on February 9, Wilson read Kosygin the U.S. phase A-phase B formula again, and this time Kosygin asked that it be put in writing for him. That evening White House aide Chester Cooper cabled a version of the formula to Washington after working it out with officials of the British Foreign Office. However, the version which was approved by President Johnson for Wilson to give to Kosygin reversed the sequence of the two phases that had been proposed previously. Now the Vietnamese were expected to assure the United States that the infiltration from North Vietnam had already stopped before the United States would stop the bombing. As the State Department's telegram to Saigon on the document makes clear, the Administration believed that the Communist forces would be "significantly weakened" by acceptance of the proposal.

2. We have provided British with text of proposal. They had already outlined a variation of it orally to Kosygin, who expressed interest today and asked for

written text to forward at once to Hanoi. This has been provided and reads as below. You may convey to Ky orally as much of digest of proposal as you deem wise in view of great necessity for secrecy.

QTE A. The United States will order a cessation of bombing of North Vietnam as soon as they are assured that infiltration from North Vietnam to South Vietnam has stopped. This assurance can be communicated in secret if North Vietnam so wishes.

B. Within a few days (with a period to be agreed with the two sides before the bombing stops) the United States will stop further augmenting their force in South Vietnam. The cessation of bombing of North Vietnam is an action which will be immediately apparent. This requires that the stoppage of infiltration become public very quickly thereafter. If Hanoi is unwilling to announce the stoppage of infiltration, the United States must do so at the time its stops augmentation of US forces. In that case, Hanoi must not deny it.

C. Any assurances from Hanoi can reach the United States direct, or through Soviet channels, or through the Soviet and British Governments. This is for North Vietnam to decide. END QUOTE.

3. In explaining about text, we believe British will have made clear that our stopping "augmenting" would still permit rotation and continued supply. Stoppage of infiltration defined as meaning that men and arms cannot move from DRV into South Vietnam. You should note also that wording of subpara A preclude any sudden last-minute reinforcements after bombing has stopped. . . .

4. . . . Deprived of additional men and of urgently needed equipment from the North, we believe NVA/VC forces would be significantly weakened in concrete terms and would probably suffer serious adverse effects on their morale. If infiltration in fact ceases and this word can be picked up by SVN and allied psychological warfare units, we believe there are big chances that Chieu Hoi and reconciliation programs would produce substantially larger returns. In short, we think proposal is defensible and forthcoming, if it should ever be surfaced, but at the same time clearly favorable in terms of its effect on the military and morale situation. . . .

221. INTELLIGENCE MEMORANDUM BY THE DIRECTORATE OF INTELLIGENCE, CIA, MAY 12, 1967 [Extract]

The CIA examined the damage inflicted on North Vietnam by U.S. bombing and found that North Vietnam had a high capability to recover from the attacks by a combination of increased imports, dispersal, and fast repair.

Summary

Through the end of April 1967 the US air campaign against North Vietnam—Rolling Thunder—had significantly eroded the capacities of North Vietnam's limited industrial and military base. These losses, however, have not meaningfully degraded North Vietnam's material ability to continue the war in South Vietnam.

SOURCE: Document declassified by the CIA.

Total damage through April 1967 was over $233 million, of which 70 percent was accounted for by damage to economic targets. The greatest amount of damage was inflicted on the so-called logistics target system—transport equipment and lines of communication.

By the end of April 1967 the US air campaign had attacked 173 fixed targets, over 70 percent of the targets on the JCS list. This campaign included extensive attacks on almost every major target system in the country. The physical results have varied widely.

All of the 13 targeted petroleum storage facilities have been attacked, with an estimated loss of 85 percent of storage capacity. Attacks on 13 of the 20 targeted electric power facilities have neutralized 70 percent of North Vietnam's power-generating capacity. The major losses in the military establishment include the neutralization of 18 ammunition depots, with a loss capacity of 70 percent. Over three fourths of the 65 JCS-targeted barracks have been attacked, with a loss of about one fourth of national capacity. Attacks on 22 of 29 targeted supply depots reduced capacity by 17 percent. Through the end of April 1967, five of North Vietnam's airfields had been attacked, with a loss of about 20 percent of national capacity.

North Vietnam's ability to recuperate from the air attacks has been of a high order. The major exception has been the electric power industry. One small plant—Co Dinh—is beyond repair. Most of the other plants would require 3–4 months to be restored to partial operations, although two plants—Haiphong East and Uong Bi—would require one year. For complete restoration, all of the plants would require at least a year. Restoration of these plants would require foreign technical assistance and equipment.

The recuperability problem is not significant for the other target systems. The destroyed petroleum storage system has been replaced by an effective system of dispersed storage and distribution. The damaged military target systems—particularly barracks and storage depots—have simply been abandoned, and supplies and troops dispersed throughout the country. The inventories of transport and military equipment have been replaced by large infusions of military and economic aid from the USSR and Communist China. Damage to bridges and lines of communications is frequently repaired within a matter of days, if not hours, or the effects are countered by an elaborate system of multiple bypasses or pre-positioned spans.

222. MEMORANDUM FOR THE SECRETARY OF DEFENSE BY THE JOINT CHIEFS OF STAFF, JCSM-286-67, MAY 20, 1967 [Extract]

The Joint Chiefs of Staff called for the "neutralization" of the Hanoi-Haiphong area, the DRV's chief logistics base, by the interdiction of land and sea lanes in and out of the area, by air attacks on the Haiphong harbor, to be followed by mining of the harbor and the intensification of the air war against roads, rail lines, and airfields.

SOURCE: Document declassifed by Department of Defense, April 3, 1978.

5. The Hanoi-Haiphong areas constitute the principal NVN logistical base. This base should be neutralized. This can be accomplished by direct attack on these areas which would increase the danger of high civilian casualties or, more preferably, by interdiction of land and sea lines of communication which enter and depart from the area. However, for such an interdiction campaign to be effective, elements of the import system in NVN must be attacked concurrently on a sustained basis. The campaign must be of sufficient weight to reduce imports to a level which will seriously impair the NVN war-supporting capability. The level of effort required to accomplish this task is within Southeast Asia force capabilities. The Joint Chiefs of Staff believe that such a campaign against the total import capability should be initiated immediately.

a. The facility which provides the prime terminal for the sea LOCs is Haiphong. While Haiphong could be attacked in several ways, in recognition of the political considerations, the Joint Chiefs of Staff propose a course of action to "shoulder out" foreign shipping and then mine the harbor and approaches. This can be accomplished by a series of air attacks commencing on the periphery of the port area and gradually moving to the center of the port complex. These successful attacks will reduce the functional efficiency of the port and could be expected to force foreign shipping out into the nearby estuaries for off-loading by lighterage.

b. At that time, with minimum likelihood of damage to shipping, the remaining elements of the port can be taken under attack and the harbor mined. The exact location of the minefields will be determined at the appropriate time as their locations will be dependent on the dispersion pattern of foreign shipping after being "shouldered out" of the immediate port area.

c. While the Haiphong port is being attacked, an intensive interdiction campaign will be initiated against the roads and railroads from China. The deep water ports of Cam Pha and Hon Gai will be attacked as required. Maximum effort will be made to keep the northeast railroad nonoperational. Coastal armed reconnaissance will be intensified to detect and destroy NVN shipping in transit and transshipment locations along the NVN coast.

d. In addition a systematic attack against the eight major operational airfields will be initiated concurrently with attacks on the surface LOCs. At present, attacks are authorized against Kien An Airfield, Kep Airfield, and Hoa Lac Airfield. Attacks against all eight of these airfields would restrict air importation of critical military supplies, reduce the capability of the air defense system by decreasing the MIG threat, and impede expansion of the NVN air order of battle.

6. Should the United States effectively close the Haiphong harbor to deep water shipping by bombing and mining, the Soviets would:

a. Probably protest such an action diplomatically by propaganda, and perhaps by seeking condemnation of the United States in the United Nations.

b. Possibly suspend current diplomatic negotiations, such as the Nuclear Proliferation Treaty and the "Proposed Freeze on ABM and ICMB Deployment."

c. Continue to avoid an active confrontation with the United States.

d. Seek alternative means for providing the required material support to the NVN war effort, including increased use of rail shipments through China and use of Chinese and possibly Cambodian ports for off-loading and further transshipment. There is a possibility that, as air attacks close in toward the Haiphong port (Target 70), some foreign shipping might choose not to leave the port and could be damaged.

7. The sequential pattern of proposed attacks on the Haiphong port complex has been initiated by the recent airstrikes on the two Haiphong thermal power plants. Current attacks against the cement plant and restrike of Haiphong POL continue the pattern. Sequential and continuing attacks are proposed as follows:

  a. Haiphong RR Yds W; Area C (Shipyard #1), Area D (Naval Base), Target 70, Haiphong port.

  b. Haiphong RR Yd/Shops; Area A (Shipyard # 1), Area F (Shipyard #2), and Area G (Shipyard North), Target 70, Haiphong port.

  c. Target 70, Haiphong port (all elements) and mining of harbor. The location of the targets and elements of the Haiphong port are depicted in the Appendix.

8. The Joint Chiefs of Staff conclude that no important element of the NVN LOC system can be permitted to function freely. They therefore recommend that, as a matter of urgency, the initiation of the attack program as outlined above be authorized. In addition to the reasons cited above, an early approval will allow attacks during the favorable May–September weather season and before onset of the unfavorable weather conditions which seriously impair operations.

9. The Joint Chiefs of Staff request that their views as contained in this memorandum be presented to the President.

223. INTELLIGENCE MEMORANDUM BY THE DIRECTORATE OF INTELLIGENCE, CIA, MAY 23, 1967 [Extract]

Responding to the JCS proposal for the mining of North Vietnam's harbors to interdict shipping, the CIA judged that it could at most reduce the existing level of imports by 25 percent. This would impose a heavy economic burden on the North, it concluded, but not prevent it from maintaining its military operations in the South.

Summary

A mining program coupled with intensified armed reconnaissance against the railroads and roads in the northern part of North Vietnam would have serious economic consequences, but it would not be likely to weaken the military establishment seriously or to prevent Hanoi from continuing its aggression in the south.

The disruption caused by mining would depend upon the type and extent of the program. A substantial portion of imports could be maintained by sea and coastal water movements despite a conventional mining program designed to prevent the discharge of deep-draft oceangoing ships in harbors. However, almost complete

---

SOURCE: Document declassified by the CIA, April 12, 1976.

denial of water access to North Vietnam could result from a mining program which also used a newly developed mine effective against shallow-draft shipping.

An optimum program against all means of land and water transportation probably could interdict at most 70 percent of North Vietnam's transport *capacity* to import, reducing it from about 14,000 tons a day at present to about 3,900 a day. Interdiction to this extent would reduce the present level of goods *actually imported* by about 25 percent.

North Vietnam could, however, reduce the flow of supplies from outside the country to manageable levels by eliminating nonessential imports. The military supplies and essential economic goods needed by Hanoi to continue with the war would not exceed an estimated 3,000 tons a day. This amount of traffic could be handled even if the capacity of North Vietnam's transport system were reduced by 70 percent.

Imports at this level would not be sufficient to continue operations of modern industrial plants or to restore operation of those which have received extensive bomb damage. The economy would be reduced to its essential subsistence character, but those modern sectors such as transportation, construction, communications and other elements essential to support the military establishment in North Vietnam and in the South could be sustained.

224. ADDRESS BY PRESIDENT JOHNSON, SAN ANTONIO, TEXAS, SEPTEMBER 29, 1967 [Extract]

In late July 1967, two Frenchmen, Dr. Herbert Marcovich and Raymond Aubrac, an old friend of Ho Chi Minh, returned from Hanoi after talks with Pham Van Dong and Ho Chi Minh, and reported to Harvard Professor Henry Kissinger a more flexible DRV position on a peace settlement than was reflected in Hanoi's public statements. Kissinger was then given a new U.S. proposal to be conveyed to Hanoi by Marcovich and Aubrac: the United States would stop the bombing in return for the start of negotiations without insisting on substantial deescalation by Hanoi. The message warned against any move by the DRV to "take advantage" of the bombing halt. In September Johnson revealed the substance of the proposal in a speech in San Antonio. The DRV, which was already beginning to plan its Tet offensive, rejected the proposal as still posing "conditions" on a bombing halt. But it brought the two adversaries a step closer to negotiations.

Our desire to negotiate peace—through the United Nations or out—has been made very, very clear to Hanoi—directly and many times through third parties.

As we have told Hanoi time and time and time again, the heart of the matter really is this: The United States is willing to stop all aerial and naval bombardment of North Viet-Nam when this will lead promptly to productive discussions. We, of

SOURCE: Department of State *Bulletin*, October 23, 1967.

course, assume that while discussions proceed, North Viet-Nam would not take advantage of the bombing cessation or limitation.

But Hanoi has not accepted any of these proposals.

So it is by Hanoi's choice, and not ours and not the rest of the world's, that the war continues.

Why, in the face of military and political progress in the South, and the burden of our bombing in the North, do they insist and persist with the war?

From the many sources the answer is the same. They still hope that the people of the United States will not see this struggle through to the very end. As one Western diplomat reported to me only this week—he had just been in Hanoi—"They believe their staying power is greater than ours and that they can't lose." A visitor from a Communist capital had this to say: "They expect the war to be long, and that the Americans in the end will be defeated by a breakdown in morale, fatigue, and psychological factors." The Premier of North Viet-Nam said as far back as 1962: "Americans do not like long, inconclusive war . . . Thus we are sure to win in the end."

Are the North Vietnamese right about us?

I think not. No. I think they are wrong. I think it is the common failing of totalitarian regimes, that they cannot really understand the nature of our democracy:

—They mistake dissent for disloyalty;
—They mistake restlessness for a rejection of policy;
—They mistake a few committees for a country;
—They misjudge individual speeches for public policy.

They are no better suited to judge the strength and perseverance of America than the Nazi and the Stalinist propagandists were able to judge it. It is a tragedy that they must discover these qualities in the American people, and discover them through a bloody war.

And, soon or late, they will discover them.

In the meantime, it shall be our policy to continue to seek negotiations, confident that reason will some day prevail, that Hanoi will realize that it just can never win, that it will turn away from fighting and start building for its own people.

225. MEMORANDUM OF CONVERSATION BETWEEN RUSK AND SOVIET DEPUTY FOREIGN MINISTER V. V. KUZNETSOV, IN WASHINGTON, NOVEMBER 3, 1967

Rusk took a very hard line on Vietnam in a talk with Deputy Foreign Minister Kuznetsov, likening South Vietnam, as an "ally" of the United States, to Czechoslovakia for the Soviet Union. All the comments by Kuznetsov were deleted from the document by the State Department before releasing.

SOURCE: Document declassified by Department of State, August 21, 1978.

[Officially deleted.]

The Secretary said there was a simple solution to the problem in Vietnam. If the North Vietnamese would agree to remain north of the 17th Parallel a solution could be found. Unfortunately no one has told us what Hanoi would do if we should stop bombing. The Secretary recognized that Kuznetsov could not speak for Hanoi, but he could certainly speak for Moscow.

[Officially deleted.]

The Secretary said this gave us no problem so long as the principle of noninterference applies to North Vietnam as well. There could be no solution and no peace, however, if Hanoi considered that it was entitled to interfere in others' internal affairs.

[Officially deleted.]

The Secretary said that this statement did not mean that we were prepared to deal with the NLF as a government. The position of the United States Government on representation in negotiations of the NLF had been made clear on numerous occasions and had not changed.

[Officially deleted.]

The Secretary said we had no problem with this at all. The Soviets, however, must be perfectly clear on one fundamental point. We will continue to oppose the spread of world revolution by force. With regard to Vietnam the Secretary saw no need for a conflict of interest between the United States and the Soviet Union. It was important that the Soviets recognize that we have a vital interest in what happens in South Vietnam, just as we recognize that the Soviets have an interest as to what happens in North Vietnam. We are prepared to stop the bombing now if the Soviet Union can tell us that the North Vietnamese will stop its infiltration.

[Officially deleted.]

The Secretary said that we were not concerned with prestige, but with what happened to South Vietnam. We have informed the North Vietnamese that we will specify the timetable of our withdrawal from South Vietnam if they will do the same. This, the Secretary said, is a reasonable proposal.

[Officially deleted.]

The Secretary then said that he wished to be perfectly frank with Kuznetsov on the problem before us. If wars of liberation should be directed against allies of the United States we would never accept the concept that the source of these wars should be treated as a sanctuary. This is fundamental, and the Soviets must have a clear understanding of our position on this question. The secretary was sure that the Soviets held the same view. If, for example, the West Germans should move "forces of liberation" into Czechoslovakia the Soviets would strike back. Similarly, if the South Vietnamese had attacked North Vietnam, a Soviet ally, the Soviets would have reacted sharply. Our position is the same with regard to our allies.

[Officially deleted.]

The Secretary said he could agree [*officially deleted*] on the need and the possibilities of cooperation. We are prepared to do what we can, but we cannot abandon our allies nor can we jeopardize our vital interests. We should both put aside ideological differences and concentrate on our national interests and see what progress we can make.

[Officially deleted.]

226. SNIE 14.3-67, "CAPABILITIES OF THE VIETNAMESE COMMUNISTS FOR FIGHTING IN SOUTH VIETNAM," NOVEMBER 13, 1967 [Extract]

Assuming a Communist strategy of attrition to convince the United States to settle the war on their terms, the intelligence community judged that it would require an increased infiltration effort to maintain Communist forces at or near 1967 levels during the next year, but said that Hanoi could adequately support its military strategy for at least another year.

Conclusions

A. During the past year, Hanoi's direct control and share of the burden of the war in South Vietnam has grown substantially. This trend will continue.

B. Manpower is a major problem confronting the Communists. Losses have been increasing and recruitment in South Vietnam is becoming more difficult. Despite heavy infiltration from North Vietnam, the strength of the Communist military forces and political organizations in South Vietnam declined in the last year.

C. The major portion of this decline has probably been felt at the lower levels, reflecting a deliberate policy of sacrificing these levels to maintain the structure of political cadres and the strength of the Regular military forces. In particular the guerrillas, now estimated to total some 70,000–90,000, have suffered a substantial reduction since the estimated peak of about early 1966. Regular force strength, now estimated at 118,000, has declined only slightly, but Viet Cong (VC) units are increasingly dependent upon North Vietnamese replacements.

D. Given current Communist strategy, and levels of operations, a major effort will be necessary if the Regular forces and the guerrillas are to be maintained at or near present levels. To do so will require both a level of infiltration much higher than that observed in 1967 and intensive VC recruitment as well. Considering all the relevant factors, however, we believe there is a fairly good chance that the overall strength and effectiveness of the military forces and the political infrastructure will continue to decline.

E. The Communist leadership is already having problems in maintaining morale and quality. These problems have not yet impaired overall military effectiveness, but they are likely to become more difficult.

F. Difficulties in internal distribution will continue to cause local shortages and interfere with Communist operations from time to time. But we believe that the Communists will be able to continue to meet at least their essential supply requirement for the level of forces and activities in South Vietnam described in this estimate.

G. Communist strategy is to sustain a protracted war of attrition and to persuade the US that it must pull out or settle on Hanoi's terms. Our judgment is that the Communists still retain adequate capabilities to support this strategy for at least

SOURCE: Document declassified by the CIA, December 1, 1975.

another year. Whether or not Hanoi does in fact persist with this strategy depends not only on its capabilities to do so, but on a number of political and international considerations not treated in this estimate.

227. ADDRESS BY COMMANDER OF U.S. FORCES IN VIETNAM, GEN. WILLIAM C. WESTMORELAND, NOVEMBER 21, 1967 [Extracts]

By late 1967, Lyndon Johnson, worried by signs of sagging public support for the U.S. war effort, ordered his Commander, General William C. Westmoreland, home from Vietnam to reassure the American people that the United States was winning and that the end was only a matter of time. Westmoreland's major address portrayed the war as having passed through two phases by the end of 1967 and entering a third phase in 1968 in which "the end begins to come into view."

Improving Vietnamese Effectiveness

With 1968, a new phase is now starting. We have reached an important point when the end begins to come into view. What is this third phase we are about to enter?

In Phase III, in 1968, we intend to do the following:

Help the Vietnamese Armed Forces to continue improving their effectiveness.

Decrease our advisers in training centers and other places where the professional competence of Vietnamese officers makes this possible.

Increase our advisory effort with the younger brothers of the Vietnamese Army: the Regional Forces and Popular Forces.

Use U.S. and free-world forces to destroy North Vietnamese forays while we assist the Vietnamese to reorganize for territorial security.

Provide the new military equipment to revitalize the Vietnamese Army and prepare it to take on an ever-increasing share of the war.

Continue pressure on North to prevent rebuilding and to make infiltration more costly.

Turn a major share of frontline DMZ defense over to the Vietnamese Army.

Increase U.S. support in the rich and populated delta.

Help the Government of Viet-Nam single out and destroy the Communist shadow government.

Continue to isolate the guerrilla from the people.

Help the new Vietnamese government to respond to popular aspirations and to reduce and eliminate corruption.

Help the Vietnamese strengthen their policy forces to enhance law and order.

Open more roads and canals.

Continue to improve the Vietnamese economy and standard of living.

SOURCE: Department of State *Bulletin,* December 11, 1967, pp. 786–788.

The Final Phase

Now for phase IV—the final phase. That period will see the conclusion of our plan to weaken the enemy and strengthen our friends until we become progressively superfluous. The object will be to show the world that guerrilla warfare and invasion do not pay as a new means of Communist aggression.

I see phase IV happening as follows:

Infiltration will slow.

The Communist infrastructure will be cut up and near collapse.

The Vietnamese Government will prove its stability, and the Vietnamese Army will show that it can handle Viet Cong.

The Regional Forces and Popular Forces will reach a higher level of professional performance.

U.S. units can begin to phase down as the Vietnamese Army is modernized and develops its capacity to the fullest.

The military physical assets, bases and ports, will be progressively turned over to the Vietnamese.

The Vietnamese will take charge of the final mopping up of the Viet Cong (which will probably last several years). The U.S., at the same time, will continue the developmental help envisaged by the President for the community of Southeast Asia.

You may ask how long phase III will take, before we reach the final phase. We have already entered part of phase III. Looking back on phases I and II, we can conclude that we have come a long way.

I see progress as I travel all over Viet-Nam.

I see it in the attitudes of the Vietnamese.

I see it in the open roads and canals.

I see it in the new crops and the new purchasing power of the farmer.

I see it in the increasing willingness of the Vietnamese Army to fight North Vietnamese units and in the victories they are winning.

Parenthetically, I might say that the U.S. press tends to report U.S. actions; so you may not be as aware as I am of the victories won by South Vietnamese forces.

The enemy has many problems:

He is losing control of the scattered population under his influence.

He is losing credibility with the population he still controls.

He is alienating the people by his increased demands and taxes, where he can impose them.

He sees the strength of his forces steadily declining.

He can no longer recruit in the South to any meaningful extent; he must plug the gap with North Vietnamese.

His monsoon offensives have been failures.

He was dealt a mortal blow by the installation of a freely elected representative government.

And he failed in his desperate effort to take the world's headlines from the inauguration by a military victory.

Lastly, the Vietnamese Army is on the road to becoming a competent force. Korean troops in Viet-Nam provide a good example for the Vietnamese. Fifteen years ago the Koreans themselves had problems now ascribed to the Vietnamese. The Koreans surmounted these problems, and so can and will the Vietnamese.

*　　*　　*

We are making progress. We know you want an honorable and early transition to the fourth and last phase. So do your sons and so do I.

It lies within our grasp—the enemy's hopes are bankrupt. With your support we will give you a success that will impact not only on South Viet-Nam but on every emerging nation in the world.

1968

228. MEMORANDUM FOR THE SECRETARY OF DEFENSE BY THE JOINT CHIEFS OF STAFF, JCSM-91-68, FEBRUARY 12, 1968

On January 31, 1968, Communist forces surprised their foes by launching the "Tet offensive"—a coordinated series of attacks on thirty-four of forty-four province capitals, some sixty-four district towns, and every autonomous city in the country. They held most of their objectives in whole or in part for periods ranging from a few hours to more than three weeks in Hue. The official optimism expressed in previous months about progress in the war was largely discredited in the United States. Secretary McNamara asked the Joint Chiefs for plans for emergency reinforcements for Vietnam, but the Joint Chiefs responded that the situation was too unclear to make recommendations. They noted serious problems in sending further deployments: the need to maintain a minimum capacity to deal with civil disorder in the United States as well as the strain it would place on the American global military posture. They called for measures to call up additional reserve units and bring existing units in the United States up to increased combat readiness.

1. Reference is made to your oral request of 9 February 1968 for three plans which would provide emergency reinforcement of COMUSMACV.

2. The three plans examined are:

　　a. *Plan One*, which is based upon prompt deployment of the 82nd Airborne Division and 6/9 Marine division/wing team, callup of some 120,000 Army and Marine Corps Reserves, and appropriate legislative action to permit

SOURCE: Document declassified by the Joint Chiefs of Staff, February 24, 1978.

extension of terms of service of active duty personnel and the recall of individual Reservists.

b. *Plan Two*, which would deploy as many Marine Corps battalions as are now available in CONUS, less one battalion in the Caribbean, the battalion in the Mediterranean, and the Guantanamo Defense Force. This plan would not be based upon a callup of Reservists or legislative action.

c. *Plan Three*, which would deploy the 82nd Airborne Division but would leave Marine Corps battalions in CONUS. This plan would likewise envisage no Reserve callup and no legislative action.

The guidelines for development of the plans and description of the airlift force mix options and movement capability are contained in Annex A. Plan One is examined in detail in Annex B, Plan Two in Annex C, and Plan Three in Annex D. Plans One and Three would require appropriate tactical air units for support of Army forces. All three plans require other support forces consistent with the duration of the augmentation.

3. *Assessment of the Situation in Vietnam*.

a. The VC/NVA forces have launched large-scale offensive operations throughout South Vietnam.

b. As of 11 February 1968, Headquarters, MACV, reports that attacks have taken place on 34 provincial towns, 64 district towns, and all of the autonomous cities.

c. The enemy has expressed his intention to continue offensive operations and to destroy the Government of Vietnam and its Armed Forces.

d. The first phase of his offensive has failed in that he does not have adequate control over any population center to install his Revolutionary Committees which he hoped to form into a coalition with the NLF.

e. He has lost between 30 and 40 thousand killed and captured, and we have seized over seven thousand weapons.

f. Reports indicate that he has committed the bulk of his VC main force elements down to platoon level throughout the country, with the exception of six to eight battalions in the general area of Saigon.

g. Thus far, he has committed only 20 to 25 percent of his North Vietnamese forces. These were employed as gap fillers where VC strength was apparently not adequate to carry out his initial thrust on the cities and towns. Since November, he has increased his NVA battalions by about 25. The bulk of these and the bulk of the uncommitted NVA forces are in the I Corps area.

h. It is not clear whether the enemy will be able to recycle his attacks on a second phase. He has indicated his intention to do so during the period from 10 to 15 February.

i. South Vietnamese forces have suffered nearly two thousand killed, over seven thousand wounded, and an unknown number of absences. MACV suspects the desertion rate may be high. The average present for duty strength of RVN infantry battalions is 50 percent and Ranger Battalions, 43 percent. Five of nine airborne battalions are judged by MACV to be combat ineffective at this time.

4. *MACV, RVNAF posture*—COMUSMACV has expressed three major concerns:

a. The ability of the weakened RVNAF to cope with additional sustained enemy offensive operations.

b. Logistic support north of Danang, because of weather and sea conditions in the Northern I Corps area, enemy interdiction of Route 1, and the probability of intensified combat in that area.

c. The forces available to him are not adequate at the moment to permit him to pursue his own campaign plans and to resume offensive operations against a weakened enemy, considering the competing requirements of reacting to enemy initiatives, assisting defending Government centers, and reinforcing weakened RVNAF units when necessary.

5. It is not clear at this time whether the enemy will be able to mount and sustain a second series of major attacks throughout the country. It is equally unclear as to how well the Vietnamese Armed Forces would be able to stand up against such a series of attacks if they were to occur. In the face of these uncertainties, a more precise assessment of USMACV's additional force requirements, if any, must await further developments. The Joint Chiefs of Staff do not exclude the possibility that additional developments could make further deployments necessary.

6. Measured against the foregoing, the only active combat-ready and readily deployable general purpose forces consist of the 82nd Airborne Division, one and one-third Marine division/wing teams, eight recalled Air National Guard tactical fighter squadrons, and nonforward-deployed Navy forces which constitute the rotation base for forward deployments. Thus, the residual CONUS-based active combat-ready ground forces that would result from the execution of each of the plans examined would be:

a. Plan One—6/9 Marine Division/Wing Team.

b. Plan Two—One Airborne Division.

c. Plan Three—One and 3/9 Marine Division/Wing Team.

These Army and Marine Corps forces are at various levels of readiness, and a high percentage of personnel assigned are Vietnam returnees or personnel close to end of obligated active service.

7. An examination was made to determine the feasibility of a more rapid acceleration in the deployment of the four infantry battalions now scheduled to deploy to Southeast Asia in March-April as a part of Program 5 forces. It was concluded that, while these units are currently undergoing an accelerated training program, they have not yet completed company-level training and should not be deployed earlier, except under the most critical circumstances.

8. In addition to examining the criticality of deployments to South Vietnam, we must look to our capacity to meet the possibility of widespread civil disorder in the United States in the months ahead. It appears that, whether or not deployments under any of these plans are directed, sufficient forces are still available for civil disorder control. These include National Guard forces deployed under State or Federal control, composite units brought together in each CONUS Army area, and some of the troops from the 1st and 2nd Armored Divisions and 5th Infantry Division (Mech).

9. Against the possible increase in force requirements in Southeast Asia as well as those to respond to contingencies elsewhere in the world, our posture of readily available combat forces is seriously strained. Consequently, any decision to deploy emergency augmentation Active forces should be accompanied by the recall

of at least an equivalent number from the Reserve components and an extension of terms of service for active duty personnel. In view of the time required to bring Reserve component forces to a combat-ready status [*officially deleted*] Marine Division/Wing Team and three or more months for Army [*officially deleted*] and the limited number of Active combat forces available for deployment, it would be prudent to call to active duty certain additional Reserve component forces.

10. While there are variations in the problems of each of the Services, the rotation/training base of each is stretched and would be incapable of supporting, under existing criteria, substantially increased unit deployments. In addition, the capability of our uncommitted general purpose forces is further constrained by shortages of critical skilled specialists and shortages in mission-essential items of materiel and equipment, such as munitions, modern combat aircraft, helicopters, and communications/electronics and heavy engineer equipment.

11. Based on the foregoing assessment of the situation and problems facing COMUSMACV and the analysis of courses of action contained in the Annexes, the Joint Chiefs of Staff conclude and recommend that:

a. A decision to deploy reinforcements to Vietnam be deferred at this time.

b. Measures be taken now to prepare the 82nd Airborne Division and 6/9 Marine division/wing team for possible deployment to Vietnam.

c. As a matter of prudence, call certain additional Reserve units to active duty now. Deployment of emergency reinforcements to Vietnam should not be made without concomitant callup of Reserves sufficient at least to replace those deployed and provide for the increased sustaining base requirements of all Services. In addition, bring selected Reserve force units to full strength and an increased state of combat readiness.

d. Legislation be sought now to (1) provide authority to call individual Reservists to active duty; (2) extend past 30 June 1968 the existing authority to call Reserve units to active duty; and (3) extend terms of service for active duty personnel.

e. Procurement and other supply actions be taken now to overcome shortages existing in certain critical items of materiel and equipment such as munitions, helicopters, and other combat aircraft.

12. The Joint Chiefs of Staff observe that many additional problems pertaining to US military capabilities—although critical—are not treated in this paper. An updated assessment of US military posture worldwide and specific recommendations for required improvements will be reported to you in the near future.

229. REPORT OF CHAIRMAN OF THE JOINT CHIEFS OF STAFF GEN. EARLE G. WHEELER ON THE SITUATION IN VIETNAM, FEBRUARY 27, 1968 [Extracts]

Gen. Earle G. Wheeler, reporting on his three-day visit to South Vietnam, said the Communists largely controlled the countryside, were probably recruiting

---

SOURCE: Document declassified by Department of Defense, no date shown.

heavily, and had the morale and the forces to attack again. ARVN was on the defensive, and pacification had suffered a "severe setback," he reported. He judged that U.S. forces would have to be used to replace ARVN units in many places in order to get ARVN troops back in the countryside. To go back on the offensive, he said, MACV wanted an additional 206,756 troops in South Vietnam by the end of 1968.

1. The Chairman, JCS and party visited SVN on 23, 24 and 25 February. This report summarizes the impressions and facts developed through conversations and briefings at MACV and with senior commanders throughout the country.

2. *Summary*

—The current situation in Vietnam is still developing and fraught with opportunities as well as dangers.

—There is no question in the mind of MACV that the enemy went all out for a general offensive and general uprising and apparently believed that he would succeed in bringing the war to an early successful conclusion.

—The enemy failed to achieve this initial objectives but is continuing his effort. Although many of his units were badly hurt, the judgment is that he has the will and the capability to continue.

—Enemy losses have been heavy; he has failed to achieve his prime objectives of mass uprisings and capture of a large number of the capital cities and towns. Morale in enemy units which were badly mauled or where the men were oversold the idea of a decisive victory at TET probably has suffered severely. However, with replacements, his indoctrination system would seem capable of maintaining morale at a generally adequate level. His determination appears to be unshaken.

—The enemy is operating with relative freedom in the countryside, probably recruiting heavily and no doubt infiltrating NVA units and personnel. His recovery is likely to be rapid; his supplies are adequate; and he is trying to maintain the momentum of his winter-spring offensive.

—The structure of the GVN held up but its effectiveness has suffered.

—The RVNAF held up against the initial assault with gratifying, and in a way, surprising strength and fortitude. However, ARVN is now in a defensive posture around towns and cities and there is concern about how well they will bear up under sustained pressure.

—The initial attack nearly succeeded in a dozen places, and defeat in those places was only averted by the timely reaction of US forces. In short, it was a very near thing.

—There is no doubt that the RD Program has suffered a severe set back.

—RVNAF was not badly hurt physically—they should recover strength and equipment rather quickly (equipment in 2–3 months—strength in 3–6 months). Their problems are more psychological than physical.

—US forces have lost none of their pre-TET capability.

—MACV has three principal problems. First, logistic support north of Danang is marginal owing to weather, enemy interdiction and harassment and the massive deployment of US forces into the DMZ/Hue area. Opening Route 1 will alleviate this problem but takes a substantial troop commitment. Second, the defensive posture of ARVN is permitting the VC to make rapid inroads in the formerly pacified countryside. ARVN, in its own words, is in a dilemma as it cannot afford another enemy thrust into the cities and towns and yet if it remains in a defensive posture against this contingency, the countryside goes by default. MACV is forced to devote much of its troop strength to this problem. Third, MACV has been forced to deploy 50% of all US maneuver battalions into I Corps, to meet the threat there, while stripping the rest of the country of adequate reserves. If the enemy synchronizes an attack against Khe Sanh/Hue-Quang Tri with an offensive in the Highlands and around Saigon while keeping the pressure on throughout the remainder of the country, MACV will be hard pressed to meet adequately all threats. Under these circumstances, we must be prepared to accept some reverses.

—For these reasons, General Westmoreland has asked for a 3 division-15 tactical fighter squadron force. This force would provide him with a theater reserve and an offensive capability which he does not now have.

3. The situation as it stands today:

    a. Enemy capabilities

       (1) The enemy has been hurt badly in the populated lowlands, but is practically intact elsewhere. He committed over 67,000 combat maneuver forces plus perhaps 25% or 17,000 more impressed men and boys, for a total of about 84,000. He lost 40,000 killed, at least 3,000 captured, and perhaps 5,000 disabled or died of wounds. He had peaked his force total to about 240,000 just before TET, by hard recruiting, infiltration, civilian impressment, and drawdowns on service and guerrilla personnel. So he has lost about one fifth of his total strength. About two-third of his trained, organized unit strength can continue offensive action. He is probably infiltrating and recruiting heavily in the countryside while allied forces are securing the urban areas. (Discussions of strengths and recruiting are in paragraphs 1, 2 and 3 of Enclosure (1)). The enemy has adequate munitions, stockpiled in-country and available through the DMZ, Laos, and Cambodia, to support major attacks and countrywide pressure; food procurement may be a problem. (Discussion is in paragraph 6 Enclosure (1)). Besides strength losses, the enemy now has morale and training problems which currently limit combat effectiveness of VC guerrilla, main and local forces. (Discussions of forces are in paragraphs 2, 5, Enclosure (1)).

       (a) I Corps Tactical Zone: Strong enemy forces in the northern two provinces threaten Quang Tri and Hue cities, and US positions at the DMZ. Two NVA divisions threaten Khe Sanh. Eight enemy battalion equivalents are in the Danang-Hoi An area. Enemy losses in I CTZ have been heavy, with about 13,000 killed; some NVA as well as VC units have been hurt badly. However, NVA replacements in the DMZ area can offset these losses fairly quickly. The enemy has an increased artillery capability at the DMZ, plus some tanks and possibly even a limited air threat in I CTZ.

       (b) II Corps Tactical Zone: The 1st NVA Division went virtually unscathed during TET offensive, and represents a strong threat in the western highlands. Seven combat battalion equivalents threaten Dak To. Elsewhere in the highlands, NVA units have been hurt and

VC units chopped up badly. On the coast, the 3rd NVA Division had already taken heavy losses just prior to the offensive. The 5th NVA Division, also located on the coast, is not in good shape. Local force strength in coastal II CTZ had dwindled long before the offensive. The enemy's strength in II CTZ is in the highlands where enemy troops are fresh and supply lines short.

(c) III CTZ: Most of the enemy's units were used in the TET effort, and suffered substantial losses. Probably the only major unit to escape heavy losses was the 7th NVA Division. However, present dispositions give the enemy the continuing capability of attacking the Saigon area with 10 to 11 combat effective battalion equivalents. His increased movement southward of supporting arms and infiltration of supplies has further developed his capacity for attacks by fire.

(d) IV Corps Tactical Zone: All enemy forces were committed in IV Corps, but losses per total strength were the lightest in the country. The enemy continues to be capable of investing or attacking cities throughout the area.

(2) New weapons or tactics:

We may see heavier rockets and tube artillery, additional armor, and the use of aircraft, particularly in the I CTZ. The only new tactic in view is infiltration and investment of cities to create chaos, to demoralize the people, to discredit the government, and to tie allied forces to urban security.

*   *   *

4. What does the future hold?

a. Probable enemy strategy. (Reference paragraph 7b, Enclosure (1)). We see the enemy pursuing a reinforced offensive to enlarge his control throughout the country and keep pressures on the government and allies. We expect him to maintain strong threats in the DMZ area, at Khe Sanh, in the highlands, and at Saigon, and to attack in force when conditions seem favorable. He is likely to try to gain control of the country's northern provinces. He will continue efforts to encircle cities and province capitals to isolate and disrupt normal activities, and infiltrate them to create chaos. He will seek maximum attrition of RVNAF elements. Against US forces, he will emphasize attacks by fire on airfields and installations, using assaults and ambushes selectively. His central objective continues to be the destruction of the Government of SVN and its armed forces. As a minimum he hopes to seize sufficient territory and gain control of enough people to support establishment of the groups and committees he proposes for participation in an NLF dominated government.

b. MACV Strategy:

(1) MACV believes that the central thrust of our strategy now must be to defeat the enemy offensive and that if this is done well, the situation overall will be greatly improved over the pre-TET condition.

(2) MACV accepts the fact that its first priority must be the security of Government of Vietnam in Saigon and provincial capitals. MACV describes its objectives as:

—First, to counter the enemy offensive and to destroy or eject the NVA invasion force in the north.

—Second, to restore security in the cities and towns.

—Third, to restore security in the heavily populated areas of the countryside.

—Fourth, to regain the initiative through offensive operations.

c. Tasks:

(1) *Security of Cities and Government*. MACV recognizes that US forces will be required to reinforce and support RVNAF in the security of cities, towns and government structure. At this time, 10 US battalions are operating in the environs of Saigon. It is clear that this task will absorb a substantial portion of US forces.

(2) *Security in the Countryside*. To a large extent the VC now control the countryside. Most of the 54 battalions formerly providing security for pacification are now defending district or province towns. MACV estimates that US forces will be required in a number of places to assist and encourage the Vietnamese Army to leave the cities and towns and reenter the country. This is especially true in the Delta.

(3) *Defense of the borders, the DMZ and the northern provinces*. MACV considers that it must meet the enemy threat in I Corps Tactical Zone and has already deployed there slightly over 50% of all US maneuver battalions. US forces have been thinned out in the highlands, notwithstanding an expected enemy offensive in the early future.

(4) *Offensive Operations*. Coupling the increased requirement for the cities and subsequent reentry into the rural areas, and the heavy requirement for defense of the I Corps Zone, MACV does not have adequate forces at this time to resume the offensive in the remainder of the country, nor does it have adequate reserves against the contingency of simultaneous large-scale enemy offensive action throughout the country.

5. Force Requirements:

a. Forces currently assigned to MACV, plus the residual Program Five forces yet to be delivered, are inadequate in numbers and balance to carry out the strategy and to accomplish the tasks described above in the proper priority. To contend with, and defeat, the new enemy threat, MACV has stated requirements for forces over the 525,000 ceiling imposed by Program Five. The add-on requested totals 206,756 spaces for a new proposed ceiling of 731,756, with all forces being deployed into country by the end of CY 68. Principal forces included in the add-on are three division equivalents, 15 tactical fighter squadrons and augmentation for current Navy programs. MACV desires that these additional forces be delivered in three packages as follows:

(1) *Immediate Increment, Priority One:* To be deployed by 1 May 68. Major elements include one brigade of the 5th Mechanized Division with a mix of one infantry, one armored and one mechanized battalion; the Fifth Marine Division (less RLT-26); one armored cavalry regiment; eight tactical fighter squadrons; and a groupment of Navy units to augment on-going programs.

(2) *Immediate Increment, Priority Two:* To be deployed as soon as possible but prior to 1 Sep. 68. Major elements include the remainder of the 5th Mechanized Division, and four tactical fighter squadrons. It is

desirable that the ROK Light Division be deployed within this time frame.

(3) *Follow-On Increment:* To be deployed by the end of CY 68. Major elements include one infantry division, three tactical fighter squadrons, and units to further augment Navy Programs.

230. LAO DONG PARTY TRAINING DOCUMENT ON COSVN RESOLUTION NO. 6, MARCH 1968 [Extract]

In the Southern Party headquarters' first major assessment of the Tet Offensive, aimed at encouraging its cadres for later offensive waves, it was asserted that the United States and Saigon had been forced into a passive and defensive position defending the towns and lines of communications, and that 1.5 million people had been liberated. But the assessment pointed to weaknesses in the plans for urban uprisings and the failure to stimulate revolt within the Saigon army. It simultaneously held out hope for a sudden change that would bring final victory and warned of the possibility of protracted struggle.

I. *Great and unprecedented successes recorded in all fields during the first-month phase of the General Offensive and General Uprising.*

Since the beginning of Spring this year, the "Anti-U.S. National Salvation" resistance war of our people in the South has entered a new phase:

In this phase of General Offensive and General Uprising, after a month of continuous offensives and simultaneous uprisings conducted on all battlefields in the South, we have recorded great and unprecedented victories in all fields, inflicting on the enemy heavier losses than those he had suffered in any previous period.

1) We wore down, annihilated and disintegrated almost one-third of the puppet troops' strength, wore down and annihilated about one-fifth of U.S. combat forces, one-third of the total number of aircraft, one-third of the total number of mechanized vehicles, and an important part of U.S. and puppet material installations; destroyed and forced to surrender or withdrawal one-third of the enemy military posts, driving the enemy into an unprecedentedly awkward situation: from the position of the aggressor striving to gain the initiative through a two-prong tactic [military action and rural pacification], the enemy has withdrawn into a purely passive and defensive position, with his forces dispersed on all battlefields in the South for the purpose of defending the towns, cities and the main lines of communications. The struggle potential and morale of U.S. and puppet troops have seriously weakened because our army and people have dealt thundering blows at them everywhere, even at their principal lairs, and because they are facing great difficulties in replenishing troops and replacing war facilities destroyed during the past month.

2) We attacked all U.S.-puppet nerve centers, occupied and exerted our control for a definite period and at varying degrees over almost all towns, cities and municipalities in the South, and destroyed and disintegrated an

---

SOURCE: *Viet-Nam Documents and Research Notes,* Document No. 38, July 1968.

important part of puppet installations at all levels, seriously damaging the puppet administrative machinery.

3) We liberated additional wide areas in the countryside containing a population of 1.5 million inhabitants; consolidated and widened our rear areas, shifted immense resources of manpower and material, which had been previously robbed by the enemy in these areas, to the support of the front-line and of victory; encircled and isolated the enemy, and reduced the enemy's reserves of human and material resources, driving him into a very difficult economic and financial situation.

4) We have quantitatively and qualitatively improved our armed forces and political forces which have become outstandingly mature during the struggle in the past month. Our armed forces have progressed in many aspects, political organizations are being consolidated and have stepped forward, much progress has been realized in leadership activities and methods and we have gained richer experiences.

The above-mentioned great and unprecedented successes in all fields have strongly encouraged and motivated compatriots in towns and cities and areas under temporary enemy control to arise to seize the state power, have created a lively and enthusiastic atmosphere and inspired a strong confidence in final victory among compatriots in both the North and South. These successes have moreover won the sympathy and support of the socialist countries and the world's progressive people (including the U.S. progressive people) for our people's revolutionary cause, seriously isolated the U.S. imperialists and their lackeys, deepened their internal contradictions and thereby weakened the U.S. will of aggression.

The above-mentioned great successes in all fields have been recorded thanks to the clear-sighted and correct policy, line and strategic determination of the Party, the wise and resolute leadership of the Party Central Committee, the correct implementation of the Party's policy and line by Nam Truong and Party committee echelons, the sacrifice and devotion of all Party cadres and members who have in an exemplary manner carried out the Party's strategic determination, the eagerness for independence and freedom of the people in the South who are ready to shed their blood in exchange for independence and freedom, the absolute loyalty to the Party's and masses' revolution of the People's armed forces who have fought with infinite courage, the great assistance from the northern rear area and brotherly socialist countries, and the sympathy and support from the world people.

We have won great successes but still have many deficiencies and weak points:

1) In the military field—From the beginning, we have not been able to annihilate much of the enemy's live force and much of the reactionary clique. Our armed forces have not fulfilled their role as "lever" and have not created favorable conditions for motivating the masses to arise in towns and cities.

2) In the political field—Organized popular forces were not broad and strong enough. We have not had specific plans for motivating the masses to the extent that they would indulge in violent armed uprisings in coordination with and supporting the military offensives.

3) The puppet troop proselyting failed to create a military revolt movement in which the troops would arise and return to the people's side. The enemy troop proselyting task to be carried out in coordination with the armed struggle and

political struggle has not been performed, and inadequate attention had been paid to this in particular.

4) There has not been enough consciousness about specific plans for the widening and development of liberated rural areas and the appropriate mobilization of manpower, material resources and the great capabilities of the masses to support the front line.

5) The building of real strength and particularly the replenishment of troops and development of political forces of the infrastructure has been slow and has not met the requirements of continuous offensives and uprisings of the new phase.

6) In providing leadership and guidance to various echelons, we failed to give them a profound and thorough understanding of the Party's policy, line and strategic determination so that they have a correct and full realization of this phase of General Offensive and General Uprising. The implementation of our policies has not been sharply and closely conducted. We lacked concreteness, our plans were simple, our coordination poor, control and prodding were absent, reporting and requests for instructions were much delayed.

The above-mentioned deficiencies and weak points have limited our successes and are, at the same time, difficulties which we must resolutely overcome.

231. MESSAGE FROM WHEELER TO ALL PACIFIC COMMANDERS, MARCH 30, 1968

In a message to Westmoreland and all other American commanders in the Pacific, Chairman of the JCS Wheeler explained Johnson's decision to cut back the bombing of North Vietnam in terms of the rapid loss of public support for continuation of the war and the need for an initiative that would reverse the trend.

1. The referenced message apprises you that combat air operations against North Vietnam north of 20° North Latitude will be discontinued effective 0800 hours 1 April 1968, Saigon time. The purpose of this message is to acquaint you with the reasons for the cessation of air strikes.

2. At 2100 hours, 31 March, Washington time, the President will make an address to the Nation in which he will announce deployment of additional forces to South Vietnam, including forces called to active duty from the Reserve Components. He feels it mandatory that, at the same time, he proclaim another initiative designed to achieve a peaceful settlement of the conflict in Southeast Asia in order to blunt accusations of escalation from the opposers of Administration policy in Southeast Asia.

3. The following factors are pertinent to his decision:

    a. Since the TET offensive support of the American public and the Congress for the war in SEA has decreased at an accelerating rate. Many of the strongest proponents of forceful action in Vietnam have reversed their positions, have moved to neutral ground, or are wavering. If this trend continues unchecked, public support of our objectives in SEA will be too frail to sustain the effort.

    b. Weather over the northern portion of North Vietnam will continue

---

SOURCE: Document declassified by the Department of Defense, no date shown.

unsuitable for air operations during the next 30 days; therefore, if a cessation of air operations is to be undertaken, now is the best time from the military viewpoint.

    c. It is hoped that this unilateral initiative to seek peace will reverse the growing dissent and opposition within our society to the war.

    d. The initiative will aid in countering foreign criticism.

    e. President Thieu has been consulted and agrees to the cessation.

4. The Joint Chiefs of Staff have been apprised of the unilateral initiative to be taken, understand the reasons therefor, and they enjoin all commanders to support the decision of the President. In this connection, addressees, without citing the source or mentioning the President, should draw on this message in talking to subordinate commanders to solicit their understanding and support. In particular, every effort should be made to discourage military personnel from expressing criticism to news media representatives. I recognize that this is a delicate matter and one which cannot be approached on the basis of issuing fiats; rather, the attitudes of commanders will probably be most influential in guiding the reaction of their subordinates.

5. For Admiral Sharp: Secretary Rusk has been requested by Secretary Clifford to discuss fully with you the situation in this country which I have sketched above and to acquaint you fully with the problems we face here.

6. Information contained in paragraphs 1 and 2 is time-sensitive. I request you use it prior to the President's address with utmost discretion. Warm regards to all.

232. TELEGRAM FROM KATZENBACH TO SEVERAL SELECTED AMBASSADORS, MARCH 30, 1968 [Extract]

Informing U.S. ambassadors in the Asia Pacific region of the president's plans to announce a bombing cutback in North Vietnam, the State Department noted that it expected Hanoi to denounce it and "free our hand" for even stronger actions. It emphasized that the United States was not giving up anything serious in the bombing cutback because of weather conditions in the North during the month of April. The North Vietnamese acceptance of talks with the United States on April 1 took the Johnson administration by surprise.

1. You should see Chief of State or Government at once to convey following:

2. After full consultation with GVN and with complete concurrence of Thieu and Ky, President plans policy announcement Sunday night that would have following major elements:

    a. Major stress on importance of GVN and ARVN increased effectiveness, with our equipment and other support as first priority in our own actions.

    b. 13,500 support forces to be called up at once in order to round out the 10,500 combat units sent in February.

    c. Replenishment of strategic reserve by calling up 48,500 additional reserves, stating that these would be designed for strategic reserve.

SOURCE: Document declassified by the Department of State, June 9, 1978

d. Related tax increases and budget cuts already largely need for non-Vietnam reasons.

3. In addition, after similar consultation and concurrence, President proposes to announce that bombing will be restricted to targets most directly engaged in the battlefield area and that this meant that there would be no bombing north of 20th parallel. Announcement would leave open how Hanoi might respond, and would be open-ended as to time. However, it would indicate that Hanoi's response could be helpful in determining whether we were justified in assumption that Hanoi would not take advantage if we stopping bombing altogether. Thus, it would to this extent foreshadow possibility of full bombing stoppage at a later point.

4. In presenting this plan, you may make following points:

a. You should call attention to force increases that would be announced at the same time and would make clear our continued resolve. Also our top priority to re-equipping ARVN forces.

b. You should make clear that Hanoi is most likely to denounce the project and thus free our hand after a short period. Nonetheless, we might wish to continue the limitation even after a formal denunciation, in order to reinforce its sincerity and put the monkey firmly on Hanoi's back for whatever follows. Of course, any major military change could compel full-scale resumption at any time.

c. With or without denunciation, Hanoi might well feel limited in conducting any major offensives at least in the northern areas. If they did so, this could ease the pressure where it is most potentially serious. If they did not, then this would give us a clear field for whatever actions were then required.

d. In view of weather limitations, bombing north of the 20th parallel will in any event be limited at least for the next four weeks or so—which we tentatively envisage as a maximum testing period in any event. Hence, we are not giving up anything really serious in this time frame. Moreover, air power now used north of 20th can probably be used in Laos (where no policy change planned) and in SVN.

e. Insofar as our announcement foreshadows any possibility of a complete bombing stoppage, in the event Hanoi really exercises reciprocal restraints, we regard this as unlikely. But in any case, the period of demonstrated restraint would probably have to continue for a period of several weeks, and we would have time to appraise the situation and to consult carefully with them before we undertook any such action.

233. TELEVISION ADDRESS BY JOHNSON, MARCH 31, 1968 [Extracts]

Following weeks of debate and turmoil within the Administration over Vietnam, Lyndon Johnson surprised the nation by announcing a partial bombing halt as a step toward beginning talks with the DRV, and his own withdrawal from the 1968 presidential race.

Tonight I renew the offer I made last August—to stop the bombardment of North Viet-Nam. We ask that talks begin promptly, that they be serious talks on the

SOURCE: Department of State *Bulletin*, April 15, 1968, pp. 481–486.

substance of peace. We assume that during those talks Hanoi will not take advantage of our restraint.

We are prepared to move immediately toward peace through negotiations.

So tonight, in the hope that this action will lead to early talks, I am taking the first step to deescalate the conflict. We are reducing—substantially reducing—the present level of hostilities. And we are doing so unilaterally and at once.

Unilateral Deescalation by United States

Tonight I have ordered our aircraft and our naval vessels to make no attacks on North Viet-Nam, except in the area north of the demilitarized zone where the continuing enemy buildup directly threatens Allied forward positions and where the movements of their troops and supplies are clearly related to that threat.

The area in which we are stopping our attacks includes almost 90 percent of North Viet-Nam's population and most of its territory. Thus there will be no attacks around the principal populated areas or in the food-producing areas of North Viet-Nam.

Even this very limited bombing of the North could come to an early end if our restraint is matched by restraint in Hanoi. But I cannot in good conscience stop all bombing so long as to do so would immediately and directly endanger the lives of our men and our allies. Whether a complete bombing halt becomes possible in the future will be determined by events.

Our purpose in this action is to bring about a reduction in the level of violence that now exists.

It is to save the lives of brave men and to save the lives of innocent women and children. It is to permit the contending forces to move closer to a political settlement.

And tonight I call upon the United Kingdom and I call upon the Soviet Union, as cochairmen of the Geneva conferences and as permanent members of the United Nations Security Council, to do all they can to move from the unilateral act of deescalation that I have just announced toward genuine peace in Southeast Asia.

Now, as in the past, the United States is ready to send its representatives to any forum, at any time, to discuss the means of bringing this ugly war to an end.

I am designating one of our most distinguished Americans, Ambassador Averell Harriman, as my personal representative for such talks. In addition, I have asked Ambassador Llewellyn Thompson, who returned from Moscow for consultation, to be available to join Ambassador Harriman at Geneva or any other suitable place just as soon as Hanoi agrees to a conference.

I call upon President Ho Chi Minh to respond positively and favorably to this new step toward peace.

But if peace does not come now through negotiations, it will come when Hanoi understands that our common resolve is unshakable and our common strength is invincible.

*　　*　　*

A Call for National Unity

Finally, my fellow Americans, let me say this:

Of those to whom much is given, much is asked. I cannot say, and no man could say, that no more will be asked of us.

Yet, I believe that now, no less than when the decade began, this generation of Americans is willing to "pay any price, bear any burden, meet any hardship, support any friend, oppose any foe to assure the survival and the success of liberty." Since those words were spoken by John F. Kennedy, the people of America have kept that compact with mankind's noblest cause.

And we shall continue to keep it.

Yet I believe that we must always be mindful of this one thing, whatever the trials and the tests ahead: The ultimate strength of our country and our cause will lie not in powerful weapons or infinite resources or boundless wealth but will lie in the unity of our people.

This I believe very deeply.

Throughout my entire public career I have followed the personal philosophy that I am a free man, an American, a public servant, and a member of my party, in that order always and only.

For 37 years in the service of our nation, first as a Congressman, as a Senator and as Vice President and now as your President, I have put the unity of the people first. I have put it ahead of any divisive partisanship.

And in these times as in times before, it is true that a house divided against itself by the spirit of faction, of party, of region, of religion, of race, is a house that cannot stand.

There is division in the American house now. There is divisiveness among us all tonight. And holding the trust that is mine, as President of all the people, I cannot disregard the peril to the progress of the American people and the hope and the prospect of peace for all peoples.

So I would ask all Americans, whatever their personal interests or concern, to guard against divisiveness and all its ugly consequences.

Fifty-two months and 10 days ago, in a moment of tragedy and trauma, the duties of this Office fell upon me. I asked then for your help and God's, that we might continue America on its course, binding up our wounds, healing our history, moving forward in new unity, to clear the American agenda and to keep the American commitment for all of our people.

United we have kept that commitment. United we have enlarged that commitment.

Through all time to come, I think America will be a stronger nation, a more just society, and a land of greater opportunity and fulfillment because of what we have all done together in these years of unparalleled achievement.

Our reward will come in the life of freedom, peace, and hope that our children will enjoy through ages ahead.

What we won when all of our people united just must not now be lost in suspicion, distrust, selfishness, and politics among any of our people.

Believing this as I do, I have concluded that I should not permit the Presidency to become involved in the partisan divisions that are developing in this political year.

With America's sons in the fields far away, with America's future under challenge right here at home, with our hopes and the world's hopes for peace in the balance every day, I do not believe that I should devote an hour or a day of my time to any personal partisan causes or to any duties other than the awesome duties of this Office—the Presidency of your country.

Accordingly, I shall not seek, and I will not accept, the nomination of my party for another term as your President.

But let men everywhere know, however, that a strong, a confident, and a vigilant America stands ready tonight to seek an honorable peace—and stands ready tonight to defend an honored cause—whatever the price, whatever the burden, whatever the sacrifices that duty may require.

Thank you for listening.

Good night and God bless all of you.

234. COSVN DIRECTIVE, JUNE 10, 1968 [Extract]

In May 1968, the Communists began the second phase of the "Spring Offensive and Uprising," which concentrated on the Saigon area. But unlike the Tet Offensive, which achieved nearly complete surprise, the May offensive was anticipated by the United States and Saigon, who were able to inflict major losses on the revolutionary forces and prevent them from achieving any major success. This assessment of the May offensive conceded that the loss of surprise had hurt the effort but still claimed that it was a significant victory, showing that the revolutionary side still held the initiative.

3. Four main weak points stood out in the second phase:

—Militarily, our attacks were concentrated upon main targets, whereas secondary targets were neglected, or were not attacked as vigorously as they should have been.

—The uprising of the people was slow and scattered.

—Troop proselyting was deplorably weak.

—Development of our political armed forces and the strengthening of rear areas was poor.

These four reasons limited our success. . . .

Viewed objectively, our second phase was launched under conditions where the enemy had been warned [*officially deleted*] and had strengthened his defensive system. We therefore met considerable difficulties created by him. In addition, we did not have enough time for the Party Branches and people to assimilate the resolutions of the Party which caused the forces of the Party, army and people to be less than fully prepared. Subjectively, these weak points and deficiencies originated from our lack of efforts which can be illustrated as follows:

First: We still did not sharply and profoundly assimilate the basic lines of the Party's policy and strategic determination. We did not fully understand the characteristics of the new phase. From the basic assumption that the General Offensive/General Uprising was a "one blow affair" to the realization that it was a phase [of operations], there was a tendency to consider it as a "protracted" struggle and a

SOURCE: Captured document released to the press by the U.S. Mission, August 21, 1968. Press release No. 163-68.

failure to view it as a phase of continuous offensives and uprising which require a positive urgency in gaining success every hour and every minute. We did not correctly take into consideration the relationship that existed between attacks and uprisings; armed forces and political forces; urban and rural areas; killing the enemy, destroying his key agencies in cities, bases and liberation of the rural areas; attack and building of strength; main points and secondary points; firmness and intrepidity, etc. . . .

Second: In the face of the rigors of war, our ideological indoctrination was not thorough, opportune or persevering, and our soldiers were not taught how to thoroughly rid themselves of their rightist and shirking attitudes.

Among cadre and Party members, including some at leadership levels, inaccurate estimations of the enemy and friendly situations still existed. (They viewed the enemy's forces without considering his serious weaknesses and remarked only on our own difficulties, without realizing the huge potential of our people and the opportunity that was increasingly open for us.) They lacked zeal in attacking the enemy and they were hesitant and sheep-like. They lost their self-confidence, feared to make sacrifices, suffered hardships and had very little sense of responsibility.

Third: The leadership plan at all levels was deficient and the performance of tasks was too simple and lackadaisical. There was no thorough understanding of the Party's policy and strategic determination in general and of the requirements of the second phase in particular. Leadership was not "total, continuous, expedient or daring. . . ." Furthermore, it failed to transform itself into a tool for the people, as it did not realize the potential of the local areas. Leadership at various levels also lacked a sense of urgency and motivation. Close coordination among various levels was poor. The Standing Committee of Nam Truong loosely coordinated with the regions, the regions with the provinces, the provinces with the districts, etc. . . .[sic]. A number of Party Committee echelons and cadre did not keep pace with the requirements of the new phase. They were slow, hesitating and reluctant.

Fourth: Two Party branches and popular organizations in the cities and rural areas were as poor in quantity as they were in quality. The Party Committee echelons did not pay enough attention to strengthening leadership and developing the Party's basic structures in accordance with the requirements of the new phase.

These four causes limited our successes, and at the same time, constitute very great obstacles to the future implementation of the strategic determination of the Party. We must do our best to overcome these obstacles with a resolute Revolutionary spirit and a very high sense of responsibility.

235. LAO DONG PARTY DIRECTIVE ON A U.S. BOMBING HALT OVER NORTH VIETNAM, OCTOBER 28, 1968 [Extract]

During the summer of 1968, the United States and the DRV carried on discussions in Paris on the circumstances under which the United States would halt the

SOURCE: Captured document released by U.S. Mission, November 8, 1968. Press Release No. 22C-68.

bombing and the DRV would enter into talks. The primary issue was whether the DRV would have to pledge any "reciprocal" actions of deescalation in return for the bombing halt. In October, Ambassador Harriman indicated that the United States would not place any conditions on its bombing halt. The Party began to prepare cadres in the South for a bombing halt. This directive, from the Ben Tre Province Party leadership, presented the prospective bombing halt as a significant factor in promoting troop morale, while warning against the erroneous tendency to believe that the United States side was stronger.

I. *Remarks on the situation:*

The Anti-US Resistance for National Salvation waged by our Army and people in North and South Viet-Nam has driven the US Imperialists into serious defeats forcing them to deescalate the war, reduce their bombings of North Viet-Nam and talk to us at the conference table. However, they are not willing to cease bombing of all of North Viet-Nam and they continue to intensify the war in South Viet-Nam in an extremely stubborn and cunning manner.

In the face of our continuous and intensified military, political and diplomatic activities, in the face of the internal troubles and failures of the US Government authorities in the general elections, and under the increasingly heavy pressure of the world and the US anti-war movement, it is possible that [President] Johnson may be compelled to stop bombing of North Viet-Nam.

This is a great fact which marks the outstanding achievements attained by our Army and people in both, North and South Viet-Nam, in the accomplishment of their revolutionary work. It is also a great achievement of the world and the US people's anti-war movement. This fact is also proof of the [US] failure to implement the war of destruction in North Viet-Nam and [illustrates] a great defeat in [their attempt] to carry out the war of aggression in our country.

This achievement will exhort our Army and people in North Viet-Nam to increase their support of the South in order to fight the Americans and gain final victory.

This achievement will highly promote the morale of the troops and people in South Viet-Nam and provide more favorable conditions for them to be determined to accomplish their mission of fighting the Americans for national salvation.

The US and Puppet troops are cruel and stubborn. However, they are becoming increasingly weak by the serious contradictions between the US and Puppet Governments, and between the Puppets themselves. All these [factors] will provide favorable conditions for us to defeat them and to attain final victory.

236. ANNOUNCEMENT BY JOHNSON OF U.S. BOMBING HALT, OCTOBER 31, 1968 [Extract]

Lyndon Johnson's announcement of the complete bombing halt over North Vietnam implied that North Vietnamese negotiators had made some commitment to Washington that made the bombing halt possible. It concealed the fact that the United States was acting unilaterally with no assurance from the other side that it

SOURCE: Department of State Bureau of Public Affairs release No. 1168, November 1968.

would reciprocate, and that the only concession made by the DRV was to drop its demand that the United States put in a written document that it was halting the bombing unconditionally.

Good evening my fellow Americans:

I speak to you this evening about very important developments in our search for peace in Vietnam. We have been engaged in discussions with the North Vietnamese in Paris since last May. The discussions began after I announced on the evening of March 31 in a television speech to the nation that the United States—in an effort to get talks started on a settlement of the Vietnam war—had stopped the bombing of North Vietnam in the area where 90 percent of the people live.

When our representatives—Ambassador Harriman and Ambassador Vance— were sent to Paris, they were instructed to insist throughout the discussions that the legitimate elected government of South Vietnam must take its place in any serious negotiations affecting the future of South Vietnam. Therefore, our Ambassadors Harriman and Vance made it abundantly clear to the representatives of North Vietnam in the beginning that—as I had indicated on the evening of March 31—we would stop the bombing of North Vietnamese territory entirely when that would lead to prompt and productive talks, meaning by that talks in which the Government of Vietnam was free to participate. Our Ambassadors also stressed that we could not stop the bombing so long as by doing so we would endanger the lives and the safety of our troops.

For a good many weeks, there was no movement in the talks at all. The talks appeared to really be deadlocked. Then a few weeks ago, they entered a new and a very much more hopeful phase. As we moved ahead. I conducted a series of very intensive discussions with our allies, and with the senior military and diplomatic officers of the U.S. Government, on the prospect for peace. The President also briefed our congressional leaders and all of the presidential candidates.

Last Sunday evening, and throughout Monday, we began to get confirmation of the essential understanding that we had been seeking with the North Vietnamese on the critical issues between us for some time. I spent most of all day Tuesday reviewing every single detail of this matter with our field commander. General Abrams, whom I had ordered home, and who arrived here at the White House at 2:30 in the morning and went into immediate conference with the President and the appropriate members of his Cabinet. We received General Abrams' judgment and we heard his recommendations at some length.

Now, as a result of all of these developments, I have now ordered that all air, naval, and artillery bombardment of North Vietnam cease as of 8 a.m., Washington time, Friday morning. I have reached this decision on the basis of the developments in the Paris talks. And I have reached it in the belief that this action can lead to progress toward a peaceful settlement of the Vietnamese war. I have already informed the three presidential candidates, as well as the congressional leaders of both the Republican and Democratic Parties of the reasons that the Government has made this decision. This decision very closely conforms to the statements that I have made in the past concerning a bombing cessation.

It was on August 19 that the President said:

"This administration does not intend to move further until it has good reasons to believe that the other side intends seriously, seriously, to join us in deescalating the war and moving seriously toward peace."

Then again on September 10, I said:

"The bombing will not stop until we are confident that it will not lead to an increase in American casualties."

The Joint Chiefs of Staff, all military men have assured me—and General Abrams firmly asserted to me on Tuesday in that early, 2:30 a.m. meeting—that in their military judgment this action should be taken now, and this action would not result in any increase in American casualties.

A regular session of the Paris talks will take place on Wednesday, November 6, at which the representatives of the Government of South Vietnam are free to participate. We are informed by the representatives of the Hanoi Government that the representatives of the National Liberation Front will also be present. I emphasize that their attendance in no way involves recognition of the National Liberation Front in any form. Yet, it conforms to the statements that we have made many times over the years that the NLF would have no difficulty making its views known.

What we now expect—what we have a right to expect—are prompt, productive, serious and intensive negotiations in an atmosphere that is conducive to progress. We have reached the stage where productive talks can begin. We have made clear to the other side that such talks cannot continue if they take military advantage of them. We cannot have productive talks in an atmosphere where the cities are being shelled and where the demilitarized zone is being abused.

I think I should caution you, my fellow Americans, that arrangements of this kind are never foolproof. For that matter, even formal treaties are never foolproof, as we have learned from our experience. But in the light of the progress that has been made in recent weeks, and after carefully considering and weighing the unanimous military and diplomatic advice and judgment rendered to the Commander in Chief, I have finally decided to take this step now and to really determine the good faith of those who have assured us that progress will result when bombing ceases and to try to ascertain if an early peace is possible. The overriding consideration that governs us at this hour is the chance and the opportunity that we might have to save human lives, save human lives on both sides of the conflict. Therefore, I have concluded that we should see if they are acting in good faith.

1969

237. NATIONAL SECURITY STUDY MEMORANDUM NO. 1, JANUARY 21, 1969 [Extracts]

Dr. Henry Kissinger's first move as presidential assistant for national security affairs was to have his staff draw up a list of twenty-eight major questions to be

SOURCE: *Congressional Record*, May 10, 1972, pp. E4977-E4981.

*answered by the various agencies involved in Vietnam policy. The answers that
came back from the agencies consisted of 548 pages. They were summarized
in the document printed here. The summary discloses that the agencies generally
divided along the lines of relative optimism (MACV, CINCPAC, JCS and Embassy
Saigon) and relative pessimism (CIA, Office of the Secretary of Defense, and State).
But there was general agreement that the Communists had not decided to negotiate
in Paris out of weakness and that they were still capable of defeating the RVN
armed forces if the United States were to withdraw from the war at any time in the
foreseeable future. This highly classified document was entered into the* Congressional Record, *without identification, in May 1972 by Congressman Ronald Dellums
(D-Cal.), who was advocating the impeachment of President Nixon because of his
Indochina policy.*

Summary of Responses to NSSM 1—The Situation in Vietnam

The responses to the questions posed regarding Vietnam show agreement on
some matters as well as very substantial differences of opinion within the U.S.
Government on many aspects of the Vietnam situation. While there are some
divergencies on the facts, the sharpest differences arise in the interpretation of those
facts, the relative weight to be given them, and the implications to be drawn. In
addition, there remain certain areas where our information remains inadequate.

There is general agreement, assuming we follow our current strategy, on the
following—

(1) The GVN and allied position in Vietnam has been strengthened recently in
many respects.

(2) The GVN has improved its political position, but it is not certain that GVN
and other non-communist groups will be able to survive a peaceful competition
with the NLF for political power in South Vietnam.

(3) The RVNAF alone cannot now, or in the foreseeable future, stand up to
the current North Vietnamese-Viet Cong forces.

(4) The enemy have suffered some reverses but they have not changed their
essential objectives and they have sufficient strength to pursue these objectives. We
are not attriting his forces faster than he can recruit or infiltrate.

(5) The enemy is not in Paris primarily out of weakness.

The disagreements within these parameters are reflected in two schools in the
government with generally consistent membership. The first school, which we will
call Group A, usually includes MACV, CINCPAC, JCS and Embassy Saigon, and
takes a hopeful view of current and future prospects in Vietnam within the parameters mentioned. The second school, Group B, usually includes OSD, CIA and (to a
lesser extent) State, and is decidedly more skeptical about the present and pessimistic about the future. There are, of course, disagreements within agencies across the
board or on specific issues.

As illustration, these schools line up as follows on some of the broader
questions:

In explaining reduced enemy military presence and activities, Group A gives
greater relative weight to allied military pressure, than does Group B.

The improvements in RVNAF are considered much more significant by Group A than Group B.

Group A underlines advancements in the pacification program, while Group B is skeptical both of the evaluation system used to measure progress and of the solidity of recent advances.

In looking at the political scene, Group A accents recent improvements while Group B highlights remaining obstacles and the relative strength of the NLF.

Group A assigns much greater effectiveness to bombing in Vietnam and Laos than Group B.

Following is a summary of the major conclusions and disagreements about each of six broad areas with regard to Vietnam: the negotiating environment, enemy capabilities, RVNAF capabilities, pacification, South Vietnamese politics, and U.S. military operations. Attached (at Tabs A-F) are summaries of the individual questions asked of the various agencies.

1. Negotiating Environment (Questions 1–4)

There is general U.S. government agreement that Hanoi is in Paris for a variety of motives but not primarily out of weakness; that Hanoi is charting a course independent of Moscow, which favors negotiations, and of Peking, which opposes them; and that our knowledge of possible political factions among North Vietnamese leaders is extremely imprecise. There continues wide disagreement about the impact on Southeast Asia of various outcomes in Vietnam.

Why is the DRV in Paris?

Various possible North Vietnamese motives for negotiating are discussed, and there is agreement that the DRV is in Paris for mixed reasons. No U.S. agency responding to the questions believes that the primary reason the DRV is in Paris is weakness. All consider it unlikely that Hanoi came to Paris either to accept a face-saving formula for defeat or to give the U.S. a face-saving way to withdraw. There is agreement that Hanoi has been subject to heavy military pressure and that a desire to end the losses and costs of war was an element in Hanoi's decision. The consensus is that Hanoi believes that it can persist long enough to obtain a relatively favorable negotiated compromise. The respondents agree that the DRV is in Paris to negotiate withdrawal of U.S. forces, to undermine GVN and USG relations and to provide a better chance for FV victory in the South. State believes that increased doubt about winning the war through continued military and international political pressure also played a major role. Hanoi's ultimate goal of a unified Vietnam under its control has not changed.

Vietnam Impact on Southeast Asia

There continues to be a sharp debate between and within agencies about the effect of the outcome in Vietnam on other nations. The most recent NIE on this subject (NIE 50-58) tended to downgrade the so-called "domino theory." It states that a settlement which would permit the Communists to take control of the Government in South Viet-Nam, not immediately but within a year or two, would be likely to bring Cambodia and Laos into Hanoi's orbit at a fairly early state, but that these developments would not necessarily unhinge the rest of Asia.

The NIE dissenters believe that an unfavorable settlement would stimulate the

Communists to become more active elsewhere and that it will be difficult to resist making some accommodation to the pressure that generated. They believe, in contrast to the Estimate, these adjustments would be relatively small and insensitive to subsequent U.S. policy.

Factors entering into the judgments are estimates of (1) Hanoi's and Peking's behavior after the settlement; (2) U.S. posture in the regions; (3) Asian leaders' estimates of future U.S. policy; (4) the reactions of the area's non-Communist leaders to the outcome in Viet-Nam; (5) vulnerabilities of the various governments to insurgency or subversion; and (6) the strengths of opposition groups within each state.

The assessments rest more on judgments and assumptions than on tangible and convincing evidence, and there are major disagreements within the same Department. Within the Defense Department, OSD and CIA support the conclusions of the NIE, while Army, Navy and Air Force Intelligence dissent. Within State, the Bureau of Intelligence supports the NIE while the East Asian Bureau dissents.

Both the majority and the dissenters reject the view that an unfavorable settlement in Viet-Nam will inevitably be followed by Communist takeovers outside Indo China.

Indeed, even the dissenters, by phrasing the adverse results in terms such as "pragmatic adjustments" by the Thais and "some means of accommodation" leave it unclear how injurious the adverse effects would be to U.S. security.

*   *   *

2. The Enemy (Questions 5–10)

Analyses of various enemy tactics and capabilities reveal both significant agreements and sharp controversies within the Government. Among the major points of consensus:

A combination of military pressures and political tacts explains recent enemy withdrawals and lower levels of activity.

Under current rules of engagement, the enemy's manpower pool and infiltration capabilities can outlast allied attrition efforts indefinitely.

The enemy basically controls both side's casualty rates.

The enemy can still launch major offensives, although not at Tet levels, or, probably, with equally dramatic effect.

Major controversies include:

CIA and State assign much higher figures to the VC Order of Battle than MACV, and they include additional categories of VC/NLF organization.

MACV/JCS and Saigon consider Cambodia (and specifically Sihanoukville) an important enemy supply channel while CIA disagrees strongly.

Recent Enemy Activities

Military pressures and political considerations are viewed as responsible for the withdrawal of some North Vietnamese units into Cambodian and Laotian sanctuaries during the summer and fall of 1968. Military factors included heavy enemy losses, effective allied tactics, material shortages, and bad weather. Political factors centered on enemy efforts to make a political virtue out of a military necessity

in a talk-fight strategy to influence the Paris negotiations, and the enemy's emphasis on the establishment of "Liberation Committees" throughout the South Vietnamese countryside.

The enemy undertook a third-wave of offensive during the week of August 17.
At a cost of 5,500 enemy KIA, the enemy tripled the number of his attacks to 300
per week and his assaults during the second half of August nearly equalled the level
of his "second wave" offensive in May. Prisoners and captured documents reported the goal of achieving a general uprising and overthrow of the GVN. The lack
of greater success was attributed to: the enemy's economy-of-forces tactics; his
desire to demonstrate initiative but at reduced risk; effective U.S. spoiling actions
and increased intelligence; and the continuing deterioration of enemy Post-Tet capabilities in terms of quality of men and officers and lack of training.

All evaluators except the Department of State and Embassy Saigon state that
VC guerillas and local forces are now relatively dormant and that levels of harassment and terror remain high. However, the Embassy notes "the current low level of
guerrilla and local forces activity," and State agrees there has been a "relative
decline." Both agree that among the reasons are the heavy casualty rates, manpower problems and loss of cadres. But according to Embassy evaluators the main
factor is that "The VC are husbanding their resources to give themselves the option
of a 'climaxing' offensive." State notes that to support the VC counter-pacification
campaign and their "Liberation Committees," "the Communists may feel that a
demonstrably strong blow against the pacification program would have wide repercussions particularly at a time of optimistic Allied claims about pacification successes."

NVN/VC Manpower

It is generally agreed that the NVN/VC manpower pool is sufficiently large to
meet the enemy's replenishment needs over an extended period of time within the
framework of current rules of engagement. According to the JCS, "The North
Vietnamese and Viet Cong have access to sufficient manpower to meet their replenishment needs—even at the high 1968 loss rate of some 291,000—for at least the
next several years. . . . Present operations are not outrunning the enemy's ability to
replenish by recruitment or infiltration." Enemy losses of 291,000 in 1968 were
roughly balanced by infiltration and recruitment of 298,000. North Vietnamese
manpower assets include 1.8 million physically fit males aged 14-34 of whom 45%
are in the regular forces (475,000) and paramilitary (400,000) forces. 120,000
physically fit males reach draft age each year and 200,000 military and labor
personnel have been freed by the bombing half from defensive work. The potential
manpower pool in SVN is estimated at half a million men and recruitment, while
down, is running at approximately 3,500 per month. Enemy maintenance of the
current commitment of 300,000 new men per year requires that the Allies inflict
losses of 25,000 KIA per month, or 7,000 more than the current rate. MACV
considers current Allied force levels adequate to inflict such casualties if the enemy
chooses to engage.

The enemy's employment of economy of forces tactics since the fall of 1968
and intelligence evidence reflect the enemy's concern about his 1968 level of
losses, which if continued another year would mean nearly 100% yearly attrition of
his full-time fighters and nearly total North Vietnamization of local fighting forces

in South Vietnam. He is judged unlikely to undertake the heavy losses of a major offensive unless he believes he could thereby achieve a breakthrough in Allied will-power in Vietnam or Paris. Yet, without a VC/NVA offensive on the scale of Tet 1968, the JCS believe "It will be exceedingly difficult in 1969 for allied forces to attrite the enemy at 1968 levels."

*   *   *

3. The South Vietnamese Armed Forces
(Questions 10A – 13)

The emphatic differences between U.S. agencies on the RVNAF outweigh the points of agreement. There is consensus that the RVNAF is getting larger, better equipped and somewhat more effective. And all agree that it could not now, or in the foreseeable future, handle both the VC and sizeable NVA forces without U.S. combat support. On other major points there is vivid controversy. The military community gives much greater weight to RVNAF statistical improvements while OSD and CIA highlight remaining obstacles, with OSD being the most pessimistic. Paradoxically, MACV/CINCPAC/JCS see RVNAF as being less capable against the VC alone than does CIA.

RVNAF Capabilities Against the Enemy

The Vietnamese Armed Forces (RVNAF) are being increased in size and re-equipped to improve their ground combat capability. The best measure of this improvement is the RVNAF's expected performance against a given enemy threat. However, there is paradoxical divergence in agency views on the RVNAF ability to handle the internal VC threat without U.S. assistance. State (both EA and INR) and CIA—who generally rate RVNAF improvement and effectiveness lowest among the respondents, and who accept the highest estimates of overall VC strength—believe that, "Without any U.S. support . . . ARVN would at least be able to hold its own and make some progress against the VC unsupported by the NVA" (i.e. the VC without NVA fillers, thought with regroupees).

In contrast is the view of MACV/CINCPAC/JCS, who rate RVNAF improvement and effectiveness highest, who accept the lowest estimates of VC armed strength and who (unlike CIA and State) do not consider VC irregular forces to be part of the VC military threat. But the military community believes that without U.S. combat support, in opposing VC main and local forces with any NVA units or fillers, RVNAF "would have to reduce the number of offensive operations and adopt more of a defensive posture," resulting in "loss of control by the Government of Vietnam over substantial rural areas." Thus, MACV/CINCPAC/JCS believe that RVNAF would not be able to cope with purely indigenous VC forces without U.S. combat support until the completion of the modernization program in 1972.

OSD, however, believes that a number of major reforms are required, in addition to the current modernization program, if this goal is to be met. "It is unlikely that the RVNAF, as presently organized and led, will ever constitute an effective political or military counter to the Viet Cong."

All agencies agree that RVNAF could not, either now or even when fully modernized, handle both the VC and a sizable level of NVA forces without U.S. combat support in the form of air, helicopters, artillery, logistics and some ground forces.

*   *   *

4. Pacification (Questions 14–20)

Two well-defined and divergent views emerged from the agencies on the pacification situation in South Vietnam. One view is held by MACV and Embassy Saigon and endorsed by CINCPAC and JCS. The other view is that of OSD, CIA and State. The two views are profoundly different in terms of factual interpretation and policy implications. Both views agree on the nature of the problem, that is, the obstacles to improvement and complete success. What distinguishes one view from the other is each's assessment of the magnitude of the problem, and the likelihood that obstacles will be overcome.

The Two Views

The first group, consisting of MACV JCS Saigon, maintains that "at the present time, the security situation is better than any time during period in question," i.e., 1961–1968. MACV cites a "dramatic change in the security situation," and finds that the GVN controls three-fourths of the population. JCS suggests that the GVN will control 90% of the population in 1969. The second group, OSD CIA State, on the other hand, is more cautious and pessimistic, their view is not inconsistent with another Tet-offensive-like shock in the countryside, for example, wiping out the much-touted gains of the 1968 Accelerated Pacification Program, or with more gradual erosion. Representing the latter view, OSD arrives at the following conclusions:

(1) "The portions of the SVN rural population aligned with the VC and aligned with the GVN are apparently the same today as in 1962 [a discouraging year]: 5,000,000 GVN aligned and nearly 3,000,000 VC aligned.

(2) "At the present, it appears that at least 50% of the total rural population is subject to significant VC presence and influence."

CIA agrees, and State (INR) goes even further, saying:

"Our best estimate is that the VC have a significant effect on at least two-thirds of the rural population."

* * *

6. U.S. Military Operations (Questions 24–28)

The only major points of agreement with the U.S. Government on these subjects are:

The description of recent US deployment and tactics;

The difficulties of assessing the results of B-52 strikes, but their known effectiveness against known troop concentrations and in close support operations;

The fact that the Soviets and Chinese supply almost all war material to Hanoi and have enabled the North Vietnamese to carry on despite all our operations.

Otherwise there are fundamental disagreements running throughout this section, including the following:

OSD believes, the MACV/JCS deny, that there is a certain amount of "fat" in our current force levels that could be cut back without significant reduction in combat capability.

MACV/JCS and, somewhat more cautiously CIA ascribe much higher casualty estimates to our B-52 strikes.

MACV/JCS assign very much greater effectiveness to our past and current Laos and North Vietnam bombing campaigns than do OSD and CIA.

MACV/JCS believe that a vigorous bombing campaign could choke off enough supplies to Hanoi to make her stop fighting, while OSD and CIA see North Vietnam continuing the struggle even against unlimited bombing.

238. TELEVISION ADDRESS BY PRESIDENT RICHARD M. NIXON, MAY 14, 1969 [Extract]

The Nixon Administration inherited a negotiating position (the San Antonio formula) which called for the withdrawal of all North Vietnamese troops in advance of U.S. military withdrawal. Kissinger recognized this as an unrealistic posture and persuaded President Nixon to accept a cease-fire and mutual troop withdrawal as his negotiating position. But Kissinger, who was opposed to the U.S. negotiating on a political settlement, offered the DRV an undefined role in South Vietnamese politics, in return for their acceptance of the U.S.-sponsored constitutional regime and a formal *acceptance of two Vietnams for a period of five years. The Kissinger formula, conveyed secretly to the Soviet Union, would have represented a surrender on fundamental principles by Hanoi. When Kissinger hastily drafted a speech for Nixon to give on May 14, to respond to the NLF ten-point proposal of May 8, it made no references to these two principles, referring only to mutual withdrawal and elections under international supervision. The actual U.S. negotiating position, as conveyed in the Kissinger formula, took a far harder line.*

This brings us, then, to the matter of negotiations.

We must recognize that peace in Vietnam cannot be achieved overnight. A war which has raged for so many years will require detailed negotiations and cannot be settled at a single stroke.

What kind of a settlement will permit the South Vietnamese people to determine freely their own political future? Such a settlement will require the withdrawal of all non-South Vietnamese forces from South Vietnam and procedures for political choice that give each significant group in South Vietnam a real opportunity to participate in the political life of the nation.

To implement these principles, I reaffirm now our willingness to withdraw our forces on a specified timetable. We ask only that North Vietnam withdraw its forces from South Vietnam, Cambodia and Laos into North Vietnam, also in accordance with a timetable.

We include Cambodia and Laos to ensure that these countries would not be used as bases for a renewed war. The Cambodian border is only 35 miles from Saigon: the Laotian border is only 25 miles from Hue.

SOURCE: Reprinted in Committee on Foreign Relations, U.S. Senate, *Background Information Relating to Southeast Asia and Vietnam* (7th rev. ed.), December 1974, pp. 345–347. Hereafter cited as *Background Information Relating to Southeast Asia and Vietnam.*

Our offer provides for a simultaneous start on withdrawal by both sides: agreement on a mutually acceptable timetable; and for the withdrawal to be accomplished quickly.

If North Vietnam wants to insist that it has no forces in South Vietnam, we will no longer debate the point—provided that its forces cease to be there, and that we have reliable assurances that they will not return.

The North Vietnamese delegates have been saying in Paris that political issues should be discussed along with military issues, and that there must be a political settlement in the South. We do not dispute this, but the military withdrawal involves outside forces, and can therefore be properly negotiated by North Vietnam and the United States, with the concurrence of its allies. The political settlement is an internal matter, which ought to be decided among the South Vietnamese themselves and not imposed by outside powers. However, if our presence at these political negotiations would be helpful, and if the South Vietnamese concerned agreed, we would be willing to participate, along with the representatives of Hanoi if that were also desired.

Recent statements by President Thieu have gone far toward opening the way to a political settlement. He has publicly declared his government's willingness to discuss a political solution with the National Liberation Front and has offered free elections. His was a dramatic step forward, a reasonable offer that could lead to a settlement. The South Vietnamese Government has offered to talk without preconditions. I believe that the other side should also be willing to talk without preconditions.

The South Vietnamese Government recognizes, as we do, that a settlement must permit all persons and groups that are prepared to renounce the use of force to participate freely in the political life of South Vietnam. To be effective, such a settlement would require two things: First, a process that would allow the South Vietnamese people to express their choice; and second, a guarantee that this process would be a fair one.

We do not insist on a particular form of guarantee. The important thing is that the guarantees should have the confidence of the South Vietnamese people, and that they should be broad enough and strong enough to protect the interests of all major South Vietnamese groups.

This, then, is the outline of the settlement that we seek to negotiate in Paris. Its basic terms are very simple: Mutual withdrawal of non-South Vietnamese forces from South Vietnam, and free choice for the people of South Vietnam. I believe that the long-term interests of peace require that we insist on no less, and that the realities of the situation require that we seek no more.

Programs and Alternatives

To make very concrete what I have said, I propose the following measures, which seem to me consistent with the principles of all parties. These proposals are made on the basis of full consultation with President Thieu.

—As soon as agreement can be reached, all non-South Vietnamese forces would begin withdrawals from South Vietnam.

—Over a period of 12 months, by agreed-upon stages, the major portions of all U.S., Allied and other non-South Vietnamese forces would be withdrawn. At the end of this 12-month period, the remaining U.S., Allied and other non-South Vietnamese forces would move into designated base areas and would not engage in combat operations.

—The remaining U.S. and Allied forces would move to complete their withdrawals as the remaining North Vietnam forces were withdrawn and returned to North Vietnam.

—An international supervisory body, acceptable to both sides, would be created for the purpose of verifying withdrawals, and for any other purposes agreed upon between the two sides.

—This international body would begin operating in accordance with an agreed timetable, and would participate in arranging supervised ceasefires.

—As soon as possible after the international body was functioning, elections would be held under agreed procedures and under the supervision of the international body.

—Arrangements would be made for the earliest possible release of prisoners of war on both sides.

—All parties would agree to observe the Geneva Accords of 1954 regarding Vietnam and Cambodia, and the Laos Accords of 1962.

I believe this proposal for peace is realistic, and takes account of the legitimate interests of all concerned. It is consistent with President Thieu's six points. It can accommodate the various programs put forth by the other side. We and the Government of South Vietnam are prepared to discuss its details with the other side. Secretary Rogers is now in Saigon and will be discussing with President Thieu how, together, we may put forward these proposed measures most usefully in Paris. He will, as well, be consulting with our other Asian allies on these measures while on his Asian trip. However, I would stress that these proposals are not offered on a take-it-or-leave-it basis. We are quite willing to consider other approaches consistent with our principles.

We are willing to talk about anybody's program—Hanoi's four points, the NLF's 10 points—provided it can be made consistent with the few basic principles I have set forth here.

239. COSVN RESOLUTION NO. 9, JULY 1969 [Extract]

The Ninth Conference of COSVN, convened in July 1969, claimed that the offensives of the previous year and a half had brought a turning point in the war, having forced the United States to begin a gradual deescalation of its military effort, including a bombing halt and negotiations with the DRV and the Provisional Revolutionary Government of the Republic of South Vietnam officially founded in June 1969. But it pointed to difficulties in maintaining confidence in the Party leadership's line, which had shifted from attacks on cities with large units to

---

SOURCE: Captured document released in English translation by the U.S Mission in Vietnam, no date.

tactics designed to conserve manpower, because of confusion about the nature of the "General Offensive and Uprising." The conference foresaw the possibility of Nixon being forced to seek an early end to the war but also warned of the possibility of renewed bombing and expansion of the war into Laos and Cambodia.

On our part, the outstanding point is that, on the basis of thoroughly under-standing the Central Committee's strategic determination, we have achieved obvi-ous progress since the Spring of 1969 to date in applying the guidelines and methods of struggling and building, both in military and political fields, and mak-ing them more fitting to the rules of the General Offensive and Uprising; especially, we have applied and developed *the direction and method of fighting with high efficiency which caused very heavy losses to the enemy at very light cost in friendly casualties; we have applied and developed the guidelines and methods for opera-tions in the three areas designed to win and hold control of the weak areas, the areas bordering the cities and parts of the cities and municipalities.* This is an improvement in the quality of our Party body's leadership and guidance aimed at securing a more thorough understanding of the Central Committee's lines, policies, and resolutions and fully applying them in a most fitting way to the practical realities of the General Offensive and Uprising in our war theater. This [improve-ment] has opened up vast possibilities for our army and people to *fight strongly and sustainedly, to become stronger as they fight, to win bigger victories as they fight, to launch strong military attacks at the same time as they launch strong political offensives in the cities and countryside, to firmly hold and expand the liberated areas, to widen our mastership, to secure our strategic positions, and to keep up and develop our offensive position and our encirclement of the enemy, especially on the major battlefield under extremely fierce and complicated [fighting] condi-tions of our war theater.*

*   *   *

However, the General Offensive and Uprising is a phase which marks a leap forward of our people's revolutionary warfare; it requires more than ever a strong impulse and improvement in leadership and guidance. Yet the reality of the recent past indicated that the leadership and guidance of our authorities at various echelons did not meet these objective requirements; worse still, in some places and at times, this leadership and guidance evolved too slowly.

a. The key issue which is the origin of all shortcomings and weak points in the leadership and guidance of our authorities at various echelons during the recent period *lies in the fact that we did not thoroughly comprehend the basic problems of the General Offensive and Uprising and problems relating to [Party] policies and guidelines; worse still, in some places and at times we made serious mistakes both in ideological concepts, viewpoints, and standpoints, and in the supervision of policy execution.* A few of our cadres and Party members, including those at Region and Province Party Committee levels, are usually superficial and narrow-minded in assessing our strength and the enemy's; they only see the manifestations [of things] and fail to see their nature, they overestimate the enemy and underesti-mate the revolutionary capacities of the masses; therefore, when faced with diffi-culties, *they become skeptical and lack resolution vis-à-vis the Central Committee's strategic determination; and they lose interest in attacking, which is the highest principle of the General Offensive and Uprising.* Because they are not firmly anchored in the working class standpoint, they lack absolute determination, and their thinking is subjective and superficial; therefore, they usually have an *erroneous conception of the transitional nature of the General Offensive and Uprising,* now thinking it is a one-blow affair and consequently lacking vigilance against the enemy plots, now thinking it is a period of protracted struggle and consequently lacking boldness and a sense of urgency; worse still, they become right-leaning and shrink back from action.

* * *

Part II. Future Enemy Schemes and Our Immediate Tasks

* * *

The Americans' subjective intention is to carry out the *precept* of deescalating [the war] step by step; to strive to seize the initiative in a passive position; to win a strong position on the battlefield as they de-escalate; *to de-escalate in order to "de-Americanize" the war but not to immediately end* the war; to reinforce the puppet army as American troops are withdrawn; to have necessary time for having appropriate de-escalation steps; and at *every de-escalation step, to strive to launch partial counter-offensives in fierce competition with our forces.*

b. At present, there is very little possibility that the enemy will carry out a massive troop build-up and expand the limited war to the whole country; however, we still need to keep our alertness. There are *two possible developments* to the war as follows:

One: In the process of de-escalating the war, the Americans may suffer increasing losses and encounter greater difficulties; therefore they may be *forced to seek an early end to the war* through a political solution which they cannot refuse. Even in this case, there will be a period of time from the signing of the agreement ending the war until all American troops are withdrawn from South Viet-Nam. During this period of time, our struggle against the enemy will go on with extreme complexity and we will have to be extremely alert.

Two: If our attacks in all aspects are not sufficiently strong and if the Americans are able to temporarily overcome part of their difficulties, they will strive to prolong the war in South Viet-Nam for a certain period of time during which they will try to de-escalate from a strong position of one sort or another, and carry out the de-Americanization in a prolonged war contest before they must admit defeat and accept a political solution.

In both these eventualities, especially in the case of a prolonged de-escalation, the Americans may, in certain circumstances, put pressure on us by threatening to broaden the war through the resumption of bombing in North Viet-Nam within a definite scope and time limit, or the expansion of the war into Laos and Cambodia.

Whether the war will develop according to the first or second eventuality *depends principally on the strength of our attacks in the military, political and diplomatic fields,* especially our military and political attacks, and on the extent of military, political, economic and financial difficulties which the war causes to the Americans in Viet-Nam, in the U.S.A. itself, and over the world.

240. ADDRESS BY NIXON,
NOVEMBER 3, 1969 [Extracts]

At the end of June, Nixon made his first major decision on Vietnam. He set a deadline of November 1, 1969, by which the DRV would have to make substantial concessions in peace negotiations or face what he termed in a private letter to Ho Chi Minh "measures of great consequence and force." Contingency plans were drawn up for the mining of North Vietnamese ports and harbors and intensive bombing of both military and economic targets in the North. But a massive nation-wide antiwar protest, the Vietnam Moratorium in October 1969, forced Nixon to face the probability that further escalation of the war would result in even broader and more intense public opposition. Nixon recognized that his "ultimatum" to Hanoi had been undercut and abandoned plans to carry out his threat. Instead, he used the speech he had scheduled for November 1 to attempt to rally public support behind him sufficiently to carry out a longer-term strategy based on "Vietnamiza- tion" of the war. It was an appeal to the "silent majority" of Americans to repudiate the protesters' demand for an end to U.S. involvement in Indochina. The response, reflected in favorable telegrams and letters and approval of the speech in public opinion polls, gave Nixon time to continue direct U.S. participation in the war for another three years.

Now, many believe that President Johnson's decision to send American com- bat forces to South Vietnam was wrong. And many others—I among them—have been strongly critical of the way the war has been conducted.

But the question facing us today is—now that we are in the war, what is the best way to end it?

In January I could only conclude that the precipitate withdrawal of American forces from Vietnam would be a disaster not only for South Vietnam but for the United States and for the cause of peace.

For the South Vietnamese, our precipitate withdrawal would inevitably allow the Communists to repeat the massacres which followed their takeover in the North 15 years before.

—They then murdered more than 50,000 people and hundreds of thousands more died in slave labor camps.

—We saw a prelude of what would happen in South Vietnam when the Communists entered the city of Hue last year. During their brief rule there, there was a bloody reign of terror in which 3,000 civilians were clubbed, shot to death, and buried in mass graves.

—With the sudden collapse of our support, these atrocities of Hue would become the nightmare of the entire nation—and particularly for the million and a half Catholic refugees who fled to South Vietnam when the Communists took over in the North.

For the United States, this first defeat in our Nation's history would result in a

SOURCE: *Background Information on Southeast Asia and Vietnam.* pp. 367–376.

collapse of confidence in American leadership, not only in Asia but throughout the world.

Three American Presidents have recognized the great stakes involved in Vietnam and understood what had to be done.

*   *   *

My fellow Americans, I am sure you can recognize from what I have said that we really only have two choices open to us if we want to end this war.

—I can order an immediate, precipitate withdrawal of all Americans from Vietnam without regard to the effects of that action.

—Or we can persist in our search for a just peace through a negotiated settlement if possible, or through continued implementation of our plan for Vietnamization if necessary—a plan in which we will withdraw all of our forces from Vietnam on a schedule in accordance with our program, as the South Vietnamese become strong enough to defend their own freedom.

I have chosen this second course.

It is not the easy way.

It is the right way.

It is a plan which will end the war and serve the cause of peace—not just in Vietnam but in the Pacific and in the world.

In speaking of the consequences of a precipitate withdrawal, I mentioned that our allies would lose confidence in America.

Far more dangerous, we would lose confidence in ourselves. Oh, the immediate reaction would be a sense of relief that our men were coming home, but as we saw the consequences of what we had done, inevitable remorse and divisive recrimination would scar our spirit as a people.

We have faced other crises in our history and have become stronger by rejecting the easy way out and taking the right way in meeting our challenges. Our greatness as a nation has been our capacity to do what had to be done when we knew our course was right.

*   *   *

And now I would like to address a word if I may to the young people of this Nation who are particularly concerned, and I understand why they are concerned, about this war.

I respect your idealism.

I share your concern for peace.

I want peace as much as you do.

There are powerful personal reasons I want to end this war. This week I will have to sign 83 letters to mothers, fathers, wives, and loved ones of men who have given their lives for America in Vietnam. It is very little satisfaction to me that this is only one-third as many letters as I signed the first week in office. There is nothing I want more than to see the day come when I do not have to write any of those letters.

—I want to end the war to save the lives of those brave young men in Vietnam.

—But I want to end it in a way which will increase the chance that their younger brothers and their sons will not have to fight in some future Vietnam someplace in the world.

—And I want to end the war for another reason. I want to end it so that the energy and dedication of you, our young people, now too often directed into bitter hatred against those responsible for the war, can be turned to the great challenges of peace, a better life for all Americans, a better life for all people on this earth.

I have chosen a plan for peace. I believe it will succeed.

If it does succeed, what the critics say now won't matter. If it does not succeed, anything I say then won't matter.

I know it may not be fashionable to speak of patriotism or national destiny these days. But I feel it is appropriate to do so on this occasion.

Two hundred years ago this Nation was weak and poor. But even then, America was the hope of millions in the world. Today we have become the strongest and richest Nation in the world. The wheel of destiny has turned so that any hope the world has for the survival of peace and freedom will be determined by whether the American people have the moral stamina and the courage to meet the challenge of free world leadership.

Let historians not record that when America was the most powerful nation in the world we passed on the other side of the road and allowed the last hopes for peace and freedom of millions of people to be suffocated by the forces of totalitarianism.

And so tonight—to you, the great silent majority of my fellow Americans—I ask for your support.

I pledged in my campaign for the Presidency to end the war in a way that we could win the peace. I have initiated a plan of action which will enable me to keep that pledge.

The more support I can have from the American people, the sooner that pledge can be redeemed; for the more divided we are at home, the less likely the enemy is to negotiate at Paris.

Let us be united for peace. Let us also be united against defeat. Because let us understand: North Vietnam cannot defeat or humiliate the United States. Only Americans can do that.

Fifty years ago, in this room and at this very desk, President Woodrow Wilson spoke words which caught the imagination of a war-weary world. He said, "This is the war to end wars." His dream for peace after World War I was shattered on the hard realities of great power politics and Woodrow Wilson died a broken man.

Tonight I do not tell you that the war in Vietnam is the war to end wars. But I do say this.

I have initiated a plan which will end this war in a way that will bring us closer to that great goal to which Woodrow Wilson and every American President in our history has been dedicated—the goal of a just and lasting peace.

As President I hold the responsibility for choosing the best path to that goal and then leading the Nation along it.

I pledge to you tonight that I shall meet this responsibility with all of the strength and wisdom I can command in accordance with your hopes, mindful of your concerns, sustained by your prayers.

Thank you and good night.

1970

241. MEMORANDUM FROM SECRETARY OF DEFENSE MELVIN LAIRD FOR THE PRESIDENT, FEBRUARY 17, 1970 [Extracts]

Following a trip to Vietnam from February 10 to February 14, 1970, Secretary of Defense Laird gave Nixon an optimistic report on the progress and future prospects for Vietnamization. Laird noted his warnings to U.S. and Saigon government officials that public opinion and fiscal restraints required the continual reduction of American forces and the transfer of combat responsibilities to the Saigon army. His report reflected the central importance of U.S. air power to the Vietnamization strategy and the idea that a residual American military presence would have to remain behind, once the bulk of U.S. combat forces had departed, to carry out what Laird suggested could be called "protective reaction" operations–a phrase that would enter the vocabulary of the war the following year.

The best characterization of the atmosphere among top US and GVN officials in South Vietnam is one of cautious optimism. I was told on this visit, just as last March, that we now have and can retain sufficient strength to keep the enemy from achieving any kind of military verdict in South Vietnam. I was also told the South Vietnamese were making satisfactory progress in Vietnamization, especially on the military front. All indicators tend to confirm these judgments.

That, in essence, is what the US and GVN leadership in South Vietnam conveyed to me. What I attempted to convey to them was, in my judgment, likewise important. I emphasized the major constraint on US involvement was now economic. Last year, the principal constraint was diminishing US public support. I assured the people with whom I talked US public support is still vital and should not be taken for granted. But, the actual and prospective diminished US funds available for national security are consistently narrowing our operational latitude in Southeast Asia. Comprehension of that problem is vital to continued progress in Vietnamization. I emphasized the key factor, if we are to (a) operate within the resources available and (b) sustain the support of the American people, is to continue shifting the burden of military combat to the South Vietnamese. The fiscal situation provides an incentive and reinforcement to the Vietnamization policy. It also introduces a new element of risk.

* * *

A more disturbing problem in the joint planning area involves political or negotiating contingencies which may arise. As I indicated earlier, one of the enemy courses of action deemed most likely by both US and GVN leadership is a sharp enemy military move, followed by a Paris initiative involving some cease-fire feature. Surprisingly, little has been done, or is being done, to think through the handling of such a situation—or of similar situations. Ambassador Bunker was candid in rendering this judgment. In fact, he reasoned, Hanoi would be smart to follow the strategy of occupying one or two towns and then appealing for a cease-fire. General Abrams concurred in that conclusion, contending such a tactic would

SOURCE: Document declassified by Department of Defense, August 18, 1977.

have been prudent for the enemy at various times during and since TET 1968. Ambassador Bunker informed us the GVN Foreign Minister was scheduled to present a paper shortly which might serve as the basis for contingency planning. I believe we must move expeditiously in this area, taking the initiative, if necessary.

* * *

There is no doubt in Saigon, among US or GVN officials, that US troop redeployments will continue. There is likewise no doubt that the ultimate goal is for a relatively small military assistance group. The question is one of force composition and timing. The South Vietnamese are perhaps more confident on the potential and feasible redeployment rates than our US leadership. Ambassador Bunker made the point cogently when he reasoned that in terms of ARVN combat power "Vietnamization [has] proceeded more rapidly than US redeployments."

General Abrams is more cautious. He makes the point that, despite an "entirely satisfactory" current military situation and an RVNAF modernization program that is "moving well," the next redeployment increment, i.e., number four, will be the "crunch" increment. He argues that RVNAF leadership is still weak in some areas. He also argues that, if military difficulties ensue in the wake of the redeployment announcement or movement, the psychological impact could be severe. Finally, he notes increasing problems in handling the logistics aspects of redeployment.

I am not certain I fully understand all of General Abrams' argument about the gravity of the next increment. While contending the RVNAF leadership is weak in some areas, which it almost certainly is, he also noted that perhaps as few as four major leadership positions now need President Thieu's attention. Furthermore, General Abrams made a convincing case for the enemy's inability in the foreseeable future to mount any wide, sustained, or decisive military moves. General Abrams speaks confidently of his ability to use air reserves as an adequate source of reserve power. Presumably, a fourth redeployment increment could be devised which impacted relatively little on that reserve power. Additionally, I have directed a full-scale effort by the logistics staffs at all echelons towards easing the postulated logistics problems. Finally, the GVN leadership spoke with confidence of their ability to fill in behind continuing US redeployments. Ambassador Bunker conveyed to me their confidence is sincere.

Therefore, the prediction the next redeployment increment will be "the crunch," at least to date, is not entirely consistent with all the other observable factors. Nevertheless, there could be an element of self-fulfillment about feelings of uncertainty and potential psychological reactions to the next US troop movements. We shall be advised, I believe, to weigh the timing, force composition, and risks carefully. I am prepared to believe redeployment increment four will be more difficult than the immediately succeeding increments.

Still another element of redeployment planning which must bear close scrutiny is the concept, at least as expressed publicly, of the role of the so-called security force after our main combat elements have departed.

As you know, there is a common, though misguided, feeling that, when our troop strengths have declined to about the 250,000 level, we shall have few or no combat troops left in South Vietnam. That is not the plan nor has it ever been the plan. While major combat elements will have departed by that juncture, the remaining force will be weighted as much as 60 percent with combat troops. They are to provide the security assurance which is absolutely vital for the remaining support elements.

General Abrams makes the valid point, with strong conviction, that such remaining combat elements—called security elements, or whatever—must be free to stay active and aggressive in the field. Without such freedom, they will lose their sharpness. Rather than holding down casualty levels, they will, under such circumstances, be apt to sustain higher casualty levels.

The point is that after our so-called combat elements have redeployed, US units must be free to maintain an active and forceful combat posture. The issue may be one of semantics. It is an important concept, however, on which we must have agreement and a common voice. I support General Abrams' view. Our field commanders should be free to use their resources in whatever way will keep US casualties low. We can and perhaps should portray the operations as "protective reaction," i.e., using whatever means are necessary to safeguard our troops properly. In any event, I repeat my conviction we should agree on the concept and present it with a common voice.

Another aspect of redeployment planning and technique which I emphasized consistently was the procedure on redeployment announcements. All the officials with whom I talked, including President Thieu and Vice President Ky, agreed we should *not* make public announcements on Vietnamization schedules more than 4–5 months in advance. The principal reasons are twofold: (a) to create doubt and uncertainty in Hanoi, and (b) to preclude unnecessary risks of credibility problems, especially in the United States.

242. TELEGRAM FROM ACTING CHAIRMAN OF THE JOINT CHIEFS OF STAFF WESTMORELAND TO COMMANDER IN CHIEF, PACIFIC FORCES, ADM. JOHN MCCAIN AND COMMANDER, U.S. MILITARY ASSISTANCE COMMAND VIETNAM GEN. CREIGHTON ABRAMS, APRIL 22, 1970

Within days of the coup against Cambodian chief of state Norodom Sihanouk, on March 18, the new government headed by Lon Nol cut off the former Communist source of supply through the port of Sihanoukville, declared it would oust all Vietnamese troops from the country, and even launched futile attacks against the Vietnamese Communist sanctuaries in the border area. At the end of March, South Vietnamese government forces, with U.S. logistical support, launched company-sized attacks on the sanctuaries, penetrating up to three miles inside Cambodia. Beginning in the first week in April, Communist forces began moving westward out of their border sanctuaries, ambushing Cambodian army units and setting up local pro-Sihanouk administrations. The Lon Nol government then systematically massacred thousands of Vietnamese civilians who had long resided in eastern Cambo-

SOURCE: Document declassified by the Joint Chiefs of Staff, September 9, 1977.

dia, and the Vietnamese Communist forces responded by taking over the towns where the Vietnamese civilian population was concentrated.

By April 21 the Vietnamese had cut the roads into Phnom Penh from three directions, and the Lon Nol government appeared to be in peril. Nixon authorized American air support for a major South Vietnamese operation against the "Parrot's Beak" area of Cambodia at a National Security Council meeting on April 22, but held off a decision on a U.S. ground offensive against the sanctuaries. In a message to Admiral McCain in Honolulu and General Abrams in Saigon that same day, General Westmoreland, then acting chairman of the Joint Chiefs, viewed the Vietnamese as "overextended" in Cambodia and saw "opportunities that we should not let slip by" to achieve the long-held JCS objective of attacking the sanctuaries and to remove other restrictions on American forces in Indochina.

Subj: Situation-in-Cambodia

1. As you are certainly aware, there is highest level concern here with respect to the situation in Cambodia. This concern has been heightened by the following:

    a. It appears that the success of NVA and VC troops to date have encouraged them to expand what may have been limited objectives initially to a current drive to isolate Phnom Penh.

    b. Most lines of communication leading into Phnom Penh from the north, east, and south have been interdicted by enemy forces and the security of Phnom Penh and the Cambodian Government appears to be seriously threatened.

2. Considerations are continuing as to how best to respond to this situation in a timely manner. As you know, limited US materiel support to the Cambodian Government has begun; however, we are of the view that this will have only minor impact on the current momentum of the VC/NVA. Further, we believe that a more direct approach through attack of enemy support areas along the South Vietnam/Cambodian border would probably have much greater effect on the enemy in the near term. With the enemy over-extended, he presents us with opportunities that we should not let slip by. Further, the threat to Phnom Penh and the present concern of higher authority may be conducive to relaxation of some of the current constraints under which we are operating. If this happens we should be prepared to take advantage of the opportunity.

3. Actions which we might consider and on which I would like your views follow:

    a. More US involvement in detailed ARVN planning for cross-border operations.

    b. Preparations to provide US fire support and logistic support for ARVN units operating cross-border.

    c. Preparation for selective use of US troops in most productive base areas, if US policy permits.

    d. Plans for employment of Khmer CIDG [Civilian Irregular Defense Groups] troops.

    e. Diversion of some of the small arms and ammunition now en route to the PSDF [People's Self-Defense Forces].

3. With respect to employment of the Khmer CIDG we could:

    a. Fly them to Phnom Penh to support the FARK. [Forces Armées Royale Khmer].

    b. Use them for cross-border operations supported from SVN.

It would appear that the later [sic] would be more productive. In this case we could relieve the Khmer of their present CIDG border post duties and concentrate them in one or more areas where they could devote full attention to cross-border operations. In this way we could continue to support them from bases in SVN. Under proper circumstances they might be accompanied by Vietnamese Special Forces (LLDB) [*Luc Luong Dac Diet*, "Special Forces" in Vietnamese] or US Special Forces. We would like your appraisal of their probable effectiveness if:

 (1) Vietnamese Special Forces remain with them; or

 (2) They operated without either Vietnamese or US Special Forces accompanying them.

 4. With respect to small arms delivery, it would appear that we might consider delivering arms by sea to Vung Tau and then by air to Phnom Penh. We would want delivery to be covert if possible; however, this may not be feasible over a long period or if large quantities are involved.

 5. We would appreciate your views on the above suggestions and any others that you believe would be effective in relieving pressure on Phnom Penh and the Cambodian Government. Whatever plans we embark on should be designed for early implementation and be effective over the next few weeks to take advantage of the remaining dry season. Highest authority is particularly interested in steps that we can take now to reflect our support for Lon Nol and to cause the North Vietnamese to reappraise their actions. We believe that the first step should be ARVN operations against critical base areas in the following target priorities:

 a. Headquarters and Communication Centers.

 b. Caches and Depots.

 c. Troop concentrations.

The US would support this initial step up to the border, working with the South Vietnamese, and should be prepared to take further actions into Cambodia if the political situation permits.

 6. (U) Since we must provide recommendations to higher authority, would appreciate your views by 0800 Washington time on 22 April.

243. ADDRESS BY NIXON ON CAMBODIA, APRIL 30, 1970 [Extracts]

Only ten days after he had given an optimistic assessment for Vietnamization in South Vietnam, Nixon announced that American and South Vietnamese troops were attacking Communist sanctuaries in Cambodia, claiming that they would attack the headquarters for the entire war effort in South Vietnam that very night. (In his background briefing for the press, Kissinger admitted that the Central Office for South Vietnam was highly mobile and that the United States did not expect to capture it intact, but Nixon had refused to eliminate the reference from his speech.) Nixon and Kissinger had agreed that the invasion was certain to provoke a major uproar at home, and that there was no assurance of military success. The nation-wide protest was the most intense and violent of the war: after four students were killed by National Guardsmen at Kent State, 450 colleges and uni-

SOURCE: *Background Information Relating to Southeast Asia and Vietnam*, pp. 412–414.

*versities went on strike and classes had to be cancelled for the remainder of
the year.*

Good evening, my fellow Americans. Ten days ago, in my report to the
Nation on Viet-Nam, I announced a decision to withdraw an additional 150,000
Americans from Viet-Nam over the next year. I said then that I was making that
decision despite our concern over increased enemy activity in Laos, in Cambodia,
and in South Viet-Nam.

At that time, I warned that if I concluded that increased enemy activity in any
of these areas endangered the lives of Americans remaining in Viet-Nam I would
not hesitate to take strong and effective measures to deal with that situation.

Despite that warning, North Viet-Nam has increased its military aggression in
all these areas, and particularly in Cambodia.

After full consultation with the National Security Council, Ambassador Bunker, General Abrams, and my other advisers, I have concluded that the actions of the
enemy in the last 10 days clearly endanger the lives of Americans who are in
Viet-Nam now and would constitute an unacceptable risk to those who will be
there after withdrawal of another 150,000.

To protect our men who are in Viet-Nam and to guarantee the continued
success of our withdrawal and Vietnamization programs, I have concluded that the
time has come for action.

*   *   *

North Viet-Nam in the last 2 weeks has stripped away all pretense of respecting the sovereignty or the neutrality of Cambodia. Thousands of their soldiers are
invading the country from the sanctuaries; they are encircling the Capital of Phnom
Penh. Coming from these sanctuaries, as you see here, they have moved into
Cambodia and are encircling the Capital.

Cambodia, as a result of this, has sent out a call to the United States, to a
number of other nations, for assistance. Because if this enemy effort succeeds,
Cambodia would become a vast enemy staging area and a springboard for attacks
on South Viet-Nam along 600 miles of frontier, a refuge where enemy troops could
return from combat without fear of retaliation.

North Vietnamese men and supplies could then be poured into that country,
jeopardizing not only the lives of our own men but the people of South Viet-Nam as
well.

Now, confronted with this situation, we have three options.

First, we can do nothing. Well, the ultimate result of that course of action is
clear. Unless we indulge in wishful thinking, the lives of Americans remaining in
Viet-Nam after our next withdrawal of 150,000 would be gravely threatened.

Let us go to the map again. Here is South Viet-Nam. Here is North Viet-Nam.
North iet-Nam already occupies this part of Laos. If North Viet-Nam also occupied this whole band in Cambodia, or the entire country, it would mean that South
Viet-Nam was completely outflanked and the forces of Americans in this area, as
well as the South Vietnamese, would be in an untenable military position.

Our second choice is to provide massive military assistance to Cambodia
itself. Now, unfortunately, while we deeply sympathize with the plight of 7
million Cambodians, whose country is being invaded, massive amounts of military
assistance could not be rapidly and effectively utilized by the small Cambodian
Army against the immediate threat.

With other nations, we shall do our best to provide the small arms and other equipment which the Cambodian Army of 40,000 needs and can use for its defense. But the aid we will provide will be limited to the purpose of enabling Cambodia to defend its neutrality and not for the purpose of making it an active belligerent on one side or the other.

Our third choice is to go to the heart of the trouble. That means cleaning out major North Vietnamese and Viet Cong occupied territories—these sanctuaries which serve as bases for attacks on both Cambodia and American and South Vietnamese forces in South Viet-Nam. Some of these, incidentally, are as close to Saigon as Baltimore is to Washington. This one, for example [*indicating*], is called the Parrot's Beak. It is only 33 miles from Saigon.

Now, faced with these three options, this is the decision I have made.

In cooperation with the armed forces of South Viet-Nam, attacks are being launched this week to clean out major enemy sanctuaries on the Cambodian-Viet-Nam border.

A major responsibility for the ground operations is being assumed by South Vietnamese forces. For example, the attacks in several areas, including the Parrot's Beak that I referred to a moment ago, are exclusively South Vietnamese ground operations under South Vietnamese command, with the United States providing air and logistical support.

There is one area, however, immediately above Parrot's Beak, where I have concluded that a combined American and South Vietnamese operation is necessary.

Tonight American and South Vietnamese units will attack the headquarters for the entire Communist military operation in South Viet-Nam. This key control center has been occupied by the North Vietnamese and Viet Cong for 5 years in blatant violation of Cambodia's neutrality.

This is not an invasion of Cambodia. The areas in which these attacks will be launched are completely occupied and controlled by North Vietnamese forces. Our purpose is not to occupy the areas. Once enemy forces are driven out of these sanctuaries and once their military supplies are destroyed, we will withdraw.

These actions are in no way directed at the security interests of any nation. Any government that chooses to use these actions as a pretext for harming relations with the United States will be doing so on its own responsibility and on its own initiative, and we will draw the appropriate conclusions.

1971

244. SUMMARY OF COSVN DIRECTIVE NO. 01/CT71, JANUARY–FEBRUARY 1971 [Extracts]

COSVN Resolution 9, passed in July 1969, apparently served as the strategic guidance for the Party organization in the South until early 1971, when COSVN

SOURCE: Viet-Nam Documents and Research Notes, No. 99, October 1971.

convened another full conference and passed Resolution 10. Although the text of that resolution never fell into U.S. or Saigon hands, a study document that summarized the resolution, undated but believed to be written at about the same time as the COSVN conference, did. This document admitted that the Saigon government and the United States had achieved temporary success in its pacification program, but argued that its policies of conscription, troop upgrading, and increased war spending would push the urban struggle movement forward. It looked to a combination of trends, including the antiwar movement in the United States and the fact that revolutionary forces were active in Laos and Cambodia as well, to turn the tide in the Indochinese theater in favor of the revolution.

Following are the characteristics particular to the struggle on the South Viet-Nam battlefield and the general characteristics of the Indochinese theater of operations.

1. Pacification and counterpacification struggles by enemy and friendly forces were and are being conducted under highly violent forms. The enemy has achieved some temporary results, but is steadily failing in implementing his basic schemes. Meanwhile, we have fought courageously and persistently, surmounted all difficulties, and are forging ahead, although some minor difficulties still exist in conducting fierce attacks against the enemy.

During the past two years, the U.S. and puppet focused their efforts on pacifying and encroaching upon rural areas, using the most barbarous schemes. They strengthened puppet forces, consolidated the puppet government, and established an outpost network and espionage and People's Self-Defense Force organizations in many hamlets and villages. They provided more technical equipment for, and increased the mobility of, puppet forces, established blocking lines, and created a new defensive and oppressive system in densely populated rural areas. As a result, they caused many difficulties to and inflicted losses on friendly forces. Generally, however, they were unable to attain their basic objectives. They failed to destroy or wipe out the revolutionary infrastructure or our local and guerrilla forces which continued to remain in their areas of operation. In some areas, we were even able to increase our forces. In spite of his oppressive control, the enemy failed to subdue our people. Along with our cadre and Party members, the people in rural areas continually attacked the enemy and constantly maintained and developed the revolutionary movement. On the other hand, enemy forces and war facilities were increasingly depleted and destroyed. Enemy military forces were thinly dispersed and many of his outposts were encircled or isolated. The noteworthy point is that in implementing his pacification and Vietnamization programs, the enemy was forced to resort to dictatorial and fascist policies which deepened the contradictions between people of various strata, including personnel of the puppet army and administration, and various political factions, on one hand and the U.S.-Thieu-Ky-Khiem clique on the other hand; this situation further aggravated the political, economic and financial crisis of the U.S.-puppets, sapped the internal unity of the puppets and isolated the U.S.-Thieu-Ky-Khiem clique. This created new favorable conditions for popular struggle movements in Saigon and other cities and rural areas.

2. The 18 March 1970 coup d'etat and the subsequent expansion of the war of aggression by the U.S. imperialists to Cambodia, which was intended to support the Vietnamization program in South Viet-Nam, failed to enable them to attain their

proposed goals of destroying our agencies, storage facilities, and base areas, destroying and depleting our main forces, halting the revolutionary movement in Cambodia, and saving the Lon Nol clique from a dangerous situation.

On the contrary, this created conditions for the Cambodian revolutionary movement to leap forward and strengthened the unity of the peoples of Laos, Cambodia, and Viet-Nam in their struggles. A unified front was established through which the Indochinese peoples are fighting their common enemy, the U.S. imperialists and their henchmen. A large strategic theater of operations was developed, binding the three countries together, linking the big frontline with the big rear area, and turning Indo-China into a unified battlefield. In this theater, Cambodia is the most vulnerable point of the U.S. and puppets, South Viet-Nam is the main war theater with a decisive bearing on the common victory, and Laos is a significant area of operations.

In 1970, the U.S. imperialists ventured to expand the war in Cambodia, but failed to save themselves from the dangerous situation. On the contrary, they suffered heavier military, political, and diplomatic failures and became further bogged down and strategically deadlocked. The U.S. withdrew its troops while puppet troops had to replace U.S. troops and concurrently play the key role in supporting the puppet Cambodian troops. Since enemy troops were forced to disperse thinly, the enemy experienced increasing difficulties in his pacification and Vietnamization plans and will certainly meet defeat.

3. Because the enemy exerted great efforts to implement the Nixon doctrine in South Viet-Nam and Indo-China, we had to surmount great difficulties and trials in the resistance against the U.S. for national salvation.

The [revolutionary] movement in the rural area was subjected to unprecedented disturbances by barbarous enemy attacks through his pacification and encroachment programs. However, we were still able to maintain the operational positions of our infrastructure and armed forces.

We managed to maintain and in some areas even expand, our control over villages and hamlets in spite of the presence of enemy outposts. In many areas, we even undermined or reduced the effectiveness of the enemy defensive and oppressive control system.

The [struggle] movement in urban areas against the burden born from the Vietnamization plan developed on a large scale with support from all social classes. They openly demanded U.S. troop withdrawals, an overthrow of the Thieu-Ky-Khiem clique, and the establishment of a Government which would restore peace. The movement was supported by uncommitted factions and many personalities of various [political] parties, including those in the puppet National Assembly and the puppet government. Such a movement has caused continual failures for the U.S.-Thieu-Ky-Khiem clique in its efforts to rally a political force to support its oppression of revolutionary forces and opposition parties.

In this extremely fierce and complicated war, our main force units effectively fulfilled their role by attracting, containing and destroying many enemy mobile forces to successfully support political and armed [struggle] movements in South Viet-Nam and Cambodia. Through their successful maintenance and expansion of our strategic bases and corridors, they have proven to be increasingly significant in the new war position of the Indochinese people.

The great victories achieved on the battlefield by the people of the three Indochinese countries, in conjunction with positive diplomatic activities, won increasingly broad support and cooperation from all democratic and peace-loving people throught the world and isolated the Nixon clique and its lackey governments.

*   *   *

Noteworthy is the fact that although they would continue to withdraw their troops, they would retain an important element of U.S: and satellite forces to operate with puppet forces which are large in number but low in morale. These troops are reinforced with equipment and given additional training and support from U.S. troops, especially the U.S. Air Force, therefore they have considerable firepower and great mobility. They have a new defensive and oppressive control system designed to safeguard both rural and urban areas therefore they have the hope to maintain and improve their position.

Nevertheless, they also have very fundamental difficulties that cannot be surmounted even with the large military and economic potentials of the ringleader imperialists. They have to deescalate the war, continue to withdraw their troops, and rely on the puppet government and Army which are increasingly demoralized and politically weakened. They have to cope with three Indochinese countries which have power and sound leadership in addition to their tradition of fighting the aggressors. They also have to face the peace movements in the U.S. and throughout the world demanding the end of the war of aggression in Viet-Nam and Indo-China.

The basic enemy weaknesses and our objective advantages are as follows:

The more the U.S. speeds up the Vietnamization program, the more the puppet government is compelled to expedite its dictatorial and fascist policies on conscription, troop upgrading, taxation and inflation, and to send puppet troops to the battlefields to die in the place of U.S. soldiers. By so doing, the puppet government would aggravate the contradictions between itself and the people of various classes, including the uncommitted class and a large number of puppet government personnel. It would make the demands for social welfare, economic improvement, freedom, democracy, culture, the end of war, and restoration of peace become more pressing. It would ripen the political awareness demanding U.S. troop withdrawals and the replacement of the Thieu-Ky-Khiem government by a new one which would restore peace; aggravate the political, economic, and financial crises; and deepen the internal dissensions in the puppet government. These are the objective conditions necessary for us to expand the struggle movement against the Americans for national salvation and rally the new forces including the uncommitted class, puppet soldiers and personnel, and a number of personalities in the puppet government to promote a new movement against the U.S. and the Thieu-Ky-Khiem clique.

245. TELEVISION INTERVIEW BY NIXON, MARCH 22, 1971 [Extract]

As the Nixon Administration looked toward continued withdrawals of American forces from South Vietnam, it planned to weaken Communist military forces by

SOURCE: Department of State *Bulletin,* April 12, 1971, pp. 499–500.

disrupting their logistics system of trail networks and base areas in Laos and Cambodia. The key strategic decision on the 1970–1971 dry season was that the Thieu government's best divisions would attack the hub of the entire trail network in southern Laos, the province town of Tchepone, then continue to interdict the trails and destroy Communist logistics structures during the remainder of the dry season. The operation, which began early in February, was supposed to have captured Tchepone in four or five days, but it bogged down and suffered very heavy casualties. According to Kissinger's account, it was terminated arbitrarily by Thieu in mid-March when ARVN forces had taken three thousand casualties out of a total of five thousand troops. After six weeks, ARVN forces were in full retreat, much to the chagrin of U.S. officials. Nixon gamely tried to put the best face on the defeat in an interview with ABC's Howard K. Smith. But there was never a report to the nation on what was supposed to have been a decisive battle in the war.

Mr. Smith: Well, now, sir, they give the impression of retreating from Laos now, and there is still a whole month of dry season before the rains come. If they retreat now, won't the Communists have plenty of time to repair their trails and repair their pipelines before the rains come?

The President: They can never gain back the time, Mr. Smith. Six weeks is a period in which the Communists not only have found, as we pointed out earlier, that the supplies to the South have been drastically cut.

During that 6-week period they have had chewed up great amounts of ammunition, great amounts of materiel that otherwise would have gone south and would have been used, incidentally, against many Americans fighting in South Viet-Nam, and also in that 6-week period the South Vietnamese have developed a considerable capability on their own and considerable confidence on their own. They are better units to handle the situation as we withdraw.

Now, insofar as what they are going to be able to do for the balance of this dry season is concerned, I can only suggest that I cannot predict what will happen today, tomorrow, or the next day. There is going to be some more severe fighting as the South Vietnamese continue to withdraw from Laos. That we expected.

But let me try to put it in perspective. I have noted a considerable amount of discussion on the networks and in the newspapers and so forth, and it is altogether, let me say, understandable and justifiable discussion, as to whether this is a victory or a defeat. And I know that that is a question perhaps that you would raise; certainly, our viewers would raise it.

Let me hit it very directly. This is not the kind of an operation that you can really describe in the traditional terms of victory or defeat, because its purpose was not to conquer territory. Its purpose was not to destroy an army. Its purpose was simply to disrupt supply lines. Its purpose, in other words, was not to conquer or occupy a part of Laos. Its purpose was to defend South Viet-Nam.

Now, let's measure this operation in terms of accomplishing that purpose. For 6 weeks the South Vietnamese have disrupted the enemy's supply lines. For 6 weeks they have tied down some of the enemy's best divisions. For 6 weeks we have seen, too, that the South Vietnamese have been able to handle themselves quite well under very, very difficult circumstances.

Now, what does this mean for the future? Well, I think when we judge whether this operation is going to be labeled a success or a failure, we cannot judge it before it is concluded, and we cannot judge it even after it is concluded. We can only see it in perspective because its goals were long range—long range being, first, to insure the continuation of the American withdrawal; second, to reduce the risk to the remaining Americans as we withdraw; and third, to insure the ability of the South Vietnamese to defend themselves after we have left. Those were the three goals of this operation.

How do we know whether or not those goals will be achieved? Well, I will say this. My interim assessment based on General Abrams' advice and the advice that I get from all people in the field is this: As far as our withdrawal is concerned, it is assured. The next withdrawal announcement will be made in April. It will be at least at the number that I have been withdrawing over the past few months; and second, as far as the danger to the American forces remaining, particularly in the northern part of South Viet-Nam, there are 100,000 there, as you know, that danger has been substantially reduced. That operation has already accomplished that much.

Third, as far as the ARVN [Army of the Republic of Viet-Nam] is concerned— and here I come back to an expert—General Abrams, who tells it like it is and says it like it is, says that some of their units did not do so well but 18 out of 22 battalions conducted themselves with high morale, with great confidence, and they are able to defend themselves man for man against the North Vietnamese.

And so that I would say insofar as achieving our goals of assuring American withdrawal, reducing the threat to the remainder of our forces, and, finally, our goal of seeing to it that the ARVN develops the capability to defend itself, that the operation in Laos at this interim period has made considerable progress in achieving those goals.

246. DRV PEACE PROPOSAL, JUNE 26, 1971

Beginning in February 1970, Lao Dong Party Political Bureau member Le Duc Tho, the "Special Adviser" to the DRV at the Paris talks, met Dr. Kissinger in Paris in a series of secret negotiating sessions. On May 31, 1971, Kissinger presented a plan offering a willingness to agree to deadline for withdrawal of U.S. troops in return for the repatriation of U.S. prisoners. (The text of that proposal has never been made public.) At the following meeting, on June 26, 1971, Le Duc Tho countered with a proposal that the U.S. troop withdrawal and release of military and civilian prisoners would be completed at the same time and demanding that the U.S. "stop supporting" the Thieu regime. The proposal, coming at a time when opposition figure General Duong Van Minh was considered a potential "peace candidate" in the 1971 South Vietnamese presidential election, was an apparent invitation to the United States to encourage a change in the Saigon government through elections.

1—The withdrawal of all the forces of the United States and those of the other foreign countries in the U.S. camp from South Vietnam and the other Indochinese countries must be achieved in 1971.

SOURCE: Paris Vietnam News Agency [VNA] in French to VNA Hanoi, January 31, 1972. Translated in FBIS, Asia and Pacific, February 1, 1972, pp. k4–5.

2—The release of all the militarymen and civilians captured in the war will be carried out at the same time and will be completed at the same moment as the withdrawal of troops mentioned in Point 1.

3—In South Vietnam, the United States ceases supporting Thieu-Ky-Khiem to allow the formation in Saigon of a new administration standing for peace, independence, neutrality and democracy. The PRGRSV will engage in talks with the said administration with a view to settling the internal affairs of South Vietnam and achieving national concord.

4—The U.S. Government must assume the entire responsibility for the damage caused by the United States to the entire Vietnamese people. The DRV Government and the PRGRSV request from the U.S. Government reparations for damage caused by the United States in the two zones of Vietnam.

5—The United States must respect the 1954 Geneva agreements on Vietnam and Indochina and those of 1962 on Laos. It must cease its aggression against and intervention in the Indochinese countries to let the Indochinese people settle their own affairs.

6—The problems existing between the Indochinese countries will be settled by the Indochinese parties on the basis of mutual respect for independence, sovereignty and territorial integrity, and for noninterference in internal affairs. For its part, the DRV is prepared to participate in the settlement of these problems.

7—All the parties will observe a cease-fire after the conclusion of agreements of the aforementioned problems.

8—An international supervision will be set up.

9—An international guarantee will be indispensable for the realization of the basic national rights of the Indochinese people, for the neutrality of South Vietnam Laos and Cambodia and for the establishment of a lasting peace in this region.

These nine points make up a whole.

247. PEACE PROPOSAL OF THE PROVISIONAL REVOLUTIONARY GOVERNMENT OF THE REPUBLIC OF SOUTH VIETNAM, JULY 1, 1971

A more detailed version of the DRV peace proposal of June 26, 1971, was made public by the Provisional Revolutionary Government on July 1, spelling out each of the points made in the private proposal. It spelled out the political settlement advocated by the Communists: a new "peace" government in Saigon with whom the PRG would negotiate for a three-segment government to carry out elections. It also called for guarantees against reprisals and restoration of democratic liberties—points not covered in U.S. proposals.

1—Regarding the deadline for the total withdrawal of U.S. forces.

The U.S. Government must put an end to its war of aggression in Viet Nam, stop its policy of "Vietnamization" of the war, withdraw from South Viet Nam all

SOURCE: Liberation Press Agency, July 1, 1971. Reprinted in *Background Information Relating to Southeast Asia, and Vietnam*, pp. 640–641.

troops, military personnel, weapons, and war materials of the United States and of the other foreign countries in the U.S. camp, and dismantle all U.S. bases in South Viet Nam, without posing any condition whatsoever.

The U.S. Government must set a terminal date for the withdrawal from South Viet Nam of the totality of U.S. forces and those of the other foreign countries in the U.S. camp.

If the U.S. Government sets a terminal date for the withdrawal from South Viet Nam in 1971 of the totality of U.S. forces and those of the other foreign countries in the U.S. camp, the parties will at the same time agree on the modalities:

A—Of the withdrawal in safety from South Vietnam of the totality of U.S. forces and those of the other foreign countries in the U.S. camp.

B—Of the release of the totality of militarymen of all parties and of the civilians captured in the war (including American pilots captured in North Viet Nam) so that they may all rapidly return to their homes.

These two operations will begin on the same date and will end on the same date.

A cease-fire will be observed between the South Viet Nam People's Liberation Armed Forces and the armed forces of the United States and of the other foreign countries in the U.S. camp as soon as the parties reach agreement on the withdrawal from South Viet Nam of the totality of U.S. forces and those of the other foreign countries in the U.S. camp.

2—Regarding the question of power in South Viet Nam.

The U.S. Government must really respect the South Viet Nam people's right to self-determination, put an end to its interference in the internal affairs of South Viet Nam, cease backing the bellicose group headed by Nguyen Van Thieu at present in office in Saigon, and stop all maneuvers, including tricks on elections, aimed at maintaining the puppet Nguyen Van Thieu.

The political, social and religious forces in South Viet Nam aspiring to peace and national concord will use various means to form in Saigon a new administration favouring peace, independence, neutrality and democracy. The Provisional Revolutionary Government of the Republic of South Viet Nam will immediately enter into talks with the administration in order to settle the following questions:

A—To form a broad three-segment government of national concord that will assume its functions during the period between the restoration of peace and the holding of general elections and organize general election in South Viet Nam.

A ceasefire will be observed between the South Viet Nam People's Liberation Armed Forces and the armed forces of the Saigon Administration as soon as a government of national concord is formed.

B—To take concrete measures with the required guarantees so as to prohibit all acts of terror, reprisal, and discrimination against persons having collaborated with one or the other party, to ensure every democratic liberty to the South Viet Nam people, to release all persons jailed for political reasons, to dissolve all concentration camps and to liquidate all forms of constraint and coercion so as to permit the people to return to their native places in complete freedom and to freely engage in their occupations.

C—To see that the people's living conditions are stabilized and gradually improve, to create conditions allowing everyone to contribute his talents and efforts to heal the war wounds and rebuild the country.

D—To agree on measures to be taken to ensure the holding of genuinely free, democratic and fair general elections in South Viet Nam.

3—Regarding the question of Vietnamese armed forces in South Viet Nam.

The Vietnamese parties will together settle the question of Vietnamese armed forces in South Viet Nam in a spirit of national concord, equality and mutual respect, without foreign interference, in accordance with the post-war situation and with a view to lightening the people's contribution.

4—Regarding the peaceful reunification of Viet Nam and the relations between the north and south zones.

A—The reunification of Viet Nam will be achieved step by step, by peaceful means, on the basis of discussions and agreements between the two zones, without constraint and annexation from either party, without foreign interference.

Pending the reunification of the country, the north and the south zones will re-establish normal relations, guarantee free movement, free correspondence, free choice of residence and maintain economic and cultural relations on the principle of mutual interests and mutual assistance.

All questions concerning the two zones will be settled by qualified representatives of the Vietnamese people in the two zones on the basis of negotiations, without foreign interference.

B—In keeping with the provisions of the 1954 Geneva agreements on Viet Nam, in the present temporary partition of the country into two zones, the north and the south zones of Viet Nam will refrain from joining any military alliance with foreign countries, from allowing any foreign country to have military bases, troops and military personnel on their soil, and from recognizing the protection of any country, of any military alliance or bloc.

5—Regarding the foreign policy of peace and neutrality of South Viet Nam.

South Viet Nam will pursue a foreign policy of peace and neutrality, establish relations with all countries regardless of their political and social regime, in accordance with the five principles of peaceful coexistence, maintain economic and cultural relations with all countries, accept the cooperation of foreign countries in the exploitation of the resources of South Viet Nam, accept from any country economic and technical aid without any political conditions attached, and participate in regional plans of economic cooperation.

On the basis of these principles, after the end of the war, South Viet Nam and the United States will establish relations in the political, economic and cultural fields.

6—Regarding the damage caused by the United States to the Vietnamese people in the two zones.

The U.S. Government must bear full responsibility for the losses and destruction it has caused to the Vietnamese people in the two zones.

7—Regarding the respect for and international guarantee of the accords that will be concluded.

The parties will find agreement on the forms of respect for and international guarantee of the accords that will be concluded.

248. U.S. PEACE PROPOSAL,
OCTOBER 11, 1971

Refusing to make any move to disturb the status quo in Saigon politics, the United States continued to give implicit backing to Thieu in the presidential campaign, with the result that the only opposition candidate, "Big Minh," withdrew from the race on August 20. Only a few days after Thieu was elected with 82 percent of the votes did the United States make a new secret proposal offering a free election to be organized and run by an independent body representing all political forces in the South. The proposal provided for the resignation of Thieu and his vice-president one month before the election. It still contained other provisions that Hanoi found objectionable: an Indochina-wide cease-fire without any political settlement for Laos or Cambodia, the absence of guarantees of democratic freedoms, and a residual U.S. military presence in South Vietnam.

1—The United States agrees to a total withdrawal from South Vietnam of all U.S. forces and other foreign forces allied with the Government of South Vietnam. The withdrawal will be carried out in the following manner:

—The U.S. and allied forces, except for a small number of personnel necessary for technical advice, logistics and observation of the cease-fire mentioned in Point 6, will be withdrawn by 1 July 1972 at the latest, on the condition that this declaration of principle is signed between now and 1 December 1971. In no case will the final date for these withdrawals exceed a period of 7 months after the signing of this declaration of principle.[x]

—The remaining personnel will be progressively withdrawn, beginning 1 month before the presidential election mentioned in Point 3 and simultaneously with the resignation of the present president and vice president of South Vietnam also provided for in Point 3. These withdrawals will be completed before the date of the presidential election.[x]

2—The release of all militarymen and innocent civilians captured throughout Indochina will be carried out in parallel with the troop withdrawals mentioned in Point 1. Both sides will present a complete list of militarymen and innocent civilians held throughout Indochina on the day this declaration of principle is signed. This release will begin on the same day the troop withdrawal begins and will be completed on 1 July 1972, on the condition that this declaration is signed by 1 December 1971 at the latest. The completion of this release will not be later than 7 months after the signing of this declaration.[x]

3—The following principles will govern the political future of South Vietnam.

The political future of South Vietnam will be left for the South Vietnamese people to decide for themselves, free from outside interference.

There will be free and democratic presidential elections in South Vietnam

---

SOURCE: Paris VNA in French to VNA Hanoi, January 31, 1972. Translated in FBIS, Asia and Pacific, February 1, 1972, pp. k3–4.

[x]Passages indicate a different content than in the eight-point proposal published by the White House on 25 January 1972 and presented to the Paris conference on Vietnam on 27 January 1972.

within 6 months after the signing of the final agreement based on the principles of this declaration.[x]

These elections will be organized and run by an independent body representing all political forces in South Vietnam which will assume its responsibilities on the date of the final agreement. This body will, among other responsibilities, determine the qualifications of candidates. All political forces in South Vietnam can participate in the elections and present candidates. There will be international supervision of these elections.

One month before the presidential election takes place, the present president and vice president of South Vietnam will resign. A caretaker government, headed by the chairman of the senate, will assume administrative responsibilities except for those pertaining to the election, which will remain with the independent election body.

The United States, for its part, declares that:

—It will support no candidate and will remain completely neutral in the election.

—It will abide by the outcome of this election and any other political processes shaped by the South Vietnamese people themselves.

—It is prepared to define its military and economic assistance relationships with any government that exists in South Vietnam.

Both sides agree that:

—South Vietnam, together with the other Indochinese countries, should adopt a foreign policy of neutrality.[x]

—The reunification of Vietnam should be decided on the basis of discussions and agreements between North and South Vietnam without constraint or annexation from either party and without foreign interference.

4—Both sides will respect the 1954 Geneva agreements on Indochina and those of 1962 on Laos. There will be no foreign intervention in the Indochinese countries and the Indochinese people will be able to settle their own affairs by themselves.

5—The problems existing among the Indochinese countries will be settled by the Indochinese parties on the basis of mutual respect for their independence, sovereignty and territorial integrity and noninterference in each other's affairs. Among the problems that will be settled is the implementation of the principle that all armed forces of the Indochinese countries must remain within their national frontiers.

6—There will be a general cease-fire throughout Indochina, to begin when the final agreement is signed.[x] Apart from the cease-fire, there will be no further infiltration of outside forces into any of the Indochinese countries.

7—There will be international supervision of the military aspects of this agreement, including the cease-fire and its provisions, the release of prisoners of war and innocent civilians and the withdrawal of outside forces from Indochina.[x]

8—There will be an international guarantee for the fundamental national rights of the Indochinese people, for the neutrality of all Indochinese countries[x] and for a lasting peace in this region.

Both sides express their willingness to participate in an international conference for this and other appropriate purposes.

1972

249. ADDRESS TO THE NATION BY NIXON, MAY 8, 1972 [Extract]

At the end of March 1972, Communist forces struck across the demilitarized zone to smash a newly formed ARVN division, then swiftly opened up two other fronts in the central highlands and northwest of Saigon. A nation-wide offensive aimed at upsetting the balance of forces and pushing for a peace agreement on more favorable terms had begun. U.S. strategic bombing of the North resumed at a much more intense level than under the Johnson Administration, but it failed to deter the offensive. At the end of April, Communist forces overran Quang Tri and advanced on Hue, whose government disintegrated and fled in panic. A few days later, Nixon announced a strategic move that had been considered by the Johnson Administration but rejected as ineffective: the mining of the port of Haiphong. He said the mining would continue until an internationally supervised cease-fire was carried out in all three countries of Indochina.

It is plain then that what appears to be a choice among three courses of action for the United States is really no choice at all. The killing in this tragic war must stop. By simply getting out, we would only worsen the bloodshed. By relying solely on negotiations, we would give an intransigent enemy the time he needs to press his aggression on the battlefield.

There is only one way to stop the killing. That is to keep the weapons of war out of the hands of the international outlaws of North Vietnam.

. . . I therefore concluded that Hanoi must be denied the weapons and supplies it needs to continue the aggression. In full coordination with the Republic of Vietnam, I have ordered the following measures which are being implemented as I am speaking to you.

All entrances to North Vietnamese ports will be mined to prevent access to these ports and North Vietnamese naval operations from these ports. United States forces have been direct to take appropriate measures within the internal and claimed territorial waters of North Vietnam to interdict the delivery of supplies. Rail and all other communications will be cut off to the maximum extent possible. Air and naval strikes against military targets in North Vietnam will continue.

These actions are not directed against any other nation. Countries with ships presently in North Vietnamese ports have already been notified that their ships will have three daylight periods to leave in safety. After that time, the mines will become active and any ships attempting to leave or enter these ports will do so at their own risk.

These actions I have ordered will cease when the following conditions are met:

First, all American prisoners of war must be returned.

Second, there must be an internationally supervised cease-fire throughout Indochina.

SOURCE: *Background Information Relating to Southeast Asia and Vietnam*, p. 473.

Once prisoners of war are released, once the internationally supervised cease-fire has begun, we will stop all acts of force throughout Indochina, and at that time we will proceed with a complete withdrawal of all American forces from Vietnam within 4 months.

Now these terms are generous terms. They are terms which would not require surrender and humiliation on the part of anybody. They would permit the United States to withdraw with honor. They would end the killing. They would bring our POW's home. They would allow negotiations on a political settlement between the Vietnamese themselves. They would permit all the nations which have suffered in this long war—Cambodia, Laos, North Vietnam, South Vietnam—to turn at last to the urgent works of healing and of peace. They deserve immediate acceptance by North Vietnam.

250. NEWS CONFERENCE OF NATIONAL SECURITY ADVISER HENRY A. KISSINGER, MAY 9, 1972 [Extract]

In an account of the diplomatic contacts with the DRV during the period preceding the start of the spring offensive and the meeting in Paris on May 2, Kissinger claimed that the DRV demanded the exclusion of all "organized non-Communist forces" from a coalition government prior to a cease-fire and negotiation of a final settlement.

What is it that the other side is asking of us that we have rejected? The other side has asked of us, prior to negotiations, prior to a cease-fire, that the following steps must be taken:

The President of South Vietnam must resign. What is called by the other side "the machinery of oppression of the government" must be disbanded. Pacification must be stopped. Vietnamization must be stopped, which means the end of American military and economic aid. All persons that have been arrested on political grounds should be set free. Then a government should be formed which is composed of all those who favor peace, independence, neutrality, and democracy, presumably by definition, including the Communists.

In that government, in other words, the Communists would be the only organized force, since all the organized non-Communist forces would have been disbanded by definition.

All of this is prior to a cease-fire. Then this government is supposed to negotiate with the Communists a final solution. In other words, this is only the thinnest veneer; this government, which already contains the Communists, is then supposed to negotiate with the Provisional Revolutionary Government, which is backed by the North Vietnamese army. It will be the only force in the country that has any physical strength, and it is supposed to negotiate with them a final settlement. And all of this, ladies and gentlemen, is before a cease-fire.

SOURCE: *Weekly Compilation of Presidential Documents,* May 15, 1972, pp. 843–844. (Washington D.C.: Office of the Federal Register; Distributed by the Superintendent of Docs., GPO)

That is what we have rejected. That is what we call the imposition, under the thinnest veneer, of a Communist government. That is the ending of American economic and military aid, the disbanding of the government that exists in South Vietnam, as a prelude to negotiations. That is the only issue on which negotiations have broken down.

251. NEWS CONFERENCE OF SPECIAL ADVISER TO THE DRV DELEGATION TO THE PARIS PEACE TALKS LE DUC THO, IN PARIS, MAY 12, 1972 [Extract]

Contradicting Kissinger's characterization of the DRV position in the May 2 meeting, Le Duc Tho, in his first press conference on the Paris negotiations, declared that the Saigon government could name its own representation to the proposed tripartite government, as long as it did not include Thieu, and that such a tripartite government would hold elections – not negotiate with the PRG for a settlement.

QUESTION: Mr. Le Duc Tho, you have many times said that you do not want to force a Communist regime on Saigon. Please clarify that point, because that is the specific point on which the negotiations have stuck.
ANSWER: As we have said the problem between us and the American side which is not yet resolved and which is rather tense, is the problem of the government of South Vietnam. This is one of the thorniest problems. The American desire is to maintain in South Vietnam a US lackey government in order to carry out the policy of "Vietnamizing the war," that is to achieve US neocolonialism in South Vietnam. Because they only want to maintain their lackeys, they have sacrificed unknown numbers of American lives to protect the warmongers and dictators who the Vietnamese and American people both hate.

For our part, we have said many times, — since I returned to Paris, this is the fifth time — we have declared clearly that the DRV government and the PRG of the Republic of South Vietnam have never wished to force a Communist government on South Vietnam. We only want that there be in South Vietnam a national reconciliation government having three segments, supporting peace, independence, neutrality and democracy. I can clarify for you what the three segments are: one segment belonging to the PRG RSV, one belonging to the Saigon government, and one segment belonging to patriots supporting peace, independence, neutrality and democracy — people who don't like the US, but who also may not support the PRG RSV. A government like this would reflect the real political situation in South Vietnam, and would be a resolution in accord with the situation and with logic.

QUESTION: Can one say that no one holding the position of general in Saigon at present can participate in a tripartite government?
ANSWER: With regard to the three segments, the segment belonging to the Saigon government is chosen by themselves. They can choose whomever they wish

SOURCE: *Doan Ket* [Solidarity] (Paris), May 31, 1972 [Translation by the editor].

in the segment reserved for them, but it can't be Thieu. The tripartite government is a national reconciliation government to achieve democratic rights of the South Vietnamese people. Therefore, whoever is in those three segments must carry out that policy.

252. EDITORIAL IN *NHAN DAN*, AUGUST 17, 1972 [Extract]

The failure of either the Soviet Union or China to make the Nixon Administration's mining of Haiphong and escalation of bombing in the North a major issue in relations with the U.S. permitted Nixon to portray his Vietnam policy at home as a major success and weakened the DRV's hand in the bargaining for a peace agreement. Hanoi, which had hoped to bring enough military-political pressure to bear on Nixon to force acceptance of a coalition government, felt betrayed by its socialist allies. In an editorial on detente, the Vietnamese Communist leaders directly criticized Moscow and Peking for helping Nixon for their own "narrow national interests."

The present *détente* is the product of a world situation which has changed: though having to overcome difficulties in their march forward, the revolutionary forces continue to develop whereas imperialism is facing a new period in its general crisis. An overall crisis is unfolding in the US—the main bastion and the last prop of imperialism. The repeated setbacks suffered by the US everywhere, including its bitter defeats in Viet Nam, have turned it into a "clay-footed colossus." In the US, the masses, especially the youth, are demanding a change in US policy.

Genuine *détente* between the nations rests on respect for the independence, sovereignty, unity and territorial integrity of all countries, big and small. But, for US imperialism, *détente* is but a perfidious policy aimed at carrying out schemes of aggression, enslavement, subversion, and peaceful regression through new means, that is, the "Nixon doctrine." The imperialists pursue a policy of *détente* with some big countries in order to have a free hand to consolidate their forces, oppose the revolutionary movement in the world, repress the revolution in their own countries, bully the small countries and stamp out the national-liberation movement while never giving up their preparations for a new world war.

With regard to the socialist countries, the defence of peace and peaceful co-existence cannot be dissociated from the movement for independence, democracy and socialism in the world. For a country to care for its immediate and narrow interests while shirking its lofty internationalist duties not only is detrimental to the revolutionary movement in the world but will also bring unfathomable harm to itself in the end. The vitality of Marxism-Leninism and proletarian internationalism manifests itself in revolutionary deeds, not in empty words. In the present-day world we can find many examples proving that very seldom do genuine national interests clash with the overall interest of world revolution. A principled policy of *détente* with imperialistic countries must aim at consolidating and strengthening the

SOURCE: *Vietnam Courier (Hanoi)*, September 1972, p. 5.

revolutionary forces, isolating and dividing the class enemy, and aiming the spear-head of the revolutionary forces at the leading imperialist warmongers. To achieve *détente* in certain concrete conditions in order to push forward the offensive of the revolutionary forces is correct; but if in order to serve one's narrow national interests, one is to help the most reactionary forces stave off dangerous blows, one is indeed throwing a life-buoy to a drowning pirate: this is a harmful compromise advantageous to the enemy, and disadvantageous to the revolution.

253. STATEMENT OF THE PRG, SEPTEMBER 11, 1972 [Extract]

In an initiative aimed at putting the Nixon Administration on the defensive only a few days before the next scheduled meeting of the two sides in Paris, the PRG released in a statement explicitly stating for the first time the idea that the settlement in South Vietnam had to reflect the "reality" of "two administrations, two armies and other political forces." It was an indication that the DRV would not demand that a tripartite "government" supersede the two existing administrations. It was only a short step from this position to the actual draft text advanced by Le Duc Tho at the meeting of October 8, which formed the basis of the Paris Agreement.

The Provisional Revolutionary Government of the Republic of South Vietnam solemnly declares as follows:

If a correct solution is to be found to the Vietnam problem, and a lasting peace ensured in Vietnam, the U.S. Government must meet the two following requirement:

1—To respect the Vietnamese people's right to true independence and the South Vietnamese people's right to effective self-determination; stop the U.S. war of aggression in Vietnam, the bombing, mining and blockade of the Democratic Republic of Vietnam; completely cease the "Vietnamization" policy; and all U.S. military activities in South Vietnam; rapidly and completely withdraw all U.S. troops, advisors, military personnel, technical personnel, weapons and war materials and those of the other foreign countries in the U.S. camp from South Vietnam; liquidate the U.S. military bases in South Vietnam; end all U.S. military involvement in Vietnam; and stop supporting the Nguyen Van Thieu stooge administration.

2—A solution to the internal problem of South Vietnam must proceed from the actual situation that there exist in South Vietnam two administrations, two armies, and other political forces. It is necessary to achieve national concord. The sides in South Vietnam must unite on the basis of equality, mutual respect and mutual nonelimination. Democratic freedoms must be guaranteed to the people. To this end, it is necessary to form in South Vietnam a provisional government of national concord with three equal segments to take charge of the affairs in the period of transition and to organize truly free and democratic general elections.

SOURCE: Hanoi Radio, September 11, 1972. Reprinted in *Background Information Relating to Southeast Asia and Vietnam*, pp. 648.

254. DOCUMENT BY RVN MINISTRY OF FOREIGN AFFAIRS ON PARIS PEACE TALKS, OCTOBER 24, 1972

Following meetings between Kissinger and Thieu October 22-23, the RVN conveyed a message to friendly foreign missions in Saigon which gave its key objections to the draft treaty that Kissinger had been on the verge of initialing with Le Duc Tho only a few days earlier. The note made it clear that Thieu was insisting that Hanoi recognize the seventeenth parallel as an international boundary, agree that its troops were in the South illegally, and recognize the existing constitutional structure of South Vietnam. All these demands were clearly unacceptable to Hanoi.

1. There have been innumerable rumors and speculations with regard to a peaceful solution of the war in Indochina and in Vietnam in particular. The speculations are all the more feverish as the US Presidential elections come closer, and feed on missions carried out by US Presidential adviser Henry Kissinger to Peking, Moscow, Paris and these days to Saigon and Phnom Penh to meet with leaders of friendly and hostile countries.

Meetings in Paris between Dr. Kissinger and Le Duc Tho resulted in agreement on a number of points between the U.S. and North Vietnam, which in turn induced a belief in some quarters of the public opinion that a ceasefire is imminent in Indochina with conditions which are unacceptable to the Republic of Vietnam.

2. The United States has informed the Republic of Vietnam progressively about the evolution of the talks with North Vietnam and the Republic of Vietnam always discussed with the US the course of action to be followed by both parties. Throughout the consultations with the US, the Government of the Republic of Vietnam has observed an absolute discretion so as not to prejudice their outcome, and in order to avoid erroneous speculations about a conflict between the Republic of Vietnam and the US. However, the international press has advanced many stories with regard to those discussions. Those news items, either accurate or misleading, have had an unsettling impact on public opinion in Vietnam.

3. In order to eliminate any doubt, the Republic of Vietnam wishes to affirm that:

Although the Government and people of the Republic of Vietnam fervently wish a return of peace in their land, they cannot accept a peace at all costs, especially a peace that would pave the way to the subjugation of 17 million South Vietnamese people by the Communists. Such a solution would be a betrayal of the many sacrifices consented by combatants of the Republic of Vietnam and the free world who have fought and died for the survival of the Republic of Vietnam.

4. For the aforementioned reasons, and after long and delicate discussion with Dr. Kissinger during the latter's stay in Saigon from October 18th to 23rd, in a frank and cordial atmosphere, President Nguyen Van Thieu had to prepare certain modifications in the cease-fire proposal put forward by North Vietnam. President

SOURCE: Telegram from Bunker to Kissinger, October 24, 1972. Document declassified by Department of State, August 15, 1978.

Nguyen Van Thieu affirmed the RVN's position after the consultations with the National Security Council.

5. The need for further negotiations is based on the consideration of three essential points of the proposed agreement, as follows:

A. North Vietnam does not explicitly recognize the demilitarized zone at the 17th parallel as established by the 1954 Geneva Agreements. The Geneva Accords recognize that the territory of Vietnam is temporarily separated into two states and as a corollary, that there exists a constitutional and legal government in South Vietnam. It must be clear that North Vietnam cannot assume for itself the right to invade South Vietnam at any moment.

B. The important question of the withdrawal of North Vietnamese forces from South Vietnam is also under negotiation. As a result of infiltrations effected in the past and of the open invasion carried out this year, North Vietnam's army has presently no less than 300,000 troops in South Vietnam, who constitute a mortal threat to the security of the Republic of Vietnam, at present as well as in the future, in case of a cease-fire.

C. Although there has been some change in the proposals previously put forward by the other side, the political arrangements are still under discussion. The Republic of Vietnam is determined to assure arrangements which reflect political realities in South Vietnam and respect basic principles of freedom and democracy as translated in the practice of "one man one vote" in the Republic of Vietnam. Any solution must maintain the constitutional and legal structure adopted by the people of the Republic of Vietnam.

6. There are many other points in the proposed cease-fire agreement which are less important but still require a thorough examination by the Government of the Republic of Vietnam. It is regrettable though that the Government of the Republic of Vietnam had been consulted in a so short period of time that it therefore has not been in a position to examine them in detail.

7. The position of the Government of the Republic of Vietnam is that the Hanoi authorities should hold direct discussions with the Republic of Vietnam to find a solution to the conflict. The Republic of Vietnam has repeatedly proposed bilateral discussions with Hanoi either open or secret, any time anywhere.

8. Problems with regard to the so-called National Liberation Front are a matter of internal affairs of the Republic of Vietnam, and the Government of the Republic of Vietnam has pledged to solve them within the democratic framework and in a spirit of national reconciliation.

255. STATEMENT OF THE DRV GOVERNMENT, OCTOBER 26, 1972 [Extract]

After the DRV received a message from Kissinger on October 23 indicating difficulties with the Saigon government and failing to reaffirm the previous U.S. pledge of a signing on October 31, its leaders decided to make public the history of

SOURCE: Radio Hanoi, October 26, 1972. Reprinted in *Background Information Relating to Southeast Asia and Vietnam*, pp. 484–487.

the last phase of the negotiations and the essential provisions of the text that had been agreed to. The accuracy of the negotiating history and of the text was not challenged by the Nixon administration.

With a view to making the negotiations progress, at the private meeting on October 8, 1972, the DRV side took a new, extremely important initiative: it put forward a draft "agreement on ending the war and restoring peace in Vietnam," and proposed that the Government of the Democratic Republic of Vietnam, with the concurrence of the Provisional Revolutionary Government of the Republic of South Vietnam, and the Government of the United States of America, with the concurrence of the Government of the Republic of Vietnam, immediately agreed upon and signed [as received] this agreement to rapidly restore peace in Vietnam. In that draft agreement, the DRV side proposed a cessation of the war throughout Vietnam, a cease-fire in South Vietnam, an end to all U.S. military involvement in Vietnam, a total withdrawal from South Vietnam of troops of the United States and those of the foreign countries allied with the United States and with the Republic of Vietnam, and the return of all captured and detained personnel of the parties. From the enforcement of the cease-fire to the installation of the government formed after free and democratic general elections, the two present administrations in South Vietnam will remain in existence with their respective domestic and external functions.

These two administrations shall immediately hold consultations with a view to the exercise of the South Vietnamese people's right to self-determination, achieving national concord, ensuring the democratic liberties of the South Vietnamese people, and forming an administration of national concord which shall have the task of promoting the South Vietnamese parties' implementation of the signed agreements and organizing general elections in South Vietnam. The two South Vietnamese parties shall settle together the internal matters of South Vietnam within three months after the cease-fire comes into effect. Thus the Vietnam problem will be settled in two stages in accordance with the oft-expressed desire of the American side: The first stage will include a cessation of the war in Vietnam, a cease-fire in South Vietnam, a cessation of the U.S. military involvement in South Vietnam and an agreement on the principles for the exercise of the South Vietnamese people's right to self-determination. In the second stage, the two South Vietnamese parties will settle together the internal matters of South Vietnam. The DRV side proposed that the Democratic Republic of Vietnam and the United States sign this agreement by mid-October 1972.

The above initiative of the Government of the Democratic Republic of Vietnam brought the negotiations on the Vietnam problem, which had dragged on for four years now, onto the path to a settlement. The American side itself admitted that the draft "agreement on ending the war and restoring peace in Vietnam" put forward by the DRV side was indeed an important and very fundamental document which opened up the way to an early settlement.

After several days of negotiations, on October 17, 1972, the Democratic Republic of Vietnam and the United States reached agreement on almost all problems on the basis of the draft agreement of the Democratic Republic of Vietnam, except for only *two unagreed issues*. With its goodwill, the DRV side did its utmost to remove the last obstacles in accepting the American side's proposals on the two remaining questions in the agreement. In his October 10, 1972 message to the premier of the Democratic Republic of Vietnam, the President of the United States appreciated the goodwill of the Democratic Republic of Vietnam, and confirmed that the formulation of the agreement could be considered complete. But in the same message, he raised a number of complex points. Desirous of rapidly ending the war and restoring peace in Vietnam, the Government of the Democratic Republic of Vietnam clearly explained its views on this subject. In his October 22, 1972 message, the President of the United States expressed satisfaction with the explanations given by the Government of the Democratic Republic of Vietnam. Thus by October 22, 1972, the formulation of the agreement was complete. The main issues of the agreement which have been agreed upon may be summarized as follows:

(1) The United States respects the independence, sovereignty, unity and territorial integrity of Vietnam as recognized by the 1954 Geneva agreements.

(2) Twenty-four hours after the signing of the agreement, *a cease-fire shall be observed throughout South Vietnam*. The United States will stop all its military activities, and end the bombing and mining in North Vietnam. Within 60 days, there will be a total withdrawal from South Vietnam of troops and military personnel of the United States and those of the foreign countries allied with the United States and with the Republic of Vietnam. The two South Vietnamese parties shall not accept the introduction of troops, military advisors and military personnel, armaments, munitions, and war material into South Vietnam.The two South Vietnamese parties shall be permitted to make periodical replacements of armaments, munitions, and war material that have been worn out or damaged after the cease-fire, on the basis of piece for piece of similar characteristics and properties. The United States will not continue its military involvement or intervene in the internal affairs of South Vietnam.

(3) The return of all captured personnel of the parties shall be carried out simultaneously with the U.S. troops withdrawal.

(4) The principles for the exercise of the South Vietnamese people's right to self-determination are as follows: The South Vietnamese people shall decide themselves the political future of South Vietnam through genuinely free and democratic general elections under international supervision: the United States is not committed to any political tendency or to any personality in South Vietnam, and it does not seek to impose a pro-American regime in Saigon: national reconciliation and concord will be achieved, the democratic liberties of the people ensured: an administrative structure called the National Council of National Reconciliation and Concord of three equal segments will be set up to promote the implementation of the signed agreements by the Provisional Revolutionary Government of the Republic of South Vietnam and the Government of the Republic of Vietnam and to organize the general elections, the two South Vietnamese parties will consult about the formation of councils at lower levels; the question of Vietnamese armed forces in South Vietnam shall be settled by the South Vietnamese parties in a spirit of national reconciliation and concord, equality and mutual respect, without foreign interference, in accordance with the post-war situation: among the questions to be discussed by the two South Vietnamese parties shall sign an agreement on the internal matters of South Vietnam as soon possible and will do their utmost to accomplish this within three months after the cease-fire comes into effect.

(5) The *reunification* of Vietnam shall be carried out step by step through peaceful means.

(6) There will be formed a four-party joint military commission, and a joint military commission of the two South Vietnamese parties.

An international commission of control and supervision shall be established.

An international guarantee conference on Vietnam will be convened within 30 days of the signing of this agreement.

(7) The Government of the Democratic Republic of Vietnam, the Provisional Revolutionary Government of the Republic of South Vietnam, the Government of the United States of America, and the Government of the Republic of Vietnam shall strictly respect the Cambodian and Lao peoples' fundamental national rights as recognized by the 1954 Geneva agreements on Indochina and the 1962 Geneva agreements on Laos, i.e., the independence, sovereignty, unity and territorial integrity of these countries. They shall respect the neutrality of Cambodia and Laos. The Government of the Democratic Republic of Vietnam, the Provisional Revolutionary Government of the Republic of South Vietnam, the Government of the United States of America and the Government of the Republic of Vietnam undertake to refrain from using the territory of Cambodia and the territory of Laos to encroach on the sovereignty and security of other countries. Foreign countries shall put an end to all military activities in Laos and Cambodia, totally withdraw from and refrain reintroducing into these two countries troops, military advisers and military personnel, armaments, munitions and war material. The internal affairs of Cambodia and Laos shall be settled by the people of each of these countries without foreign interference.

The problems existing between the *three Indochinese countries* shall be settled by the Indochinese parties on the basis of respect for each other's independence, sovereignty, and territorial integrity, and non-interference in each other's internal affairs.

(8) The ending of the war, the restoration of peace in Vietnam will create conditions for establishing a new, equal, and mutually beneficial relationship between the Democratic Republic of Vietnam and the United States. The United States will contribute to healing the wounds of war and to post-war reconstruction in the Democratic Republic of Vietnam and throughout Indochina.

(9) This agreement shall come into force as of its signing. It will be strictly implemented by all the parties concerned.

The two parties have also agreed on a schedule for the signing of the agreement. On October 9, 1972, at the proposal of the U.S. side, it was agreed that on October 18, 1972, the United States would stop the bombing and mining in North Vietnam; on October 19, 1972, *the two parties* would initial the text of the agreement in Hanoi: on October 26, 1972, the foreign ministers of the two countries would formally sign the agreement in Paris.

On October 11, 1972, the U.S. side proposed the following change to the schedule: On October 21, 1972, the United States would stop the bombing and mining in North Vietnam; on October 22, 1972, *the two parties* would initial the text of the agreement in Hanoi; on October 30, 1972, the foreign ministers of the two countries would formally sign the agreement in Paris. The Democratic Republic of Vietnam agreed to the new U.S. schedule.

On October 20, 1972, under the pretext that there still remained a number of unagreed points, the U.S. side again put forth another schedule: On October 23, 1972, the United States would stop the bombing and mining in North Vietnam; on October 24, 1972, the *two parties* would initial the text of the agreement in Hanoi; on October 31, 1972, the foreign ministers of the two countries would formally sign the agreement in Paris. Despite the fact that the U.S. side had changed many times what had been agreed upon, the DRV side with its goodwill again agreed to the U.S. proposal while stressing that the U.S. side should not under any pretext change the agreed schedule.

Thus, by October 22, 1972, the DRV side and the U.S. side had agreed both on the full text of the "agreement on ending the war and restoring peace in Vietnam" and on a schedule to be observed for the formal signing of the agreement on October 31, 1972. Obviously, the *two sides had agreed upon an agreement* of extremely important significance, which meets the wishes of the peoples in Vietnam, the United States and the world.

But on October 23, 1972, contrary to its pledges, the U.S. side again referred to difficulties in Saigon, demanded that the negotiations be continued for resolving new problems, and did not say anything about the implementation of its commitments under the agreed schedule. This behaviour of the U.S. side has brought about a very serious situation which risks to jeopardize the signing of the "agreement on ending the war and restoring peace in Vietnam."

The so-called difficulties in Saigon represent a mere pretext to delay the implementation of the U.S. commitments, because it is public knowledge that the Saigon administration has been rigged up and fostered by the United States. With a mercenary army equipped and paid by the United States, this administration is a tool for carrying out the "Vietnamization" policy and the neocolonialist policy of the United States in violation of the South Vietnamese people's national rights. It is an instrument for the United States to sabotage all peaceful settlement of the Vietnam problem.

256. NEWS CONFERENCE OF KISSINGER, OCTOBER 26, 1972 [Extract]

The DRV broadcast of the outline of the agreed text forced the Nixon Administration to explain its demand for further negotiations. Kissinger declared that there remained "six or seven" issues to be resolved, citing the need to put international machinery in place simultaneous with a cease-fire, the need to shorten the time between cease-fires in Vietnam and those in Cambodia and Laos, and other "linguistic" and "technical" problems. Kissinger did not mention the Nixon October 23 message to Hanoi pledging to sign the agreement as it then stood, nor the fact that the United States intended to introduce significant new demands that would have changed the character of the draft agreement.

SOURCE: *Background Information Relating to Southeast Asia and Vietnam*, pp. 487–495.

Now, what is it, then, that prevents the completion of the agreement? Why is it that we have asked for one more meeting with the North Vietnamese to work out a final text? The principal reason is that in a negotiation that was stalemated for five years, and which did not really make a breakthrough until October 8, many of the general principles were clearly understood before the breakthrough, but as one elaborated the text, many of the nuances on which the implementation will ultimately depend became more and more apparent.

It was obvious, it was natural, that when we were talking about the abstract desirability of a cease-fire that neither side was perhaps as precise as it had to become later about the timing and staging of a cease-fire in a country in which there are no clear frontlines. And also the acceptance on our part of the North Vietnamese insistence on an accelerated schedule meant that texts could never be conformed, that English and Vietnamese texts tended to lag behind each other, and that ambiguities in formulation arose that require one more meeting to straighten out.

Let me give you a few examples, and I think you will understand that we are talking here of a different problem than what occupied us in the many sessions I have had with you ladies and gentlemen about the problem of peace in Vietnam, sessions which concerned abstract theories of what approach might succeed.

We are talking here about six or seven very concrete issues that, with anything like the good will that has already been shown, can easily be settled. For example, it has become apparent to us that there will be great temptation for the cease-fire to be paralled by a last effort to seize as much territory as possible and perhaps to extend operations for long enough to establish political control over a given area.

We would like to avoid the dangers of the loss of life, perhaps in some areas even of the massacre that may be inherent in this, and we therefore want to discuss methods by which the international supervisory body can be put in place at the same time that the cease-fire is promulgated.

The Secretary of State has already had preliminary conversations with some of the countries that are being asked to join this body in order to speed up this process.

Secondly, because of the different political circumstances in each of the Indochinese countries, the relationship of military operations there to the end of the war in Viet-Nam, or cease-fires there in relation to the end of the war in Viet-Nam, is somewhat complex; and we would like to discuss more concretely how to compress this time as much as possible.

There were certain ambiguities that were raised by the interview that the North Vietnamese Prime Minister, Pham Van Dong, gave to one of the weekly journals in which he seemed to be, with respect to one or two points, under a misapprehension as to what the agreement contained, and at any rate, we would like to have that clarified.

There are linguistic problems. For example, we call the National Council of Reconciliation an administrative structure in order to make clear that we do not see it as anything comparable to a coalition government. We want to make sure that the Vietnamese text conveys the same meaning.

I must add that the words "administrative structure" were given to us in English by the Vietnamese, so this is not a maneuver on our part.

There are some technical problems as to what clauses of the Geneva accords to refer to in certain sections of the document, and there is a problem which was never settled in which the North Vietnamese, as they have pointed out in their broadcast, have proposed that the agreement be signed by the United States and North Viet-Nam—we on behalf of Saigon, they on behalf of their allies in South Viet-Nam.

We have always held the view that we would leave it up to our allies whether they wanted a two-power document or whether they wanted to sign themselves a document that establishes peace in their country. Now, they prefer to participate in the signing of the peace, and it seems to us not an unreasonable proposal that a country on whose territory a war has been fought and whose population has been uprooted and has suffered so greatly—that it should have the right to sign its own peace treaty. This, again, strikes us as a not insuperable difficulty, but its acceptance will require the redrafting of certain sections of the document, and that, again, is a job that will require several hours of work.

We have asked the North Vietnamese to meet with us on any date of their choice. We have, as has been reported, restricted our bombing, in effect, to the battle area in order to show our good will and to indicate that we are working within the framework of existing agreements.

We remain convinced that the issues that I have mentioned are soluble in a very brief period of time. We have undertaken, and I repeat it here publicly, to settle them at one more meeting and to remain at that meeting for as long as is necessary to complete the agreement.

257. LETTER FROM NIXON TO RVN PRESIDENT NGUYEN VAN THIEU, NOVEMBER 14, 1972

Nixon assured Thieu that the United States would press Hanoi for a series of changes in the October text, including a new provision for reduction and demobilization of troops on a one-for-one basis and return of those personnel to their "homes." Nixon also warned Thieu that the United States did not expect to secure all the changes Thieu wanted, and hinted that a refusal by Thieu to sign the final text would jeopardize American assistance to him.

I was pleased to learn from General Haig that you held useful and constructive discussions with him in Saigon in preparation for Dr. Kissinger's forthcoming meeting with North Vietnam's negotiations in Paris.

After studying your letter of November 11 with great care I have concluded that we have made substantial progress towards reaching a common understanding on many of the important issues before us. You can be sure that we will pursue the proposed changes in the draft agreement that General Haig discussed with you with the utmost firmness and that, as these discussions proceed, we shall keep you fully informed through your Ambassador to the Paris Conference on Vietnam who will be briefed daily by Dr. Kissinger.

I understand from your letter and from General Haig's personal report that

SOURCE: Document released by Dr. Nguyen Tien Hung, former minister of planning under Thieu, at a press conference in Washington, D.C., April 30, 1975.

your principal remaining concern with respect to the draft agreement is the status of North Vietnamese forces now in South Vietnam. As General Haig explained to you, it is our intention to deal with this problem first by seeking to insert a reference to respect for the demilitarized zone in the proposed agreement and, second, by proposing a clause which provides for the reduction and demobilization of forces on both sides in South Vietnam on a one-to-one basis and to have demobilized personnel return to their homes.

Upon reviewing this proposed language, it is my conviction that such a provision can go a long way towards dealing with your concern with respect to North Vietnamese forces. General Haig tells me, however, that you are also seriously concerned about the timing and verification of such reductions. In light of this, I have asked Dr. Kissinger to convey to you, through Ambassador Bunker, some additional clauses we would propose adding to the agreement dealing with each of these points. In addition, I have asked that Dr. Kissinger send you the other technical and less important substantive changes which General Haig did not have the opportunity to discuss with you because they had not yet been fully developed in Washington. With these proposed modifications, I think you will agree that we have done everything we can to improve the existing draft while remaining within its general framework.

You also raise in your letter the question of participation by other Asian countries in the International Conference. As you know, the presently contemplated composition are the permanent members of the United Nations Security Council, the members of the ICCS, the parties to the Paris Conference on Vietnam and the Secretary General of the United Nations. We seriously considered Cambodian and Laotian participation but decided that these would be unnecessary complications with respect to representation. We do not, however, exclude the possibility of delegations from these countries participating in an observer status at the invitation of the conference. As for Japan, this question was raised earlier in our negotiations with Hanoi and set aside because it inevitably raises the possibility of Indian participation. I have, however, asked that Dr. Kissinger raise this matter again in Paris and he will inform your representative what progress we make on this. What we must recognize as a practical matter is that participation of Japan is very likely to lead to the participation of India. We would appreciate hearing your preference on whether it is better to include both countries or neither of them.

Finally, in respect to the composition of the ICCS, I must say in all candor that I do not share your view that its contemplated membership is unbalanced. I am hopeful that it will prove to be a useful mechanism in detecting and reporting violations of the agreement. In any event, what we both must recognize is that the supervisory mechanism in itself is in no measure as important as our own firm determination to see to it that the agreement works and our vigilance with respect to the prospect of its violation.

I will not repeat here all that I said to you in my letter of November 8, but I do wish to reaffirm its essential content and stress again my determination to work towards an early agreement along the lines of the schedule which General Haig explained to you. I must explain in all frankness that while we will do our very best to secure the changes in the agreement which General Haig discussed with you and those additional ones which Ambassador Bunker will bring you, we cannot expect to secure them all. For example, it is unrealistic to assume that we will be able to secure the absolute assurances which you would hope to have on the troop issue.

But far more important than what we say in the agreement on this issue is what we do in the event the enemy renews its aggression. You have my absolute assurance that if Hanoi fails to abide by the terms of this agreement it is my intention to take swift and severe retaliatory action.

I believe the existing agreement to be an essentially sound one which should become even more so if we succeed in obtaining some of the changes we have discussed. Our best assurance of success is to move into this new situation with confidence and cooperation.

With this attitude and the inherent strength of your government and army on the ground in South Vietnam, I am confident this agreement will be a successful one.

If, on the other hand, we are unable to agree on the course that I have outlined, it is difficult for me to see how we will be able to continue our common effort towards securing a just and honorable peace. As General Haig told you I would with great reluctance be forced to consider other alternatives. For this reason, it is essential that we have your agreement as we proceed into our next meeting with Hanoi's negotiators. And I strongly urge you and your advisors to work promptly with Ambassador Bunker and our Mission in Saigon on the many practical problems which will face us in implementing the agreement. I cannot overemphasize the urgency of the task at hand nor my unalterable determination to proceed along the course which we have outlined.

Above all we must bear in mind what will really maintain the agreement. It is not any particular clause in the agreement but our joint willingness to maintain its clauses. I repeat my personal assurances to you that the United States will react very strongly and rapidly to any violation of the agreement. But in order to do this effectively it is essential that I have public support and that your Government does not emerge as the obstacle to a peace which American public now universally desires. It is for this reason that I am pressing for the acceptance of an agreement which I am convinced is honorable and fair and which can be made essentially secure by our joint determination.

Mrs. Nixon joins me in extending our warmest personal regards to Madame Thieu and to you. We look forward to seeing you again at our home in California once the just peace we have both fought for so long is finally achieved.

258. NEWS CONFERENCE OF KISSINGER, DECEMBER 16, 1972 [Extract]

The negotiations resumed on November 20, with Kissinger demanding all sixty-nine changes demanded by Thieu. Le Duc Tho retaliated by withdrawing Hanoi's key concession in the October round—separating the release of American prisoners from the release of Vietnamese political prisoners. When Kissinger continued to press for several major changes, Tho made new demands for changes in Hanoi's favor as well. On November 25, as the talks recessed, the United States opened new issues when it submitted its draft proposals on the protocols to the agreement. Again, the DRV retaliated by introducing new demands of its own when the negotiations resumed on December 4. While most of these new demands were

SOURCE: *Background Information Relating to Southeast Asia and Vietnam*, pp. 495–502.

negotiated away, the United States continued to demand some change in the October draft that would make North Vietnamese military presence in the South illegitimate. Le Duc Tho refused to accept such a change, and Nixon decided to carry out a major bombing campaign against Hanoi and Haiphong with B-52's for "shock" effect on DRV leaders. Kissinger again went before the press to blame the North Vietnamese for the failure to reach agreement in Paris. His account obscured the degree to which the United States had been pushing for a very different agreement from the October draft as the talks went into the December round.

The first time we saw the North Vietnamese protocols was on the evening of December 12th, the night before I was supposed to leave Paris, six weeks after we had stated what our aim was, five weeks after the cease-fire was supposed to be signed, a cease-fire which called for that machinery to be set up immediately.

These protocols were not technical instruments, but reopened a whole list of issues that had been settled, or we thought had been settled, in the agreement. They contained provisions that were not in the original agreement, and they excluded provisions that were in the original agreement. They are now in the process of being discussed by the technical experts in Paris, but some effort will be needed to remove the political provisions from them and to return them to a technical status.

Secondly, I think it is safe to say that the North Vietnamese perception of international machinery and our perception of international machinery is at drastic variance, and that, ladies and gentlemen, is an understatement.

We had thought that an effective machinery required, in effect, some freedom of movement, and our estimate was that several thousand people were needed to monitor the many provisions of the agreement. The North Vietnamese perception is that the total force should be no more than 250, of which nearly half should be located at headquarters; that it would be dependent for its communications, logistics, and even physical necessities entirely on the party in whose area it was located.

So it would have no jeeps, no telephones, no radios of its own; that it could not move without being accompanied by liaison officers of the party that was to be investigated, if that party decided to give it the jeeps to get to where the violation was taking place and if that party would then let it communicate what it found.

It is our impression that the members of this commission will not exhaust themselves in frenzies of activity if this procedure were adopted.

Now, thirdly, the substance of the agreement. The negotiations since November 20th really have taken place in two phases. The first phase, which lasted for three days, continued the spirit and the attitude of the meetings in October. We presented our proposals. Some were accepted; others were rejected.

But by the end of the third day we had made very substantial progress, and all of us thought that we were within a day or two of completing arrangements. We do not know what decisions were made in Hanoi at that point, but from that point on, the negotiations have had the character where a settlement was always just within our reach, and was always pulled just beyond our reach when we attempted to grasp it.

I do not think it is proper for me to go into the details of the specific issues, but I think I should give you a general atmosphere and a general sense of the procedures that were followed.

When we returned on December 4th, we of the American team, we thought that the meetings could not last more than two or three days because there were only two or three issues left to be resolved. You all know that the meetings lasted nine days. They began with Hanoi withdrawing every change that had been agreed to two weeks previously.

We then spent the rest of the week getting back to where we had already been two weeks before. By Saturday, we thought we had narrowed the issues sufficiently where, if the other side had accepted again one section they already had agreed to two weeks previously, the agreement could have been completed.

At that point, the President ordered General Haig to return to Washington so that he would be available for the mission, that would then follow, of presenting the agreement to our allies. At that point, we thought we were sufficiently close so that experts could meet to conform the texts so that we would not again encounter the linguistic difficulties which we had experienced previously, and so that we could make sure that the changes that had been negotiated in English would also be reflected in Vietnamese.

When the experts met, they were presented with 17 new changes in the guise of linguistic changes. When I met again with the Special Advisor, the one problem which we thought remained on Saturday had grown to two, and a new demand was presented. When we accepted that, it was withdrawn the next day and sharpened up. So we spent our time going through the 17 linguistic changes and reduced them again to two.

Then, on the last day of the meeting, we asked our experts to meet to compare whether the 15 changes that had been settled, of the 17 that had been proposed, now conformed in the two texts. At that point we were presented with 16 new changes, including four substantive ones, some of which now still remain unsettled.

Now, I will not go into the details or into the merits of these changes. The major difficulty that we now face is that provisions that were settled in the agreement appear again in a different form in the protocols; that matters of technical implementation which were implicit in the agreement from the beginning have not been addressed and were not presented to us until the very last day of a series of sessions that had been specifically designed to discuss them; and that as soon as one issue was settled, a new issue was raised.

It was very tempting for us to continue the process which is so close to everybody's heart, implicit in the many meetings, of indicating great progress, but the President decided that we could not engage in a charade with the American people.

We now are in this curious position: Great progress has been made, even in the talks. The only thing that is lacking is one decision in Hanoi, to settle the remaining issues in terms that two weeks previously they had already agreed to.

So, we are not talking of an issue of principle that is totally unacceptable.

Secondly, to compete the work that is required to bring the international machinery into being in the spirit that both sides have an interest of not ending the war in such a way that it is just the beginning of another round of conflict. So, we are in a position where peace can be near, but peace requires a decision. This is why we wanted to restate once more what our basic attitude is.

With respect to Saigon, we have sympathy and compassion for the anguish of their people and for the concerns of their government. But if we can get an agreement that the President considers just, we will proceed with it.

With respect to Hanoi, our basic objective was stated in the press conference of October 26th. We want an end to the war that is something more than an armistice. We want to move from hostility to normalization and from normalization to cooperation. But we will not make a settlement which is a disguised form of continued warfare and which brings about, by indirection, what we have always said we would not tolerate.

We have always stated that a fair solution cannot possibly give either side everything that it wants. We are not continuing a war in order to give total victory to our allies. We want to give them a reasonable opportunity to participate in a political structure, but we also will not make a settlement which is a disguised form of victory for the other side.

Therefore, we are at a point where we are again perhaps closer to an agreement than we were at the end of October, if the other side is willing to deal with us in good faith and with good will. But it cannot do that if every day an issue is settled a new one is raised, that when an issue is settled in an agreement, it is raised again as an understanding and if it is settled in an understanding, it is raised again as a protocol. We will not be blackmailed into an agreement. We will not be stampeded into an agreement, and, if I may say so, we will not be charmed into an agreement until its conditions are right.

259. PRESS CONFERENCE STATEMENT BY DRV DELEGATION CHIEF, XUAN THUY, PARIS, DECEMBER 19, 1972 [Extract]

In response to Kissinger's version of the reasons for delay in signing a peace agreement, the DRV delegation chief charged that the United States had proposed many major changes during the November and December talks, including protocols differing in substance from the principles of the October text. He said the Vietnamese terms referred to by Kissinger had been agreed to by both sides well before Kissinger's October 26 "Peace is at hand" speech.

During these private meetings, the D.R.V.N. side repeatedly expounded its stand that the two parties should maintain the text of the Agreement reached on October 20, 1972. But the U.S. side proposed a large number of changes in the text of the Agreement. Counting in the manner applied by the Americans, it can be said that up to December 13, 1972 the U.S. side had proposed changes in all the nine Chapters of the Agreement, 126 changes in all. Except for a number of proposals for technical changes regarding details, most of the changes were substantive ones; several were changes which would violate the principle of the Vietnamese people's fundamental national rights and the South Vietnamese people's right to self-determination; several would ignore the realities—which have been recognized by

SOURCE: Original text in mimeograph.

the United States—that in South Viet Nam there are two governments, two armies, three political forces, and seek to permanently divide Viet Nam. Most of these proposals were rejected only to be put forth again by the U.S. side. A number of terms in the Vietnamese version which were used as early as October 8, 1972 have been agreed to by the experts of both sides on October 12; now the U.S. insist on changing them, considering the proposed changes as linguistic ones although they are actually substantive ones.

At his Dec. 16, 1972, press conference, Dr. Kissinger spoke lengthily about the I.C. [intentional omission]. As a matter of fact, as reflected in the Agreement, the two parties have agreed on the formation of the Joint Military Commissions and the International Commission, the composition and the task of these Commissions regarding the implementation of the Agreement, and the operation principles of these Commissions. The Agreement has also explicitly stipulated that the implementation of the Agreement is the responsibility of the signatories; the Joint Military Commissions composed of the representatives of the parties to the Agreement have the task of ensuring joint action of the parties in implementing the provisions of the Agreement, whereas the International Commission has the task of supervising and controlling the implementation of the Agreement. If the parties respect the Agreement and base themselves on the principles mentioned in the Agreement to decide on the organization and the operation of those Commissions, a settlement will come rapidly. However, as the press has reported, the U.S. side put forward proposal with a view to forming an International Commission with several thousand armed militarymen who will be free to move all over South Viet Nam. The U.S. intention is to install a foreign occupation corps in South Viet Nam, grossly trampling underfoot South Viet Nam's sovereignty; at variance with the agreed principles mentioned in the Agreement.

In a word, the fact about the recent rounds of private meetings is that the D.R.V.N. side has endeavoured to maintain the principles, the substance, and the text of the Agreement reached on October 20, 1972; at the same time, it has shown good will with a view to rapidly concluding the Agreement, in the interest of the Vietnamese people, the American people, and world peace. On the contrary, the U.S. side is deliberately delaying the signing of the Agreement on Ending the War and Restoring Peace in Viet Nam.

The deliberate distortion by the U.S. side of facts related to the private meetings since November 20, 1972 is aimed at deceiving U.S. and world opinion, in an attempt to lay the blame on the D.R.V.N. side and concealing the wicked U.S. scheme of intensifying the bombing of North Viet Nam, continuing the Vietnamization policy in South Viet Nam, using military force in order to force the Vietnamese people to accept the terms imposed by the United States. This scheme is evidenced by the massive introduction into South Viet Nam of armaments, war material and military personnel disguised as civilians since October 1972, the frenzied intensification of the aggressive war in the two zones of Viet Nam, in Laos and Cambodia, the U.S. condoning of the Saigon Administration's arrogant demands and preparations for the sabotage of the Agreement even before its signing. What is called "a massive communist effort to launch an attack throughout South Viet Nam before the cease-fire" is nothing but a brazen fabrication to conceal the dark designs of the White House.

1973

260. LETTER FROM NIXON TO THIEU, JANUARY 5, 1973

In another direct communication with Thieu before the final round of the negotiations, Nixon repeated his warning that a refusal to sign the final agreement would endanger U.S. support and pledged to respond to any North Vietnamese violation "with full force."

This will acknowledge your letter of December 20, 1972.

There is nothing substantial that I can add to my many previous messages, including my December 17 letter, which clearly stated my opinions and intentions. With respect to the question of North Vietnamese troops, we will again present your views to the Communists as we have done vigorously at every other opportunity in the negotiations. The result is certain to be once more the rejection of our position. We have explained to you repeatedly why we believe the problem of North Vietnamese troops is manageable under the agreement, and I see no reason to repeat all the arguments.

We will proceed next week in Paris along the lines that General Haig explained to you. Accordingly, if the North Vietnamese meet our concerns on the two outstanding substantive issues in the agreement, concerning the DMZ and the method of signing, and if we can arrange acceptable supervisory machinery, we will proceed to conclude the settlement. The gravest consequences would then ensue if your government chose to reject the agreement and split off from the United States. As I said in my December 17 letter, "I am convinced that your refusal to join us would be an invitation to disaster—to the loss of all that we together have fought for over the past decade. It would be inexcusable above all because we will have lost a just and honorable alternative."

As we enter this new round of talks, I hope that our countries will now show a united front. It is imperative for our common objectives that your government take no further actions that complicate our task and would make more difficult the acceptance of the settlement by all parties. We will keep you informed of the negotiations in Paris through daily briefings of Ambassador Lam.

I can only repeat what I have so often said: The best guarantee for the survival of South Vietnam is the unity of our two countries which would be gravely jeopardized if you persist in your present course. The actions of our Congress since its return have clearly borne out the many warnings we have made.

Should you decide, as I trust you will, to go with us, you have my assurance of continued assistance in the post-settlement period and that we will respond with full force should the settlement be violated by North Vietnam. So once more I conclude with an appeal to you to close ranks with us.

SOURCE: Document released by Dr. Nguyen Tien Hung, former Minister of Planning under Thieu, at a press conference in Washington, D.C., April 30, 1975.

261. COSVN DIRECTIVE 02/73 "ON POLICIES RELATED TO THE POLITICAL SETTLEMENT AND CEASE-FIRE," JANUARY 19, 1973 [Extract]

On January 19, 1973, even before the final substantive issues had been resolved between Dr. Kissinger and Le Duc Tho in Paris, the Party's Central Office for South Vietnam, informed that an agreement was imminent, prepared a directive establishing the basic political-military line of the Party on implementing the peace agreement. The directive argued that the United States and Saigon would sabotage the implementation of the agreement and provoke armed conflict, but that the revolutionary side could, by relying primarily on political struggle, create conditions for the implementation of the agreement.

II. Direction of Our Policies in the Event the Agreement is Signed and the Cease-Fire Goes Into Effect

1. In the face of the new situation, in order to ensure the fulfillment of our basic mission which is to achieve the national democratic revolution in the South as a step toward peacefully unifying our country, the direction of our immediate mission when the Agreement is signed is as follows:

"To mobilize the entire Party and people to bring our victory into full play by taking part in the high political movement in the three areas using the slogans calling for "peace, independence, democracy, rice and clothing for the people, national concord" and demanding the implementation of the Agreement. To disintegrate and seriously collapse the puppet army and government, take over control of the rural area, seize power at the base level; simultaneously, to build and develop our political and armed forces, build and strengthen the revolutionary administration and liberated area in all aspects, smash all enemy schemes to sabotage the Agreement, prevent large scale conflicts, maintain peace, hold general elections as provided for in the Agreement, bring the South Viet-Nam revolution toward the fulfillment of its basic objectives, at the same time, maintain constant alertness and readiness to deal with the U.S. imperialists' plot to resume hostilities."

In order to fulfill this immediate mission, we must strive to meet the following key requirements:

First, we must reach unity of mind in the entire Party with regard to the victory already gained. We must confidently strive to carry out the Party's immediate political mission at all costs and, at the same time, remain firm in the event the *Americans obdurately renege their commitments, sabotage the implementation of the Agreement or even resume hostilities.*

Second, we must concentrate efforts to turn the political struggle movement

---

SOURCE: U.S. Mission in Viet Nam, *Viet-Nam Documents and Research Notes*, Document No. 113, June 1973, pp. 1–8.

into a high revolutionary movement focussing on the principal slogans mentioned above.

Third, we must strive to severely disintegrate and collapse the puppet army and government, especially at the base level.

Fourth, we must build our forces in every aspect so they become strong, stable and present everywhere, especially in prosperous and populated areas, in the cities, in the religious communities. Development [of our forces] must go hand in hand with consolidation and preservation of forces, cadres and base organizations.

Fifth, we must strengthen our base areas and liberated areas in all aspects, consolidate and expand the revolutionary administration in all areas, and continue to bring the enemy-controlled area and cities to a new step of evolution.

Sixth, we must maintain firmly and improve the development of our armed forces in the new situation, strive to strengthen our three-troop-category forces and make sure that they are ready in any circumstance.

Seventh, we must build up the Party's strength, especially the strength of base-level Party chapters.

2. *Strategic principles and struggle guidelines* [*which*] *we must fully grasp in the new phase.*

a. The following strategic principles must be fully grasped:

One: *We must fully grasp the objective of the national democratic revolution and closely combine the national mission with the democratic mission in the new situation.*

Therefore, the slogans calling for "peace, independence, democracy, rice and clothing, national concord" are not only principal slogans to be used in the immediate future but also strategic slogans to be used during the whole new phase.

Two: We must fully grasp the *offensive strategy of pushing back the enemy step by step and winning victory bit by bit before achieving complete victory.* On the basis of persisting in the thought of unceasing and continuous revolution, we must create opportunities and grasp the opportunities in order to accelerate the development of the revolution in the new phase.

Three: We must fully grasp the *concept of violence* in the context of the new situation, in the political struggle phase. We must absolutely bring into play the masses' political violence, and stand ready to surmount fierceness and bloodshed in the course of promoting the political movement into a high tide. At the same time, we must not neglect military violence. On the contrary, we must stand constantly ready, especially we must unceasingly build up our three-troop-category armed forces as a firm support for our political struggle.

Four: We must *closely assciate the mission of achieving the national democratic revolution in the South with the mission of protecting and building socialism in the North as a step toward the unification of our country.*

Five: We must coordinate the revolutionary movement in South Viet-Nam with the revolutionary movements in Kampuchea and Laos and the Indochinese revolution in general, coordinate the struggle movement for peace, independence, democracy, improvement of living standards with the movement for peace, national liberation and socialism all over the world.

b. We must fully grasp the following guideline and method of operation:

One: We must closely combine political struggle with armed struggle and legalistic struggle, using political struggle as the base, armed struggle as support, while bringing into full play the legalistic effects of the Agreement.

Two: We must closely combine the overt form of organization with the semi-overt and clandestine forms of organization, using the clandestine form as a base.

Three: We must closely coordinate our offensive activities with activities to build our forces in all aspects for the purpose of creating a new position, strength and situation.

Four: We must closely coordinate the masses' struggle in the three strategic areas with the struggle of the overt organizations which are provided for in the Agreement [the Joint Military Commission, the National Council of National Reconciliation and Concord, the Prisoner Exchange Commission], using the masses' struggle as a base while bringing into full play the struggling effects of the overt organizations.

262. LETTER FROM NIXON TO PHAM VAN DONG, FEBRUARY 1, 1973

During the final phase of the negotiations, Le Duc Tho and Kissinger agreed on the text of a letter to be sent by Nixon to Premier Pham Van Dong which would elaborate on and make more concrete the U.S. commitment in Article 21 to provide postwar reconstruction aid to the DRV. The letter, which was not revealed publicly until 1977, provided for the establishment of a Joint Economic Commission to negotiate an aid program and established a "preliminary" figure of $3.25 billion in grant aid over a five-year period, with other forms of aid to be negotiated.

The President wishes to inform the Democratic Republic of Vietnam of the principles which will govern United States participation in the postwar reconstruction of North Vietnam. As indicated in Article 21 of the Agreement on Ending the War and Restoring Peace in Vietnam signed in Paris on Jan. 27, 1973, the United States undertakes this participation in accordance with its traditional policies. These principles are as follows:

1. The Government of the United States of America will contribute to postwar reconstruction in North Vietnam without any political conditions.

2. Preliminary United States studies indicate that the appropriate programs for the United States contribution to postwar reconstruction will fall in the range of $3.25 billion of grant aid over five years. Other forms of aid will be agreed upon between the two parties. This estimate is subject to revision and to detailed discussion between the Government of the United States and the Government of the Democratic Republic [of] Vietnam.

3. The United States will propose to the Democratic Republic of Vietnam the

SOURCE: *Aid to North Vietnam,* Hearing before the Subcommittee on Asian and Pacific Affairs of the Committee on International Relations, House of Representatives, 95th Congress, 1st Session, (Washington: Government Printing Office, 1979). Appendix 2, p. 25.

establishment of a United States-North Vietnamese Joint Economic Commission within 30 days from the date of this message.

4. The function of the commission will be to develop programs for the United States contribution to reconstruction of North Vietnam. This United States contribution will be based upon such factors as:

(a) The needs of North Vietnam arising from the dislocation of war; .

(b) The requirements for postwar reconstruction in the agricultural and industrial sectors of North Vietnam's economy.

5. The Joint Economic Commission will have an equal number of representatives from each side. It will agree upon a mechanism to administer the program which will constitute the United States contribution to the reconstruction of North Vietnam. The commission will attempt to complete this agreement within 60 days after its establishment.

6. The two members of the commission will function on the principle of respect for each other's sovereignty, noninterference in each other's internal affairs, equality and mutual benefit. The offices of the commission will be located at a place to be agreed upon by the United States and the Democratic Republic of Vietnam.

7. The United States considers that the implementation of the foregoing principles will prompt economic, trade and other relations between the United States of America and the Democratic Republic of Vietnam and will contribute to the spirit of Chapter VIII of the Agreement on Ending the War and Restoring Peace in Vietnam which was signed in Paris on Jan. 27, 1973.

Understanding Regarding Economic Reconstruction Program

It is understood that the recommendations of the Joint Economic Commission mentioned in the President's note to the Prime Minister will be implemented by each member in accordance with its own constitutional provisions.

Note Regarding Other Forms of Aid

In regard to other forms of aid, United States studies indicate that the appropriate programs could fall in the range of $1 billion to $1.5 billion, depending on food and other commodity needs of the Democratic Republic of Vietnam.

263. TELEGRAM FROM SECRETARY OF STATE WILLIAM ROGERS TO AMBASSADOR ELLSWORTH BUNKER, FEBRUARY 8, 1973

Early in February, the U.S. Embassy picked up reports that the RVN was considering organizing demonstrations against DRV and PRG delegations to the Joint Military Commission, set up by the Paris Agreement to implement the cease-

SOURCE: Document declassified by Department of State, July 19, 1978.

fire provisions of the Agreement. The State Department directed the Embassy's chief officer in Danang, Frederick Brown, to intervene with RVN officials in Hue and Danang. The day the telegram was sent, a rock-throwing demonstration against DRV and PRG delegates took place in Banmethuot, in the Central Highlands, and similar demonstrations took place on February 25 in both Hue and Danang.

We find disturbing the reports (Reftel) of possible demonstrations in Hue and Danang against the Communist elements of the JMC and against the Paris Agreement. We would regard any such demonstrations as unhelpful, particularly at this early point in the process of trying to foster a viable cease-fire. Request you convey this view at appropriately high level of GVN. Suggest also that Brown see [*officially deleted*] and other key officials Hue and Danang in effort to forestall untoward action.

264. BRIEFING PAPER ON INTERPRETATIONS OF THE PARIS PEACE AGREEMENT BY STATE DEPARTMENT LEGAL ADVISER GEORGE ALDRICH, FEBRUARY 1973 [Extract]

To guide U.S. negotiators involved in implementing the Paris Agreement in the Four-Party Joint Military Commission, the State Department's legal adviser, George Aldrich, wrote a paper explaining how the U.S. government interpreted various provisions of the Agreement. The paper reveals that, contrary to arguments made by Nixon Administration officials in the spring of 1973, Article 20 of the Agreement calling for withdrawal of foreign troops from Laos and Cambodia was clearly understood to be applicable only after cease-fire and troop withdrawal arrangements were worked out by the parties to the conflict in each of the two countries. (The full text of the Paris Peace Agreement, which is not published here because of space limitations, may be found in the Weekly Compilation of Presidential Documents, *January 29, 1973, pp. 45–64.)*

9. Withdrawal of Foreign Forces from Laos and Cambodia—Timing.
The obligation to withdraw foreign forces from Laos and Cambodia is stated in Article 20(b) of the Agreement. However, this obligation constitutes an agreement in principle and no time is stated for it to become an effective obligation. It was recognized that this, as other obligations of Article 20, should become effective at the earliest possible time, but it was also recognized that the precise timing would depend upon the timing of agreements among the contesting parties in Laos and Cambodia. We made it clear to the North Vietnamese that we intended to continue our air strikes in Laos until there was a cease-fire there, at which time they would of course be prohibited.
Thus, the provisions of Article 20(b) should be understood as agreements in

SOURCE: Document declassified by Department of State, no date shown.

principles which the United States and the DRV would endeavor to see were included in cease-fire or other settlement agreements in Laos and Cambodia. Only when such agreements are concluded will the obligation to withdraw become operational.

265. COSVN DIRECTIVE 03/CT 73, MARCH 1973 [Extracts]

Despite the wide-ranging military-pacification efforts by the RVN to expand its zone of control in February and March and Thieu's hostility toward the Joint Military Commission, the Party's Central Office for South Vietnam issued a direc-tive in March indicating that the Party still believed that the United States and Thieu could be forced eventually to carry out the agreement. It admitted that ARVN had inflicted "a number of losses and difficulties" on the revolutionary side but promised that, if the Saigon side could be held back militarily and the political struggle stepped up within its army and population, the peace agreement would bring victories for the revolution. Both the Two-Party Joint Military Committee and the National Council for National Reconciliation and Concord were portrayed as important to the success of the revolutionary strategy. But the directive also called for an increase in the revolutionary armed forces.

I. *The Nature of the Situation, the Form of the Struggle between Us and the Enemy at this Time, the Enemy's Plots, and Facts Concerning the Possibilities for Development of the Situation after 60 Days of Implementation of the Ceasefire Agreement.*

1. Message No. 775 of 25 February 1973 made it clear that: The main feature of the situation at this time is that the Agreement to End the War and Restore Peace in Viet-Nam (VN) has been signed, and the U.S. must withdraw all its troops and must cease the bombing and shelling of our people with its fleet. However, the U.S. is, on the other hand, shielding its puppets in their not implementing the Ceasefire order and in violating the Agreement.

The situation in South Viet-Nam (SVN) is not yet stable. The insta-bility and complexity of the situation is seen clearly in the following points: Although there is an Agreement to End the War and Restore Peace in VN, in truth in SVN there are many places where the shooting and bombing and shelling continue, and in some places more than prior to the Agreement.

Armed conflict continues without pause because of the enemy's police operations and aggression and infringement, but the scale and the methods are not what they were when the war was still going on and are concentrated in a limited number of areas. There are no B-52's, artillery, fleet, or, actions by aircraft and infantry of the U.S. and satellites.

SOURCE: U.S. Mission in Viet-Nam, *Viet-Nam Documents and Research Notes*, Document No. 115, September 1973, 4–10, 11–13.

The puppets are applying pressure and violating the agreement in this way, but they are still bound by the Paris Agreement. They can postpone and delay the implementation of the Agreement, but they cannot altogether not implement it, as in the cases of the initiation of the FPJMC [Four-Party Joint Military Commission], and the TPJMC [Two-Party Joint Military Commission], the International Commission for Control and Supervision (ICCS), the exchange of POW's.

The form of the struggle between us and the enemy is: The enemy distorts the Ceasefire Agreement, impedes the implementation of the Agreement, creates suspicion and divisions and hatred among the people, and maintains the tense situation.

We disseminate the Agreement broadly, bring out the significance of the Agreement as a great victory, open up the movement of struggle to demand that the enemy implement the Agreement, and follow the trend in demanding peace and national concord among all classes of people—even within the puppet army and puppet government—and this forms our new struggle position in the new situation.

The enemy launches police operations and oppresses and terrorizes the people, not permitting them freedom of movement in order to make their living. At the same time, he launches military operations with air and artillery support, tries to reoccupy the areas he has lost, does damage to the fields and gardens, gathers the people up, and builds additional outposts.

We are determined to foil enemy oppression and aggression by mobilizing the masses to engage in political, armed and military-proselyting [sic] struggle in coordination with legality to defend the lives and property of the people, to defend the liberated areas, to defeat the enemy's plots of obstruction and destruction, and to force the enemy to implement the agreement.

The enemy is delaying, creating problems and even engaging in physical abuse with regard to the initiation of the organizations for the implementation of the Agreement (the ICCS, the JMC's, the negotiations between the two SVN parties). The enemy is fabricating and distorting the provisions of the Cease-fire Agreement and its Protocols. We are determined to struggle to initiate the above-named organizations in order to guarantee the implementation of the Agreement according to the time-schedule and the scope of responsibility set forth in the Agreement and its Protocols.

*   *   *

After 60 days, the situation may change as follows: Firstly, if we evaluate the situation of ourselves and the enemy correctly and in good time, exploit quickly the effects of the Ceasefire Agreement, apply the principles and methods for struggles, prevent the enemy from striking into our territory, bring the political and military-proselyting movements of the masses up to meet requirements, and coordinate the military victories which have forced the enemy to cease his advances and to implement the Cease-fire Agreement—then the situation will develop every day more to our advantage. We will repel the enemy's plot to impede the Ceasefire Agreement and advance our movement another step, continuing to win new victories. As in reality there are two governments, two armies and two areas of control, it is not possible to avoid having scattered, small military engagements, but we must try hard to hold the enemy back and we must know how to defeat the enemy and to force him to implement the Agreement. Secondly, if we make the changes in directions too slowly and are not resolute in attacking the enemy, the enemy will continue to infringe further on us and to create a tense situation to cause us greater difficulties, to limit and paralyze the actions of the TPJMC, and to draw out the talks concerning the establishment of the National Council for National Reconciliation and Concord (NCNRC); the enemy will create a political and military situation to his advantage. Thirdly, it is also possible that, because of his collapse and isolation from which recovery is impossible, the enemy will draw out matters and the current situation will collapse entirely; or, because they hope to achieve victory by arms, we cannot exclude the possibility the enemy may initiate an adventurous civil war. We must be prepared to smother any such action by the enemy and to win a great victory for the nationalist democratic revolution in SVN.

How the situation develops will depend on our subjective efforts, particularly on whether or not we can control our thinking so we can retain the initiative, on whether or not we can change the directions of our policies and methods for struggle to be appropriate, and on whether or not we have the resolve to develop ourselves in every way in order to change the ratio of forces between us and the enemy.

*　　*　　*

C) We have the Paris Agreement as the new element in the current situation and as the new weapon with which to attack the enemy and to develop our strength. We need to avoid two attitudes:

1. Holding that the Paris Agreement is a complete weapon and can replace the other types of struggle, imagining that with the Agreement we can solve all our problems, not seeing that the ratio of forces is actually the decisive factor. With the Paris Agreement, we have an additional sharp weapon with which to attack the enemy. The agreement creates more advantageous circumstances for us to develop more power and better position and to change the ratio of forces between us and the enemy in our favor.

2. Holding that the enemy has so seriously broken the Agreement that it no longer is valid and has no value, feeling that the current situation is "a return to normal war" as before, or "undeclared war" and, when the U.S. has withdrawn completely they will resume the war immediately. This attitude leads to the idea of going back a step and engaging in armed operations as before; it does not see that the Agreement has been achieved only by the blood of our people in struggle, and the Agreement opens for us a new phase and creates for us a new weapon and new circumstances in our favor for attack upon the enemy. This attitude

is the main mistaken attitude at this time. It must be recognized that we have the strength of the masses, the strength of all our armed forces, and now we have the legal sanction to apply to give us the cutting edge of the three strengths in all our struggles, and so we have obtained a new considerable strength for attack upon the enemy. This strength must be shown concretely in the activities of our armed forces and in the three prongs in the villages, in order to develop the new assault posture in the new situation.

D) Because of a lack of deep awareness of the enemy's so very stubborn plots and because of simplistic assessments when the Ceasefire Agreement went into effect, our mental and material preparations to contend steadfastly with the enemy have not been sufficient. In many places the people who have come forth are still confused about the application of the struggle principles and methods in the new situation, while the enemy is infringing on us in many places and is secretly causing us a number of losses and difficulties, but in general the trend of the development of the situation is in our favor. The enemy builds more outposts in many places, but he is drawn-out and has many shortcomings—his soldiers and a large number of the outpost commanders and personnel of the puppet government are now suffering from low morale, are tired and disgusted, and want peace. We must calmly and correctly evaluate the nature of the situation in our own areas, make plans for implementation, and avoid two wrong attitudes:

1. Anxiety and subjectivity in wanting to contend with the enemy's incursions by expanding the scope of military attacks on all the battlefields, as the only way quickly to recover lost territory.

2. Passivity, feeling that even use of the military cannot restore the previous position, and acceptance of Ceasefire Agreement violations just to maintain our position "whereafter we can advance step by step": The essence of this attitude is acceptance of enemy infringements. The above two attitudes: anxiety and subjectivity, and passivity and loss of confidence and struggle orientation, are both in essence rightist; they are wrong evaluations of the situation and represent a failure to recognize strong and weak points and the enemy's new shortcomings, a loss of firm thinking concerning attacks upon the enemy by the right means and in the right form, and a lack of knowledge of the use of the armed forces in conjunction with the political and military-proselitizing and of the new weapon, i.e., the Ceasefire Agreement, in each prong of attack as they are joined tightly together.

266. NEWS CONFERENCE OF NIXON, MARCH 15, 1973 [Extract]

In early March, President Nixon tried to put pressure on Hanoi to reduce significantly, if not halt completely, its resupply to troops in the South, even though

SOURCE: *The Nixon Presidential Press Conferences* (New York: Earl M. Coleman Enterprises, 1978), pp. 323–24.

a high level of military conflict was continuing there. As the first in a series of Administration moves, on March 10 the Defense Department said that some 250 tanks, some weapons, and "about 30,000 troops" had been seen moving through Laos and some across the demilitarized zone to South Vietnam, without saying how many had actually crossed into the South or when. Three days later, the State Department issued a statement expressing "concern" over the movement of troops and supplies. On March 15, Nixon himself carried the campaign a step further, threatening unilateral U.S. action if the DRV did not stop its use of the trail network and the DMZ to move military equipment into the South. Interestingly, Nixon conceded that the personnel going South could be "replacements," rather than additional troops. Any plan to use military force against North Vietnam, however, was effectively blocked by rising Congressional opposition to further U.S. military involvement in Indochina, and the unraveling of Nixon's Watergate cover-up.

Q. *Mr. President, can you say, sir, how concerned you are about the reports of cease-fire violations in Vietnam.*

A. Well, I am concerned about the cease-fire violations. As you ladies and gentlemen will recall, I have consistently pointed out in meetings with you, that we would expect violations because of the nature of the war, the guerrilla nature, and that even in Korea, in which we do not have a guerrilla war, we still have violations. They recede each year, but we still have them. Long, 15, 20 years after the war is over.

In the case of these violations, we are concerned about them on two scores. One, because they occur, but two, we are concerned because of another violation that could lead to, we think, rather serious consequences. We do not believe it will. We hope that it will not. And that is the report that you ladies and gentlemen have been receiving from your colleagues in Vietnam with regard to infiltration.

You will note that there have been reports of infiltration by the North Vietnamese into South Vietnam of equipment exceeding the amounts that were agreed upon in the settlement.

Now, some equipment can come in. In other words, replacement equipment, but no new equipment, nothing, which steps up the capacity of the North Vietnamese or the Vietcong to wage war in the South. No new equipment is allowed under the agreement.

Now, as far as that concern is concerned, particularly on the infiltration, that is the more important point, rather than the cease-fire violations which we think, over a period of time, will be reduced—but in terms of the infiltration, I am not going to say publicly what we have said.

I only suggest this: That we have informed the North Vietnamese of our concern about this infiltration and what we believe it to be, a violation of the cease-fire, the cease-fire and the peace agreements. Our concern has also been expressed to other interested parties and I would only suggest that based on my actions over the past four years, that the North Vietnamese should not lightly disregard such expressions of concern, when they are made, with regard to violation. That is all I will say about it.

Q. *Mr. President, in connection with this matter, there is a report also that not just equipment, but a new infusion of North Vietnamese combat personnel have been introduced into South Vietnam, which is apart from just equipment. Can you confirm this? Is this partly what you are talking about?*

A. Mr. Theis, the reports that we get with regard to infiltration, as you know, are always either too little or too much. And I am not going to confirm that one, except to say that we have noted the report having been made. We, however, are primarily concerned about the equipment, because as far as the personnel are concerned, they could be simply replacement personnel.

267. STAFF REPORT BY THE SUBCOMMITTEE ON U.S. SECURITY OF THE SENATE COMMITTEE ON FOREIGN RELATIONS, APRIL 1973 [Extract]

Senate staff investigators discovered from interviews with U.S. intelligence personnel in Thailand that the impression conveyed by the Nixon Administration in Washington that North Vietnam was violating the peace agreement by uilding up its manpower and weaponry in the South was misleading. They learned that the North Vietnamese were believed to be simply holding their own when casualties in the post-cease-fire fighting were taken into account, and that most of the weapons entered South Vietnam before the cease-fire.

D. Enemy Forces

The CIA estimate of North Vietnamese/Viet Cong strength as of April 15, 1973 was 253,000—142,000 North Vietnamese and 110,900 Viet Cong. Of the 142,000 North Vietnamese 80,600 were in Military Region I, 24,600 in Military Region II, 22,500 in Military Region III and 14,300 in Military Region IV. Of the 110,900 Viet Cong, 25,700 were in Military Region I, 19,500 in Military Region II, 42,400 in Military Region III and 23,300 in Military Region IV. As of January 31, 1973, total North Vietnamese strength had been 120,500. That estimate rose to 142,000 as of April 15 by adding 28,200 infiltration arrivals and 9,800 returned prisoners of war and by subtracting 5,100 in one departing division and 11,400 casualties.

The infiltration picture is confused. Before we left Washington we were told at the Defense Department that enemy tank strength had increased from between about 300 on March 31, 1972 to over 400 as of March 19, 1973; that enemy artillery had increased slightly in the same period; and that infiltration which, in the period January 28-March 19, 1972 had been about 21,000, had been about 25,000 in the same period in 1973 with about 10,000 personnel entering the pipeline after the cease-fire.

At USSAG Headquarters in Thailand we were told that since the cease-fire 9,300 North Vietnamese had begun to infiltrate—7,000 of whom were infantry—and

SOURCE: *Thailand, Laos, Cambodia and Vietnam: April 1973*, Staff Report, Subcommittee on U.S. Security Agreements, Committee on Foreign Relations, U.S. Senate, 93rd Congress, 1st Session, pp. 36–37.

that the net result has been that the North Vietnamese were holding their own against casualties. In Saigon we were told that 341 tanks, 27 armored personnel carriers, 173 artillery pieces and 146 anti-aircraft weapons were sent down the trail in the 1972–73 dry season; that most of this equipment was already on the trail before the cease-fire and relatively little had arrived in Vietnam since the cease-fire; that, as far as infiltration of personnel was concerned, about 25,000 were in the pipeline at the time the cease-fire was declared; that some 5,200 (half regular infantry groups and half special purpose groups) had entered the pipeline since the cease-fire was declared; that a total of 15,100 had arrived since the cease-fire and there were no replacements in the pipeline; that last year there were between 90,000 and 100,000 in the pipeline at this time; and that North Vietnamese draft calls were down in December and January and are even lower in March. By contrast at the South Vietnamese Joint General Staff headquarters we were told that 60,000 men had entered the pipeline between January 1 and the end of March.

It would appear that in terms of personnel in South Vietnam, North Vietnamese strength, taking account of infiltration, released prisoners and casualties, is almost exactly equal to the lower range of the CIA estimate of one year ago. In May 1972 the CIA in Saigon estimate of North Vietnamese in the South was 145–165,000. In terms of armored vehicles and heavy artillery and anti-aircraft, however, the current inventory of the North Vietnamese is greater than that in the South at the time of the 1972 spring offensive. It appears, incidentally, that most of the new equipment brought south during the 1972–1973 dry season entered North Vietnam during the period of the intensive U.S. air and naval interdiction of North Vietnam in 1972.

We were also told in Saigon that all the supplies that had been stockpiled in Cambodian storage areas were used up in 1972 and early 1973 and that the kinds of supplies being brought down now were those required to maintain troops in place—food, clothing and medical supplies—not ammunition and other items indicating immediate offensive intentions. CIA analysts thus had concluded that there will be no general offensive in the next four months. In September, however, they expect the North Vietnamese to emphasize ammunition in their supply flow and if they now preposition armor and artillery, and there is no bombing on the trail so that men could be moved quickly down it by truck, by late next fall they could again be in a position to launch a major offensive similar to that in the spring of 1972.

268. TELEGRAM FROM CHIEF OF THE U.S. DELEGATION TO THE JOINT ECONOMIC COMMISSION MAURICE J. WILLIAMS TO ROGERS, JUNE 18, 1973

The U.S. DRV talks on economic relations in the Joint Economic Commission had been making rapid progress until they were suspended in April. When the Joint Economic Commission resumed its discussions on June 18, the U.S. delegation chief, Maurice J. Williams, informed his counterpart, DRV Finance Minister Dang

SOURCE: Document declassified by Department of State, November 13, 1978.

*Viet Chau, that there would be no final agreement on assistance unless DRV
"performance" on Laos and Cambodia was satisfactory. This was an apparent
reference to the American insistence during negotiations between the United States
and the DRV in Paris on the implementation of the peace agreement during May
and June that the DRV ensure a cease-fire in Cambodia—something the DRV
negotiators rejected as neither possible nor required under the terms of Article 20.
It was over this issue that the United States finally refused to complete an agreement for postwar assistance.*

1. Most of the nearly two-hour meeting was devoted to the procedural question of scheduling the Commission's work during the fifteen-day period prescribed
by the Joint Communique. Min CHAU and LE KHAC attended, but not THACH
(who had told USDEL officers last week he was leaving Paris).

2. Chau led off with a stern [*officially deleted*] statement full of self-righteous
indignation which chastised the US for having unilaterally suspended JEC activities.
Williams responded by reminding Chau we had continually emphasized that Article
21 could not be taken in isolation from other provisions of the Agreement. Thus
unilateral DRV interpretations of Articles 7 and 20 had greatly concerned the U.S.
Williams drove home that their performance on Laos and Cambodia under Article
20 was essential before the work of the JEC could result in a fruitful conclusion.
Chau, finding his own moralistic stance unproductive, gradually changed to a more
cordial approach.

3. Chau's substantive suggestion was that the Commission adopt a fixed
agenda in advance, to include discussions on DRV purchases outside the U.S., size
and content of program, etc. Chau continually stressed urgency, and sought to
speed up review for completion of all major substantive issues this week. He also
stressed the importance of the form and level of signature of a US-DRV agreement
incorporating final JEC decisions.

4. Williams insisted that the JEC resume by taking up the DRV revised
five-year program, with detailed emphasis on the first year, which the DRV was
about to transmit April 19 (USDEL JEC 10910). This would provide a practical
basis from which meetings could evolve progressively.

5. After some reiteration of DRV objectives, especially that of reaching agreement with urgency, Chau accepted Williams' proposed modus operandi. It was
agreed to reconvene June 19.

269. FULBRIGHT-AIKEN
AMENDMENT—PUBLIC LAW 93-52,
SECTION 108, JULY 1, 1973

*In the single most important legislation passed by Congress relating to U.S.
policy in Indochina, the Nixon Administration was forbidden to resume bombing or
any other combat activity in Indochina. That legal restriction, passed as Nixon
himself began to lose his political clout because of the Watergate coverup coming*

SOURCE: *Background Information Relating to Southeast Asia and Vietnam,* p. 577.

unravelled, prevented the United States from following up on the bombing threat made by Nixon in March. From then on, reintervention by the United States in any form, was only a distant possibility.

SEC. 108. Notwithstanding any other provision of law, on or after August 15, 1973, no funds herein or heretofore appropriated may be obligated or expended to finance directly or indirectly combat activities by United States military forces in or over or from off the shores of North Vietnam, South Vietnam, Laos or Cambodia.

Approved July 1, 1973.

270. PEOPLE'S LIBERATION ARMED FORCES COMMAND ORDER, OCTOBER 15, 1973.

During the first eight months of the Paris Agreement, the Communist strategy had been to resist ARVN operations to extend territorial control with guerrillas and local troops, refraining from any coordinated counteroffensive. But in October 1973, after a significant chunk of PRG territory had been seized by the RVN, the Party authorized the PLAF main force units to strike back at Saigon's rear bases and at other points of its own choosing. This change in military posture was followed by a new escalation of military force on the Saigon side in late 1973 and early 1974.

U.S. imperialism, defeated in its war of aggression in Vietnam has been forced to sign the Agreement on Ending the War and Restoring Peace in Vietnam.

Yet, the United States does not want yet to give up the design to impose neocolonialism on South Vietnam; and the Saigon administration, encouraged and supported by it, is acting in opposition to our people's desire for peace, independence, democracy and national concord.

U.S. imperialism and the Saigon administration have never seriously implemented the agreement all through the past 8 months. They have violated and sabotaged the most vital provisions of the agreement all-sidedly and in a systematic and utterly serious manner.

The Saigon administration has never observed the ceasefire; it just goes on with war acts against our people.

It has frantically conducted a "special pacification program" by subjecting our compatriots, in the towns and the countryside alike, to arrests, terror and very savage massacres.

It has been nibbling at many areas controlled by the PRGRSV in western Thuan Thien, in the central plains, in western Kontum, and in Cai Lay and Chuong Thien, Nam Bo [South Vietnam—ed.]. Right now it is mustering a big force to nibble at the liberated areas in western Pleiku.

SOURCE: Vietnam News Agency in English, October 15, 1973, in Foreign Broadcast Information Service, Asia and Pacific, October 15, 1973, pp. L2–L3.

Most recently on October 3 and 11, it used aircraft to conduct wanton bombings on many populous areas deep in the PRG's territory in Tay Ninh and Thu Dau Mot.

This is a very grave step taken to further the general scheme of sabotage hatched by the U.S. and the Saigon administration against the Paris agreement on Vietnam.

The U.S. and the Saigon administration are held completely responsible for these war acts, and must bear all the serious consequences of their own deeds.

The command of the South Vietnam People's Liberation Armed Forces now orders all officers and men of the main forces army, the regional army, the militia, and all guerrilla, home-guard and security forces across South Vietnam to:

1. Sharpen their vigilance and counter in a fitting manner all war acts of the Saigon administration in order to defend the liberated zone and the lives and property of its population and preserve the Paris agreement on Vietnam; and

2. Fight back at the Saigon administration, as long as its has not discontinued its war acts, any place and with appropriate forms and force, thus compelling the other side to implement the Paris agreement seriously and scrupulously and to put a complete stop to all its acts of war and sabotage.

The PLAF command calls upon the entire people to give the greatest assistance to the PLAF and join them closely in the struggle for the maintenance of peace and the materialization of national concord by meting out due punishment to the U.S. and Saigon for any of their acts of sabotage against the Paris agreement and forcing them to implement the agreement strictly, so that the gains our people have made in revolution may be preserved.

1974

271. STATEMENT BY PRG MILITARY DELEGATION TO THE TWO PARTY JOINT MILITARY COMMISSION, MAY 10, 1974

In the spring of 1974, the escalation of fighting was reflected in the breakdown of negotiations on implementation of the agreement in Saigon. After Saigon evacuated a major ranger base at Tong Le Chan, which had been surrounded by Communist forces for many weeks, it charged that it had been overrun in a major operation heralding a Communist offensive which destroyed the Paris Agreement. Saigon then withdrew the privileges and immunities previously granted to the PRG delegates, leaving them in isolation from the press, cutting telephone lines, and ending liaison flights. Three weeks later, the PRG delegation walked out of the JMC

SOURCE: Mimeographed copy of original text.

meeting in protest, and despite conditional restoration of the privileges, Saigon still claimed the right to withdraw them again at any time. In June the PRG delegation resumed negotiations at the Two Party Joint Military Commission (TPJMC), but only on the privileges and immunities question. When the RVN refused its demand for a new agreement confirming the equal status of its delegates, the PRG delegation announced on June 21, 1974, that it would suspend its participation in the TPJMC as well as the Four Party Joint Military Team [FPJMT], which was to search for missing personnel.

The Military Delegation of the Provisional Revolutionary Government of the Republic of South Viet Nam to the Central Two-Party Joint Military Commission (J.M.C.) May 10, issued the following statement:

Since the signing of the Paris Agreement on Viet Nam, the Saigon administration, commanded and backed by the United States, has ceaselessly escalated its sabotage of the cease-fire and the Agreement in a global, systematic and aggravated manner, thus causing an extremely tense situation in South Viet Nam.

The Saigon administration has mustered all its armed forces to conduct repeated land-grabbing operations throughout South Viet Nam, carry out bombings and shellings against heavily populated areas, and illegally erect posts in areas controlled by the P.R.G. of the R.S.V.N. At the same time, in contested areas and areas under its control, the Saigon administration has stepped up its extremely barbarous "pacification" policy, repeatedly launched police raids and campaigns of repression and terror to kill civilians, loot their property and herd them into concentration camps thus piling up crimes against the people.

To cover up and serve its schemes of intensifying the war and sabotaging the Agreement, the Saigon administration has mounted slanderous campaigns against the P.R.G. and the Government of the D.R.V.N. It has on many occasions, fooled public opinion about the so-called "coming major offensive of the Communists," repeatedly committed massacres like the Cai Lay, Tam Soc, Gia Binh, Cay Dua, Song Phu, etc. cases, then slandered the People's Liberation Armed Forces with a view to covering up its crimes. It has continuously and systematically sabotaged the organizations set up to implement and supervise the Agreement. Of late, along with delaying and unilateral suspending the Consultative conference between the two South-Vietnamese parties in La Celle Saint-Cloud, it has taken a new and very serious step in undermining the central two-party J.M.C.

The Saigon administration has repeatedly torpedoed the meetings of the central two-party J.M.C. and arbitrarily imposed absurd conditions for making speeches at the conference table—relying on that pretext to brazenly interrupt speeches of the P.R.G.'s delegates, with a view to eluding all remarks and condemnations of its actions of sabotage of the Agreement. As a result, no discussion can be carried out on any problem.

The Saigon side has tried by all means to hinder the normal activities of the military delegation of the P.R.G. It has seriously undermined the privileges and diplomatic immunities agreed upon by the two sides, arbitrarily cancelled all Saigon-Loc Ninh regular liaison flights, prevented all press conferences of the P.R.G. military delegation, disconnected all the telephone lines of the delegation and prevented all contacts between the delegation and the outside, even with the I.C.C.S.

With the above-mentioned acts of sabotage, the Saigon administration has paralyzed both the organization and activities of the central two party J.M.C., destroyed all capacities of negotiation and cooperation between the two South-Vietnamese parties in the implementation of the Agreement and, at the same time, undermined the possibility of cooperation between the J.M.C., and the I.C.C.S. thus placing the I.C.C.S. before a danger of being completely paralyzed and threatening the Paris Agreement on Viet Nam as a whole.

In the past as in the present, relying on its government's constant position—namely to honour, thoroughly implement and resolutely defend the Agreement—the military delegation of the P.R.G. has persisted in its efforts to promote the work of the central two-party J.M.C. On many occasions, it has put forward constructive, realistic, fair and reasonable proposals so as to reach rapidly an agreement on the measures which the two-party J.M.C. has the responsibility to implement.

Of late, relying on the March 22, 1974, 6-point Statement of its government, the P.R.G. military delegation of the R.S.V.N. put forward, at the conference table of the central two-party J.M.C., concrete initiatives on two urgent problems belonging to the responsibility of the two-party J.M.C., namely to strictly observe the cease-fire throughout South Viet Nam and release all the Vietnamese military and civilian personnel captured and detained. But the Saigon administration side has not only obstinately refused to accept those initiatives, but eluded them by brazenly sabotaging all discussions. With its goodwill and very persistent attitude, at all the successive sessions of the central two-party J.M.C. in the past month, especially at the two delegation-heads' regular sessions held on the morning of May 7, and 10, 1974, the military delegation of the P.R.G. drew the Saigon administration side's attention to the serious situation of the central two-party J.M.C. (a situation for which the Saigon administration must be held responsible) and resolutely demanded that it end completely all acts of sabotage against this body, adopt a serious attitude at the conference table, restore and fully carry out the privileges and diplomatic immunities, guarantee the normal activities of the military delegation of the P.R.G. in strict application of Articles 16 and 17 of the Protocol on the cease-fire in South Viet Nam, and on the J.M.C., and Article 11(A) of the June 13, 1973, Joint Communiqué, and on that basis, restore the normal activities of the central two-party J.M.C. Only by doing so can the J.M.C. discuss and settle urgent problems, such as the strict observance of the cease-fire, and the return of all civilians and military personnel still detained. etc. . . .

The Saigon administration did not respond to these correct demands, instead, it systematically distorted and slandered the P.R.G. and the D.R.V.N. Government, while arrogantly pleading for its erroneous actions. Besides, the Saigon administration imposed insolent conditions for the restoration and application of the privileges and diplomatic immunities. It does not regard it as an obligation to the Agreement, but as a matter that it can re-examine, lift or refuse to carry out at will.

It is clear that the Saigon administration obstinately moves ahead along the path of war and sabotage of the Agreement. It has ever more seriously torpedoed the J.M.C., and is intentionally maintaining this body in an impasse as far as its organization and activities, are concerned thus causing a complete deadlock in the implementation of the Agreement.

In face of this serious fact, and because no question can be seriously discussed and solved at the conference table, the military delegation of the P.R.G. has had to suspend its participation at the sessions of the central two-party J.M.C. at delegation-head level as well as at the sessions of the J.M.C. sub-commissions till the Saigon administration accepts to restore and guarantee the full application of the privileges and diplomatic immunities and adopts a serious attitude in the negotiations. The Saigon administration and the United States must bear full responsibility for all the consequences arising from their actions of sabotage.

272. COSVN DIRECTIVE 08/CT 74,
AUGUST 1974 [Extract]

In July and early August 1974, Communist forces overran a heavily fortified ARVN base complex and the district town of Thuong Duc in their first major offensive in the lowland area. Almost immediately after these moves, Richard Nixon was forced to resign from the presidency. The United States did not respond with threats to bomb North Vietnam, as Nixon had done in the spring of 1973 to put pressure on DRV officials in connection with replacement and resupply of Communist troops in the South and Cambodia. Meeting shortly after the Nixon resignation, the Party leadership analyzed the situation and formulated a new line for South Vietnam. Based on this assessment, COSVN issued a new directive surveying the gains of the previous six months and establishing guidelines for the next several months. It noted that the possibility of U.S. intervention was slim but suggested a cautious approach to the military offensive. It suggested that Saigon might switch to a policy of carrying out the agreement in part, but said basic provisions could not be implemented as long as Thieu's regime was intact.

The following conclusion can be drawn from the real situation of the movement in the last six months.

1. During the first six months of the year we *scored major full-scale and firm gains,* blunted the enemy-initiated dry-season rice-looting plan, and set back and defeated by one major step his pacification and encroaching project. Those facts were evidence of the "Central" and COSVN resolutions that deeply reflect the realities of the movement and can produce major strength-generating effects.

A number of shortcomings and weaknesses adversely affecting our gains were the slow building-up of our forces that failed to meet the requirements, spotty three-pronged offensive at the grassroots, imbalance among the three types of forces, slow growth of the movement at urban centers and weak areas.

The enemy still has strong points such as a numerically large army and control over populous and rich areas. This thus permits him to continue sweeping off resources and pressing people into his army. The U.S. is still striving to provide aid to Thieu (Those strengths definitely hamper the development of the revolution.). *However, developments resulting from the evolution of the situation are greatly in our favor.* Our weaknesses can be entirely overcome and they are being effectively reduced step-by-step. The enemy's strong points are temporary ones with internal conflicts. [These strengths] can not develop and become weaker than before.

SOURCE: Mimeographed copy of the translated directive, with commentary, released by the State Department, no date shown.

2. *Our posture and force is being developed steadily, stronger than at the time we embarked on the '73–'74 dry season, stronger even than at the time we made preparations for the offensives in 1968 and 1972.* Meantime, U.S. aggressor troops are no longer present on the battlefield; enemy air and artillery support has presently decreased a great deal as compared with that received in the days of the Americans' presence. With our steadily increasing material facilities for battle-fields, (our liberated areas and bases being connected with the "greater rear base" [translation: North Vietnam] and receiving large assistance from it), *we have achieved a very high level of unity of spirit within the whole Party, the whole army, and the whole people revolving around the resolutions of* the Party's Central Committee and COSVN. The Party's policies correctly reflect the aspirations and pressing needs of the masses such as those in "weak" *areas inhabited by the refugees and ethnic minorities,* where up to now, revolutionary activities have been weak be-cause of the small and inadequate number of our infrastructures. New develop-ments have taken place there; the masses hate the enemy, have a better understanding of the revolution, and are ready to help and support our infrastructures. This is a condition greatly advantageous to the stronger and larger development of our posture and force.

3. *The Nguyen Van Thieu's puppet army and government although not yet being reduced to collapse, continue to face increasing difficulties in all respects and keep on declining both quantitatively and qualitatively in terms of posture and force.* However, the U.S. and the puppet government are very stubborn; they continue to brazenly display their reactionary intent of aggression and (working) class hatred.

Although they have *tried to regain freedom of action from their defensive posture and changed tactics and schemes to cope with the new situation, their schemes and tactics have been conceived from a defensive posture* and conse-quently present numerous shortcomings and weaknesses.

The material facilities for the survival of the Nguyen Van Thieu's puppet government are being seriously shaken as they have to nurture an excessively heavy war and administrative machinery with over one and a half million nonproductive personnel, with expenses for military requirements that keep increasing in the face of our concerted offensives on all battlefields, and with measures to meet the living needs of the population in areas under enemy control and of the people gathered in large numbers by the enemy. Meantime, production in agriculture and industry has declined seriously, and the life of the Thieu's regime depends entirely on U.S. aid which in the near future will be further reduced. To remedy this situation, the Saigon puppet government has only one alternative—to resort to inflation and robbery practices to the utmost at the expense of people from all social strata (practices that are carried on concurrently with brazenly-conducted forced induc-tion). To this end, there is the *need to further apply fascism to its oppressive machinery,* to put down whatever opposition (opposition that may come from the people or from the Third Force), and as a consequence, this generates bitter and irreconciliable antagonisms between every social class and the Saigon government and will certainly lead sooner or later to a new, widespread and strong movement of the people of all social strata. The possibility that the enemy's internal differences might become so critical that internecine strife could happen within his den is not ruled out.

4. The current contest of strength between us and the enemy is occurring within the context of the world's situation, of the situation in Indochina, and even in the U.S., and is *highly favorable to our side and greatly disadvantageous to the enemy.*

*   *   *

We must fully understand the realistic situation up to the present time despite the above enemy scheme. However, in keeping abreast of the situation we come to realize that recently when we stepped up the people's warfare in the lowlands and the border area, raiding their bases or destroying their subsectors, district seats, infantry battalions and battle groups the puppet army met with lots of difficulties and the U.S. did not dare intervene openly.

If in coming years we alter the balance of forces in our favor and the puppet side is weakened and encounters additional troubles they may either partially carry out the Agreement to bide time, seek accommodation, overcome their difficulties only to later resume the sabotage of the Accord by all possible means, (or) keep on attacking us to resume war in South Vietnam. In short, so long as the mandarinistic, militarist, fascist, U.S. lackey administration has not been toppled yet they surely cannot implement the Agreement's basic provisions and will try to renew the hostilities. In case the enemy risks being reduced to a crumbling state U.S. Air Force and Navy can be called for to come to his rescue. Though the possibility of an intervention in the South and an offensive against the North by U.S. ground forces is slim, we must, nevertheless, be on the look-out and make sound estimates. We must apply preventive measures and an appropriate strategy so as not to leave room for a U.S. intervention or a U.S. timely intervention. However, we must not entertain defeatism in the eventuality of an American involvement in the hostilities. We must resolutely defeat them to have the Revolution in the South continually take a step ahead.

*   *   *

Section III. Policy and Missions in the Coming Period

A. *The basic mission of the Revolution in the South in the forthcoming stage is to carry on with the strategy of people's democratic and national revolution, unite all people in a struggle against U.S. imperialists and against mandarinistic, militarist, fascist, U.S. lackey, mercantile bourgeois, eradicate neo-colonialism, set up a national, genuinely democratic administration, carry out national concord, entirely get rid of U.S. dependence and achieve a peaceful, independent, democratic, neutral and prosperous South Vietnam to advance toward peace and national reunification.*

B. Our immediate mission is to unite all people in the political, military and diplomatic fronts in the most active and flexible way, and, depending on the conditions at each place or each period, appropriately coordinate these fronts to force the enemy to correctly implement the Paris Agreement on Vietnam. We must maintain and develop the revolutionary force in all respects, win victories step-by-step and keep the initiative under all circumstances so as to help the Revolution in the South proceed forward.

C. There exist two capabilities in the development of the Revolution in the South. They are:

—If in the coming period the balance of force between the enemy and us tilts to our side and the enemy meets with increased difficulties they are compelled to cling to the Agreement and implement small parts of it to impede our advancement, save their deteriorating situation and sabotage the Accord.

—In case they do not want to carry out the Accord and the present war gradually widens into a large scale one we again have to wage a decisive revolutionary war to defeat the enemy to win total victory.

—These two capabilities exist side by side and are in the process of development. We must take advantage of Capability 1 and ready ourselves for Capability 2 and grasp revolutionary violence to secure victory regardless of what development will happen. The road to success for the Revolution in the South is the road of violence based on political and military forces.

1975

273. STATEMENT BY SECRETARY OF STATE KISSINGER TO THE SENATE COMMITTEE ON APPROPRIATIONS, APRIL 15, 1975 [Extracts]

At an October 1974 meeting of the Vietnamese Party Political Bureau, Party Military Committee, and General Staff, it was agreed that the United States was unlikely to reintervene, and that even if it did, it would not be able to save the Thieu regime. The Political Bureau met from December 18, 1974, to January 8, 1975, and decided on a two-year strategic plan for defeating the Thieu regime. The spring offensive launched in March 1975 in the central highlands triggered a withdrawal of Saigon forces from the region; this swiftly turned into the disintegration of the army. The Ford Administration asked Congress in early April for an additional $300 million in military assistance to help Saigon make a last stand against the rapidly advancing North Vietnamese forces. In his last appearance before Congress during the war, Kissinger argued that the United States had a "moral obligation" to continue to fund the war effort. Kissinger blamed the military imbalance in the South, largely on cuts in U.S. military assistance to Saigon in 1973 and 1974. The CIA-State Department estimate of military assistance to North Vietnam for 1973 and 1974 was $730 million, compared to a total of $3.3 billion in military assistance to South Vietnam by the United States in the same years.

SOURCE: Department of State *Bulletin*, May 5, 1975, pp. 584–586.

While North Viet-Nam had available several reserve divisions which it could commit to battle at times and places of its choosing, the South had no strategic reserves. Its forces were stretched thin, defending lines of communication and population centers throughout the country.

While North Viet-Nam, by early this year, had accumulated in South Viet-Nam enough ammunition for two years of intensive combat, South Vietnamese commanders had to ration ammunition as their stocks declined and were not replenished.

While North Viet-Nam had enough fuel in the South to operate its tanks and armored vehicles for at least 18 months, South Viet-Nam faced stringent shortages.

In sum, while Hanoi was strengthening its army in the South, the combat effectiveness of South Viet-Nam's army gradually grew weaker. While Hanoi built up its reserve divisions and accumulated ammunition, fuel, and other military supplies, U.S. aid levels to Viet-Nam were cut—first by half in 1973 and then by another third in 1974. This coincided with a worldwide inflation and a fourfold increase in fuel prices. As a result almost all of our military aid had to be devoted to ammunition and fuel. Very little was available for spare parts, and none for new equipment.

These imbalances became painfully evident when the offensive broke full force, and they contributed to the tragedy which unfolded. Moreover, the steady diminution in the resources available to the Army of South Viet-Nam unquestionably affected the morale of its officers and men. South Vietnamese units in the northern and central provinces knew full well that they faced an enemy superior both in numbers and in firepower. They knew that reinforcements and resupply would not be forthcoming. When the fighting began they also knew, as they had begun to suspect, that the United States would not respond. I would suggest that all of these factors added significantly to the sense of helplessness, despair, and, eventually, panic which we witnessed in late March and early April.

I would add that it is both inaccurate and unfair to hold South Viet-Nam responsible for blocking progress toward a political solution to the conflict. Saigon's proposals in its conversations with PRG [Provisional Revolutionary Government] representatives in Paris were in general constructive and conciliatory. There was no progress toward a compromise political settlement because Hanoi intended that there should not be. Instead, North Viet-Nam's strategy was to lay the groundwork for an eventual military offensive, one which would either bring outright victory or at least allow Hanoi to dictate the terms of a political solution.

Neither the United States nor South Viet-Nam entered into the Paris agreement with the expectation that Hanoi would abide by it in every respect. We did believe, however, that the agreement was sufficiently equitable to both sides that its major provisions could be accepted and acted upon by Hanoi and that the contest could be shifted thereby from a military to a political track. However, our two governments also recognized that, since the agreement manifestly was not self-enforcing, Hanoi's adherence depended heavily on maintaining a military parity in South Viet-Nam. So long as North Viet-Nam confronted a strong South Vietnamese army and so long as the possibility existed of U.S. intervention to offset the strategic advantages of the North, Hanoi could be expected to forgo major military action. Both of those essential conditions were dissipated over the past two years. Hanoi attained a clear military superiority, and it became increasingly convinced that U.S. intervention could be ruled out. It therefore returned to a military course, with the results we have seen.

The present situation in Viet-Nam is ominous. North Viet-Nam's combat forces far outnumber those of the South, and they are better armed. Perhaps more important, they enjoy a psychological momentum which can be as decisive as armaments in battle. South Viet-Nam must reorganize and reequip its forces, and it must restore the morale of its army and its people. These tasks will be difficult, and they can be performed only by the South Vietnamese. However, a successful defense will also require resources—arms, fuel, ammunition, and medical supplies— and these can come only from the United States.

Large quantities of equipment and supplies, totaling perhaps $800 million, were lost in South Viet-Nam's precipitous retreat from the northern and central areas. Much of this should not have been lost, and we regret that it happened. But South Viet-Nam is now faced with a different strategic and tactical situation and different military requirements. Although the amount of military assistance the President has requested is of the same general magnitude as the value of the equipment lost, we are not attempting simply to replace those losses. The President's request, based on General Weyand's [Gen. Frederick C. Weyand, Chief of Staff, United States Army] assessment, represents our best judgment as to what is needed now, in this new situation, to defend what is left of South Viet-Nam. Weapons, ammunition, and supplies to reequip four divisions, to form a number of ranger groups into divisional units, and to upgrade some territorial forces into infantry regiments will require some $326 million. The balance of our request is for ammunition, fuel, spare parts, and medical supplies to sustain up to 60 days of intensive combat and to pay for the cost of transporting those items. These are minimum requirements, and they are needed urgently.

The human tragedy of Viet-Nam has never been more acute than it now is. Hundreds of thousands of South Vietnamese have sought to flee Communist control and are homeless refugees. They have our compassion, and they must also have our help. Despite commendable efforts by the South Vietnamese Government, the burden of caring for these innocent victims is beyond its capacity. The United States has already done much to assist these people, but many remain without adequate food, shelter, or medical care. The President has asked that additional efforts and additional resources be devoted to this humanitarian effort. I ask that the Congress respond generously and quickly.

The objectives of the United States in this immensely difficult situation remain as they were when the Paris agreement was signed—to end the military conflict and establish conditions which will allow a fair political solution to be achieved. We believe that despite the tragic experience to date, the Paris agreement remains a valid framework within which to proceed toward such a solution. However, today, as in 1973, battlefield conditions will affect political perceptions and the outcome of negotiations. We therefore believe that in order for a political settlement to be reached which preserves any degree of self-determination for the people of South Viet-Nam, the present military situation must be stabilized. It is for these reasons that the President has asked Congress to appropriate urgently additional funds for military assistance for Viet-Nam.

I am acutely aware of the emotions aroused in this country by our long and difficult involvement in Viet-Nam. I understand what the cost has been for this nation and why frustration and anger continue to dominate our national debate. Many will argue that we have done more than enough for the Government and the people of South Viet-Nam. I do not agree with that proposition, however, nor do I believe that to review endlessly the wisdom of our original involvement serves a useful purpose now. For despite the agony of this nation's experience in Indochina and the substantial reappraisal which has taken place concerning our proper role there, few would deny that we are still involved or that what we do—or fail to do—will still weigh heavily in the outcome. We cannot by our actions alone insure the survival of South Viet-Nam. But we can, alone, by our inaction assure its demise.

The United States has no legal obligation to the Government and the people of South Viet-Nam of which the Congress is not aware. But we do have a deep moral obligation—rooted in the history of our involvement and sustained by the continuing efforts of our friends. We cannot easily set it aside. In addition to the obvious consequences for the people of Viet-Nam, our failure to act in accordance with that obligation would inevitably influence other nations' perceptions of our constancy and our determination. American credibility would not collapse, and American honor would not be destroyed. But both would be weakened, to the detriment of this nation and of the peaceful world order we have sought to build.

274. EDITORIAL IN *HOC TAP*, APRIL 1975 [Extract]

By the time Kissinger made his plea for supplementary military assistance for Saigon, Communist troops were already beginning to position themselves for the final assault on Saigon. In an editorial in the Party's theoretical journal—the last before the end of the war—the Party leadership attributed its victories and the collapse of Saigon's army in Central Vietnam to the change in the balance of forces within South Vietnam as well as to a "deep, all-round crisis" in the United States. But it also hailed the development of the "military art" of Vietnam, in the tradition of great Vietnamese military strategists of the past.

The Causes of Victory

Why have the victories recorded by our southern armed forces and people been so big and so quick? All the victories recorded by our people's revolutionary struggle and all the defeats suffered by the U.S. neocolonialist policy of aggression, from the past to the present, have occurred according to the rules of history. The victory of the current offensive and uprising staged by the southern armed forces is a successful continuation and development of the great victory of the resistance against the U.S. aggressors and for national salvation. This time, the offensives and uprisings are the culmination of more than 2 years of fierce struggle by our people to safeguard and implement the Paris agreement and firmly maintain and develop the southern revolutionary gains. These great and quick victories recorded by the southern armed forces and people are due, first of all, to the correct

SOURCE: FBIS, Asia and Pacific, April 24, 1975, pp. K9–11.

and creative political and military lines of the NFLSV and the PRGRSV. Correctly assessing the situation at home and abroad since the Paris agreement, the NFLSV and the PRGRSV have drawn up judicious policies and correct methods of struggle suitable for the new conditions.

The southern armed forces and people have scrupulously implemented the Paris agreement; held aloft the banner of peace, independence, democracy and national concord; and resolutely punished the enemy for stubbornly dragging on the war and sabotaging the agreement. Firmly grasping the concept of revolutionary violence and thoroughly imbued with the idea of revolutionary offensive, the southern armed forces and people have combined their struggle against the enemy on three fronts—political, military and diplomatic—safeguarded and implemented the Paris agreement and gradually defeated and repelled the enemy's war schemes and activities. This correct and creative revolutionary line has succeeded in motivating all forces throughout the country and developing the extremely great combined strength of the southern revolution, while winning ever broader and stronger sympathy and support of public opinion the world over and utterly isolating the U.S. imperialists and their lackey clique.

The victories in the current offensives and uprisings are due to the great solidarity and heroism and the ability to fight and to win of the southern armed forces and people. Unable to live under the extremely cruel oppression imposed by Nguyen Van Thieu and burning with resentment against the Vietnamization policy, the southern compatriots in areas under temporary enemy control have resolutely risen up to overthrow the puppet administration, eliminate the U.S. neocolonialist yoke and achieve peace, freedom and a decent life. Even the puppet troops and puppet administrative officials have also realized ever more clearly the country-selling people-harming nature of the Thieu clique and have resolutely refused to die in the place of the U.S.-Thieu clique.

The southern armed forces and people have developed the national unity tradition to determinedly sruggle against both the external and internal enemies. In the military field our armed forces and people have successfully grasped and improved the military art of their ancestors; have smoothly combined such strong points as the ingenious stratagems of the Tran Dynasty, the patience and endurance of the Le Dynasty and the valiant and lightning attacks of the Nguyen-Quang Trung Dynasty; and have brought into full play the experience gained from the two resistances against the French and the Americans, from the armed uprisings of the August revolution and from modern people's war. Therefore, they have scored glorious armed exploits in this 1975 spring of great victories. The enormous impetus, daring actions and the tempestuous strength of this offensive and uprising movement have manifested gloriously our nation's revolutionary heroism and the "determined-to-fight-and-win" spirit of the southern compatriots and combatants and of our entire people.

The liberation armed forces have clearly displayed the spirit of gallantry and sacrifice and their know-how in employing resourceful and creative fighting methods to attack continuously and determinedly and acting in a daring and timely manner with a strong impetus and high intensity. The outstandingly successful large-scale annihilating battles in the Central Highlands, Hue and Danang mark the extraordinary maturity of the heroic southern liberation forces in terms of combat might in general and efficiency in performing combat with coordination among various armed branches in particular. The southern forces and people have adroitly combined offensives with uprisings, thereby not allowing the enemy troops to react and subjecting them to annihilation, surrender, disintegration or retreat in disarray.

This offensive and uprising movement has recorded such great victories in so short a time because the balance of forces between ourselves and the enemy has changed completely to our advantage and to the disadvantage of the enemy. The southern armed forces and people have not only won great victories but have done it in record time, so that now both their position and strength are superior to those of the enemy. They have creatively employed revolutionary methods under new conditions and successfully developed to such a point that it helps our armed forces and people overpower the enemy in major directions and areas in the current offensive and uprising movement, thus strengthening the revolutionary forces many times and causing a rapid deterioration of the enemy forces, which are now declining.

This offensive and uprising movement has recorded quick and great victories because it occurred at the right time. After 2 years of concentrating all-out efforts on the neocolonialist war and frenziedly violating the agreement, the Nguyen Van Thieu clique had been gravely defeated in the military field, highly isolated in the political field and driven into an economic quandry. At that time, Thieu's ally—the puppet Lon Nol Clique—was facing a desperate situation in Phnom Penh. Meanwhile, the United States was caught in a deep, all-round crisis at home and faced mounting difficulties abroad. The southern revolution faced new advantages and had new capabilities to win total victory. In this situation, the southern armed forces' and people's offensive and uprising movement caused extreme dismay and consternation among the puppet administration and armed forces. Their spirit and their willpower collapsed and their fighting strength deteriorated rapidly. They fled in panic.

275. DIRECTIVE FROM THE POLITICAL BUREAU, VIETNAM WORKERS PARTY, APRIL 29, 1975

On April 21, under pressure from the U.S. Embassy, RVN President Thieu resigned in favor of his vice-president, Tran Van Huong. But it was already too late to negotiate with the forces surrounding the capital. As Communist troops began moving on Saigon, the Political Bureau sent a final directive urging the troops to quickly eliminate resistance in the city, preparing for the task of ending resistance in the rest of the Mekong Delta and supplying food to the poorest Saigon families. Communist forces marched in to capture Saigon without a battle, and a thirty year political-military struggle was finally over.

1. We warmly commend all units for having made great armed exploits in the past few days by smashing the enemy defense groups north, east, northwest and southwest of Saigon, severing Route 4, attacking major enemy airbases and satisfactorily operating in Saigon and its surrounding areas.

SOURCE: Van Tien Dung, "Great Spring Victory," *Nhan Dan*, May 17, 1976, p. 3. Translated in Foreign Broadcast Information Service, Asia and Pacific, Daily Report, July 7, 1976, Supplement 42, p. 110.

All cadres, combatants and party and youth union members are called on to display their highest determination to launch a quick and direct attack on the enemy's last den and to use the powerful force of an invincible army to smash all enemy resistance, combining an offensive with an uprising to completely liberate Saigon-Gia Dinh municipality.

At the same time, they must strictly observe discipline, comply with all directives and orders, protect the people's lives and property, enhance the revolutionary qualities and the determined-to-win tradition of our army, outstandingly do all tasks and win a total victory for the historic campaign bearing great Uncle Ho's name.

2. While concentrating command and guidance to satisfactorily liberate Saigon-Gia Dinh, it is necessary to plan for armed assignments and preparatory tasks aimed at quickly developing advantageous positions, completely eradicating all residual enemy forces in other areas, especially in the Mekong Delta and on Con Son and Phu Quoc islands, and totally liberating South Vietnam.

The revolutionary and combat spirit of the troops must be strictly and continually developed to overcome all feelings of complacency until we win total victory.

3. Once entering the municipality, cadres at all echelons must pay immediate attention to the laboring people's livelihood, the former regime's exploitative policies and the monopoly of the comprador bourgeoisie. Among the working class and the laboring people there are some starving people, and many families have neither rice nor money to buy rice. Enemy rice supplies must immediately be distributed to starving families, or if need be, troops will share their rations with the people.

Chronology of Events Relating to the Vietnam War

1940

SEPTEMBER. Japanese troops, with French cooperation, occupy Indochina.

1941

MAY. Vietnam Doc Lap Dong Minh Hoi (Viet Minh) founded.

1945

MARCH 9. Japanese stage a coup d'etat against French and seize power directly in Vietnam.

AUGUST. Viet Minh seize power throughout Vietnam.

SEPTEMBER 2. Ho Chi Minh proclaims the founding of the Democratic Republic of Vietnam (DRV).

SEPTEMBER 13. British troops land in Saigon to disarm Japanese troops south of the sixteenth parallel on behalf of Allied forces.

SEPTEMBER 14. Chiang Kai-Shek's *Kuomintang* troops enter Vietnam to disarm Japanese troops north of the sixteenth parallel on behalf of Allied forces.

SEPTEMBER 23. French troops, released by the British, reoccupy Saigon and take power in southern cities.

1946

FEBRUARY 20. French and Chiang Kai-Shek governments reach accord permitting French troops to replace Chinese troops north of the sixteenth parallel.

MARCH 6. DRV and France agree on a "Preliminary Convention" under which Vietnam is proclaimed a "Free State" within the French Union.

APRIL 3. French and Vietnamese general staffs reach agreement on stationing of French troops in Vietnam.

APRIL 17. Franco-Vietnamese negotiations open at Dalat, but fail to progress in the issue of Cochinchina.

JUNE 1. French High Commissioner for Indochina sets up a puppet "Provisional Government of the Republic of Cochinchina."

JULY 6. Franco-Vietnamese negotiations begin in Fontainebleau.

SEPTEMBER 14. Franco-Vietnamese *Modus Vivendi* signed.

NOVEMBER 22. French unilaterally demand control of Haiphong and kill thousands of Vietnamese civilians in naval bombardment of the city.

DECEMBER 19. Franco-Vietnamese war begins.

1947

MAY 12. French envoy Professor Paul Mus meets with Ho Chi Minh and presents nonnegotiable demands.

OCTOBER. French launch offensive aimed at destroying DRV main forces and capturing its top officials, which fails after two months.

1948

JANUARY 15–16. Indochinese Communist Party Central Committee decides to shift from the defensive stage to the contention stage of the resistance war.

JUNE 5. French High Commissioner signs Baie d'Along Agreement with Gen. Nguyen Van Xuan, head of the Republic of Cochinchina, to establish the State of Vietnam, with Bao Dai as chief of state.

1949

MARCH 8. Elysée Agreements establish principals affecting French relations with the state of Vietnam.

JULY 1. State of Vietnam formally established by decrees by Bao Dai.

JULY 19. French conclude agreement with the kingdom of Laos confirming French powers over foreign and military policy, judicial, fiscal, and monetary matters.

1950

JANUARY 18. People's Republic of China extends diplomatic recognition to the DRV.

FEBRUARY 7. Great Britain and the United States extend *de jure* recognition to the State of Vietnam.

MARCH 6. U.S. mission arrives in Saigon to study economic assistance to the Bao Dai government.

MAY 8. United States announces plans to extend economic and military aid to the French in Indochina, beginning with a $10 million grant.

MAY 30. U.S. Economic Mission under Robert Blum established in Saigon.

JUNE 27. President Truman announces acceleration of military aid to French Union forces in Indochina and dispatch of a military mission to Indochina.

OCTOBER 10. U.S. Military Assistance Advisory Group (MAAG) established in Saigon under Gen. Francis L. Brink.

DECEMBER 23. United States signs Mutual Defense Assistance Agreement with France, Vietnam, Cambodia, and Laos.

1951

FEBRUARY 11–19. Indochinese Communist Party convenes Second National Congress and changes its name to the Vietnam Workers Party.

SEPTEMBER 7. United States signs agreement with Vietnam for direct economic assistance.

NOVEMBER 18. Vietnamese forces launch the Hoa Binh Campaign, the largest offensive since the border campaign of 1950.

1952

FEBRUARY 23. French are driven from the town of Hoa Binh, south of Hanoi, at the conclusion of the Hoa Binh Campaign.

OCTOBER 14. Vietnamese forces begin the Northwest Campaign, which lasts three months.

1953

JANUARY 25–30. Vietnam Workers Party Central Committee Conference decides to lay the groundwork for land redistribution by putting rent reduction program into effect.

APRIL 13. Vietnamese troops and the Lao Liberation Army seize all of Sam Neua Province in Laos from the French.

JUNE 20. Gen. John O'Daniel, appointed chief of U.S. Military Mission in Indochina, arrives in Saigon to assess French war plans and participate in day-to-day military planning.

JULY 3. French Premier Joseph Laniel announces intention to "complete the independence" of the Associated States by negotiations with each of them.

SEPTEMBER 29. United States and France reach a supplementary aid agreement for an additional $385 million in assistance.

1954

MARCH 13. The Vietnam People's Army launches its offensive against the entrenched French position at Dienbienphu.

MARCH 20. Gen. Paul Ely, chief of the General Staff of the French Army, arrives in Washington to seek assistance for the French garrison at Dienbienphu.

MARCH 29. Dulles calls for "united action" to save Indochina from Communist victory.

APRIL 13. Dulles arrives in Britain to hold conversations with British Foreign Minister Anthony Eden on intervention in Indochina.

APRIL 14. Dulles arrives in Paris for talks with French Foreign Minister Bidault on internationalization of the war.

MAY 8. Geneva Conference on Indochina opens.

JUNE 26. Ngo Dinh Diem, appointed premier of the State of Vietnam by Bao Dai, arrives in Saigon.

JULY 21. Geneva Conference issues three cease-fire agreements and one final declaration.

SEPTEMBER 8. Southeast Asia Collective Defense Treaty and Protocol are signed in Manila.

OCTOBER 24. President Eisenhower writes to Diem promising direct assistance to his government, now in control of South Vietnam.

1955

JANUARY 1. United States begins channeling aid directly to the Diem Government in South Vietnam.

FEBRUARY 12. U.S. Military Assistance Advisory Group takes over full responsibility for training and organization of the South Vietnamese government army from the French.

JULY 19. DRV Government sends a diplomatic note to the Diem government proposing the naming of representatives for the conference to negotiate the general elections provided for in the Geneva Agreement.

JULY 20. Several hundred rioters ransack the headquarters of the International Control Commission (ICC) in Saigon, while Diem's police look on. India protests the failure of the South Vietnamese government to provide protection.

AUGUST 9. The government of South Vietnam (GVN) declares that it will not enter into negotiations with the DRV on elections as long as the Communist government remains in the North.

AUGUST 31. Secretary of State John Foster Dulles supports the position of the government of Vietnam in refusing consultations on the Geneva elections.

OCTOBER 23. A "referendum" organized by Ngo Dinh Diem with the covert participation of CIA psychological warfare officers deposes Bao Dai and makes Diem "chief of state."

OCTOBER 26. Diem proclaims South Vietnam a republic and becomes its first president.

1956

JANUARY 11. Diem's Republic of Vietnam (RVN) issues Ordinance No. 6, allowing the arrest and detention of anyone "considered dangerous to national defense and common security" in concentration camps.

APRIL 6. RVN again declares that it is a "non-signatory to the Geneva Agreements" and "continues not to recognize their provisions."

APRIL 28. French Expeditionary Corps officially leaves Vietnam, and MAAG officially assumes responsibility for training the Vietnamese army.

MAY 11. DRV again proposes the convening of the Consultative Conference on elections called for in the Geneva Agreement.

MAY 22. RVN, in a note to the British government, again says that it will not negotiate on nation-wide elections.

JULY. Land reform completed in North Vietnam.

SEPTEMBER. Tenth Central Committee Plenum of the Vietnam Workers Party, meeting secretly, concludes that "serious errors" were committed in the land reform program.

1957

JANUARY 3. International Control Commission report says neither North Vietnam nor South Vietnam fulfilled its obligations under the Geneva Agreement during the period from December 1955 to August 1956.

FEBRUARY 9. The Vietnam People's Army of the DRV requests that the International Control Commission investigate the detention of 1,700 former resistance fighters by RVN authorities at Hoi An, Quang Nam Province.

MAY 5–19. President Diem visits the United States and addresses a joint session of Congress.

1958

JUNE 14. Gen. Vo Nguyen Giap sends a letter to the Co-Chairmen of the Geneva Conference protesting RVN's request for new armaments in replacement for French Expeditionary Corps war equipment and ICC approval of the request.

DECEMBER 22. Premier Dong sends another letter to Diem repeating his proposals for mutual force reductions, economic exchanges, free movement between zones, and an end to hostile propaganda.

1959

JANUARY. Fifteenth Enlarged Plenum of the Vietnam Workers Party Central Committee meets secretly and approves limited use of armed force, to support political struggle against Diem.

FEBRUARY 6. ICC concludes that former resistance members in Quang Nam Province of South Vietnam were subjected to reprisals by RVN authorities.

MAY. At the request of the RVN, U.S. advisers are ordered to Vietnam at infantry regiment, artillery, armored, and separate Marine battalion level.

MAY 6. Diem proclaims law "10/59" providing for special military tribunals with power to execute those accused of "sabotage and offense to national security."

1960

APRIL 30. Eighteen opposition politicians, calling themselves the Committee for Progress and Liberty, send a letter to Diem demanding economic, administrative, and military reforms.

MAY 5. United States announces increase of MAAG strength from 327 to 685 by the end of the year.

SEPTEMBER 10. Vietnam Workers Party's Third National Congress reaffirms the primacy of socialist construction for North Vietnam and calls for "united bloc" against Diem in the South.

NOVEMBER 11. A group of military officers takes over Presidential Palace and accuses Diem of autocratic rule and nepotism, but loyal troops save Diem the following day.

DECEMBER 20. South Vietnam National Liberation Front (NLF) is established to overthrow the RVN and establish a coalition government.

1961

APRIL 9. Diem reelected president with 89 percent of the total vote.

MAY 5. President Kennedy declares that consideration is being given to the use of U.S. troops, if necessary, in South Vietnam.

MAY 15. State Department tells allies it will increase MAAG personnel beyond Geneva limit, citing North Vietnamese violations of the agreement.

JUNE 3. First group of South Vietnamese commandos, dropped over North Vietnam for espionage-sabotage mission, is captured.

JUNE 9. Diem sends a letter to Kennedy saying RVN would require 100,000 additional troops beyond the 20,000-man increase already planned.

JUNE 19. A U.S. mission under Dr. Eugene Staley arrives in Saigon to determine financial measures required to support counterinsurgency plan.

NOVEMBER 16. Kennedy announces U.S. decision to increase South Vietnamese military strength but not to commit U.S. combat forces.

NOVEMBER 22. National Security Action Memorandum No. 111 authorizes Diem be informed United States would provide additional helicopters, transport planes, and warplanes as well as personnel to carry out instruction and actual combat missions. That decision is kept secret from the American public.

DECEMBER 8. United States publishes "white paper" accusing North Vietnam of aggression against the South and warning of a "clear and present danger" of Communist victory.

1962

FEBRUARY 7. Two U.S. army air support companies totalling 300 men arrive in Saigon, increasing total U.S. military personnel to 4,000.

FEBRUARY 8. United States reorganizes its South Vietnam military command, establishing the U.S. Military Assistance Command, Vietnam, (MACV) under Gen. Paul D. Harkins.

FEBRUARY 24. People's Republic of China demands United States withdraw its military personnel and equipment from South Vietnam, charging "undeclared war" threatens China's security.

FEBRUARY 28. DRV Ministry of Foreign Affairs publishes a memorandum denouncing U.S. military agression in South Vietnam.

MARCH 17. Soviet Foreign Ministry note to Geneva Agreement signatories charges United States with creating a "serious danger to peace" by its "interference" in South Vietnam, in violation of the agreements.

MAY. Communist forces in Laos gain control of large area, as about 2,000 Royal Lao Army troops flee into Thailand with their commanders.

MAY 15. Kennedy announces United States is sending troops to Thailand, at the Thai government's request, because of Communist offensive in Laos and subsequent movement of Communist forces toward the Thai border.

JUNE 2. Canadian and Indian members of the ICC find the DRV guilty of carrying out "hostile activities, including armed attacks" against the RVN armed forces and administration, in violation of the Geneva Agreement. All three members of the ICC find RVN guilty of violating Articles 16 and 17 of the agreement by receiving additional military aid and entering into a "factual military alliance" with the U.S.

JULY 23. Declaration and protocol on the neutrality of Laos is signed by fourteen-nation conference in Geneva.

1963

MAY 8. Riot erupts in Hue during Buddha's birthday celebration. Buddhists charge Government troops fired into the crowd, killing twelve.

JUNE 3. Martial law declared in Hue after Buddhist antigovernment protest.

JULY 17. Armed policemen use clubs to break up a Buddhist protest demonstration against alleged religious discrimination in Saigon. Kennedy declares the religious crisis is interfering with the war effort and expresses hope for agreement to halt civil disturbances.

AUGUST 21. Martial law proclaimed throughout South Vietnam, as Special Forces loyal to Diem's brother Nho Dinh Nhu attack pagodas, arresting 1,400 Buddhists. Washington deplores the raids as a direct violation of Diem's assurances.

AUGUST 24. State Department cable to Saigon Embassy acknowledges Nhu's responsibility for raids on Buddhist pagodas and says generals should be told United States is prepared to discontinue economic and military aid to Diem and promised support in any interim breakdown of government.

AUGUST 26. At a National Security Council (NSC) meeting, senior advisors express reservations about the August 24 cable, drafted when they were all out of town.

AUGUST 29. Gen. Duong Van Minh meets with a CIA agent and says the United States should suspend economic aid to the regime as a signal of support for a coup.

SEPTEMBER 2. Kennedy, in an interview with CBS, says the war cannot be won "unless the people support the effort," adding "in my opinion, in the last two months, the Government has gotten out of touch with the people."

SEPTEMBER 12. Senator Church, with White House approval, introduces a resolution condeming the South Vietnamese government for repression of Buddhists and calling for an end to American aid unless the repressions are abandoned.

OCTOBER 2. After a visit to South Vietnam, Secretary of Defense Robert McNamara and White House Defense Adviser Maxwell Taylor recommend pressures against Diem to bring political changes, including selective aid suspension and aloofness toward the regime by Lodge. Gen. Tran Van Don tells a CIA contact there is an active plot among the generals for a coup.

OCTOBER 5. General Minh meets with CIA contact and discusses three possible coup plans, one involving assassination, demanding to know the U.S. position.

OCTOBER 10. CIA agent meets with Minh and conveys U.S. position that it will neither encourage nor thwart a coup attempt, but wants to be kept informed.

OCTOBER 17. U.S. Embassy informs GVN of suspension of assistance to Special Forces, pending their transfer to the field under command of the Joint General Staff (JGS).

NOVEMBER 1. Military coup overthrows Diem regime, killing Diem and Nhu.

NOVEMBER 2. Military leaders set up a provisional government, suspend the Constitution, and dissolve the National Assembly.

NOVEMBER 23. One day after Kennedy's assassination, President Lyndon Johnson reaffirms the U.S. commitment to defeat the Communists in South Vietnam and authorizes clandestine operations against North Vietnam and in Laos.

1964

JANUARY 30. Military coup by Maj. Gen. Nguyen Khanh ousts government of Maj. Gen. Duong Van Minh.

MAY 21. Rusk says expansion of the war could result "if the Communists persist in their course of aggression."

JUNE 12. French President Charles de Gaulle calls for an end to all foreign intervention in South Vietnam.

JUNE 4. Ambassador Henry Cabot Lodge indicates to Khanh that the United States will prepare American public opinion for actions against North Vietnam.

JUNE 30. United States and RVN agree to joint planning for cross-border operations in Laos.

JULY 19. Khanh and Air Marshall Nguyen Cao Ky call publicly for cross-border operations and air strikes into Laos and North Vietnam.

JULY 25. Soviet Union calls for reconvening of the Geneva Conference on Laos.

JULY 30–31. South Vietnamese naval forces, using American "swiftboats," carry out commando raid on Hon Me and Non Nhieu islands, twelve and four kilometers off the North Vietnamese coast. DRV accuses United States and RVN of "extremely serious" violation of the Geneva Agreement.

AUGUST 2. North Vietnamese patrol boats intercept the U.S. destroyer *Maddox* twenty-eight miles from the coast and launch a single torpedo at it. U.S. planes from the *Ticonderoga* destroy one North Vietnamese patrol boat and damage two.

AUGUST 3. DRV endorses call for reconvening of Geneva Conference to "preserve the peace of Indochina and Southeast Asia."

AUGUST 4. One day after the shelling of two points on the North Vietnamese coast, the *Maddox* and *C. Turner Joy* are attacked by North Vietnamese patrol boats. President Johnson orders U.S. air strikes against "gunboats and certain supporting facilities in North Vietnam."

AUGUST 7. Tonkin Gulf Resolution, authorizing "all necessary steps, including the use of armed force" in Southeast Asia, is passed by Congress 88-2 (Senate) and 416-0 (House). Nguyen Khanh declares a "state of emergency" in South Vietnam.

AUGUST 16. Khanh is elected president by the Military Council, ousts Duong Van Minh as chief of state, and installs a new constitution, which the U.S. Embassy helped draft.

AUGUST 21. Student demonstration against Khanh and military government begin, turning into rioting within days.

AUGUST 27. New constitution is withdrawn; Revolutionary Council dissolved. "Triumvirate" of Khanh, Minh, and Gen. Tran Thien Khiem created.

AUGUST 29. Nguyen Xuan Oanh, a former professor at Trinity College, Hartford, Connecticut, named Acting Premier, says Khanh has suffered mental and physical breakdown.

SEPTEMBER 5. DRV Minister of Foreign Affairs renews appeal to Geneva Conference Co-Chairman to reconvene the Conference.

SEPTEMBER 13. Bloodless coup by Brig. Gen. Lam Van Phat is abortive.

SEPTEMBER 26. Provisional legislature ("High National Council") inaugurated in Saigon.

SEPTEMBER 30. William Bundy says bombing North Vietnam would cut down the threat to the RVN within months.

OCTOBER 31. Tran Van Huong is named Premier.

DECEMBER 8–20. Student and Buddhist demonstrations threaten the military-supported government of Tran Van Huong.

DECEMBER 20. Khanh and generals dissolve the High National Council, arrest oppositionists and conduct purge of military leadership, despite opposition by Ambassador Maxwell Taylor.

DECEMBER 24. Taylor tells the press Khanh has outlived his usefulness.

1965

JANUARY 7. Armed Forces Council (AFC) and Khanh restore civilian government under Tran Van Huong.

JANUARY 19–24. Buddhist demonstrations include sacking of United States Information Service (USIS) buildings in Saigon and Hue, as Buddhists demand military ouster of the Huong government.

JANUARY 27. Armed Forces Council ousts the Huong government, putting Khanh openly back in power.

FEBRUARY 7. Communist attack on U.S. advisers' compound near Pleiku kills nine, wounds seventy-six. U.S. planes strike targets in North Vietnam in retaliation.

FEBRUARY 9. U.S. Marine Corps Hawk air defense missile battalion deployed at Danang.

FEBRUARY 15. People's Republic of China threatens to enter the war if United States invades North Vietnam.

FEBRUARY 18. South Vietnamese army and marine units stage a bloodless coup and oust Khanh.

FEBRUARY 20. After forces loyal to the Armed Forces Council regain control, AFC demands Khanh's resignation.

FEBRUARY 27. State Department issues "white paper" detailing its case against North Vietnamese "aggression."

FEBRUARY 28. U.S. and RVN officials declare President Johnson has decided to begin continuous reprisal attacks against North Vietnam to bring about a negotiated settlement.

MARCH 8. United Nations Secretary General U Thant proposes a preliminary conference, with the United States, Soviet Union, Great Britain, France, China, and North and South Vietnam.

MARCH 9. United States rejects U Thant's proposal until North Vietnam ends the war in the South. Two battalions of U.S. marines land at Danang.

APRIL 2. United States announces it will send several thousand more troops to South Vietnam.

APRIL 7. Johnson, in a speech at Johns Hopkins University, says United States is willing to hold "unconditional discussions" with North Vietnam and suggests a $1 billion economic aid program for Southeast Asia.

APRIL 8. DRV Premier Pham Van Dong announces four-point position on peace; including settlement of South Vietnam's internal affairs "in accordance with the program of the National Liberation Front of South Vietnam, without any foreign interference."

MAY 13. United States begins six-day bombing pause over North Vietnam.

JUNE 8. State Department reveals U.S. troops are authorized to participate in combat.

JUNE 4. RVN "National Directorate," comprised of ten military leaders forms a "war cabinet" headed by Air Marshall Nguyen Kao Ky.

JUNE 16. McNamara announces new troop deployments to South Vietnam, bringing total there to 70,000.

OCTOBER 15–16. Student-run National Coordinating Committee to End the War in Vietnam sponsors a series of nation-wide demonstrations.

NOVEMBER 27. March for peace in Vietnam draws 15,000 to 35,000 marchers in Washington.

DECEMBER 24. United States begins second bombing pause.

1966

JANUARY 31. Johnson announces resumption of American air strikes against North Vietnam.

FEBRUARY 1. UN Security Council meets to consider an American draft resolution calling for council action to arrange an international conference to bring about peace in South Vietnam and Southeast Asia.

FEBRUARY 2. North Vietnamese Foreign Ministry formally rejects UN action on Vietnam.

MARCH 12. Buddhists and students begin demonstrations in Hue and Danang to protest ouster of Corps Commander Gen. Nguyen Chanh Thi and to demand elections for a new national assembly.

MARCH 23. General strikes occur in Danang and Hue.

MARCH 16–20. Mass Buddhist protests in Saigon against Thieu-Ky government.

APRIL 2–5. Ky threatens to use troops to quell antigovernment rebellion in Danang, then flies two Ranger battalions to Danang.

APRIL 11. B-52's used to bomb North Vietnam for the first time; press reports Pentagon decision to use them regularly against the North.

APRIL 12–14. "National Directorate" promises elections for a constituent assembly within three to five months, and Buddhists demonstrations end.

MAY 15. Ky airlifts 1,000 marines to Danang and begins to seize key points, including Buddhist Youth headquarters.

JUNE 1. Students burn the U.S. consulate in Hue, after earlier sacking and burning the U.S. cultural center there.

JUNE 19. "National Directorate" schedules assembly elections for September 11.

JUNE 23. RVN troops seize the principle Buddhist stronghold in Saigon, the United Buddhist Church's Secular Affairs Institute.

JUNE 29. U.S. planes conduct the first attack on oil installations in the Hanoi and Haiphong urban areas.

JULY 8. South Vietnamese Chief of State Lt. Gen. Nguyen Van Thieu, states that the allies should invade North Vietnam if necessary to end the war.

SEPTEMBER 11. 117-member constituent assembly elected in South Vietnam from among officially approved anti-Communist slates. Buddhists denounce the election as "completely crooked."

OCTOBER 25. In Manila the United States and five other nations assisting South Vietnam offer to withdraw their troops from South Vietnam six months after Hanoi disengages itself from the war.

NOVEMBER 5. McNamara says the number of U.S. troops in Vietnam will continue to grow in 1967 but at a lower rate of increase than in 1966.

NOVEMBER 30. Polish International Control Commission representative Janusz Lewandowski formulates a ten-point U.S. peace position on which basis North Vietnam would negotiate seriously with the United States.

DECEMBER 2. State Department decides to contact DRV representative in Warsaw about secret talks.

DECEMBER 2–5. U.S. bombers carry out raids on truck depots, rail yards, and fuel dumps in the immediate environs of Hanoi.

DECEMBER 9. Lewandowski informs Lodge no contact could take place in Warsaw in the face of escalation of bombing.

DECEMBER 14–15. U.S. planes attack military targets two miles from Hanoi city limits.

DECEMBER 25. Responding to reports by Harrision Salisbury of the *New York Times*, officials admit U.S. planes have "accidentally struck civilian areas while attempting to bomb military targets."

1967

JANUARY 10. Johnson asks for a 6 percent surcharge on income taxes to support the war.

FEBRUARY 7. Johnson sends a proposal to British Prime Minister Harold Wilson for an "assured stoppage" of infiltration by the DRV in return for a bombing halt and to further augmentation of American forces in South Vietnam. United States begins a six-day bombing pause.

FEBRUARY 10. White House insists Wilson formula for the talks with Kosygin requires that North Vietnamese infiltration stop *before a* bombing halt, not after, as Wilson had suggested in an oral presentation.

MARCH 21. DRV Foreign Ministry releases Johnson-Ho exchange in February, in which Ho rejected peace talks unless the United States unconditionally halted bombing and all other acts of war against North Vietnam.

APRIL. Massive antiwar demonstrations throughout the United States.

APRIL 20. U.S. planes bomb two power plants in Hanoi for the first time.

APRIL 24. U.S. planes attack two North Vietnamese MIG bases for the first time.

MAY 13. Premier Ky says he might respond "militarily" if a civilian whose policies he disagreed with is elected president.

MAY 14. Chief of State Thieu says he believes 50,000 American or allied troops will be needed for ten to twenty years after the end of the war.

JUNE 30. After three days of meetings of the ruling Armed Forces Council, Ky withdraws from the presidential race, agreeing to be vice-presidential candidate with Thieu.

JULY 16. United States admits in a diplomatic note to the USSR that its planes may have bombed the Soviet ship *Mikhail Frunze* in Haiphong Harbor June 29.

JULY 18–19. Constituent Assembly approves eleven slates of candidates for the presidential election but rejects peace candidate Au Truong Thanh, on trumped-up charges of Communist links, and exiled Gen. Duong Van Minh.

AUGUST 31. U.S. Senate Preparedness Subcommittee says McNamara has "shackled" the air war against North Vietnam and calls for "closure, neutralization, or isolation of Haiphong."

SEPTEMBER 3. Thieu-Ky slate elected with 35 percent of the vote.

SEPTEMBER 29. Johnson declares in a speech at San Antonio that the United States will stop the bombing of North Vietnam "when this will lead promptly to productive discussions" and adds, "We would assume that while discussions proceed, North Vietnam would not take advantage of the bombing cessation or limitation."

OCTOBER 12. Rusk says the Vietnam war is a test of Asia's ability to withstand the threat of "a billion Chinese . . . armed with nuclear weapons."

OCTOBER 1967. Massive antiwar rally in Washington includes march on the Pentagon.

NOVEMBER 21. Commander of U.S. forces in Vietnam Gen. William West-moreland, in a speech at the National Press Club, says the war has reached the point "when the end begins to come into view."

1968

JANUARY 1. DRV Foreign Minister Nguyen Duy Trinh says for the first time North Vietnam "will hold talks with the United States" after the United States has "unconditionally" halted the bombing and other acts of war against North Vietnam.

JANUARY 25. Clark Clifford, Johnson's nominee as Secretary of Defense, tells Senate Armed Services Committee the "no advantage" clause of the San Antonio speech means the North could continue to transport the "normal" level of goods and men to the South after a bombing halt.

JANUARY 30–31. Communist forces launch simultaneous attacks on major South Vietnamese cities, including an invasion of the U.S. Embassy grounds in Saigon. More than half of the province capitals are attacked, as well as twenty-five air-fields.

FEBRUARY 20. McNamara testifies before the Senate Foreign Relations Committee on the 1964 Gulf of Tonkin incident, denying any provocation by the United States. Senators Fulbright and Morse charge the Defense Department had withheld information on U.S. naval activities in the Gulf that could have provoked the North.

FEBRUARY 24. South Vietnamese forces recapture Hue after twenty-five days of occupation by Communist troops.

FEBRUARY 25. Westmoreland states that additional troops "will probably be required" in Vietnam.

MARCH 31. Johnson announces a bombing halt over North Vietnam except for "the area north of the demilitarized zone," calls on the DRV to agree to peace talks, and announces he is withdrawing from the Presidential race.

APRIL 3. DRV offers to send representatives to meet with the United States "with a view to determining with the American side the unconditional cessation of the U.S. bombing raids and all other acts of war against the Democratic Republic of Vietnam so that talks may start." Johnson agrees and suggests Geneva as a meeting site.

MAY 3. Johnson announces U.S. acceptance of North Vietnamese offer to meet in Paris for preliminary talks May 10 or soon afterwards.

JUNE 27. U.S. troops withdraw from their base at Khe Sanh near the DMZ after a 77-day siege that began in January 1968.

OCTOBER 31. Johnson announces cessation of "all air, naval, and artillery bombardment of North Vietnam" as of November 1.

NOVEMBER 1. DRV delegation at Paris says a meeting including representatives of the DRV, the South Vietnam National Front for Liberation, the United States, and the RVN, will be held in Paris some time after November 6.

NOVEMBER 2. Thieu says his government will not attend the Paris negotiations.

NOVEMBER 12. Defense Secretary Clifford says United States will eventually have to decide whether to proceed with Paris negotiations without Thieu government participation, but that United States could only negotiate on military issues, not a political settlement.

NOVEMBER 27. RVN announces it would take part in the Paris peace talks, after United States reiterates its nonrecognition of the NLF as a separate entity.

1969

JANUARY 16. The United States and DRV announce agreement on a round conference table.

FEBRUARY 23–24. Communist forces launch mortar and rocket attacks on 115 targets in South Vietnam, including Saigon, Danang, Hue, and the American base at Bien Hoa.

MARCH 27. In Paris, Ambassador Lodge and RVN Delegation Chief Pham Dang Lam declare that the price of a peace settlement includes withdrawal of all North Vietnamese "regular and subversive forces" from Laos and Cambodia as well as from South Vietnam.

APRIL 7. Thieu says he would ask allies to remove their forces after a North Vietnamese withdrawal of regular troops as well as "auxiliary troops and cadres."

MAY 8. NLF Delegate Tran Buu Kiem demands unconditional U.S. troop withdrawal and settlement of remaining military and political issues among Vietnamese parties.

MAY 14. President Nixon's first major speech on Vietnam calls for withdrawal of "all non-South Vietnamese forces" from South Vietnam and praises Thieu's April proposal.

JUNE 10. Provisional Revolutionary Government of the Republic of South Vietnam (PRGRSV) is formed by the NLF and other pro-NLF, anti-RVN organizations and individuals.

JULY 11. Thieu offers internationally supervised elections and Communist participation in an "electoral commission," provided they first renounce violence, but does not yield the administration of the election to anyone else.

SEPTEMBER 3. DRV's first and only president, Ho Chi Minh, dies.

OCTOBER 15. Vietnam Moratorium demonstrations involve hundreds of thousands of people around the United States.

OCTOBER 16. Secretary of Defense Melvin Laird says the plans are to keep "residual force" of more than six or seven thousand troops in South Vietnam after hostilities end.

NOVEMBER 3. In his second major address on Vietnam, Nixon appeals to the "silent majority," arguing that "precipitate withdrawal would lead to a disaster of immense magnitude."

NOVEMBER 12. The Army announces it is investigating a charge that a U.S. unit shot over one-hundred Vietnamese civilians in My Lai Village in March 1968.

NOVEMBER 15. Mass antiwar demonstration at the Washington Monument, the largest ever seen in Washington, draws an estimated 250,000 people.

DECEMBER 4. The Louis Harris survey reports that 46 percent of those polled indicated sympathy with the goals of the November Moratorium demonstrations, while 45 percent disagreed with its goals.

1970

JANUARY 28. A Gallup Poll shows that 65 percent of those interviewed said they approved of Nixon's handling of the war, his highest level of approval to date.

MARCH 13. With Prince Norodom Sihanouk out of the country, the Cambodian government demands that North Vietnamese and South Vietnamese Communist troops withdraw from Cambodia immediately, while Cambodians sack Vietnamese Communist Embassies in Phnom Penh.

MARCH 17. Cambodian troops attack Vietnamese Communist sanctuaries along the Cambodia-Vietnam border, supported by Saigon army artillery.

MARCH 18. Sihanouk is deposed by the National Assembly after a coup d'etat and Lt. Gen. Lon Nol is designated interim chief of state. Thieu says he hopes to work with the new Cambodian government to control Communist activity along their border.

MARCH 23. Sihanouk declares in Peking that he will form a "national union government" and a "national liberation army." The DRV, PRG, and Pathet Lao declare their support for his resistance government.

MARCH 27-28. RVN forces launch their first major attack against Communist base areas in Cambodia, supported by U.S. helicopters. RVN and Cambodian military officers hold an informal meeting on the border in the presence of an American Colonel.

APRIL 5. Two RVN battalions push more than ten miles into Cambodia in an operation against Communist sanctuaries, this time without U.S. air support.

APRIL 8. Cambodian government forces are driven back by Vietnamese Communist troops in heavy fighting nine miles from the South Vietnamese border.

APRIL 11. Cambodian government troops begin to massacre several thousand Vietnamese civilians in towns in Southeast Cambodia, while some forty-thousand Vietnamese in Phnom Penh are herded into concentration camps.

APRIL 21. RVN troops cross the Cambodian border for the third time in a week to strike at Communist base areas.

APRIL 30. Nixon announces that American troops are attacking Communist sanctuaries in Cambodia, with the immediate objective being the location of the Communist Central Office of South Vietnam (COSVN) in the Fish Hook area.

MAY 3. The Pentagon confirms that the United States has conducted heavy bombing of targets in North Vietnam, the first major bombing of the North since the bombing halt in November 1968, calling them "protective reaction" strikes.

MAY 4. Ohio National Guardsmen fire on student demonstrators at Kent State University, killing four.

MAY 9. Seventy-five thousand to one-hundred thousand people gather in Washington, D.C., in a hastily organized protest against the U.S. invasion of Cambodia. More than two-hundred colleges and universities close, and about four hundred organize strikes protesting the Cambodia invasion and the killing of four students at Kent State.

MAY 12. RVN Vice-President Ky reveals that RVN and U.S. vessels began on May 9 to blockade a one-hundred mile stretch of Cambodian coastline to prevent the Vietnamese Communists from resupplying their troops by sea.

MAY 21. Ky says RVN forces will remain in Cambodia after the withdrawal of American troops from the operation.

JUNE 7. Secretary of State William Rogers says no U.S. troops will be used to protect Lon Nol's government, even if its existence is threatened by Communist forces.

JUNE 30. Senate approves the Cooper-Church Amendment aimed at limiting future presidential action in Cambodia by prohibiting military personnel in either combat or advisory roles in Cambodia or air activity in direct support of Cambodian forces. It nevertheless allows strategic bombing in Cambodia.

SEPTEMBER 17. PRG delegation in Paris proposes an eight-point peace plan, calling for complete U.S. withdrawal by June 30, 1971, and political settlement between the PRG and an interim government excluding Thieu, Ky, and Premier Tran Thien Khiem.

SEPTEMBER 26. A Gallup Poll shows that 55 percent of those surveyed favor the Hatfield-McGovern amendment to cut off funds for continued U.S. military activities in Vietnam, Laos and Cambodia unless there was a declaration of war, with 36 percent opposed.

OCTOBER 7. Nixon makes a new five-point proposal to end the war, based on a cease-fire in place in all three countries.

NOVEMBER 20. A U.S. rescue team raids Son Tay prisoner-of-war compound twenty miles west of Hanoi but finds it empty.

1971

FEBRUARY 8. Thieu orders RVN forces into southern Laos to disrupt the Communist supply and infiltration network. American officials in Saigon say the United States is providing full combat air support for the operation.

FEBRUARY 20–21. RVN troops suffer heavy casualties and are forced to abandon a fire base in southern Laos.

MARCH 25. The RVN drive in Southern Laos ends with the withdrawal of all but five-hundred troops, long before expected, due to strength of enemy resistance.

APRIL 16. Nixon says a residual American force will remain in Vietnam "as long as there is still time needed for the South Vietnamese to develop the capacity for self-defense."

APRIL 24. An estimated five-hundred thousand participate in a Washington rally to protest the war.

MAY 31. The United States secretly proposes to the DRV a deadline for the withdrawal of all American troops in return for the repatriation of American prisoners and a cease-fire.

JUNE 26. The DRV offers to release American prisoners at the same time as the release of civilian prisoners and withdrawal of U.S. forces, but demands that the United States stop supporting Thieu.

JULY 1. The PRG delegation in Paris proposes a plan under which it would negotiate with a neutral coalition government excluding Thieu, Ky, and Khiem.

AUGUST 20. Retired Gen. Duong Van Minh, the only opposition candidate in the RVN presidential election, withdraws from the race, charging that it was already rigged in Thieu's favor, due to American political support for Thieu.

OCTOBER 3. Thieu is elected to another four-year term with more than 80 percent of the vote.

OCTOBER 11. United States made a new proposal offering free elections to be organized by an independent body representing all political forces in the South, with Thieu and his vice-president resigning one month before the elections.

DECEMBER 26–30. U.S. planes stage heavy attacks on targets in North Vietnam; government again refers to them as "protective reaction" strikes.

1972

JANUARY 25. Nixon reveals details of Kissinger's thirteen secret trips to Paris and the text of the last U.S. peace proposal of October 11, 1971.

FEBRUARY 3. The PRG presents a revised version of the July 1971 peace proposal, calling for immediate resignation of President Thieu in exchange for immediate discussion of a political settlement; a specific date for total U.S. withdrawal and release of all military and civilian prisoners; and an end to Saigon's "warlike policy."

MARCH 30. North Vietnamese troops attack and overrun South Vietnamese bases south of the DMZ, in their first major ground offensive since 1968.

APRIL 6. Communist troops open a new offensive in the area of Loc Ninh, north of Saigon.

APRIL 16. U.S. Command announces that B-52's and tactical aircraft have struck "military targets in the vicinity of Haiphong and other areas of North Vietnam."

APRIL 22. Antiwar demonstrators hold marches and rallies throughout the United States to protest new bombing of North Vietnam.

APRIL 26. Nixon announces that 10,000 troops per month will be withdrawn from Vietnam in the next two months, bringing the total to forty-nine thousand by July 1.

APRIL 30. Nixon warns North Vietnam is "taking a very great risk if they continue their offensive in the South."

MAY 1. Quang Tri, the northernmost province capital of South Vietnam, is abandoned by RVN forces and their American advisers after five days of intensive fighting.

MAY 8. Nixon, in a broadcast address, announces mining of all North Vietnamese ports, interdiction of all rail and other communications, and strikes against military targets in North Vietnam, until return of American prisoners and an internationally supervised cease-fire throughout Indochina.

SEPTEMBER 11. The PRG says a settlement in South Vietnam has to reflect the "reality" of "two administrations, two armies and other political forces," suggesting that it was abandoning the idea of a coalition government.

OCTOBER 8. DRV presents its first draft peace agreement in Paris, in which two separate administrations would remain in South Vietnam and negotiate general elections.

OCTOBER 20. Nixon sends a message to Pham Van Dong confirming that the agreement was complete and pledging that it would be signed by the two foreign ministers on October 31, but asking for clarification on several points.

OCTOBER 22. Nixon's message to Pham Van Dong expresses satisfaction with DRV replies to his questions of October 20.

OCTOBER 23. A U.S. message to Hanoi asks for further negotiations, citing difficulties with Saigon.

OCTOBER 26. Hanoi broadcasts a summary of the peace agreement. Kissinger says "Peace is at hand," and that only one more meeting is needed to complete the agreement.

NOVEMBER 1. Thieu publicly objects to the draft agreement's provisions permitting North Vietnamese troops to remain in the South, and providing for a three-segment "administrative structure" to preside over the political settlement and elections.

NOVEMBER 16. Nixon sends a letter to Thieu pledging to press Hanoi for a series of changes demanded by Thieu.

NOVEMBER 20. Kissinger and Le Duc Tho begin another round of secret negotiations near Paris.

DECEMBER 16. Kissinger holds a press conference to blame North Vietnam for the stalemate in the negotiations.

DECEMBER 18. United States begins bombing of the Hanoi-Haiphong area, using B-52's as well as fighter-bombers. The White House says it will continue until "a settlement is arrived at."

DECEMBER 22. White House says that bombing will continue until Hanoi agrees to negotiate "in a spirit of good will and in a constructive attitude."

DECEMBER 30. White House announces that negotiations between Kissinger and Tho will resume January 2 and that the President has ordered a halt to the bombing above the twentieth parallel.

1973

JANUARY 8. Kissinger and Tho resume private negotiations in Paris.

JANUARY 17. Nixon warns Thieu in a private letter that his refusal to sign the agreement would make it impossible to continue assistance to RVN.

JANUARY 20. Nixon sends an ultimatum to Thieu on signing the peace agreement, demanding an answer by January 21.

JANUARY 23. Kissinger and Tho initial a peace agreement.

JANUARY 25. The foreign ministers of the United States, DRV, RVN, and PRG sign two-party and four-party versions of the peace agreement.

JANUARY 27. Cease-fire agreement goes into effect, as RVN forces continue to take back villages occupied by Communists in the two days before the cease-fire deadline.

FEBRUARY 1. In a secret letter to Pham Van Dong, Nixon pledges to contribute to "postwar reconstruction in North Vietnam" in the "range of $3.25 billion of grand aid over five years."

FEBRUARY 17. United States and DRV issue a joint communiqué after a four-day visit by Henry Kissinger to Hanoi, announcing agreement to establish a Joint Economic Commission (JEC) to develop economic relations, particularly an American contribution to "healing the wounds of war" in North Vietnam.

FEBRUARY 16. Four-Party Joint Military Commission issues an appeal to the military commands of both South Vietnamese parties to strictly respect the cease-fire and reaffirms the prohibition on air combat missions.

MARCH 15. Nixon threatens in a press conference to take unilateral action to force the DRV to suspend or reduce the use of the trail network to move military equipment into South Vietnam.

MARCH 28. Nixon again warns that North Vietnamese "should have no doubt as to the consequences if they fail to comply with the agreement."

MARCH 29. The last sixty-seven American prisoners of war held by North Vietnam fly out of Hanoi, and the last American troops leave South Vietnam.

APRIL 3. A Nixon-Thieu joint communiqué issued from San Clemente charge DRV violations of the cease-fire agreement by infiltration and warns that continued violations "would call for appropriately vigorous reactions." Defense Secretary Elliot Richardson says the United States would not renew the bombing unless there were a "flagrant" violation of the agreement, such as a full-scale invasion of the South.

APRIL 24. State Department makes public texts of North Vietnam and U.S. notes accusing each other of violating the Paris Peace Agreement.

APRIL 25. RVN and PRG delegations to the political talks in Paris offer incompatible proposals for a political settlement.

MAY 10. The House passes the second supplemental appropriations bill with an amendment deleting the authorization for transfer of $430 million by the Defense Department for the bombing of Cambodia, and another amendment prohibiting use of funds for combat activities in or over Cambodia by U.S. forces.

JUNE 9. While Kissinger and Tho negotiate a new agreement for implementation of the Paris peace agreement, fighting in South Vietnam reaches its highest level since mid-February.

JUNE 13. Signatories to the Paris agreement issue a joint communiqué on implementation of the agreement, calling for resumption of the processes interrupted in April, including the meetings of the United States-DRV Joint Economic Commission. Kissinger refers to a "satisfactory conclusion" on points of concern to the United States.

JUNE 20. Documents declassified by the Defense Department show that 3.2 million tons of bombs have been dropped on South Vietnam, 2.1 million on Laos, and 340,000 tons on North Vietnam, in seven years of war.

JUNE 26. House passes a continuing appropriations resolution for FY 1974 after agreeing to an amendment prohibiting all funds appropriated by the resolution and all funds previously appropriated from being used for combat activities in Cambodia and Laos. The Senate agrees to conference report on the second supplemental appropriations bill with the prohibition on funds for the bombing of Cambodia.

JUNE 29. House passes a compromise bill with an August 15 deadline for cessation of bombing, and adding North and South Vietnam to the areas included in the ban on combat activities. Nixon signs the bill into law three days later.

JULY 26. House passes the Foreign Assistance Bill after agreeing to an amendment prohibiting use of authorized funds to aid in reconstruction of North Vietnam unless specifically authorized by Congress.

AUGUST 15. American bombing of Cambodia ends.

SEPTEMBER 10. RVN protests the construction of air bases in the PRG zone, on the ground that all air space over South Vietnam belongs to the RVN.

OCTOBER 1. Thieu declares that the Communists are planning a "general offensive" in the Spring and calls for "preemptive attacks" against Communist forces.

OCTOBER 3–7. RVN Air Force planes carry out heavy bombing raids against the PRG zone in Tay Ninh Province, initiating a bombing campaign throughout the Third Military Region.

OCTOBER 15. The Communist command in the South, the People's Liberation Armed Forces, issues orders to begin counterattacking RVN rear bases and other points of its own choosing, in retaliation for Saigon's offensive operations earlier in the year.

1974

JANUARY 4. Thieu declares, "The war has restarted."

FEBRUARY. RVN forces launch major offensive operations in PRG areas of Quang Ngai and the Cu Chi-Trang Bang area west of Saigon.

MARCH. Communist Party's Central Military Committee passes resolution that, if United States and Thieu "do not implement the agreement," it must "destroy the enemy and liberate the South."

MARCH 22. PRG offers to hold elections within one year of the establishment of the National Council of National Reconciliation and Concord in the last major political initiative by either side.

APRIL 11. RVN Ranger base at Tong Le Chan, surrounded by Communist troops since the cease-fire, is evacuated. RVN immediately claims it has been overrun by the Communists.

APRIL 16. RVN withdraws diplomatic "privileges and immunities" of the PRG delegation to the Joint Military Commission (JMC), including access to the press, telephone service, and weekly liaison flights.

MAY 10. PRG delegation walks out of the JMC and refuses to return until privileges and immunities have been restored.

MAY 13. PRG delegation suspends its participation in the political talks in Paris, citing the earlier suspension of the conference by Saigon, the withdrawal of diplomatic privileges for the PRG delegation in Saigon, and land-grabbing operations.

JULY–AUGUST. Communist forces regain major areas of Quang Nam and Quang Ngai in its first major offensive in the lowlands.

AUGUST 6. The House cuts U.S. military aid appropriations for RVN from $1 billion to $700 million by a 233 to 157 vote.

OCTOBER 8. PRG issues a statement calling on public figures and organizations in South Vietnam to work for the overthrow of the Thieu regime and establishment of a new regime in Saigon.

OCTOBER. The Political Bureau, Party Military Committee and General Staff agree that the United States is unlikely to intervene and could not save Thieu even if it did.

DECEMBER 18. Political Bureau opens a series of meetings during the next three weeks to determine a two-year strategic plan for defeating the Thieu regime.

1975

MARCH 10. Communist forces attack Banmethuot, opening the Spring Offensive.

MARCH 15. RVN forces begin a retreat from Kontum and Pleiku, which turns into a debacle, as the 23rd division is destroyed before reaching the coast.

MARCH 19. Communist forces attack and capture Quang Tri, as RVN withdrawal toward Danang turns into a rout, and the First Division disintegrates.

MARCH 25. Hue falls to Communist troops. The Political Bureau decides to "liberate Saigon before the rainy season."

MARCH 30. Danang, already abandoned in chaos for three days, is taken over by Communist forces without resistance. The remaining coastal cities are taken over from fleeing RVN troops.

MARCH 31. Political Bureau decides to carry out the "general offensive and general uprising" in April, if possible.

APRIL 11. The Ford Administration asks Congress for an additional $722 million in military aid. Kissinger, in a background briefing, suggests that public support for Thieu regime is necessary to get Thieu's cooperation in the evacuation of Americans from Saigon.

APRIL 14. Political Bureau approves the proposal from the command at the front to name the campaign to take Saigon, set for the last week in April, the Ho Chi Minh Campaign.

APRIL 18. Kissinger issues orders for the immediate evacuation of Americans from Saigon.

APRIL 21. Thieu announces his resignation and leaves for Taiwan.

APRIL 22. Political Bureau cables the command near Saigon that the general offensive should be launched "without delay."

APRIL 26. Ho Chi Minh Campaign begins against Saigon.

APRIL 27. RVN National Assembly votes unanimously to turn power over to Duong Van Minh.

APRIL 30. Communist forces drive into Saigon, as the RVN army melts away.

INDEX